EDUGORILLA
PUBLICATION

NABARD Development Assistant

Preliminary Exam

Latest Edition
Practice Kit

14 Tests
08 Mock Test
06 Sectional Test

Based On Real Exam Pattern

✓ Thoroughly Revised and Updated

✓ Detailed Analysis of all MCQs

<table>
<tr><td>Title</td><td>: NABARD Development Assistant Preliminary Exam</td></tr>
<tr><td>Author Name</td><td>: Mr. Rohit Manglik</td></tr>
<tr><td>Published By</td><td>: EduGorilla Community Pvt. Ltd.</td></tr>
<tr><td>Publishers Address</td><td>: 12/651, First Floor Opp. Arvindo Park, Near Jama Masjid,
Indira Nagar, Lucknow, Uttar Pradesh-226016, India</td></tr>
</table>

Copyright EduGorilla

Disclaimer EduGorilla

ROHIT MANGLIK
CEO, EduGorilla

Dear Applicants,

People say *"Success comes to those who work hard."* But I've seen people working hard for their exams day in and day out for marginal success. While others succeed in their examinations by putting in just half the work. So are they God Gifted? No! I believe that it's because they work *smart* and not just *hard*. Similarly, for your exams, you should strategize your preparation so as to increase the likelihood of success. Well with EduGorilla get ready to increase your *chances of selection* in your exam by *16x*.

EduGorilla helps you in not only working *hard* but also working in a *smart and strategic* manner. With EduGorilla's preparation package, you get a chance to make your exam preparation easy, and a fun learning path towards selection. Finding the right path to your preparations can be difficult if you don't know in which direction to head. Don't worry, we have you covered! EduGorilla will be your guide to success in your journey. With our Preparation Package, you can prepare strategically and beat the exam in just one attempt.

EduGorilla's Preparation Package includes-

• Test Series   **• Books**

Our preparation package is handcrafted as per the latest changes, expert opinions, and students' discretion. Thus, enabling you to get through each stage of the selection process for your exam.

Our Books are designed by the teachers and experts of the respective exam with a combined 150+ years of experience; to provide you with easy, efficient, and effective learning. Our books are smart, in the sense that not only do they give you the answers to the questions but also provide similar questions for practice.

EduGorilla's competent Test Series gives you real-time experience and confidence through which you can clear your offline or online exam in just one attempt. We currently host 83,000+ mock tests for 1,440+ competitive and academic exams.

Thus, EduGorilla misses no chance to assist you in your preparation and covers all stages of the exam, so that you don't have to look anywhere else.

We provide complete preparation packages for defense, banking, teaching, and other National & State-Level exams. Hence, it doesn't matter which exam you aspire to because you will reach your success.

ALL THE BEST !
Let EduGorilla be your Guide to Success.

Rohit Manglik,
Founder and CEO, EduGorilla

INTRODUCTION

EduGorilla focuses on guiding students to succeed in their examinations. With that in mind, our book, titled "NABARD Development Assistant : Preliminary Exam", has been drafted through the collective efforts of our distinguished experts with 150+ years of combined experience. This book consists of questions that are created following the latest changes in the syllabus and exam pattern. We compiled the book on the basis of questions that are most likely to appear in the NABARD Development Assistant. Through EduGorilla's "NABARD Development Assistant : Preliminary Exam" your chances of success will increase 16x.

EduGorilla does this through our Complete Preparation Package. This package consists of well-conceptualized and structured content in the form of questions that are tailor-made according to your needs and will help you practice for exams in a smart way by pinpointing all the necessary information. It also provides hints and solutions, along with a smart answer sheet for your self-evaluation. You can assess your shortcomings and work accordingly on areas that may require more of your attention.

EduGorilla promises to help you succeed in your examination and accomplish your dream goals. We believe in our aspirants and see them at the top of the merit list. And the first step towards the top is to start preparing with us. EduGorilla's "NABARD Development Assistant : Preliminary Exam" includes the following attributes.

➤ Well-Researched Content

➤ Top-Notch Quality

➤ Detailed Answers and Analysis

➤ Smart Answer Sheet

➤ Exam Relevant Questions

Therefore, EduGorilla fortifies your preparation and makes it durable enough to help you stand tall and beat the examination.

NABARD Development Assistant
Scan QR code for Eligibility, Exam Pattern, Syllabus and more.

Book ID: 0792

TABLE OF CONTENTS

Test of English Language

Q.1 Direction: Read the following sentence and determine whether there is an error in it. The error, if any, will be in one part of the sentence. If the sentence is error-free, select 'No Error' as your answer.

When it comes to playing (A) cricket, Amisha is better then (B) Samuel yet no one (C) selects her for the team. (D)

A. (A)   **B.** (B)   **C.** (C)   **D.** (D)
E. No error

Q.2 Direction: In this question, a sentence has been divided into four parts (A), (B), (C), (D). Read the sentence to find out whether there is any grammatical error in it. The error, if any, will be in one part of the sentence. Mark that part as your answer. If there is no error, the answer is 'No error'.

The brother-in-laws (A) / were very helpful (B) / and supportive of (C) / their choices. (D)

A. (A)   **B.** (B)   **C.** (C)   **D.** (D)
E. No error

Ques (3-4):Direction: In the following sentence, four words printed in bold are given. One of these words printed in bold might either be wrongly spelt or inappropriate to the context of the sentence. Find out that word that is inappropriate or wrongly spelt, if any. If all of the words in bold are correct, then mark 'No error' as your answer.

Q.3 Rahul **screamed** because Riya asked him to **acknowledge** that his suggestion of an **accumulation** of coins was **revolving**.

[SBI Clerk, 2021]

A. Screamed   **B.** Acknowledge
C. Acknowledge   **D.** Revolving
E. No error

Q.4
The **application** with the particularly **detrimental** effect on **operators**' jobs was the biscuit **dough** mixing automation.

[SBI Clerk, 2021]

A. Detrimental   **B.** Application
C. Operators   **D.** Dough
E. No error

Ques (5-9):Direction: The following question has two blanks, each blank indicating that something has been omitted. Choose the set of words for each blank that best fits in the context of the sentence.

Q.5 The boost to the Infrastructure sector was ________ ahead of the Union Budget and does play a key role in ________ demand in the economy.

A. inspired, revived
B. anticipating, revisit

C. erected, relate
D. anticipated, reviving
E. erased, expect

Q.6 Democracy needs to be ________not for perpetuation of power but for the perpetuation of democratic ________.

A. abandoned, efficacy   **B.** related, efficacy
C. requested, values   **D.** endured, evaluation
E. preserved, values

Q.7 Only MSMEs are well placed with ________, flexibility, local market understanding, and ________ to bring about this rural revolution.

A. apathetic, solution
B. dormant, evaluate
C. progression, decay
D. familiarity, advancement
E. competency, experience

Q.8 Growing ________ towards environment protection and the quest for an alternative, clean energy has created the right ________ for the electric vehicle industry in India.

A. insensibility, passion
B. fondness, drag
C. consciousness, push
D. credibility, trend
E. apprehension, flaw

Q.9 In order to ________ the quality and effectiveness of internal audit system, the RBI ________ guidelines on RBIA system for selecting non bank leaders and UCBs.

A. strong, issuing   **B.** strengthen, issued
C. strengthen, process   **D.** comprehend, issue
E. transfer, emerge

Q.10 Direction: In the following question, a sentence is given with four words marked as (A), (B) (C), and (D). These words may or may not be placed in the correct order. Five options with different arrangements of these words have been provided. Mark the option with the correct arrangement as the answer.

Smita was **jobless(A)** happy with the **conditions(B)** of the women in her **district(C)** as most were poor and **never(D)**, so she planned to do something

A. (A)-(B)   **B.** (A)-(C)   **C.** (B)-(C)   **D.** (A)-(D)
E. (B)-(D)

Ques (11-12):Direction: In the following question, a sentence is given with four words marked as (A), (B) (C), and (D). These words may or may not be placed in the correct order. Five options with different arrangements of these words have been provided. Mark the option with the correct arrangement as the answer.

Q.11 Taylor's husband **repent(A)** to **continues(B)** for cheating in the **past(C)**, but she isn't sure that his **apologies(D)** are sincere.

[SBI Apprentice, 2021], [IBPS Clerk, 2021]

A. (A) - (C) **B.** (C) - (D) **C.** (A) - (B) **D.** (B) - (C)
E. (A) - (C)

Q.12 More police **officers(A)** are needed
to **protest(B)** the **populace(C)** calm during the **keep(D)** march.

[IBPS Clerk, 2021]

A. (A) - (C) **B.** (B) - (D) **C.** (A) - (B) **D.** (C) - (D)
E. (A) - (D)

Ques (13-17):Direction: A passage is given below with five blanks labelled (A)-(E). Below the passage, five options are given for each blank. Choose the word that fits each blank most appropriately in the context of the passage, and mark the corresponding answer.

The end of World War II was not just the end of a war, but also the __(A)__ of a tense and dynamic period that affected society on all levels. This "postwar" period, as it became known, shaped the world as we know it today; likewise, the period was shaped itself both by the war that had __(B)__ it, and the powerful forces that surrounded it. As the energy of fundamentally different ideologies—Communism and Democracy—collided with advances in science such as the nuclear bomb, a dangerous environment ensued that created an atmosphere of __(C)__ throughout the world and especially, within America.

This atmosphere is known broadly as the "Cold War." While the Cold War played out step-by-step between the United States and the Soviet Union, it was __(D)__ playing out in the everyday lives of the masses within their borders. Paranoia, nevertheless, was not an effect that followed immediately after the close of the War. In fact, the United States had enjoyed an extended period of economic __(E)__ during the war, and following the war, the U.S. economy continued with great strength for more than a decade.

Q.13 Which of the following words most appropriately fits the blank labelled (A)?

[SBI Clerk, 2021]

A. Significant **B.** Advantage
C. Beginning **D.** Successfully
E. Staff

Q.14 Which of the following words most appropriately fits the blank labelled (B)?

[SBI Clerk, 2021]

A. Preceded **B.** Damper
C. Subsequent **D.** Arming
E. Static

Q.15 Which of the following words most appropriately fits the blank labelled (C)?

[SBI Clerk, 2021]

A. Public **B.** Radical
C. Politically **D.** Paranoia
E. Symbolic

Q.16 Which of the following words most appropriately fits the blank labelled (D)?

[SBI Clerk, 2021]

A. Warheads **B.** Separated
C. Simultaneously **D.** Hiding
E. Seek

Q.17 Which of the following words most appropriately fits the blank labelled (E)?

[SBI Clerk, 2021]

A. Expansion **B.** Retrospect
C. Behind **D.** Repressive
E. Subject

Ques (18-22):Direction: Rearrange the following five sentences/group of sentences (A), (B), (C), (D), and (E) in the proper sequence to form a meaningful paragraph; then answer the questions given below them.

(A) Bud-break — which is when trees leaf out — has undergone a change.

(B) This is why understanding the genetics of bud-break helps scientists modify or select crop varieties that can be more resilient to the climate threat.

(C) Several trees initiate bud-break too early or too late, which affects the harvest.

(D) Changing climate has transformed the time spring unfolds in front of us.

(E) Spring, for example, arrived earlier than usual in Kashmir this year due to higher temperatures in February and March.

Q.18 Which of the following should be the FIRST sentence after rearrangement?

[SBI PO, 2021], [IBPS Clerk, 2021]

A. (A) **B.** (C) **C.** (D) **D.** (B)
E. (E)

Q.19 Which of the following should be the SECOND sentence after rearrangement?

[SBI PO, 2021], [IBPS Clerk, 2021]

A. (A) **B.** (B) **C.** (C) **D.** (D)
E. (E)

Q.20 Which of the following should be the THIRD sentence after rearrangement?

[IBPS Clerk, 2021]

A. (A) **B.** (B) **C.** (D) **D.** (C)
E. (E)

Q.21 Which of the following should be the FOURTH sentence after rearrangement?

[IBPS Clerk, 2021]

A. (A) **B.** (B) **C.** (C) **D.** (D)
E. (E)

Q.22 Which of the following should be the LAST sentence after rearrangement?

[IBPS Clerk, 2021]

A. (A)   **B.** (B)   **C.** (C)   **D.** (D)
E. (E)

Ques (23-24):Direction: Three sentences are given. You need to find if they are grammatically correct or incorrect and mark the answer accordingly.

Q.23 P. From the first, he had a driving curiosity along with a bright mind.

Q. She took him on trips, bought him telescopes, microscopes, cameras, mounting materials, and other equipment, and helped him in many other ways.

R. Richie was my hole life after his father died when Richie was in third grade.

A. Only P is incorrect
B. Only Q is incorrect
C. Only P and Q are incorrect
D. Only R is incorrect
E. All are correct

Q.24 P. He broke open boxes and wrappers and fitted himself out with warm clothes

Q. Soon, with shoes, an overcoat, and a wide-brimmed hat, he became a fully dressed and visible person.

R. If only Griffin had managed to wake up in good time all may have been well.

A. Only P is incorrect
B. Only Q is incorrect
C. Both P and Q are incorrect
D. Only R is incorrect
E. All are correct

Q.25 Direction: Read the following sentence and determine whether there is an error in it. The error, if any, will be in one part of the sentence. If the sentence is error-free, select 'No Error' as your answer.

Samantha felt it was more better (A) if she chose the job in London (B) as compared to Dubai (C) as it was closer to home. (D)

A. (A)   **B.** (B)   **C.** (C)   **D.** (D)
E. No error

Ques (26-28):Direction: In the following question, two columns are given containing three phrases each. In the first column, phrases are A, B, and C, and in the second column, the phrases are D, E, and F. A phrase from the first column may or may not connect with a phrase from the second column to make a grammatically and contextually correct sentence. There are five options, four of which display the sequence(s) in which the phrases can be joined to form a grammatically and contextually correct sentence. If none of the options forms a correct sentence after combination, select 'None of these' as your answer.

Q.26

Column (1)	Column (2)
A. Local officials in 15 areas around the capital were also asked	D. was built to protect the land of the natives.

B. Volvo cars are understandably superior to their	E. to remove anything lying in the streets that could be used as projectiles.
C. Kohli remains the highest run scorer in	F. indeed needed but wasn't given to the poor in time.

[IBPS PO, 2021]

A. A-F
B. C-D
C. A-E
D. B-D
E. None of these

Q.27

Column (1)	Column (2)
A. We talk and plan and dream about nothing but	D. a big part of who I am and I have no desire to trade any of it away.
B. There were many people in his dream, and	E. excited to see her dressed up for the occasion
C. Everything I found in books that pleased me I retained in my memory	F. he thought he should remember them.

[IBPS PO, 2021]

A. B -E and C-F
B. A-E, B-F and C-D
C. A-F and C-D
D. B-F
E. None of these

Q.28

Column (1)	Column (2)
A. The Consumer Protection Act should be implemented more strictly	D. but there are many dark sides to it once you enter into this
B. The music industry is now saturated with too many singers	E. so that the businessmen become alert and are compelled to stop the unfair practice
C. The showbiz business is not all rosy as it seems	F. and the lifetime of a singer is hence reduced to one or two songs only

[IBPS PO, 2021]

A. A-F
B. B-F and C-D
C. A-E, B-F and C-D
D. B-F and C-E
E. None of these

Ques (29-30):Direction: In the following question, two columns are given containing three phrases each. In the first column, phrases are A, B, and C, and in the second column, the phrases are D, E, and F. A phrase from the first column may or may not connect with a phrase from the second column to make a grammatically and contextually correct sentence. There are five options, four of which display the sequence(s) in which the phrases can be joined to form a grammatically and contextually correct sentence. If none of the options forms a correct sentence after combination, select 'None of these' as your answer.

Q.29

Column (1)	Column (2)
(A) It was in his nature, and it was	(D) you at the conference tomorrow
(B) Sometimes we have to	(E) because they don't fit into

accept change,	someone else's plans
(C) It is indeed my pleasure to introduce	(F) something that wasn't going to change.

A. B-Eand C-F

B. A-E, B-F and C-D

C. A-F and C-D

D. B-F

E. None of these

Q.30

Column (1)	Column (2)
(A) The extreme positive and the extreme	(D) water to make their own food.
(B) There were	(E) a tiny squirrel.
(C) Plants need sunlight and	(F) negative are always similar.

A. A-D

B. A-E and B-F

C. A-F and C-D

D. B-D and C-E

E. None of these

Ques (31-40):Direction: Read the following passage carefully and answer the questions given below it.

Most people spend (on average) half of their day tapping away at their hand-held devices. Either, surfing the net or checking notifications. Facebook ranks the highest in all social networking platforms, followed by Twitter, Instagram and so forth.

Social media is addictive- which is why so many people are 'hooked'. Often referred to as Social networking addiction, this phrase is often used to describe someone who spends too much time on Facebook, Twitter, Instagram and other channels. A blog post, Instagram post, tweet, or youtube video can be produced easily by anyone and shared, which can then be viewed by millions for free. Psychologists and scientists have now taken the time to study social media in terms of why they believe it interferes with aspects of our daily life.There is no official medical term that identifies addiction and social networking. It cannot be deemed as a disease or disorder as the cases are not severe and the habit can easily be maintained or prevented. Furthermore, instead of spending long periods of time on social media, we dip into and out of these sites all day long. We check for updates from friends and family as well as news and information. However, the behavior associated with the excessive use of these channels has become the subject of much public and sociological debate.We actively post, like, comment and share personal posts. Not only that, we tend to share and reshare expressions (of either negative or positive) contagiously. But, why?

Scientists believed some years ago that, dopamine was simply a pleasure chemical in the brain. Recent studies have shown that; dopamine actually produces the desire in people to 'want' by drawing out the need for us to -seek and search. Creating the ultimate drive to find what is that what we want.

Dopamine is spontaneous. It's stimulated by unpredictability and small bits of information as well as reward cues which are the same conditions that social media presents to all users. In addition, the pull of dopamine is so strong that recent studies have shown that tweeting, for example, can be harder to resist than cigarettes and alcohol!

Researchers at Chicago University studied the effects of social media. They concluded quite quickly that people presented higher levels of addiction to social media than the need to smoke or drink. Media cravings ranked higher.

And, let's not forget oxytocin, many call it the cuddle chemical because the brain releases pleasure chemicals that transpire usually when you kiss and hug- or tweet. It is also known as the hormone that builds the strong yet unique bond between mothers and their babies. Oxytocin is now regarded as the human stimulant of empathy, generosity, trust, and more. These are factors which many advertisers and marketers play on when promoting a brand or business over social media.

Nevertheless, problems have arisen most commonly with school kids - whereby mobile phone devices have been confiscated because exam results have fallen severely due to lack of attention on homework or studies. Schools in many westernized countries have had to take drastic action - banning smartphones, iPad and most portable devices from school premises- as it is claimed to be a huge distraction. Whereas, other schools use it for educational purposes and as a rewards system for their pupils.

Research has also indicated unsurprisingly that Facebook is the most common activity that university students switch to, when studying. Worryingly, it has also found that those who most engage in this type of internet browsing tend to have lower levels of educational achievement.

Also, there have been many cases of students posting or sharing content that is unethical, which has caused parents and academic institutions to limit the use of these online networking channels.

Q.31 Which is the most common activity that university students switch to when studying?

[IBPS PO, 2021]

A. Youtube

B. Facebook

C. Twitter

D. Twitter

E. All of the above

Q.32 Why is there no real medical term that identifies addiction and social networking?

[IBPS PO, 2021]

A. Research is not yet done on the subject

B. It cannot be deemed as a disease or disorder as cases are not severe

C. The habit can easily be maintained or prevented

D. (A) and (B)

E. (B) and (C)

Q.33 What stands true about Dopamine in the present scenario?

[IBPS PO, 2021]

A. It creates the ultimate drive to find what is that what we want.

B. It's stimulated by unpredictability and small bits of information as well as reward cues.

C. Dopamine was simply a pleasure chemical in the brain.

D. (A) and (B)

Q.63 Find the total number of women who visited the zoo on Sunday, Friday and Saturday.

[IBPS Clerk, 2021]

A. 135
B. 435
C. 335
D. 235
E. None of these

Q.64 What is the average number of women who visited the zoo on Tuesday and Saturday?

[IBPS Clerk, 2021]

A. 75
B. 65
C. 95
D. 85
E. 55

Q.65 Find the ratio of men who came on Sunday to the total number of men who came on Friday and Saturday together

[IBPS Clerk, 2021]

A. $10:57$
B. $57:10$
C. $47:20$
D. $20:47$
E. None of these

Q.66 The number of men who visited the zoo on Sunday and Tuesday together is approximately what percent more or less than the number of women who visited the zoo on Friday and Saturday together?

[IBPS Clerk, 2021]

A. 37% more
B. 37% less
C. 47% more
D. 47% less
E. None of these

Q.67 Find the difference between the total number of women who visited the zoo on Sunday and Saturday together and the total number of men who visited the zoo on Tuesday and Friday together.

[IBPS Clerk, 2021]

A. 150
B. 160
C. 140
D. 180
E. None of these

Q.68 The sum of the radius and height of a cylinder is $19m$. The total surface area of the cylinder is $1672m^2$. What is the volume of the cylinder?

[IBPS Clerk, 2021]

A. $3080m^3$
B. $2940m^3$
C. $3420m^3$
D. $2860m^3$
E. None of these

Ques (69-70):Direction: What will come in the place of the question mark '?' in the following question?

Q.69 $? \times 22 = 2740 \div 20 - [\left(\frac{100}{9}\right)\% \text{ of } 729 - 10]$

[SBI Clerk, 2021]

A. 2
B. 5
C. 3
D. 4
E. None of these

Q.70 $?^{\frac{2}{3}} = 64\% \text{ of } 150 + 7 \times 3 - 9^2$

[SBI Clerk, 2021]

A. 1296
B. 36
C. 36
D. 216
E. None of these

Test of Reasoning

Ques (71-72):Direction: In the following question, Few statements are given which are followed by some conclusions. According to the given statements, which conclusion is/are follows?

Q.71 Statements: $P \geq A \geq B > C; E < F \leq G = C$
Conclusions:
I. $B > F$
II. $P \geq G$

A. Only II follows
B. Only I follows
C. Both I and II follow
D. Either I or II follow
E. Neither I nor II follows

Q.72 Statements:
$R = S, K < R, L < K$
Conclusions:
I) $S > L$
II) $K < S$

A. Only conclusion I is follow
B. Only conclusion II is follows
C. Either conclusion I or II is follows
D. Neither conclusion I nor II is follows
E. Both conclusions I and II are follow

Ques (73-77):Directions: Study the following information carefully and answer the given questions.

In a certain code language 'hi ta mi si' means 'raghu plays rugby today', 'gi ti ta ha' means 'raghu goes to school', 'si ki ha li' means 'tapan plays in school'.

Q.73 Which of the following means 'in' in that code language?
A. ki
B. li
C. ti
D. si
E. Either (A) or (B)

Q.74 Code 'ha' is for which word in the given language?
A. raghu
B. school
C. to
D. goes
E. None of the above

Q.75 What would be the code for 'tapan plays Rugby in school today'?
A. ki si mi li ha hi
B. ta si mi li ha hi
C. ta ki li hi ha gi
D. li si ta li ha si
E. ki si hi gi ha hi

Q.76 What would be the code for the word 'goes'?
A. gi
B. ti

C. ta   **D.** ha
E. Either (A) or (B)

Q.77 Code 'si ta li ha' is for which of the following sentence in the given language?
A. tapan plays in school
B. tapan goes to school
C. raghu plays in school
D. raghu plays with tapan
E. tapan goes to raghu

Ques (78-83):Directions: Study the following information carefully and answer the questions based on it.

Eight people L, M, N, O, P, Q, R and S are sitting around a circular table. Each of them works in different banks viz., Canara, Bank of India (BOI), Central Bank of India (CBI), Bank of Baroda (BOB), Indian Bank (IB), Union Bank of India (UBI), Oriental Bank of Commerce (OBC) and Dena Bank (DB), not necessarily in the same order. Four of them are facing towards the center while others face outside the center.

O is third to the right of S. The one who is working in Indian Bank is to the immediate left of O, who is not working in Dena Bank. R is fourth to the left of Q. Neither R nor Q is an immediate neighbor of O. L is working in Canara Bank and sits third to the right of the one who is working in Indian Bank. The one who is working in Union Bank of India sits second to the left of the one who is working in Canara Bank. The one who is working in Oriental Bank of Commerce sits second to the right of O. The one who works in Bank of India sits exactly between L and Q and adjacent to them. The one who works in the Central Bank of India sits second to the right of the one who works in the Bank of India. P sits third to the left of L. N is facing the center and is to the immediate right of both L and Q. M and R faces the same direction. L is facing the opposite direction of N.

Q.78 In which bank does O works?
A. Oriental bank of Commerce
B. Bank of India
C. Canara Bank
D. Bank of Baroda
E. Union Bank of India

Q.79 Who is sitting to the immediate left of the one who works in the Indian Bank?
A. R   **B.** L   **C.** M   **D.** N
E. O

Q.80 Who is sitting opposite to Q?
A. R   **B.** O   **C.** L   **D.** N
E. M

Q.81 In which bank do L works?
A. Oriental bank of Commerce
B. Bank of India
C. Canara Bank
D. Bank of Baroda
E. Union Bank of India

Q.82 Who is sitting to the immediate left of the one who works in the Oriental Bank of Commerce?

A. R   **B.** L   **C.** M   **D.** N
E. O

Q.83 In which company S works?
A. Oriental Bank of Commerce
B. Indian Bank
C. Dena Bank
D. Central Bank of India
E. None of these

Ques (84-86):Directions: Study the information given below carefully and answer the questions that follow.

Two buses, F and G starts from their respective terminals D and H respectively. F goes 4 km north before turning right and travelling 6 km east to reach city T. From there it goes 3 km north then turns left and travels 4 km more to finally stop at city U. Bus G starts from terminal H goes 9 km north to reach city S. From there it turns left to travel 4 km more before turning south and travelling 2 km more to reach city A. Terminal H is 10 km to the east of terminal D.

Q.84 What is total distance covered by the bus F?
A. 15 km   **B.** 13 km
C. 17 km   **D.** 19 km
E. None of these

Q.85 If bus P is standing 2 km to the west of terminal point H, what is distance between point D and bus P?
A. 15 km   **B.** 13 km
C. 17 km   **D.** 19 km
E. None of these

Q.86 According to the route map, which city they both have to cross?
A. T
B. U
C. A
D. S
E. They have no common city

Q.87 Direction: In the question below are given some statements followed by two conclusions numbered I and II. You have to take the given statements to be true even if they seem to be at variance with commonly known facts. Read all the conclusions and then decide which of the given conclusions logically follows from the given statements disregarding commonly known facts.
Statements:
All ice cream is chocolate.
Some mango is vanilla.
Some ice cream is vanilla.
Conclusions:
I. Some ice cream being vanilla is a possibility.
II. Some mango is chocolate.
A. Only conclusion I follow
B. Only conclusion II follows
C. Either conclusion I or II follows
D. Neither conclusion I nor II follows.

E. Both conclusions I and II follow

Q.88 Direction: In the question below are given some statements followed by three conclusions numbered I, II and III. You have to take the given statements to be true even if they seem to be at variance with commonly known facts. Read all the conclusions and then decide which of the given conclusions logically follows from the given statements disregarding commonly known facts.

Statements:

All Clocks are Digital.

Some Watches are Calculator.

No Clock is a Watch.

Conclusions:

I. All Watches being Digital is a possibility.

II. No calculator is a Clock.

III. Some Digitals are Clocks.

A. Only II follows

B. Only III follows

C. Only I and III follows

D. Either II or III follows

E. None of these

Q.89 Direction: In the question below are given some statements followed by two conclusions numbered I and II. You have to take the given statements to be true even if they seem to be at variance with commonly known facts. Read all the conclusions and then decide which of the given conclusions logically follows from the given statements disregarding commonly known facts.

Statements:

All chairs are locks.

All locks are key.

Some key are box.

Conclusions:

I. Some chairs are key.

II. Some box are chairs.

A. Only conclusion I follow

B. Only conclusion II follows

C. Either conclusion I or II follows

D. Neither conclusion I nor II follows

E. Both conclusions I and II follow

Q.90 Direction: In the questions given below statements are followed by some conclusions. You have to take the given statements to be True even if they seem to be at variance from commonly known facts. Read all the conclusions and then decide which of the given conclusions logically follows from the given statements disregarding commonly known facts.

Statement:

Frequently Silver is Black.

None Black is White.

Occasionally Gold is Silver.

More of the White is Yellow.

Conclusion:

I) some Yellow is not Black.

II) Few silver is black.

III) All White can never be Silver.

A. Only III and II follows

B. Only I follows

C. Only I and II follows

D. All follows

E. Only II follows

Q.91 Direction: In the question below are given some statements followed by some conclusions. You have to take given statements to be true even if they seem to be at variance with commonly known facts. Read all the conclusions and then decide which of the given conclusions logically follows from the given statements disregarding commonly known facts.

Statements:

Some Painter are Artist.

Only few brush are paints.

All artists are paints.

No frame is Paints.

Conclusions:

I. Some Paints are Painter.

II. Some Brush are not Paint.

III. Some Brush are Artist.

A. Only I and II follows

B. Only I and Either II or III follows

C. Either II or III follows

D. Only III follows

E. Only I follows

Ques (92-94):Direction: In the following question assuming the given statements to be true, find which of the conclusion among the given conclusions is/are definitely true and then give your answers accordingly.

Q.92 Statements:

K ≤ D, H ≥ R < P < K

Conclusions:

I. R < D

II. H > K

III. D > P

[IBPS SO HR Officer, 2019], [IBPS SO Marketing Officer, 2019], [IBPS SO Law Officer, 2019]

A. Only conclusion III is True

B. Either conclusion I and II is True

C. Only conclusion I is True

D. Neither conclusion I nor II is True

E. Only conclusions I and III are True

Q.93 Statement: U < V, W > X ≥ Y, Y = V

Conclusion:

I. X > V

II. U < W

[IBPS SO HR Officer, 2019], [IBPS SO Marketing Officer, 2019], [IBPS SO Law Officer, 2019]

A. Both I and II are true

B. None is true

C. Only I is true
D. Only II is true
E. Either I or II is true

Q.94 Statements: X > P < Z, P < J = O > M
Conclusions:
I. P > M
II. X < J

[IBPS SO HR Officer, 2019], [IBPS SO Marketing Officer, 2019], [IBPS SO Law Officer, 2019]

A. Only I is true
B. Only II is true
C. Both I and II are true
D. Neither I nor II is true
E. Either I or II is true

Ques (95-100):Direction: Study the following information to answer the given Question.

Seven boxes K, D, S, M, G, C and N are kept one above the other, not necessarily in the same order.

The box of N is three boxes above the box of K. The box of G is the topmost box. The box of C is just above the box of N. The box of D is just below box of S. There is one box between the box of D and the box of M.

Q.95 Which is the bottommost box?

[IBPS Clerk, 2021]

A. D   **B.** N   **C.** S   **D.** C
E. M

Q.96 How many boxes are above the box of K?

[IBPS Clerk, 2021]

A. One   **B.** Two   **C.** Three   **D.** Four
E. Five

Q.97 Which among the following box is just above C?

[IBPS Clerk, 2021]

A. K   **B.** N
C. G   **D.** S
E. None of these

Q.98 How many boxes are there between M and N?

[IBPS Clerk, 2021]

A. One   **B.** Two   **C.** Three   **D.** Five
E. None

Q.99 Which of the following pair does not belong to the group?

[IBPS Clerk, 2021]

A. S - C   **B.** M - D   **C.** G - C   **D.** D - N
E. K - S

Q.100 How many boxes are there below the box of N?
A. 2   **B.** 3   **C.** 4   **D.** 6
E. 5

// Smart Answer Sheet //

Correct Indicates percentage of students who answered questions correctly.

Skipped Indicates percentage of students who skipped questions.

Q.	Ans.	Correct / Skipped
1	B	35.52 % / 27.76 %
2	A	23.88 % / 26.57 %
3	D	21.79 % / 21.2 %
4	E	11.94 % / 18.21 %
5	D	43.28 % / 26.57 %
6	E	41.49 % / 26.57 %
7	E	24.48 % / 25.37 %
8	C	35.52 % / 26.57 %
9	B	54.63 % / 25.97 %
10	D	51.64 % / 22.69 %
11	C	47.16 % / 27.17 %
12	B	47.46 % / 27.76 %
13	C	45.97 % / 31.34 %
14	A	35.22 % / 32.24 %
15	D	35.22 % / 30.45 %
16	C	42.09 % / 31.64 %
17	A	37.01 % / 31.95 %
18	C	24.78 % / 34.03 %
19	A	6.27 % / 34.33 %
20	D	14.03 % / 36.12 %
21	E	8.06 % / 35.82 %
22	B	25.07 % / 36.72 %
23	D	29.25 % / 25.38 %
24	D	9.85 % / 26.27 %
25	A	37.91 % / 28.66 %
26	C	53.13 % / 24.18 %
27	D	34.93 % / 24.77 %
28	C	45.97 % / 24.48 %
29	C	45.37 % / 27.76 %
30	C	58.51 % / 28.95 %
31	B	30.75 % / 32.24 %
32	E	28.06 % / 30.75 %
33	D	16.72 % / 29.25 %
34	A	8.06 % / 31.34 %
35	D	13.13 % / 30.45 %
36	E	13.13 % / 32.24 %
37	E	29.25 % / 28.36 %
38	E	34.03 % / 26.27 %
39	D	43.88 % / 32.24 %
40	A	31.94 % / 31.34 %
41	E	35.82 % / 29.55 %
42	C	43.58 % / 24.18 %
43	A	32.54 % / 26.27 %
44	A	30.75 % / 25.97 %
45	D	8.66 % / 20.59 %
46	B	27.16 % / 23.88 %
47	A	36.72 % / 23.58 %
48	C	24.18 % / 31.34 %
49	C	17.61 % / 30.75 %
50	A	12.54 % / 31.04 %
51	D	27.16 % / 27.77 %
52	C	21.19 % / 28.36 %
53	D	48.06 % / 18.51 %
54	B	56.12 % / 18.81 %
55	B	57.61 % / 17.61 %
56	A	55.52 % / 18.81 %
57	B	62.99 % / 18.5 %
58	B	62.39 % / 18.21 %
59	A	19.4 % / 24.18 %
60	B	8.36 % / 24.77 %
61	E	14.93 % / 24.17 %
62	B	38.51 % / 20.89 %
63	C	43.28 % / 31.05 %
64	D	42.39 % / 28.95 %
65	A	43.88 % / 29.55 %
66	B	26.27 % / 31.04 %
67	D	37.61 % / 31.05 %
68	A	7.16 % / 31.65 %
69	C	43.88 % / 25.97 %
70	D	23.88 % / 26.27 %
71	B	45.67 % / 21.49 %
72	E	52.84 % / 21.19 %
73	E	48.66 % / 25.97 %
74	B	56.42 % / 26.86 %
75	A	37.31 % / 24.18 %
76	E	51.34 % / 25.67 %
77	C	48.06 % / 25.07 %
78	D	11.64 % / 31.05 %
79	E	12.84 % / 25.37 %
80	A	13.73 % / 32.24 %

Q.	Ans.	Correct		Q.	Ans.	Correct		Q.	Ans.	Correct		Q.	Ans.	Correct		Q.	Ans.	Correct
		Skipped				Skipped				Skipped				Skipped				Skipped
81	C	16.12 %		85	E	17.91 %		89	A	42.39 %		93	D	39.1 %		97	C	60.3 %
		29.25 %				28.66 %				21.79 %				23.89 %				22.69 %
82	D	2.69 %		86	C	12.84 %		90	C	20.9 %		94	D	57.61 %		98	C	51.04 %
		34.62 %				28.65 %				26.56 %				23.58 %				23.89 %
83	D	12.54 %		87	D	27.16 %		91	A	31.64 %		95	E	50.15 %		99	C	52.84 %
		26.27 %				23.88 %				23.58 %				24.18 %				23.28 %
84	C	27.46 %		88	C	40.0 %		92	E	53.73 %		96	E	52.54 %		100	C	57.01 %
		29.26 %				22.69 %				23.28 %				23.58 %				25.08 %

Performance Analysis

Avg. Score (%)	29.0%
Toppers Score (%)	85.0%
Your Score	

//Hints and Solutions//

1. 'Then' is an adverb that is used to refers to a particular time period. Example: It was then that Ashley decided to leave her job and move to another city.

'Than' is a conjunction that means 'used to introduce the second element in a comparison. Example: Saurabh was richer than Mayuri and yet they led a very happy life.

The current sentence compares 2 people, Amisha and Samuel in terms of their cricket playing skills.

The sentence is not referring to any particular time period and thus the use of the adverb 'then' does not seem correct.

Thus, the adverb 'then' needs to be replaced with the conjunction 'than' in order to make it grammatically correct.

Thus, the correct sentence is: 'When it comes to playing cricket, Amisha is better than Samuel yet no one selects for the team.'

Hence, the correct option is (B).

2. In the given sentence, the error in the part is the inappropriate use of the noun number.

Nouns are words used to name person, place, animal, thing, emotion, or state.

In the given statement, the incorrect plural form of 'brother-in-law' is being used.

Compound nouns are made plural by adding 's' to the main word.

For example: Commander-in-chief - Commanders-in-chief, brother-in-law - brothers-in-law etc.

Therefore, we will replace 'brother-in-laws' with 'brothers-in-law' to make the sentence grammatically correct.

The correct sentence will be: 'The brothers-in-law were very helpful and supportive to their choices.'

Hence, the correct option is (A).

3. The word "Revolving" is out of context here as the correct word should be "Revolting".

Meaning of "Revolting" and "Revolving":

- Revolting: causing intense disgust; disgusting.
- Revolving: move in a circle on a central axis.

Hence, the correct option is (D).

4. The given sentence has no grammatically incorrect words.

The meanings of words:

- Detrimental - obviously harmful
- Application - a formal request to be considered for a position or to be allowed to do or have something, submitted to an authority, institution, or organization.
- Operators - a person who operates equipment or a machine.
- Dough - a mixture that consists essentially of flour or meal and a liquid and is stiff enough to knead or roll.

Hence, the correct option is (E).

5. Option (D) is the best fit given blanks in sentences.

The boost to the Infrastructure sector was **anticipated** ahead of the Union Budget and does play a key role in **reviving** demand in the economy.

What happened ahead of the Union Budget is mentioned in the given sentence.

- The meaning of the word 'inspired' is 'to motivate' and it is not making the sentence contextually meaningful. So, we cannot choose the word 'inspired' for the first blank.
- The meaning of the word 'erect' is 'to build'. It is not appropriate for the first blank because the word is not making the sentence grammatically or contextually correct.
- The meaning of the word 'erased' is 'wiped out' and it is not appropriate for the first blank.
- The meaning of the word 'anticipated' is 'expected or predicted' and we can say that something was predicted ahead of the budget.
- The meaning of the word 'reviving' is 'to restore to life' and it is appropriate for the second blank.

Hence, the correct option is (D).

6. Option (E) is the best fit given blanks in sentences. Democracy needs to be **preserved** not for perpetuation of power but for the perpetuation of democratic **values**.

The given sentence is about democracy.

- The meaning of the word 'abandoned' is 'left'. It is clear that the word 'abandoned' is not suitable for the first blank.
- The meaning of the word 'related' is 'connected' and it is not making any meaningful sentence.
- The meaning of the word 'requested' is 'asked politely' and it is not relevant to the context. So we cannot choose this word for the first blank.
- The meaning of the word 'endured' is 'suffered patiently'.
- The word 'endure' is not making any meaningful sentence. So, we cannot choose this word for the first blank.
- The meaning of the word 'preserved' is 'maintained or took care of'. The word 'preserved' is appropriate for the first blank because democracy should be protected.
- The meaning of the word 'values' is 'moral principles'. The word 'values' is appropriate for the second blank because democracy should be preserved for democratic values.

Hence, the correct option is (E).

7. Option (E) is the best fit given blanks in sentences. Only MSMEs are well placed with **competency**, flexibility, local market understanding, and **experience** to bring about this rural revolution.

The given sentence discusses certain features of MSMEs.

- The meaning of the word 'apathetic' is 'showing no interest or enthusiasm'. The word 'apathetic' is not an appropriate word to describe MSMEs. So, we cannot choose this word for the first blank.

- The meaning of the word 'dormant' is 'sleeping or asleep'. The word 'dormant' cannot be used here to describe MSMEs.

- The meaning of the word 'progression' is 'the process of moving towards a more advanced state'. The word 'progression' is not appropriate for the first blank because it is a process.

- The meaning of the word 'familiarity' is 'knowledge of something'. The word 'familiarity' is not a trait of MSMEs. So, we cannot choose this word.

- The meaning of the word 'competency' is 'ability to do something efficiently'. The word 'competency' is an appropriate feature of MSMEs. So, we can choose this word for the first blank.

- The meaning of the word 'experience' is 'practical contact with facts or events'. We can say that the word 'experience' is another trait of MSMEs.

Hence, the correct option is (E).

8. Option (C) is the best fit given blanks in sentences. Growing **consciousness** towards environment protection and the quest for an alternative, clean energy has created the right **push** for the electric vehicle industry in India.

The given sentence talks about the impact of different factors on the electric vehicle industry in India.

- The meaning of the word 'consciousness' is 'the state of being aware of'.

- The word 'consciousness' is relevant to the context as people are being aware of 'environment protection'. So, it is suitable for the first blank.

- The meaning of the word 'push' is 'the act of moving something'.

- The factors which are mentioned in the sentence have pushed forward the 'electric vehicle industry in India'.

- Therefore, 'push' is the correct word for the second blank.

Hence, the correct option is (C).

9. Option (B) is the best fit given blanks in sentences. In order to **strengthen** the quality and effectiveness of internal audit system, the RBI **issued** guidelines on RBIA system for selecting non bank leaders and UCBs.

The given sentence mentions what did RBI do for the internal audit system.

- We need a verb for the first blank and the word 'strong' is an adjective.

- The meaning of the word 'strengthen' is 'to make stronger' is appropriate for the first blank because RBI may have taken some action to strengthen the internal audit system.

- The meaning of the word 'issued' is 'released' and guidelines are released or issued. So, the word 'issued' is appropriate for the second blank.

Hence, the correct option is (B).

10. The words 'jobless' and 'never' have been placed incorrectly, they have to be replaced with each other to make the sentence meaningful and contextually correct.

- Jobless means unemployed.

- Never means at no time; not ever.

The correct sentence will be: Smita was never happy with the conditions of the women in her district as most were poor and jobless, so she planned to do something.

Hence, the correct option is (D).

11. The meaning of the given words:

- Continues: persist in an activity or process.

- Repent: feel or express sincere regret or remorse about one's wrongdoing or sin.

- Past: gone by in time and no longer existing.

- Apology: a regretful acknowledgment of an offence or failure

Look at the given sentence in the following manner:

- Taylor's husband ______(A) to _____(B) for cheating in the _____(C), but she isn't sure that his _____(D) are sincere.

- In (B) husband repent and in (D) continues for cheating both are incorrect phrases.

- The sentence tells us that her husband regrets cheating on her but she isn't sure that his apologies are sincere.

- So, (A) and (B) should be interchanged to make the sentence correct.

Therefore the correct sentence is: Taylor's husband continues to repent for cheating in the past, but she isn't sure that his apologies are sincere.

Hence, the correct option is (C).

12. The meaning of the given words:

- Officers: people who hold a position of authority

- Protest: a statement or action expressing disapproval of or objection to something

- Populace: the people living in a particular country or area.

- Keep: to have or to retain possession of.

Look at the given sentence in the following manner:

- More police _____(A) are needed
  to ____(B) the _____(C) calm during
  the _____(D) march.
- In (B) protest the populace and in (D) keep march both
  are incorrect phrases.
- The sentence tells us that during the protest march,
  many police officers were needed to keep people
  calm.
- So, (B) and (D) should be interchanged to make the
  sentence correct.

Therefore the correct sentence is: More police officers are needed
to keep the populace calm during the protest march.

Hence, the correct option is (B).

13. The sentence mentions 'tense and dynamic period that
affected society on all levels', therefore, ruling-out words like
'significant' and 'advantage' as these terms do not fit the context.

The word 'successfully' disturbs the meaning of the sentence.

The word 'beginning' that means 'to start' fits the blank best.

Therefore making 'beginning' is the best fit to fill the blank.

Hence, the correct option is (C).

14. The meaning of the given words:

- Preceded: to happen, come or go before
  somebody/something.
- Damper: a little wet
- Subsequent: coming after or later
- Arming: the act of taking arms or providing with arms
- Static: not moving, changing or developing

The word 'damper' cannot be used with respect to 'war', as
mentioned in the sentence.

The words 'subsequent' and 'arming' are grammatically incorrect
and therefore making 'preceded' as the best fit to fill the blank.

Hence, the correct option is (A).

15. The sentence mentions 'Communism and Democracy', which
should be used as a hint while picking up the word fitting the
blank.

As the sentence indicates a negative remark, 'public' and 'radical'
gets omitted.

The word 'politically' is grammatically incorrect.

The word 'paranoia' fits the blank along with appropriately
conveying the meaning of the sentence too.

Therefore making 'Paranoia' is the best fit to fill the blank.

Hence, the correct option is (D).

16. The words 'separated' and 'hiding' are grammatically
incorrect.

The word 'warheads' do not make a strong option to fit the blank
as it doesn't fit the context of the sentence.

The word 'simultaneously' makes the best fit for the blank as it
conveys the most appropriate meaning.

Hence, the correct option is (C).

17. The words 'behind' and 'repressive' gets omitted due to being
grammatically incorrect.

The word 'retrospect' does not fit the context of the sentence.

'Expansion' not just carries the required message fitting the sense
of the statement, but also make the sentence meaningful.

Hence, the correct option is (A).

Ques (18-22): The given passage is about the effect of changing
climate on the time spring unfolds.

- The first sentence is (D) because it mentions that the
  time spring unfolds in front of us has changed because
  of changing climate.
- The second sentence is (A) because it mentions that
  the time when the trees leaf out is no longer the same.
- The third sentence is (C) because it mentions that the
  harvest is being affected by the bud-break which is
  either too early or too late.
- The fourth sentence is (E) because it gives an example
  of the early arrival of spring.
- The last sentence is (B) because it concludes the
  passage by mentioning the way the scientists can deal
  with this issue.

After arranging the five sentences in proper sequence:

Changing climate has transformed the time spring unfolds in
front of us. Bud-break — which is when trees leaf out - has
undergone a change. Several trees initiate bud-break too early or
too late, which affects the harvest. Spring, for example, arrived
earlier than in in due to higher temperatures in February and
March. This is why understanding the genetics of bud-break
helps scientists modify or select crop varieties that can be more
resilient to the climate threat.

So, the correct sequence is DACEB.

18. (D) should be the first sentence after rearrangement.

Hence, the correct option is (C).

19. (A) should be the second sentence after rearrangement.

Hence, the correct option is (A).

20. (C) should be the third sentence after rearrangement.

Hence, the correct option is (D).

21. (E) should be the fourth sentence after rearrangement.

Hence, the correct option is (E).

22. (B) should be the last sentence after rearrangement.

Hence, the correct option is (B).

23. In the sentence R,

- The word hole does not fit the context of the sentence.

- It should be replaced with the word 'whole'

- hole means: a hollow place in a solid body or surface.

- Whole means: all of; entire.

- Therefore the correct sentence is,

- Richie was my whole life after his father died when Richie was in third grade.

So, only R is incorrect

Hence, the correct option is (D).

24. In sentence R,

- May should be replaced with might.

- There is a slight difference between the usage of may and might

- May is used to express what is possible, factual, or could be factual. For example, He may lose his job.

- Might is used to expressing what is hypothetical, counterfactual, or remotely possible. For example, If you hurry, you might get there on time.

- The correct word that should be used here is, might.

- Therefore, the correct sentence is,

- If only Griffin had managed to wake up in good time all might have been well.

Hence, the correct option is (D).

25. The given sentence is in the past tense as can be seen from the use of the verbs 'felt' and 'chose' in the past tense.

'Better' is an adjective which means 'of a more excellent or effective type or quality'.

By referring to something as 'more' in a certain quality than something else automatically means it is a comparison.

Example: Dean was better than his brother at hunting.

'More' is also a determiner which means 'a greater or additional amount or degree of'

Example: Patrick was more talented at carrom than Stewart.

Both of them mean the same thing and thus using both of them at the same time becomes redundant.

Thus, the 'more' needs to be removed from the sentence in order to make the sentence grammatically correct.

Thus, the correct sentence: 'Samantha felt it was better if she chose the job in London as compared to Dubai as it was closer to home.'

Hence, the correct option is (A).

26. We need to join the sentence segments in column 1 with those in column 2 to create sentences that are contextually and grammatically correct. Let us see how the parts of the sentence can join.

- PART A joins with PART E to make a contextually correct sentence. Part A states that the local officials were asked to do something and Part E explains what

they were asked to do.(remove anything lying in the streets that could be used as projectiles)

- Rest of the combinations don't make sense.

Hence, the correct option is (C).

27. We need to join the sentence segments in column 1 with those in column 2 to create sentences that are contextually and grammatically correct. Let us see how the parts of the sentence can join.

- PART B & PART F can be used to form a single sentence as PART B talks of a dream and PART F justifies it by stating that he should remember them.

- PART A has the subject 'we', but none of the options in column 2 actually have a plural subject.

- PART C is a complete sentence itself and would require a conjunction in the next part. PART B has a conjunction but B and C can't be formed together.(both belong to the same column)

- PART B has a conjunction which means the next part of B should start with a noun or pronoun. PART F stars with the pronoun 'he'. So, B & F go together.

Hence, the correct option is (D).

28. We need to join the sentence segments in column 1 with those in column 2 to create sentences that are contextually and grammatically correct. Let us see how the parts of the sentence can join.

- Part A and Part E: Part A talks about the strict implementation of The Consumer Protection Act and Part E justifies its implementation by saying "so that the businessmen become alert and are compelled to stop unfair trade practice". Hence, these two fragments can be combined together to form a sentence both meaningful and grammatically correct. This pair is correct.

- Part B talks about the music industry being saturated with too many singers and Part F shows the effect of having so many singers by saying that the lifetime of a singer is hence reduced to one or two songs only. These two fragments can also be combined in order to form a meaningful statement both contextually and grammatically correct.

- Part C talks about the showbiz business not being as rosy as it seems and Part D specifies the dark sides to it once you enter into this. Thus, These two fragments can be combined to form a grammatically and contextually correct sentence.

Hence, the correct option is (C).

29. We need to join the sentence segments in column 1 with those in column 2 to create sentences that are contextually and grammatically correct. Let us see how the parts of the sentence can join.

- When we use the verb 'introduce', we need to mention what is to be introduced. Both 'something' and 'you' can be introduced. But, 'you' is more appropriate as introductions are generally done for humans rather

than some unchangeable entity. So, Part C & Part D go together.

- When we say 'in his nature', we are actually describing a distinct character trait, which is more unlikely to change. Also, character traits don't 'fit into someone's plans. So, Part A & Part F go together.

- Part B & Part E, even though when joined, will be grammatically correct, but they do not make any sense. ("Sometimes we have to accept change because they don't fit into someone else's plans".)

Hence, the correct option is (C).

30. We need to join the sentence segments in column 1 with those in column 2 to create sentences that are contextually and grammatically correct. Let us see how the parts of the sentence can join.

- In Part A there is a repetition of the word 'extreme'. It is used as an adjective and describes the noun 'positive'. So, to maintain continuity, part A should be followed by part F, which starts with the noun 'negative'. So, A-F.

- Part B is a phrase that is plural(were). It is being used to indicate the existence of something. But the only segment that can meaningfully join with part B is part E which is singular(a tiny squirrel) in nature. So, grammatically, they cannot be joined.

- Part C talks about plants needing sunlight and so it should be joined with part D that mentions what else plants need and why. So, C-D.

Hence, the correct option is (C).

31. According to the passage, "Facebook is the most common activity that university students switch to when studying."

Hence, the correct option is (B).

32. According to the passage, "There is no official medical term that identifies addiction and social networking because it cannot be deemed as a disease or disorder as cases are not severe and the habit can easily be maintained or prevented."

Hence, the correct option is (E).

33. According to the passage, "Recent studies have shown that; dopamine actually produces the desire in people to 'want' by drawing out the need for us to -seek and search. Creating the ultimate drive to find what is that what we want"

According to the passage, "It's stimulated by unpredictability and small bits of information as well as reward cues which are the same conditions that social media presents to all users"

So, it is concluded that statement (A) and (B) is true.

Hence, the correct option is (D).

34. According to the passage, "Many call it the cuddle chemical because the brain releases pleasure chemicals that transpire usually when you kiss and hug- or tweet."

So, it is concluded that oxytocin regarded as the cuddle chemical because the brain releases pleasure chemicals that transpire usually when you kiss and hug- or tweet.

Hence, the correct option is (A).

35. The meaning of the given words:

- Contagiously: (an emotion, feeling, or attitude) likely to spread to and affect others

- Malignant: very virulent or infectious

- Assail: to criticize strongly

- Ambivalent: having mixed feelings or contradictory ideas about something or someone

- Arboreal: related to trees

- Cogent: clear, logical, and convincing

From the meanings of the given words, we can conclude that Malignant is the most appropriate synonym of contagiously.

Hence, the correct option is (D).

36. The meaning of the given words:

- Confiscated: to steal or seize

- Relinquish: voluntarily cease to keep or claim or give up

- Cognizant: having knowledge or awareness

- Covet: yearning to possess

- Expiate: to make amends or reparation for (guilt or wrongdoing)

- Pithy: terse and vigorously expressive

From the meanings of the given words, we can conclude that relinquish is the most appropriate antonym of confiscated.

Hence, the correct option is (E).

37. According to the passage, "Researchers at Chicago University studied the effects of social media. They concluded quite quickly that people presented higher levels of addiction to social media than the need to smoke or drink. Media cravings ranked higher."

Hence, the correct option is (E).

38. According to the passage, "Schools in many westernized countries have had to take drastic action- banning smartphones, iPad, and most portable devices from school premises- as it is claimed to be a huge distraction. Whereas, other schools use it for educational purposes and as a rewards system for their pupils."

Hence, the correct option is (E).

39. 'Social Networking Addiction' mean someone who spends too much time on social websites.

Hence, the correct option is (D).

40. The passage can be divided into four subheadings:

- It begins with the Science behind Social Addiction talking about how it interferes with the basic aspects of our life.

- It continues telling that there is no medical term that identifies addiction and social networking.

- Furthermore, it talks about Dopamine and Oxytocin and how they contribute to social media addiction.

- The passage ends with a brief discussion of addiction in students nowadays.

Thus, all these subsections can be put together into one major heading which would be 'The Psychology of Social Addiction'.

Hence, the correct option is (A).

41. Follow BODMAS rule to solve this question, as per the order given below,

Step-1- Parts of an equation enclosed in 'Brackets' must be solved first, and in the bracket,

Step-2- Any mathematical 'Of' or 'Exponent' must be solved next,

Step-3- Next, the parts of the equation that contain 'Division' and 'Multiplication' are calculated,

Step-4- Last but not least, the parts of the equation that contain 'Addition' and 'Subtraction' should be calculated.

Given expression is,

$$\left(7\frac{5}{2} + 4\frac{7}{2}\right) \div 7\frac{3}{2} = 11\frac{5}{3} - \frac{2}{3} - ?$$

$$\Rightarrow \left(\frac{19}{2} + \frac{15}{2}\right) \div \frac{17}{2} = \frac{38}{3} - \frac{2}{3} - ?$$

$$\Rightarrow 17 \times \frac{2}{17} = \frac{38}{3} - \frac{2}{3} - ?$$

$$\Rightarrow 2 = \frac{(38 - 2)}{3} - ?$$

$$\Rightarrow 2 = 12 - ?$$

$$? = 10$$

Hence, the correct option is (E).

42. Use the BODMAS rule to solve this question:

Given:

$$4\frac{2}{5} \div 1\frac{7}{15} + 5\frac{5}{3} \times 3\frac{3}{2} = ?$$

$$\Rightarrow \frac{22}{5} \div \frac{22}{15} + \frac{20}{3} \times \frac{9}{2} = ?$$

$$\Rightarrow \frac{22}{5} \times \frac{15}{22} + 10 \times 3 = ?$$

$$\Rightarrow 3 + 30 = 33 = ?$$

$\therefore$ The value of '?' is 33.

Hence, the correct option is (C).

43. Given:

First discount $= 20\%$

Second discount $= 30\%$

Third discount $= 50\%$

Marked price $=$ Rs. 2000

So, Revised Price $=$ Marked Price $\times$ $\left(1 - \frac{\text{(Discount Percentage)}}{100}\right)$

Revised Price $= 2000 \times \left(1 - \frac{20}{100}\right) = 2000 \times 0.8 = 1600$

New Revised Price $=$ Revised Price $\times \left(1 - \frac{30}{100}\right) = 1600 \times 0.7 = 1120$

Final Selling Price $=$ New Revised Price $\times \left(1 - \frac{50}{100}\right) = 1120 \times 0.5 = 560$

$\therefore$ Selling price of a pair of jeans $=$ Rs. 560

Hence, the correct option is (A).

44. Given,

The ratio of income of A and B $= 4:3$

The ratio of annual expenses of A and B $= 3:2$

Savings $=$ Rs. 60000 each

As we know,

Income $=$ Expenditure $+$ Saving

Let the income of A and B be $4x$ and $3x$ respectively.

Their expenditure $= \frac{(4x-60000)}{(3x-60000)} = \frac{3}{2}$

$$\Rightarrow 2 \times (4x - 60000) = 3 \times (3x - 60000)$$

$$\Rightarrow 8x - 120000 = 9x - 180000$$

$$\Rightarrow 9x - 8x = 180000 - 120000$$

$$\Rightarrow x = 60000$$

Income of A $= 4x$

$$= 4 \times 60000$$

$$= 240000$$

$\therefore$ The income of A is Rs. 240000.

Hence, the correct option is (A).

45. The average of 9 digits is given as 11

Now, each of these digits is multiplied by 5

We know, if each quantity is multiplied by certain value 'k', then the new average is also multiplied by 'k'

Here, k = 5

New average = Old average × k

$\Rightarrow$ New average = 11 × 5

$\Rightarrow$ New average = 55

Again, each of these digits is added by 8 now

Similarly, if each quantity is increased/decreased by "k", the new average is increased/decreased by "k"

Here, k = 8

New average = Old average + k

$\Rightarrow$ New average = 55 + 8

$\therefore$ The new average is 63

Hence, the correct option is (D).

46. Given,

The speed of the boat in still water $= 10m/s$

The speed of the stream $= 20\%$ of the speed of the boat

Let the speed of the boat in still water is u m/s and the speed of the stream is v m/s

Then,

The speed of the boat in still water $= 10m/s$

The speed of the stream $= 20\%$ of $10m/s$

$$= 10 \times \frac{20}{100}$$

$$= 2m/s$$

Downstream speed = speed of the boat in still water + speed of the stream

Downstream speed $= (10 + 2)$

$$= 12m/s$$

Hence, the correct option is (B).

47. Given:

Sanju complete a work $= 12$ days

Suraj complete a work $= 16$ days

Sanjay complete a work $= 24$ days

As we know,

Total Wok Done $=$ Number of Days $\times$ Efficiency

Let the efficiencies (work is done per day) of Sanju, Suraj and Sanjay be ' a', ' b' and ' c' respectively.

Let total work be 1 unit.

Then, $(a \times 12) = 1$

$$\Rightarrow a = \frac{1}{12}$$

Then, $(b \times 16) = 1$

$$\Rightarrow b = \frac{1}{16}$$

Then, $(c \times 24) = 1$

$$c = \frac{1}{24}$$

Time Taken by Sanju, Suraj and Sanjay together $= \dfrac{\text{Total work done}}{\text{Efficiency}}$

$$= \frac{1}{\{\left(\frac{1}{12}\right)+\left(\frac{1}{16}\right)+\left(\frac{1}{24}\right)\}}$$

$$= \frac{48}{(4+3+2)}$$

$$= \frac{48}{9} \text{ days}$$

$$= \frac{16}{3}\text{days}$$

$\therefore$ Sanju, Suraj and Sanjay together complete the whole work in $\dfrac{16}{3}$ days.

Hence, the correct option is (A).

48. The series follows the following pattern:

72.9 - 71.5 = 1.4

71.5 - 68.7 = 2.8

68.7 - 64.5 = 4.2 $\neq$ (68.7 - 64 = 4.7)

64.5 - 58.9 = 5.6

58.9 - 51.9 = 7.0

Since 64.5 will come in place of 64.

$\therefore$ Wrong number is 64.

Hence, the correct option is (C).

49. The series follows the following pattern:

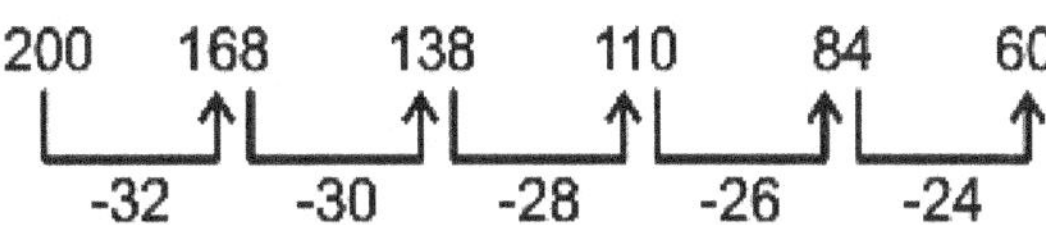

Since 138 will come in place of 140.

$\therefore$ Wrong number is 140.

Hence, the correct option is (C).

50. The series follows the following pattern:

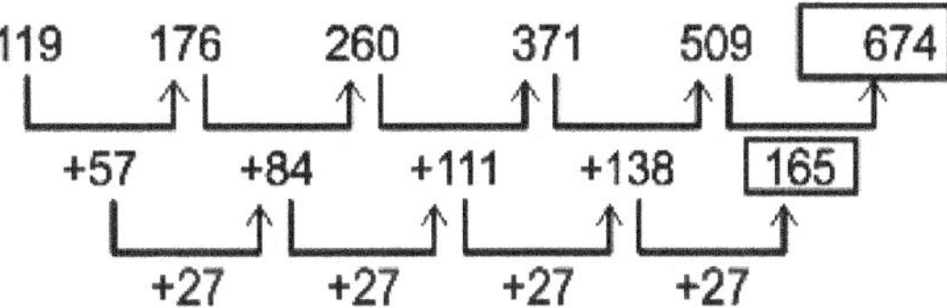

Since 674 will come in place of 675.

$\therefore$ Wrong number is 675.

Hence, the correct option is (A).

51. The series follows the following pattern:

$7 + 1^2 = 8$

$8 + 3^2 = 17$

$17 + 5^2 = 42$

$42 + 7^2 = 91$

$91 + 9^2 = 172$

Since 42 will come in place of 45.

$\therefore$ Wrong number is 45.

Hence, the correct option is (D).

52. The series follows the following pattern:

$8 + 4 \times 1 = 12$

$12 + 4 \times 3 = 24$

$24 + 4 \times 5 = 44 \neq 46$

$44 + 4 \times 7 = 72$

$72 + 4 \times 9 = 108$

Since 44 will come in place of 46.

$\therefore$ Wrong number is 46.

Hence, the correct option is (C).

53. Given,

$$\sqrt{6561} + \sqrt{289} \times 2 + 45\% \text{ of } 80 =? +1$$

$$\Rightarrow 81 + 17 \times 2 + 36 =? +1$$

$$\Rightarrow 81 + 34 + 36 - 1 =?$$

$$\Rightarrow ? = 150$$

$\therefore$ The value of $?$ is 150.

Hence, the correct option is (D).

54. Given,

$$25\% \times 676 - 10\% \times 810 + 60 \div 6 =? \times 70 \div 5$$

$$\Rightarrow 169 - 81 + 10 =? \times 14$$

$$\Rightarrow 98 =? \times 14$$

$$\Rightarrow \frac{98}{14} =?$$

$$\Rightarrow ? = 7$$

$\therefore$ The value of $?$ is 7.

Hence, the correct option is (B).

55. Given,

$$8888 \div 22 \times 4 - 316 =?^2 + 400$$

$$\Rightarrow 404 \times 4 - 316 =?^2 + 400$$

$$\Rightarrow 1616 - 316 - 400 =?^2$$

$$\Rightarrow 900 =?^2$$

$$\Rightarrow ? = 30$$

$\therefore$ The value of $?$ is 30.

Hence, the correct option is (B).

56. Given,

$$240 \div 6 + \sqrt{529} \times 17 =? + 150\% \text{ of } 80$$

$$\Rightarrow 40 + 23 \times 17 =? + 120$$

$$\Rightarrow 40 + 391 =? + 120$$

$$\Rightarrow 431 - 120 =?$$

$$\Rightarrow ? = 311$$

$\therefore$ The value of $?$ is 311.

Hence, the correct option is (A).

57. Given,

$$\sqrt{400} \times 2 - 30 = \sqrt{256} - 12 +?$$

$$\Rightarrow 20 \times 2 - 30 = 16 - 12 +?$$

$$\Rightarrow 40 - 30 = 4 +?$$

$$\Rightarrow 10 - 4 =?$$

$$\Rightarrow ? = 6$$

$\therefore$ The value of $?$ is 6.

Hence, the correct option is (B).

58. Given,

$$99 - 9^2 =?^2 + 9$$

$$\Rightarrow 99 - 81 =?^2 + 9$$

$$\Rightarrow 18 =?^2 + 9$$

$$\Rightarrow ?^2 = 18 - 9$$

$$\Rightarrow ?^2 = 9$$

$$\Rightarrow ? = \sqrt{9}$$

$$\Rightarrow ? = 3$$

$\therefore$ The value of $?$ is 3.

Hence, the correct option is (B).

59. Given,

Principal $=$ Rs. 48000

Amount $=$ Rs. 55560

Time $= 2$ year and 3 months

As we know,

$$\text{S.I} = A - P$$

$$S.I = \frac{(P \times R \times T)}{100}$$

$$S.I = 55560 - 48000 = 7560$$

$$\text{Time} = 2\frac{1}{4} = \frac{9}{4} \text{ year}$$

$$S.I = \frac{\left(48000 \times R \times \frac{9}{4}\right)}{100}$$

$$\Rightarrow 7560 = \frac{\left(48000 \times R \times \frac{9}{4}\right)}{100}$$

$$\Rightarrow 756000 = 108000 \times R$$

$$\Rightarrow R = \frac{756}{108} = 7\%$$

$\therefore$ The rate of interest per year is 7%.

Hence, the correct option is (A).

60. Given,

$$S = 16 km/h$$

$$D = 40 km$$

Rest time $= 4$ min after every km

As we know,

$$\text{Speed} = \frac{Distance}{Time}$$

Time taken without break $= \frac{40}{16} = 2.5 hrs$

Interval in distance of $40 km = 39$

Resting time $= 39 \times 4 = 156$

$$= 2hr\ 36min$$

Total time $= 5hrs\ 6min$

$\therefore$ The time taken is $5hrs\ 6min$.

Hence, the correct option is (B).

61. Ratio of profit $=$ Ratio of Amit's capital $\times$ time: Ratio of Sumit's capital $\times$ time

$$\Rightarrow 5:1 = 80000 \times 12 : 48000 \times t$$

$$\Rightarrow 5:1 = 20:t$$

$$\Rightarrow \frac{5}{1} = \frac{20}{t}$$

$$\Rightarrow t = 4$$

$\therefore$ Sumit entered in business after $(12 - 4 = 8)$ months.

Hence, the correct option is (E).

62. Given,

Difference between the ages of Aditya and his mother $= 20$ years

Age of his mother after 5 years $=$ Twice of Aditya's age after 5 years

Let the age of Aditya be x years.

Age of mother $= (x + 20)$ years

Age of Aditya after 5 years $= (x + 5)$ years

Age of his mother after 5 years $= (x + 20 + 5)$ years

According to the question,

$$(x + 25) = 2 \times (x + 5)$$

$$\Rightarrow x + 25 = 2x + 10$$

$$\Rightarrow 15 = x$$

$\therefore$ The present age of Aditya is 15 years.

Hence, the correct option is (B).

Ques (63-67): Given,

Day	Total number of Men	Total number of women =Total number of people visited − Total number of Men	Total number of people visited
Sunday	20% of 250 = 50	$250 - 50 = 200$	250
Tuesday	35% of 100 = 35	$100 - 35 = 65$	100
Friday	75% of 120 = 90	$120 - 90 = 30$	120
Saturday	65% of 300 = 195	$300 - 195 = 105$	300

63. The number of women who visited the zoo on Sunday $= 200$

The number of women who visited the zoo on Friday $= 30$

The number of women who visited the zoo on Saturday $= 105$

Total number of women who visited the zoo on the above mentioned days $= (200 + 30 + 105) = 335$

$\therefore$ The total number of women who visited on Sunday, Friday and Saturday are 335.

Hence, the correct option is (C).

64. The total number of women who visited the zoo on Tuesday and Saturday $= (65 + 105)$

$= 170$

Average number of women who visited the zoo on Tuesday and Saturday $= \frac{170}{2} = 85$

$\therefore$ The average number of women who visited the zoo on Tuesday and Saturday is 85.

Hence, the correct option is (D).

65. Total number of men who came on Friday and Saturday together $= (90 + 195) = 285$

Required ratio $= 50 : 285 = 10 : 57$

$\therefore$ The ratio of men who came on Sunday to the total number of men who came on Friday and Saturday together is $10 : 57$.

Hence, the correct option is (A).

66. The total number of men who visited the zoo on Sunday and Tuesday $= (50 + 35)$

$= 85$

The total number of women who visited the zoo on Friday and Saturday $= (30 + 105)$

$= 135$

Difference between them $= (135 - 85)$

$= 50$

Required percentage $= \{\left(\frac{50}{135}\right) \times 100\}$

$= 37.03\% \approx 37\%$

$\therefore$ The number of men who visited the zoo on Sunday and Tuesday together is 37% less than the number of women who visited the zoo on Friday and Saturday together.

Hence, the correct option is (B).

67. The total number of women who visited the zoo on Sunday and Saturday $= (200 + 105)$

$= 305$

The total number of men who visited the zoo on Tuesday and Friday $= (35 + 90)$

$= 125$

Difference between them $= (305 - 125)$

$= 180$

$\therefore$ The difference between the total number of women who visited the zoo on Sunday and Saturday together and the total number of men who visited the zoo on Tuesday and Friday together is 180.

Hence, the correct option is (D).

68. Given,

Surface area of the cylinder $= 1672 m^2$

As we know,

Surface area of the cylinder $= 2\pi r(r + h)$

According to the question,

$\Rightarrow 2\pi r(r + h) = 1672 m^2$

$\Rightarrow 2 \times \frac{22}{7} \times r \times 19 = 1672 m^2$

$\Rightarrow r = \frac{(1672 \times 7)}{(2 \times 22 \times 19)}$

$\Rightarrow r = 14$

$\therefore h = 19 - 14 = 5m$

Volume of the cylinder $= \pi r^2 h$

$= \frac{22}{7} \times 14 \times 14 \times 5$

$= 3080 m^3$

Hence, the correct option is (A).

69. Given,

$? \times 22 = 2740 \div 20 - [\left(\frac{100}{9}\right) \% \text{ of } 729 - 10]$

$\Rightarrow ? \times 22 = 137 - [\frac{\left(\frac{100}{9}\right)}{100} \times 729 - 10]$

$\Rightarrow ? \times 22 = 137 - [\frac{100}{9} \times \frac{1}{100} \times 729 - 10]$

$\Rightarrow ? \times 22 = 137 - [81 - 10]$

$\Rightarrow ? \times 22 = 137 - 71$

$\Rightarrow ? \times 22 = 66$

$\Rightarrow ? = \frac{66}{22}$

$\Rightarrow ? = 3$

$\therefore$ The value of ? is 3.

Hence, the correct option is (C).

70. Given,

$?^{\frac{2}{3}} = 64\% \text{ of } 150 + 7 \times 3 - 9^2$

$\Rightarrow ?^{\frac{2}{3}} = \frac{64}{100} \times 150 + 7 \times 3 - 9^2$

$\Rightarrow ?^{\frac{2}{3}} = 96 + 21 - 81$

$\Rightarrow ?^{\frac{2}{3}} = 117 - 81$

$\Rightarrow ?^{\frac{2}{3}} = 36$

$$\Rightarrow ? \; \frac{2}{3} \times \frac{1}{2} = \sqrt{36}$$

$$\Rightarrow ? \; \frac{1}{3} = 6$$

$$\Rightarrow ? \; \frac{1}{3} \times 3 = 6^3$$

$$\Rightarrow ? \; ^1 = 216$$

$$\Rightarrow ? = 216$$

∴ The value of ? is 216.

Hence, the correct option is (D).

71. Given statement: P ≥ A ≥ B > C; E < F ≤ G = C

On combining: P ≥ A ≥ B > C = G ≥ F > E

Conclusion:

I. B > F → True (as B > C → C = G → G ≥ F → So, B > F)

II. P ≥ G → False (as P ≥ A → A ≥ B → B > C → C = G) ' > ' symbol is used between P and G. Hence, the relation between P and G is P > G.

Therefore, only conclusion I follows.

Hence, the correct option is (B).

72. Given Statements: R = S, K < R, L < K

When added: L < K < R = S

Conclusion:

I) S > L → True (Since S = R > K > L → S > L)

II) K < S → True (Since K < R = S → K < S)

So, both conclusions I and II follow.

Hence, the correct option is (E).

Ques (73-77): In certain coding languages,

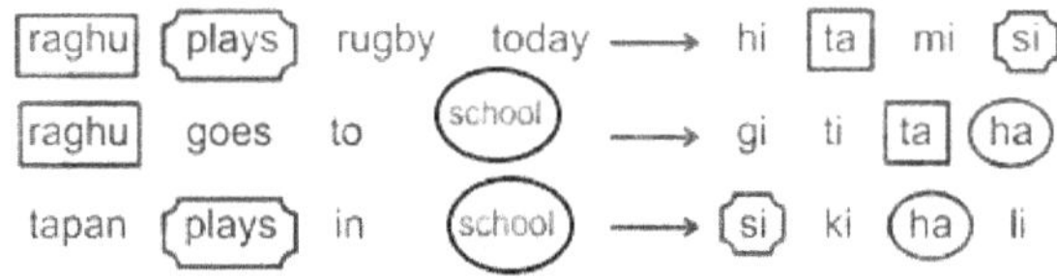

73. So, 'in' is coded as "either 'ki' or 'li'".

Hence, the correct option is (E).

74. So, 'ha' is the code for 'school'.

Hence, the correct option is (B).

75. Code for 'tapan' is either 'ki' or 'li',

Code for 'plays' is 'si',

Code for 'rugby' is either 'hi' or 'mi',

Code for 'in' is either 'ki' or 'li',

Code for 'school' is 'ha'.

Code for 'today' is either 'hi' or 'mi'.

So, the possible answer is 'ki si mi li ha hi'.

Hence, the correct option is (A).

76. Code for 'goes' is either 'gi' or 'ti'.

So, 'either (A) or (B)' is the correct answer.

Hence, the correct option is (E).

77. Code 'si' corresponds to 'plays',

Code 'ta' corresponds to 'raghu',

Code 'li' corresponds to either 'tapan' or 'in',

Code 'ha' corresponds to 'school'.

So, the only possible answer is 'raghu plays in school.

Hence, the correct option is (C).

Ques (78-83):Given:

People: L, M, N, O, P, Q, R, and S are sitting around a circular table. E

Bank: Canara, Bank of India (BOI), Central Bank of India (CBI), Bank of Baroda (BOB), Indian Bank (IB), Union Bank of India (UBI), Oriental Bank of Commerce (OBC) and Dena Bank (DB).

Four of them are facing towards the center while others are facing outside the center.

1) N is facing the center and is to the immediate right of both L and Q. L is facing the opposite direction of N.

2) R is fourth to the left of Q.

3) Neither R nor Q is an immediate neighbor of O.

4) L is working in Canara Bank and sits third to the right of the one who is working in Indian Bank.

5) The one who is working in Union Bank of India sits second to the left of the one who is working in Canara Bank.

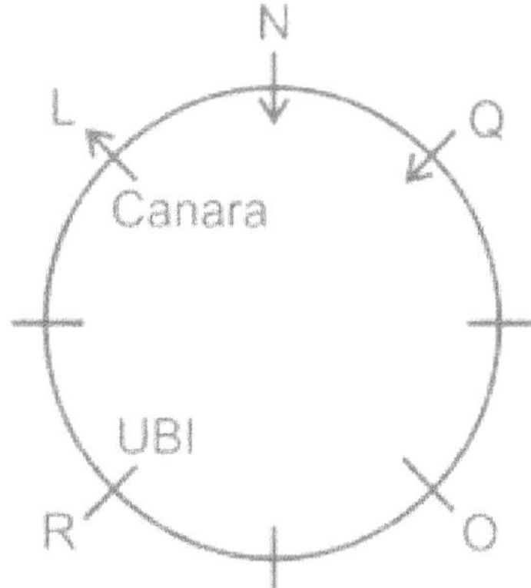

6) The one who works in Bank of India sits exactly between L and Q and adjacent to them.

7) The one who is working in Oriental Bank of Commerce sits second to the right of O.

8) P sits third to the left of L.

9) O is third to the right of S.

10) M and R faces the same direction.

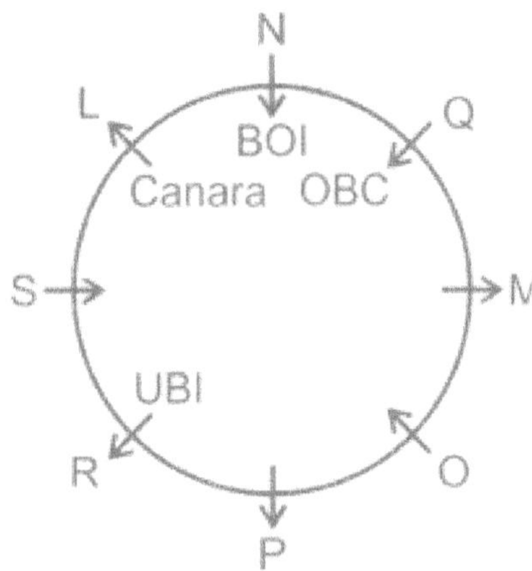

11) The one who is working in Indian Bank is to the immediate left of O, who is not working in Dena Bank.

12) The one who works in the Central Bank of India sits second to the right of the one who works in the Bank of India.

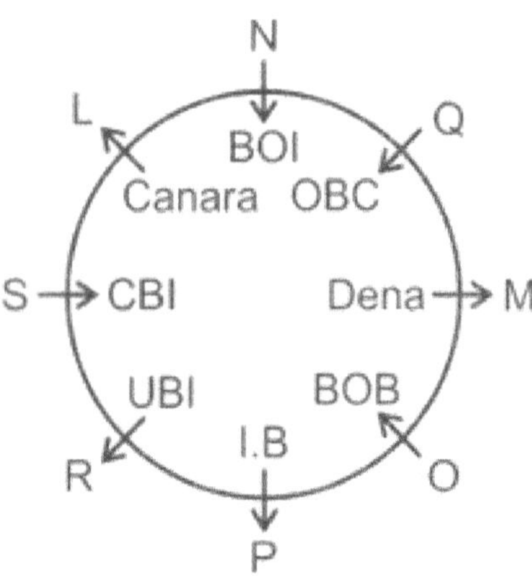

78. So, O works in the Bank of Baroda.

Hence, the correct option is (D).

79. So, O is sitting to the immediate left of the one who works in the Indian Bank.

Hence, the correct option is (E).

80. So, R is sitting opposite to Q.

Hence, the correct option is (A).

81. So, L works in the Canara Bank.

Hence, the correct option is (C).

82. So, N is sitting to the immediate left of the one who works in the Oriental Bank of Commerce.

Hence, the correct option is (D).

83. Clearly, S works in Central Bank of India.

Hence, the correct option is (D).

Ques (84-86): Here dotted line indicates bus F and solid line indicates bus G.

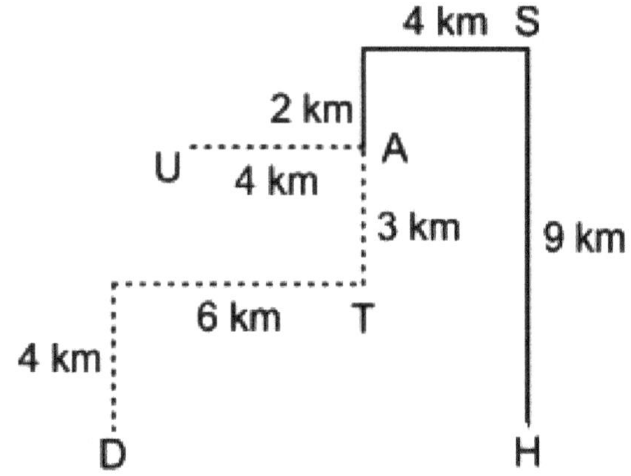

84. Total distance covered by bus F = 4 km + 6 km + 3 km + 4 km = 17 km

Hence, the correct option is (C).

85. According to the questions,

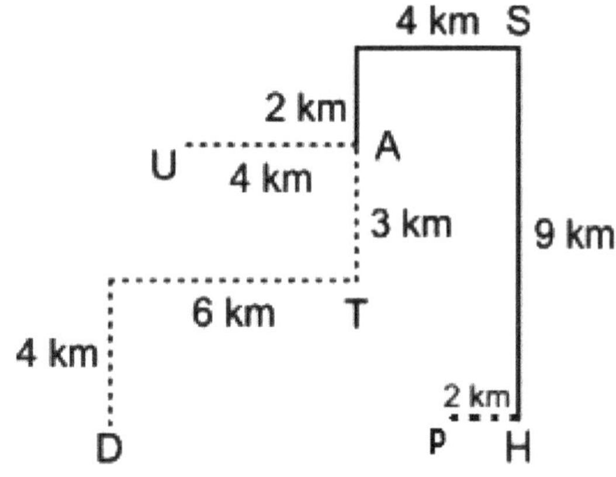

Thus, the distance between point D and bus P = 10 - 2 = 8 km

Hence, the correct option is (E).

86. From the figure we can see that city A falls in both of their route.

Hence, the correct option is (C).

87. We draw the least possible Venn diagram:

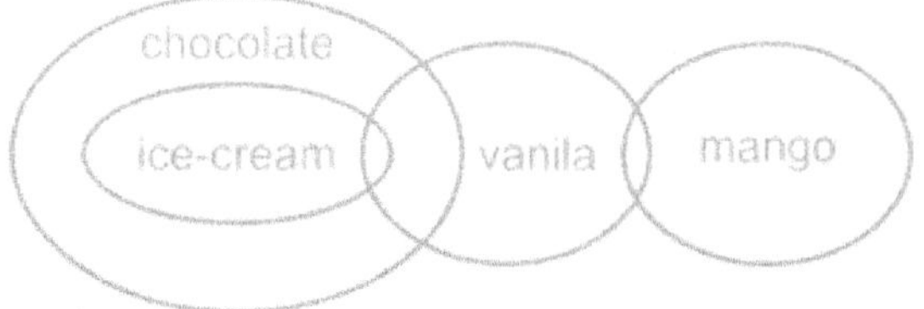

Conclusions:

I. Some ice cream being vanilla is a possibility → False (Some ice cream is definitely vanilla. Hence, the possibility is false) wrong

II. Some mango is chocolate → It's possible but not definite.

So, Neither conclusion I nor II follows.

Hence, the correct option is (D).

88. The least possible Venn diagram for the given statements is as follows,

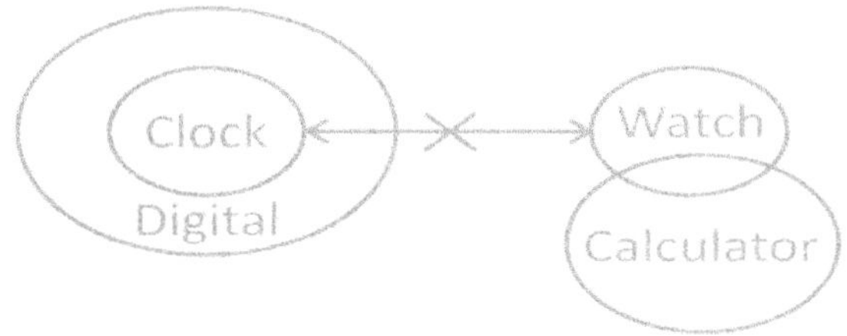

Conclusions:

I. All Watches being Digital is a possibility → Possibility is true.

II. No calculator is a Clock → False.

III. Some Digitals are Clocks → it's true.

So, the conclusion I and III follow.

Hence, the correct option is (C).

89. The possible Venn diagram is:

I. Some chairs are key → It is a definite case, hence true.

II. Some box are chairs → It is not a definite case, hence false.

Thus, only conclusion I follow.

Hence, the correct option is (A).

90. The least possible Venn diagram is given below:

I) some Yellow is not Black → True (As some yellow is white and no white is black, so some yellow is not black is true).

II) Few silver is black → True(It is True as directly seen in the figure).

III) All White can never be Silver → False

So, the correct answer is the conclusion I and II follow.

Hence, the correct option is (C).

91. The least possible Venn diagram is shown below:

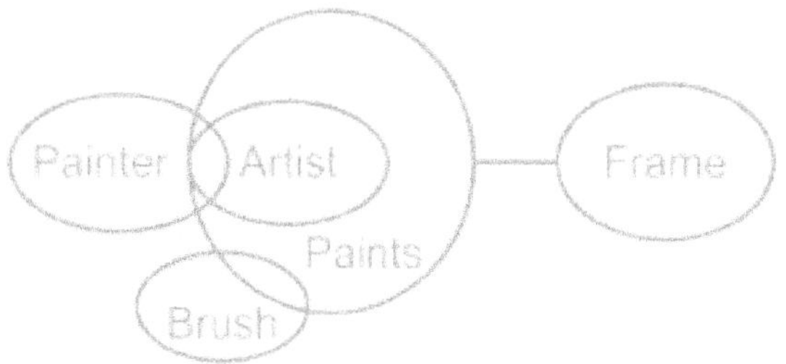

I. Some Paints are Painter → True

II. Some Brush are not Paint → True (Because in the statement it is given that strictly only a few brush are paint which indicates that there are some brush which are not paint)

III. Some Brush are Artist → false

So, only I and II follows.

Hence, the correct option is (A).

92. Given statement: K ≤ D, H ≥ R < P < K

On combining: H ≥ R < P < K ≤ D

Conclusions:

I. R < D → True (As, R < P < K ≤ D)

II. H > K → False (As, H ≥ R < P < K)

III. D > P → True (As, D ≥ K > P)

Therefore, only conclusions I and III are True.

Hence, the correct option is (E).

93. Given Statements: U < V, W > X ≥ Y, Y = V

On combining: U < V = Y ≤ X < W

Conclusion:

I. X > V → False (as V = Y ≤ X → X ≥ V)

II. U < W → True (as U < V = Y ≤ X < W → U < W)

So, only II is true.

Hence, the correct option is (D).

94. Given statements: X > P < Z; P < J = O > M

On combining: X > P < J = O > M; P < Z

Conclusions:

I. P > M → False (as P < O and O > M → thus clear relation between P and M cannot be established)

II. X < J → False (as X > P and P < J → thus clear relation between X and J cannot be established)

So, Neither conclusion I nor II is true.

Hence, the correct option is (D).

Ques (95-100):1) The box of N is three boxes above the box of K.

2) The box of G is the topmost box.

3) The box of C is just above the box of N,

Box	Case 1	Case 2
1	G	G
2	C	
3	N	C
4		N
5		
6	K	
7		K

4) The box of D is just below box of S

Box	Case 1	Case 2
1	G	G
2	C	
3	N	C
4	S	N
5	D	S
6	K	D
7		K

5) There is one box between the box of D and the box of M. So, case 2 is rejected.

So, the final arrangement is:

1	G
2	C
3	N
4	S
5	D
6	K
7	M

95. M is the bottom most box.

Hence, the correct option is (E).

96. So, five boxes are above K.

Hence, the correct option is (E).

97. So, G is just above C.

Hence, the correct option is (C).

98. So, there are three boxes between M and N.

Hence, the correct option is (C).

99. All having one box in between except G - C.

So, G - C does not belong to the group.

Hence, the correct option is (C).

100. So, 4 boxes are below the box of N.

Hence, the correct option is (C).

Test of English Language

Ques (1-5):Direction: In the question below, a sentence is given with two blanks that indicate that some parts are missing. Identify the correct pair of words that fit in the sentence to make it grammatically and contextually correct.

Q.1 Only a third in India are _______ saving for their retirement while just 33 percent of working-age respondents globally are _______ anything aside for their later life.

A. hardly, saving
B. regularly, putting
C. constantly, setting
D. continuously, debating
E. diligently, meticulously

Q.2 If you consider the number of districts, then the areas under the _______ of left-wing extremism have shrunk _______ more than 40% in the last three years.

A. existence, with   B. ecstasy, about
C. influence, by   D. confidence, off
E. installation, about

Q.3 Chaotic traffic has become the _______ of the day at major junctions in Puducherry thanks to poor traffic management, _______ posting of police personnel and disregard of rules by motorists and vehicle owner.

A. dynamics, frequent
B. diabolical, often
C. order, inadequate
D. access, uncontrollable
E. attention, unassailable

Q.4 Pedestrians complain that there is no _______ left for them to walk at pedestrian crossings near major junctions as they are _______ upon by motorists.

A. road, encircled   B. place, accustomed
C. figures, crossed   D. space, encroached
E. None of the above

Q.5 While the demand is _______ for clay idols, people also prefer moulded idols _______ in bulk from other cities.

A. low, manufactured   B. few, transferred
C. small, distributed   D. high, procured
E. None of the above

Ques (6-10):Direction: In the following question, some of the words have been left out. Read the passage carefully and select the correct answer for the given blank out of the five alternatives given in the questions that follow:

__________ (1) is a measure of the market value of all the final goods and services produced in a period of time. It is a very important factor in estimating the total income being produced in the country in a given year. It defines, if you will, the size of the cake. But there is a whole bunch of other __________ (2).

After all, the size of the cake is only one part of the story. How that cake is divided into different groups of people, sectors, that is equally important. When you talk of jobless growth, the growth part is coming from the GDP estimate and the __________ (3) part is coming from employment data. The GDP data is critical to understand the pattern of growth you are seeing that is leading to the lack of jobs. __________ (4) is another big indicator. As a country, we have neglected employment data for far too long. It's only in the last decade or so that we have started to say it is important, and finally got around to doing something about it only last year. The second, which is simply not produced, is the damage we are doing to our natural _______ (5). There is scattered data on forest cover, air pollution, water pollution, but you don't have a measure of the state of our natural capital. Are you getting high-income growth but at the cost of the environment? Is that trade-off worth it? The third is to know how income is distributed. Poverty measures, for instance, are important. Because they tell you, is this increase in income benefiting the poor?

Q.6 Which of the following words most appropriately fits the blank labelled (1)?

A. Guanosine Diphosphate
B. Gross Double Product
C. Group of Dispersed Products
D. Gross Domestic Progression
E. Gross Domestic Product

Q.7 Which of the following words most appropriately fits the blank labelled (2)?

A. Indicating   B. Indicators
C. Indication   D. Indicater
E. Indicate

Q.8 Which of the following words most appropriately fits the blank labelled (3)?

A. Conscientious   B. Obligation
C. Dutiful   D. Jobless
E. Joblessness

Q.9 Which of the following words most appropriately fits the blank labelled (4)?

A. Transport   B. Farming
C. Agriculture   D. Employment
E. Rigorous

Q.10 Which of the following words most appropriately fits the blank labelled (5)?

A. GDP   B. NDP   C. GNP   D. GATT
E. Growth

Ques (11-15):Direction: The following sentences form a paragraph. The second and fifth sentences of the paragraph are given. The rest are numbered as P, Q, R, S, and T. These five parts are not given in their proper order. Arrange them in the correct order to make the paragraph meaningful and then answer the questions given below.

P. By the early 1960s, calls to reform U.S. immigration policy had mounted, thanks in no small part to the growing strength of the civil rights movement.

At the time, immigration was based on the national-origins quota system in place since the 1920s, under which each nationality was assigned a quota based on its representation in past U.S. census figures.

Q. President John F. Kennedy even took up the immigration reform cause, giving a speech in June 1963 calling the quota system "intolerable."

R. The civil rights movement's focus on equal treatment regardless of race or nationality led many to view the quota system as backward and discriminatory.

The Immigration and Naturalization Act of 1965, also known as the Hart-Celler Act, abolished an earlier quota system based on national origin and established a new immigration policy based on reuniting immigrant families and attracting skilled labor to the United States.

S. Immigrants entering the United States under the new legislation now came increasingly from countries in Asia, Africa and Latin America, as opposed to Europe.

T. Over the next four decades, the policies put into effect in 1965 would greatly change the demographic makeup of the American population.

Q.11 Which of the following should be the FIRST sentence in the correct order?

A. P   **B.** Q   **C.** R   **D.** S
E. T

Q.12 Which of the following should be the THIRD sentence in the correct order?

A. P   **B.** Q   **C.** R   **D.** S
E. T

Q.13 Which of the following should be the FOURTH sentence in the correct order?

A. Q   **B.** P   **C.** R   **D.** S
E. T

Q.14 Which of the following should be the SIXTH sentence in the correct order?

A. P   **B.** Q   **C.** R   **D.** S
E. T

Q.15 Which of the following should be the SEVENTH or last sentence in the correct order?

A. P   **B.** Q   **C.** R   **D.** S
E. T

Ques (16-17):Direction: In following question, a sentence with four words printed in bold type is given. These are numbered as A, B, C and D. One of these four words printed in bold may be either wrongly spelled or inappropriate in context of the sentence. Find out the word which is wrongly spelled or

inappropriate if any. The number of that word is your answer. If all the words printed in bold are correctly spelled and also appropriate in the context of the sentence, mark (E) "All are correct" as your answer.

Q.16 The **effeminet (A)** young man was **bullied (B) throughout (C)** his school days, still he never complained against his **persecutors (D)** to the schools authority.

A. Effeminet   **B.** Bullied
C. Throughout   **D.** Persecutors
E. All are correct

Q.17 The hospital super **initiated (A)** the **investigation (B)** to **ascertein (C)** if the newborn baby's death was indeed caused due to the **negligence (D)** of the doctor.

A. Initiated   **B.** Investigation
C. Ascertein   **D.** Negligence
E. All are correct

Ques (18-20):Direction: In the following question given below, four words are given in bold. These four words may or may not be in their correct position. The sentence is then followed by options with the correct combination of words that should replace each other in order to make the sentence grammatically and contextually correct. Find the correct combination of words that replace each other. If the sentence is correct as it is, select '(E)' as your option.

Q.18 The mural — in a town which **contentious (A)** voted to leave and is one of Britain's main crossing points to the continent — gained much **elusive (B)** after it emerged that it was the work of Banksy, the **attention (C)** artist, who till this time had not made known his political views on the **overwhelmingly (D)** Brexit referendum.

A. Both A-D and B-C
B. Only (A)-(C)
C. Only (B)-(D)
D. Both (A)-(B) and (C)-(D)
E. The sentence is correct

Q.19 While Mahindra will **balance (A)** 60% stake in the new **company (B)** named Mahindra **Summit (C)** Agriscience Limited, the **hold (D)** will be with Sumitomo Corporation.

A. Only (B)-(C)
B. Both (A)-(D) and (B)-(C)
C. Only (A)-(D)
D. Both (A)-(C) and (B)-(D)
E. The sentence is correct

Q.20 China and the United States have **slapped (A)** tit-for-tat tariffs over the past few months, **rattling (B)** financial markets as investors worried the **escalating (C)** trade war could **knock (D)** global trade and investment.

A. Only (B)-(C)
B. Both (A)-(D) and (B)-(C)
C. Only (A)-(D)
D. Both (A)-(C) and (B)-(D)
E. The sentence is correct

Ques (21-22):Direction: In the following question, a sentence is given, divided into 5 parts. Part (1) is grammatically correct.

Out of the other four parts, one part contains an error. Mark the option containing the part with the error. If none of the parts have errors, mark 'No error' as your answer.

Q.21 Women's badminton has (1) been a display of exquisite skill, wrist turns,(A) / drop shots and exhausting (B) rallies that spectator love, (C) but drain contestants physically. (D)

A. A   **B.** B   **C.** C   **D.** D
E. No error

Q.22 The Amazon tussle highlights (1) the precarious balance that must (A) / have been achieved between national (B) / concerns and international efforts (C) / to protect the global commons. (D)

A. A   **B.** B   **C.** C   **D.** D
E. No error

Q.23 Direction: A statement has been divided into five parts- (A), (B), (C), (D) and (E). Part (E) is fixed and grammatically correct. Out of the other parts, only one is without error. You are required to find the error-free part and mark it as your answer. If none of the parts have errors, mark- 'no error' as your answer while if all the parts have an error, mark- 'all have errors'.

Over the last 15 years, but more (A)/ so for 2013, the Serious Fraud Investigation Office (SFIO) (B)/ has emerged as India's premier (C)/ corporate fraud investigation agencies, (D)/ **investigating several high-profile cases. (E)**

A. A   **B.** B
C. C   **D.** D
E. All have errors

Ques (24-28):Direction: You are required to match statements from columns 1 and 2 and find which of the following pairs of statement make sense meaningfully and grammatically.

Q.24

	Column (1)		Column (2)
A	The eagle was afraid to fly into the sky	D	in spite of the Internet has a plethora of options.
B	The shrewd businessman quickly .	E	after remain in captivity for two years.
C	Freelancing has always been a popular way to earn money online	F	grabbed beneath the opportunity and earned a huge pile of money.

A. Only A-E and C-D   **B.** Only B-F and C-D
C. Only A-E and B-F   **D.** Only C-D
E. None of these

Q.25

	Column (1)		Column (2)
A	The audience gave the veteran musician	D	in the country today and covers over 50 per cent of Kerala households.
B	Kudumbashree is one of the largest women-empowerment projects	E	a standing ovation.
C	Children who have been victims of violence are more	F	likely to drop out of high school before graduation than their peers.

A. Only A-E   **B.** Only A-E and B-D
C. Only B-D and C-F   **D.** A-E, B-D and C-F
E. None of these

Q.26

	Column (1)		Column (2)
A	The tsunami swept over the island	D	will spur more Indian entrepreneurship.
B	The printer was out of ink and	E	hence showed promise of growth and vitality.
C	Hopefully the momentum at both PhonePe and Paytm	F	and destroyed over 2 billion dollars of property.

A. Only A-F   **B.** Only A-F and B-E
C. Only A-F and C-D   **D.** Only C-D
E. None of these

Q.27

	Column (1)		Column (2)
A	The angry mob	D	on the lines of defense public sector undertakings.
B	The Centre is considering converting the factories into multiple companies	E	beat upon the thief mercilessly.
C	The four indicators for the hunger index	F	are undernourishment, child stunting, child wasting and child mortality.

A. Only A-E   **B.** Only B-D
C. Only C-F   **D.** Only B-D and C-F
E. None of these

Q.28

	Column (1)		Column (2)
A	My sister fought with two boys	D	his son failed to secure good marks of Mathematics.
B	The anguished cricketer lashed out	E	and won the surprise tests.
C	The father was deeply pained as	F	at the journalists when they went to ask him questions.

A. Only A-E   **B.** Only B-F
C. Only C-D   **D.** Only A-E and C-D
E. None of these

Ques (29-38):Direction: Read the passage and answer the following question.

Ever since the first gleaming towers sprang out of the desert, Dubai has gotten used to rapid change. It's no stranger to **boom-and-bust**. What's happening now is different: a slow bleed. The city's iconic builders are ploughing ahead. Cranes are everywhere. But no one is sure who'll occupy all that new retail and office space. Already, Dubai's malls are noticeably less full of stores and restaurants than they once were. Expatriates, the lifeblood of the economy, have started to pack up and go home -- or at least talk about it, as the cost of living and doing business surges. Corporate mainstays, from Emirates airline to developer Emaar Properties, just reported disappointing third-quarter profits. The stock market is having its worst year since 2008. Business unease was already apparent in April when Sheikh Mohammed bin Rashid Al Maktoum

convened a meeting with more than 100 executives in his palace overlooking the Persian Gulf. The bosses raised issues including hefty government fees -- which are eroding the comparative advantage of tax-free Dubai -- to strict visa rules that push foreigners out when they lose their jobs. The conclave was followed by a flurry of decisions, still working their way through the system. But a fix for what's **ailing** Dubai may be beyond the powers of its ruler. Sheikh Mohammed and his predecessors built a fishing village into a hub for finance, trade and tourism in the region -- but now that region is changing, perhaps for good.

The oil slump since 2014 hit big spenders from neighbouring Gulf states who used to flock to Dubai (tourists from China and India are filling the gap, but they're more price-conscious). Saudis, in particular, are feeling the pinch, as their own government imposes fiscal **austerity** and confiscates private wealth. The city's role as a trading post is being undermined by a global tariff war -- and in particular by the U.S. drive to shut down commerce with nearby Iran. Now that the state of Dubai is part of the UAE, has become an active player in those conflicts, fighting in civil wars from Libya to Yemen and joining the Saudi-led boycott of Qatar.

Dubai also faces consequences of its own success. Lacking energy resources of its own, the city had little choice but to build a non-oil economy. The 2014 crash jolted other Gulf countries into following suit. They're all planning for a post-crude era and trying to emulate their thriving neighbour by marketing their own capitals as regional hubs. Dubai remains preeminent in that role. But it's an increasingly high-cost base. In 2013, it ranked as the 90th most expensive place for ex-pats to live, according to New York-based consultant Mercer. It's now vaulted to 26th on the list.

Government, builders and businesses alike are all looking to one event on the horizon that may come to the rescue. Dubai will host the World Expo fair in 2020. Meant to **showcase** the city's future prospects, it's become almost an end in itself, a reason to keep the cranes at work. "The biggest saving grace," Haque calls it.

Q.29 What is the main context of the passage?

A. Lack of natural resources in Dubai

B. Dependence of Dubai on other countries

C. Dubai's stagnant position and its efforts to regain its sheen

D. Commercial problems in Dubai increase conflicts in the region

E. The problems in Dubai caused by the USA

Q.30 Which of the following can be inferred about the present state of Dubai?

I. People are moving out of the country thereby leading to lesser business.

II. Businesses present in Dubai are suffering from losses and are not being able to earn profits like before.

III. Excessive number of shopping malls filled with stores are present but not bringing much profit.

A. Only II

B. Both I and II

C. Both II and III

D. Only I

E. All of the above

Q.31 Which of the following was the scenario in Dubai earlier?

A. The government made business easy in Dubai and laws were not stringent

B. Dubai was a place of growth and a hub of business

C. The government was strict with the laws earlier which had made profits for Dubai

D. Business thrived there but in different forms, especially related to oil and malls were lesser in number

E. Both (A) and (B)

Q.32 Which of the following is not a reason for declining business in Dubai?

I. Consequential involvement of Dubai in regional conflicts.

II. Strict visa rules that push foreigners out when they lose their jobs.

III. Too much of people rushing into the place to do business but not knowing the appropriate sector.

IV. Stringent laws by the government and confiscation of private property.

A. Only III

B. Only II

C. Both II and III

D. Both I and IV

E. All of the above

Q.33 Which of the following is/are true according to the passage?

I. Lower cost of living in Dubai can attract more people to do business here.

II. Indians and Chinese are price-conscious tourists.

III. The Gulf countries are trying to walk on the same path as that Dubai and are creating similar businesses.

A. Only II

B. Both I and II

C. Both II and III

D. Only I

E. All of the above

Q.34 Which of the following is the purpose of holding the World Expo fair in 2020?

A. To remove the obstacles it has faced in business for some years

B. To shift the idea of an oil-dependent economy to a non-oil one

C. To make up for the scarcity of resources it has

D. To end regional conflicts

E. To show the world the ability that Dubai has in the field of business

Q.35 What do you mean by boom and bust?

A. Glamour and power of money

B. Achieving prosperity all of a sudden

C. Sudden prosperity followed by an abrupt decline

D. Celebration after a long time

E. Respite from poverty

Q.36 Which of the following is OPPOSITE in meaning to the word 'ailing'?

A. Prosperous

B. Frivolous

C. Smart

D. Healthy

E. None of these

Q.37 Which of the following is SIMILAR in meaning to the word 'austerity'?

A. Sternness **B.** Growth
C. Rudeness **D.** Greed
E. Wisdom

Q.38 Which of the following is SIMILAR in meaning to the word 'showcase'?

A. Initiate **B.** Strengthen
C. Justify **D.** Focus
E. Display

Ques (39-40):Direction: The given question contains three statements, one or more of which may not be grammatically correct. You are required to identify the incorrect statements from the options given below and mark that as your answer.

Q.39 I. There should be special places in hell for those which promoted Brexit.

II. The reason May's plan failed was her effort to avoid any possibility of a hard border.

III. A soft border was an essential feature of the agreement that ended 40 years of terrorist violence.

A. Only II **B.** Only I and II
C. Only I and III **D.** Only I
E. All are correct

Q.40 I. Global warming is on track to transform the frigid mountain peaks in empty rocks shortly.

II. People living in the downstream areas of this river basins benefit directly and indirectly from its resources.

III. The projected shortage in pre-monsoon river flows will hit the hardest.

A. Only II **B.** Only I and II
C. Only I and III **D.** Only III
E. All are correct

Test of Numerical Ability

Q.41 A money lender borrows money at 4% per annum and pays the interest at the end of the year. He lends it at 6% per annum compound interest compounded half yearly and receives the interest at the end of the year. In this way, he gains Rs. 104.50, a year. The amount of money be borrows, is:

A. Rs. 4500 **B.** Rs. 5000 **C.** Rs. 5500 **D.** Rs. 6000
E. Rs. 2000

Q.42 Direction: What will come in place of the question mark (?) in the following question?

$$64 \div \sqrt{?} + 12 = 20$$

[RBI Assistant, 2020]

A. 81 **B.** 64 **C.** 49 **D.** 25
E. 121

Q.43 Direction: What will come in place of the question mark (?) in the following question?

$$28 + 5 \times (?) \div 3 = 73$$

[RBI Assistant, 2020]

A. 27 **B.** 24 **C.** 29 **D.** 33
E. 39

Q.44 Direction: What will come in place of the question mark (?) in the following question?

$$\sqrt{676} \times \sqrt{576} - ? \times 18 = 300$$

[RBI Assistant, 2020]

A. 14 **B.** 16 **C.** 18 **D.** 20
E. 22

Q.45 If $x = 5 + \sqrt{79 + \sqrt{11 - \sqrt{49}}}$, then find $2x + 3$.

A. 31 **B.** 41 **C.** 29 **D.** 37
E. 32

Q.46 Direction: What will come in place of question mark (?) in the following question?

$$\left(\sqrt{64} + 3\right)^3 = 750 + ?$$

[RBI Assistant, 2020]

A. 576 **B.** 581 **C.** 588 **D.** 590
E. 622

Q.47 Direction: What will come in place of question mark (?) in the following question?

$$\frac{(220 \div 20 \times 135 \div 15)}{3} = ?$$

[RBI Assistant, 2020]

A. 31 **B.** 44 **C.** 33 **D.** 42
E. 28

Q.48 Direction: What will come in place of the question mark (?) in the following question?

$$24 + \sqrt{81} \div 3 \times ? = 30$$

[RBI Assistant, 2020]

A. 1 **B.** 2 **C.** 3 **D.** 4
E. 5

Q.49 Direction: What will come in place of question mark (?) in the following question?

$$4 \times \left(\frac{?}{100}\right) \times 210 + 225 = 351$$

[RBI Assistant, 2020]

A. 15 **B.** 21 **C.** 25 **D.** 12
E. 18

Q.50 Direction: What will come in place of question mark (?) in the following question?

$$\frac{(\sqrt{36} \times \sqrt{64})}{4} = ?$$

[RBI Assistant, 2020]

A. 14 **B.** 6 **C.** 8 **D.** 10
E. 12

Q.51 Direction: What will come in place of the question mark (?) in the following question?

40% of 180 + 70% of ? = 121

[RBI Assistant, 2020]

A. 81   **B.** 77   **C.** 65   **D.** 70
E. 75

Q.52 A shopkeeper has two items of same cost price. One item sold at 10% profit and other sold at 5% loss. He gets total profit of Rs.200. Find the total profit percentage earned.
A. 8%   **B.** 1.5%   **C.** 3%   **D.** 2%
E. 2.5%

Q.53 The average age of workers in field and in documentation in a factory was 45 year. The average age of all the 16 documentation workers was 38 years and average age of field workers was 52 years. If 7 field workers were married then the number of unmarried field workers was:
A. 5   **B.** 6   **C.** 7   **D.** 8
E. 9

Q.54 Akshara was travelling in her boat when the wind blew her hat and hat started floating back stream. The boat continued to travel upstream for twelve minutes after which Akshara realized that her hat had fallen off and turned back downstream. She caught up with that as soon as it reached the starting point. Find the speed of river if Akshara's hat flew off exactly 3 km from where she started?
A. 7.5 km/hr   **B.** 25 km/hr
C. 15 km/hr   **D.** 9 km/hr
E. 12 km/hr

Q.55 The ratio of the salaries of Adam and Ponting is 5 : 7 and that of the salaries of Ponting and Marsh is 3 : 5. The salary of Adam is Rs. 16,500, and Marsh spends 28.4% of his salary on his basic needs. How much money is left with Marsh after the expenditure on basic needs?
A. Rs. 38,500   **B.** Rs. 10,934
C. Rs. 27,566   **D.** Rs. 16,500
E. Rs. 16,000

Q.56 Three pipes A, B, and C can fill a tank from empty to full in 30 minutes, 20 minutes, and 10 minutes respectively. When the tank is empty, all three pipes are opened. A, B, and C discharge chemical solutions P, Q, and R respectively. What is the proportion of the solution R in the liquid in the tank after 3 minutes?
A. $\frac{5}{11}$ **B.** $\frac{6}{11}$ **C.** $\frac{7}{11}$ **D.** $\frac{8}{11}$
E. $\frac{9}{11}$

Ques (57-61):Direction: Read the following line graph carefully and answer the questions given below.

The given Line graph shows the number of shoes sold by 3 brands in 4 different months.

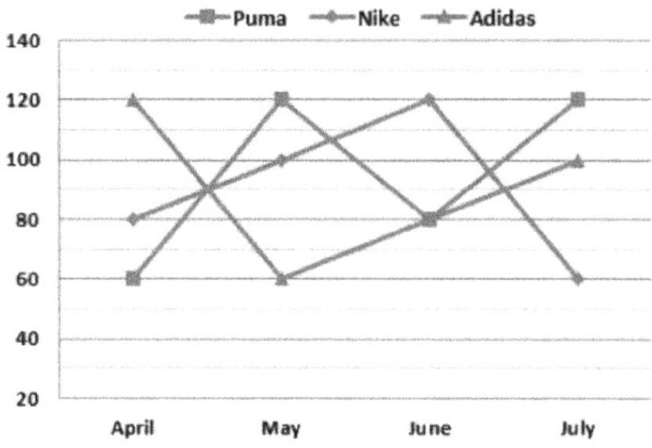

Q.57 What is the ratio of the number of total shoes sold of Puma in April and June to the number of shoes sold of Adidas in May and July?
A. 7 : 8   **B.** 7 : 9   **C.** 5 : 8   **D.** 6 : 7
E. 4 : 5

Q.58 The number of shoes sold in May and June of all companies is what percent more/less than the number of total shoes sold of Adidas in all months?
A. $64\frac{2}{7}\%$ **B.** $48\frac{5}{9}\%$ **C.** $53\frac{5}{9}\%$ **D.** $55\frac{5}{9}\%$
E. $54\frac{2}{7}\%$

Q.59 What is the average number of shoes sold of Puma in April, Nike in June, and Adidas in May?
A. 78   **B.** 80   **C.** 76   **D.** 82
E. 84

Q.60 What is the difference between the number of shoes sold by Puma in all months and the number of shoes sold by all companies in June?
A. 90   **B.** 80   **C.** 60   **D.** 120
E. 100

Q.61 The number of shoes sold in April of all companies is approximately what percent of the number of shoes sold by all companies in July?
A. 117%   **B.** 86%   **C.** 93%   **D.** 107%
E. 99%

Q.62 The product of the ages of Swati and Aparna is 120. If thrice the age of Aparna is more than Swati's age by 2 years, find the age of Swati.
A. 18   **B.** 21   **C.** 24   **D.** 16
E. 25

Q.63 The perimeter of a rectangle is 8936 m and the area is 4203987 sq. m Given that the length of the rectangle is greater than the breadth, what is the ratio of the length to the breadth?
A. 3111 : 1357   **B.** 3121 : 1347
C. 2922 : 1546   **D.** 2546 : 1922
E. Can't be determined

Q.64 In an election, 80% of the people casted their votes and 45% of the voters who casted votes are employed and 66.67% of employed voters are engineers. Find the percentage of non-engineers among total voters?

A. 12% **B.** 24% **C.** 50% **D.** 76%
E. 48%

Ques (65-69):Direction: In the following number series, only one number is wrong. Find out the wrong number.

Q.65 48, 72, 108, 162, 243, 366
A. 72   **B.** 108
C. 162   **D.** 243
E. None of these

Q.66 150, 450, 750, 1060, 1350, 1650, 1950
A. 1060 **B.** 1950 **C.** 450 **D.** 1350
E. 750

Q.67 32, 39, 65, 128, 253, 467, 809, 1320
A. 39 **B.** 65 **C.** 253 **D.** 467
E. 32

Q.68 38, 49, 62, 72, 77, 91, 101
A. 49 **B.** 72 **C.** 77 **D.** 91
E. 38

Q.69 19, 22, 32, 46, 73, 108, 158
A. 22 **B.** 46 **C.** 73 **D.** 19
E. 158

Q.70 A, B and C invested respectively Rs. 5000, Rs. 7000 and Rs. 6000 in a business. If at the end of two years, they got a profit of Rs. 10,800. The share of B in this total profit is:
A. Rs. 4500 **B.** Rs. 4200 **C.** Rs. 1800 **D.** Rs. 1500
E. Rs. 3600

Test of Reasoning

Ques (71-76):

Directions: Study the following information carefully and answer the question given below:

Eight books A, B, C, D, P, Q, R and S are kept in racks one above the other. There are three 3 books kept between A & R. Book P is just below to book R. There are two books kept between P & S. There are as many books between B & D as R & A. Book B is above book D. Book C is immediate above to D and neither D nor A at the lowermost rack.

Q.71 How many books are kept between book R and Q?
A. One **B.** Three **C.** Four **D.** Five
E. Zero

Q.72 Which of the following statement is False?
A. Book C is kept 3 Books above to book A.
B. Two books kept between D and R
C. Book B is kept immediately above to R.
D. Book Q kept in lowermost rack.
E. Book S is kept in topmost rack.

Q.73 How many books kept above to the book Q?
A. Six **B.** Five **C.** Four **D.** Seven
E. Zero

Q.74 Choose the odd one?

A. A **B.** B **C.** R **D.** C
E. S

Q.75 Which did Book keep in the lowermost rack?
A. R **B.** A **C.** C **D.** Q
E. P

Q.76 Which did Book keep in the second lowest rack?
A. R **B.** A **C.** C **D.** Q
E. P

Ques (77-81):Direction: In the following question assuming the given statements to be True, find which of the conclusion among given conclusions is/are definitely true and then give your answers accordingly.

Q.77 Statements: A > B < C < D; K ≥ L > M = D; G > H ≥ I ≤ J < A

Conclusions:

I. G > A

II. A ≥ G

III. K > I

A. Only I is true **B.** Only II is true
C. Only III is true **D.** None true
E. Either I or II true

Q.78 Statements: R ≤ D ≤ X; K > V ≥ I; R = O ≥ K
Conclusions:
I. D ≤ V
II. X > K
III. I < O
A. Only III is True
B. Both I and III are True
C. Either I or II is True
D. Both II and III are True
E. Only II is True

Q.79 Statements: X < M ≤ W; B ≥ L ≥ O; O = X
Conclusions:
I. B > M
II. M ≥ B
III. L < W
A. Only III is True
B. Both I and III are True
C. Either I or II is True
D. Both II and III are True
E. Only II is True

Q.80 Statements: R ≤ A < N ≤ I; K ≥ I; V > A
Conclusions:
I) K ≥ A
II) V > I
III) R ≤ K
A. Only I and II is true
B. Only I is true
C. Only II and III is true
D. Only III is true

E. None of these

Q.81 Statements: W < X, Y = Z , V < U, X > Z, G ≥ Y, W > U, H = V

Conclusions:

(i). G > X

(ii). W > H

(iii). Y = H

A. Only conclusion (i) follows

B. Both conclusions (i) and (iii) follow

C. Only conclusion (ii) follows

D. Either conclusion (i) or (ii) follows

E. None of the conclusions follow

Ques (82-84):Direction: Study the information given below carefully and answer the question that follow.

Nine friends A, B, C, D, E, F, G, H, and I lives at a certain distance from each other. C is 6 km West of B. A is 3 km South of B and H is 5 km north of A. G is 3 km East of H while D is 7 km West of G and F is 3 km South of G. I is situated just in middle of B and C while E is just in middle of H and D.

Q.82 Minimum Distance between E and I is?

A. 4 km   **B.** 2.5 km   **C.** 2.23 km   **D.** 7.12 km
E. 5.1 km

Q.83 How far is I from C and B?

A. 1km   **B.** 2km   **C.** 3km   **D.** 4km
E. 5km

Q.84 Point D is in which direction from point C?

A. South – West   **B.** East
C. North   **D.** North – East
E. None of these

Q.85 Direction: In the question below are given three statements followed by three conclusions numbered I, II, and III. You have to take the given statements to be true even if they seem to be at variance with commonly known facts. Read all the conclusions and then decide which of the given conclusions logically follows from the given statements disregarding commonly known facts.

Statements:

Some men are cow.

All men and cow are genius.

Some men which are not cow are rich.

Conclusion:

I. Some genius are rich.

II. Some rich are cow.

III. Some cow are genius.

A. Only I and II follows

B. Only II and III follows

C. Only I and III follows

D. All follows

E. None follows

Ques (86-89):Direction: In each of the questions below are given some statements followed by two conclusions. You have to take the given statements to be true even if they seem to be at variance with commonly known facts. Read all the conclusions and then decide which of the given conclusions logically follows from the given statements, disregarding commonly known facts. Give answer.

Q.86 Statements:

Only a few Gmail are yahoo.

Some yahoo are windows.

Conclusions:

I. Some gmail are windows.

II. No gmail are windows.

A. Only I follows

B. Only II follows

C. Either I or II follows

D. Neither I nor II follows

E. Both I and II follows

Q.87 Statements:

Only a few speaker are special.

Only speaker are spear.

Conclusions:

I. Some spear are special is a possibility.

II. only a few spear are special.

A. Only I follows

B. Only II follows

C. Either I or II follows

D. Neither I nor II follows

E. Both I and II follows

Q.88 Statements:

All studious are student.

Some studious are teacher.

Conclusions:

I. Some teacher are student.

II. No student are teacher.

A. Only I follows

B. Only II follows

C. Either I or II follows

D. Neither I nor II follows

E. Both I and II follows

Q.89 Statements:

Only a few seven are eight.

Only eight are nine.

Conclusions:

I. Some seven are nine.

II. All nine are eight.

A. Only I follows

B. Only II follows

C. Either I or II follows

D. Neither I nor II follows

E. Both I and II follows

Ques (90-95):Direction: Read the following information carefully and answer the question given beside.

Eight persons are sitting around a circular table such that some of them are facing towards the centre while some are facing away from centre. M is third to the right of S, who sits second to the left of Y. P sits on the immediate right of X, who faces the same direction as faced by M. Neither X nor P is adjacent to M. C is third to the left of Y. Not more than 4 persons face outside. B and S face same direction. C is third to the right of B. J is second to the left of M. C and J face opposite direction to that of B. Immediate neighbors of C face opposite directions.

Q.90 How many persons face towards the centre?

A. 2   **B.** 3   **C.** 4   **D.** 5

E. 6

Q.91 What is the position of J with respect to P?

A. Sixth to the right   **B.** Third to the left

C. Third to the right   **D.** Second to the right

E. None of these

Q.92 Find the odd one out.

A. X   **B.** S   **C.** M   **D.** Y

E. P

Q.93 Who is second to the right of C?

A. X   **B.** P

C. J   **D.** S

E. Can't be determined

Q.94 How many persons sit between J and B when counted from the right of former?

A. 2   **B.** 3

C. 5   **D.** 4

E. None of these

Q.95 Who is second to the left of C?

A. J   **B.** S   **C.** Y   **D.** P

E. X

Ques (96-100):Direction: Read the following information carefully and answer the question given beside.

"Backlog disc live heavily" is coded as " 2$A 4#I 8$E 12#I ".

"Innocent band actress salute" is coded as " 2#A 1$C 9%N 19&A".

"Notify selfish model change" is coded as "14&O 13!O 19$E 3&H".

"Langer hill external limelight" is coded as "12&A 12@I 8#I 5%X".

Q.96 Find the code for "Easy goals fulfilled".

A. 5#A 6!O 7@U   **B.** 7$A 8!O 6@U

C. 5#A 7!O 6@U   **D.** 5$A 7!O 6%U

E. None of these

Q.97 Find the code for "Take advance receipt".

A. 20#A 1$D 18$E   **B.** 2#A 1$D 7$E

C. 20#A 11#D 17$E   **D.** 20$A 1$D 17$E

E. None of these

Q.98 Find the code for "Advertise your product".

A. 1@D 5#O 6$R   **B.** 1@D 25#O 16$R

C. 1@D 25#O 16#R   **D.** 1@D 25#O 16@R

E. None of these

Q.99 Find the code for "Great gesture".

A. 7!E 7$S   **B.** 7!R 7$A   **C.** 7!R 7$E   **D.** 7!G 7$E

E. 7$R 7$E

Q.100 Find the code for "Travel with wander".

A. 20&R 23#I 23#A   **B.** 20&R 23&I 23&A

C. 23&R 23#I 23&A   **D.** 20&R 23#I 23&A

E. None of these

// Smart Answer Sheet //

Correct   Indicates percentage of students who answered questions correctly.

Skipped   Indicates percentage of students who skipped questions.

Q.	Ans.	Correct / Skipped	Q.	Ans.	Correct / Skipped	Q.	Ans.	Correct / Skipped	Q.	Ans.	Correct / Skipped	Q.	Ans.	Correct / Skipped
1	B	28.76 % / 69.43 %	17	C	60.16 % / 31.74 %	33	E	28.48 % / 70.86 %	49	A	65.43 % / 32.87 %	65	E	24.34 % / 72.24 %
2	C	41.25 % / 46.33 %	18	A	40.72 % / 37.29 %	34	E	54.63 % / 33.15 %	50	E	79.54 % / 11.15 %	66	A	79.74 % / 10.51 %
3	C	57.44 % / 38.76 %	19	C	56.63 % / 37.52 %	35	C	46.74 % / 30.13 %	51	D	63.29 % / 31.78 %	67	C	56.9 % / 30.88 %
4	D	66.92 % / 31.58 %	20	E	65.58 % / 33.45 %	36	D	50.61 % / 47.31 %	52	E	40.1 % / 57.49 %	68	C	46.88 % / 34.62 %
5	D	78.12 % / 15.5 %	21	C	61.4 % / 35.73 %	37	A	53.38 % / 42.67 %	53	E	53.17 % / 36.93 %	69	B	58.85 % / 33.92 %
6	E	87.91 % / 11.35 %	22	B	42.72 % / 36.03 %	38	E	76.22 % / 15.56 %	54	A	51.44 % / 44.8 %	70	B	69.03 % / 30.89 %
7	B	55.2 % / 32.77 %	23	A	44.85 % / 40.36 %	39	D	40.01 % / 47.66 %	55	C	64.61 % / 33.09 %	71	C	31.47 % / 68.08 %
8	E	52.73 % / 44.99 %	24	E	47.78 % / 46.8 %	40	B	66.35 % / 31.85 %	56	B	41.34 % / 52.86 %	72	A	49.77 % / 43.05 %
9	D	21.3 % / 67.22 %	25	D	43.39 % / 47.76 %	41	B	66.18 % / 32.09 %	57	A	40.25 % / 54.28 %	73	D	56.28 % / 38.41 %
10	A	47.85 % / 46.58 %	26	C	41.28 % / 49.36 %	42	B	87.04 % / 10.38 %	58	D	51.72 % / 39.85 %	74	B	46.87 % / 52.71 %
11	A	54.82 % / 43.76 %	27	D	42.59 % / 49.66 %	43	A	63.02 % / 30.86 %	59	B	54.95 % / 41.66 %	75	D	69.82 % / 30.07 %
12	C	63.26 % / 33.94 %	28	B	61.36 % / 30.27 %	44	C	24.65 % / 67.4 %	60	E	47.49 % / 31.42 %	76	B	45.45 % / 39.57 %
13	A	50.88 % / 32.03 %	29	C	46.74 % / 33.23 %	45	A	40.47 % / 35.66 %	61	C	69.31 % / 30.09 %	77	E	45.44 % / 50.53 %
14	E	52.97 % / 45.02 %	30	B	56.71 % / 32.24 %	46	B	77.62 % / 10.3 %	62	A	58.79 % / 40.34 %	78	A	85.04 % / 13.7 %
15	D	55.61 % / 42.83 %	31	B	59.65 % / 35.1 %	47	C	77.15 % / 13.19 %	63	B	89.62 % / 10.28 %	79	C	58.54 % / 33.38 %
16	A	59.77 % / 32.24 %	32	A	43.17 % / 40.43 %	48	B	66.22 % / 31.23 %	64	A	45.62 % / 35.63 %	80	E	16.64 % / 77.88 %

Q.	Ans.	Correct		Q.	Ans.	Correct		Q.	Ans.	Correct		Q.	Ans.	Correct		Q.	Ans.	Correct
		Skipped				Skipped				Skipped				Skipped				Skipped
81	C	77.82 %		85	C	64.71 %		89	B	49.23 %		93	A	11.7 %		97	A	43.43 %
		19.5 %				34.39 %				39.78 %				87.9 %				32.42 %
82	C	89.08 %		86	B	52.35 %		90	D	15.86 %		94	D	61.7 %		98	B	62.48 %
		10.72 %				39.07 %				82.03 %				34.51 %				34.04 %
83	C	88.43 %		87	D	54.57 %		91	B	11.56 %		95	A	50.57 %		99	C	86.79 %
		10.85 %				33.06 %				79.64 %				31.3 %				12.54 %
84	D	62.13 %		88	A	43.64 %		92	E	18.16 %		96	C	62.07 %		100	D	52.81 %
		37.6 %				36.72 %				74.58 %				30.95 %				30.23 %

Performance Analysis

Avg. Score (%)	57.0%
Toppers Score (%)	63.0%
Your Score	

//Hints and Solutions//

1. The correct sentence is,

Only a third in India are regularly saving for their retirement while just 33 percent of working-age respondents globally are putting anything aside for their later life.

The context says something about the savings of Indians for the retirement age and the comparison of Indians with respect to the global scenario in terms of savings for life after retirement.

Since now we have understood the context of the sentence, it is now necessary to weigh the options according to their suitability in the blanks. Coming to option (A), hardly is still okay for the first blank but saving is not fit for the second blank.

Option (C) is not correct since the second word is not correct for the blank.

Option (D) is not correct because of the same reason as Option (C) whereas Option (E) is also not correct due to the second word being not correct for the respective blank.

Option (B) is correct since both the words fit perfectly in the respective blanks.

This makes option (B) the correct choice among the given options.

Hence, the correct option is (B).

2. The correct sentence is,

If you consider the number of districts, then the areas under the influence, of left-wing extremism have shrunk by more than 40% in the last three years.

The given sentence is about the data regarding the influence of left-wing extremism in India in the last three years in which it has seen a downfall.

Among the given options, option (A) is not correct since existence does not fit in the context and the same can be said about the second word also.

Option (B) is not correct since both the words are not fit for the blanks in the sentence. The same can be said about options (D) and (E).

Only option (C) implies the actual meaning intended in the sentence and it explains the meaning that the number of districts affected by left-wing extremism has decreased the last few years.

This makes option (C) the correct choice among the given options.

Hence, the correct option is (C).

3. The correct sentence is,

Chaotic traffic has become the order, of the day at major junctions in Puducherry thanks to poor traffic management, inadequate posting of police personnel and disregard of rules by motorists and vehicle owner.

It is clear from the given sentence that chaotic traffic is very common in Puducherry because of reasons such as poor traffic management, disregard of rules by motorists and vehicle drivers etc. The words in blank should reflect the meaning as intended.

Option (A) is not correct since both the words do not fit in the given context. The same can be said about options (B), (D) and (E).

Option (C) fits in the blanks since it is implied that chaotic traffic is very common in the union Territory whereas one of the reasons can be the posting of the insufficient number of policemen in the major areas of the U.T.

This makes option (C) the correct choice among the given options.

Hence, the correct option is (C).

4. The correct sentence is,

Pedestrians complain that there is no space left for them to walk at pedestrian crossings near major junctions as they are encroached upon by motorists.

From the given sentence, it is very clear that the pedestrians do not have enough space left on the roads to move because there are motorists everywhere on the roads.

Among the given options, option (A) is not correct since encircled cannot be placed in the blank.

Option (B) is also not correct because accustomed cannot fit in the context in any manner. The same can be said about option (C) where figures are not a fit word for the first blank. Only (D) is the option where both the words fit perfectly in the given context.

This makes option (D) the correct choice among the given options.

Hence, the correct option is (D).

5. The correct sentence is,

While the demand is high for clay idols, people also prefer moulded idols procured in bulk from other cities.

The given statement gives the impression that people prefer clay idols but they also prefer moulded idols from other cities.

Among the given options, (A) is not correct since low itself gives the opposite impression to the one actually intended in the sentence.

Option (B) is not correct since few is not the correct word for the first blank whereas small is also not correct in option (C) for the first blank in the sentence. Option (D) is correct because both the words fit perfectly in the given sentence as high implies that the demand for clay idols is good but people are also preferring moulded idols procured from other cities.

This makes option (D) the correct choice among the given options.

Hence, the correct option is (D).

6. Here, a bit of general awareness is required. Upon reading the sentence will give you an idea that the paragraph is about the economy and so option (A) does not fit in.

Option (A),(B) and (C) are wrong options.

The complete sentence is:

Gross Domestic Product is a measure of the market value of all the final goods and services produced in a period of time.

Hence, the correct option is (E).

7. Here, different forms of the verb indicate are given. You have to choose the right word that is grammatically correct with the statement.

Gerund: **Indicating**

Noun: **Indication**

Noun: **Indicators**; (s) is for plural and singular is an indicator

Verb: **Indicate**

And in Indicater, there is a spelling error. So it is incorrect.

The sentence here refers to the indicators and in the latter part of the passage, employment and environment are used as indicators, not indications.

The complete sentence is:

But there is a whole bunch of other indicators.

Hence, the correct option is (B).

8. In the former part of the sentence, jobless growth is taken as a subject where growth is related to GDP and joblessness part is from the employment.

The words in options (A),(B) and (C) are somewhat similar in a sense but are incorrect for the given question.

Conscientious means to follow one's part or duty well and thoroughly.

Obligation means morally bound to something.

Only joblessness is right for the given question. One may get confused with jobless and joblessness but the thing here is the requirement of a word that tells you about the state being jobless that has already been referred in the sentence.

"A noun ending in 'ness' literally means the state of the original adjective".

The complete sentence is:

When you talk of jobless growth, the growth part is coming from the GDP estimate and the joblessness part is coming from employment data.

Hence, the correct option is (E).

9. Here, to answer this question one has to read the sentence after this. It has been clearly mentioned there that employment has been neglected for a long as an indicator. Now, for the past few years, it is being taken as an important factor and plays an essential role in GDP.

Farming and agriculture are synonyms and refer to growing crops

Transport refers to the movement of goods from place to place

Rigorous refers to hard strenuous work

The complete sentence is:

Employment is another big indicator.

Hence, the correct option is (D).

10. Here, one can understand the context of the statement and find the correct answer to the question. The blank must contain that term which is the main topic of discussion in the passage.

The Gross Domestic Product (GDP)measures the value of economic activity within a country.

The Net Domestic Product (NDP) is an annual measure of the economic output of a nation that is adjusted to account for depreciation.

Gross national product (GNP) is the value of all finished goods and services or the market value of all goods and services produced

The General Agreement on Tariffs and Trade (GATT) is a multilateral agreement regulating international trade

One can easily understand that the sentence is talking about GDP, its estimation and various other factors that involve GDP.

Hence, the correct option is (A).

11. The first sentence of a paragraph introduces a topic. The second sentence usually provides more information about the first.

Here, the second sentence mentions 'At that time' and only sentence P mentions another time frame – 'By the early 1960s.'

So, **P must be the first sentence.**

The third sentence must logically follow from the second sentence. Only sentence R mentions the change – 'equal treatment' instead of the 'quota system' mentioned in sentence 2.

So, **R must be the third sentence.**

The fourth sentence must follow from the third. Only sentence Q further reiterates the need for reform by President Kennedy calling the old quota system 'intolerable.'

So, **Q must be the fourth sentence.**

Sixth and seventh sentences would follow the earlier sentences, with the last giving some kind of conclusion to the above sentences. Out of the remaining sentences, T mentions change in demography after the immigration rules were changed and S with 'now' concludes the paragraph by stating that immigrants now increasingly came from Asia, Africa and South America instead of from Europe.

So, T must be the sixth sentence while S is the last sentence of the paragraph. The correct order is: PRQTS or P2RQ5TS.

The complete paragraph is: By the early 1960s, calls to reform U.S. immigration policy had mounted, thanks in no small part to the growing strength of the civil rights movement. At the time, immigration was based on the national-origins quota system in place since the 1920s, under which each nationality was assigned a quota based on its representation in past U.S. census figures. The civil rights movement's focus on equal treatment regardless of race or nationality led many to view the quota system as backward and discriminatory. President John F. Kennedy even took up the immigration reform cause, giving a speech in June 1963 calling the quota system "intolerable." The Immigration and Naturalization Act of 1965, also known as the Hart-Celler Act, abolished an earlier quota system based on national origin and established a new immigration policy based on reuniting immigrant families and attracting skilled labor to the United States. Over the next four decades, the policies put into effect in 1965 would greatly change the demographic makeup of the American population. Immigrants entering the United States under the new legislation now came increasingly from countries in Asia, Africa and Latin America, as opposed to Europe.

Hence, the correct option is (A).

12. The first sentence of a paragraph introduces a topic. The second sentence usually provides more information about the first.

Here, the second sentence mentions 'At that time' and only sentence P mentions another time frame – 'By the early 1960s.'

So, **P must be the first sentence.**

The third sentence must logically follow from the second sentence. Only sentence R mentions the change – 'equal treatment' instead of the 'quota system' mentioned in sentence 2.

So, **R must be the third sentence.**

The fourth sentence must follow from the third. Only sentence Q further reiterates the need for reform by President Kennedy calling the old quota system 'intolerable.'

So, **Q must be the fourth sentence.**

Sixth and seventh sentences would follow the earlier sentences, with the last giving some kind of conclusion to the above sentences. Out of the remaining sentences, T mentions change in demography after the immigration rules were changed and S with 'now' concludes the paragraph by stating that immigrants now increasingly came from Asia, Africa and South America instead of from Europe.

So, T must be the sixth sentence while S is the last sentence of the paragraph. The correct order is: PRQTS or P2RQ5TS.

The complete paragraph is: By the early 1960s, calls to reform U.S. immigration policy had mounted, thanks in no small part to the growing strength of the civil rights movement. At the time, immigration was based on the national-origins quota system in place since the 1920s, under which each nationality was assigned a quota based on its representation in past U.S. census figures. The civil rights movement's focus on equal treatment regardless of race or nationality led many to view the quota system as backward and discriminatory. President John F. Kennedy even took up the immigration reform cause, giving a speech in June 1963 calling the quota system "intolerable." The Immigration and Naturalization Act of 1965, also known as the Hart-Celler Act, abolished an earlier quota system based on national origin and established a new immigration policy based on reuniting immigrant families and attracting skilled labor to the United States. Over the next four decades, the policies put into effect in

1965 would greatly change the demographic makeup of the American population. Immigrants entering the United States under the new legislation now came increasingly from countries in Asia, Africa and Latin America, as opposed to Europe.

Hence, the correct option is (C).

13. The first sentence of a paragraph introduces a topic. The second sentence usually provides more information about the first.

Here, the second sentence mentions 'At that time' and only sentence P mentions another time frame – 'By the early 1960s.'

So, **P must be the first sentence.**

The third sentence must logically follow from the second sentence. Only sentence R mentions the change – 'equal treatment' instead of the 'quota system' mentioned in sentence 2.

So, **R must be the third sentence.**

The fourth sentence must follow from the third. Only sentence Q further reiterates the need for reform by President Kennedy calling the old quota system 'intolerable.'

So, **Q must be the fourth sentence.**

Sixth and seventh sentences would follow the earlier sentences, with the last giving some kind of conclusion to the above sentences. Out of the remaining sentences, T mentions change in demography after the immigration rules were changed and S with 'now' concludes the paragraph by stating that immigrants now increasingly came from Asia, Africa and South America instead of from Europe.

So, T must be the sixth sentence while S is the last sentence of the paragraph. The correct order is: PRQTS or P2RQ5TS.

The complete paragraph is: By the early 1960s, calls to reform U.S. immigration policy had mounted, thanks in no small part to the growing strength of the civil rights movement. At the time, immigration was based on the national-origins quota system in place since the 1920s, under which each nationality was assigned a quota based on its representation in past U.S. census figures. The civil rights movement's focus on equal treatment regardless of race or nationality led many to view the quota system as backward and discriminatory. President John F. Kennedy even took up the immigration reform cause, giving a speech in June 1963 calling the quota system "intolerable." The Immigration and Naturalization Act of 1965, also known as the Hart-Celler Act, abolished an earlier quota system based on national origin and established a new immigration policy based on reuniting immigrant families and attracting skilled labor to the United States. Over the next four decades, the policies put into effect in 1965 would greatly change the demographic makeup of the American population. Immigrants entering the United States under the new legislation now came increasingly from countries in Asia, Africa and Latin America, as opposed to Europe.

Hence, the correct option is (A).

14. The first sentence of a paragraph introduces a topic. The second sentence usually provides more information about the first.

Here, the second sentence mentions 'At that time' and only sentence P mentions another time frame – 'By the early 1960s.'

So, **P must be the first sentence.**

The third sentence must logically follow from the second sentence. Only sentence R mentions the change – 'equal treatment' instead of the 'quota system' mentioned in sentence 2.

So, **R must be the third sentence.**

The fourth sentence must follow from the third. Only sentence Q further reiterates the need for reform by President Kennedy calling the old quota system 'intolerable.'

So, **Q must be the fourth sentence.**

Sixth and seventh sentences would follow the earlier sentences, with the last giving some kind of conclusion to the above sentences. Out of the remaining sentences, T mentions change in demography after the immigration rules were changed and S with 'now' concludes the paragraph by stating that immigrants now increasingly came from Asia, Africa and South America instead of from Europe.

So, T must be the sixth sentence while S is the last sentence of the paragraph. The correct order is: PRQTS or P2RQ5TS.

The complete paragraph is: By the early 1960s, calls to reform U.S. immigration policy had mounted, thanks in no small part to the growing strength of the civil rights movement. At the time, immigration was based on the national-origins quota system in place since the 1920s, under which each nationality was assigned a quota based on its representation in past U.S. census figures. The civil rights movement's focus on equal treatment regardless of race or nationality led many to view the quota system as backward and discriminatory. President John F. Kennedy even took up the immigration reform cause, giving a speech in June 1963 calling the quota system "intolerable." The Immigration and Naturalization Act of 1965, also known as the Hart-Celler Act, abolished an earlier quota system based on national origin and established a new immigration policy based on reuniting immigrant families and attracting skilled labor to the United States. Over the next four decades, the policies put into effect in 1965 would greatly change the demographic makeup of the American population. Immigrants entering the United States under the new legislation now came increasingly from countries in Asia, Africa and Latin America, as opposed to Europe.

Hence, the correct option is (E).

15. The first sentence of a paragraph introduces a topic. The second sentence usually provides more information about the first.

Here, the second sentence mentions 'At that time' and only sentence P mentions another time frame – 'By the early 1960s.'

So, **P must be the first sentence.**

The third sentence must logically follow from the second sentence. Only sentence R mentions the change – 'equal treatment' instead of the 'quota system' mentioned in sentence 2.

So, **R must be the third sentence.**

The fourth sentence must follow from the third. Only sentence Q further reiterates the need for reform by President Kennedy calling the old quota system 'intolerable.'

So, **Q must be the fourth sentence.**

Sixth and seventh sentences would follow the earlier sentences, with the last giving some kind of conclusion to the above sentences. Out of the remaining sentences, T mentions change in demography after the immigration rules were changed and S with 'now' concludes the paragraph by stating that immigrants now increasingly came from Asia, Africa and South America instead of from Europe.

So, T must be the sixth sentence while S is the last sentence of the paragraph. The correct order is: PRQTS or P2RQ5TS.

The complete paragraph is: By the early 1960s, calls to reform U.S. immigration policy had mounted, thanks in no small part to the growing strength of the civil rights movement. At the time, immigration was based on the national-origins quota system in place since the 1920s, under which each nationality was assigned a quota based on its representation in past U.S. census figures. The civil rights movement's focus on equal treatment regardless of race or nationality led many to view the quota system as backward and discriminatory. President John F. Kennedy even took up the immigration reform cause, giving a speech in June 1963 calling the quota system "intolerable." The Immigration and Naturalization Act of 1965, also known as the Hart-Celler Act, abolished an earlier quota system based on national origin and established a new immigration policy based on reuniting immigrant families and attracting skilled labor to the United States. Over the next four decades, the policies put into effect in 1965 would greatly change the demographic makeup of the American population. Immigrants entering the United States under the new legislation now came increasingly from countries in Asia, Africa and Latin America, as opposed to Europe.

Hence, the correct option is (D).

16. The word 'effeminet' has been wrongly spelled.

The correct spelling of the word is 'effeminate'.

All other words are correct from every aspect.

Effeminate : (of a man) Having characteristics regarded as typical of a woman; unmanly

Bully : Seek to harm, intimidate, or coerce (someone perceived as vulnerable)/ a person who habitually seeks to harm or intimidate those whom they perceive as vulnerable

Throughout : From beginning to end of (an event or period of time)

Persecutor : A person who persecutes someone, especially for their race or political or religious beliefs

Hence, the correct option is (A).

17. The word 'ascertein' has been wrongly spelled.

The correct spelling of the word is 'ascertain'.

All other words are correct from every aspect.

Ascertain : Find (something) out for certain; make sure of

Initiate : Cause (a process or action) to begin

Investigation : The action of investigating something or someone; formal or systematic examination or research

Negligence : Failure to take proper care over something

Hence, the correct option is (C).

18. While solving such a question, what we should do is to check if the statement is correct in its present form given the fact that the statement is a long one. However, the sentence is not correct and is not making any sense also if we just see the first word which seems completely out of context.

Now, we have to weigh the options. If we go through option A, A and D are interchanged, we can find that the change is making sense and there is no error with this. So, we can move ahead with the next set in this option. Now, after interchanging B and C, we shall get a statement which will imply the intended meaning of the statement.

Therefore, the other options are not required to be considered.

The correct statement would be:

The mural — in a town which overwhelmingly voted to leave and is one of Britain's main crossing points to the continent — gained much attention after it emerged that it was the work of Banksy, the elusive artist, who till this time had not made known his political views on the contentious Brexit referendum.

Hence, the correct option is (A).

19. If we go through the statement, it may seem correct at the first glance but it is not since the intended meaning is not being explained by the existing statement. This rules out option (E).

Coming to the given options now, A can be ruled out since with the interchanging of (B) and (C), the statement will not make any sense whereas for option (B), if we carry out the interchanging of (A) and (D), it will imply the correct meaning of the sentence but as we have seen (B) and (C) should not be interchanged. So, it is certain that our option should have (A)-(D) as the pair and not (B)-(C). There is only one option that will explain this and the same is option (C).

The correct statement would be:

While Mahindra will hold 60% stake in the new company named Mahindra Summit Agriscience Limited, the balance will be with Sumitomo Corporation.

Hence, the correct option is (C).

20. The sentence is correct in its present form and all the bold words are in correct places making it unnecessary to interchange any of the given pairs.

Hence, the correct option is (E).

21. The error lies in the fragment C of the sentence.

Reason:

Usage of the verb 'love' shows that it is in plural form and must take a plural subject with it. Instead of the single subject 'spectator', the plural subject 'spectators' should be used in order to make it a grammatically correct sentence.

Correct Sentence:

Women's badminton has been a display of exquisite skill, wrist turns, drop shots and exhausting rallies that spectators love, but drain contestants physically.

Hence, the correct option is (C).

22. The error lies in the fragment B of the sentence.

Reason :

The given sentence is in simple present tense. Therefore, the fragment B should also be in simple present instead of present perfect tense in order to make it a grammatically correct sentence.

Correct Sentence :

The Amazon tussle highlights the precarious balance that must be achieved between national concerns and international efforts to protect the global commons.

Hence, the correct option is (B).

23. Fragment B: so for 2013, the Serious Fraud Investigation Office (SFIO)

The statement tries to convey that from/since 2013 onwards, the SFIO has emerged as a leading fraud investigation agency. For makes it sound as if it was the leading agency just for 2013 which is incorrect.

Correct: so since 2013, the Serious Fraud Investigation Office (SFIO)

Fragment C: has emerged as Indias premier

The apostrophe is missing.

Correct: has emerged as India's premier

Fragment D: corporate fraud investigation agencies,

Only one agency- SFIO- is being talked about here.

Correct: corporate fraud investigation agency,

Hence, the correct option is (A).

24. Checking A-E:

The eagle was afraid to fly into the sky after remain in captivity for two years.

The above sentence is grammatically erroneous. The usage of 'remain' is incorrect. It should have been 'remaining' instead of 'remain'. Hence, the pair A-E is invalid.

Checking B-F:

The shrewd businessman quickly grabbed beneath the opportunity and earned a huge pile of money.

The above sentence is grammatically erroneous. The correct preposition after 'grabbed' would be 'onto'. Hence, the pair B-F is invalid.

Checking C-D:

Freelancing has always been a popular way to earn money online in spite of the Internet has a plethora of options.

The above sentence is grammatically erroneous. The usage of 'in spite of' in the above sentence is incorrect. The correct word in front of 'the internet' would be 'and' instead of the expression 'in spite of'. So, the pair C-D is invalid.

Hence, the correct option is (E).

25. Checking A-E:

The audience gave the veteran musician a standing ovation.

The above sentence is correct both grammatically and contextually. Hence, the pair A-E is valid.

Checking B-D:

Kudumbashree is one of the largest women- empowerment projects in the country today and covers over 50 per cent of Kerala households.

The above sentence is correct both grammatically and contextually. Hence, the pair B-D is valid.

Checking C-F:

Children who have been victims of violence are more likely to drop out of high school before graduation than their peers.

The above sentence is correct both grammatically and contextually. Hence, the pair C-F is valid.

Hence, the correct option is (D).

26. Checking A-F:

The tsunami swept over the island and destroyed over 2 billion dollars of property.

The above sentence is correct both grammatically and contextually. Hence, the pair A-F is valid.

Checking B-E:

The printer was out of ink and hence showed promise of growth and vitality.

Contextually speaking, the above sentence does not make any sense. Hence, the pair B-E is invalid.

Checking C-D:

Hopefully the momentum at both PhonePe and Paytm will spur more Indian entrepreneurship.

The above sentence is correct both grammatically and contextually. Hence, the pair C-D is valid.

Hence, the correct option is (C).

27. Checking A-E:

The angry mob beat upon the thief mercilessly.

The sentence is grammatically erroneous. The correct preposition after 'beat' should have been 'up' instead of 'upon'. The pair A-E is hence invalid.

Checking B-D:

The Centre is considering converting the factories into multiple companies on the lines of defense public sector undertakings.

The above sentence is correct both grammatically and contextually. Hence, the pair B-D is valid.

Checking C-F:

The four indicators for the hunger index are undernourishment, child stunting, child wasting and child mortality.

The above sentence is correct both grammatically and contextually. Hence, the pair C-F is valid.

Hence, the correct option is (D).

28. Checking A-E:

My sister fought with two boys and won the surprise tests.

The sentence does not make any sense contextually. The pair A-E is hence invalid.

Checking B-F:

The anguished cricketer lashed out at the journalists when they went to ask him questions.

The above sentence is correct both grammatically and contextually. Hence, the pair B-F is valid.

Checking C-D:

The father was deeply pained as his son failed to secure good marks of Mathematics.

The sentence does not make any sense grammatically. The correct preposition in front of "Mathematics" should have been 'in' instead of 'of'. The pair C-D is hence invalid.

Hence, the correct option is (B).

29. According to the passage, the idea of declining business in Dubai and the place losing its previous shine and glamour. The author has stated the reasons and Dubai's efforts to regain the lost position.

Hence, the correct option is (C).

30. According to the passage, the expatriates are moving out of the place due to the high cost of living. This has hampered business like never before. Thus I is correct. It is mentioned that 'Corporate mainstays, from Emirates airline to developer Emaar Properties, just reported disappointing third-quarter profits. The stock market is having its worst year since 2008.' Thus II is correct too. Statement III is incorrect as the passage states that there are malls present but they do not have sufficient stores and most of them are empty.

Hence, the correct option is (B).

31. According to the passage, Option (A) cannot be determined as anywhere in the passage has it been mentioned that the laws are stricter now, or they were lenient earlier. It was a place of fast growth and development was conspicuously present everywhere. Option (A) and (C) are thus ruled out. Option (D) and (E) are also incorrect.

Hence, the correct option is (B).

32. According to the passage, all the options are valid except for statement III. The scenario is totally different than what is mentioned in statement III. People are moving out of the country due to the high cost of living.

Hence, the correct option is (A).

33. All the statements are mentioned in the passage. It is mentioned that the high cost of living drives people out of the country. Thus, a lower cost of living will definitely help people to come and do business in Dubai.

'The oil slump since 2014 hit big spenders from neighbouring Gulf states who used to flock to Dubai (tourists from China and India are filling the gap, but they're more price-conscious). Saudis, in particular, are feeling the pinch, as their own government imposes fiscal austerity and confiscates private wealth.' Thus, statement II can be inferred from the passage.

'Dubai also faces consequences of its own success. Lacking energy resources of its own, the city had little choice but to build a non-oil economy. The 2014 crash jolted other Gulf countries into following suit. They're all planning for a post-crude era and trying to emulate their thriving neighbor by marketing their own capitals as regional hubs.' Thus, statement III is correct.

All the options are therefore correct.

Hence, the correct option is (E).

34. It is mentioned in the passage 'Government, builders and business alike are all looking to one event on the horizon that may come to the rescue. Dubai will host the World Expo fair in 2020. Meant to showcase the city's future prospects.'

Thus, the purpose of holding the World Expo fair in 2020 is to show the world the ability that Dubai has in the field of business.

Hence, the correct option is (E).

35. The phrase 'boom and bust' means 'a situation in which a period of great prosperity or rapid economic growth is abruptly followed by one of economic decline.'

Hence, the correct option is (C).

36. The word 'ailing' means 'sick; unwell.' The meanings of the words are:

Prosperous: wealthy

Frivolous: not having any serious purpose or value.

Healthy: in a good physical or mental condition; in good health

Hence, the correct option is (D).

37. The word 'austerity' means 'sternness.'

Growth: the process of increasing in size

Rudeness: lack of manners; discourteousness

Greed: an intense and selfish desire for something, especially wealth, power, or food.

Wisdom: the quality of having experience, knowledge, and good judgment; the quality of being wise

Hence, the correct option is (A).

38. The word 'showcase' means 'exhibit; display.'

Initiate: cause (a process or action) to begin

Strengthen: make or become stronger

Justify: show or prove to be right or reasonable

Focus: pay particular attention to

Hence, the correct option is (E).

39. I. is grammatically incorrect. As the ones who have promoted Brexit were the human beings and for living-beings 'who' is used instead of 'which'.

Correct sentence: There should be special places in hell for those who promoted Brexit.

And, II and III are correct.

Hence, the correct option is (D).

40. I. is grammatically incorrect as it uses incorrect preposition with the verb 'transform', which is accompanied by prepositions 'to' or 'into'.

Correct sentence: Global warming is on track to transform the frigid mountain peaks into empty rocks shortly.

II. is also grammatically incorrect with respect to use of singular pronoun 'this' along with the plural subject basins.

Correct sentence: People living in the downstream areas of these river basins benefit directly and indirectly from its resources.

And III is absolutely correct.

Hence, the correct option is (B).

41. Let the sum Rs. x

Then,

C.I. when compounded half yearly

$$= \text{Rs. } \left[x \times \left(1 + \frac{3}{100} \right)^2 - x \right]$$

$$= \text{Rs. } \left(\frac{10609}{10000} x - x \right)$$

$$= \text{Rs. } \left(\frac{609x}{10000} \right)$$

C.I. when compounded yearly

$$= \text{Rs. } \left[x \times \left(1 + \frac{4}{100} \right) - x \right]$$

$$= \text{Rs. } \left(\frac{26x}{25} - x \right)$$

$$= \text{Rs. } \frac{x}{25}$$

$$\therefore \frac{609x}{10000} - \frac{x}{25} = 104.50$$

$$\Rightarrow \frac{209x}{10000} = 104.50$$

$$\Rightarrow x = \left(\frac{104.50 \times 10000}{209} \right)$$

$\Rightarrow x = 5000$

Hence, the correct option is (B).

42. Given,

$64 \div \sqrt{?} + 12 = 20$

$\Rightarrow 64 \div \sqrt{?} = 8$

$\Rightarrow 64 \div 8 = \sqrt{?}$

$\Rightarrow 8 = \sqrt{?}$

$\therefore ? = 8^2$

$= 64$

Hence, the correct option is (B).

43. Given:

$28 + 5 \times (?) \div 3 = 73$

$\Rightarrow 5 \times (?) \div 3 = 45$

$\Rightarrow ? = 45 \times \dfrac{3}{5}$

$\therefore ? = 27$

Hence, the correct option is (A).

44. Given:

$\sqrt{676} \times \sqrt{576} - ? \times 18 = 300$

$\Rightarrow 26 \times 24 - ? \times 18 = 300$

$\Rightarrow 624 - ? \times 18 = 300$

$\Rightarrow ? \times 18 = 324$

$\therefore ? = 18$

Hence, the correct option is (C).

45. Given:

$x = 5 + \sqrt{79 + \sqrt{11 - \sqrt{49}}}$

$\Rightarrow x = 5 + \sqrt{79 + \sqrt{11 - 7}}$

$\Rightarrow x = 5 + \sqrt{79 + \sqrt{4}}$

$\Rightarrow x = 5 + \sqrt{79 + 2}$

$\Rightarrow x = 5 + \sqrt{81}$

$\Rightarrow x = 5 + 9$

$\Rightarrow x = 14$

Now, $2x + 3$

$\Rightarrow 2 \times 14 + 3$

$\Rightarrow 31$

Hence, the correct option is (A).

46. Given

$\left(\sqrt{64} + 3\right)^3 = 750 + ?$

$\Rightarrow (8 + 3)^3 = 750 + ?$

$\Rightarrow 11^3 = 750 + ?$

$\Rightarrow 1331 = 750 + ?$

$\therefore ? = 581$

Hence, the correct option is (B).

47. Given:

$\dfrac{(220 \div 20 \times 135 \div 15)}{3} = ?$

$\Rightarrow \dfrac{(11 \times 9)}{3} = ?$

$\therefore ? = 33$

Hence, the correct option is (C).

48. Given

$24 + \sqrt{81} \div 3 \times ? = 30$

$\Rightarrow 9 \div 3 \times ? = 6$

$\Rightarrow 3 \times ? = 6$

$\therefore ? = 2$

Hence, the correct option is (B).

49. Given

$4 \times \left(\dfrac{?}{100}\right) \times 210 + 225 = 351$

$\Rightarrow 4 \times \left(\dfrac{?}{100}\right) \times 210 = 126$

$\Rightarrow ? = \dfrac{(126 \times 100)}{(4 \times 210)}$

$\therefore ? = 15$

Hence, the correct option is (A).

50. Given:

$\dfrac{\left(\sqrt{36} \times \sqrt{64}\right)}{4} = ?$

$\Rightarrow \dfrac{(6 \times 8)}{4} = ?$

$\therefore ? = 12$

Hence, the correct option is (E).

51. Given:

$$40\% \text{ of } 180 + 70\% \text{ of } ? = 121$$

$$\Rightarrow \left(\frac{40}{100} \times 180\right) + \left(\frac{70}{100} \times ?\right) = 121$$

$$\Rightarrow 72 + \left(\frac{70}{100} \times ?\right) = 121$$

$$\Rightarrow \left(\frac{70}{100} \times ?\right) = 49$$

$$\therefore ? = 49 \times \frac{100}{70}$$

$$= 70$$

Hence, the correct option is (D).

52. Given:

Let the cost price of an item be Rs.a

$$\Rightarrow \text{Selling price of one item} = a \times \frac{110}{100} = \text{Rs. } \frac{11a}{10}$$

$$\Rightarrow \text{Selling price of other item} = a \times \frac{95}{100} = \text{Rs. } \frac{19a}{20}$$

$$\Rightarrow \left(\frac{11a}{10} + \frac{19a}{20}\right) - 2a = 200$$

$$\Rightarrow a = 4000$$

Total cost price of two items = 4000 × 2 = Rs.8000

$$\therefore \text{Required percentage} = \frac{200}{8000} \times 100 = 2.5\%$$

Hence, the correct option is (E).

53. Let the number of field workers be x.

There are 16 documentation workers.

Given total average = 45

$$\frac{Total\ age\ of\ all\ workers}{(16 + x)} = 45$$

Total age of all the workers = 45(16 + x)

The average age of 16 documentation workers = 38

Total age of documentation workers = 38 × 16

Total age of field workers = x × 52

Total age of all the workers = total age of field workers + total age of documentation workers

45(16 + x) = x × 52 + 38 × 16

$$\Rightarrow 45 \times 16 + 45x = 52x + 38 \times 16$$

$$\Rightarrow 720 - 608 = 7x$$

$$\Rightarrow 7x = 112$$

$$\Rightarrow x = 16$$

∴ Unmarried field workers = (16 – 7) = 9

Hence, the correct option is (E).

54. Let x km/hr be the speed of boat and y km/hr be the speed of stream

D be the total distance covered in 12 minutes together by hat and Akshara when Akshara realized that her at had fallen off

Here, the speed of the hat will be equal to speed of stream

As the hat and Akshara are travelling in the opposite direction for 12 minutes before realization and Akshara is travelling upstream

$$D = \frac{12y}{60} + \frac{12(x - y)}{60}$$

$$\Rightarrow D = \frac{12x}{60}$$

Now, Akshara realised that her hat is fallen off return in the downstream to take his hat

Akshara and hat are moving in the same direction and the distance between them is D so Akshara will catch the hat at the stating point in

$$\Rightarrow \frac{\frac{12x}{60}}{(x + y - y)}$$

$$\Rightarrow 12 \text{ minutes}$$

Total distance covered by hat to reach the staring point is 3 km

Total time taken to reach the starting point = 12 minutes + 12 minutes = 24 minutes

$$\Rightarrow \text{speed of stream} = \frac{3}{\left(\frac{24}{60}\right)} = 7.5 \text{ km/hr}$$

Hence, the correct option is (A).

55. Given:

The ratio of the salaries of Adam and Ponting = 5 : 7

The ratio of the salaries of Ponting and Marsh = 3 : 5

The salary of Adam = Rs. 16,500

Marsh spends 28.4% of his salary on his basic needs

Calculation:

The ratio of the salaries of Adam and Ponting = 5 : 7   ----(i)

The ratio of the salaries of Ponting and Marsh = 3 : 5   ----(ii)

Now we multiply equation (i) by 3 and equation (ii) by 7, we get

So the ratio of the salaries of Adam, Ponting, and Marsh

= 15 : 21 : 35

Now the ratio of the salaries of Adam and Marsh = 15 : 35 = 3 : 7

The salary of Adam = Rs. 16,500

Now let the salaries of Adam and Marsh be 3x and 7x.

So, 3x = 16,500

$$\Rightarrow x = 5,500$$

So the salary of Marsh = 7x = 7 × 5500 = Rs. 38,500

Marsh's expenditure on basic needs = 28.4% of 38,500 = $\frac{28.4}{100}$ × 38,500 = Rs. 10,934

So the money is left with Marsh = 38,500 – 10,934 = Rs. 27,566

∴ The money is left with Marsh after the expenditure on basic needs is Rs. 27,566

Hence, the correct option is (C).

56. Given,

Time taken by pipe A to fill the tank with chemical P = 30 minutes

Time taken by pipe B to fill the tank with chemical Q = 20 minutes

Time taken by pipe C to fill the tank with chemical R = 10 minutes

Part filled by A, B and C in 3 minutes $= 3 \times \left(\frac{1}{30} + \frac{1}{20} + \frac{1}{10}\right)$

$= 3 \times \frac{11}{60}$

$= \frac{11}{20}$

Part filled by C in 3 minutes $= \frac{3}{10}$

∴ Required ratio $= \frac{3}{10} \times \frac{20}{11}$

$= \frac{6}{11}$

Hence, the correct option is (B).

57. Number of shoes sold of Puma in April and June = 60 + 80 = 140

Number of shoes sold of Adidas in May and July = 60 + 100 = 160

∴ Required ratio = 140 : 160 = 7 : 8

Hence, the correct option is (A).

58. Number of shoes sold of all companies in May and June = (120 + 100 + 60) + (80 + 120 + 80)

= 560

Number of shoes sold of Adidas in all months = 120 + 60 + 80 + 100 = 360

∴ Required percent = $\frac{(560-360)}{360} \times 100 = 55\frac{5}{9}\%$

Hence, the correct option is (D).

59. Number of shoes sold of Puma in April, Nike in June, and Adidas in May = 60 + 120 + 60 = 240

∴ Required average = $\frac{240}{3}$ = 80

Hence, the correct option is (B).

60. Number of shoes sold of Puma in all months = 60 + 120 + 80 + 120 = 380

Number of shoes sold in June of all companies = 80 + 120 + 80 = 280

∴ Required difference = 380 – 280 = 100

Hence, the correct option is (E).

61. Number of shoes sold of all companies in July = 120 + 60 + 100 = 280

Number of shoes sold of companies in April = 60 + 80 + 120 = 260

∴ Required percent = $\frac{260}{280}$ × 100 = 92.85% ≈ 93%

Hence, the correct option is (C).

62. Let the ages of Swati and Aparna be x and y respectively.

The product of the ages of Swati and Aparna = xy = 120   ----- (1)

According to the given information,

3y = x + 2

⇒ x = 3y – 2

Substitute the above value of x in (1).

⇒ (3y – 2) × y = 120

⇒ 3y² – 2y – 120 = 0

⇒ 3y² + 18y – 20y – 120 = 0

⇒ 3y(y + 6) – 20(y + 6) = 0

⇒ (y + 6)(3y – 20) = 0

⇒ y = -6 or y = $\frac{20}{3}$

(∵ Age can't be negative)

⇒ y = $\frac{20}{3}$

x = 3 × $\left(\frac{20}{3}\right)$ – 2 = 20 – 2 = 18

∴ Age of Swati = 18 years

Hence, the correct option is (A).

63. As we know,

P = 2L+2B or 2(L+B)

Where L and B are the lengths of the rectangle's sides (length and breadth).

Let the length of the rectangle be L and its breadth be equal to B.

Therefore, 2(L+B) = 8936 and L×B = 4203987

Solving the two equations, we get,

B = 1347 and L = 3121 and their ratio equals 3121 : 1347

Hence, the correct option is (B).

64. Given:

80% of the people casted their votes

45% of the voters who casted votes are employed

66.67% of employed voters are engineers

Let the total number of voters be 100

80% of the voters casted their votes

$$\left(\frac{80}{100}\right) \times 100 = 80$$

80 people casted their votes

45% of 80 = $\left(\frac{45}{100} \times 80\right) = 36$

36 voters were employed

Among employed voters 66.67% are engineers

$\Rightarrow 36 \times 66.67\% = 24$

24% voters were the engineer

Number of non – engineers among total voters = 36 – 24 = 12

$\therefore$ Required percentage = $\dfrac{12}{100} \times 100 = 12\%$

Hence, the correct option is (A).

65. The series follows the following pattern:

$$48 \times \frac{3}{2} = 72$$

$$72 \times \frac{3}{2} = 108$$

$$108 \times \frac{3}{2} = 162$$

$$162 \times \frac{3}{2} = 243$$

$$243 \times \frac{3}{2} = 364.5 \neq 366$$

Since 364.5 will come in place of 366.

$\therefore$ Wrong number is 366.

Hence, the correct option is (E).

66. The series follows the following pattern:

150+300 = 420

450+300 = 750

750+300 = 1050

1050+300 = 1350

1350+300 = 1650

1650+300 = 1950

Since 1050 will come in place of 1060.

$\therefore$ Wrong number is 1060.

Hence, the correct option is (A).

67. The series follows the following pattern:

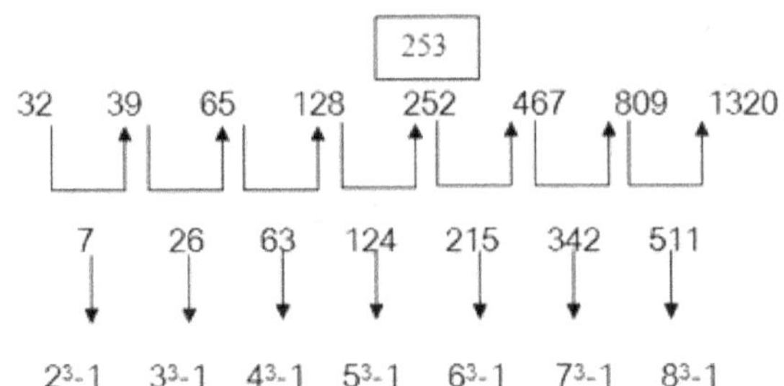

Since 252 will come in place of 253.

$\therefore$ Wrong number is 253.

Hence, the correct option is (C).

68. The series follows the following pattern:

38 + 11 = 49   ($\because$ 3 + 8 = 11)

49 + 13 = 62   ($\because$ 4 + 9 = 13)

62 + 8 = 70 $\neq$ 72   ($\because$ 6 + 2 = 8)

70 + 7 = 77   ($\because$ 7 + 0 = 7)

77 + 14 = 91   ($\because$ 7 + 7 = 14)

91 + 10 = 101   ($\because$ 9 + 1 = 10)

Since 70 will come in place of 77.

$\therefore$ Wrong number is 77.

Hence, the correct option is (C).

69. The series follows the following pattern:

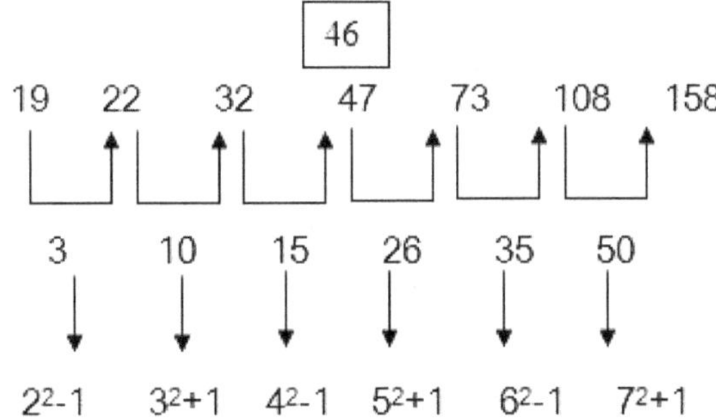

Since 47 will come in place of 46.

$\therefore$ Wrong number is 46.

Hence, the correct option is (B).

70. Ratio of shares of A, B and C = Ratio of their investments for 2 years

= [(5000 × 2): (7000 × 2): (6000 × 2)]

= [10000: 14000: 12000]

= 5: 7: 6

Given: Net profit earned = Rs. 10,800

$\therefore$ B's share = $\dfrac{7}{18} \times 10800$ = Rs. 4,200

Hence, the correct option is (B).

Ques (71-76): Books: A, B, C, D, P, Q, R and S.

1) There are three 3 books kept between A & R.

2) Book P is just below to book R.

Case – 1	Case – 2	Case – 3	Case – 4	Case – 5	Case – 6
A			R		
	A		P	R	
		A		P	R
					P
R			A		
P	R			A	
	P	R			A
		P			

3) There are two books kept between P & S.

(Here case – 4 and 5 will gets eliminated)

Case – 1	Case – 2	Case – 3	Case – 6
A			S
	A		
S		A	R
	S		P
R		S	
P	R		
	P	R	A
		P	

4) There are as many books between B & D as R & A.

5) Book B is above book D.

Case – 1	Case – 2	Case – 3	Case – 6
A	B		S
	A	B	B
S		A	R
B	S		P
R	D	S	
P	R	D	D
	P	R	A
D		P	

6) Book C is immediate above to D and neither D nor A is at the lowermost rack.

Case – 6
S
B
R
P
C
D
A
Q

71. Above combination will be the final combination.

As we can see in the above table there are four books between R and Q.

Hence, the correct option is (C).

72. 1) Book C is kept 3 Book above to book A. ⇒ False

2) Two books kept between D and R ⇒ True

3) Book B is kept immediately above to R. ⇒ True

4) Book Q kept in the lowermost rack. ⇒ True

5) Book S is kept in the topmost rack. ⇒ True

Therefore, "Book C is kept 3 Book above to book A" is an only a false statement.

Hence, the correct option is (A).

73. As Q is kept in lowermost rack therefore there will be 7 books above to the book Q.

Hence, the correct option is (D).

74. As we can see in the above arrangement Books A, C, R and S are at even number rack but book B is at odd number rack. (Considering bottom to top)

Therefore, B is an odd one here.

Hence, the correct option is (B).

75. Therefore, Q is at the lowermost rack.

Hence, the correct option is (D).

76. Therefore, A is in the second lowest rack.

Hence, the correct option is (B).

77. Given Statements: A > B < C < D; K ≥ L > M = D; G > H ≥ I ≤ J < A

On combining: G > H ≥ I ≤ J < A > B < C < D = M < L ≤ K

Conclusions:

I. G > A → False (Given G > H ≥ I ≤ J < A thus clear relation between G and A cannot be determined)

II. A ≥ G → False (Given G > H ≥ I ≤ J < A thus clear relation between G and A cannot be determined)

III. K > I → False (Given I ≤ J < A > B < C < D = M < L ≤ K so K> B but the relation between B and I is not clear thus clear relation between K and I cannot be determined)

Hence, the correct option is (E).

78. Given statements: R ≤ D ≤ X; K > V ≥ I; R = O ≥ K

On combining: X ≥ D ≥ R = O ≥ K > V ≥ I

Conclusions:

I. D ≤ V → False (D > R = O ≥ K > V → D > V)

II. X > K → False (X ≥ D > R = O ≥ K → X > K)

III. I ≤ O → True (O ≥ K > V ≥ I → O > I)

Thus, Only III is True.

Hence, the correct option is (A).

79. Given statements: X< M ≤ W; B ≥ L ≥ O; O = X

On combining: B ≥ L ≥ O = X; W ≥ M >O = X

Conclusions:

I. B >M → False (B ≥ L ≥ O and M >O → relation between B and M cannot be determined.)

II. M ≥ B → False (B ≥ L ≥ O and M >O → relation between B and M cannot be determined.)

III. L< W → False (L ≥ O and W ≥ M >O → relation between L and W can't be determined.)

None of the conclusions are true but conclusions I and II form a complementary pair.

Thus, either conclusion I or conclusion II is true.

Hence, the correct option is (C).

80. Given Statements: R ≤ A < N ≤ I; K ≥ I; V > A

On combining: R ≤ A < N ≤ I ≤ K and V > A

Conclusions:

I) K ≥ A → False (A < N ≤ I ≤ K implies that K is greater than A)

II) V > I → False (V > A < N ≤ I here we don't have the clear relation between V and I)

III) R ≤ K → False (R ≤ A < N ≤ I ≤ K here we have R is less than K)

Thus, the correct answer is None of these.

Hence, the correct option is (E).

81. Given statements: W < X, Y = Z , V < U, X > Z, G ≥ Y, W > U, H = V

on combining : G ≥ Y = Z < X > W > U > V = H

Conclusions:

(i): G > X

Here we can see the opposite signs between G and X, thus no relationship can be established between them.

So conclusion (i) does not follow.

(ii): W > H

Here, the common sign between W and H is '>'. Thus W > H.

So conclusion (ii) follows.

(iii): Y = H

Here we can see the opposite signs between Y and H, thus no relationship can be established between them.

Therefore conclusion (iii) does not follow.

Hence, the correct option is (C).

82. We have drawn the figure according to the information given in the question,

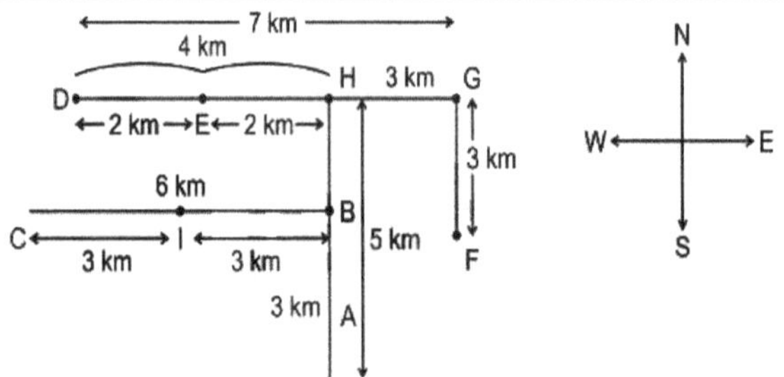

To find distance between E and I:

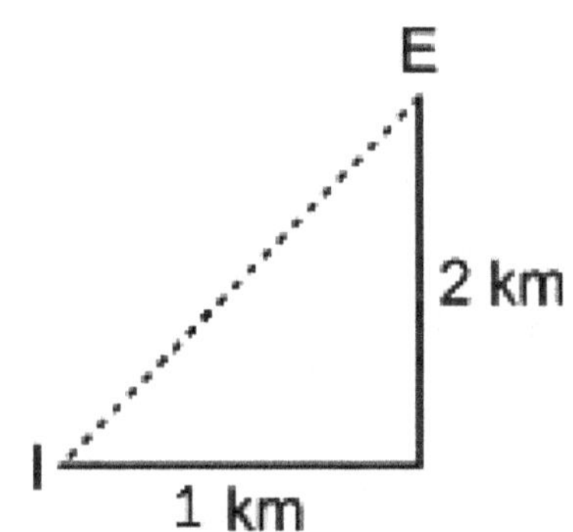

From the figure, it is clear that the distance between E and I =

$$EI = \sqrt{2^2 + 1^2}$$

$$= \sqrt{5} = 2.23 \text{ km}$$

Hence, the correct option is (C).

83. We have drawn the figure according to the information given in the question,

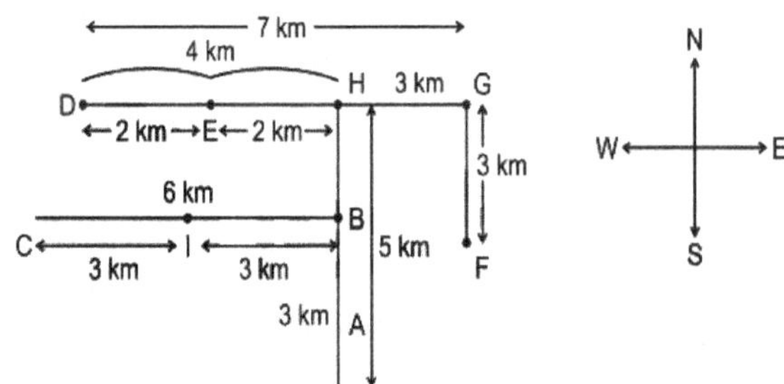

From the figure, it is clear that the distance of I from B and C is 3 km.

Hence, the correct option is (C).

84. We have drawn the figure according to the information given in the question,

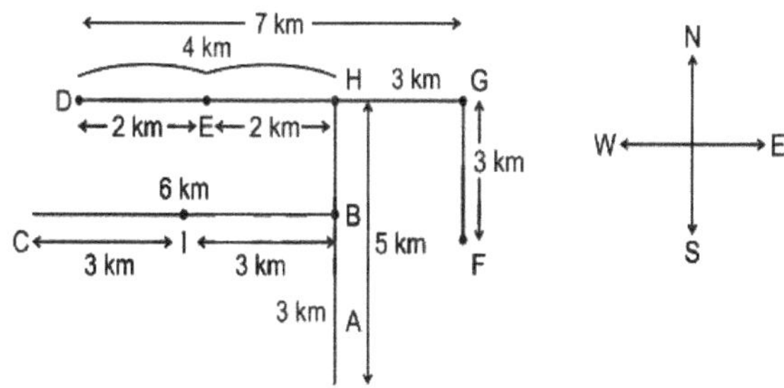

From the figure it is clear that the point D is North – East Direction from Point C.

Hence, the correct option is (D).

85. The least possible Venn diagram for the given statements is as follows,

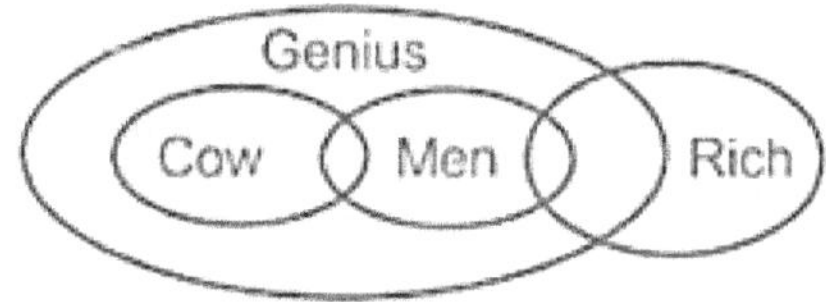

Conclusion:

I. Some genius are rich → True (All men are genius and some men which are not cow are rich)

II. Some rich are cow → False (It is possible but not definite)

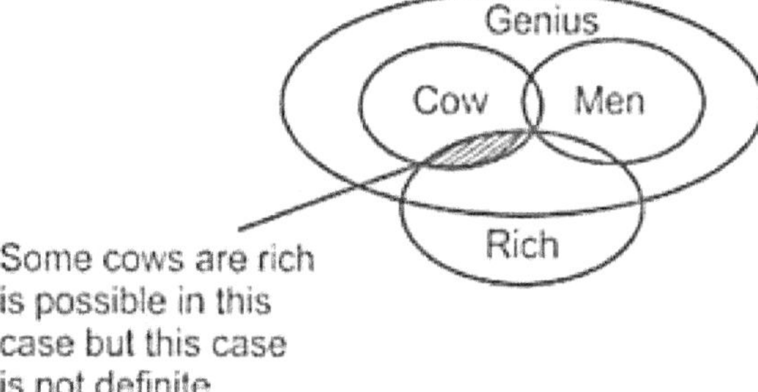

Some cows are rich is possible in this case but this case is not definite

III. Some cow are genius → True (All men and cow are genius)

Thus, only conclusion I and III follows.

Hence, the correct option is (C).

86. The least possible Venn diagram is as follows-

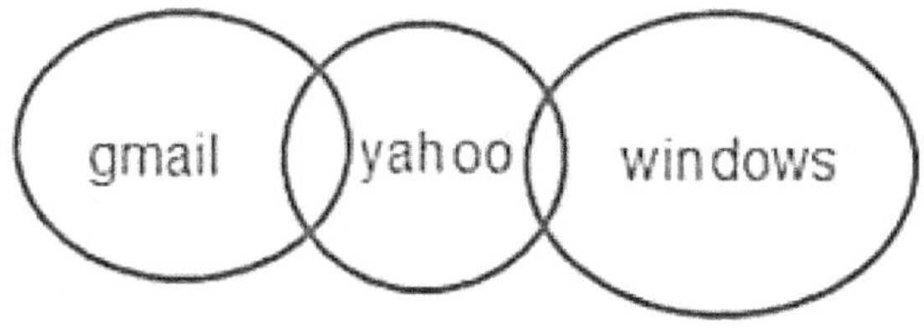

Conclusions – I Some gmail are windows – False

Conclusions – II No gmail are windows.– True

So, only II follows

Hence, the correct option is (B).

87. The least possible Venn diagram is as follows-

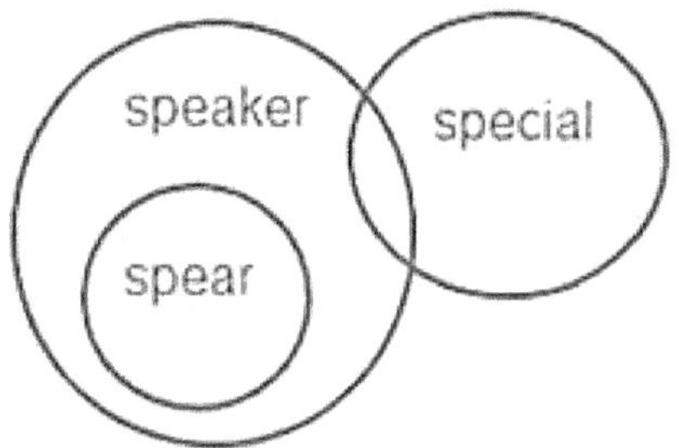

Conclusions – I some spear are special is a possibility – False (as only speaker is spear there is no relation possible between spear and any other except Speaker)

Conclusions – II only a few spear are special – False (Only a few speaker are special, Only speaker are spear)

So, neither I nor II follows.

Hence, the correct option is (D).

88. The least possible Venn diagram is as follows-

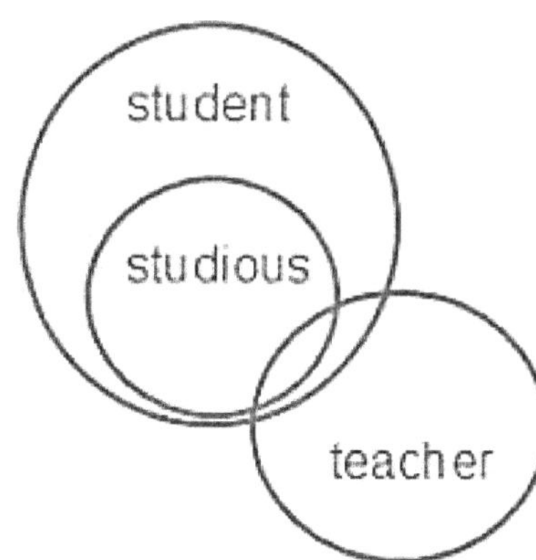

Conclusions – I Some teacher are student – True (All studious are student)

Conclusions – II No student are teacher – False (All studious are student)

So, only conclusions – I follows.

Hence, the correct option is (A).

89. The least possible Venn diagram is as follows-

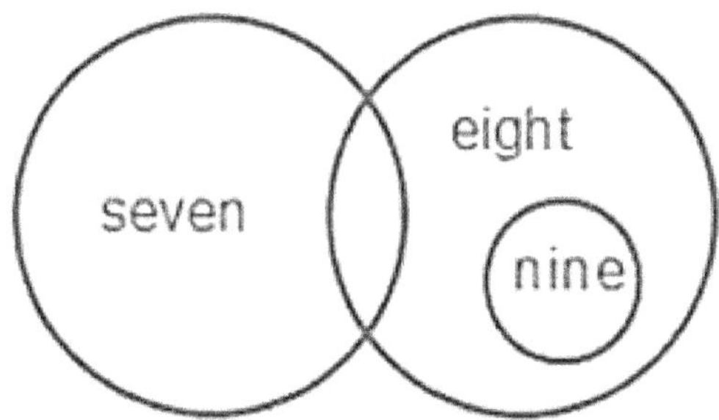

Conclusions – I some seven are nine – False (it is possible but not definite)

Conclusions – II All nine are eight – True (Only eight are nine)

So, only II follows.

Hence, the correct option is (B).

Ques (90-95):M is third to the right of S, who sits second to the left of Y.

C is third to the left of Y.

Following cases can be prepared with the given hints.

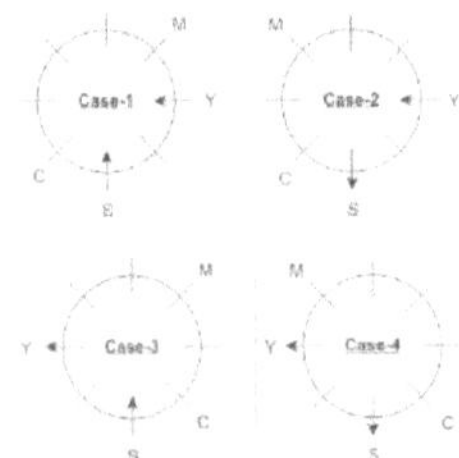

P sits on the immediate right of X, who faces the same direction as faced by M.

Neither X nor P is adjacent to M.

Case2 and 3 fail to satisfy the given hints. Further two cases arise from Case-1 and Case-4 which are named as Case-1A and Case-4A.

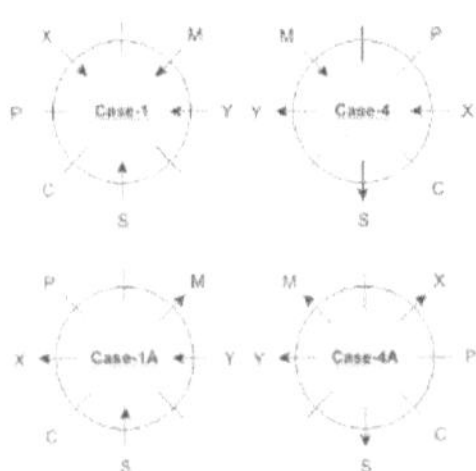

C is third to the right of B.

J is second to the left of M.

B and S face same direction.

Immediate neighbors of C face opposite directions.

Not more than 4 persons face outside.

Case-4A eliminated as it violates the last hint.

Case-1A and 4 eliminated as they violate the second hint where J is to be placed second to the left of M.

Thus only Case-1 fulfills all the given hints.

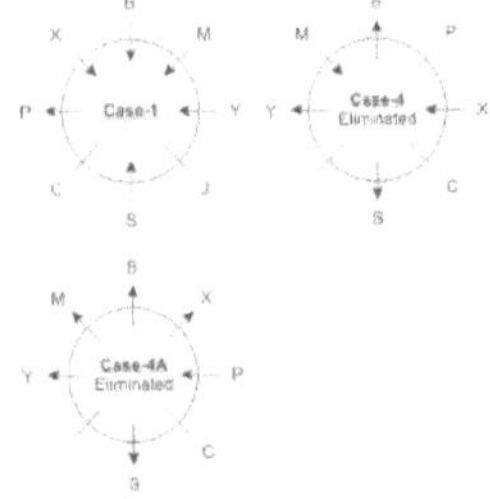

C and J face opposite direction to that of B.

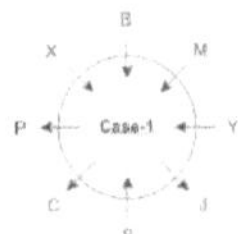

90. Thus, 5 persons face towards centre.

Hence, the correct option is (D).

91. Thus, J is third to the left of P.

Hence, the correct option is (B).

92. Thus, P is the odd one out as all others except P face towards centre.

Hence, the correct option is (E).

93. Thus, X is second to the right of C.

Hence, the correct option is (A).

94. Thus, 4 persons sit between J and B when counted from the right of former.

Hence, the correct option is (D).

95. Thus, J is second to the left of C.

Hence, the correct option is (A).

Ques (96-100): The first element of the code represents the numerical value of first letter, considering A-Z as 1-26.

For Example: Disk

The first element would be 4, which represents the numeric value of D.

The second element of the code represents the codes as per number of letters as shown in the following table.

Number of letters Code:

Number of letters	Code
4	#
5	!
6	&
7	$
8	%
9	@

Disk has 4 letters, so its middle code would be # as per the table.

The third element represents the second letter of the respective word.

Second letter in the word Disk is 'i', so the last element would be 'I'.

Thus code for Disk would be 4#I.

96. By following the above explanation, we can get the code for "Easy goals fulfilled" as 5#A 7!O 6@U.

Hence, the correct option is (C).

97. By following the above explanation, we can get the code for "Take advance receipt" as 20#A 1$D 18$E.

Hence, the correct option is (A).

98. By following the above explanation, we can get the code for "Advertise your product" as 1@D 25#O 16$R.

Hence, the correct option is (B).

99. By following the above explanation, we can get the code for "Great gesture" as 7!R 7$E.

Hence, the correct option is (C).

100. By following the above explanation, we can get the code for "Travel with wander" as 20&R 23#I 23&A.

Hence, the correct option is (D).

Test of English Language

Ques (1-5):Direction: A passage is given below with five blanks labelled (A)-(E). Below the passage, five options are given for each blank. Choose the word that fits each blank most appropriately in the context of the passage, and mark the corresponding answer.

Almost one-third of the world's population consists of children. Therefore they need to be cared for and __(A)__. Children are an important component of the social __(B)__. Finding a single definition to describe a 'child' is becoming an __(C)__ task. The dictionary defines the word 'child' as a young person, especially __(D)__ infancy and youth.

Biologically, a child is anyone between the stages of infancy and adulthood, or a child is a human being between the stages of birth and puberty. The legal definition of 'child' refers to a minor, or somebody who is yet to become an adult. The only __(E)__ is that the child should be unable to maintain himself. Hence a child, though not a minor, is still a child as long as it is unable to maintain himself.

Q.1 Which of the following words most appropriately fits the blank labelled (A)?

A. Emotional   **B.** Protected
C. Democratic   **D.** Abused
E. None of these

Q.2 Which of the following words most appropriately fits the blank labelled (B)?

A. Structure   **B.** Fullness
C. Statutory   **D.** Contrast
E. None of these

Q.3 Which of the following words most appropriately fits the blank labelled (C)?

A. Qualified   **B.** Pleasant
C. Uphill   **D.** Untoward
E. None of these

Q.4 Which of the following words most appropriately fits the blank labelled (D)?

A. Between   **B.** Among
C. Amidst   **D.** Along
E. None of these

Q.5 Which of the following words most appropriately fits the blank labelled (E)?

A. Surprise   **B.** Policies
C. Qualification   **D.** Adopt
E. None of these

Ques (6-10):Direction: The following question has two blanks, each blank indicating that something has been omitted.

Choose the set of words for each blank that best fits in the context of the sentence.

Q.6 Problems of exclusion will be eliminated if the payer-insurer is the state, the ___________ is done through public taxes, and coverage is ___________.

A. loading, unreal
B. funding, imaginary
C. financing, universal
D. projection, hazy
E. sponsoring, questionable

Q.7 Investors can think of putting in at least 10 per cent of their savings in gold as it has the ___________ to be an ___________ for the portfolio in a fragile trade environment.

A. purpose, disturbance
B. status, inspiration
C. potential, insurance
D. possibility, indictment
E. reasoning, arrangement

Q.8 Central banks across the globe are preparing to loosen monetary policies, to ___________ their respective economies and it is expected that gold will continue the ongoing ___________.

A. spur, momentum   **B.** inspire, synergy
C. enervate, juncture   **D.** encourage, matches
E. design, cooperation

Q.9 Promoters of MSMEs must have ___________ in the game to ensure that funds — venture capital, as well as bank loans made liberal by fiat — are not ___________ off.

A. interest, taken   **B.** name, bought
C. skin, siphoned   **D.** feet, stolen
E. hands, signed

Q.10 In mature economies, central banks accept corporate bonds as ___________ for their liquidity management operations, so as to purposefully ___________ the bond market.

A. security, undermine
B. collateral, develop
C. woeful, work
D. insurance, accentuate
E. baggage, strengthen

Ques (11-13):Direction: In the given question, four words are printed in bold and are marked as A, B, C and D. Of these, the positions of two of these words may be incorrect and need to be exchanged to make the sentence correct. Find the two words which need to be exchanged. In case the given sentence is correct, your answer is (E), i.e., 'No Interchange required'.

Q.11 The NCLAT's **(A) findings** lay emphasis on greater **(B) transparency** and adherence to governance norms especially in the conduct of affairs at the **(C) controlling** company of a large **(D) diversified** conglomerate.

A. A-D
B. B-C
C. A-C
D. B-D
E. No Interchange Required

Q.12 The telecom industry has been increasingly **(A) bruising** about India's **(B) daunting** high spectrum costs, which are all the more **(C) disproportionately** as the companies have gone through a **(D) vocal** price war that left finances stretched.

A. A-D
B. B-C
C. A-C
D. B-D and A-C
E. No Interchange required

Q.13 The government **(A) distracted** to **(B) urgently** focus on the economic crisis, but it is increasingly **(C) needs** by a gathering storm on the political **(D) front.**

A. A-D
B. B-C
C. A-C
D. B-D
E. No Interchange Required

Ques (14-23):Direction: Read the following passage to answer the given questions based on it. Some words/phrases are printed in bold to help you locate them while answering some of the questions.

"Rivers should link, not divide us," said the Indian prime Minister expressing concern over interstate disputes and urged state governments to show "understanding and consideration, statesmanship and an appreciation of the other point of view."

Water conflicts in India now reach every level; divide every segment of our society, political parties, states, regions and sub-regions within states, districts, castes and groups and individual farmers. Water conflicts within and between many developing countries are also taking a serious turn. Fortunately, the "water wars", forecast by so many, have not yet **materialized**. War has taken place, but over oil, not water. Water is **radically** altering and affecting political boundaries all over the world, between as well as within countries. In India, water conflicts are likely to **worsen** before they being to be resolved. Till then they pose a significant threat to economic growth, security and health of the ecosystem and the victims are likely to be the poorest of the poor as well as the very sources of water - rivers, wetlands and aquifers.

Conflicts might sound bad or negative, but they are logical developments in the absence of proper democratic, legal and administrative mechanisms to handle issues at the root of water conflicts. Part of the problem steams from the specific nature of water, namely that water is divisible and amenable to sharing; one unit of water is used by one is a unit **denied** to others; it has multiple uses and users and involves resultant trade-offs. Excludability is an **inherent** problem and very often exclusion costs involved are very high: it involves the issue of graded scales and boundaries and need for evolving a corresponding understanding around them. Finally the way

water is planned, used and managed causes externalities, both positive and negative, and many of them are unidirectional and **asymmetric**.

There is a relatively greater visibility as well as a greater body of experience in evolving policies, frameworks, legal set-ups and administrative mechanisms dealing with immobile natural resources, however contested the space may be Reformist as well as revolutionary movements are rooted in issues related to land. Several political and legal interventions addressing the issue of equity and societal justice have been attempted. Most countries have gone through land reforms of one type or another. Issues related to forests have also generated a body of comprehensive literature on forest resources and rights. Though conflicts over them have not necessarily been effectively or adequately resolved, they have received much more serious attentation, have been studied in their own right and practical as well as theoretical means of dealing with them have been sought. In contrast, water conflicts have not received the same kind of attention.

Q.14 According to the author which of the following is/are consequences of water conflicts?

1. Trans-border conflicts between developing countries.

2. Water bodies will remain unused and unaffected till the conflict is resolved.

3. Water conflicts have altered the political boundaries within countries.

A. Only 1   **B.** Only 2
C. Only 3   **D.** Both 1 & 3
E. None of these

Q.15 Why dose the author ask readers not to view conflicts too negatively?

1. Most countries have survived them easily.

2. They bring political parties together.

3. They only affect the grass root levels.

A. Only 1   **B.** Only 2
C. Only 3   **D.** All 1, 2 & 3
E. None of 1, 2 and 3

Q.16 The author's main objective in writing the passage is to:

A. Showcase government commitment to solve the water distribution problem.

B. Make a strong case for war as the logical resolution for water conflicts.

C. Point out the seriousness of the threat posed by unresolved water conflicts.

D. Describe how the very nature of water contributes to water struggles.

E. Criticise governmental efforts for water conflict resolution.

Q.17 Which of the following is TRUE in the context of the passage?

A. Water wars are taking place between many developing countries.

B. There have been several legal interventions in India to govern the use of water resources.

C. The poor people are worst affected by water conflicts.

D. Water diversion by Indian states has helped resolve water

disputes.
E. None of these

Q.18 What is the prime Minister's advice to resolve water disputes?
A. Link all rivers to make national grid.
B. Politicians alone can solve the problem.
C. Bridges and dams can resolve water issues.
D. Make consensual and conscious efforts.
E. Create public awareness.

Q.19 Which of the following is NOT TRUE in the context of the passage?
A. Deeper problems exist at the root of all water conflicts
B. Competing usage of water is a cause of water conflict.
C. In India water conflicts affect all levels.
D. Only social stability is unaffected by water disputes.
E. All are true.

Q.20 According to the passage, which of the following is a limitation of water resulting in disputes?
A. Water is not a divisible resource.
B. Manipulation of water distribution is easy.
C. Water is an interconnected resource.
D. Water is an immobile resource.
E. None of these

Q.21 Pick out the word which is the closest in meaning to the printed in bold as used in the passage.
Radically
A. Suddenly　　　　**B.** Equally
C. Completely　　　**D.** Moderately
E. Concurrently

Q.22 Pick out the word which is the closest in meaning to the printed in bold as used in the passage.
Inherent
A. Functional　　　**B.** Intense
C. Feasible　　　　**D.** Intrinsic
E. Genetic

Q.23 Pick out the word which is opposite in meaning to the printed in bold as used in the passage.
Denied
A. Considered　　　**B.** Assigned
C. Concerned　　　**D.** Fined
E. Acknowledged

Ques (24-28):Direction: Five statements are given below, which are jumbled in any random order. These statements will form a coherent and meaningful paragraph, when arranged in the correct sequence. Arrange the sentences in the right order and answer the questions that follow.

The World Health Organization has declared India as polio-free since no new polio case has been reported in the country in the last couple of years.

A. It also gives an idea regarding the effective implementation of the government schemes in the country so that they give the desired result

B. Without participation from the general public, it would not have been possible to achieve this tremendous feat with the government schemes only.

C. India can take heart from this success and can replicate the same model for eradication of other diseases also from the country.

D. The thrust should be on educating the mass regarding the harmful effects of insects and the reasons for the growth of such insects.

E. This underlines the efforts by the Ministry of Health and Family Welfare along with the staff members at the ground level.

Q.24 Which among the following will be the FIRST sentence of the paragraph after the rearrangement?
A. A　　**B.** B　　**C.** D　　**D.** E
E. B

Q.25 Which among the following will be the second sentence of the paragraph after the rearrangement?
A. D　　**B.** C　　**C.** B　　**D.** A
E. E

Q.26 Which among the following will be the third sentence of the paragraph after the rearrangement?
A. A　　**B.** B　　**C.** D　　**D.** E
E. C

Q.27 Which among the following will be the fourth sentence of the paragraph after the rearrangement?
A. H　　　　　　**B.** D
C. B　　　　　　**D.** A
E. None of the above

Q.28 Which among the following will be the fifth sentence of the paragraph after the rearrangement?
A. D　　**B.** B　　**C.** E　　**D.** C
E. A

Ques (29-31):Direction: The given sentence has been broken up into four different parts. The error, if any, will be in one or more parts of the sentence. Select the option which contains the part/parts of the sentence which has/have an error (spelling, grammatical or contextual). If there is no error, choose option E.

Q.29 Parliament is not competing to (A) / enacts any law which is inconsistent (B) / with a fundamental rights (C) / enshrined in Part III of the Constitution. (D) / No Error (E)
A. Only B　　　　　　**B.** Only A and C
C. Only A, B and C　　**D.** Only B, C and D
E. No error

Q.30 An ordinance is a constitutionally sanctioned (A) / ad hoc mechanism for which critically (B) / urgent situations are meet when Parliament (C) / or a State Assembly is not in session. (D) / No Error (E)
A. Only C　　　　　　**B.** Only B and C
C. Only A, B and D　　**D.** Only B, C and D
E. No error

Q.31 Given there limited attention and (A) / computational capacity, people gravitate (B) / towards the status quo, which often results (C) / in a gap between a policy's intent and action. (D) / No Error (E)

A. Only A
B. Only D
C. Only A and C
D. Only B and D
E. No error

Ques (32-33):Direction: Two sentences are given below. Five options are given below for two sentences. Choose the correct option.

Q.32 1. These novels that I have ordered online after much wait during yesterday's flash sale are for you and me, they are coming tomorrow.

2. Each of the participants get a gift hamper for the participation as it's the 50th anniversary of the company and we have registered a net profit of 100 million this year.

A. If only sentence 1 has error
B. If only sentence 2 has error
C. If there is an error in both 1 and 2
D. If there is no error in both sentences
E. If there is more than one error in either of the two sentences

Q.33 1. There is nothing that can be done to stop the girl from filing a report against a crime she witnessed.

2. The plays who leave a lasting impression on the minds of the spectators are those which strive to create a change in theatre.

A. If only sentence 1 has error
B. If only sentence 2 has error
C. If there is an error in both 1 and 2
D. If there is no error in both sentences
E. If there is more than one error in either of the two sentences

Ques (34-35):Direction: In each of these questions, a sentence with four words printed in bold type is given. These are numbered as A, B, C and D. One of these four words printed in bold may be either wrongly spelled or inappropriate in context of the sentence. Find out the word which is wrongly spelled or inappropriate if any. The number of that word is your answer. If all the words printed in bold are correctly spelled and also appropriate in the context of the sentence, mark (5) "All are correct" as your answer.

Q.34 The **misogynist (A)** was **publicly (B) humiliated** (C) by a group of women in front of our house the day before **yesterday (D).**

A. Misogynist
B. Publicly
C. Humiliated
D. Yesterday
E. All are correct

Q.35 The young **bureaucrat's (A) unflinching (B)** decision to root out corruption brought him **acolades (C)** from his **subordinates (D).**

A. Bureaucrat's
B. Unflinching
C. Acolades
D. Subordinates
E. All are correct

Ques (36-40):Direction: In the following questions, some part of the sentence is highlighted in bold. Which of the options given below the sentence should replace the part printed in bold to make the sentence grammatically correct? If the sentence is correct as it is given then choose option E 'No Correction required' as the answer.

Q.36 Maslow's Hierarchy of needs states that we must satisfy each need in turn <u>starting with the first, dealing in the most obvious needs of survival itself.</u>

A. Starting with the first, which deals with the most obvious needs of survival itself.
B. First starting with the one that deals with the most obvious needs of survival itself.
C. Starting with the first, which is dealt with the most obvious needs of survival itself.
D. Starting with the first one that deals in the most obvious need of survival itself.
E. No Correction required

Q.37 An individual's behaviour may change over time, becoming bizarre if medication is stopped <u>and returns closer to normal when receiving appropriate treatment.</u>

A. And can return closer to normal when receiving appropriate treatment.
B. While returned closer to normal when receiving appropriate treatment.
C. And returning closer to normal when receiving appropriate treatment.
D. After returning close to normal when receiving appropriate treatment.
E. No Correction required

Q.38 Opposing free trade, some argue, <u>is tantamount to support economic injustice.</u>

A. Is tantamount of supporting economic injustice.
B. Is tantamount with supporting economic injustice.
C. Is tantamountly supporting economic injustice.
D. Is tantamount to supporting economic injustice.
E. No Correction required

Q.39 The Indian Air Force has played a vital role in the nation's defense and our glorious history is <u>replete of numerous counts</u> of valour and fortitude in the face of extreme odds.

A. Replete of numerous accounts
B. Replete with numerous accounts
C. Replete by numerous account
D. Replete through numerous counts
E. No correction required

Q.40 Everyone around Sachin in 1988 knew that he would play for India but never thought <u>he would end up</u> with all the cricketing records possible.

A. He would end
B. He would end in
C. He would end with
D. He would end into
E. No correction required

Test of Numerical Ability

Q.41 A certain sum of money amounts to Rs. 720 in 2 years and Rs. 870 in 4.5 years, with same rate of simple interest. Find the rate of interest.

A. 12%   **B.** 15%   **C.** 10%   **D.** 8%
E. 11%

Ques (42-44):Direction: What will come in the place of question $(?)$ mark?

Q.42 $26 \times 15 + 310 - (15)^2 = 25\%$ of ?

[RBI Assistant, 2019]

A. 1500   **B.** 1800   **C.** 1700   **D.** 1900
E. 1600

Q.43 $20 \times 168 \div 14 - 40 = ? + 110$

[RBI Assistant, 2019]

A. 84   **B.** 75   **C.** 90   **D.** 87
E. 94

Q.44 $\sqrt{625} \div \sqrt{16} \times 6 = ?\%$ of 300

[RBI Assistant, 2019]

A. 8.5   **B.** 15   **C.** 17.5   **D.** 10
E. 12.5

Q.45 Direction: Simplify the given expression.

$(4698 - 3625 - 857) = ?^3 - 42 - \sqrt{7225}$

A. 49   **B.** 14   **C.** 7   **D.** 343
E. 326

Q.46 A person divides a certain amount among his three sons in the ratio of $3:4:5$. If he had divided this amount in the ratio of $\frac{1}{3}, \frac{1}{4}, \frac{1}{5}$ his son, who had got the lowest share earlier, would get Rs. 1188 more. Find the amount (in Rs).

[SSC CGL, 2020]

A. 5640   **B.** 6840
C. 6768   **D.** 7008
E. None of these

Q.47 Rohan started a garage to provide the services for the old cars and after giving the labor charges of 10% per month, he was saving 15% per car which was Rs. 15000 then and on average he was selling 20 cars per month. What was the selling price of 20 cars?

A. Rs. 1200000   **B.** Rs. 2000000
C. Rs. 3000000   **D.** Rs. 2200000
E. None of these

Q.48 A man can row 5 km along the stream in 25 minutes and return in 50 miuutes. Find the speed of current (in km/h).

A. 2 km/h   **B.** 3 km/h   **C.** 4 km/h   **D.** 5 km/h
E. 6 km/h

Ques (49-53):Direction: In the following number series, only one number is wrong. Find out the wrong number.

Q.49 72, 73, 59, 78, 62, 87, 51

A. 73   **B.** 59   **C.** 78   **D.** 62
E. 51

Q.50 11, 35, 65, 119, 191, 281

A. 191   **B.** 65   **C.** 35   **D.** 119
E. 120

Q.51 8, 8, 12, 22, 60, 180, 630

A. 12   **B.** 22   **C.** 60   **D.** 180
E. 630

Q.52 1, 6, 23, 60, 125, 225, 371

A. 6   **B.** 23   **C.** 60   **D.** 225
E. 371

Q.53 171, 172, 346, 1031, 4168, 20845

[IDBI Bank Assistant Manager, 2021]

A. 171   **B.** 1031   **C.** 4168   **D.** 20845
E. 346

Q.54 The marks scored by Sam, by Geeta and by Radha in a competitive exam for Mathematics section out of 150 is 94, 85 and 120 respectively. For Science section, the scores for Sam, Geeta and Radha out of 150 is 135, 80 and 90 respectively. Find the average scores in percent of Sam, Geeta and Radha.

A. 76.33%, 55%, 70%   **B.** 55%, 46%, 59%
C. 78%, 57.33%, 82%   **D.** 70%, 60%, 62%
E. 80%, 65%, 91%

Q.55 A boat takes 90 minutes less to travel 36 miles downstream than to travel the same distance upstream. If the speed of the boat in still water is 10 mph, the speed of the stream is:

A. 2 mph   **B.** 2.5 mph
C. 3 mph   **D.** 4 mph
E. None of these

Q.56 The altitude of trapezium is 10 cm and the area of the trapezium is 195 cm². If the parallel sides are in the ratio of 5 : 8, find the length of longer side.

A. 15   **B.** 25   **C.** 29   **D.** 23
E. 24

Q.57 A started a business with a capital of Rs. 1,00,000. One year later, B joined him with a capital of Rs. 2,00,000. At the end of 3 years from the start of the business, the profit earned was 84,000. The share of B in the profit exceeded the share of A by

A. Rs. 18,000   **B.** Rs. 14,000
C. Rs. 12,000   **D.** Rs. 16,000
E. None of these

Ques (58-62):Direction: Following bar graph show the number of units produced and sold by different companies.

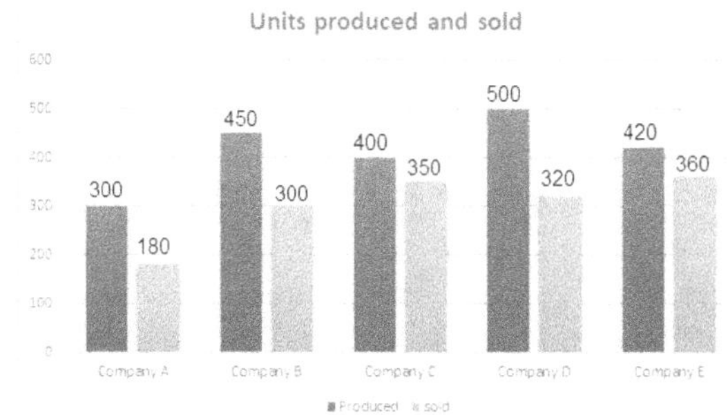

Q.58 What is the ratio of unsold units of Company E and D together to the sold units of company A and B together?

A. $1:2$ **B.** $2:1$ **C.** $3:2$ **D.** $4:3$
E. $5:7$

Q.59 Units produced by company C is how much percent more/less than that of the units sold by company B?

A. 25% **B.** 20% **C.** 30% **D.** 33.33%
E. 37.5%

Q.60 What is the average unit of all the companies that remain unsold?

A. 118 **B.** 120 **C.** 112 **D.** 150
E. 130

Q.61 If company F produces 10% more unit that was produced by company A and sells 20% fewer units that were sold by Company C. How many units of company F remain unsold?

A. 60 **B.** 50 **C.** 70 **D.** 90
E. 80

Q.62 What is the difference between the total produced and total sold units by all the companies?

A. 500 **B.** 560 **C.** 550 **D.** 600
E. 650

Q.63 When 75 is added to 75% of a number, the result obtained is the number itself. Find the number.

A. 50 **B.** 60 **C.** 300 **D.** 400
E. 500

Q.64 A alone can complete the work in 12 days and B alone can complete the work in 24 days. When A, B and C worked together then work will be completed in $\dfrac{72}{11}$ days. In how many days C alone can complete the half of the work?

A. 18 days **B.** 72 days **C.** 36 days **D.** 40 days
E. 45 days

Ques (65-68): What value should come in place of question mark (?) in the following question?

Q.65 $\sqrt{225} + (1500 \text{ of } 55\%) - \{(45)^2 \div 81 \times 4\} + 20 - 16 =?$

A. 744 **B.** 748 **C.** 746 **D.** 752
E. 742

Q.66 $(8375 \div 67)^{\frac{1}{3}} + (7.84 \times 25)^{\frac{1}{2}} = (?)^{\frac{1}{2}}$

A. 456 **B.** 361 **C.** 324 **D.** 338
E. 432

Q.67 $57\dfrac{1}{7}\%$ of $490 + 22.22\%$ of $729 - \sqrt{2500} \times \sqrt{25} \div 5^2 =?$

A. 440 **B.** 322 **C.** 432 **D.** 452
E. 462

Q.68 $\sqrt{[(6.25)^2 \times 100]} + \dfrac{7}{2} =? \times 11$

A. 6 **B.** 7 **C.** 8 **D.** 10
E. 12

Q.69 Direction: Simplify the given expression.

$\sqrt{1024} \times 40 + 20^2 + 0.5\%$ of $9600 + 469 =?^3$

A. 23 **B.** 13 **C.** 17 **D.** 19
E. 21

Q.70 Direction: Simplify the given expression.

$\left(\sqrt{8} \times \sqrt{8}\right)^{\frac{1}{2}} + 9^{\frac{1}{2}} =?^3 + \sqrt{8} - 340$

A. 7 **B.** 19 **C.** 18 **D.** 9
E. 8

Test of Reasoning

Q.71 Direction: Read the following information carefully and answer the questions that follow:

In a shop, there are 7 boxes A, B, C, D, E, F, and G kept one above another but not necessarily in the same order. The box at topmost position is numbered 1 and the box at the bottommost position is numbered 7.There are 3 boxes between D and E. Box E is kept above box D. There are 2 boxes between box G and box F. Box B is kept above the box G. Box C is kept just above box E. Box A is kept in an odd number place.

How many boxes are there between box B and box D?

A. 1 **B.** 2 **C.** 3 **D.** 4
E. 5

Ques (72-76):Direction: Read the following information carefully and answer the questions that follow:

In a shop, there are 7 boxes A, B, C, D, E, F, and G kept one above another but not necessarily in the same order. The box at topmost position is numbered 1 and the box at the bottommost position is numbered 7.There are 3 boxes between D and E. Box E is kept above box D. There are 2 boxes between box G and box F. Box B is kept above the box G. Box C is kept just above box E. Box A is kept in an odd number place.

Q.72 What is the position of box C?

A. First **B.** Second **C.** Third **D.** Fourth
E. Fifth

Q.73 How many boxes are kept above the box A?

A. 2 **B.** 4 **C.** 5 **D.** 6
E. 1

Q.74 How many boxes are there between box C and box G?

A. 2   **B.** 3   **C.** 4   **D.** 5

E. 6

Q.75 How many boxes are kept below the box F?

A. One   **B.** Two   **C.** Three   **D.** Four

E. Zero

Q.76 Choose the odd one out?

A. F   **B.** A   **C.** G   **D.** B

E. C

Ques (77-81):Directions: In the following question assuming the given statements to be True, find which of the conclusion among given conclusions is/are definitely true and then give your answers accordingly.

Q.77 Statements: $B \leq E \leq M; A > P \geq X; A = B$

Conclusions:

I. $X \leq E$

II. $M \geq P$

A. Only II is true

B. Only I is true

C. Both I and II are true

D. None is true

E. Either I or II is true

Q.78 Statements: $T < H \leq W; D > S \geq M; T > D$

Conclusions:

I. $W > D$

II. $M < T$

III. $H > S$

A. Only I is true

B. Both I and III are true

C. Either I or III is true

D. Both II and III are true

E. All are true

Q.79 Statements: $F \geq W > P; G \leq J \leq Y; W \geq Y$

Conclusions:

I. $P > J$

II. $Y < F$

III. $J \geq P$

A. Only I is true

B. Both I and III are true

C. Either I or III is true

D. Both II and III are true

E. All are true

Q.80 Statements: $Y \leq P < K; F > H \geq U \geq M; M = K$

Conclusions:

I. $F \geq K$

II. $Y < U$

A. Only II is true

B. Only I is true

C. Both I and II are true

D. None is true

E. Either I or II is true

Q.81 Statements: $C > T \geq W; J < Q \leq W; K > C$

Conclusions:

I. $C > J$

II. $Q \leq T$

A. Only II is true

B. Only I is true

C. Both I and II are true

D. None is true

E. Either I or II is true

Q.82 Direction: Study the following information carefully and answer the given questions:

In a certain code language:

'bees are making honey' is written as 'tu lu du su'

'honey is very sweet' is written as 'pu lu bu fu'

'children are sweet enough' is written as 'bu tu zu yu'

'bees are chasing children' is written as 'tu yu su mu'

What is the code for 'honey' in that language?

A. su   **B.** tu   **C.** du   **D.** lu

E. bu

Ques (83-86):Direction: Study the following information carefully and answer the given questions:

In a certain code language:

'bees are making honey' is written as 'tu lu du su'

'honey is very sweet' is written as 'pu lu bu fu'

'children are sweet enough' is written as 'bu tu zu yu'

'bees are chasing children' is written as 'tu yu su mu'

Q.83 What is the code for 'chasing' in that language?

A. yu   **B.** tu   **C.** mu   **D.** su

E. bu

Q.84 Code 'yu' is for which word in that given code language?

A. making   **B.** bees   **C.** honey   **D.** children

E. sweet

Q.85 What would be the code for 'children chasing sweet honey' in that code language?

A. su bu tu lu   **B.** zu tu yu mu

C. bu tu yu su   **D.** tu lu bu mu

E. yu mu bu lu

Q.86 Code 'su du zu lu' is for which of the following sentence in the following code language?

A. bees are making honey

B. bees making enough honey

C. bees making sweet honey

D. children making enough honey

E. children making sweet honey

Ques (87-92):Directions: Read the information given below and answer the questions that follow:

Eight people A, B, C, D, L, M, N and O are sitting around a circular table with equal distance between each other but not necessarily in the same order. Some of them are facing the centre while some are facing outside. B sits third to the left of A. Only three people sit between B and O. L sits to the immediate right of O. Immediate neighbor of L faces the opposite direction. Only one person sits between L and D. N sits second to the right of D. Both N and C face the same direction as O. Immediate neighbors of M face opposite directions to each other. L does not face outside. D faces a direction opposite to that of B.

Q.87 How many people sit between A and M when counted from the left of M?

A. Five   **B.** None   **C.** Four   **D.** One
E. Two

Q.88 Which of the following statements is true as per the given arrangement?

A. M faces the centre
B. Only three people sit between L and A
C. N sits to the immediate right of C
D. C is an immediate neighbour of D
E. None of these

Q.89 Who amongst the following sits third to the left of L?

A. M   **B.** C   **C.** B   **D.** A
E. N

Q.90 Which of the following pair represents the immediate neighbours of C?

A. L and A   **B.** A and N   **C.** M and B   **D.** D and N
E. D and L

Q.91 How many person sits between B and L when counted from left of L?

A. 4   **B.** 3
C. 2   **D.** 5
E. None of these

Q.92 Who sits at the exact opposite of O?

A. B   **B.** N   **C.** C   **D.** D
E. M

Ques (93-95):Direction: Study the information given below carefully and answer the questions that follow.

Sara goes 10 km South from the Market, takes a right turn and goes 24 km to meet Karan. She then goes 15 km North and meets Shaan. She then turns right and goes 30 km to meet Parush. She further goes 9 km South to reach her house and stops there.

Q.93 What is the shortest distance between the market and Karan?

A. 26 km   **B.** 25 km   **C.** 26√2 km   **D.** 24√2 km
E. 27 km

Q.94 What is the direction of Parush from the Market?

A. South West   **B.** North East
C. South East   **D.** East
E. North-West

Q.95 What is the shortest distance between Shaan and Sara's House?

A. 3√105 km   **B.** 2√109 km
C. 3√107 km   **D.** 3√109 km
E. 2√107 km

Q.96 Direction: In the question below are given four statements followed by three conclusions I, II, III. You have to take the given statements to be true even if they seem to be at variance from commonly known facts. Read all the conclusions and then decide which of the given conclusions logically follows from the given statements disregarding commonly known facts.

Statements:

Some Pizza's are fries.

All fries are burgers.

No burger is Tacos.

Some Tacos are Wraps.

Conclusions:

I. All Pizza's being Tacos is a possibility.

II. No fries is Tacos.

III. Some Pizza are burgers.

A. Only II follows
B. Only III follows
C. Only I and III follow
D. Only II and III follows
E. None follows

Q.97 Direction: In the question below are given three statements followed by two conclusions numbered I and II. You have to take the given statements to be true even if they seem to be at variance with commonly known facts. Read all the conclusions and then decide which of the given conclusions logically follows from the given statements disregarding commonly known facts.

Statement:

All alphas are betas.

Some gammas are betas.

No gamma is a theta.

Conclusion:

I. Some theta's can be alpha's.

II. No gamma is alpha.

A. Only conclusion I follows.
B. Only conclusion II follows.
C. Either conclusion I or conclusion II follows.
D. Neither conclusion I nor conclusion II follows.
E. Both conclusion I and conclusion II follow.

Q.98 Direction: In the question below are given two statements followed by two conclusions numbered I and II. You have to take the given statements to be true even if they seem to be at variance with commonly known facts. Read all the conclusions and then decide which of the given conclusions logically follows from the given statements disregarding commonly known facts.

Statement:

All short is cute.

Some cute is not tall.

Conclusion:

I. Some short is tall is a possibility

II. All tall is short is a possibility.

A. only conclusion I follows

B. only conclusion II follows

C. either I or II follow

D. neither I nor II follow

E. both conclusion I and II follow

Q.99 Direction: In the question below are given three statements followed by three conclusions numbered I, II and III. You have to take the given statements to be true even if they seem to be at variance with commonly known facts. Read all the conclusions and then decide which of the given conclusions logically follows from the given statements disregarding commonly known facts.

Statements:

Some Japaneses are Indians.

All Chinese are Mexicans.

Some Chinese are not Indians.

Conclusions:

I. Some Indians are not Mexicans.

II. Some Mexicans are not Chinese

III. Some Mexicans are Japanese.

A. Only I follows

B. Both I and II follow

C. Only II follows

D. Both I and III follow

E. None follows

Q.100 Direction: In the question below are given some statements followed by some conclusions. You have to take the given statements to be true even if they seem to be at variance with commonly known facts. Read all the conclusions and then decide which of the given conclusions logically follows from the given statements disregarding commonly known facts.

Statements:

All vegetables are fruit

No fruit are drink

Some drink are honey.

Conclusions:

I. Some honey is not fruit.

II. No vegetables are drink.

A. Only conclusion II is true

B. Only conclusion I is true

C. Both conclusions I and II are true

D. Either conclusion I or II is true

E. Neither conclusion I nor II is true

// Smart Answer Sheet //

Correct — Indicates percentage of students who answered questions correctly.

Skipped — Indicates percentage of students who skipped questions.

Q.	Ans.	Correct / Skipped	Q.	Ans.	Correct / Skipped	Q.	Ans.	Correct / Skipped	Q.	Ans.	Correct / Skipped	Q.	Ans.	Correct / Skipped
1	B	69.54 % / 30.14 %	17	C	58.68 % / 30.07 %	33	B	62.62 % / 35.15 %	49	B	79.88 % / 11.21 %	65	A	64.05 % / 32.6 %
2	A	61.91 % / 30.73 %	18	D	45.98 % / 32.69 %	34	E	51.37 % / 39.97 %	50	C	88.04 % / 11.59 %	66	B	60.36 % / 36.27 %
3	C	60.34 % / 36.63 %	19	D	47.63 % / 44.72 %	35	C	68.85 % / 30.65 %	51	B	50.22 % / 49.07 %	67	C	46.14 % / 46.1 %
4	A	64.33 % / 34.96 %	20	C	83.07 % / 10.29 %	36	A	48.55 % / 46.43 %	52	D	16.11 % / 77.63 %	68	A	68.12 % / 30.49 %
5	C	47.49 % / 50.22 %	21	C	51.11 % / 48.3 %	37	C	31.19 % / 68.05 %	53	B	59.14 % / 38.82 %	69	B	55.11 % / 38.53 %
6	C	53.84 % / 39.02 %	22	D	84.64 % / 12.21 %	38	D	40.43 % / 51.98 %	54	A	43.91 % / 30.38 %	70	A	48.41 % / 32.07 %
7	C	40.34 % / 59.01 %	23	B	63.05 % / 33.72 %	39	B	52.35 % / 45.43 %	55	A	56.23 % / 38.88 %	71	B	55.59 % / 31.94 %
8	A	64.67 % / 34.56 %	24	D	50.03 % / 46.21 %	40	E	59.92 % / 30.86 %	56	E	60.95 % / 34.48 %	72	A	40.11 % / 33.37 %
9	C	50.73 % / 35.07 %	25	B	65.57 % / 32.8 %	41	C	41.63 % / 32.72 %	57	C	77.27 % / 21.29 %	73	B	55.48 % / 33.4 %
10	B	47.38 % / 43.69 %	26	C	44.81 % / 54.21 %	42	D	54.5 % / 44.49 %	58	A	77.45 % / 13.37 %	74	A	67.26 % / 31.48 %
11	E	58.02 % / 37.35 %	27	C	63.21 % / 36.18 %	43	C	64.08 % / 31.9 %	59	D	81.95 % / 16.85 %	75	E	43.02 % / 50.12 %
12	E	53.42 % / 31.44 %	28	E	42.01 % / 42.89 %	44	E	41.94 % / 34.97 %	60	C	79.85 % / 11.83 %	76	C	68.97 % / 30.89 %
13	C	62.09 % / 33.89 %	29	C	86.76 % / 11.74 %	45	C	61.9 % / 30.03 %	61	B	63.28 % / 31.92 %	77	D	62.08 % / 34.68 %
14	D	58.37 % / 30.24 %	30	B	63.78 % / 30.33 %	46	C	67.54 % / 32.18 %	62	B	88.93 % / 10.13 %	78	E	46.06 % / 45.56 %
15	E	40.27 % / 49.82 %	31	A	59.43 % / 39.67 %	47	D	44.64 % / 55.24 %	63	C	76.05 % / 13.17 %	79	C	53.93 % / 45.17 %
16	C	31.25 % / 68.06 %	32	B	44.08 % / 38.36 %	48	B	44.74 % / 52.28 %	64	A	48.31 % / 44.01 %	80	A	48.04 % / 37.68 %

Q.	Ans.	Correct / Skipped		Q.	Ans.	Correct / Skipped		Q.	Ans.	Correct / Skipped		Q.	Ans.	Correct / Skipped		Q.	Ans.	Correct / Skipped
81	C	47.07 % / 34.31 %		85	E	48.82 % / 43.4 %		89	C	53.05 % / 45.27 %		93	A	54.5 % / 41.17 %		97	A	77.7 % / 13.12 %
82	D	47.92 % / 37.25 %		86	B	41.49 % / 52.27 %		90	B	63.57 % / 36.08 %		94	B	64.51 % / 32.59 %		98	E	89.53 % / 10.2 %
83	C	41.17 % / 58.04 %		87	C	46.06 % / 51.06 %		91	C	52.06 % / 39.26 %		95	D	60.14 % / 32.05 %		99	E	85.42 % / 10.6 %
84	E	51.39 % / 35.03 %		88	A	47.57 % / 33.28 %		92	A	49.5 % / 48.11 %		96	D	87.43 % / 10.34 %		100	C	44.89 % / 52.98 %

Performance Analysis

Avg. Score (%)	52.0%
Toppers Score (%)	66.0%
Your Score	

//Hints and Solutions//

1. The sentence mentions 'need to be cared for', therefore, ruling-out the word 'abused' as it would make the sentence vague. The word 'democratic' disturbs the meaning of the sentence. Using the word 'emotional' would be grammatically incorrect. The word 'protected' that means to keep someone safe from any kind of harm or injury fits the blank best.

Hence, the correct option is (B).

2. The words 'statutory' and 'contrast' cannot be used with the word 'social' mentioned in the sentence. Using the word 'fullness' would not provide any meaning to the sentence, therefore, making 'structure' as the best fit to fill the blank.

Statutory: required, permitted, or enacted by statute.

Hence, the correct option is (A).

3. The sentence mentions the word 'task', which should be used as a hint while picking up the word fitting the blank. As the sentence indicates a negative remark, 'qualified' and 'pleasant' gets omitted for being positive words. 'Untoward' does not make a proper sentence. When used with 'task', it does not convey an appropriate meaning to the sentence in the above passage. The word 'uphill' fits the word 'task' along with appropriately conveying the meaning of the sentence too.

Hence, the correct option is (C).

4. The reading of the sentence with the inclusive phrase 'infancy and youth' gives us the hint that the word that needs to fit the blank must be talking about both these terms i.e. 'infancy' and 'youth' separately. Out of the given words, 'among' is used to talk about a group or crowd or mass of objects and thus, is rejected. 'Along' means to move in a constant direction and thus, it does not fit the context of the sentence. 'Amidst' means to be in the middle of or to be surrounded by something and therefore, gets ruled out. The word 'between' makes the best fit for the blank as it is used to refer to two separate things.

Hence, the correct option is (A).

5. The words 'policies' and 'adopt' gets omitted due to being grammatically incorrect. 'Surprise' cannot be used as it makes the sentence vague and does not provide an appropriate meaning.The word 'qualification' carries the required message fitting the sense of the statement.

Hence, the correct option is (C).,

6. The first blank refers to what should be done through "public taxes" and so, "funding", "financing" or "sponsoring" may fit the first blank. However, "loading" and "projection" do not reflect this meaning. So, options (A) and (D) can be eliminated.

For the second blank, the appropriate word should be something that fits with the overall theme of eliminating the problem of exclusion. So, only "universal" meaning 'widespread or collective' fits the second blank.

Correct Sentence: Problems of exclusion will be eliminated if the payer-insurer is the state, the <u>financing</u> is done through public taxes, and coverage is <u>universal</u>.

Hence, the correct option is (C).

7. In the context of the sentence, "potential" or "probability" can fit the first blank and this eliminates options (A), (B) and (E). Further, as diversification of the portfolio by investing in gold provides a protection, "insurance" is the most appropriate choice for the second blank. Thus, option (D) gets eliminated as well.

Correct Sentence: Investors can think of putting in at least 10 per cent of their savings in gold as it has the <u>potential</u> to be an <u>insurance</u> for the portfolio in a fragile trade environment.

Hence, the correct option is (C).

8. Central banks "loosen monetary policies" so as to 'stimulate' economies. In the context of the sentence, the only possible words that can fit the first blank are "spur", "inspire" or "encourage". This eliminates the options (C) and (E).

The word "ongoing" before the second blank, implies that a force has already been set in motion and would be continued. In other words, the "momentum" would be continued. This eliminated options (B) and (D).

Correct Sentence: Central banks across the globe are preparing to loosen monetary policies, to <u>spur</u> their respective economies and it is expected that gold will continue the ongoing <u>momentum</u>.

Hence, the correct option is (A).

9. In the context of the sentence, the word that is most suitable for the first blank is "skin" and that for the second blank is "siphoned". All the other options are grammatically and contextually incorrect.

Skin in the game (Idiom)

Meaning: to be at risk financially because you have invested in something that you want to happen

E.g.: You take more ownership of something when you have some skin in the game.

Siphoned off (Phrasal verb)

Meaning: to gradually steal money or goods, usually from a business or government

E.g.: Over the years, she siphoned off hundreds of thousands of dollars from various accounts.

Correct Sentence: Promoters of MSMEs must have <u>skin</u> in the game to ensure that funds — venture capital, as well as bank loans made liberal by fiat — are not <u>siphoned</u> off.

Hence, the correct option is (C).

10. The sentence conveys that in mature countries bonds are accepted as 'guarantee' for their liquidity management operations. In the context of the sentence, the words which are suitable for the first blank are "security", "collateral" and "insurance". So, options (C) and (E) are eliminated.

The word "purposefully" before the second blank indicates that the central banks have done something with a positive effect. The only word that makes the sentence meaningfully correct is "develop". The word "undermine" has the opposite meaning and "accentuate" is irrelevant to the context of this sentence. This eliminates options (A) and (D) as well.

Correct Sentence: In mature economies, central banks accept corporate bonds as <u>collateral</u> for their liquidity management operations, so as to purposefully <u>develop</u> the bond market.

Hence, the correct option is (B).

11. The usage of all the words is correct in the given sentence.

No interchange of any word is hence required.

Hence, the correct option is (E).

12. The usage of 'daunting' and 'disproportionately' is erroneous in the given sentence.

These two words should change places with each other.

Similarly, the usage of 'bruising' and 'vocal' is also erroneous.

These two words should change places with each other.

The telecom industry has been increasingly **vocal** about India's **disproportionately** high spectrum costs, which are all the more **daunting** as the companies have gone through a **bruising** price war that left finances stretched.

Now the sentence is correct.

Hence, the correct option is (E).

13. The usage of 'distracted' and 'needs' is erroneous in the given sentence.

The sentence would be correct if these two words are interchanged.

The government **needs** to **urgently** focus on the economic crisis, but it is increasingly **distracted** by a gathering storm on the political **front**.

The usage of the other words is absolutely correct.

Hence, the correct option is (C).

14. Water conflicts in India now reach every level; divide every segment of our society, **political parties**, states, regions and sub-regions **within states, districts**, castes and groups and individual farmers. **Water conflicts within and between many developing countries are also taking a serious turn.**

The first two sentences of the 2nd paragraph clearly confirm the writer's views and the same can be found in the given Statement 1 and 3.

Hence, the correct option is (D).

15. Conflicts might sound bad or negative, but they are logical developments in the absence of proper democratic, legal and administrative mechanisms to handle issues at the root of water conflicts.

It is evident from the first sentence of the 3rd paragraph that none of the given statements echos what is stated by the writer.

Hence, the correct option is (E).

16. Till then they pose a significant threat to economic growth, security and health of the ecosystem and the victims

are likely to be the poorest of the poor as well as the very sources of water - rivers, wetlands and aquifers.

From the last sentence of the 2nd paragraph it is evident that the writer's main objective in writing this passage is to point out the seriousness of the threat posed by unresolved water conflicts.

Hence, the correct option is (C).

17. Till then they pose a significant threat to economic growth, security and health of the ecosystem **and the victims are likely to be the poorest of the poor** as well as the very sources of water - rivers, wetlands and aquifers.

Out of the given options, option C can clearly be inferred from the last sentence of the 2nd paragraph.

Hence, the correct option is (C).

18. "Rivers should link, not divide us," **said the Indian prime Minister expressing concern over interstate disputes and urged state governments to show "understanding and consideration, statesmanship and an appreciation of the other point of view."**

In the opening sentence of the passage it's clearly stated that the PM is urging state governments to be considerate and to show wisdom in public affairs like water conflicts.

Hence, the correct option is (D).

19. Water conflicts in India now reach every level; **divide every segment of our society**, political parties, states, regions and sub-regions within states, districts, castes and groups and individual farmers.

The first sentence of the 2nd paragraph clearly expresses that water conflicts divide the society and thus the option D doesn't hold true in the context.

Hence, the correct option is (D).

20. Part of the problem steams from the specific nature of water, namely that water is divisible and amenable to sharing; **one unit of water is used by one is a unit denied to others**; it has multiple uses and users and involves resultant trade-offs.

We can infer from the 2nd sentence of the 3rd paragraph that because water is an interconnected resource it results in disputes between those that can access it and those that can't.

Hence, the correct option is (C).

21. The adverb radically is a great way to say "in an extreme way."

Example: When your formerly long-haired friend shows up at work with a crew cut, you could say that she looks radically or completely different.

Hence, the correct option is (C).

22. We use the adjective **inherent** for qualities that are considered intrinsic, permanent or cannot be separated from an essential character.

For example, if you have never been able to eat spinach, you have an inherent dislike of it.

Hence, the correct option is (D).

23. To deny is to refuse to let have.

- Ex. He denies her her weekly allowance.

To assign is to give out or to allot.

- Ex. We were assigned new uniforms.

The most suitable opposite to the word 'denied' would be 'assigned'.

Hence, the correct option is (B).

Ques (24-28): Since the first sentence is given of the paragraph, it is very easy to understand the topic of the passage which is regarding the achievement of India in eradicating polio from the country. This is the premise on which the sentences are based and they have to be rearranged accordingly.

After the given sentence, the next sentence should be based on the reason behind the success of the polio eradication scheme of the government in the country when most of the other schemes do not generally become successful in the country. Among the given options, Statement E explains the reason of such a feat as the contribution of the government as well as the ground level workers of the organization.

Connectors:

First sentence and E:

1. The World Health Organization **has declared India as polio-free** since no new polio case has been reported in the country in the last couple of years.

E. **This** underlines the efforts by the Ministry of Health and Family Welfare along with the staff members at the ground level.

E should be followed by a statement in which there is some inference for the government from the success of the polio eradication program of the government. C should come after that since it explains in detail that the government should think of replicating the same model in case of other diseases also.

Connectors:

E and C:

E: **This underlines the efforts by the Ministry of Health and Family Welfare along with the staff members at the ground level.**

C: India can take heart from **this success** and can replicate the same model for eradication of other diseases also from the country.

Now, C has explained the lesson that should be learnt from this step of the government. This must be followed by something that denotes the main issue behind such problems and the mantra for success behind such programs of the government. D explains that and comes after C.

Connectors:

C: India can take heart from this success and **can replicate the same model** for eradication of other diseases also from the country.

D: **The thrust should be on educating the mass** regarding the harmful effects of insects and the reasons for the growth of such insects.

D should be followed by a statement that denotes the importance of the step explained in this sentence i.e. the participation of general public in the eradication drive of any program. B explains the importance of participation of people and should follow D.

Connectors:

D: **The thrust should be on educating the mass** regarding the harmful effects of insects and the reasons for the growth of such insects.

B: **Without participation from the general public, it would not have been possible** to achieve this tremendous feat with the government schemes only.

A will come at the end of the passage as it underlines the lesson that should be internalized by the government from the model in which polio eradication drive has been launched in the country.

This makes the correct sequence of statements as: **ECDBA**

24. So, E is the first sentence of the paragraph after the rearrangement.

Hence, the correct option is (D).

25. So, C is the second sentence of the paragraph after the rearrangement.

Hence, the correct option is (B).

26. So, D is the third sentence of the paragraph after the rearrangement.

Hence, the correct option is (C).

27. So, B is the fourth sentence of the paragraph after the rearrangement.

Hence, the correct option is (C).

28. So, A is the fifth sentence of the paragraph after the rearrangement.

Hence, the correct option is (E).

29. Fragment A: Parliament is not **competing** to

Competing is incorrect as the statement talks about competency of the Parliament to indulge in certain acts.

Correct: Parliament is not **competent** to

Fragment B: **enacts** any law which is inconsistent

Here, the error is with respect to subject-verb disagreement.

Correct: **enact** any law which is inconsistent

Fragment C: with **a** fundamental rights

Specific rights are being spoken about here and thus, article 'the' would be used.

Correct: with **the** fundamental rights

Correct: Parliament is not competent to enact any law which is inconsistent with the fundamental rights enshrined in Part III of the Constitution.

Hence, the correct option is (C).

30. Fragment B: ad hoc mechanism **for** which critically

The preposition used here is incorrect and the correct one would be **by**.

Correct: ad hoc mechanism **by** which critically

Fragment C: urgent situations are **meet** when Parliament

The tense here is incorrect.

Correct: urgent situations are **met** when Parliament

Correct: An ordinance is a constitutionally sanctioned ad hoc mechanism by which critically urgent situations are met when Parliament or a State Assembly is not in session.

Hence, the correct option is (B).

31. Fragment A: Given **there** limited attention and

Correct: Given **their** limited attention and

Correct: Given their limited attention and computational capacity, people gravitate towards the status quo, which often results in a gap between the policy's intent and action.

Hence, the correct option is (A).

32. There is an error in sentence 2.

The error lies in the wrong usage of the verb 'get' with the Distributive Pronoun 'each'.

The plural verb 'get' should be replaced by the singular verb 'gets' because the verb that is used with the Distributive Pronoun should be in the Singular Number.

- Example- Each of the attackers is arrested.

Therefore, 'gets' should be used instead of 'get'.

So, the correct sentence is:

"Each of the participants gets a gift hamper for the participation as it's the 50th anniversary of the company and we have registered a net profit of 100 million this year."

Hence, the correct option is (B).

33. There is an error in sentence 2.

The error lies in the wrong usage of the relative pronoun 'who'.

'Who' should be replaced by the relative pronoun 'which' because for inanimate objects and animals, the relative pronoun 'which' is used.

- Example- The book which I bought yesterday is a rare collection.

Therefore, 'which' should be used instead of 'who'.

So, the correct sentence is:

"The plays which leave a lasting impression on the minds of the spectators are those which strive to create a change in theatre."

Hence, the correct option is (B).

34. All the words are spelled correctly in the given sentence.

Their usages are also correct in every aspect.

Misogynist : a person who dislikes, despises, or is strongly prejudiced against women

Hence, the correct option is (E).

35. The word 'acolades' has been spelled incorrectly.

The correct spelling of the word is 'accolades'.

All other words are correct from every aspect.

- **Bureaucrat** : an official in a government department, in particular one perceived as being concerned with procedural correctness at the expense of people's needs
- **Accolade** : an award or privilege granted as a special honour or as an acknowledgement of merit
- **Unflinching** : not showing fear or hesitation in the face of danger or difficulty
- **Subordinate** : lower in rank or position

Hence, the correct option is (C).

36. Option D can be immediately eliminated because the phrasal verb 'deal in' which refers to 'buying and selling something' is not appropriate in the context.

Option B is verbose as "first starting with the one" is a repetition which can be avoided with 'starting with the first'.

In option C, usage of passive voice (which is dealt with) doesn't make any sense and is hence erroneous. This eliminates option C as well.

Hence, the correct option is (A).

37. Option A and B are erroneous because 'can return' and 'returned' are verb phrases which aren't parallel with the gerund phrase 'becoming bizarre'. Options A and B hence get eliminated.

Option D, though, takes care of the parallel structure yet deviates the meaning of the sentence.

Option C is the perfect choice among the given ones and must replace the bold part to make it a grammatically correct sentence.

Hence, the correct option is (C).

38. The adjective 'tantamount' which refers to 'being essentially equal to something' is generally followed by the preposition 'to' and not by 'of' or 'with'. The correct expression is 'tantamount to'. This immediately eliminates options A and B.

- Ex. His statement was tantamount to an admission of guilt.

Option C can be eliminated as well because the English language doesn't have a word 'tantamountly'.

Option D is the best choice among the available ones as in it the expression 'tantamount to' is followed by the gerund and thus forms a meaningful statement.

Hence, the correct option is (D).

39. Replete (Adjective):

filled or well-supplied with something. The adjective is generally followed by the proposition 'with'.

- Ex. Earth's climate system is replete with potential surprises.

Synonyms:

full, loaded, crowded, abounding, etc.

Moreover, the noun 'account' refers to a report or description of an event or experience and its plural form 'accounts' should be used here in the context.

Option B would hence make the best choice out of the given options.

Hence, the correct option is (B).

40. To end up with someone or something (Idiom):

to finish with the possession of someone or something or in the company of someone or something.

- Ex. I thought my date was with Ayesha, but I ended up with her twin sister.

The sentence is absolutely correct and hence requires no correction.

Hence, the correct option is (E).

41. Given:

Amount in 2 years $=$ Rs. 720

Amount in 4.5 years = Rs. 870

Formula used:

$$\text{Simple interest(SI)} = \frac{[\text{ Principal }(P)\times \text{ Rate }\times \text{ Time }]}{100}$$ And Amount

$=$ Principal $+$ SI

Let the sum(principal) be P and the rate of interest be R

So, $720 =$ Principal $+SI$

$\Rightarrow 720 = P + \frac{(P\times R\times 2)}{100}$ ... (i)

And $870 = P + SI$

$\Rightarrow 870 = P + \frac{(P\times R\times 4.5)}{100}$ ... (ii)

Equation (ii) - (i)

$\frac{(2.5\times P\times R)}{100} = 150$

$\Rightarrow P \times R = 6000$ ... (iii)

Now, from eq.(i),

$720 = P + \frac{(6000\times 2)}{100}$

$\Rightarrow P = 720 - 120 =$ Rs. 600

From eq. (iii)

$600 \times R = 6000$

$\Rightarrow R = 10\%$

$\therefore$ The rate of interest is 10%.

Hence, the correct option is (C).

42. Given:

$26 \times 15 + 310 - (15)^2 = 25\%$ of ?

$\Rightarrow 26 \times 15 + 310 - 225 = 25 \times \frac{1}{100}$ of ?

$\Rightarrow 390 + 310 - 225 = ? \times \frac{1}{4}$

$\Rightarrow ? = 475 \times 4$

$\Rightarrow ? = 1900$

Hence, the correct option is (D).

43. Given:

$20 \times 168 \div 14 - 40 = ? + 110$

$\Rightarrow 20 \times \frac{168}{14} - 40 = ? + 110$

$\Rightarrow 20 \times 12 - 40 = ? + 110$

$\Rightarrow 240 - 40 = ? + 110$

$\Rightarrow 200 = ? + 110$

$\Rightarrow 200 - 110 = ?$

$= 90$

Hence, the correct option is (C).

44. Given:

$\sqrt{625} \div \sqrt{16} \times 6 = ? \%$ of 300

$\Rightarrow 25 \div 4 \times 6 = ? \% \times 300$

$\Rightarrow 25 \div 4 \times 6 = ? \times \frac{1}{100} \times 300$

$\Rightarrow 25 \div 4 \times 6 = ? \times 3$

$\Rightarrow \frac{25}{4} \times 6 = ? \times 3$

$\Rightarrow \frac{25}{2} = ?$

$\Rightarrow ? = 12.5$

Hence, the correct option is (E).

45. Given,

$(4698 - 3625 - 857) = ?^3 - 42 - \sqrt{7225}$

$\Rightarrow 4698 - 4482 = ?^3 - 42 - 85$

$\Rightarrow 216 = ?^3 - 127$

$\Rightarrow ?^3 = 216 + 127$

$\Rightarrow ?^3 = 343$

$\Rightarrow ? = 7$

Hence, the correct option is (C).

46. Given:

A person divides a certain amount among his three sons in the ratio $= 3:4:5$

If he had divided this amount in the ratio $= \dfrac{1}{3}:\dfrac{1}{4}:\dfrac{1}{5}$

The person who had got the lowest share earlier would get Rs. 1188 more

Let money get by first, second and third son be $3x, 4x$ and $5x$ respectively

Total share $= 3x + 4x + 5x = 12x$

Here first son got minimum share $= 3x$

If person had divided total amount in the ratio $= \dfrac{1}{3}:\dfrac{1}{4}:\dfrac{1}{5}$

LCM of 3,4 and $5 = 60$

Ratio of First, second and third $= \left(\dfrac{1}{3}\right) \times 60 : \left(\dfrac{1}{4}\right) \times 60 : \left(\dfrac{1}{5}\right) \times 60 = 20:15:12$

Share of first student $= \left(\dfrac{12x}{47}\right) \times 20 = \dfrac{240x}{47}$

According to the question,

$\Rightarrow \left(\dfrac{240x}{47}\right) - (3x) = 1188$

$\Rightarrow \dfrac{(240x - 141x)}{47} = 1188$

$\Rightarrow \dfrac{99x}{47} = 1188$

$\Rightarrow x = 12 \times 47$

$\Rightarrow x = 564$

Total amount $= 12x$

$= 12 \times 564$

$= \text{Rs. } 6768$

∴ The total amount is Rs. 6768 .

Hence, the correct option is (C).

47. Let x be the cost price of a car.

So, according to the question,

15% of x = Rs. 15000

So, x = 15000 × $\dfrac{100}{15}$ = Rs. 100000

On this amount, he is giving 10% labour charge.

So, selling price of 1 car = C.P + 10% of C.P = 100000 + 10000 = Rs. 110000

Therefore, total selling price of 20 cars = 110000 × 20 = Rs. 2200000

Hence, the correct option is (D).

48. Given:

Distance travelled = 5 km

Time required along the stream = 25 mimutes

Time required against the stream = 50 minutes

Speed of current = $\dfrac{(downstream\ speed\ -\ upstream\ speed)}{2}$

Downstream speed = $\dfrac{5}{\left[\left(\frac{25}{60}\right)\right]}$ = 12 km/h

Upstream speed = $\dfrac{5}{\left[\left(\frac{50}{60}\right)\right]}$ = 6 km/h

Speed of current = $\dfrac{(12-6)}{2}$ = 3 km/h

Hence, the correct option is (B).

49. The series follows the following pattern:

$72 + 1^2 = 73$

$73 - 2^2 = 69 \neq 59$

$69 + 3^2 = 78$

$78 - 4^2 = 62$

$62 + 5^2 = 87$

$87 - 6^2 = 51$

Since 69 will come in place of 59.

∴ Wrong number is 59.

Hence, the correct option is (B).

50. The series follows the following pattern:

11 + 18 = 29   (∵ 18 = 18 × 1)

29 + 36 = 65   (∵ 36 = 18 × 2)

65 + 54 = 119   (∵ 54 = 18 × 3)

119 + 72 = 191   (∵ 72 = 18 × 4)

191 + 90 = 281   (∵ 90 = 18 × 5)

Since 29 will come in place of 35.

∴ Wrong number is 35.

Hence, the correct option is (C).

51. The series follows the following pattern:

8 × 1 = 8

8 × 1.5 = 12

12 × 2 = 24 ≠ 22

24 × 2.5 = 60

60 × 3 = 180

180 × 3.5 = 630

Since 24 will come in place of 22.

∴ Wrong number is 22.

Hence, the correct option is (B).

52. The series follows the following pattern:

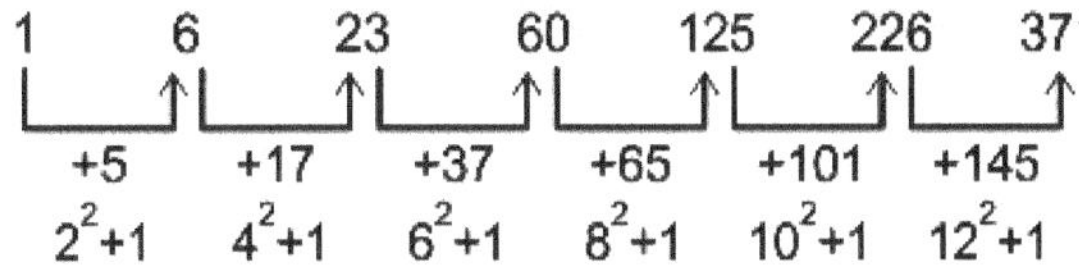

Since 226 will come in place of 225.

∴ Wrong number is 225.

Hence, the correct option is (D).

53. The series follows the following pattern:

171 × 1 + 1 = 172

172 × 2 + 2 = 346

346 × 3 + 3 = 1041

1041 × 4 + 4 = 4168

4168 × 5 + 5 = 20845

Since 1041 will come in place of 1031.

∴ Wrong number is 1031.

Hence, the correct option is (B).

54. Average = $\dfrac{(sum\ of\ elements)}{(number\ of\ elements)}$

Given,

The scores of Sam, Geeta and Radha out of 150

For Mathematics section = 94, 85 and 120 respectively

For Science section = 135, 80 and 90 respectively.

Sam's total score out of 300

= 94 + 135

= 229

The average percent = $\left\{\dfrac{229}{300}\right\} \times 100$

= 76.33%

Geeta's total score out of 300

= 85 + 80

= 165

The average percent = $\left(\dfrac{165}{300}\right) \times 100$

= 55%

Radha's total score out of 300

= 120 + 90

= 210

The average percent = $\left(\dfrac{210}{300}\right) \times 100$

= 70%

∴ The average percent of Sam, Geeta and Radha are 76.33%, 55% and 70% respectively.

Hence, the correct option is (A).

55. Given,

Speed of boat in still water $= 10mph$

Distance covered by boat in downstream and upstream $= 36$ miles

Let the speed of the stream be x mph.

Then,

Speed in downstream $= (10 + x)mph$

Speed in upstream $= (10 - x)mph$

Therefore,

$$\dfrac{36}{10-x} - \dfrac{36}{10+x} = \dfrac{90}{60}$$

$$\Rightarrow \dfrac{36\times(10+x)-36\times(10-x)}{(10-x)\times(10+x)} = \dfrac{90}{60}$$

$$\Rightarrow \dfrac{72x}{(100-x^2)} = \dfrac{90}{60}$$

$$\Rightarrow 72x \times 60 = 90(100 - x^2)$$

$$\Rightarrow x^2 + 48x - 100 = 0$$

$$\Rightarrow (x + 50)(x - 2) = 0$$

$$\Rightarrow x = 2mph$$

Hence, the correct option is (A).

56. Area of trapezium = (sum of parallel side) × $\dfrac{height}{2}$

Here, height = altitude = 10 cm

⇒ Area of trapezium = 195 cm²

⇒ 345 = (sum of parallel side) × $\left(\dfrac{10}{2}\right)$

⇒ Sum of parallel side = $\dfrac{195}{5}$ = 39 cm

Parallel side are in the ratio of 5 : 8,

$\Rightarrow$ 5x + 8x = 39

$\Rightarrow$ 13x = 39

$\Rightarrow$ x = 3

$\therefore$ Longest line = 8x = 8 × 3 = 24 cm

Hence, the correct option is (E).

57. The ratio of equivalent capitals of A and B for 1 month = 100000×36 : 200000×24

= 36 : 48 = 3 : 4

Part of profit gained by A $= \dfrac{3}{7}$

Part of profit gained by B $= \dfrac{4}{7}$

$\therefore$ Required difference $= \left(\dfrac{4}{7} - \dfrac{3}{7}\right) \times 84000 =$ Rs. 12000

Hence, the correct option is (C).

58. Unsold unit of company E $= 420 - 360 = 60$

Unsold unit of company D $= 500 - 320 = 180$

Unsold units of Company E and D together $= 180 + 60 = 240$

Sold units of company A $= 180$

Sold units of company B $= 300$

Sold units of company A and B together $= 180 + 300 = 480$

Required ratio $= 240 : 480$

$= 1 : 2$

Hence, the correct option is (A).

59. Unit produced by Company C $= 400$

Units sold by Company B $= 300$

$\therefore$ Required percentage $= \dfrac{(400-300)}{300} \times 100$

= 33.33%

Hence, the correct option is (D).

60. Unsold unit of company A $= 120$

Unsold unit of company B $= 150$

Unsold unit of company C $= 50$

Unsold unit of company D $= 180$

Unsold unit of company E $= 60$

Average unit remain unsold $= \dfrac{(120+150+50+180+60)}{5}$

= 112

Hence, the correct option is (C).

61. Units produced by A = 300

So, units produced by company F $= 300 \times \dfrac{110}{100} = 330$

Units sold by company C = 350

So, units sold by company F $= 350 \times \dfrac{80}{100} = 280$

Unsold unit of company F = 330 - 280

= 50

Hence, the correct option is (B).

62. Total produced units = 300 + 450 + 400 + 500 + 420 = 2070

Total sold units = 180 + 300 + 350 + 320 + 360 = 1510

$\therefore$ Required difference = 2070 - 1510

= 560

Hence, the correct option is (B).

63. Given-

75 is added to 75% of a number and the result obtained is the number itself.

Let the number be a.

$\Rightarrow 75 + (75\% \times a) = a$

$\Rightarrow 75 + \left(\dfrac{75}{100} \times a\right) = a$

$\Rightarrow 75 + \dfrac{3a}{4} = a$

$\Rightarrow 75 = a - \dfrac{3a}{4}$

$\Rightarrow 75 = \dfrac{a}{4}$

$\Rightarrow 75 \times 4 = a$

$\Rightarrow a = 300$

Hence, the correct option is (C).

64. A can do the work in 12 days.

B can do the work in 24 days.

A, B, C can do the work in $\dfrac{72}{11}$ days.

A's 1 days work $= \dfrac{1}{12}$

B's 1 days work $= \dfrac{1}{24}$

$\Rightarrow (A + B + C)$'s 1 days work $= \dfrac{1}{12} + \dfrac{1}{24} + \dfrac{1}{C}$

$\Rightarrow \dfrac{1}{12} + \dfrac{1}{24} + \dfrac{1}{C} = \dfrac{11}{72}$

$$\Rightarrow \frac{1}{C} = \frac{1}{36}$$

C alone can complete the work in 36 days.

$\therefore$ Time taken by C to complete half of work $= 36 \times \frac{1}{2} =$ 18 days

Hence, the correct option is (A).

65. Using the BODMAS rule:

$\sqrt{225} + (1500 \text{ of } 55\%) - \{(45)^2 \div 81 \times 4\} + 20 - 16 = ?$

$= 15 + 825 - 25 \times 4 + 20 - 16$

$= 15 + 825 - 100 + 20 - 16$

$= 840 - 100 + 20 - 16$

$= 740 + 4$

$= 744$

$\therefore$ Answer is 744

Hence, the correct option is (A).

66. Using the BODMAS rule:

$(8375 \div 67)^{\frac{1}{3}} + (7.84 \times 25)^{\frac{1}{2}} = (?)^{\frac{1}{2}}$

$\Rightarrow (125)^{\frac{1}{3}} + (7.84 \times 25)^{\frac{1}{2}} = (?)^{\frac{1}{2}}$

$\Rightarrow (125)^{\frac{1}{2}} + (196)^{\frac{1}{2}} = (?)^{\frac{1}{2}}$

$\Rightarrow 5 + 14 = (?)^{\frac{1}{2}}$

$\Rightarrow (?)^{\frac{1}{2}} = 19$

Squaring both sides,

$? = 19^2$

$= 361$

$\therefore$ 361 will come in place of '?'

Hence, the correct option is (B).

67. According to BODMAS:

$57\frac{1}{7}\% \text{ of } 490 + 22.22\% \text{ of } 729 - \sqrt{2500} \times \sqrt{25} \div 5^2 = ?$

$\Rightarrow \left(\frac{4}{7}\right) \times 490 + \left(\frac{2}{9}\right) \times 729 - 50 \times 5 \div 25 = ?$

$\Rightarrow 4 \times 70 + 2 \times 81 - 10 = ?$

$\Rightarrow 280 + 162 - 10 = ?$

$\Rightarrow 442 - 10 = ?$

$\Rightarrow ? = 432$

$\therefore$ The value of '?' Is 432 .

Hence, the correct option is (C).

68. According to BODMAS:

$\sqrt{[(6.25)^2 \times 100]} + \frac{7}{2} = ? \times 11$

$\sqrt{[(6.25)^2 \times 100]} + 3.5 = ? \times 11$

$\Rightarrow \sqrt{(6.25 \times 6.25 \times 100)} + 3.5 = ? \times 119$

$\Rightarrow \sqrt{(6.25 \times 6.25 \times 10 \times 10)} + 3.5 = ? \times 11$

$\Rightarrow 62.5 + 3.5 = ? \times 11$

$\Rightarrow 66 = ? \times 11$

$\Rightarrow 6 = ?$

$\therefore$ The required value is 6 .

Hence, the correct option is (A).

69. Given,

$\sqrt{1024} \times 40 + 20^2 + 0.5\% \text{ of } 9600 + 469 = ?^3$

$\Rightarrow 32 \times 40 + 400 + 9600 \times \frac{0.5}{100} + 469 = ?^3$

$\Rightarrow 32 \times 40 + 400 + 48 + 469 = ?^3$

$\Rightarrow 1280 + 400 + 48 + 469 = ?^3$

$\Rightarrow 1280 + 448 + 469 = ?^3$

$\Rightarrow 2197 = ?^3$

$\Rightarrow ? = \sqrt[3]{2197}$

$\Rightarrow ? = 13$

Hence, the correct option is (B).

70. Given,

$\left(\sqrt{8} \times \sqrt{8}\right)^{\frac{1}{2}} + 9^{\frac{1}{2}} = ?^3 + \sqrt{8} - 340$

$\Rightarrow \left(\left(\sqrt{8}\right)^2\right)^{\frac{1}{2}} + 9^{\frac{1}{2}} = ?^3 + \sqrt{8} - 340$

$\Rightarrow (8)^{\frac{1}{2}} + 9^{\frac{1}{2}} = ?^3 + \sqrt{8} - 340$

$\Rightarrow (4 \times 2)^{\frac{1}{2}} + 9^{\frac{1}{2}} = ?^3 + \sqrt{(4 \times 2)} - 340$

$\Rightarrow 2\sqrt{2} + 3 = ?^3 + 2\sqrt{2} - 340$

$\Rightarrow 3 = ?^3 + (-340)$

$\Rightarrow ?^3 = 340 + 3$

$\Rightarrow ?^3 = 343$

$$\Rightarrow ? = \sqrt[3]{343}$$

$$\Rightarrow ? = 7$$

Hence, the correct option is (A).

Q.71 Boxes: A, B, C, D, E, F, and G.

1) There are 3 boxes between D and E.

2) Box E is kept above box D.

3) Box C is kept just above the box E.

S.N	Case 1	Case 2
1	C	
2	E	C
3		E
4		
5		
6	D	
7		D

4) There are 2 boxes between box G and box F.

S.N	Case 1	Case 2
1	C	G/F
2	E	C
3		E
4	G/F	F/G
5		
6	D	
7	F/G	D

5) Box A is kept in an odd number place.

6) Box B is kept above the box G.

Now case 2 did not follow the above-mentioned information, so terminated, as B can't be placed above G as no space left for B to be placed.

Box B will be place at 3rd position as It is given Box B is placed one box above the box G, which means Box B will be placed immediately above box G, which is possible only when Box B is placed at 3rd position.

Now only position is left that is 5th position so Box A will be placed on 5th position and also 5 is a odd number so this condition is also satisfied here.

S.N	Boxes
1	C
2	E
3	B
4	G
5	A
6	D
7	F

So, 2 boxes are present between box B and box D.

Hence, the correct option is (B).

Ques (72-76): Boxes: A, B, C, D, E, F, and G.

1) There are 3 boxes between D and E.

2) Box E is kept above box D.

3) Box C is kept just above the box E.

S.N	Case 1	Case 2
1	C	
2	E	C
3		E
4		
5		
6	D	
7		D

4) There are 2 boxes between box G and box F.

S.N	Case 1	Case 2
1	C	G/F
2	E	C
3		E
4	G/F	F/G
5		
6	D	
7	F/G	D

5) Box A is kept in an odd number place.

6) Box B is kept above the box G.

Now case 2 did not follow the above-mentioned information, so terminated, as B can't be placed above G as no space left for B to be placed.

Box B will be place at 3rd position as It is given Box B is placed one box above the box G, which means Box B will be placed immediately above box G, which is possible only when Box B is placed at 3rd position.

Now only position is left that is 5th position so Box A will be placed on 5th position and also 5 is a odd number so this condition is also satisfied here.

S.N	Boxes
1	C
2	E
3	B
4	G
5	A
6	D
7	F

72. So, box C is kept on the first position.

Hence, the correct option is (A).

73. So, 4 boxes are kept above box A.

Hence, the correct option is (B).

74. So, 2 boxes are present between box C and G.

Hence, the correct option is (A).

75. So, zero boxes are kept below box F.

Hence, the correct option is (E).

76. Four of the following are placed in odd places so they form a group but box G is kept in an even place.

So, box G is an odd one.

Hence, the correct option is (C).

77. Given statements: B ≤ E ≤ M; A > P ≥ X; A = B

On combining: X ≤ P < A = B ≤ E ≤ M

Conclusions:

I. X ≤ E → False (X ≤ P < A = B ≤ E → X < E)

II. M ≥ P → False (P < A = B ≤ E ≤ M → P < M)

Thus, neither conclusion I nor conclusion II is true.

Hence, the correct option is (D).

78. Given statements: T < H ≤ W; D > S ≥ M; T > D

On combining: W ≥ H > T > D > S ≥ M

Conclusions:

I. W > D → True (W ≥ H > T > D → W > D)

II. M < T → True (T > D > S ≥ M → T > M)

III. H > S → True (H > T > D > S → H > S)

Thus, all the conclusions are true.

Hence, the correct option is (E).

79. Given statements: F ≥ W > P; G ≤ J ≤ Y; W ≥ Y

On combining: F ≥ W > P; F ≥ W ≥ Y ≥ J ≥ G

Conclusions:

I. P > J → False (W > P and W ≥ Y ≥ J → relation between P and J cannot be determined.)

II. Y < F → False (F ≥ W ≥ Y → F ≥ Y)

III. J ≥ P → False (W > P and W ≥ Y ≥ J → relation between P and J cannot be determined.)

None of the conclusions are true but conclusions I and III form complementary pair.)

Thus, either conclusion I or III is true.

Hence, the correct option is (C).

80. Given statements: Y ≤ P < K; F > H ≥ U ≥ M; M = K

On combining: F > H ≥ U ≥ M = K > P ≥ Y

Conclusions:

I. F ≥ K → False (F > H ≥ U ≥ M = K → F > K)

II. Y < U → True (U ≥ M = K > P ≥ Y → U > Y)

Thus, only conclusion II is true.

Hence, the correct option is (A).

81. Given statements: C > T ≥ W; J < Q ≤ W; K > C

On combining: K > C > T ≥ W ≥ Q > J

Conclusions:

I. C > J → True (C > T ≥ W ≥ Q > J → C > J)

II. Q ≤ T → True (T ≥ W ≥ Q → T ≥ Q)

Thus, both conclusions I and II are true.

Q.82 The given codes are represented as follows:

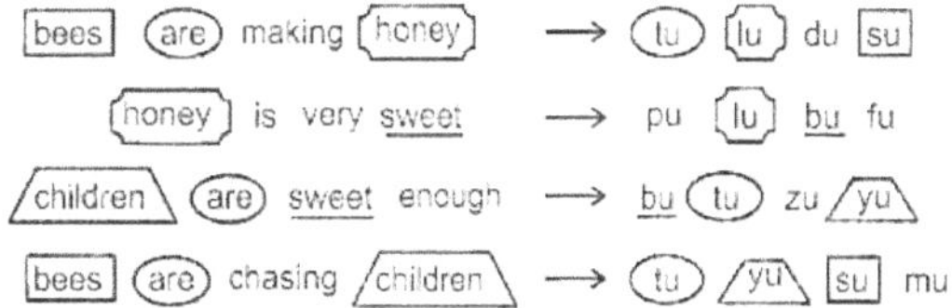

Word	Code
bees	su
are	tu
making	du
honey	lu
is	pu/fu
very	pu/fu
sweet	bu
children	yu
enough	zu
chasing	mu

So, the code for honey is 'lu'.

Hence, the correct option is (D).

Ques (83-86): The given codes are represented as follows:

Word	Code
bees	su
are	tu
making	du
honey	lu
is	pu/fu
very	pu/fu
sweet	bu
children	yu
enough	zu
chasing	mu

83. So, the code for chasing is 'mu'.

Hence, the correct option is (C).

84. Thus, the code 'yu' is for the word 'children'.

Hence, the correct option is (E).

85. Code 'yu' represents 'children'

Code 'mu' represents 'chasing'

Code 'bu' represents 'sweet'

Code 'lu' represents 'honey'

So, the code for 'children chasing sweet honey' is 'yu mu bu lu'.

Hence, the correct option is (E).

86. Code 'su' represents 'bees'

Code 'du' represents 'making'

Code 'zu' represents 'enough'

Code 'lu' represents 'honey'

So, the word for the code 'su du zu lu' is for the sentence 'bees making enough honey'.

Hence, the correct option is (B).

Ques (87-92): Eight people are A, B, C, D, L, M, N, and O. Some are facing centre, and some are facing outside.

i) Only three people sit between B and O.

ii) L sits to the immediate right of O.

iii) B sits third to the left of A.

Case 1.
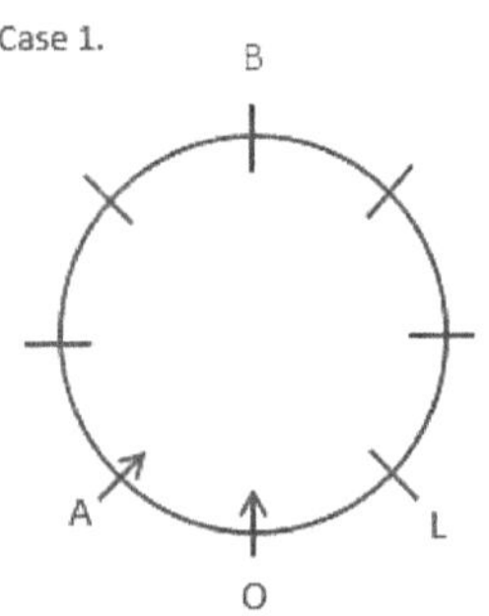

Case 2.
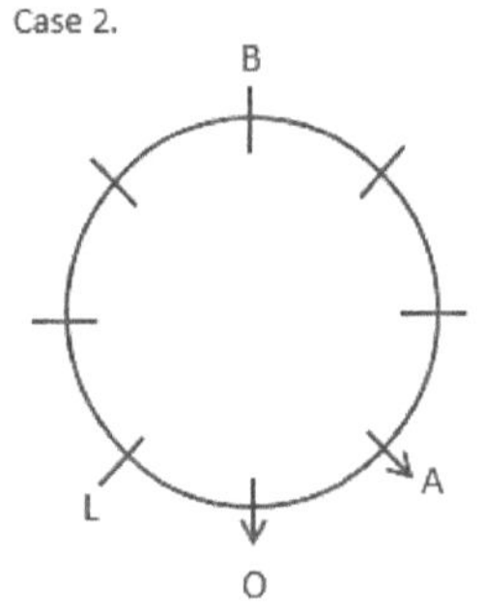

iv) Only one person sits between L and D.

v) Immediate neighbours of L face opposite directions.

vi) L does not face outside.

vii) N sits second to the right of D.

Case 1.
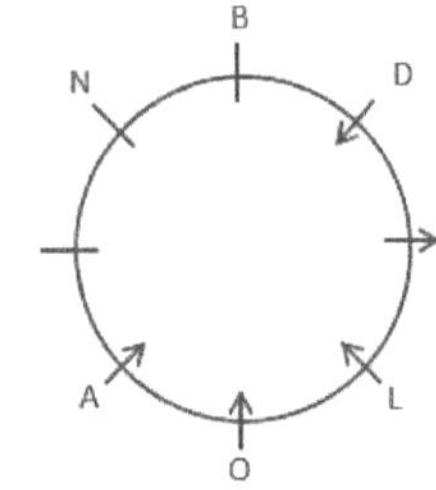

Case 2.
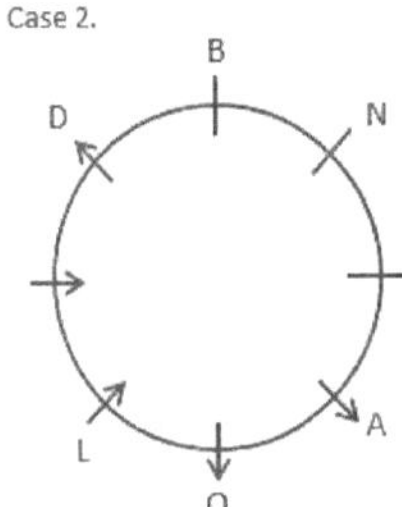

viii) Both N and C face the same direction as O.

ix) Immediate neighbours of M face opposite directions to each other.

In Case 1. Both N and C will face towards centre. Thus, M will sit between L and D. Both L and D face the same direction. So, Case 1 gets eliminated.

x) D faces a direction opposite to that of B.

Case 2.

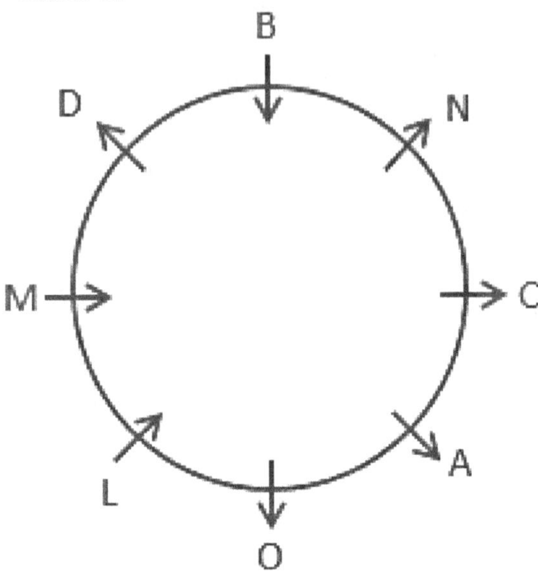

87. Clearly, 4 people sit between A and M if counted from left of M.

Hence, the correct option is (C).

88. So, M faces the centre is true.

Hence, the correct option is (A).

89. B sits third to the left of L.

Hence, the correct option is (C).

90. So, A and N are immediate neighbours of C.

Hence, the correct option is (B).

91. So, when counted from left of L two persons sits between B and L

Hence, the correct option is (C).

92. So, B is sitting at the exact opposite of O.

Hence, the correct option is (A).

93. The figure according to the information given in the question will be as follows:

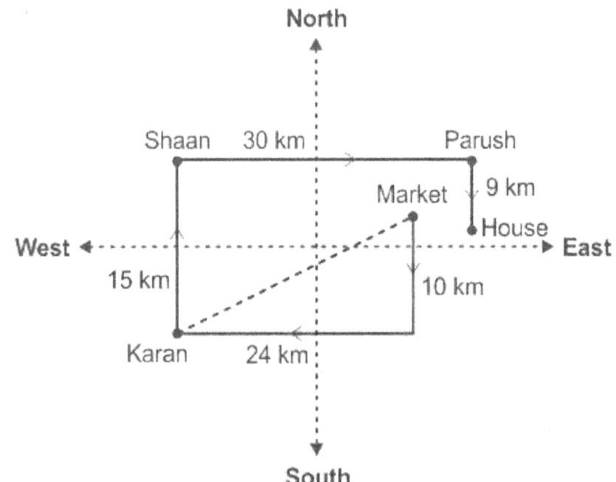

Applying Pythagoras Theorem,

The shortest distance between the market and Karan will be

$$= \sqrt{(24)^2 + (10)^2}$$

$$= \sqrt{576 + 100} \text{ km}$$

$$= \sqrt{676} = 26 \text{ km}$$

So, the shortest distance between the market and Karan is 26 km.

Hence, the correct option is (A).

94. The figure according to the information given in the question will be as follows:

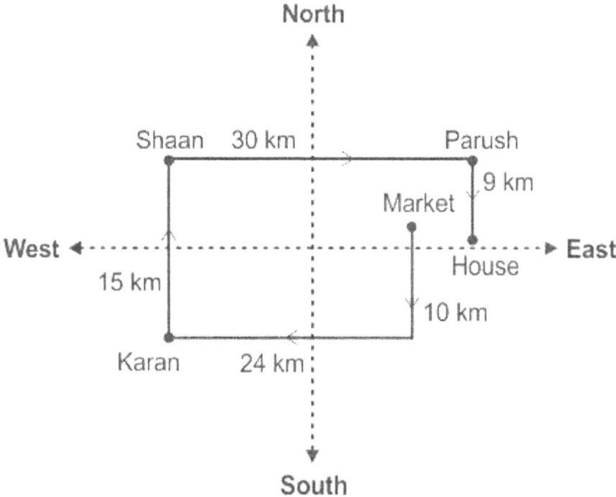

So, the direction of Parush from the market is North-East.

Hence, the correct option is (B).

95. The figure according to the information given in the question will be as follows:

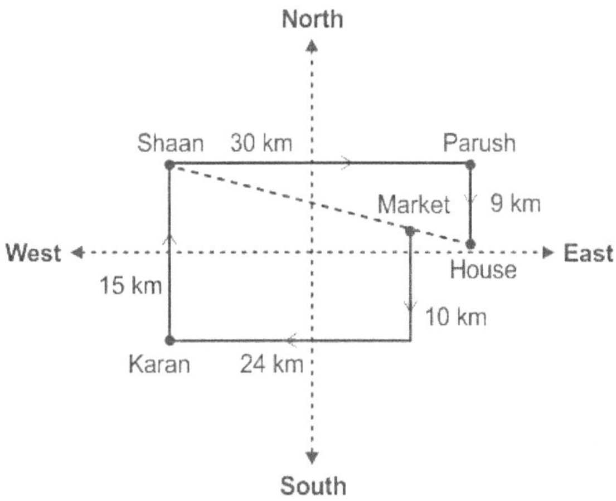

Applying Pythagoras Theorem,

The shortest distance between Shaan and Sara's House will be

$$= \sqrt{(30)^2 + (9)^2}$$

$$= \sqrt{900 + 81}$$

$$= \sqrt{981} = 3\sqrt{109} \ km$$

So, the shortest distance between Shaan and Sara's House is $3\sqrt{109}$ km.

Hence, the correct option is (D).

96. The least possible Venn diagram for the given statements is as follows,

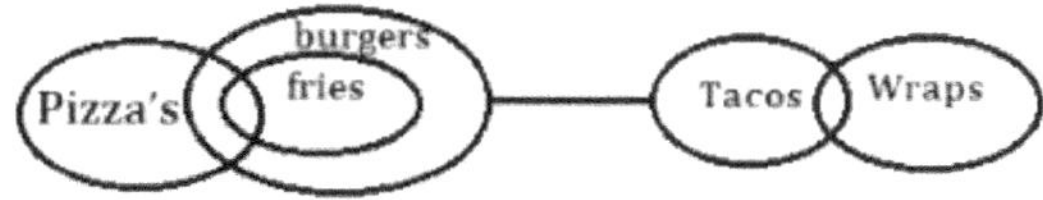

Conclusion:

I. All Pizza's being Tacos is a possibility. → False (It is not possible since no burger is Tacos)

II. No fries is Tacos → True (It is possible since no burger is Tacos)

III. Some Pizza's are burgers → True (It is possible as shown in the figure above)

So, only II and III follows.

Hence, the correct option is (D).

97. The least possible diagram of this question is as follows,

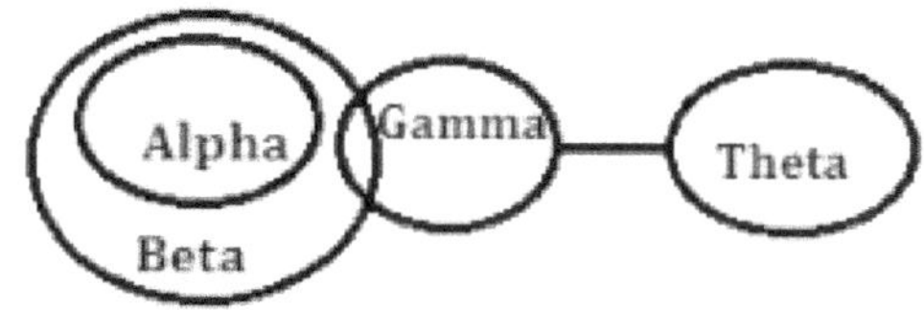

I. Some thetas can be alpha's → True (possibility is true)

II. No gamma is alpha → False (it is possible but not definite)

So, the only conclusion I follows.

Hence, the correct option is (A).

98. The given statement can be represented by using the following Venn Diagram.

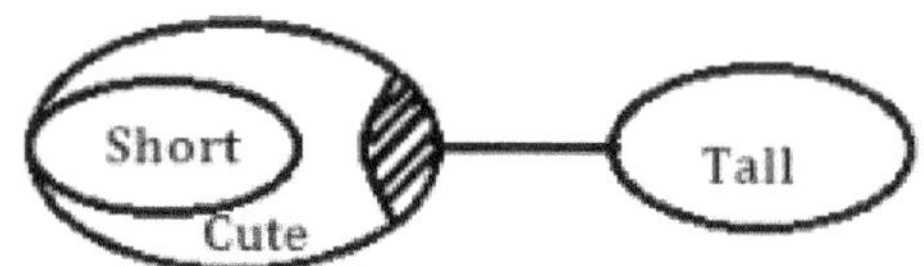

Conclusion:

I. Some short is tall is a possibility → Possibility is true.

II. All tall is short is a possibility → Possibility is true.

So, both I and II follow.

Hence, the correct option is (E).

99. The least possible Venn diagram for the given statements is as follows.

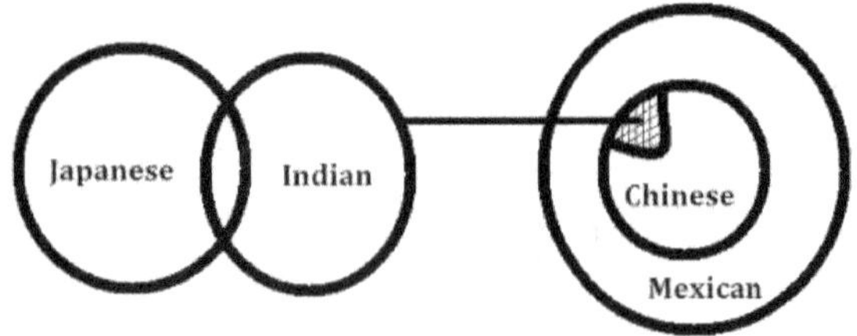

Conclusions:

I. Some Indians are not Mexicans → False (All Indians being Mexicans is a possibility, therefore the definite case is false).

II. Some Mexicans are not Chinese → False (It is possible but not definite)

III. Some Mexicans are Japaneses → False (It is possible but not definite)

So, none follows.

Hence, the correct option is (E).

100. The Venn diagram for all the given statements:

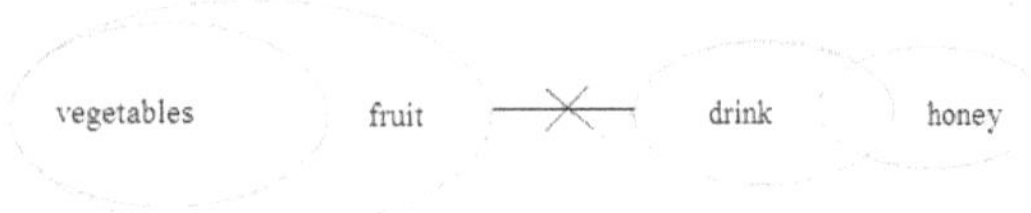

Conclusions:

I. Some honey is not fruit → definitely true.

II. No vegetables are drink → definitely true.

Clearly, both conclusions I and II follow.

Hence, the correct option is (C).

Test of English Language

Ques (1-5):Direction: Fill in the blanks with the suitable words in the given sentence.

Q.1 In addition, growing ___________ of society on ideological lines has made the job of ___________ fake news easier.

A. masses, observing
B. divergence, collecting
C. numbers, sorting
D. polarization, spreading
E. multitude, financing

Q.2 Basic principles of credit ___________ and monitoring are obviated in PSBs and must be sharpened to ___________ defects of capital, business purpose and character.

A. lending, reduce
B. assessment, emphasize
C. evaluation, clarify
D. appraisal, diagnose
E. prevention, roughen

Q.3 While all these forms exist in India, ___________ and ___________ content are gaining steam, leading to the possibility of potential violence and impacting society.

A. fabricated, manipulated
B. irrelevant, useless
C. joyous, exalted
D. unnecessary, neutral
E. dangerous, exuberant

Q.4 While predatory journals are not a uniquely Indian problem, the problem appears to be more grave here, and has possibly been aggravated by the UGC's policy of ___________ recommendations for ___________ of journals in its approved list.

A. seeking, exclusion
B. denying, publishing
C. soliciting, inclusion
D. facing, projection
E. handing, seeking

Q.5 While media researchers around the world are ___________ the fake news scene, little ___________ information is available on the creators and the intention behind it.

A. investigating, credible
B. innovating, sound
C. instigating, genuine
D. obscuring, relevant
E. obliterating, believable

Ques (6-10):Direction: In the following passage, some of the words have been left out. Read the passage carefully and select the correct answer for the given blanks out of the given alternatives.

The pockets of methane trapped within Canada's frozen Lake Abraham are a natural wonder, ___1___ yet with a deadly core. These beautiful, ethereal blue orbs indeed have a dark side. Although produced by a natural process, the alluring ice-encased bubbles enclose a ___2___ greenhouse gas and therefore a threat to the planet.

The story of how the bubbles come into being is far from appealing and, as with many a horror story, it ___3___ with dead bodies. Microbes feeding on the decomposing organic matter at the bottom of the lake release methane, which floats to the surface in bubbles. When the water freezes in winter, these bubbles become trapped, producing magical landscapes. But come the spring thaw, the bubbles pop, releasing the methane within them to the atmosphere. Methane is highly inflammable and so the bubbles explode when set ___4___. Its real danger lies in its impact on Earth's temperature. Although methane doesn't stick around in the atmosphere like carbon dioxide, its heat-trapping effect is 34 times stronger, making it potentially far more ___5___ to our climate.

Q.6 Choose the correct word to fill the blank 1.

A. absolute
B. dazzling
C. lethal
D. salubrious
E. fatal

Q.7 Choose the correct word to fill the blank 2.

A. nocuous
B. vital
C. requisite
D. conducive
E. None of these

Q.8 Choose the correct word to fill the blank 3.

A. depicts
B. narrates
C. starts
D. entails
E. concludes

Q.9 Choose the correct word to fill the blank 4.

A. intense
B. aside
C. shining
D. frozen
E. alight

Q.10 Choose the correct word to fill the blank 5.

A. deleterious
B. affecting
C. pervasive
D. invisible
E. invisible

Ques (11-20):Direction: Read the passage and answer the following questions.

The Central Board of Film Certification (CBFC) is a statutory body formed under the Cinematograph Act 1952. It is a statutory body under the Ministry of Information and Broadcasting. The Cinematograph Act manufactures a regime of pre-censorship which is, in technical terms, called a regime of "prior restraint". The main responsibility of the board is to ensure that any content of any film does not fall into any of the categories of "reasonable restrictions upon free speech". These restrictions are mentioned under Article 19(2) of the

Constitution. Article 19(2) of the constitution consists of a set of abstract phrases such as "defamation", "decency or morality, "public order", and so on. The CBFC has certain guidelines that have been changed from time to time.

The central government appoints a Chairman and the non-official members who constitute the Board. Headquarters of the board are located in Mumbai. The CBFC has nine regional offices which include Mumbai, Kolkata, Bangalore Chennai, Hyderabad, Thiruvananthapuram, New Delhi, Guwahati and Cuttack. The advisory panels assist the regional offices in the examination of the films. The members of the advisory panels belong to different walks of life. These members are nominated by the Central government for a tenure of two years. There are 25 members and 60 advisory panel members on the board from across India. All these members are appointed by the Information & Broadcasting Ministry. The CEO is mainly responsible for administrative functions, and regional officers are responsible for the examining committees that certify films.

For general films, the committee consists of an examining officer and four members of the advisory panel and. Two members of the committee must be women. If the applicant isn't satisfied with the list of changes and the certification, he or she can apply to the Revising Committee for a review. The revising committee has the chairperson, a mix of the Board and the Advisory, and up to nine committee members. Any member who was part of the committee who viewed the film is not included in the revising committee. A similar process is adopted at this stage too, and the chairman has the final say on the matter. The goal of the CBFC is to ascertain that healthy entertainment is provided to the general public of the country. The certification process is usually kept very transparent. Any film, be it Indian or Foreign, must get certified by the CBFC before being screened in India.

Q.11 What is the main goal of the CBFC?

A. to provide healthy entertainment to the general public

B. promotion of all kinds of movies

C. criticizing every movie application

D. withholding the certificate if the movie is average

E. promoting Indian movies to the foreign audience

Q.12 What happens if the applicant is not satisfied with the changes and the certification?

A. he/she cancel the whole production of the movie

B. he/she make the changes all over again

C. he/she release the movie anyway

D. he/she can apply to the Revising Committee for a review

E. he/she revolt against the board

Q.13 Which committee appoints the board members?

A. Information & Broadcasting Ministry

B. Central Board of Film Certification

C. The Film & Television Producers Guild of India Ltd.

D. The ITA School of Performing Arts

E. Cinematograph Act of 1918

Q.14 How many advisory members are present in the board?

A. 25   B. 60   C. 31   D. 15

E. 10

Q.15 Where are the CBFC's regional offices located?

A. Guwahati

B. Mumbai

C. Chennai

A. All except 1   **B.** all except 2

C. all except 3   **D.** All of these

E. None of these

Q.16 Under which act is the Central Board of Film Certification (CBFC) formed?

A. Article 19(2)

B. Draft Cinematograph Bill, 2010

C. The Film & Television Producers Guild of India Ltd.

D. The Cinematograph Act, 1952

E. Cinematograph Act of 1918

Q.17 According to the passage, the word 'ensure' means-

A. to protect yourself against risk by regularly paying a special company

B. prove that (someone) is wrong.

C. make certain of obtaining or providing (something).

D. make certain of obtaining or providing (something).

E. a person or thing providing protection.

Q.18 For general films, who among the given options is one of the correct constituents of the committee?

A. examining officer

B. two members from the advisory panel

C. only male members

A. Only 1   **B.** Only 2

C. Only 3   **D.** All of these

E. None of these

Q.19 According to the passage, the word 'certify' means-

A. give a practical exhibition and explanation of something

B. performing fictional roles in plays, films, or television

C. officially recognize as possessing certain qualifications or meeting certain standards.

D. dismiss as inadequate, unacceptable, or faulty.

E. not in accordance with accepted standards, especially of morality or honesty.

Q.20 What are the restrictions mentioned under Article 19(2)?

A. defamation

B. decency or morality

C. public order

A. only 1   **B.** only 2

C. all except 1   **D.** all except 3

E. all of these

Q.21 Direction: In each of the following questions a sentence is given with four of its words printed in bold. One of the four bold words may be misspelt or inappropriate. You have to identify that word and choose the appropriate option as your answer. If all words given in the bold are correctly spelt and also apppropriate in the context of the sentence. Then 'All Correct' is your answer.

Lucien could not **andure** the thought of appearing **barefaced** in front of a stranger, **especially** a person of great **status**.

A. barefaced
B. especially
C. status
D. andure
E. All Correct

Q.22 Direction: In each of the following questions a sentence is given with four of its words printed in bold. One of the four bold words may be misspelt or inappropriate. You have to identify that word and choose the appropriate option as your answer. If all words given in the bold are correctly spelt and also apppropriate in the context of the sentence. Then 'All Correct' is your answer.

Selfhood is not imagined as an **abstract** concept, but the **struggle** for space begins with physical **existence** and the right to ownership.

A. Selfhood
B. Abstract
C. Struggle
D. Existence
E. All Correct

Q.23 Direction: Arrange these parts so as to form a complete meaningful sentence/paragraph and then choose the correct combination.

A : disintegrates some part of the old truths, and

B : there by upsets the way of men's thinking and the ways of their lives

C : science does not merely add new truths to the old ones, but

D : sometimes the new truth it discovers

Which of the sequences present the most logical sentence?

A. ACBD
B. CDAB
C. ABCD
D. CBAD
E. None of these

Q.24 Direction: In the following question, sentences of a paragraph have been jumbled and labeled as A, B, C and D. You are required to rearrange the jumbled sentences of the paragraph and mark your response accordingly by selecting the correct option.

A. The element symbol for Plutonium is Pu, rather than Pl.

B. They later withdrew it as they realized it could also be used for an atomic bomb.

C. The researchers submitted the proposed name and symbol to the journal Physical Review.

D. This is because Pu was a more amusing symbol of the two.

A. DCAB
B. ADCB
C. CDAB
D. BCAD
E. None of these

Q.25 Directions: Given below are four sentences in jumbled order. Select the option that gives their correct order.

A. This flight takes place on a hot summer day.

B. It has a pair of wings but bites them off after its 'wedding' flight.

C. In the heat, the queen leaves the nest and goes out to meet a drone, high up in the air.

D. The queen is the mother of the entire population of a colony of ants.

A. DBAC
B. BACD
C. CABD
D. ACBD
E. None of these

Q.26 Directions: Given below are four sentences in jumbled order. Pick the option that gives their correct order.

A. Someone had been smart enough to remove it before I went on the rampage.

B. My hands had been itching to tear down that collage from my bedroom wall.

C. But I found the wall bare.

D. So, I entered my room in a hurry.

A. DABC
B. CBAD
C. ABCD
D. BDCA
E. None of these

Q.27 Directions: In the following question, sentences of a paragraph have been jumbled and labelled as A, B, C, and D. You are required to rearrange the jumbled sentences of the paragraph and mark your response accordingly by selecting the correct option.

A: The Bihar Legislative Assembly election will be held to elect members of the Legislative Assembly of the Indian State of Bihar.

B: Finally, he results will be announced on 10 November 2020.

C: The elections will be conducted amid the COVID-19 pandemic with the necessary guidelines issued by the Election Commission of India.

D: The election will be held in three phases for a total of 243 seats.

A. ACDB
B. CABD
C. DCAB
D. ADCB
E. None of these

Q.28 Direction: Read the sentence below to find out if there is any error in it. The error, if any, will be in one part of the sentence. The letter of that part is the answer. If there is no error the answer is (E)

As I reached the hospital (A) / I had found, a great rush of visitor (B) / whose relatives had been admitted there (C) / for one or the other ailment. (D) / No error (E)

A. As I reached the hospital
B. I had found, a great rush of visitor
C. whose relatives had been admitted there
D. for one or the other ailment
E. No error

Q.29 Direction: Read the sentence below to find out if there is any error in it. The error, if any, will be in one part of the sentence. The letter of that part is the answer. If there is no error the answer is (E)

Sharing a room helps kids and (A)/ teenagers learn how to cooperate together (B)/ with one another, pick up (C)/ after themselves, and make compromises (D)/ when things don't go their way. (E)/.

A. A
B. B
C. C
D. D
E. E

Q.30 Direction: Read the sentence below to find out if there is any error in it. The error, if any, will be in one part of the sentence. The letter of that part is the answer. If there is no error the answer is (E)

With a burning desire to (A)/ achieve the dream as a backing, so that (B)/ the desire to become enthusiastic, (C)/ let it become your brain in one of (D)/ the most important thing. (E)/.

A. A   **B.** B   **C.** C   **D.** D

E. E

Ques (31-32):Directions: Each question contains three statements, one or more of which may not be grammatically correct. You are required to identify the incorrect statements from the options given below and mark that as your answer.

Q.31 I. The Rafale issue was raised before the Supreme Court, which did not find any substance in the allegations.

II. Finance Secretary is only a designation given to the senior most secretary in the finance ministry.

III. Under the original proposal, 18 warplanes were to be procured in a fly-away condition.

A. Only II   **B.** Only I and II
C. Only I and III   **D.** Only III
E. All are correct

Q.32 I. Chabahar port enjoy special strategic status and is the gateway to Afghanistan.

II. We must translate these good intentions to actions.

III. We need some drivers and incentives in much areas such as biotechnology, IT and so on.

A. Only II   **B.** Only I and II
C. Only I and III   **D.** Only III
E. All are correct

Ques (33-35):Directions: A sentence is given below with three words highlighted in bold. Select the option that gives the correct set of words. In case the sentence is correct, select 'No improvement required'.

Q.33 Under tremendous **trying** (A) from the media and the Congress for taking some action against Saudi Arabia, after the sudden **disappearance** (B) of Saudi dissident and journalist Jamal Khashoggi in Turkey, Mr. Trump told reporters that he is **pressure** (C) to get at the bottom of the issue and has sought **details** (D) of it from Saudi Arabia.

A. Both A-D and B-C
B. Both A-C and B-D
C. Only A-C
D. Both A-B and C-D
E. No improvement required

Q.34 The Election Commission has **announced (A)** second installment of 1,100 more VVPATs **ensuing (B)** the State for the **to (C)** elections in the first **week (D)** of December.

A. Both B-D and A-C
B. Both A-B and C-D
C. Both B-C and A-D
D. Only B-C
E. No improvement required

Q.35 China and the United States have **slapped** (A) tit-for-tat tariffs over the past few months, **rattling** (B) financial markets as investors worried the **escalating** (C) trade war could **knock** (D) global trade and investment.

A. Both A-C and B-D
B. Both A-D and B-C
C. Both A-B and C-D
D. Only B-D
E. No improvement required

Ques (36-40):Direction: In the following question, out of the four alternatives, select the alternative which will improve the underlined part of the sentence. In case no improvement is needed, select "No Improvement".

Q.36 Prime Minister assured the house that <u>before signing the WTO agreement, every aspects will be discussed thoroughly.</u>

A. before signing WTO agreement, every aspects would be discussed thoroughly.
B. before signing the WTO agreement, every aspects will be thoroughly discussed.
C. before being signed, the WTO agreement will be discussed thoroughly.
D. before signing the WTO agreement, every aspect would be discussed thoroughly.
E. No Improvement.

Q.37 Since the military take over in Pakistan, the family members of deposed the Prime Minister <u>are confined within their houses.</u>

A. are confined to their houses.
B. are confined in their houses.
C. is confined within their houses.
D. is confined to his houses.
E. No Improvement.

Q.38 For a whole, the alternative to big dams suggested by experts,<u> appear to be superior and more feasible than any other alternative that one can think of.</u>

A. appear to be superior to and more feasible.
B. appear to be more superior and more feasible.
C. appears to be more superior and feasible.
D. appears to be superior to and more feasible.
E. No Improvement.

Q.39 Now HRD minister has come up with the proposal to make elementary education a fundamental right <u>as if it is the panacea for all ill afflicting the education system.</u>

A. as if it were a panacea for all ills afflicting
B. as if it were the panacea for all ill afflicting`
C. as if it were a panacea for all ill afflicting
D. as if it were the panacea for all ills afflicting
E. No Improvement.

Q.40 <u>Her supporters rallied for her defence</u> when the government brought the bill seeking to bar any person of foreign origin from holding the high offices.

A. Her supporters rallied of her defence
B. Her supporters rallied in her defence

C.   Her supporters rallied up in her defence
D.   Her supporters rallied to her defence
E.   No Improvement.

Test of Numerical Ability

Q.41 Sunil invested a sum of Rs. 6600 on simple interest at 9% per annum for 5 years. He then invested only the interest obtained after 5 years on another plan at 5% simple interest for an additional 8 years. What is the total amount that Sunil has after 13 years?

A. Rs. 7778   B. Rs. 8788
C. Rs. 9778   D. Rs. 10758
E. Rs. 1075

Q.42 What will come in place of the question mark (?) in the following question?

$4^3 + [(11^2 + 24) + (8^2 \div 4)] = ?$

A. 125   B. 225   C. 202   D. 145
E. 545

Q.43 What will come in place of the question mark (?) in the following question?

$31\% \text{ of } 200 + 21\% \text{ of } 300 = 25 \times 5 + ?^2 - 40\% \text{ of } 90$

A. 7   B. 4   C. 6   D. 5
E. 8

Q.44 What will come in place of the question mark (?) in the following equation?

30% of ? + 10% of 90 = 150

A. 370   B. 650   C. 520   D. 390
E. 470

Q.45 What will come in place of the question mark (?) in the following equation?

80% of 750 + 60% of 800 = ?

A. 980   B. 960   C. 1060   D. 1080
E. 1160

Q.46 What will come in place of the question mark (?) in the following equation?

$\{45 - (66 - 54 \div 9 \times 8)\} = ?$

A. 32   B. 22   C. 24   D. 36
E. 27

Q.47 Directions: What should come in place of the question mark '?' in the following number series?

$1728 - \sqrt{169} + (2 - 3 + 5)^2 + 12 = ?$

A. 1741   B. 1743
C. 1742   D. 1751
E. None of these

Q.48 What will come in place of question mark (?) in the following equation?

$5 \times \sqrt{25} + 300 - 100 = ?^2$

A. 12   B. 20   C. 15   D. 25
E. 30

Q.49 What will come in place of question mark (?) in the following equation.

$\sqrt{784} \times \sqrt{6.25} + 56\% \, of \, 450 = ? + 186$

A. 54855   B. 54967   C. 54352   D. 55041
E. 54043

Q.50 What will come in place of the question mark (?) in the following equation?

$5.8 \times 2.5 + 0.6 \times 6.75 + 139.25 = ?$

A. 139.80   B. 157.80   C. 156.70   D. 170.70
E. 176.60

Q.51 What will come in place of the question mark (?) in the following equation?

$4\frac{5}{7} \times 4\frac{2}{3} + ? = 35\% \text{ of } 158$

A. 23.3   B. 33.3
C. 31.3   D. 19.3
E. None of these

Q.52 A book was successively sold by three book-sellers gaining a profit of 10% each. By how much percentage the price of the book has increased?

A. 10%   B. 15.5%   C. 30%   D. 31.2%
E. 33.1%

Q.53 An amount was divided among three brothers - Neel, Nitin, and Mukesh. The ratio of Neel's share to that of Mukesh's share is _______. Mukesh got half as much as Neel and Nitin together got. Neel got $\frac{1}{3}$rd of what Nitin and Mukesh together got.

A. 4 : 5   B. 5 : 6
C. 6 : 5   D. 3 : 4
E. None of these

Q.54 A tank is filled by three pipes with uniform flow. The first two pipes operating simultaneously fill the tank at the same time during which the tank is filled by the third pipe alone. The second pipe fills the tank 5 hours faster than the first pipe and 4 hours slower than the third pipe. The time required by the first pipe is:

A. 6 hours   B. 10 hours   C. 15 hours   D. 30 hours
E. 5 hours

Q.55 Age of Umesh will be 4 times the age of Reena in 6 years from today. If ages of Umesh and Mahesh are 7 times and 6 times the age of Reena respectively, what is present age of Umesh?

A. 64 years   B. 30 years   C. 48 years   D. 42 years
E. 52 years

Q.56 A metallic spherical shell has its inner and outer radii in the ratio 2 : 3. The total amount of metal used in this shell is 79546.67 cubic cm. Find the outer radius of the shell.(in cm) (Use π = 3.14)

A. 18   B. 30   C. 24   D. 15
E. 36

Q.57 Amar can buy a certain number of mangoes for a certain amount. If the price of mangoes increases by $\dfrac{100}{3}$ %, what is the % change in the number of mangoes bought which Amar can buy in the same amount?

A. +20%   **B.** +25%   **C.** -20%   **D.** -25%
E. -40%

Ques (58-60):Direction: In the following number series, only one number is wrong. Find out the wrong number.

Q.58 1.21, 2.69, 4.25, 5.98, 7.61, 9.41
A. 2.69   **B.** 7.61   **C.** 4.25   **D.** 9.41
E. 5.98

Q.59 47, 44, 45, 46, 33, 57, 3, 88
A. 44   **B.** 57   **C.** 46   **D.** 3
E. 47

Q.60 3, 5, 13, 53, 177, 891
A. 3   **B.** 5   **C.** 891   **D.** 177
E. 53

Ques (61-62):Direction: In the following number series, only one number is wrong. Find out the wrong number.

Q.61 10, 14, 23, 39, 54, 100
A. 10   **B.** 14   **C.** 39   **D.** 54
E. 100

Q.62 45, 131, 228, 338, 466, 619, 800
A. 131   **B.** 466   **C.** 619   **D.** 45
E. 800

Q.63 Jigna invest Rs. 2000 more than Esha in a business of restaurant. They found third partner named Pinky with the investment of 25% more than Esha. If the total investment amount is Rs. 12,50,000. The amount invested by Esha is-

A. 2,76,000   **B.** 3,84,000
C. 4,15,000   **D.** 5,74,000
E. None of the above

Ques (64-68):Direction: Following data shows the number of people (in thousand) from different age group who likes 7 different kind of music in a city.

Music	Age Group		
	15-20	21-30	>30
Classical	6	4	17
Pop	7	5	5
Rock	6	12	14
Jazz	1	4	11
Blues	2	3	15
Hip-Hop	9	3	4
Ambient	2	2	2
Total	33	33	68

Q.64 Which kind of music people like most?
A. Classical   **B.** Pop
C. Rock   **D.** Blues
E. None of these

Q.65 People from which age group like hip-hop the most?
A. 15 - 20   **B.** 21 - 30
C. > 30   **D.** 20 -15
E. None of these

Q.66 The ratio of number of people who like Rock to that who likes Jazz is:
A. 4 : 3   **B.** 3 : 1
C. 5 : 3   **D.** 2 : 1
E. None of these

Q.67 What is the average number of people from an age group who likes classical?
A. 9000   **B.** 7500
C. 12000   **D.** 14500
E. None of these

Q.68 What percent of people from age group 21 - 30 likes pop or hip-hop or blues?
A. 33%   **B.** $33\dfrac{1}{3}$%
C. 13%   **D.** 25%
E. None of these

Q.69 The average weight of 48 students of a class is 36 kg. If the weights of teacher and principal are included, then the average becomes 36.76 kg. Find the sum of the weights of teacher and principal?
A. 108 kg   **B.** 112 kg
C. 110 kg   **D.** 114 kg
E. None of these

Q.70 A man leaves from P at 6 AM and reaches Q at 2 PM on the same day. Another man leaves Q at 8 AM and reaches P at 3 PM on the same day. At what time do they meet?
A. 11 : 46 AM   **B.** 11 : 24 AM
C. 10 : 48 AM   **D.** 11 : 00 AM
E. None of these

Test of Reasoning

Q.71 Direction: Study the following information carefully to answer the given questions.

Six boxes M, N, O, P, Q, and R are placed one above the other not necessarily in same order with 6 being the topmost and 1 is the bottommost. These boxes contains different electronic items viz laptop, camera, phone, webcam, router, and charger. Only two boxes are placed between O and P, which has camera in it. Box O placed above Box P. The box which is at top contains laptop. Box O placed at even numbered position and is not placed at top. Only one box is placed between O and the one which contains router. Box Q contains webcam. Box N placed immediately below Box R, which contains charger.

Which box contains webcam?
A. Box Q   **B.** Box M
C. Box P   **D.** Box O
E. None of these

Ques (72-76):Direction: Study the following information carefully to answer the given questions.

Six boxes M, N, O, P, Q, and R are placed one above the other not necessarily in same order with 6 being the topmost and 1 is the bottommost. These boxes contains different electronic items viz laptop, camera, phone, webcam, router, and charger. Only two boxes are placed between O and P, which has camera in it. Box O placed above Box P. The box which is at top contains laptop. Box O placed at even numbered position and is not placed at top. Only one box is placed between O and the one which contains router. Box Q contains webcam. Box N placed immediately below Box R, which contains charger.

Q.72 Box M contains which electronic item?

A. Webcam   **B.** Laptop
C. Router   **D.** Camera
E. None of the above

Q.73 How many boxes are placed between the one which contains Phone and Box N?

A. Four   **B.** Three
C. Two   **D.** One
E. None of the above

Q.74 What is the position of Box Q?

A. Third from the bottom
B. Second from the top
C. Top most position
D. Third from the top
E. Second from bottom

Q.75 How many boxes are placed between M and N?

[IBPS Clerk, 2021]

A. Three   **B.** Two
C. One   **D.** Four
E. None of the above

Q.76 Which box contains Phone?

A. M   **B.** O   **C.** Q   **D.** P
E. N

Q.77 Direction: In the following question assuming the given statement to be true. Find which of the following conclusion(s) among the given conclusions is/are definitely true and then give your answer accordingly.

Statement:

$S > M \geq O, O \geq P \geq N > K$

Conclusion:

I. $O > N$

II. $N \leq M$

A. None is true
B. Only II is true
C. Both I and II are true
D. Only I is true
E. Either I or II is true

Ques (78-81):Direction: In the following question assuming the given statements to be True, find which of the conclusion among the given conclusion(s) is/are definitely True and then give your answers accordingly.

Q.78 Statements: $M \geq T; M < P; S > T$

Conclusions:

I. $S = M$

II. $T < P$

III. $P > S$

A. Only I is true   **B.** I, II and III are True
C. Only II is True   **D.** II and III are True
E. None is true

Q.79 Statements:

$X > C \geq V > Y; U = V < T \leq H; T < B$

Conclusions:

I. $Y < X$

II. $X \geq B$

III. $V < B$

A. None
B. Only conclusion I follows
C. None of these
D. Both conclusion I and III follow
E. Only conclusion III follows

Q.80 Statements:

$P \leq Q > R = S; S < T; T = P > U; V < U$

Conclusions:

I. $Q = P$

II. $Q > P$

III. $P < V$

A. Only III is True
B. Both I and II are True
C. Only II is True
D. Only I is True
E. Either I or II is True

Q.81 Statements: $A > P \geq K; Q > M > T; P > T$

Conclusions:

I. $T < K$

II. $K > A$

III. $A > K$

A. Only I is true
B. Only II is true
C. Only I and II are true
D. Only II and III are true
E. Only III is true

Ques (82-87):Directions: Study the following information carefully to answer the given questions:

Nine persons A, B, C, D, E, F, G, H and J are sitting around a circular table but not necessarily in the same order. All are facing towards the center. A sits 2nd to the right of B. F sits 4th to the left of A. C sits third to the right of F. G is immediate neighbor of J. G sits 2nd to the right of H. D sits 2nd to the left of E. E is not an immediate neighbor of A.

Q.82 Who among the following person sits 3rd to the right of E?

A. B   **B.** A
C. C   **D.** F

E. None of these

Q.83 How many persons sit between from left of E to F?

A. Two
B. One
C. Three
D. None
E. More than three

Q.84 Who among the following person sit exactly between E and C?

A. B
B. D
C. A
D. F
E. None of these

Q.85 Who among the following persons sits immediate right of A?

A. B
B. C
C. D
D. G
E. H

Q.86 Four of the following five are alike in certain way based from a group, find the one which does not belong to that group?

A. E – C
B. B – F
C. D – J
D. A – C
E. C – H

Q.87 Who sits eits 2nd to the right of H?

A. B
B. G
C. C
D. D
E. None of these

Ques (88-90):Direction: Study the given information to answer the following question.

There are 10 cities A, B, Z, Y, K, T, R, J, M, and P in a state. City A is 10 km to the north of city K which is 10 km to the west of city M. City J is 5 km to the south of city M and city R is 5 km to the west of city J. City T is 5 km to the south of city K. City B is 15 km to the north of city M and city Y is 10 km to the south of city P which is 5 km to the south of city Z which is 10 km to the east of city B.

Q.88 What is the distance between city T and city R?

A. 10 km
B. 5 km
C. 15 km
D. 20 km
E. None of these

Q.89 What is the distance between city M and city Y?

A. 15 km
B. 20 km
C. 5 km
D. 10 km
E. None of these

Q.90 What is the distance between city A and city P?

A. 10 km
B. 20 km
C. 15 km
D. None of these
E. Cannot be determined

Q.91 In the question below are given three statements, followed by conclusions: I, II and III. You have to take the given statements to be true even if they seem to be at variance from commonly known facts. Read the conclusions and then decide which of the given conclusions logically follows from the given statements disregarding commonly known facts.

Statements:

Some Lions are Tigers.

All Tigers are Bears.

No Bears are Parrot.

Conclusions:

I. Some Lions are Parrot.

II. Some Lions are Bears.

III. Some Parrot are Bears.

A. Only I follows.
B. Only II follows.
C. Only III follows.
D. All I, II and III follows.
E. None follows.

Ques (92-95):Direction: In these questions, the relationship between different elements is shown in the statements. These statements are followed by two conclusions. Study the conclusions based on the given statements and select the appropriate answer.

Q.92 Statement:

All cars are bikes.

Some boats are bikes.

No car is a boat.

Conclusions:

I. All bikes can be boats.

II. All bikes cannot be cars.

A. Only conclusion I follows
B. Only conclusion II follows
C. Either conclusion I or II follows
D. Neither of the conclusions follow
E. Both the conclusions follow

Q.93 Statements:

Some sky are blue.

No blue is red.

Some red are water.

Conclusions:

I. Some blue can be water.

II. All water cannot be sky.

A. Only conclusion I follows
B. Only conclusion II follows
C. Either conclusion I or II follows
D. Neither of the conclusions follow
E. Both the conclusions follow

Q.94 Statements:

All dogs are dragons.

All cats are dragons.

No dragon is a lion.

Conclusions:

I. No dog can be a lion.

II. No cat can be a lion.

A. Only conclusion I follows
B. Only conclusion II follows
C. Either conclusion I or II follows
D. Neither of the conclusions follow
E. Both the conclusions follow

E. cd ap ha

Q.95 Statements:

No tree is a herb.

Some shrubs are grass.

No grass is a herb.

Conclusions:

I. No shrub can be a herb.

II. No grass can be a tree.

A. Only conclusion I follows
B. Only conclusion II follows
C. Either conclusion I or II follows
D. Neither of the conclusions follow
E. Both the conclusions follow

Ques (96-100):Directions: Study the following information carefully and answer the questions given beside:

In certain coded language:

'Worst Thing To Happen' is coded as 'ip tn bl rm'

'Stay Close To Heart' is coded as 'pc ap ha bl'

'Your Stay Was Worst' is coded as 'jr rm ha pi'

'Thing Stay In Heart' is coded as 'ma pc ha tn'

Q.96 What does the code 'jr' stand for in the given code language?

A. Heart
B. Stay
C. Either 'Stay' or 'Close'
D. Worst
E. Either 'Your' or 'Was'

Q.97 Which of the following is the code for 'Happen' in the given code language?

A. rm
B. ip
C. tn
D. bl
E. None of these

Q.98 Which of the following is the code for 'Heart' in the given code language?

A. ma
B. ha
C. bl
D. pc
E. None of these

Q.99 Which of the following is the code for 'Worst Stay' in the given code language?

A. rm ha
B. ap bl
C. pi jr
D. rm pi
E. None of these

Q.100 If 'In Your Dreams' is written as 'cd ma pi' then what would be the code of 'Dreams Close Thing'?

A. cd bl rm
B. ma pc tn
C. cd tn ap
D. jr ha rm

// Smart Answer Sheet //

Correct — Indicates percentage of students who answered questions correctly.

Skipped — Indicates percentage of students who skipped questions.

Q.	Ans.	Correct / Skipped
1	D	64.82 % / 30.49 %
2	D	41.32 % / 48.93 %
3	A	67.6 % / 30.04 %
4	C	61.17 % / 38.09 %
5	A	61.65 % / 32.59 %
6	B	79.21 % / 12.0 %
7	A	53.24 % / 37.35 %
8	C	57.6 % / 36.8 %
9	E	24.9 % / 71.97 %
10	A	15.35 % / 84.29 %
11	A	51.91 % / 34.13 %
12	D	56.95 % / 34.41 %
13	A	40.43 % / 59.28 %
14	B	54.15 % / 44.69 %
15	D	41.85 % / 43.81 %
16	D	51.15 % / 35.2 %

Q.	Ans.	Correct / Skipped
17	C	57.64 % / 31.18 %
18	A	44.73 % / 30.54 %
19	C	67.11 % / 31.7 %
20	E	49.74 % / 46.34 %
21	D	61.0 % / 35.92 %
22	E	57.24 % / 40.87 %
23	B	52.76 % / 47.18 %
24	B	68.72 % / 31.11 %
25	A	53.8 % / 43.77 %
26	D	46.65 % / 48.82 %
27	D	47.14 % / 36.42 %
28	E	60.79 % / 30.63 %
29	B	44.53 % / 49.52 %
30	E	65.92 % / 32.32 %
31	E	66.53 % / 33.43 %
32	C	66.19 % / 30.89 %

Q.	Ans.	Correct / Skipped
33	C	42.21 % / 35.5 %
34	D	49.83 % / 32.94 %
35	E	68.63 % / 31.23 %
36	D	60.46 % / 30.42 %
37	A	55.76 % / 38.6 %
38	D	66.02 % / 30.43 %
39	D	46.84 % / 50.26 %
40	D	45.11 % / 39.85 %
41	D	48.89 % / 43.3 %
42	B	49.18 % / 39.1 %
43	C	87.65 % / 10.71 %
44	E	84.08 % / 14.37 %
45	D	44.33 % / 44.66 %
46	E	53.07 % / 44.43 %
47	B	46.12 % / 52.25 %
48	C	22.46 % / 69.91 %

Q.	Ans.	Correct / Skipped
49	D	69.28 % / 30.47 %
50	B	80.53 % / 11.24 %
51	B	89.11 % / 10.59 %
52	E	69.98 % / 30.01 %
53	D	89.66 % / 10.08 %
54	C	54.63 % / 33.17 %
55	D	50.93 % / 31.29 %
56	B	58.92 % / 38.61 %
57	D	58.18 % / 31.02 %
58	E	51.37 % / 36.29 %
59	B	68.91 % / 30.41 %
60	E	83.06 % / 15.12 %
61	D	83.53 % / 12.13 %
62	B	51.54 % / 34.29 %
63	B	55.66 % / 32.88 %
64	C	49.26 % / 30.59 %

Q.	Ans.	Correct / Skipped
65	A	69.07 % / 30.85 %
66	D	61.56 % / 36.3 %
67	A	42.64 % / 46.44 %
68	B	69.56 % / 30.43 %
69	C	48.34 % / 38.13 %
70	C	64.85 % / 34.01 %
71	A	27.77 % / 70.89 %
72	B	46.85 % / 39.45 %
73	D	60.36 % / 33.78 %
74	B	50.12 % / 46.92 %
75	A	45.99 % / 48.03 %
76	B	56.51 % / 31.46 %
77	B	31.73 % / 67.2 %
78	C	54.7 % / 33.88 %
79	D	59.44 % / 32.76 %
80	E	68.32 % / 30.28 %

Q.	Ans.	Correct		Q.	Ans.	Correct		Q.	Ans.	Correct		Q.	Ans.	Correct		Q.	Ans.	Correct
		Skipped				Skipped				Skipped				Skipped				Skipped
81	E	87.09 %		85	E	55.52 %		89	D	40.6 %		93	A	58.94 %		97	B	47.26 %
		12.12 %				42.83 %				39.75 %				30.76 %				51.05 %
82	B	17.05 %		86	D	60.24 %		90	B	65.08 %		94	E	52.0 %		98	D	67.19 %
		72.03 %				33.4 %				31.56 %				43.67 %				32.34 %
83	D	63.65 %		87	B	41.84 %		91	B	42.21 %		95	D	59.43 %		99	A	40.86 %
		31.63 %				53.05 %				54.26 %				33.91 %				57.57 %
84	A	51.69 %		88	B	58.47 %		92	B	48.36 %		96	E	50.44 %		100	C	57.06 %
		31.84 %				31.02 %				31.14 %				32.48 %				34.06 %

Performance Analysis

Avg. Score (%)	64.0%
Toppers Score (%)	65.0%
Your Score	

//Hints and Solutions//

1. The sentence talks about the increasing 'division' of society "on ideological grounds". In the context of the sentence, the only possible word that can fit the first blank is either "divergence" or "polarization". This eliminates the options (A), (C) and (E).

For the second blank, a word that implies that the 'circulation' of fake news has become "easier" is most appropriate. Only the word "spreading" is apt for the second blank.

Hence, the correct option is (D).

2. The word "monitoring" indicates that the sentence refers to 'credit review.' In the context of the sentence, the words that are suitable for the first blank are "assessment", "evaluation" and appraisal". So, options (A) and (E) are eliminated.

In order to eliminate the "defects of capital", the shortcomings must first be identified and analyzed. The only word that aptly conveys this meaning is "diagnose". "Emphasize" or "clarify" defects does not indicate this meaning and this eliminates options (B) and (C) as well.

Hence, the correct option is (D).

3. The blanks refer to the type of content that is spreading rapidly and is "leading to the possibility of potential violence". This indicates that the adjectives describing this type of content must be strongly negative.

In the context of the sentence, the only combination of words that lead to a meaningful sentence is "fabricated" and "manipulated". All other combinations are incorrect either contextually or grammatically as both the words need to be strongly negative.

Hence, the correct option is (A).

4. From the given sentence, we can infer that the problem has been made worse by UGC's policy of asking for recommendations. In the context of the sentence, the words that are suitable for the first blank are "seeking" and "soliciting". So, options (B), (D) and (E) are eliminated.

For the second blank, we can infer that the aforementioned recommendations were sought for the addition of journals in the whitelist. The only word that aptly conveys this meaning is "inclusion". The word "exclusion" means the opposite and this eliminates option (A) as well.

Hence, the correct option is (C).

5. In the context of the sentence, the only combination of words that lead to a meaningful sentence is "investigating" and "credible". All other options are incorrect either contextually or grammatically. Therefore, options (B), (C), (D) and (E) are eliminated. The sentence conveys that despite media researchers trying to inspect the fake news scenario, no reliable information has been found regarding those who have generated the false information.

Hence, the correct option is (A).

6. The passage begins by mentioning the pockets of methane that are tapped within Canada's frozen lake Abraham. They are described as a natural wonder. Further, looking at that part of the sentence with the blank 1, it is followed by the conjunction 'yet' which is usually used to show contrast.

Therefore, we need to find a word that contrasts with the 'deadly' core or sets off the negative connotation of the same.

Considering the meanings of the words in the options, "dazzling" which means extremely attractive or exciting, is the correct word. The pockets of methane are a natural wonder and thus can be attractive/interesting. Also, "dazzling" contrasts the connotation of 'wonder' with that of 'the deadly core' to make the sentence coherent.

Hence, the correct option is (B).

7. looking at the sentence with the blank 2, the word 'therefore' which is used after the blank implies that the threat is due to an attribute of the greenhouse gas. So, we can infer that the gas might be dangerous.

Therefore, we need to find a word that is similar in meaning to dangerous or harmful.

Considering the meanings of the words in the options, "nocuous" which means harmful or noxious, is the correct word. It completes the sentence, conveying the meaning precisely.

Hence, the correct option is (A).

8. The sentence with the blank 3 conveys that the story of the formation of bubbles is rather pleasant and like any horror story, it involves dead bodies. As we read further, the next sentence describes the same process that begins with microbes feeding on decomposing matter. So, we can infer that the story possibly 'begins' with dead bodies.

Therefore, we need to find a word similar in meaning to 'begins'.

Considering the meanings of the words in the options, "starts" which means 'begins' is the correct word.

Hence, the correct option is (C).

9. The sentence with the blank 4 says that Methane is highly inflammable i.e. capable of being easily ignited. So, it is clear that it explodes when set on fire.

Therefore, we need to find a word that is similar in meaning to 'on fire'.

Considering the meanings of the words given in the options, "alight" which means 'burning' or 'on fire', is the correct word. As Methane can easily catch fire, evidently it explodes when it is set on fire.

Hence, the correct option is (E).

10. The sentence with the blank 5 mentions the impact of Methane on the earth's atmosphere and climate, in comparison with carbon dioxide. It says that though Methane does not stick around in the atmosphere, its heat-trapping effect is 34 times stronger. Thus, we can infer that it is more harmful to our climate.

Therefore, we need to find a word that is similar in meaning to the word 'harmful'.Considering the meanings of the words given in the options, "deleterious" which means harmful often in a subtle or unexpected way, is the correct answer. It is most appropriate in the context too, as methane does not remain in the atmosphere like carbon dioxide, it is not expected to be more harmful. However, the fact is otherwise owing to methane's heat-trapping effect.

Hence, the correct option is (A).

11. The passage is about the role of the Central Board of Film Certification with regard to Indian cinema. It generally describes the procedures through which certification of films is carried out.

- The following is stated in the passage: "The goal of the CBFC is to ascertain that healthy entertainment is provided to the general public of the country."
- Although the other options may not completely be untrue, they are not a part of the main objective of the CBFC.

Hence, the correct option is (A).

12. The following is stated in the passage: "If the applicant isn't satisfied with the list of changes and the certification he or she can apply to the Revising Committee for a review."

Hence, the correct option is (D).

13. The following is stated in the passage: "All these members are appointed by the Information & Broadcasting Ministry."

Hence, the correct option is (A).

14. The following is stated in the passage: "There are 25 members and 60 advisory panel members in the board from across India."

Hence, the correct option is (B).

15. The following is stated in the passage: "The CBFC has nine regional offices which include Mumbai, Kolkata, Bangalore, Chennai, Hyderabad, Thiruvananthapuram, New Delhi, Guwahati and Cuttack."

Hence, the correct option is (D).

16. The following is stated in the passage: "The Central Board of Film Certification (CBFC) is a statutory body formed under the Cinematograph Act 1952."

Hence, the correct option is (D).

17. The sentence in the passage containing the above word is: "The main responsibility of the board is to ensure that any content of any film does not fall into any of the categories of "reasonable restrictions upon free speech."

Here, it refers to making sure or certain that the content of any film does not fall into the restrictions categories.

Example: I will ensure that the car arrives at six o'clock.

Hence, the correct option is (C).

18. The following is stated in the passage: "For general films, the committee consists of an examining officer and four members of the advisory panel and. Two members of the committee must be women."

Out of all these members, only 'examining officer' has been mentioned in the question.

Hence, the correct option is (A).

19. The sentence in the passage containing the above word is "...regional officers are responsible for the examining committees that certify films."

This means that the regional officers are responsible for the examining committees who officially recognize the film as meeting certain standards and qualifications.

Example: We can certify for his competence as an editor.

Hence, the correct option is (C).

20. The following is stated in the passage: "Article 19(2) of the constitution consists of a set of abstract phrases such as "defamation", "decency or morality, "public order", and so on.

Hence, the correct option is (E).

21. In the sentence, out of all the bold parts 'andure' is the word that has no meaning.

- So, 'andure' is incorrectly spelt word.
- The correct spelling is 'endure' which means suffer (something painful or difficult) patiently.
- Let us know the meanings of other words:

Option A barefaced - shameless and undisguised.

Option B especially - used to single out one person or thing over all others.

Option C status - position or rank in relation to others

So, the correct sentence is - Lucien could not endure the thought of appearing barefaced in front of a stranger, especially a person of great status.

Hence, the correct option is (D).

22. Reading the above sentence we find that all the words given in bold are correctly spelled.

Let's look at the meanings of some of the emboldened words.

Selfhood: the quality that constitutes one's individuality; the state of having an individual identity.

Abstract: Existing in thought or as an idea; not having physical or concrete existence.

Struggle: to make strenuous or violent efforts in the face of difficulties or opposition struggling with the problem.

Existence : the state or fact of having being especially independently of human consciousness and as contrasted with nonexistence.

Hence, the correct option is (E).

23. C is the opening part containing the subject because the conjunction at the end of C is but the following sentence must be opposite to D in intent, that is A. But the subject of A is in D so CDAB is the right sequence.

Hence, the correct option is (B).

24. When ordering the sentences, it is easier to find the first few and then eliminate the options. The first sentence is always independent and introduces a topic. Here, only sentence A is independent and introduces the topic of 'Plutonium'. Out of the given options, only option (B) begins with A.

Thus, the correct sequence is: ADCB.

Hence, the correct option is (B).

25. The sentence 'D' is independent of any other sentence as it is giving general information about "the queen of ants". Hence, 'D' is the first part.

Sentence B will come after D because it explains what the queen of ants does with the pair of wings.

Sentence A will come after B because it explains when the wedding flight takes place.

The sentence 'C' is the concluding part because it mentions what the queen of ants does in the heat.

So, the correct sequence is DBAC.

Hence, the correct option is (A).

26. We know that the first statement of a sentence jumbled question is usually an independent general statement, a noun, a universal fact, starting of an incident, or it starts with 'most' or 'once'.

Part B will be the first sentence because it is the starting of an incident.

Part D will be used next because Part B talks about 'tearing down' of the collage and Part D further tell what the author did to tear down that collage.

Part C will be used next because it further explains what the author found when he entered that room.

Lastly, Part A will be used to give a possible explanation the author thinks of the wall being bare.

So, the correct sequence is BDCA.

Hence, the correct option is (D).

27. Sentence 'A' is independent of any other sentences as it is giving general information about the "Bihar Legislative Assembly election". Hence, 'A' is the first sentence.

The 'election' mentioned in the sentence 'D' refers back to the "Bihar election" in the sentence 'A' and is further describing the election. Hence, 'D' follows 'A'.

Sentence 'C' talks about the conduction of the elections according to the guidelines and it follows D.

Sentence 'B' concludes the paragraph by starting with 'finally' and by giving some additional information about the election. It talks about the results. Hence, 'C' makes the last sentence.

So, the correct sequence is ADCB.

Hence, the correct option is (D).

28. In the fifth part of the given sentence, the use of the preposition 'to' is incorrect.

The preposition 'to' is used for expressing motion in the direction of a particular location.

Also, "to a picnic" means that you are going to an event, maybe a large, organized family picnic.

The preposition 'for' is used for stating the purpose of an object or action.

Also, "for a picnic" means that you are going for the purpose of having a picnic.

Therefore, the preposition 'for' should be used in place of the preposition 'to'.

Hence, the correct option is (E).

29. In the B part of the given sentence, the words 'cooperate' and 'together' are used side by side, thus the sentence is corrupted by redundancy.

The meaning of 'cooperate' is to work or act together.

The word 'together' is included in the meaning of 'cooperate'.

So, both 'cooperate' and 'together' can't be used in a single sentence.

Therefore, we can say that using the word 'together' along with 'cooperate' is redundant.

Hence, the correct option is (B).

30. In the E part of the given sentence, the singular form of the noun 'thing' is incorrect.

The phrase "one of" in the given sentence is a singular term and generally used to talk about a noun or a pronoun.

The noun or a pronoun used after the phrase "one of" is always in the plural form (as we are talking of one person/place/thing out of many).

Therefore, the plural form of the noun 'things' should be used in place of the singular form 'thing'.

Correct sentence : With a burning desire to achieve the dream as a backing, so that the desire to become enthusiastic, let it become your brain in one of the most important things.

Hence, the correct option is (E).

31. All the given statements are absolutely correct.

Hence, the correct option is (E).

32. I. Chabahar port is a singular subject, thus the verb should also be singular i.e. instead of 'enjoy', "enjoys" should be the correct helping verb.

Correct sentence: Chabahar port enjoys special strategic status and is the gateway to Afghanistan.

II. is absolutely correct.

III. is grammatically incorrect as wrong quantifier is used here. 'areas' is countable, so instead of 'much', use of "many" is preferred.

Correct sentence: We need some drivers and incentives in many areas such as biotechnology, IT and so on.

Hence, the correct option is (C).

33. The sentence is not correct in its present form and it requires to be corrected by interchanging the words in the sentence. Therefore, option E can be eliminated easily.
Coming to option A, if we carry out the first interchanging of A and D, the resultant statement is not making any sense and therefore, there is no requirement to try with the second combination. This option can be ruled out easily.
Moving on to option B, if A and C are interchanged, it is making sense and therefore, we have to go ahead with the next also. Here, it is clear that B and D cannot be interchanged to make the statement correct. But A and C should be interchanged in order to make the statement meaningful.
It implies that our correct choice should contain A-C as a pair and we have option C with that. Since the remaining pair of B-D is not applicable here, we can consider this as our correct pair.
The correct statement would be:
Under tremendous pressure from the media and the Congress for taking some action against Saudi Arabia, after the
sudden disappearance of Saudi dissident and journalist Jamal Khashoggi in Turkey, Mr. Trump told reporters that he is trying to get at the bottom of the issue and has sought details of it from Saudi Arabia.

Hence, the correct option is (C).

34. The given statement is not correct since it is not making any sense if we go with the given statement. It should be changed by changing the words in certain places or by interchanging the same. Now, according to the context of the statement, it is talking something about the new VVPAT machines to be introduced in the upcoming elections in December by the Election Commission of India.

Coming to the given options, If we follow option A, it will not make any sense whereas the same can be said about option B where A and B are to be interchanged thereby making the sentence grammatically incorrect also. Option C is not correct since A and D cannot be interchanged as that will render the whole sentence meaningless but B-C can be interchanged. Option D is the choice that will make sure that the statement is making some sense as has been observed in the preceding statement.

The correct statement would be:

The Election Commission has announced second installment of 1,100 more VVPATs to the State for the ensuing elections in the first week of December.

Hence, the correct option is (D).

35. The sentence is correct in its present form and all the bold words are in correct places making it unnecessary to interchange any of the given pairs.

Correct: China and the United States have slapped tit-for-tat tariffs over the past few months, rattling financial markets as investors worried the escalating trade war could knock global trade and investment.

Hence, the correct option is (E).

36. Correct the error of number and tense. Adjective 'every' should be followed by singular noun (aspect), while the verb 'will' should be 'would' to agree with the tense of the verb of principal clause (assured).

Correct sentence : Prime Minister assured the house that before signing the WTO agreement, every aspects would be discussed thoroughly.

Hence, the correct option is (D).

37. 'Confined' is followed by preposition 'to'.

Correct sentence : Since the military take over in Pakistan, the family members of deposed the Prime Ministers are confined to their houses.

Hence, the correct option is (A).

38. The alternative' is the subject for the verb 'appear' and since the subject is singular in form the verb must be 'appears' instead of 'appear'.

Besides, 'superior' or 'inferior' has the force of comparative degree and is followed by 'to' and not 'than'.

When two adjectives require different prepositions, appropriate prepositions should be used with both adjectives. e.g.,

Ex. He is senior and older than I. (Use 'to' after 'senior')

Ex. His dress is different and cheaper than mine. (Use 'from' after 'different')

Ex. She is stronger and younger than her sister. (Correct)

Correct sentence : For a whole, the alternative to big dams suggested by experts, appears to be superior to and more feasible.

Hence, the correct option is (D).

39. Corrects the error of past subjunctive mood and plural noun. The verb should be 'were', in the clause beginning with 'as if/as though' and refers to a situation contrary to fact or unreal past. 'All' in the sentence is used as 'indefinite determiner', and it is followed by a plural noun (ills).

Correct sentence: Now HRD minister has come up with the proposal to make elementary education a fundamental right as if it were the panacea for all ills afflicting.

Hence, the correct option is (D).

40. When people rally to something or when something rallies them, they unite to support it.

Ex. His supporters have rallied to his defence.

Ex. He rallied his own supporters for a fight.

The preposition 'in/at' is followed by the verb 'rally' only in a context of a place.

Ex. Ian Smith, a 24-year-old who works with adolescents in drug and mental health rehab, showed up at the same Trump rally in suburban Southern California.

Ex. Fistfights broke out among protesters who were rallying at the JNU, prompting the management to cancel the event.

Correct sentence: Her supporters rallied to her defence when the government brought the bill seeking to bar any person of foreign origin from holding the high offices.

Hence, the correct option is (D).

41. Formula to calculate Simple Interest (SI) = $\dfrac{PRT}{100}$

(where P = Principal/Sum, T = Time Period, R = Rate of Interest)

Simple Interest on Rs. 6600 at 9% per annum for 5 years

$= \dfrac{6600 \times 9 \times 5}{100}$

$= (66 \times 9 \times 5)$

= Rs. 2970

Simple Interest on Rs. 2970 at 5% per annum for 8 years

$= \dfrac{2970 \times 5 \times 8}{100}$

$= (297 \times 4)$

= Rs. 1188

Total money which Sunil will have after 13 years = 6600 + 2970 + 1188 = Rs. 10758

∴ Total money with Sunil after 13 years = Rs. 10758

Hence, the correct option is (D).

42. Given:

$4^3 + [(11^2 + 24) + (8^2 \div 4)] = ?$

This can be solved by BODMAS rule:

$\Rightarrow 64 + [(121 + 24) + (64 \div 4)] = ?$

$\Rightarrow 64 + (145 + 16) = ?$

$\Rightarrow 64 + 161 = ?$

$\Rightarrow ? = 225$

∴ The value of ? is 225.

Hence, the correct option is (B).

43. $31\% \text{of } 200 + 21\% \text{ of } 300 = 25 \times 5 + ?^2 - 40\% \text{of } 90$

$\Rightarrow \left(\frac{31}{100}\right) \times 200 + \left(\frac{21}{100}\right) \times 300 = 125 + ?^2 - \left(\frac{40}{100}\right) \times 90$

$\Rightarrow 62 + 63 = 125 + ?^2 - 36$

$\Rightarrow ?^2 = 36$

$\Rightarrow ? = 6$

∴ The value of ? is 6

Hence, the correct option is (C).

44. Given:

30% of ? + 10% of 90 = 150

$\Rightarrow \dfrac{30}{100}$ of ? + $\dfrac{10}{100}$ of 90 = 150

$\Rightarrow 0.3 \times ? + 9 = 150$

$\Rightarrow 0.3 \times ? = 150 - 9$

$\Rightarrow 0.3 \times ? = 141$

$\Rightarrow ? = \dfrac{141}{0.3}$

$\Rightarrow ? = 470$

∴ The required value of "?" in the given equation is 470.

Hence, the correct option is (E).

45. Given:

80% of 750 + 60% of 800 = ?

$\Rightarrow \left(\dfrac{80}{100}\right) \times 750 + \left(\dfrac{60}{100}\right) \times 800 = ?$

$\Rightarrow 600 + 480 = ?$

∴ ? = 1080

Hence, the correct option is (D).

46. Given:

{45 − (66 − 54 ÷ 9 × 8)} = ?

$\Rightarrow$ {45 − (66 − 6 × 8)} = ?

$\Rightarrow$ {45 − (66 − 48)} = ?

$\Rightarrow$ {45 − 18} = ?

∴ ? = 27

Hence, the correct option is (E).

47. This type of question can be solved with the help of BODMAS:

$1728 - \sqrt{169} + (2 - 3 + 5)^2 + 12 = ?$

$\Rightarrow 1728 - 13 + (-1 + 5)^2 + 12 = ?$

$\Rightarrow 1728 - 13 + (4)^2 + 12 = ?$

$\Rightarrow 1728 - 13 + 16 + 12 = ?$

$\Rightarrow 1728 + 3 + 12 = ?$

$\Rightarrow 1743 = ?$

The value of ? is 1743 .

Hence, the correct option is (B).

48. Given:

$5 \times \sqrt{25} + 300 - 100 = ?^2$

$\Rightarrow 5 \times 5 + 200 = ?^2$

$\Rightarrow 225 = ?^2$

∴ $15 = ?$

Hence, the correct option is (C).

49. Given,

$$13^2 \times \frac{210}{28} \times 44 =? +27^2$$

$$\Rightarrow 169 \times 7.5 \times 44 =? +729$$

$$\Rightarrow 169 \times 330 =? +729$$

$$\Rightarrow 55770 - 729 =?$$

$$\Rightarrow ? = 55041$$

Hence, the correct option is (D).

50. $5.8 \times 2.5 + 0.6 \times 6.75 + 139.25 =?$

$$= 14.5 + 4.05 + 139.25$$

$$= 157.80$$

Hence, the correct option is (B).

51. Given:

$$4\frac{5}{7} \times 4\frac{2}{3} +? = 35\% \text{ of } 158$$

$$\left(\frac{33}{7}\right) \times \left(\frac{14}{3}\right) +? = \left(\frac{35}{100}\right) \times 158$$

$$22 +? = 55.3$$

$$? = 55.3 - 22$$

$$= 33.3$$

Hence, the correct option is (B).

52. Let the original price of the painting be Rs. 'x'

Selling price of 1st seller = (100 + 10)% of x

$\Rightarrow$ 110% of x

$\Rightarrow$ 1.1x

Selling price of 2nd seller = (100 + 10)% of 1.1x

$\Rightarrow$ 110% of 1.1x

$\Rightarrow$ 1.1 × 1.1x

$\Rightarrow$ 1.21x

Selling price of 3rd seller = (100 + 10)% of 1.21x

$\Rightarrow$ 110% of 1.21x

$\Rightarrow$ 1.1 × 1.21x

$\Rightarrow$ 1.331x

$\therefore$ The price of the book increased by = 1.331x - x = 0.331x = 33.1% of x

Hence, the correct option is (E).

53. According to question,

Neel + Nitin = 2 Mukesh ....(i)

And, Nitin + Mukesh = 3 × Neel ....(ii)

From (i) and (ii), we get

4 × Neel = 3 × Mukesh

$\therefore$ Required ratio = $\dfrac{Neel}{Mukesh}$ = 3 : 4

Hence, the correct option is (D).

54. Given,

Time taken by first two pipes = Time taken by third pipe alone

Let the first pipe alone takes x hours to fill the tank.

Then, time taken by second pipe = $(x - 5)$ hours

Time taken by third pipe = $(x - 9)$ hours

According to question,

Time taken by first two pipes = Time taken by third pipe alone

$$\frac{1}{x} + \frac{1}{x-5} = \frac{1}{x-9}$$

$$\Rightarrow \frac{x-5+x}{x(x-5)} = \frac{1}{x-9}$$

$$\Rightarrow (2x-5)(x-9) = x(x-5)$$

$$\Rightarrow x^2 - 18x + 45 = 0$$

$$\Rightarrow (x-15)(x-3) = 0$$

We will not take x as 3 because this will give the negative value of an hour which is not possible.

Therefore,

$$x - 15 = 0$$

$$\Rightarrow x = 15$$

$\therefore$ The time required by the first pipe is 15 hours.

Hence, the correct option is (C).

55. Let, present age of Umesh $= U$ years, Mahesh $= M$ years and Reena $= R$ years

According to the question, $U = 7R$ and $M = 6R$

Also after 6 years,

$$U + 6 = 4(R + 6)$$

$$7R + 6 = 4R + 24$$

$\therefore R = 6$ years $=$ Present age of Reena. Present age of Umesh $= 7R = 7 \times 6 = 42$ years

Hence, the correct option is (D).

56. Let the inner and outer radii be 2T and 3T cm, respectively.

$\Rightarrow$ Amount of metal used = Volume of shell

$\Rightarrow 79546.67 = \left(\dfrac{4}{3}\right) \pi \, [(3T)^3 - (2T)^3]$

$\Rightarrow \dfrac{59660}{3.14} = [19(T)^3]$

$\Rightarrow (T)^3 = 1000$

$\Rightarrow T = 10$

$\therefore$ Outer radii = 3T = 30 cm

Hence, the correct option is (B).

57. Let the price per mango be x and the number of mangoes bought initially be y.

$\therefore$ Amount spent = x × y

$\Rightarrow$ Now the price is increased by $\dfrac{100}{3}$%.

$\therefore$ Price per mango= 1.33 × x and the number of mangoes be y′.

$\Rightarrow$ Amount spent is same in both cases.

$\Rightarrow$ x × y = 1.33x × y′

$\Rightarrow y' = \dfrac{y}{1.33}$

$\therefore y' = \dfrac{3}{4} \times y$

$\Rightarrow$ Percentage change in y = $\dfrac{\left(\dfrac{3y}{4-y}\right)}{y} \times 100 \times 100 = -25\%$

Hence, the correct option is (D).

58. Given series:

1.21, 2.69, 4.25, 5.98, 7.61, 9.41

The pattern is:

$$0 + (1.1)^2 = 1.21$$
$$1 + (1.3)^2 = 2.69$$
$$2 + (1.5)^2 = 4.25$$
$$3 + (1.7)^2 = 5.89$$
$$4 + (1.9)^2 = 7.61$$
$$5 + (2.1)^2 = 9.41$$

So, the wrong number is 5.98.

Hence, the correct option is (E).

59. The series follows the following pattern:

First series: 47, 45, 33, 3

47 - (1 × 2) = 45

45 - (3 × 4) = 33

33 - (5 × 6) = 3

Second series: 44, 46, 57, 88

44 + (1 × 2) = 46

46 + (3 × 4) = 58 ≠ 57

58 + (5 × 6) = 88

Since 58 will come in place of 57.

$\therefore$ Wrong number is 57.

Hence, the correct option is (B).

60. The series follows the following pattern:

3 × 1 + 2 = 5

5 × 2 + 3 = 13

13 × 3 + 4 = 43 ≠ 53

43 × 4 + 5 = 177

177 × 5 + 6 = 891

Since 43 will come in place of 53.

$\therefore$ Wrong number is 53.

Hence, the correct option is (E).

61. The series follows the following pattern:

$10 + 4 = 14 \quad (\because 2^2 = 4\,)$

$14 + 9 = 23 \quad (\because 3^2 = 9\,)$

$23 + 16 = 39 \quad (\because 4^2 = 16\,)$

$39 + 25 = 64 \quad (\because 5^2 = 25\,)$

$64 + 36 = 100 \quad (\because 6^2 = 36\,)$

Since 64 will come in place of 54.

$\therefore$ Wrong number is 54.

Hence, the correct option is (D).

62. The series follows the following pattern:

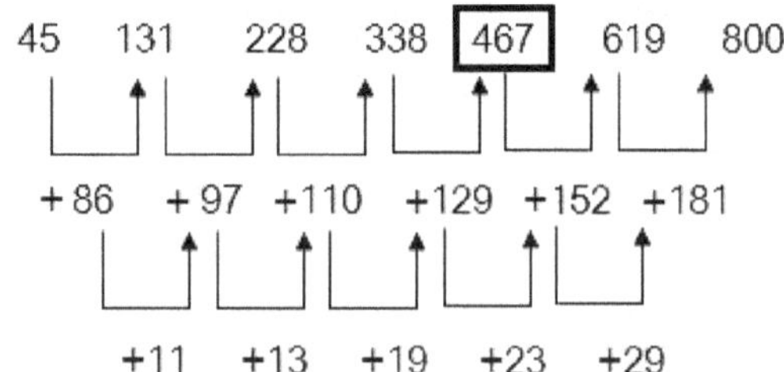

Since 467 will come in place of 466.

$\therefore$ Wrong number is 466.

Hence, the correct option is (B).

63. Let assume, Investment of Esha be Rs. x

Investment of Jigna = 2000 more than Esha's investment,

$\Rightarrow$ Investment of Jigna = 2000 + x

Investment of Pinky = 25% more investment compare to Esha,

$\Rightarrow$ Investment of Pinky = 125% of Esha = $\left(\dfrac{125}{100}\right) \times x = 1.25x$

Total investment amount = Rs. 1250000

$\Rightarrow$ 2000 + x + x + 1.25x = 1250000

$\Rightarrow$ 3.25x = 1250000 - 2000

$\Rightarrow$ x = Rs. 384000

$\therefore$ The amount invested by Esha = Rs. 384000

Hence, the correct option is (B).

64. Classical $= 6 + 4 + 17 = 27$

Pop $= 7 + 5 + 5 = 17$

Rock $= 6 + 12 + 14 = 32$ (Maximum)

Blues $= 2 + 3 + 15 = 20$

Hence, the correct option is (C).

65. Age group $15 - 20 \rightarrow 9$ thousand

Age group $21 - 30 \rightarrow 3$ thousand

Age group $> 30 \rightarrow 4$ thousand

So, age group $15 - 20$ are mostly like the hip- hop.

Hence, the correct option is (A).

66. People who like Rock $= 6 + 12 + 14 = 32$

People who like Jazz $= 1 + 4 + 11 = 16$

So, the required ratio who like Rock and who like Jazz $= \dfrac{32}{16} = \dfrac{2}{1}$

Therefore the ratio is $2:1$.

Hence, the correct option is (D).

67. The people who like the classical $= 6,4,17$ Required average $= \dfrac{6+4+17}{3}$

$= \dfrac{27}{3} = 9000$

Hence, the correct option is (A).

68. Total number of people in age group $21 - 30$ is 33 thousand.

And, the number of people who like age group is $5 + 3 + 3 = 11$ thousand.

So, required percent $\dfrac{11}{33} \times 100$

$= 33\dfrac{1}{3}\%$

Hence, the correct option is (B).

69. Sum of weights of teacher and principal

$\Rightarrow$ New avg. × No. of students – Existing avg. × No. of students

$\Rightarrow$ 36.76 × 50 – 36 × 48 = 1838 – 1728

$\Rightarrow$ 110 kg

$\therefore$ Sum of weight of teacher and principle is 110 kg

Hence, the correct option is (C).

70. Calculation:

Time taken by first man to cover journey = 2 PM – 6 AM = 8 hours

Time taken by another man to cover journey = 3 PM – 8 AM = 7 hours

Let total distance from P to Q be 56x km (LCM of 8 & 7)

$\Rightarrow$ Speed of first man = 7x km/hr

$\Rightarrow$ Speed of second man = 8x km/hr

$\Rightarrow$ Distance covered by first man in 2 hours = 14x km

$\Rightarrow$ Remaining distance = 56x – 14x = 42x km

$\Rightarrow$ Time taken to meet each other = 42x/ (7x + 8x) = 42/15 hrs

= 2 hrs 48 min

$\Rightarrow$ Time of meeting = 8:00 + 2:48 = 10:48 AM

Hence, the correct option is (C).

71. Boxes: M, N, O, P, Q, and R

Electronic items: laptop, camera, phone, webcam, router, and charger

1) Only two boxes are placed between O and P, which has camera in it.

2) Box O placed above Box P.

3) Box O placed at even numbered position and is not placed at top.

Number	Box	Electronic Item
6		
5		
4	O	
3		
2		
1	P	Camera

4) The box which is at top contains laptop.

5) Box N placed immediately below Box R, which contains charger.

6) Box Q contains webcam

7) Only one box is placed between O and the one which contains router.

Number	Box	Electronic Item
6	M	Laptop
5	Q	Webcam
4	O	Phone

3	R	Charger
2	N	Router
1	P	Camera

Box Q contains Webcam.

Hence, the correct option is (A).

Ques (72-76):Boxes: M, N, O, P, Q, and R

Electronic items: laptop, camera, phone, webcam, router, and charger

1) Only two boxes are placed between O and P, which has camera in it.

2) Box O placed above Box P.

3) Box O placed at even numbered position and is not placed at top.

Number	Box	Electronic Item
6		
5		
4	O	
3		
2		
1	P	Camera

4) The box which is at top contains laptop.

5) Box N placed immediately below Box R, which contains charger.

6) Box Q contains webcam

7) Only one box is placed between O and the one which contains router.

Number	Box	Electronic Item
6	M	Laptop
5	Q	Webcam
4	O	Phone
3	R	Charger
2	N	Router
1	P	Camera

72. So, Box M contains Laptop.

Hence, the correct option is (B).

73. So, one box is placed between the one which contains Phone and Box N.

Hence, the correct option is (D).

74. So, position of Box Q is "Second from the top".

Hence, the correct option is (B).

75. So, three boxes are placed between M and N.

Hence, the correct option is (A).

76. So, Box O contains Phone.

Hence, the correct option is (B).

77. Given Statements: S > M ≥ O, O ≥ P ≥ N > K

On combining: S > M ≥ O ≥ P ≥ N > K

Conclusions:

I. O > N → False (as O ≥ P ≥ N → O ≥ N)

II. N ≤ M → True (as M ≥ O ≥ P ≥ N → M ≥ N)

Thus, only II is true.

Hence, the correct option is (B).

78. Given statements: M ≥ T; M < P; S > T

On combining: P > M ≥ T < S

Conclusions:

I. S = M → False (as P > M ≥ T < S → thus clear relation between S and M cannot be determined)

II. T < P → True (as P > M ≥ T → P > T)

III. P > S → False (as P > M ≥ T < S → thus clear relation between P and S cannot be determined)

So, only conclusion II is true.

Hence, the correct option is (C).

79. Given Statements:

X > C ≥ V > Y; U = V < T ≤ H; T < B

On Combining:

X > C ≥ V > Y, X > C ≥ U = V < T ≤ H, B > T ≤ H

Conclusions:

I. Y < X → True (as X > C ≥ V > Y → X > Y)

II. X ≥ B → False (as X > C ≥ U = V < T < B → thus clear relation between X and B cannot be determined)

III. V < B → True (as U = V < T < B → V < B)

So, only conclusion I and III follow.

Hence, the correct option is (D).

80. Given statements: P ≤ Q > R = S; S < T; T = P > U; V < U

On combining: Q ≥ P = T > S = R; T = P > U > V

Conclusions:

I. Q = P → False (as R = S < T → R < T and T = P > U → U < T → thus clear relation between R and U cannot be determined)

II. Q > P → False (as Q ≥ P > U > V → Q > V)

III. P < V → False (as V < U < P = T → V < P)

Note: conclusion I and II forms complementary pair.

So, either I or II follows.

Hence, the correct option is (E).

81. Given statements: A > P ≥ K; Q > M > T; P > T

On combining: A > P > T < M < Q; P ≥ K

Conclusions:

I. T < K → False (as P > T; P ≥ K; relation between T and K cannot be determined)

II. K > A → False (as A > P; P ≥ K; A > P ≥ K; A > K)

III. A > K → True (as A > P; P ≥ K; A > P ≥ K; A > K)

So, only III is true.

Hence, the correct option is (E).

Ques (82-87): Persons: A, B, C, D, E, F, G, H and J.

(1) A sits 2nd to the right of B.

(2) F sits 4th to the left of A.

(3) C sits third to the right of F.

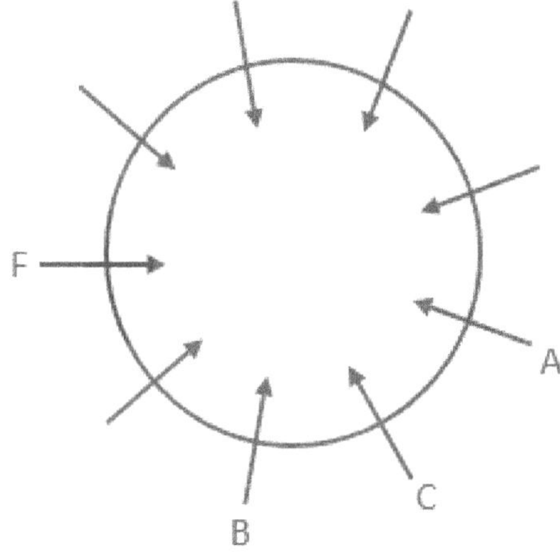

(4) G sits 2nd to the right of H.

(5) G is immediate neighbor of J.

Since G is immediate neighbor of J and sits second to the right of H, two possible cases can be made.

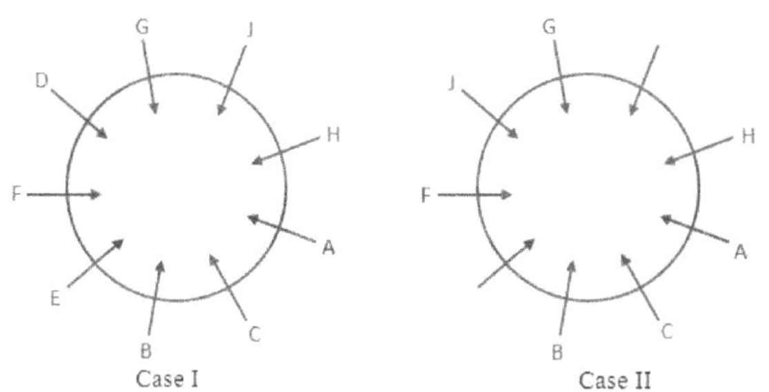

Case II can be further categorized as Case II (a) and Case II (b) as per the position of J.

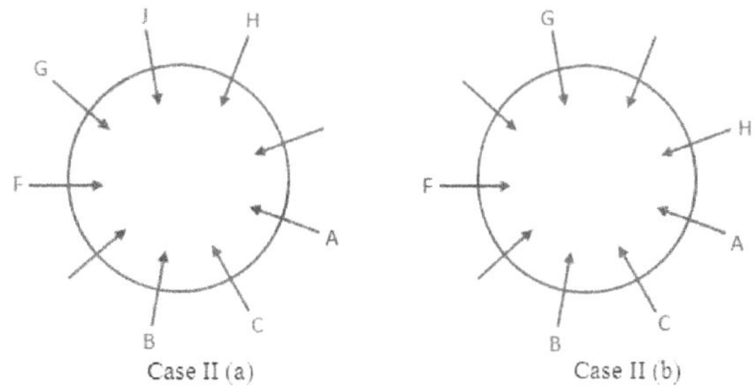

(6) D sits 2nd to the left of E.

Case I gets eliminated as no such arrangements can be made.

(7) E is not an immediate neighbor of A.

Case II (b) gets eliminated as no such arrangement is possible.

So, the final arrangement is Case II (a).

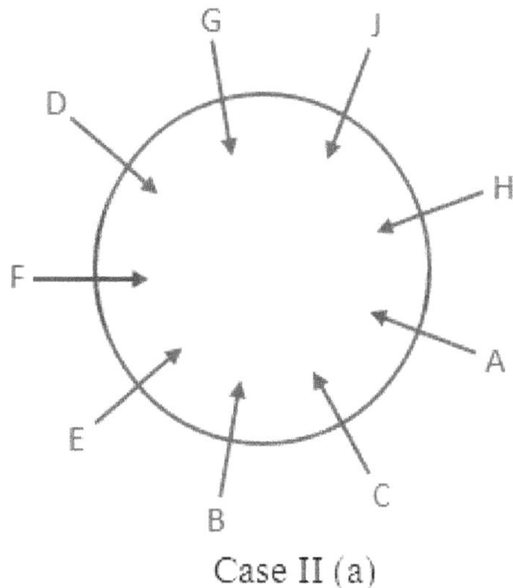

82. Thus, A sits third to the right of E.

Hence, the correct option is (B).

83. Thus, nobody sits between E and F.

Hence, the correct option is (D).

84. Thus, B sits between E and C.

Hence, the correct option is (A).

85. Thus, H sits immediate right of A.

Hence, the correct option is (E).

86. Persons: A, B, C, D, E, F, G, H and J.

(1) A sits 2nd to the right of B.

(2) F sits 4th to the left of A.

(3) C sits third to the right of F.

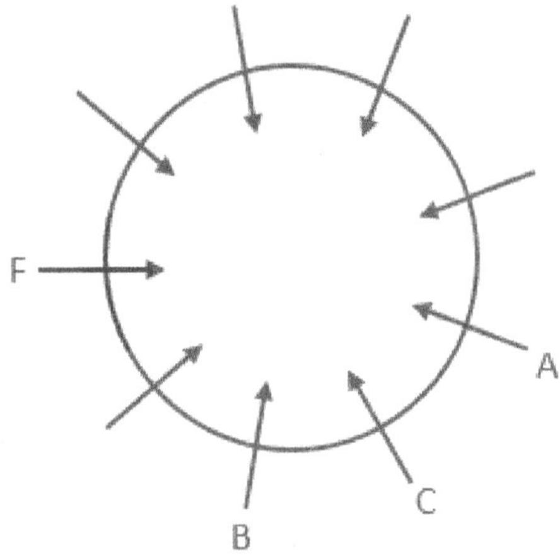

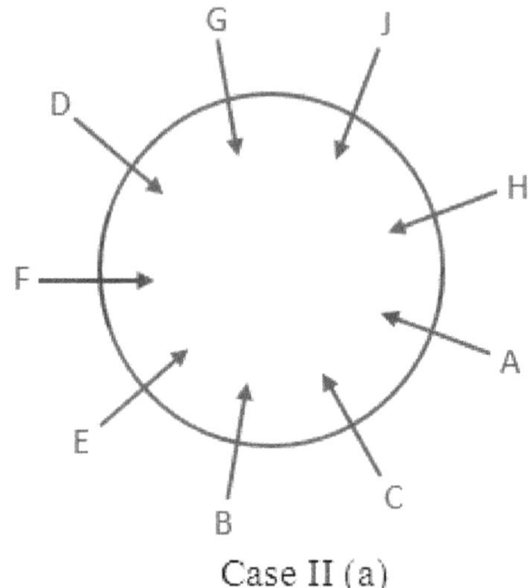

(4) G sits 2nd to the right of H.

(5) G is immediate neighbor of J.

Since G is immediate neighbor of J and sits second to the right of H, two possible cases can be made.

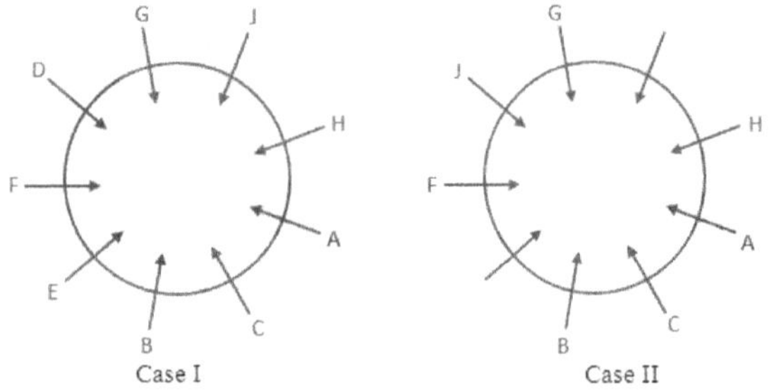

Case II can be further categorized as Case II (a) and Case II (b) as per the position of J.

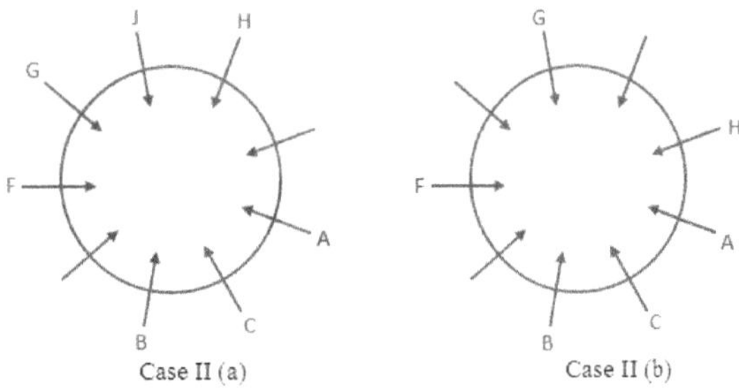

(6) D sits 2nd to the left of E.

Case I gets eliminated as no such arrangements can be made.

(7) E is not an immediate neighbor of A.

Case II (b) gets eliminated as no such arrangement is possible.

So, the final arrangement is Case II (a).

Case II (a)

Thus, A-C is the odd one out as the rest of the pairs are not immediate neighbors of each other.

Hence, the correct option is (D).

87. G sits eits 2nd to the right of H.

Hence, the correct option is (B).

Ques (88-90): City: A, B, Z, Y, K, T, R, J, M and P

1) City A is 10 km to the north of city K, which is 10 km to the west of city M.

2) City J is 5 km to the south of city M and city R is 5 km to the west of city J.

3) City B is 15 km to the north of city M and city Y is 10 km to the south of city P, which is 5 km to the south of city Z, which is 10 km to the east of city B.

4) City T is 5 km to the south of city K.

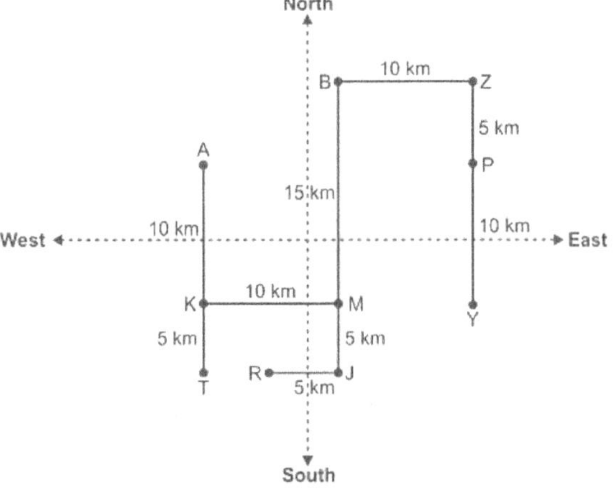

88. So, the distance between city T and city R is 5 km.

Hence, the correct option is (B).

89. So, the distance between city M and city Y is 10 km.

Hence, the correct option is (D).

90. So, the distance between city A and city P is 20 km.

Hence, the correct option is (B).

91. Following is the least possible Venn diagram for the given statements:

Conclusions:

I. Some Lions are Parrot → It's definitely not possible, hence false.

II. Some Lions are Bears → It's definitely possible, hence true.

III. Some Parrot are Bears → It's definitely not possible, hence false.

Thus, only conclusion II follows.

Hence, the correct option is (B).

92. The best possible Venn diagram for the given statements is as follows:

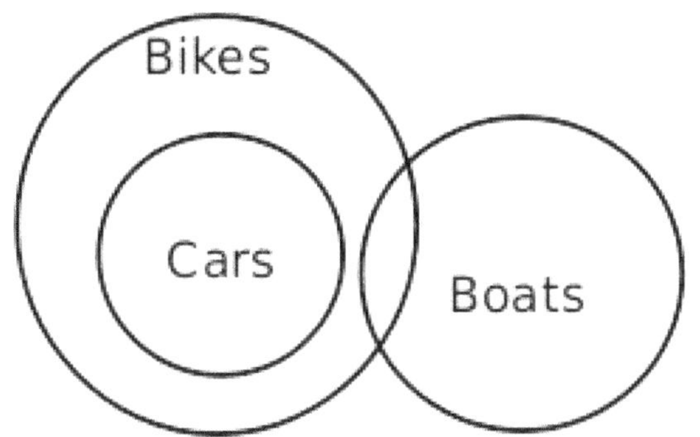

Since some bikes are cars and no car is a boat, all bikes cannot be boats. Thus, the conclusion I is not possible.

Since some bikes are boats and no car is a boat, all bikes cannot be boats. Thus, conclusion II follows.

Hence, the correct option is (B).

93.

The best possible Venn diagram for the given statements is as follows:

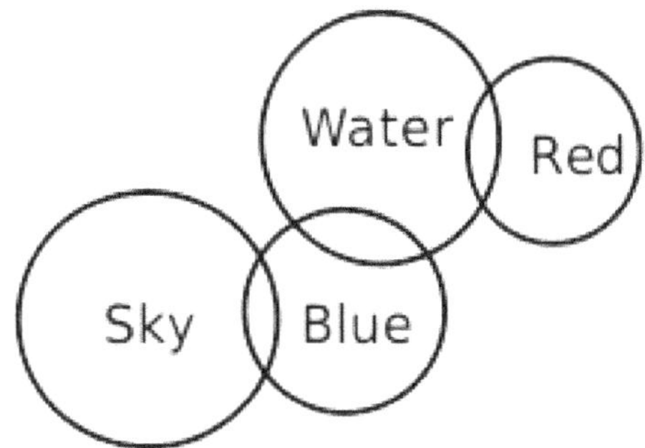

From the Venn diagram, we can see that conclusion I is possible.

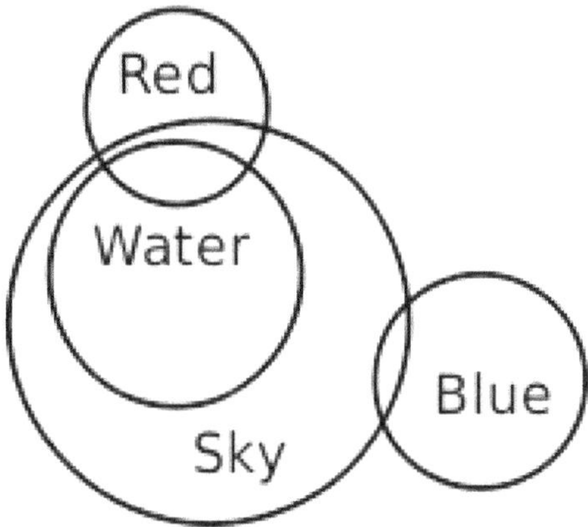

From the Venn diagram, we can see that all water can be sky. Conclusion II does not follow.

Hence, the correct option is (A).

94.

The best possible Venn diagram for the given statements is as follows:

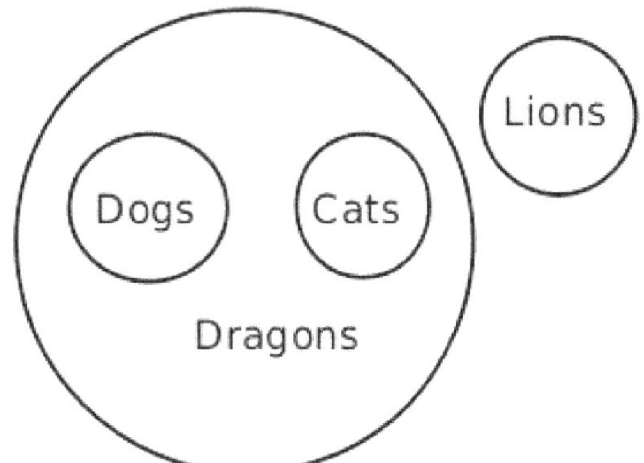

Since all cats are dragons and no dragon is a lion, no cat can be a lion. Thus, conclusion II follows.

Hence, the correct option is (E).

95. The given statements can be expressed diagrammatically as follows without violating any condition.

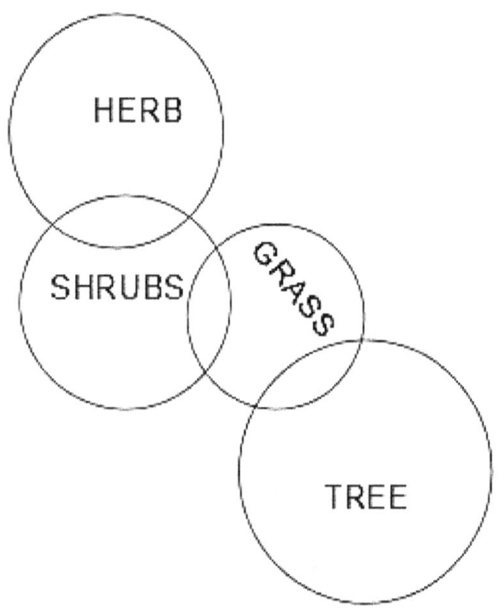

As we can see, neither of the conclusions follow.

Hence, the correct option is (D).

96. Common Explanation:

Worst Thing To Happen → ip tn bl rm ....(i)

Stay Close To Heart → pc ap ha bl ....(ii)

Your Stay Was Worst → jr rm ha pi ....(iii)

Thing Stay In Heart → pi ma ha tn ....(iv)

From the equations (i) and (ii), we get:

To → bl ....(v)

From the equations (i), and (iii), we get:

Worst → rm ....(vi)

From the equations (i) and (iv), we get:

Thing → tn ....(vii)

From the equations (i), (v), (vi) and (vii), we get:

Happen → ip ....(viii)

From the equations (ii) and (iii), we get:

Stay → ha ....(ix)

From the equations (ii), (iv) and (ix), we get:

Heart → pc ....(x)

From the equations (ii), (v), (ix) and (x), we get:

Close → ap ....(xi)

From the equations (iii), (vi) and (ix), we get:

Your/Was → pi/jr ....(xii)

From the equations (iv) (vi), (vii) and (xi), we get:

In → ma ....(xiii)

Hence, the correct option is (E).

97. Common Explanation:

Worst Thing To Happen → ip tn bl rm ....(i)

Stay Close To Heart → pc ap ha bl ....(ii)

Your Stay Was Worst → jr rm ha pi ....(iii)

Thing Stay In Heart → pi ma ha tn ....(iv)

From the equations (i) and (ii), we get:

To → bl ....(v)

From the equations (i), and (iii), we get:

Worst → rm ....(vi)

From the equations (i) and (iv), we get:

Thing → tn ....(vii)

From the equations (i), (v), (vi) and (vii), we get:

Happen → ip ....(viii)

From the equations (ii) and (iii), we get:

Stay → ha ....(ix)

From the equations (ii), (iv) and (ix), we get:

Heart → pc ....(x)

From the equations (ii), (v), (ix) and (x), we get:

Close → ap ....(xi)

From the equations (iii), (vi) and (ix), we get:

Your/Was → pi/jr ....(xii)

From the equations (iv) (vi), (vii) and (xi), we get:

In → ma ....(xii)

Hence, the correct option is (B).

98. Common Explanation:

Worst Thing To Happen → ip tn bl rm ....(i)

Stay Close To Heart → pc ap ha bl ....(ii)

Your Stay Was Worst → jr rm ha pi ....(iii)

Thing Stay In Heart → pi ma ha tn ....(iv)

From the equations (i) and (ii), we get:

To → bl ....(v)

From the equations (i), and (iii), we get:

Worst → rm ....(vi)

From the equations (i) and (iv), we get:

Thing → tn ....(vii)

From the equations (i), (v), (vi) and (vii), we get:

Happen → ip ....(viii)

From the equations (ii) and (iii), we get:

Stay → ha ....(ix)

From the equations (ii), (iv) and (ix), we get:

Heart → pc ....(x)

From the equations (ii), (v), (ix) and (x), we get:

Close → ap ....(xi)

From the equations (iii), (vi) and (ix), we get:

Your/Was → pi/jr ....(xii)

From the equations (iv) (vi), (vii) and (xi), we get:

In → ma ....(xii)

Hence, the correct option is (D).

99. Common Explanation:

Worst Thing To Happen → ip tn bl rm ....(i)

Stay Close To Heart → pc ap ha bl ....(ii)

Your Stay Was Worst → jr rm ha pi ....(iii)

Thing Stay In Heart → pi ma ha tn ....(iv)

From the equations (i) and (ii), we get:

To → bl ....(v)

From the equations (i), and (iii), we get:

Worst → rm ....(vi)

From the equations (i) and (iv), we get:

Thing → tn ....(vii)

From the equations (i), (v), (vi) and (vii), we get:

Happen → ip ....(viii)

From the equations (ii) and (iii), we get:

Stay → ha ....(ix)

From the equations (ii), (iv) and (ix), we get:

Heart → pc ....(x)

From the equations (ii), (v), (ix) and (x), we get:

Close → ap ....(xi)

From the equations (iii), (vi) and (ix), we get:

Your/Was → pi/jr ....(xii)

From the equations (iv) (vi), (vii) and (xi), we get:

In → ma ....(xii)

Hence, the correct option is (A).

100. Common Explanation:

Worst Thing To Happen → ip tn bl rm ....(i)

Stay Close To Heart → pc ap ha bl ....(ii)

Your Stay Was Worst → jr rm ha pi ....(iii)

Thing Stay In Heart → pi ma ha tn ....(iv)

From the equations (i) and (ii), we get:

To → bl ....(v)

From the equations (i), and (iii), we get:

Worst → rm ....(vi)

From the equations (i) and (iv), we get:

Thing → tn ....(vii)

From the equations (i), (v), (vi) and (vii), we get:

Happen → ip ....(viii)

From the equations (ii) and (iii), we get:

Stay → ha ....(ix)

From the equations (ii), (iv) and (ix), we get:

Heart → pc ....(x)

From the equations (ii), (v), (ix) and (x), we get:

Close → ap ....(xi)

From the equations (iii), (vi) and (ix), we get:

Your/Was → pi/jr ....(xii)

From the equations (iv) (vi), (vii) and (xi), we get:

In → ma ....(xii)

Hence, the correct option is (C).

Test of English Language

Ques (1-3):Direction: Read the sentence to find outwhether there is any error in it. The error,if any, will be in one part of the sentence.The number corresponding to that part isyour answer. If the given sentence iscorrect as given, mark the answer as "Noerror". Ignore the errors of punctuation,if any.

Q.1 The defence minister thought (1)/that each veteran (2)/ was as respectfulas himself and (3)/ should be given duepreference as well. (4)

[RBI Assistant, 2017]

A. 1   **B.** 2   **C.** 3   **D.** 4
E. No error

Q.2 Unfortunately, India continues to beone of the backward countries (1)/ withrespect to literacy, despite of the fact (2)/that successive governments have beentrying (3)/ their best to promoteeducation. (4)

[RBI Assistant, 2017]

A. 1   **B.** 2   **C.** 3   **D.** 4
E. No error

Q.3 Appropriation of assets have become(1)/ increasingly important due to (2)/the willingness of those in power (3)/ toabuse authority for personal gains. (4)

[RBI Assistant, 2017]

A. 1   **B.** 2   **C.** 3   **D.** 4
E. No error

Ques (4-8):Directions: In each of the questions below, a sentence is given with two blanks that indicate that some parts are missing. Identify the correct pair of words that fit in the sentence to make it grammatically and contextually correct.

Q.4 The shephered separated _______ and _______ from their foal in order to sell them to a circus.

A. horse, mare   **B.** colt, horse
C. lion, lioness   **D.** jenny, horse
E. donkey, mare

Q.5 My grandmother used to tell me tales of _______ and _______ to make me fall asleep.

A. fairies, angels   **B.** witches, fairies
C. witches, cupids   **D.** fairies, devils
E. wizards, witches

Q.6 Terrorist organization ISIS killed more than twenty _______ and _______ in a mass execution.

A. natives, foreigners   **B.** men, women
C. children, people   **D.** women, children
E. soldiers, policemen

Q.7 A _______ and a _______ can never be just friends.
A. father, son   **B.** mother, daughter
C. boy, girl   **D.** man, pet
E. father, daughter

Q.8 This award encourages young _______ and _______ to write great stories.
A. authors, novelists
B. poets, authors
C. writers, poets
D. authors, authoresses
E. authoresses, poetesses

Ques (9-13):Direction: A passage is given below with five blanks labelled (A)-(E). Below the passage, five options are given for each blank. Choose the word that fits each blank most appropriately in the context of the passage, and mark the corresponding answer.

Reforms have not been able to benefit agriculture, where the growth rate has been decelerating. Public investment in agriculture sector especially in infrastructure, which includes irrigation, power, roads, market linkages and research and extension has ___(A)___ in the reform period. Further, the partial removal of fertiliser subsidy has led to an increase in the cost of production, which has severely ___(B)___ the small and marginal farmers. This sector has been ___(C)___ a number of policy changes such as the reduction in import duties on agricultural products, low minimum support price and lifting of quantitative restrictions on the imports of agricultural products. These have ___(D)___ affected Indian farmers as they now have to face increased international competition. Moreover, because of export-oriented policy ___(E)___ in agriculture, there has been a shift from production for the domestic market towards production for the export market focusing on cash crops in lieu of production of food grains. This puts pressure on the prices of food grains.

Q.9 Which of the following words would most appropriately fit in the blank **(A)**?
A. Surged   **B.** Sharpened
C. Culminated   **D.** Frightened
E. Fallen

Q.10 Which of the following words would most appropriately fit in the blank **(B)**?
A. Effect   **B.** Efficacy
C. Affected   **D.** Eliminated
E. Emphasized

Q.11 Which of the following words would most appropriately fit in the blank **(C)**?
A. Experiencing   **B.** Experimenting
C. Trembling   **D.** Inciting
E. Inexperience

Q.12 Which of the following words would most appropriately fit in the blank **(D)**?

A. Positively   **B.** Adversely
C. Metaphorically   **D.** Rarely
E. Strangely

Q.13 Which of the following words would most appropriately fit in the blank **(E)**?

A. Obstacles   **B.** Prescription
C. Fatalities   **D.** Strategies
E. None of the above

Q.14 In the following question, A and H statements are in the correct order. Rearrange the remaining statements and answer the question which follows.

A. The Gurukul was a type of school in ancient education system.

B. The history of Gurukulam can be traced back to the Vedic age.

C. There was no discrimination based on their social standards.

D. At the Gurukulam, the Gurus used to train their students in many domains such as meditations, Yoga, Shastra and etc.

E. The Gurukul system refers to an ancient learning method and in Sanskrit, it was called Gurukulam.

F. The main motto of Gurukulam, since the Vedic age, was to develop the knowledge of the young students.

G. During the training, the students were treated respectfully by their teachers.

H. Thus, the Gurukulam initiated a new tradition known as the Guru-Shishya tradition.

Which of the following should be the THIRD sentence after rearrangement?

A. H   **B.** C   **C.** F   **D.** B
E. E

Q.15 In the following question, A and H statements are in the correct order. Rearrange the remaining statements and answer the question which follows.

A. The Gurukul was a type of school in ancient education system.

B. The history of Gurukulam can be traced back to the Vedic age.

C. There was no discrimination based on their social standards.

D. At the Gurukulam, the Gurus used to train their students in many domains such as meditations, Yoga, Shastra and etc.

E. The Gurukul system refers to an ancient learning method and in Sanskrit, it was called Gurukulam.

F. The main motto of Gurukulam, since the Vedic age, was to develop the knowledge of the young students.

G. During the training, the students were treated respectfully by their teachers.

H. Thus, the Gurukulam initiated a new tradition known as the Guru-Shishya tradition.

Which of the following should be the SECOND sentence after rearrangement?

A. B   **B.** F   **C.** G   **D.** C
E. E

Q.16 In the following question, A and H statements are in the correct order. Rearrange the remaining statements and answer the question which follows.

A. The Gurukul was a type of school in ancient education system.

B. The history of Gurukulam can be traced back to the Vedic age.

C. There was no discrimination based on their social standards.

D. At the Gurukulam, the Gurus used to train their students in many domains such as meditations, Yoga, Shastra and etc.

E. The Gurukul system refers to an ancient learning method and in Sanskrit, it was called Gurukulam.

F. The main motto of Gurukulam, since the Vedic age, was to develop the knowledge of the young students.

G. During the training, the students were treated respectfully by their teachers.

H. Thus, the Gurukulam initiated a new tradition known as the Guru-Shishya tradition.

Which of the following should be the FIFTH sentence after rearrangement?

A. E   **B.** F   **C.** B   **D.** D
E. C

Q.17 In the following question, A and H statements are in the correct order. Rearrange the remaining statements and answer the question which follows.

A. The Gurukul was a type of school in ancient education system.

B. The history of Gurukulam can be traced back to the Vedic age.

C. There was no discrimination based on their social standards.

D. At the Gurukulam, the Gurus used to train their students in many domains such as meditations, Yoga, Shastra and etc.

E. The Gurukul system refers to an ancient learning method and in Sanskrit, it was called Gurukulam.

F. The main motto of Gurukulam, since the Vedic age, was to develop the knowledge of the young students.

G. During the training, the students were treated respectfully by their teachers.

H. Thus, the Gurukulam initiated a new tradition known as the Guru-Shishya tradition.

Which of the following should be the SIXTH sentence after rearrangement?

A. E   **B.** D   **C.** G   **D.** C
E. B

Q.18 In the following question, A and H statements are in the correct order. Rearrange the remaining statements and answer the question which follows.

A. The Gurukul was a type of school in ancient education system.

B. The history of Gurukulam can be traced back to the Vedic age.

C. There was no discrimination based on their social standards.

D. At the Gurukulam, the Gurus used to train their students in many domains such as meditations, Yoga, Shastra and etc.

E. The Gurukul system refers to an ancient learning method and in Sanskrit, it was called Gurukulam.

F. The main motto of Gurukulam, since the Vedic age, was to develop the knowledge of the young students.

G. During the training, the students were treated respectfully by their teachers.

H. Thus, the Gurukulam initiated a new tradition known as the Guru-Shishya tradition.

Which of the following should be the SEVENTH sentence after rearrangement?

A. G   **B.** C   **C.** B   **D.** E
E. F

Ques (19-21):Direction: In the question given below, three words are given in bold. These three words may or may not be in their correct positions. The sentence is then followed by options with the correct combination of words that should replace each other in order to make the sentence grammatically and contextually correct. Find the correct combination of words that replace each other. If the sentence is correct as it is, select option (E) as your answer.

Q.19 Approved (A) on Saturday **said (B)** a third coronavirus vaccine for domestic use, Prime Minister Mikhail Mishustin **Russia (C)** on state TV.

[IBPS PO, 2021]

A. ACB   **B.** CAB
C. BAD   **D.** ABC
E. None of the above

Q.20 It is **mind (A)** that people should keep in **asserted (B)** the importance of adherence to COVID-19 appropriate **behaviour (C)**.

[IBPS PO, 2021]

A. BAC   **B.** CAB
C. ABC   **D.** CBA
E. None of the above

Q.21 The AstraZeneca company is going to **vaccine (A)** in Japan doses of the coronavirus **produce (B)** enough for 40 million **people (C)**, the executive director of the Japanese department of the firm said.

[IBPS PO, 2021]

A. CAB   **B.** ACB
C. ABC   **D.** BAC
E. None of the above

Ques (22-31):Direction: Read the following passage and answer the question given below. Some words may be highlighted and read carefully.

The Bronze Age in the Indian subcontinent began around 3300 BCE. Along with Ancient Egypt and Mesopotamia, the Indus valley region was one of three early **cradles** of the **civilization** of the Old World. Of the three, the Indus Valley Civilization was the most **expansive**, and at its peak, may have had a population of over five million. The civilization was primarily centered in modern-day Pakistan, in the Indus river basin, and secondarily in the Ghaggar-Hakra river basin in eastern Pakistan and northwestern India. The Mature Indus civilization

flourished from about 2600 to 1900 BCE, marking the beginning of urban civilization on the Indian subcontinent. The civilization included cities such as Harappa, Ganeriwala, and Mohenjo-Daro in modern-day Pakistan, and Dholavira, Kalibangan, Rakhigarhi, and Lothal in modern-day India. Inhabitants of the ancient Indus river valley, the Harappans, developed new techniques in **metallurgy** and handicraft (carneol products, seal carving), and produced copper, bronze, lead, and tin. The civilization is noted for its cities built of brick, roadside drainage systems, and multi-storeyed houses and is thought to have had some kind of municipal organization. After the **collapse** of the Indus Valley civilization, the inhabitants of the Indus Valley civilization migrated from the river valleys of Indus and Ghaggar-Hakra, towards the Himalayan foothills of the Ganga-Yamuna basin.

Q.22 What is the meaning of the word metallurgy highlighted in the given passage?
A. Study of metals
B. Study of soil
C. Study of environment
D. Study of water
E. None of the above

Q.23 Which word is similar in meaning to the word 'Collapse' highlighted in the given passage?
A. Disintegration   **B.** Rise
C. Swell   **D.** Succeed
E. None of the above

Q.24 What is the main context discussed in the passage?
A. Indus Valley Civilization
B. Iron Age
C. Copper age
D. Stone age
E. None of the above

Q.25 What was the population of the Indus Valley Civilization?
A. Over five million   **B.** Over two million
C. Over one million   **D.** Over three million
E. None of the above

Q.26 Which of the following cities was a part of the Indus Valley Civilization?
A. Ceylon   **B.** Sparta
C. Harappa   **D.** Rome
E. None of the above

Q.27 Which of the following were not produced by Harappans?
A. Copper   **B.** Bronze
C. Lead   **D.** Tin
E. None of the above

Q.28 What part of speech is 'flourished' highlighted in the given passage?
A. Verb   **B.** Noun
C. Pronoun   **D.** Adjective
E. Adverb

Q.29 What part of speech is the word 'Civilization' highlighted in the given passage?

A. Noun
B. Adjective
C. Verb
D. Adverb
E. None of the above

Q.30 Which of the following is the antonym of the word 'Expansive' highlighted in the given passage?

A. Extensive
B. Limited
C. Sweeping
D. Spacious
E. None of the above

Q.31 Which of the following are not similar in meaning to the word 'Cradle' highlighted in the passage?

A. Bassinet
B. Crib
C. Carrycot
D. Cot
E. None of the above

Ques (32-33):Direction: From the options given below, select the option which states the correct combination of incorrect/correct sentences.

Q.32 I. It is impossible to believe that the government does not know how to handle the situation with sincerity and effectiveness.

II. But it is also true that they are unable to decide the best among the two options available in front of them.

III. It seems that the perpetrators of the crime are smarter than brave.

IV. However, the police are of the opinion that they will be able to nab the criminals very soon.

A. Both I and IV are correct
B. Both I and II are correct
C. Both II and III are correct
D. All I, II, and III are incorrect
E. All I, II, III, and IV are correct

Q.33 I. The International Monetary Fund have decided that it will dole out subsidies to the developing countries in the present financial year.

II. The President of IMF announced it during the press interaction with the central bank governors last month.

III. The reason is to create the framework for the Trade Facilitation Agreement of the World Trade Organization to come into existence.

IV. The main contention regarding that agreement was that the developing countries and the developed countries were not on the same page regarding the subsidies.

A. I and IV are incorrect
B. II and III are incorrect
C. Only I is incorrect
D. Both II and IV are incorrect
E. All I, II, III, and IV are incorrect

Ques (34-38):Direction: In the following question, two columns are given containing three phrases each. In the first column phrases are A, B, and C and in the second column, the phrases are D, E, and F. A phrase from the first column may or may not connect with a phrase from the second column to make a grammatically and contextually correct sentence. There are five options, four of which display the sequence(s) in which phrases can be joined to form a grammatically and contextually correct sentence. If none of the options given forms a correct sentence after combination, select 'None of these' as your answer.

Q.34

Column (1)	Column (2)
(A) We spent the afternoon meandering	(D) if you want to succeed in business.
(B) You have to be a bit devious	(E) piece of work.
(C) This essay is the most conscientious	(F) around the streets of the old town.

A. A-E
B. B-E
C. C-E
D. A-D
E. None of these

Q.35

Column (1)	Column (2)
(A) Rome combined aspects of ancient Greek civilization	(D) by human activity.
(B) Their nesting sites were disturbed	(E) with its own contributions in new areas.
(C) Students meet with the department chairperson	(F) to plan their course work.

A. A-D and B-F
B. A-F, B-E, and C-D
C. C-D
D. A-E, B-D, and C-F
E. None of these

Q.36

Column (1)	Column (2)
(A) Liquid water may have	(D) exist on some parts of Mars' surface for long periods of time.
(B) The ancient oceans that formed on Mars dried up	(E) during periods of cold, dry weather.
(C) They could read and write a	(F) Greek language.

A. A-D
B. B-E
C. C-F
D. A-E and C-D
E. None of these

Q.37

Column (1)	Column (2)
(A) A region that had once supported many people	(D) were becoming a desert where few could survive.
(B) Access to metal tools and weapons created	(E) the power of warriors.
(C) Metal weapons increased	(F) greater social equality.

A. A-F and B-D
B. A-E and C-D
C. B-F and C-E
D. B-E and C-D
E. None of these

Q.38

Column (1)	Column (2)
(A) She thinks the answer	(D) the use of bicycles on campus.
(B) The campus sidewalks are	(E) and receive heavy

intended for pedestrians	pedestrian traffic.
(C) Beginning next semester, the University will not allow	(F) to her question is obvious.

A. A-F, B-E, and C-D
B. A-D, B-E, and C-F
C. B-F and C-E
D. A-E and C-F
E. None of these

Ques (39-40):Direction: In the following questions, a sentence with four words printed in bold type is given. These are numbered as A, B, C and D. One of these four words printed in bold may be either wrongly spelled or inappropriate in context of the sentence. Find out the word which is wrongly spelled or inappropriate if any. The number of that word is your answer. If all the words printed in bold are correctly spelled and also appropriate in the context of the sentence, mark (E) "All correct" as your answer.

Q.39 What makes the 2019 election **unprecedented** is not that **inappropriate** words were used and misinformation **spread**, but the fact that India **witnesses** an increasing tendency to normalise these.

A. Unprecedented
B. Inappropriate
C. Spread
D. Witnesses
E. All are correct

Q.40 With stronger **headwind** ahead in the form of an **escalating** trade war between the U.S. and China, and the **imbroglio** in the Middle East, the outlook for export demand is far from **reassuring**.

A. Headwind
B. Escalating
C. Imbroglio
D. Reassuring
E. All are correct

Test of Numerical Ability

Ques (41-43):Direction: In the following number series, only one number is wrong. Find out the wrong number.

Q.41 7, 29, 61, 128, 211, 349
A. 7
B. 61
C. 29
D. 349
E. 128

Q.42 4, 7, 12, 22, 34, 49
A. 22
B. 49
C. 7
D. 4
E. 12

Q.43 34, 38, 47, 63, 90, 124
A. 47
B. 90
C. 38
D. 63
E. 124

Q.44 Direction: In the following number series, only one number is wrong. Find out the wrong number.

2, 3, 10, 40, 172, 885, 5346
A. 3
B. 855
C. 40
D. 172
E. 10

Q.45 Atul started a business with investing Rs. 8000 and after some months, Balu joined with investing Rs. 6000. At the end of one year, the total profit was Rs. 4375 and the share of Atul is Rs. 2800. For how many months did Balu joined the business?
A. 4
B. 9

C. 5
D. 2
E. None of these

Q.46 Ram and Shyam's average age is 65 years. The average age of Ram, Shyam and John is 53 years. What is the age of John?
A. 29 years
B. 31 years
C. 59 years
D. 45 years
E. 50 years

Ques (47-56): What will come in the place of the question mark ' ?' in the following question?

Q.47 40% of 50% of $\frac{3}{4}$ of $2400 =?$

[IBPS RRB Office Assistant, 2021]

A. 3600
B. 36
C. 360
D. 366
E. None of these

Q.48 $24 \times 32 \div 6 + 25\%$ of $64 =?^2$
A. 11
B. 13
C. 14
D. 12
E. 21

Q.49 $450 \times 30 + 1500 \times 20 =? \% \times 43500$
A. 100
B. 50
C. 200
D. 150
E. 250

Q.50 37.5% of $(64)^2 - 62.5\%$ of 50% of $160 =?$
A. 1586
B. 1536
C. 1486
D. 1496
E. 1476

Q.51 $30\% \times 400 + 200 \times 3 + 100 \div 2 =?$
A. 770
B. 780
C. 750
D. 725
E. None of these

Q.52 20% of $420 - 33\frac{1}{3}\%$ of $? = 25 \times 42 \div 15$
A. 14
B. 28
C. 42
D. 56
E. None of these

Q.53 25% of $480 + 200 +? = 800$
A. 360
B. 520
C. 240
D. 480
E. 500

Q.54 40% of $1500 - 276 = (?)^2$
A. 22
B. 12
C. 18
D. 8
E. 20

Q.55 60% of $500 \div 0.25 + \sqrt{169} =?$
A. 1162
B. 1262
C. 1194
D. 1213
E. 1254

Q.56 15% of $40 - 20\%$ of $75 + 12.5\%$ of $80 =?$
A. 0
B. 1
C. 15
D. 5
E. 10

Ques (57-61):Direction: Study the following data and answer the following question.

The following line graph shows the literate and illiterate population of five villages.

Total population $=$ literate population $+$ illiterate population

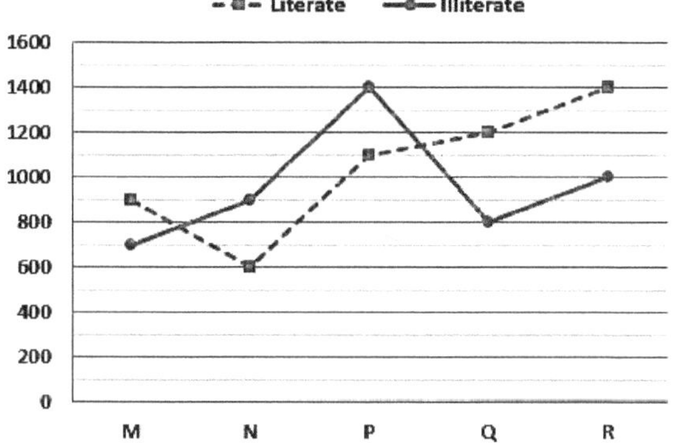

Q.57 Find the average Literate population of five villages.
A. 1100
B. 1200
C. 1250
D. 1360
E. 1040

Q.58 The literate population of village Q is approximately what percent of the total population of village Q?
A. 75%
B. 55%
C. 65%
D. 60%
E. 70%

Q.59 Find the ratio between the total population of village N and village R.
A. 1:3
B. 6:7
C. 9:1
D. 5:8
E. 8:9

Q.60 The illiterate population of village P is approximately what percent more than the literate population of the same village?
A. 27%
B. 29%
C. 30%
D. 33%
E. 36%

Q.61 Find the difference between the literate and illiterate populations of five villages.
A. 300
B. 550
C. 750
D. 600
E. 400

Q.62 A man had to drive 42 km to reach his office in 54 min. If he covers half of the distance at 35 km/hr, what should be his speed for the remaining distance so as to reach the office on time?
A. 50 km/hr
B. 60 km/hr
C. 70 km/hr
D. 80 km/hr
E. 90 km/hr

Q.63 In the following number series, the wrong number is given, find out that number.

$25,26,54,165,674,3325$

A. 674
B. 54
C. 3325
D. 165
E. 26

Q.64 If Rs. 8544 is divides between A, B and C in ratio $6:11:15$. If B increase the rupees by 50% and A spent 20% of his rupees. Find the new ratio of rupees.
A. $16:55:50$
B. $17:58:49$
C. $18:55:50$
D. $17:55:49$
E. Data Inadequate

Q.65 A can do a work in 24 days, B can do the same work in 48 days and C can do the same work in 72 days. Unfortunately, B could not become the part of the work so the work was completed by A and C only, so in this case how much more money is earned by A than the previous situation, if total amount distributed to them in both the cases was 4400 rupees.
A. Rs. 600
B. Rs. 700
C. Rs. 800
D. Rs. 900
E. Rs. 1000

Q.66 The cost price of item A is equal to the cost price of item B. If marked price of item A is Rs____ after increased by 60% of its cost price and marked price of B is Rs 600 after increased by 50% of its cost price. The difference between the selling price of item B and item A is Rs____ if 10% of discount given on the marked price of both the items.
A. 680,80
B. 640,36
C. 540,28
D. 720,240
E. 480,120

Q.67 Ayush's father gave Rs. $20,000$ to Ayush. Ayush lent some money to Arnab for 2 year at 20% simple interest. And remaining money to Ravish for same time but at the increased rate of 24%. After 2 years, interest received from Arnab was Rs. 729 more as interest received from Ravish. Find the amount of money which Ayush lent to Ravish.
A. 16524.5
B. 15000
C. 14625.5
D. 8,262.5
E. None of these

Q.68 The breadth of the rectangle when multiplied by 4 exceeds the 3 times the length of the rectangle by 5 and 3 times the length exceeds the 2 times of breadth by 35. Find the cost of carpeting the field at the rate of Rs. $40/$ cm ^{2}.
A. Rs. 16000
B. Rs. 24000
C. Rs. 20000
D. Rs. 22000
E. Rs. 18000

Q.69 Two pipes can fill a tank in 10 and 12 minutes respectively and a third pipe can empty 2 gallons per minute. All three pipes working together can fill the tank in 6 minutes. The capacity of the tank is:
A. 120 gallons
B. 100 gallons
C. 150 gallons
D. 200 gallons
E. None of these

Q.70 The average weight of 20 students of a class is 60 kg. A student whose weight was 45 kg left the class and new student replaced the old one. So, the average weight of students increased by 1 kg. Find the ratio of old and new student's weight.

A. $9:13$

B. $13:9$

C. $8:7$

D. $7:8$

E. None of these

Test of Reasoning

Q.71 Direction: In the following question assuming the given statements to be True, find which of the conclusion among given conclusions is/are definitely true and then give your answers accordingly.

Statements: $A > B > C = D; D \le E \le F \ge G \ge H; I \ge H$

Conclusions:

I. $C > G$

II. $F > I$

A. None is true

B. Both I and II are true

C. Only II is true

D. Only I is true

E. Either I and II is true

Ques (72-75):Direction: In the following question assuming the given statements to be true, find which of the conclusion among given conclusions is/are definitely true and then give your answers accordingly.

Q.72 Statements:

$A > B > C = P, R < B > Q, P \ge S = T$

Conclusions:

I. $A > R$

II. $C = T$

III. $B > S$

A. All follow

B. Only I follow

C. Only II follows

D. Only I and III follow

E. None follow

Q.73 Statement:

$N \ge T > J \le R, J \ge P \ge M$

Conclusions:

I. $M < R$

II. $N = P$

III. $R = M$

A. Only III is true

B. Only either I or III is true

C. Only II is true

D. Only I is true

E. None is true

Q.74 Statements:

$B \ge Q, O = M, E \le O, Q \le E$

Conclusions:

I. $O \ge Q$

II. $O < B$

III. $B < E$

A. Neither I nor II conclusion are true

B. Neither I nor III conclusion are true

C. Only III is true

D. Only I is true

E. Only II is true

Q.75 Statements: $K \le L \le M = N, P \ge O \ge N$

Conclusions:

I. $K < O$

II. $K = N$

III. $K \le M$

A. None is true

B. Only I is true

C. Only I and II is true

D. Only II and III is true

E. Only III is true

Ques (76-78):Direction: Study the information given below and answer the questions given below it:

Two persons, Neha and Yogita are standing at point A and B respectively and are facing each other. The distance between point A and B is 20 m. Neha is facing north. They turned to their respective left and then walked 10m to reach point N and point P respectively. From point N, Neha turned and walked 20 m in the south-west direction to reach point M. From point P, Yogita turned right and walked 30 m to reach point Z which is 20 m to the east the point L.

Q.76 Point Z is in which direction with respect to the point M?

A. North-east

B. South-east

C. East

D. West

E. Can't say

Q.77 If point C is 10 m to the north of the point N then point C is in which direction with respect to the point P?

A. South-east

B. North-east

C. South-west

D. North-west

E. East

Q.78 If a point G is in the middle of the point B and the point P then what is the minimum distance between the point G and the point A?

A. 15 m

B. $5\sqrt{7}$ m

C. $2\sqrt{7}$ m

D. $5\sqrt{17}$ m

E. Can't be determined

Ques (79-82):Direction: In the questions, two statements are given, followed by two conclusions, I and II. You have to consider the statements to be true even if it seems to be at variance from commonly known facts. You have to decide which of the given conclusions, if any, follows from the given statements.

Q.79 Statements:

No computer is a tablet.

Only a few bands are computers.

Conclusions:

I: Some bands are tablets.

II: All bands are computers.

A. Only conclusion I follows
B. Only conclusion II follows
C. Either conclusion I or II follows
D. Neither conclusion I nor II follows
E. Both conclusion I and II follow

Q.80 Statements:

All cage are bar.

Only few fence are bar.

Conclusions:

I: All cage are fence.

II: Some fence are cage.

A. Only conclusion I follows
B. Only conclusion II follows
C. Either conclusion I or II follows
D. Neither conclusion I nor II follows
E. Both conclusion I and II follow

Q.81 Statements:

Only few building are chalk.

No chalk is toffee.

Conclusions:

I: Some buildings are toffee

II: All building being chalk is a possibility

A. Only conclusion I follows
B. Only conclusion II follows
C. Either conclusion I or II follows
D. Neither conclusion I nor II follows
E. Both conclusion I and II follow

Q.82 Statements:

Only few colleague are smart.

All father are smart.

Conclusions:

I: Some colleague are father.

II: Some smart are colleague.

A. Only conclusion I follows
B. Only conclusion II follows
C. Either conclusion I or II follows
D. Neither conclusion I nor II follows
E. Both conclusion I and II follow

Q.83 Direction: In the question below are given three statements followed by two conclusions numbered (i) and (ii). You have to take the given statements to be true even if they seem to be at variance with commonly known facts. Read all the conclusions and then decide which of the given conclusions logically follows from the given statements disregarding commonly known facts.

Statements:

Only A are B.

Only C are D.

Some A are C.

Conclusions:

(i) Some B can be C.

(ii) Some D are A.

A. Only (i) follows
B. Only (ii) follows
C. Either (i) and (ii) follows
D. Both (i) and (ii) follow
E. None follows

Ques (84-88):Direction: Study the following information carefully and answer the given question.

In a certain code language

'se ma to' means 'India is beautiful'

'si fe ma' means 'Rohan is smart'

'ra fe si to' means 'Smart Rohan visits India'

'si kn ma' means 'Village is smart'

Q.84 What will be the code of Village?

A. ma   **B.** si

C. kn   **D.** to

E. Either ma or si

Q.85 What could be the code of 'Rohan is going Village'?

A. kn sa si fe   **B.** si ma se fe

C. kn ra se fe   **D.** kn ma fe kr

E. kn ma to ra

Q.86 Code 'kn ma se lk to' is for which of the following sentence in given language?

A. smart India is beautiful
B. Village in India is beautiful
C. India is smart village
D. Village in India is smart
E. Rohan is very smart

Q.87 What could be the code for 'smart city?

A. ma si   **B.** si cm   **C.** fe si   **D.** se to

E. kn ck

Q.88 What will be the code for 'smart India'?

A. si kn   **B.** se fe   **C.** ma to   **D.** si to

E. to na

Ques (89-94):Direction: Study the following information carefully and answer the question given below.

Eight boxes are kept one above another to make up a stack. The topmost box is numbered as 8 while the bottommost box is numbered as 1. Each box is filled with different colours: Blue, Yellow, Black, Pink, Green, Red and Purple, But not necessarily in the same order. One of the boxes in the arrangement is empty.

Green colour box is immediately above Red colour box. Red colour box is an even number box below box number 5. Three boxes are kept between Red colour box and Yellow colour box. Two boxes are kept between Pink colour box and Purple colour box. Purple Coloured box is not kept at the top. Blue colour box is immediately below Pink colour box. One of the boxes above box number 5 is empty. Black colour box is an odd number box.

Q.89 Which of the following condition is true?
A. Red - 2nd   **B.** Yellow - 8th
C. Black - 4th   **D.** Purple - 5th
E. None of these

Q.90 How many boxes are there between Yellow colour box and Pink colour box?
A. 6   **B.** 3
C. 5   **D.** 4
E. None of these

Q.91 How many boxes are there between Violet and Pink?
A. 6   **B.** 3
C. 5   **D.** 2
E. None of these

Q.92 Which colour box is at the bottom?
A. Black   **B.** Red
C. Blue   **D.** Pink
E. None of these

Q.93 Which colour is filled in box number 5?
A. Purple   **B.** Pink
C. Green   **D.** Blue
E. None of these

Q.94 Which number box is empty?
A. 8   **B.** 7
C. 6   **D.** 5
E. None of these

Ques (95-100):Direction: Study the following information to answer the given questions:

Eight persons M, N, O, P, Q, R, S and T sit around the circular table such that some of them face towards the center while some face away from the center.

S does not face away from the center. M faces towards the center. P sits immediate left of R and both face in same direction. Q sits second to the left of N, who sits immediate left of T. Two persons sit between Q and S. T faces away from the center. S and N are not adjacent to each other. P does not sit adjacent to Q. Neither P nor R sits opposite to Q.M does not sit adjacent to S. Immediate neighbours of S face in same direction but opposite to that of S. Person opposite to O faces towards the center.

Q.95 Who sits immediate left of S?
A. R   **B.** Q   **C.** T   **D.** O
E. P

Q.96 Who sits opposite to T?
A. R   **B.** M   **C.** O   **D.** Q
E. S

Q.97 Four are the same in a certain way thus forms a group. Which among the following does not belong to the group?
A. N   **B.** Q   **C.** O   **D.** T
E. P

Q.98 Who sits third to the right of Q?

A. P   **B.** O   **C.** N   **D.** S
E. T

Q.99 _____ sits immediate right of T.
A. O   **B.** N   **C.** M   **D.** R
E. Q

Q.100 _____ sits immediate right of Q.
A. O   **B.** R   **C.** N   **D.** M
E. T

// Smart Answer Sheet //

Correct — Indicates percentage of students who answered questions correctly.

Skipped — Indicates percentage of students who skipped questions.

Q.	Ans.	Correct / Skipped	Q.	Ans.	Correct / Skipped	Q.	Ans.	Correct / Skipped	Q.	Ans.	Correct / Skipped	Q.	Ans.	Correct / Skipped
1	E	81.03 % / 12.73 %	17	C	52.08 % / 46.32 %	33	C	55.11 % / 41.34 %	49	A	48.14 % / 37.92 %	65	D	21.59 % / 67.08 %
2	B	60.75 % / 33.18 %	18	B	53.34 % / 43.0 %	34	C	62.09 % / 34.23 %	50	C	58.29 % / 36.71 %	66	B	49.97 % / 42.56 %
3	A	29.79 % / 67.32 %	19	B	56.28 % / 37.44 %	35	D	40.34 % / 55.79 %	51	A	53.0 % / 30.25 %	67	D	65.61 % / 31.16 %
4	A	45.49 % / 32.91 %	20	A	51.54 % / 45.09 %	36	B	67.51 % / 31.96 %	52	C	56.64 % / 36.11 %	68	C	61.02 % / 34.64 %
5	E	63.66 % / 30.2 %	21	D	55.33 % / 37.33 %	37	C	56.56 % / 33.13 %	53	D	53.47 % / 39.43 %	69	A	40.97 % / 37.44 %
6	B	65.79 % / 30.52 %	22	A	58.47 % / 41.24 %	38	A	66.2 % / 31.42 %	54	C	59.13 % / 39.72 %	70	A	53.67 % / 44.21 %
7	C	55.89 % / 36.79 %	23	A	69.92 % / 30.01 %	39	D	59.59 % / 31.74 %	55	D	44.15 % / 42.06 %	71	A	66.16 % / 33.36 %
8	D	58.56 % / 37.63 %	24	A	44.75 % / 37.13 %	40	A	45.46 % / 33.72 %	56	B	58.85 % / 31.9 %	72	D	42.79 % / 46.45 %
9	E	31.08 % / 68.19 %	25	A	64.05 % / 31.24 %	41	E	51.89 % / 46.68 %	57	E	69.0 % / 30.23 %	73	B	19.11 % / 73.01 %
10	C	58.94 % / 37.56 %	26	C	64.81 % / 33.82 %	42	E	85.77 % / 13.25 %	58	D	42.63 % / 37.71 %	74	D	58.62 % / 34.54 %
11	A	40.33 % / 43.24 %	27	E	65.83 % / 30.64 %	43	B	84.59 % / 10.66 %	59	D	42.82 % / 41.81 %	75	E	26.17 % / 72.11 %
12	B	11.67 % / 79.87 %	28	A	47.26 % / 32.69 %	44	C	23.23 % / 69.66 %	60	A	53.92 % / 44.83 %	76	A	48.31 % / 42.4 %
13	D	43.65 % / 47.27 %	29	A	55.81 % / 36.6 %	45	B	56.95 % / 37.62 %	61	E	53.77 % / 34.96 %	77	C	52.65 % / 40.81 %
14	D	53.54 % / 34.31 %	30	B	55.44 % / 37.1 %	46	A	82.57 % / 12.1 %	62	C	69.4 % / 30.43 %	78	D	47.81 % / 41.17 %
15	E	69.24 % / 30.47 %	31	E	49.26 % / 47.23 %	47	C	55.97 % / 36.04 %	63	A	45.73 % / 31.7 %	79	D	50.68 % / 35.33 %
16	D	52.16 % / 41.01 %	32	A	69.92 % / 30.08 %	48	D	48.76 % / 51.1 %	64	A	19.64 % / 68.44 %	80	D	69.79 % / 30.01 %

Q.	Ans.	Correct / Skipped
81	D	48.08 %
		31.4 %
82	B	46.77 %
		51.16 %
83	E	80.7 %
		11.25 %
84	C	53.0 %
		39.8 %

Q.	Ans.	Correct / Skipped
85	D	68.6 %
		30.16 %
86	B	64.22 %
		31.3 %
87	B	58.26 %
		39.9 %
88	D	55.73 %
		39.39 %

Q.	Ans.	Correct / Skipped
89	B	58.52 %
		37.19 %
90	D	58.71 %
		37.85 %
91	D	64.85 %
		31.23 %
92	A	69.4 %
		30.52 %

Q.	Ans.	Correct / Skipped
93	C	27.66 %
		70.87 %
94	B	55.63 %
		30.01 %
95	E	63.28 %
		31.06 %
96	A	82.02 %
		17.04 %

Q.	Ans.	Correct / Skipped
97	B	14.75 %
		81.25 %
98	D	57.84 %
		40.82 %
99	A	61.02 %
		32.86 %
100	B	55.43 %
		43.75 %

Performance Analysis

Avg. Score (%)	35.0%
Toppers Score (%)	67.0%
Your Score	

//Hints and Solutions//

1. There is no error in the given sentence.

Therefore the correct sentence is "The defence minister thought that each veteran was as respectful as himself and should be given due preference as well."

Hence, the correct option is (E).

2. The error lies in the second part of thestatement because 'of' cannot be used with 'despite'. "Despite" itself means 'inspite of'.

Unfortunately, India continues to be one of the backward countries with respect to literacy, despite the fact that successive governments have been trying their best to promote education.

Hence, the correct option is (B).

3. The error lies in the first part of thesentence. The subject is 'appropriation',which is singular, thus the helping verb'have' should be replaced with 'has'.

The correct sentence will be "Appropriation of assets has become increasingly important due to the willingness of those in power to abuse authority for personal gains.

Hence, the correct option is (A).

4. Foal is the youngone of horse.

Let us check each of the options one by one.

Option (A) - Horse and mare denote masculine and feminine genders of same species (horse) respectively.

Option (B) - This is wrong because "colt" is used for a young male horse, thus both the pairs denote masculine genders.

Option (C) - This is incorrect because youngone of lion is called cub and not foal.

Option (D) - This is wrong because it contains feminine gender of donkey and masculine gender of horse.

Option (E) - This is also incorrect as it uses, feminine gender of horse along with masculine gender of Donkey.

Hence, the correct option is (A).

5. Let us check each of the options one by one.

Option (A) - This is wrong because the pair contains persons of the same gender.

Option (B) - This is wrong because the pair contains opposites.

Option (C) - This is incorrect because witches and cupids do not belong to same species or type.

Option (D) - This is wrong because the pair contains opposites.

Option (E) - This is absolutely correct because wizards and witches denote masculine and feminine genders.

Hence, the correct option is (E).

6. Let us check each of the options one by one.

Option (A) - This is wrong because the pair contains opposites but not persons of different gender of the same class.

Option (B) - This is absolutely correct as 'women' denotes the feminine of "men".

Option (C) - This is wrong because the pair contains persons of two different classes.

Option (D) - This is wrong because the pair contains persons of two different classes.

Option (E) - This is wrong because soldiers are neutral in gender and does not denote the masculine or feminine gender of policemen.

Hence, the correct option is (B).

7. All the options, except option (C) has the pairs where persons do not denote masculine or feminine of the same class or type.

Only option (C) has a pair where boy and girl belong to masculine and feminine genders respectively.

Hence, the correct option is (C).

8. In all other options except options (D) and (E), both the pairs denote masculine gender.

In option (E), both the pairs are of the feminine gender.

Only authors and authoresses in option (D) are the ones that denote masculine and feminine genders.

Hence, the correct option is (D).

9. Fallen is the most appropriate fit in the blank **(A)**.

The passage is about the current challenges in the agriculture sector.

Let us try to find the usage of the words given in the options:

Frightened: (verb) made someone afraid or anxious. It is the past and the past participle form of the verb "frighten".

Surged: (verb) increased suddenly and powerfully. It is the past and the past participle form of the verb "surge".

Sharpened: (verb) improved or cause to improve. It is the past and the past participle form of the verb "sharpen".

Culminated: (verb) reached a climax or point of highest development. It is the past and the past participle form of the verb "culminate".

Fallen: (verb) moved from a higher to a lower level, typically rapidly and without control. It is the past and the past participle form of the verb "fall".

Hence, the correct option is (E).

10. Affected is the most appropriate fit in the blank **(B)**.

The passage is about the current challenges in the agriculture sector.

Let us try to find the usage of the words given in the options:

Effect: (noun) a change which is a result or consequence of an action or other cause.

Efficacy: (noun) the ability to produce a desired or intended result.

Affected: (verb) had an effect on; make a difference to. It is the past and the past participle form of the verb "affect".

Emphasized: (verb) gave special importance or value to (something) in speaking or writing.

Eliminated: (verb) completely removed or got rid of something.

Hence, the correct option is (C).

11. Experiencing is the most appropriate fit in the blank **(C)**.

Let us try to find the usage of the words given in the options:

Experiencing: encountering or undergoing (an event or occurrence).

Trembling: (verb) shaking involuntarily, typically as a result of anxiety, excitement, or frailty.

Inciting: (verb) encouraging or stirring up (violent or unlawful behaviour).

Inexperience: (noun) lacking experience.

Experimenting: trying out new ideas or methods.

Hence, the correct option is (A).

12. Adversely is the most appropriate fit in the blank **(D)**.

Let us try to find the usage of the words given in the options:

Positively: (adjective) in a positive way, especially by expressing optimism, agreement, or acceptance.

Adversely: (adjective) in a way that prevents success or development; harmfully or unfavourably.

Strangely: (adjective) in an unusual or surprising way.

Rarely: (adjective) not often; seldom.

Metaphorically: (adjective) in a way that uses or relates to metaphor; figuratively.

Hence, the correct option is (B).

13. Strategies is the most appropriate fit in the blank **(E)**.

Let us try to find the usage of the words given in the options:

Obstacles: (noun) things that block one's way or prevent or hinder progress.

Prescription: (noun) an instruction written by a medical practitioner that authorizes a patient to be issued with a medicine or treatment.

Strategies: (noun) plans of action designed to achieve a long-term or overall aim.

Fatalities: (noun) occurrences of death by accident, in war, or from the disease.

Hence, the correct option is (D).

14. The second sentence should be E as it reiterates the same fact as sentence A. The sentence that should succeed E is B. We can confirm the fact from the usage of the word Gurukulam in the third sentence. The word Gurukulam first appears in the second sentence E and the third sentence, B traces back the history of Gurukulam. Therefore, we can conclude that B should be the third sentence after rearrangement.

Hence, the correct option is (D).

15. The second sentence should be E as it reiterates the same fact as sentence A. The sentence that should succeed E is B. We can confirm the fact from the usage of the word Gurukulam in the third sentence. The word Gurukulam first appears in the second sentence E and the third sentence, B traces back the history of Gurukulam.

Hence, the correct option is (E).

16. The second sentence should be E as it reiterates the same fact as sentence A. The sentence that should succeed E is B. We can confirm the fact from the usage of the word Gurukulam in the third sentence. The word Gurukulam first appears in the second sentence E and the third sentence, B traces back the history of Gurukulam.

The sentence that should succeed the third sentence (B), is F. We can confirm it because, in sentence F, the fact regarding the initiation of Gurukulam (Vedic Age) reappears, after appearing for the first time in sentence B, the sentence which precedes F. Therefore, we can conclude that F should be the fourth sentence.

The sentence which should succeed the fourth sentence (F), is D because we have already seen that F talks about the chief purpose of Gurukulam i.e training the young minds. And D should succeed F because D further explains in detail, the various domains in which the students were usually trained in.

Hence, the correct option is (D).

17. The second sentence should be E as it reiterates the same fact as sentence A. The sentence that should succeed E is B. We can confirm the fact from the usage of the word Gurukulam in the third sentence. The word Gurukulam first appears in the second sentence E and the third sentence, B traces back the history of Gurukulam.

The sentence that should succeed the third sentence (B), is F. We can confirm it because, in sentence F, the fact regarding the initiation of Gurukulam (Vedic Age) reappears, after appearing for the first time in sentence B, the sentence which precedes F. Therefore, we can conclude that F should be the fourth sentence.

The sentence which should succeed the fourth sentence (F), is D because we have already seen that F talks about the chief purpose of Gurukulam i.e training the young minds. And D should succeed F because D further explains in detail, the various domains in which the students were usually trained in.

The sentence that should succeed D is G. The phrase 'during the training' at the beginning of the sentence G makes a strong indication here that it should be the sixth sentence. The fifth sentence ends with referring to the training and the next sentence opens with the reference. Therefore, G should come after the fifth sentence i.e D.

Hence, the correct option is (C).

18. The second sentence should be E as it reiterates the same fact as sentence A. The sentence that should succeed E is B. We can confirm the fact from the usage of the word Gurukulam in the

third sentence. The word Gurukulam first appears in the second sentence E and the third sentence, B traces back the history of Gurukulam.

The sentence that should succeed the third sentence (B), is F. We can confirm it because, in sentence F, the fact regarding the initiation of Gurukulam (Vedic Age) reappears, after appearing for the first time in sentence B, the sentence which precedes F. Therefore, we can conclude that F should be the fourth sentence.

The sentence which should succeed the fourth sentence (F), is D because we have already seen that F talks about the chief purpose of Gurukulam i.e training the young minds. And D should succeed F because D further explains in detail, the various domains in which the students were usually trained in.

The sentence that should succeed D is G. The phrase 'during the training' at the beginning of the sentence G makes a strong indication here that it should be the sixth sentence. The fifth sentence ends with referring to the training and the next sentence opens with the reference. Therefore, G should come after the fifth sentence i.e D.

The remaining sentence i.e C, therefore, should be the seventh sentence. Also, it should be the seventh sentence because it explains how the teachers and students maintained a respectful relationship among them (the previous sentence only states the fact that there was a respectful relationship among them) and how there was no discrimination based on social standards.

Hence, the correct option is (B).

19. Russia on Saturday **approved** a third coronavirus vaccine for domestic use, Prime Minister Mikhail Mishustin **said** on state TV.

- 'Approved' is a verb and is not a physical entity that can 'do' something or take any action as it by itself is an action. Thus, this blank requires a noun, this could be 'Russia'.
- 'Said' is not an action a country can take, it has to be replaced by a doable action like 'approved'.
- 'Russia' is not something that can be 'on' state TV, it is not an action that can be done by Prime Minister Mikhail Mishustin. The blank requires a verb, like 'said'.

Hence, the correct option is (B).

20. It is **asserted** that people should keep in **mind** the importance of adherence to COVID-19 appropriate **behaviour**.

- 'Mind' is not something that can be done, the blank requires a verb. Thus, 'asserted' is appropriate for the blank.
- 'Asserted' is an action, it is not a physical entity in which something can be 'kept'. This blank requires a noun. Thus, the appropriate word is 'mind'.
- 'Behaviour' can be appropriate, and since it has been established that A and B need to be interchanged, blank C remains unchanged.

Hence, the correct option is (A).

21. The AstraZeneca company is going to **produce** in Japan doses of the coronavirus **vaccine** enough for 40 million **people**,

the executive director of the Japanese department of the firm said.

- 'Vaccine' is a noun, it is not an action that someone can 'do'. The blank requires a verb in the present tense. Thus, the correct answer is 'produce'.
- 'Produce' is a verb it cannot be a type of something, it is an action and hence cannot have 'doses'. 'Product' is the noun form and can be a type of coronavirus vaccine. The blank requires a noun and thus the answer is 'vaccine'.
- We've already established that A and B will be interchanged and also '40 million' is a quality that can be used to describe people. Thus, the answer will be 'people'.

Hence, the correct option is (D).

22. The meaning of the word metallurgy is the study of metals.

Metallurgy is a domain of materials science and engineering. It studies the physical and chemical behavior of metallic elements. It also studies the physical and chemical behavior of inter-metallic compounds.

Hence, the correct option is (A).

23. The word similar in meaning to the word 'Collapse' is 'Disintegration'.

- Collapse means to fall or shrink together abruptly and completely.
- Disintegration means breaking up into small parts.

Hence, the correct option is (A).

24. 'Indus Valley Civilization' is the main context discussed in the passage.

- After the collapse of the Indus Valley civilization, the inhabitants,
- The Indus Valley Civilization was the most expansive,
- The Mature Indus civilization flourished.

Hence, the correct option is (A).

25. The population of the Indus Valley Civilization was over five million.

- A million is equivalent to 10 lakh.
- A million is 1000 thousand.
- A billion is 1000 million.
- A trillion is 1000 billion.

Hence, the correct option is (A).

26. Harappa city was a part of the Indus Valley Civilization.

Let us have a look at the other options:

- Ceylon was the British Crown colony of present-day Sri Lanka.
- Sparta was a prominent city-state in ancient Greece.
- Rome is the capital city and a special comune of Italy.

Hence, the correct option is (C).

27. Copper, bronze, lead, and tin were produced by Harappans.

Hence, the correct option is (E).

28. Flourished means grow or develop in a healthy or vigorous way. A verb denotes an action.

Hence, the correct option is (A).

29. A civilization is a complex human society usually made up of different cities. A noun is the name of a person, place, thing, animal, or idea.

Hence, the correct option is (A).

30. 'Limited' is the antonym of the word 'Expansive'.

- Expansive means covering a wide area in terms of space or scope.
- Limited means restricted.

Hence, the correct option is (B).

31. Cradle is a small bed for a baby, especially one that moves from side to side.

Let us understand the meaning of the given options:

- A bassinet is a bed for babies designed to work with fixed legs.
- A crib is a small, cozy bed that has high sides.
- A carrycot is a small portable bed for a baby.
- A cot is a small bed with high barred sides for a baby or very young child.

All four options have a similar meaning.

Hence, the correct option is (E).

32. Coming to Statement I, there is no error in the sentence since it is grammatically and contextually right. Therefore, it is a correct sentence.

Statement II is not correct since there is an error in the degree of the comparison used in the sentence. There are two options and the comparison is between two things. This means comparative degree should be used and not the superlative degree as used in the sentence. The correct sentence would have been: But it is also true that they are unable to decide the better among the two options available in front of them.

Statement III is not correct since there is an error in the degree of the comparison in the sentence. When two qualities of the same person are compared, the comparative degree as in –er is not used but more + Adjective is used. Here, the correct statement would have been: It seems that the perpetrators of the crime are more wise than brave.

Statement IV is correct since there is no grammatical error in the sentence. Therefore, there is no correction required in it.

Only II and III are incorrect whereas the rest of the two are correct statement.

Hence, the correct option is (A).

33. Statement I is not correct since has should have been used with the International Monetary Fund since it is a single organization and have used in this statement is not right. The correct sentence would have been: The International Monetary Fund has decided that it will dole out subsidies to the developing countries in the present financial year.

All the other statements II, III, and IV are correct as there is no grammatical and contextual error in those sentences.

Hence, the correct option is (C).

34. Part A and part F should join conceptually. Part A states that 'We spent the afternoon meandering' and part F states 'around the streets of the old town'. So, A-F is the correct combination.

Part B and part D should join conceptually. Part B talks about 'You have to be a bit devious' and part D completes the sentence stating 'if you want to succeed in business'. So, B-F is the correct combination.

Part C and part E should be joined conceptually. Part C talks about 'This essay is the most conscientious' and part E completes the sentence stating 'piece of work'. So, C-D is the correct combination.

Hence, the correct option is (C).

35. Part A talks about Rome 'combining' something with another civilization. Their part is further explained in part E. So, A-E.

Part B talks about something disturbing the nesting sites. What disturbed their nesting sites is further explained in part D. So, B-D.

Part C talks about students meeting the department chairperson. For what purpose is explained in part F. So, C-F.

Hence, the correct option is (D).

36. Part B talks about how ancient oceans on Mars dried up. Conceptually it should join with part E which points out when this drying up occurred (periods of cold dry weather). So, B-E. Combining the rest of the parts is grammatically incorrect.

Hence, the correct option is (B).

37. Part B talks about access to metal tools and weapons creating something. Conceptually it should join with part F which talks about social equality becoming greater. So, B-F.

Part C talks about how metal weapons help to increase something. So it should join with part E which talks about the power of warriors, as warriors use weapons. So, C-E.

Hence, the correct option is (C).

38. Part A and part F should join conceptually as they together make a sentence which points out how the subject (she) thinks that the answer to her question is obvious. So, A-F.

Part B and part E should join conceptually as part B talks about how sidewalks are for pedestrians and part E reconfirms this statement by pointing out how they receive heavy pedestrian traffic. So, B-E.

Part C and part D should join conceptually as part C talks about a decision taken by the University for next semester, while part D points out what this decision is. So, C-D.

Hence, the correct option is (A).

39. The entire statement is in the past tense wherein events have already occurred. The word 'witnesses' is in the present continuous tense and is inappropriate in the current context.

Correct: What makes the 2019 election unprecedented is not that inappropriate words were used and misinformation spread, but the fact that India **witnessed** an increasing tendency to normalise these.

Hence, the correct option is (D).

40. The correct word here is headwinds in plural form. A headwind is something that makes progress or moving forward difficult. Basically, it is a wind which blows in the opposite direction to the one in which you are moving. The form here should be plural as there are multiple events listed in the statement.

Correct: With stronger **headwinds** ahead in the form of an escalating trade war between the U.S. and China, and the imbroglio in the Middle East, the outlook for export demand is far from reassuring.

Hence, the correct option is (A).

41. The series follows the following pattern:

$2^3 - 1 = 7$

$3^3 + 2 = 29$

$4^3 - 3 = 61$

$5^3 + 4 = 129 \neq 128$

$6^3 - 5 = 211$

$7^3 + 6 = 349$

Since 128 will come in place of 129.

∴ Wrong number is 129.

Hence, the correct option is (E).

42. The series follows the following pattern:

$4 + 3 \times 1 = 7$

$7 + 3 \times 2 = 13$

$13 + 3 \times 3 = 22$

$22 + 3 \times 4 = 34$

$34 + 3 \times 5 = 49$

Since 13 will come in place of 12.

∴ Wrong number is 12.

Hence, the correct option is (E).

43. The series follows the following pattern:

$34 + 2^2 = 38$

$38 + 3^2 = 47$

$47 + 4^2 = 63$

$63 + 5^2 = 88$

$88 + 6^2 = 124$

Since 88 will come in place of 90.

∴ Wrong number is 90.

Hence, the correct option is (B).

44. The series follows the following pattern:

$2 \times 1 + 1^2 = 3$

$3 \times 2 + 2^2 = 10$

$10 \times 3 + 3^2 = 39$

$39 \times 4 + 4^2 = 172$

$172 \times 5 + 5^2 = 885$

$885 \times 6 + 6^2 = 5346$

Since 39 will come in place of 40.

∴ Wrong number is 40.

Hence, the correct option is (C).

45. Let Balu joined for x months.

The ration of their share:

Atul : Balu

12 × 8000 : x × 6000

= 96 : 6x

Now Share of Balu = Rs. (4375 - 2800) = Rs. 1575

According to the question,

$$\frac{6x}{(96+6x)} \times 4375 = 1575$$

$$\Rightarrow \frac{6x}{(96+6x)} = \frac{1575}{4375}$$

$\Rightarrow$ 26250x = 151200 + 9450x

$\Rightarrow$ 16800x = 151200

$\Rightarrow$ x = 9

Hence, the correct option is (B).

46. Average age of Ram and Shyam $=$
$$\frac{\text{Ram's age + Shyam's age}}{2} = 65$$

∴ Ram's age $+$ Shyam's age $= 130$

Average age of Ram, Shyam and John $=$
$$\frac{\text{Ram's age + Shyam's age + john's age}}{3} = 53$$

∴ $\frac{130 + John's\ age}{3} = 53$

∴ John's age $= 29$ years

Hence, the correct option is (A).

Ques (47-56): Follow the BODMAS rule according to the table given below:

B	Brackets in order (), {}, []
O	of
D	Division (÷)
M	Multiplication (×)
A	Addition (+)
S	Subtraction (-)

47. Now,

40% of 50% of $\frac{3}{4}$ of $2400 =?$

$\Rightarrow 40\% \times 50\% \times \frac{3}{4} \times 2400 =?$

$\Rightarrow \left(\frac{40}{100}\right) \times \left(\frac{50}{100}\right) \times \frac{3}{4} \times 2400 =?$

$\Rightarrow \frac{2}{5} \times \frac{1}{2} \times \frac{3}{4} \times 2400 =?$

$\Rightarrow \left(\frac{6}{40}\right) \times 2400 =?$

$\Rightarrow ? = 360$

Hence, the correct option is (C).

48. Now,

$24 \times 32 \div 6 + 25\%$ of $64 =?^2$

$\Rightarrow 4 \times 32 + \left(\frac{25}{100}\right) \times 64 =?^2$

$\Rightarrow 128 + 16 =?^2$

$\Rightarrow ?^2 = 144$

$\Rightarrow ? = 12$

Hence, the correct option is (D).

49. Now,

$450 \times 30 + 1500 \times 20 =? \% \times 43500$

$\Rightarrow 13500 + 30000 = \left(\frac{?}{100}\right) \times 43500$

$\Rightarrow 43500 =? \times 435$

$\Rightarrow ? = 100$

Hence, the correct option is (A).

50. Now,

37.5% of $(64)^2 - 62.5\%$ of 50% of $160 =?$

$\Rightarrow \left(\frac{3}{8}\right)$ of $4096 - \left(\frac{5}{8}\right)$ of $\left(\frac{1}{2}\right)$ of $160 =?$

$\Rightarrow 1536 - 50 =?$

$\Rightarrow 1486 =?$

Hence, the correct option is (C).

51. Now,

$30\% \times 400 + 200 \times 3 + 100 \div 2 =?$

$\Rightarrow \left(\frac{30}{100}\right) \times 400 + 600 + 50 =?$

$\Rightarrow 120 + 600 + 50 =?$

$\Rightarrow ? = 770$

Hence, the correct option is (A).

52. Now,

20% of $420 - 33\frac{1}{3}\%$ of $? = 25 \times 42 \div 15$

$\Rightarrow \left(\frac{20}{100}\right) \times 420 - \left(\frac{100}{300}\right)$ of $? = 1050 \times 15$

$\Rightarrow 84 - \frac{?}{3} = 70$

$\Rightarrow \frac{?}{3} = 14$

$\Rightarrow ? = 42$

Hence, the correct option is (C).

53. Now,

25% of $480 + 200 +? = 800$

$\Rightarrow 120 + 200 +? = 800$

$\Rightarrow 320 +? = 800$

$\Rightarrow ? = 800 - 320$

$\Rightarrow ? = 480$

Hence, the correct option is (D).

54. Now,

40% of $1500 - 276 = (?)^2$

$\Rightarrow 600 - 276 =?^2$

$\Rightarrow 324 =?^2$

$\Rightarrow ? = \sqrt{324}$

$\Rightarrow ? = 18$

Hence, the correct option is (C).

55. Now,

60% of $500 \div 0.25 + \sqrt{169} =?$

$\Rightarrow 60 \times 5 \div 0.25 + 13 =?$

$\Rightarrow 60 \times 5 \times 4 + 13 =?$

$\Rightarrow 1200 + 13 =?$

$\Rightarrow 1213 =?$

Hence, the correct option is (D).

56. Now,

15% of $40 - 20\%$ of $75 + 12.5\%$ of $80 =?$

$\Rightarrow \left(\dfrac{15}{100}\right) \times 40 - \left(\dfrac{20}{100}\right) \times 75 + \left(\dfrac{12.5}{100}\right) \times 80 =?$

$\Rightarrow 6 - 15 + 10 =?$

$\Rightarrow ? = 1$

Hence, the correct option is (B).

57. Given:

The total literate population of five villages,

$= 900 + 600 + 1100 + 1200 + 1400 = 5200$

Required average $= \dfrac{5200}{5} = 1040$

Hence, the correct option is (E).

58. Given:

Total population of village $Q = 1200 + 800 = 2000$

The total literate population of village $Q = 1200$

Required percentage,

$= \dfrac{1200}{2000} \times 100$

$= 60\%$

Hence, the correct option is (D).

59. Given:

Total population of village $N = 600 + 900 = 1500$

Total population of village $R = 1400 + 1000 = 2400$

Required ratio,

$= 1500 : 2400$

$= 5 : 8$

Hence, the correct option is (D).

60. Given:

The literate population of village $P = 1100$

Illiterate population of village $P = 1400$

Difference $= 1400 - 1100 = 300$

Required percentage $= \left(\dfrac{300}{1100}\right) \times 100$

$\Rightarrow ? = 27.27\% \approx 27\%$

Hence, the correct option is (A).

61. Given:

Total literate population of five villages $= 900 + 600 + 1100 + 1200 + 1400 = 5200$

Total illiterate population of five villages $= 700 + 900 + 1400 + 800 + 1000 = 4800$

Required difference,

$= 5200 - 4800$

$= 400$

Hence, the correct option is (E).

62. When speed $= 35$ km/hr

Time taken to cover half the distance $= \dfrac{21}{35} = 0.6$ hr $= 0.6 \times 60 = 36$ min

Remaining time $= 54 - 36 = 18$ min $= \dfrac{18}{60} = 0.3$ hr

Distance to cover $= \dfrac{42}{2} = 21$ km

$\therefore$ Required speed $= \dfrac{21}{0.3} = 70$ km/hr

Hence, the correct option is (C).

63. The series follows the following pattern:

$25 \times 1 + 1 = 26$

$26 \times 2 + 2 = 54$

$54 \times 3 + 3 = 165$

$165 \times 4 + 4 = 664$

$664 \times 5 + 5 = 3325$

$\therefore$ The wrong term in the series is 674.

Hence, the correct option is (A).

64. Given:

Total rupees $=$ Rs. 8544

Let the ratio be x

Ratio is the smallest digits of that number

Formula:

Percentage $= \left(\dfrac{\text{Actual value}}{\text{Original value}}\right) \times 100$

So numbers ratio are $6x$, $11x$ and $15x$

According to question,

$\Rightarrow 6x + 11x + 15x = 8544$

$\Rightarrow 32x = 8544$

$\Rightarrow x = 267$

So,

A's Rupees $= 6 \times 267 = 1602$

A's spend his money $= 20\% \times 1602 = 320.4$

A's left with rupees $= 1281.6$

B's rupees $= 11 \times 267 = 2937$

B's increased his money by $50\% = 50\% \times 2937 = 1468.5$

B's rupees becomes Rs. 4405.5

C's rupees $= 15 \times 267 = 4005$

No change in C' rupees

Required ratio of new rupees in A, B and C $=$ $1281.6 : 4405.5 : 4005$

$\Rightarrow 12816 : 44055 : 40050$

$\therefore$ Ratio of rupees A, B and C $= 12816 : 44055 : 40050 = 16 : 55 : 50$

Hence, the correct option is (A).

65. Given:

A can do a work in 24 days, B can do the same work in 48 days and C can do the same work in 72 days.

In first case

A can do the work in 24 days

B can do the work in 48 days

C can do the work in 72 days

The ratio of their efficiency will be A : B : C $= \dfrac{1}{24} : \dfrac{1}{48} : \dfrac{1}{72} = $ $6 : 3 : 2$

A will get $\dfrac{6}{(6+3+2)} = \dfrac{6}{11}$

$= \left(\dfrac{6}{11} \times 4400\right)$ of the total amount which will be equal to Rs. 2400

But in second case only A and C work

The efficiency of A : C $= \dfrac{1}{24} : \dfrac{1}{72} = 3 : 1$

So A will get now $\dfrac{3}{(1+3)} = \dfrac{3}{4}$

$= \left(\dfrac{3}{4} \times 4400\right)$ of the total amount which will be equal to Rs. 3300

$\therefore$ extra money earned by A = Rs. $(3300 - 2400)$ = Rs. 900

Hence, the correct option is (D).

66. Given:

Cost price of item A is equal to the cost price of item B

MP of item A $= 160\%$ of CP

MP of item B $= 150\%$ of CP

Marked price of item B is 600 after increased by 50% CP of item B

$\text{CP} \times \dfrac{150}{100} = 600$

Cost price of item B $=$ Rs. 400

CP of A $=$ CP of B

Marked price of item A $= 400 \times \dfrac{160}{100}$

MP of item A $=$ Rs. 640

MP of item B $=$ Rs. 600

Selling price of item A and item B after giving 10% discount

SP of Item A $= 640 \times \dfrac{90}{100} = 576$

SP of Item B $= 600 \times \dfrac{90}{100} = 540$

Difference between selling price of item A and item B $=$ $576 - 540$

$\Rightarrow$ Rs. 36

Hence, the correct option is (B).

67. Let the money lent to Arnab be ' a'

Then, money lent to Ravish will be ' $20,000 - a$'

$\Rightarrow$ Simple interest for Arnab $= a \times \dfrac{20}{100} \times 2$

$\Rightarrow$ Simple interest for $Arnab = \dfrac{2a}{5}$

$\Rightarrow$ Simple interest for Ravish $= (20,000 - a) \times \dfrac{24}{100} \times 2$

$\Rightarrow$ Simple interest for Ravish $= (20,000 - a)\dfrac{12}{25}$

According to the question,

SI from Arnab - SI from Ravish = Rs. 729

$\Rightarrow \dfrac{2a}{5} - (20,000 - a)\dfrac{12}{25} = 729$

$\Rightarrow \dfrac{2a}{5} - 9,600 + \dfrac{12a}{25} = 729$

$\Rightarrow \dfrac{22a}{25} - 9,600 = 729$

$\Rightarrow \dfrac{22a}{25} = 10,329$

$$\Rightarrow a = 10,329 \times \frac{25}{22}$$

$$\Rightarrow a = 11,737.5$$

Amount lent to Ravish $= 20,000 - 11,737.5 =$ Rs. 8,262.5

$\therefore$ The amount of money which Ayush lent to Ravish is Rs. 8,262.5.

Hence, the correct option is (D).

68. Let the breadth and length be x cm and y cm respectively.

Now, 4 times the breadth exceeds the 3 times the length by $5 = 4x - 3y = 5$ ... (1)

And, 3 times the length exceeds the 2 times of breadth by $35 = 3y - 2x = 35$ ... (2)

Now, adding equation (1) and (2), we get,

$$2x = 40$$

$$\Rightarrow x = 20$$

Putting the value of x in equation (1), we get,

$$y = 25$$

So, Breadth $= 20$ cm

Length $= 25$ cm

Now, Area $=$ Length $\times$ Breadth

$$= (25 \times 20) \text{ cm}^2$$

$$= 500 \text{ cm}^2$$

Cost of carpeting $=$ Rs. $40/$ cm^2

The total cost of carpeting $= 500 \times 40$

$$\Rightarrow \text{Rs. } 20000$$

Hence the correct option is (C).

69. Given:

The first pipe can fill the tank in 10 minutes

The second pipe can fill the tank in 12 minutes

The third pipe can empty 2 gallons per minute

All the three pipes working together can fill the tank in 6 minutes

We know that,

$(A + B + C)$'s 1 hour work $= \dfrac{1}{A} + \dfrac{1}{B} - \dfrac{1}{C}$

Let us consider filling pipes as $A, B,$ and third pipe as C

Let the time taken by the third pipe to empty a full tank alone be x minutes

So we get:

$$\left(\frac{1}{10}\right) + \left(\frac{1}{12}\right) - \left(\frac{1}{x}\right) = \frac{1}{6}$$

$$\Rightarrow \frac{1}{x} = \frac{1}{60}$$

$$\Rightarrow x = 60 \text{ minutes}$$

Therefore, the tank capacity is obtained as:

$$60 \times 2 = 120 \text{ gallons}$$

Hence, the correct option is (A).

70. Given:

Average weight of 20 students of a class $= 60$ kg

Weight of old student who left $= 45$ kg

Increase in average weight of students $= 1$ kg

We know that,

Average $= \left(\dfrac{\text{Sum of observation}}{\text{No. of observation}}\right)$

Total weight of 20 students $= 20 \times 60$ kg $= 1200$ kg

The new average of the weight of the students will be $= 60 + 1 = 61$

Let the weight of the new student $= x$ kg

So According to the question,

The new average weight of students $= 61$

$$\Rightarrow \frac{(1200 - 45 + x)}{20} = 61$$

$$\Rightarrow 1200 - 45 + x = 61 \times 20$$

$$\Rightarrow x = 1220 - 1200 + 45$$

$$\Rightarrow x = 65 \text{ kg}$$

The ratio of old and new student's weight $= 45 : 65 = 9 : 13$

Hence, the correct option is (A).

71. Given statements: A > B > C = D; D ≤ E ≤ F ≥ G ≥ H; I ≥ H

On combining: A > B > C = D ≤ E ≤ F ≥ G ≥ H ≤ I

Conclusions:

I. C > G → False (as C = D ≤ E ≤ F ≥ G → therefore we cannot determine the relationship between C and G)

II. F > I → False (as F ≥ G ≥ H ≤ I → therefore we cannot determine the relationship between F and I)

Thus, none is true.

Hence, the correct option is (A).

72. Given statements: - A > B > C = P, R < B > Q, P ≥ S = T

On combining: A > B > C = P ≥ S = T, R < B > Q

Conclusions:

A > R → True (because A > B > R, implies A > R)

C = T → False (as C = P ≥ S =T, implies C ≥ T, thus C = T is not definite)

B > S → True (because B > C = P ≥ S, implies B > S)

So, only I and III follow.

Hence, the correct option is (D).

73. Given: N ≥ T > J ≤ R, J ≥ P ≥ M

On Combining: R ≥ J ≥ P ≥ M, N ≥ T > J ≥ P ≥ M

Conclusions:

I. M < R → False (as R ≥ J ≥ P ≥ M, therefore R ≥ M).

II. N = P → False (as N ≥ T > J ≥ P, therefore N > P).

III. R = M → False (as R ≥ J ≥ P ≥ M, therefore R ≥ M)

Conclusion I and III form a complementary pair.

So, either conclusion I or III is true.

Hence, the correct option is (B).

74. Given statement: B ≥ Q, O = M, E ≤ O, Q ≤ E

On Combining: B ≥ Q ≤ E ≤ O = M

Conclusions:

I. O ≥ Q → True (as Q ≤ E ≤ O → O ≥ Q)

II. O < B → False (as B ≥ Q ≤ E ≤ O → clear relation between O and B cannot be determined

III. B < E → False (as B ≥ Q ≤ E → clear relation between B and E cannot be determined)

Since only conclusion I is true and conclusion II and III are false.

Hence, the correct option is (D).

75. Given statements: K ≤ L ≤ M = N, P ≥ O ≥ N

On combining: K ≤ L ≤ M = N ≤ O ≤ P

Conclusions:

I. K < O → False (as K ≤ L ≤ M = N ≤ O → K ≤ O)

II. K = N → False (this can only be true if K = L and L = M, and so K = N is not definitely true)

III. K ≤ M → True (as K ≤ L and L ≤ M→ thus it can be concluded that K ≤ M)

Therefore, only conclusion III is true.

Hence, the correct option is (E).

Ques (76-78): Based on the given information direction diagram can be traced as,

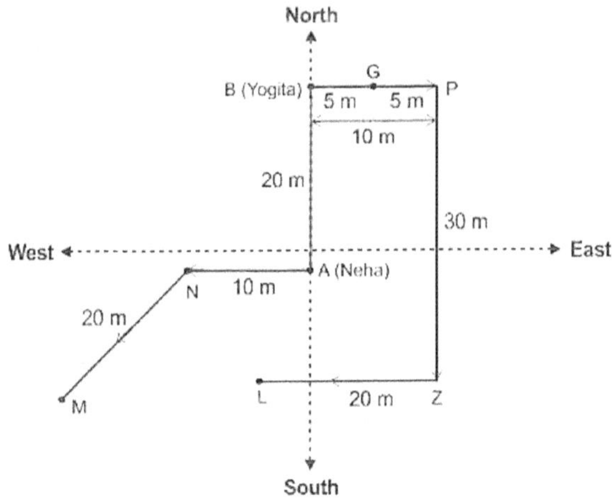

76. Therefore, point Z is in North-east direction with respect to the point M.

Hence, the correct option is (A).

77. Therefore, point C is in South-west direction with respect to the point P.

Hence, the correct option is (C).

78. The distance between A to B is 20 m.

The distance between B to G is 5m.

Using pythagoras theorem,

The minimum distance between A and G = $\sqrt{(5^2 + 20^2)}$

$= 5\sqrt{17}$ m

Hence, the correct option is (D).

79. The least possible Venn diagram is given below:

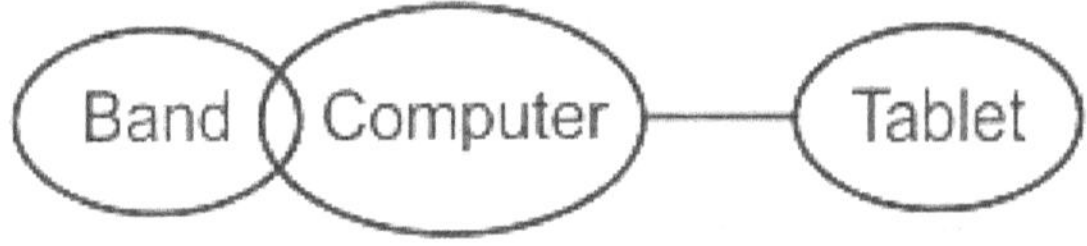

Conclusions:

I: Some bands are tablets → False (it is possible but not definite)

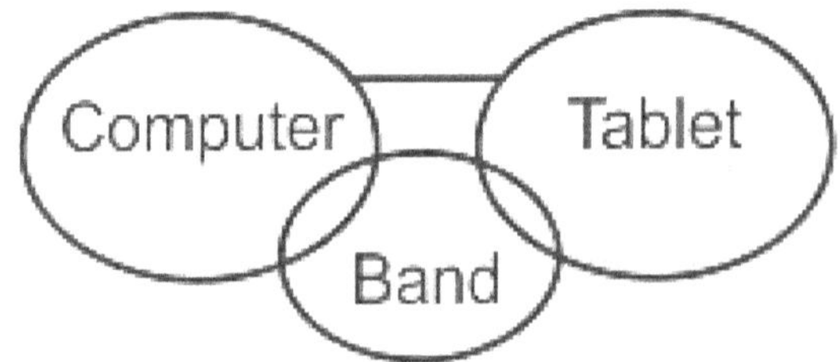

This diagram shows that some band being tablet is a possibility.

II: All bands are computers → False (only a few bands are computers)

So, neither conclusion I nor II follows.

Hence, the correct option is (D).

80. The least possible Venn diagram is given below:

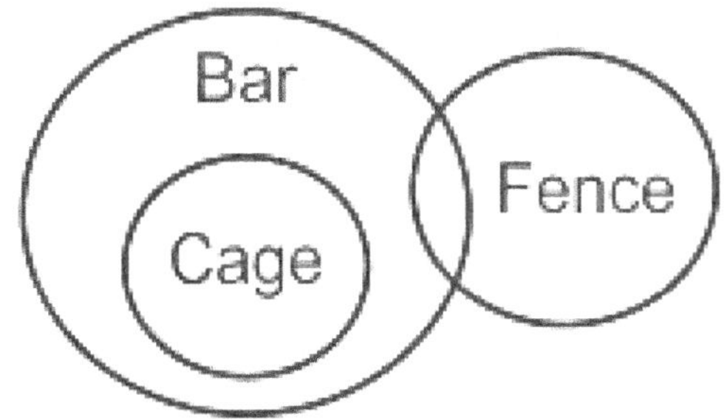

Conclusions:

I: All cage are fence → False (it is possible but not definite)

The possibility diagram is shown below:

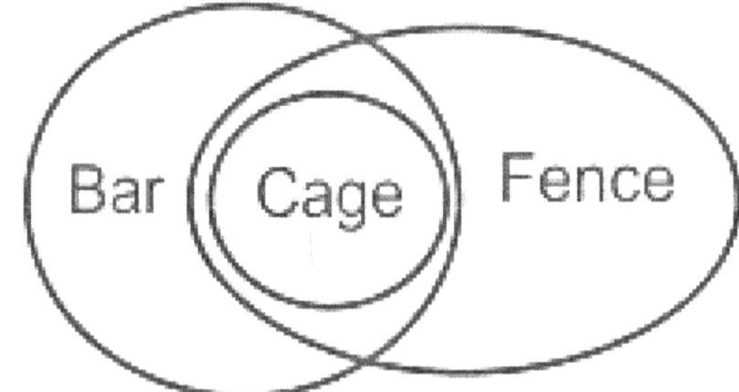

II: Some fence are cage → False (it is possible but not definite)

The possibility diagram is shown below:

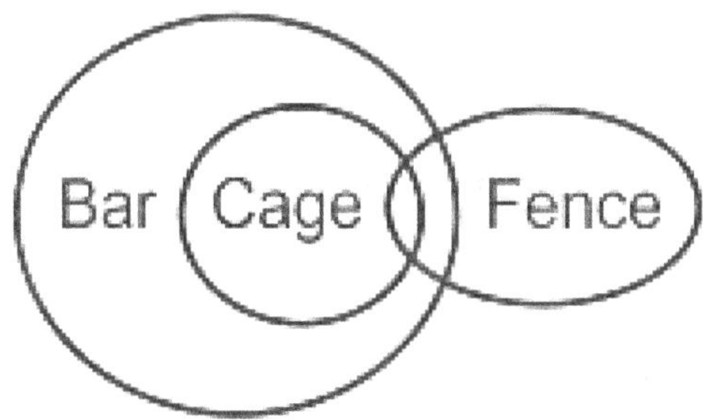

So, neither conclusion I nor II follows.

Hence, the correct option is (D).

81. The least possible Venn diagram is given below:

Conclusions:

I: Some building are toffee → False (it is possible but not definite)

The possibility diagram is shown below:

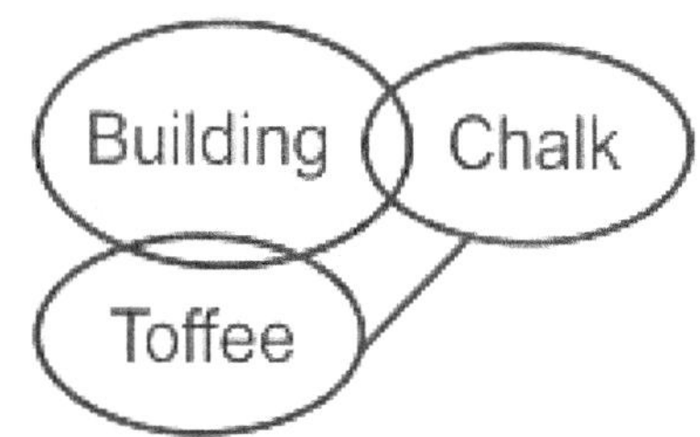

II: All building being chalk is a possibility → False (only few building are chalk)

So, neither conclusion I nor II follows.

Hence, the correct option is (D).

82. The least possible Venn diagram is given below:

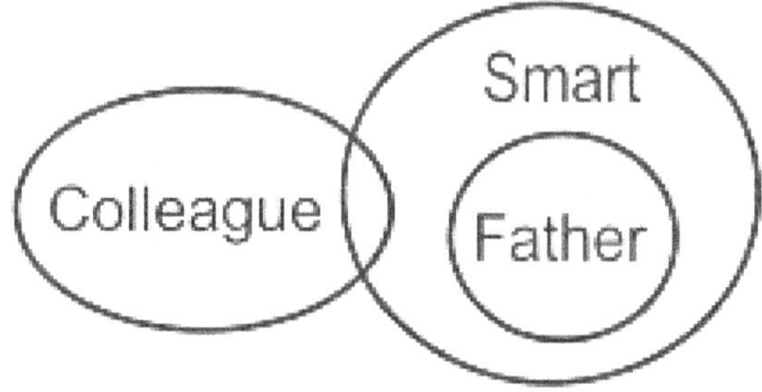

Conclusions:

I: Some colleague are father → False (it is possible but not definite)

The possibility diagram is shown below:

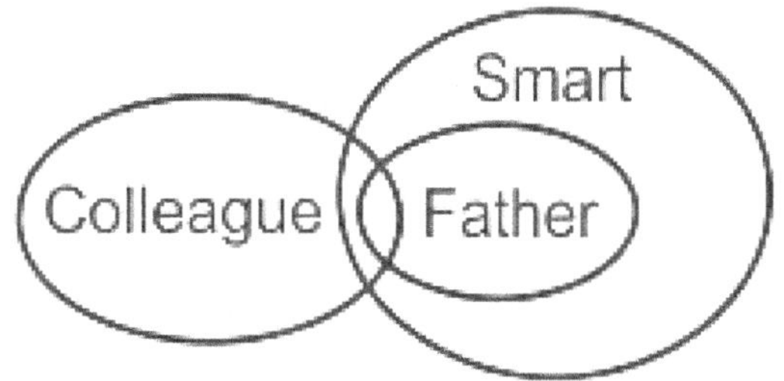

II: Some smart are colleague → True (only few colleague are smart)

So, only conclusion II follows.

Hence, the correct option is (B).

83. The least possible Venn diagram for the given statements is as follows

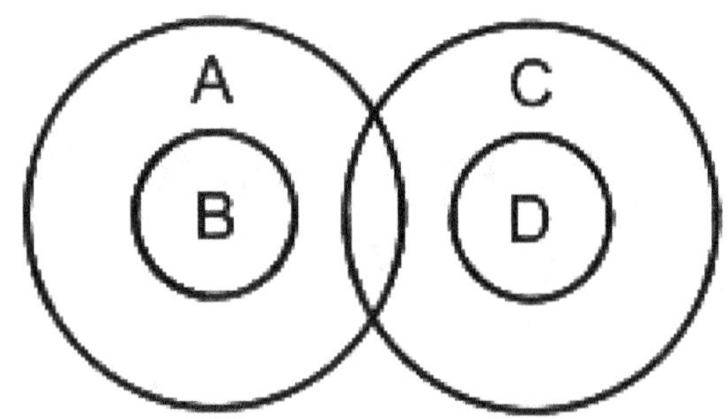

Conclusions:

(i) Some B can be C → False (only A are B, nothing else can be B)

(ii) Some D are A → False (Only C are D, nothing else can be D)

Therefore, both conclusion (i) and (ii) follow.

Hence, the correct option is (E).

Ques (84-88):

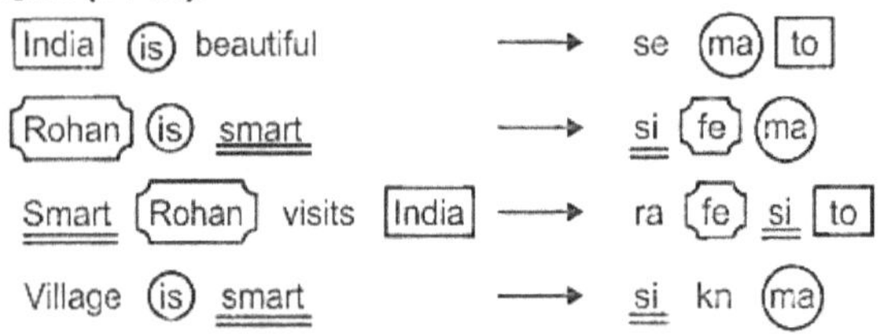

84. So, the code for village is kn.

Hence, the correct option is (C).

85. Code for 'Rohan' is 'fe'

Code for 'is' is 'ma'

Code for 'village' is 'kn'

Possible code for 'going' is 'kr'

So, code for 'Rohan is going village' is 'kn ma fe kr'.

Hence, the correct option is (D).

86. 'kn' stands for 'Village'

'ma' stands for 'is'

'se' stands for 'beautiful'

'to' stands for 'India'

'lk' can possibly stands for 'in'

So, 'kn ma se lk to' means 'Village in India is beautiful'.

Hence, the correct option is (B).

87. Code for 'smart' is 'si'

Code for 'city' can be 'cm'

So, code for 'smart city' is 'si cm'.

Hence, the correct option is (B).

88. Code for 'smart' is 'si'

Code for 'India' is 'to'

So, code for 'smart India' is 'si to'.

Hence, the correct option is (D).

Ques (89-94): Boxes: 1 to 8 in descending order

Colours: Blue, Yellow, Black, Pink, Green, Red and Purple

1) Green colour box is above Red colour box.

2) Red colour box is an even number box below box number 5.

3) Three boxes are kept between Red colour box and Yellow colour box.

Box	Case 1	Case 2
8	Yellow	
7		
6		Yellow
5	Green	
4	Red	
3		Green
2		Red
1		

4) Two boxes are kept between Pink colour box and Purple colour box.

5) Blue colour box is immediately below Pink colour box.

Box	Case 1	Case 2
8	Yellow	Pink
7		Blue
6	Purple	Yellow
5	Green	Purple
4	Red	
3	Pink	Green
2	Blue	Red
1		

6) One of the boxes above box number 5 is empty.

7) Black colour box is an odd number box.

Box	Case 1	Case 2
8	Yellow	Pink
7		Blue
6	Purple	Yellow
5	Green	Purple
4	Red	
3	Pink	Green
2	Blue	Red
1	Black	Black

As case 2 does not fulfil the above condition, it is thus eliminated. The final arrangement will be:

Box	Colour
8	Yellow
7	
6	Purple
5	Green
4	Red
3	Pink
2	Blue

1	Black

89. As Yellow colour is filled in 8th number box.

So, the condition Yellow - 8th is true and the other conditions are false.

Hence, the correct option is (B).

90. So, 4 boxes are there between Yellow colour box and Pink colour box.

Hence, the correct option is (D).

91. There are 2 (Green and Red) boxes between Violet and Pink.

Hence, the correct option is (D).

92. So, Black colour box is at the bottom.

Hence, the correct option is (A).

93. So, Green colour is filled in box number 5.

Hence, the correct option is (C).

94. So, 7 number box is an empty box.

Hence, the correct option is (B).

Ques (95-100): Persons: M, N, O, P, Q, R, S and T.

1) Q sits second to the left of N, who sits immediate left of T.

2) Two persons sit between Q and S.

3) T faces away from the center.

4) S and N are not adjacent to each other.

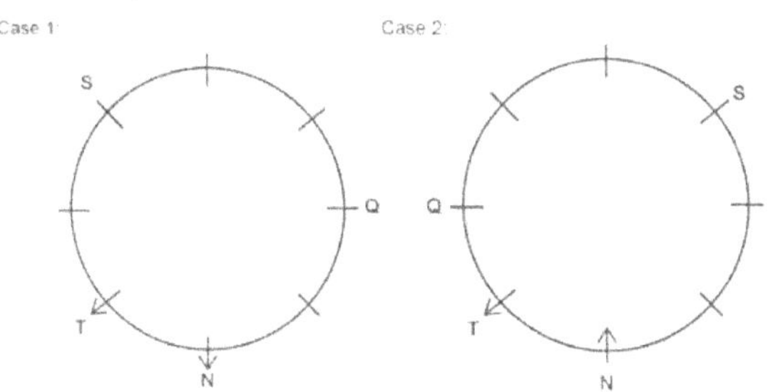

5) P sits immediate left of R and both face in same direction.

6) Immediate neighbours of S face in same direction but opposite to that of S.

7) S does not face away from the center. So, S must be facing towards the center. 8) Neither P nor R sits opposite to Q

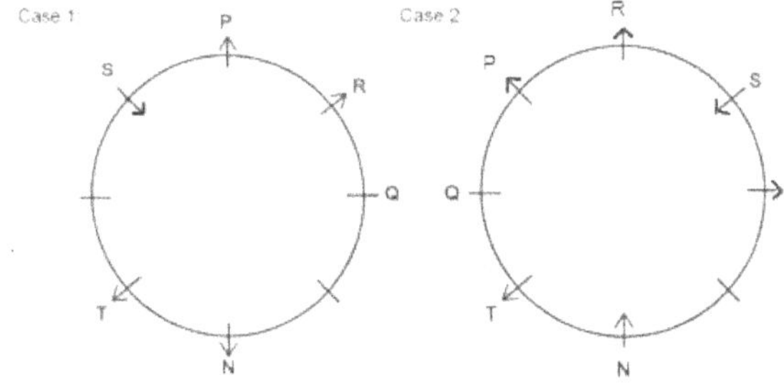

9) P does not sit adjacent to Q.

So, case 2 is not possible.

10) M faces towards the center.

11) M does not sit adjacent to S.

12) Person opposite to O faces towards the center.

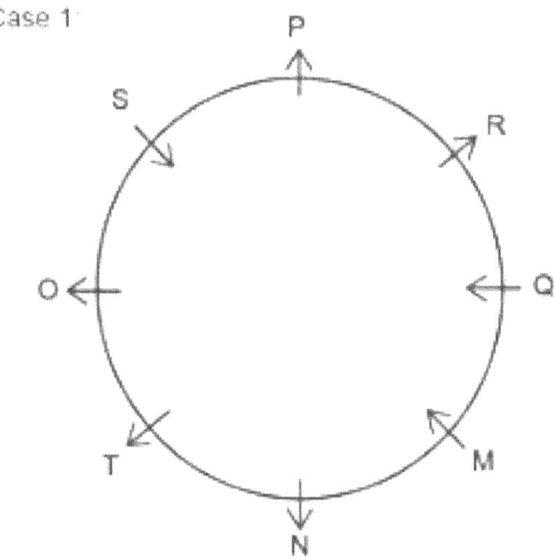

95. Hence, P sits immediate left of S.

Hence, the correct option is (E).

96. Hence, R sits opposite to T.

Hence, the correct option is (A).

97. All face away from the center except Q.

Hence, Q does not belong to the group.

Hence, the correct option is (B).

98. Hence, S sits third to the right of Q.

Hence, the correct option is (D).

99. Hence, O sits immediate right of T.

Hence, the correct option is (A).

100. Hence, R sits immediate right of Q.

Hence, the correct option is (B).

Test of English Language

Ques (1-5):Direction: Rearrange the following six sentences (A), (B), (C), (D), (E) and (F) in the proper sequence to form a meaningful paragraph and then answer the question given beside.

(A) Last June, ISRO had come close to NASA's record by launching 20 satellites in one mission.

(B) The Indian Space Research Organisation boosted its reputation further when it successfully launched a record 104 satellites in one mission from Sriharikota a few days ago.

(C) Of the 101 foreign satellites launched, 96 were from the U.S. and one each from the other five countries.

(D) An earth observation Cartosat-2 series satellite and two other nano satellites were the only Indian satellites launched: the remaining were from the United States, Israel, the UAE, the Netherlands, Kazakhstan and Switzerland.

(E) The launch is particularly significant as ISRO now cements its position as a key player in the lucrative commercial space launch market by providing a cheaper yet highly reliable alternative.

(F) But ISRO views the launch not as a mission to set a world record but as an opportunity to make full use of the capacity of the launch vehicle.

Q.1 Which of the following would be the first sentence after rearrangement?

A. (E) **B.** (A) **C.** (C) **D.** (B)
E. (D)

Q.2 Which of the following would be the second sentence after rearrangement?

A. (D) **B.** (E) **C.** (A) **D.** (F)
E. (B)

Q.3 Which of the following would be the third sentence after rearrangement?

A. (D) **B.** (C) **C.** (A) **D.** (F)
E. (E)

Q.4 Which of the following would be the fourth sentence after rearrangement?

A. (D) **B.** (F) **C.** (E) **D.** (A)
E. (C)

Q.5 Which of the following would be the last but one sentence after rearrangement?

A. (A) **B.** (C) **C.** (D) **D.** (E)
E. (F)

Q.6 Direction: In the following sentence, some parts have been printed in bold. One of the bold parts is incorrectly spelt. Pick up that part and choose its number. If there is no error in the bold parts, choose option (E)- no error as the answer.

The **application** with the particularly **detrimental** effect on **operators**' jobs was the biscuit **dough** mixing automation.

A. Detrimental **B.** Application
C. Operators **D.** Dough
E. No error

Q.7 Direction: In the following sentence, four words printed in bold are given. One of these words printed in bold might either be wrongly spelt or inappropriate to the context of the sentence. Find out that word that is inappropriate or wrongly spelt, if any. If all of the words in bold are correct, then mark 'No error' as your answer.

Rahul **screamed** because Riya asked him to **acknowledge** that his suggestion of an **accumulation** of coins was **revolving**.

A. Screamed **B.** Acknowledge
C. Accumulation **D.** Revolving
E. No error

Ques (8-12):Direction: Which of the following phrases (A), (B), (C) and (D) can replace the phrase in bold so as to make the statement correct grammatically and contextually? If the statement does not need any replacement, mark option (E) as your answer.

Q.8 The Bar Council of Delhi's directive to the Big Four accountancy firms not to offer legal services to their clients in India **has been a responsive move that is transparent protectionist in intent.**

A. is a rhetoric move that is transparent protectionist in intent
B. is a retrograde move that is transparently protectionist of intent
C. is a rhetoric move that is transparently puerile in intent
D. is a retrograde move that is transparently protectionist in intent
E. No replacement required

Q.9 An ad hoc committee, following an informal procedure, has concluded that the **allegations have no substance against the Chief Justice of India, but the finding** will not be made public.

A. alleging against the Chief Justice of India has not substance, but the findings
B. allegations has no substance against the Chief Justice of India, but the findings
C. allegations against the Chief Justice of India have no substance, but the findings
D. alleging the Chief Justice of India has not substances, but the findings
E. No replacement required

Q.10 It is essential for an entrepreneur **to keep his cheek upwards despite** failures and setbacks.

A. to keep his chin upwards despite
B. to keep his cheek up despite

C. to keep his chin up despite
D. to keep his chin up despite of
E. No replacement required

Q.11 India **being at enmity without China** weakens not only the Asian economy but also the global economy as a whole.

A. be at enmity within China
B. being at enmity within China
C. be at enmity without China
D. being at enmity with China
E. No replacement required

Q.12 Hecklers generally hurt themselves and their party the most because they **showed both under a bad light.**

A. showed both in a bad light
B. show both under a bad light
C. show both in a bad light
D. show both in front of a bad light
E. No replacement required

Ques (13-15):Direction: In each of the questions given below, four words are given in bold. These four words may or may not be in their correct position. The sentence is then followed by options with the correct combination of words that should replace each other in order to make the sentence grammatically and contextually correct. Find the correct combination of words that replace each other. If the sentence is correct as it is, select '(E)' as your option.

Q.13 The government has **collections** (A) a committee of officers to **suggest** (B) measures to **augment** (C) GST revenue **constituted** (D) and administration.

[IBPS PO, 2019]

A. B-D
B. C-D
C. A-D
D. B-C
E. None of these

Q.14 A land with a rich **invaders** (A), a people reduced to slavery, its wealth **plundered** (B) by successive bands of **civilization** (C) was awakened by the **call** (D) of Vivekananda.

[IBPS PO, 2019]

A. B-D
B. A-C
C. B-C
D. C-D
E. A-D

Q.15 There is a view that the **depreciation** (A) of the rupee has been the **appreciation** (B) of a general **result** (C) of the dollar **across** (D) all currencies.

[IBPS PO, 2019]

A. A-D
B. B-C
C. C-D
D. B-D
E. None of these

Ques (16-17):Direction: Each question contains three statements, one or more of which may not be grammatically correct. You are required to identify the incorrect statements from the options given below and mark that as your answer.

Q.16 I. Pulwama is no long just a national security or foreign policy issue.

II. Informal trade generally takes place due to restrictions on import of specific items.

III. The aftermaths of a terror attack in a democracy follows a pattern.

A. Only I
B. Only I and II
C. Only I and III
D. Only II and III
E. All are correct

Q.17 I. There is a realisation in the top ranks of the party that replicating 2014 majority is difficult.

II. The other party has demanded an equal and respectable share for the alliance.

III. A similar exercise in coalition building was witnessed in Tamil Nadu too.

A. Only I
B. Only I and II
C. Only I and III
D. Only II and III
E. All are correct

Q.18 Direction: In the given question, a sentence is divided into five parts out of which the last part is correct. Out of the remaining four, three parts have errors. Choose the part which doesn't have an error. If all the four parts are correct, mark E i.e. 'All are correct' as the answer.

War crimes include grave breaches of Geneva Conventions (A)/ and other violations serious of the laws and customs (B)/ that can applied in international armed conflict, (C)/ and in armed conflict "not of an international character", as listed in the Statute, (D)/ when they are committed as part of a plan or policy or on a large scale. (E)

A. A
B. B
C. C
D. D
E. All are correct

Q.19 Direction: A statement has been divided into five parts- A, B, C, D, and E. Part E is fixed and grammatically correct. Out of the other parts, only one is without error. You are required to find the error-free part and mark it as your answer. If none of the parts have errors, mark 'No Error' as your answer.

According to the officer, the investigating team (A)/ have already written to Google seeking details (B)/ for both the toolkit documents to ascertain where they (C)/were actually created, who all drafted and edited it (D)/, and to whom all the documents were circulated. (E)

A. A
B. B
C. C
D. D
E. No Error

Ques (20-24):Direction: Read the following passage and complete it using the words given in the options.

The threat of traditional "blood and iron" wars may have _______(A) [succumbed]- though its resurgence will always remain a possibility, particularly at a time of national weakness. However, the new ways of warfare inject "a different kind of _____(B)[languid] and cultural violence" that can be no less devastating. Its instrumentalities span the entire spectrum of human activity that can be _____(C)[instilled] to inflict harm on the target system, including _____(D)[condone] economics and trade, criminal and terrorist activities, cyber warfare, media manipulation and _____(E)[latency], technological and environmental conflict, as well as a wide array of patterns of social and political Subversion.

Q.20 Which of the following fits in the blank labelled (A)?

A. Receded   **B.** Susceptible

C. Contrived   **D.** Consorted

E. No improvement

Q.21 Which of the following fits in the blank labelled (B)?

A. Capitulate   **B.** Lascivious

C. Congenital   **D.** Cognitive

E. No improvement

Q.22 Which of the following fits in the blank labelled (C)?

A. Dandled   **B.** Deployed

C. Estranged   **D.** Dainty

E. No improvement

Q.23 Which of the following fits in the blank labelled (D)?

A. Predatory   **B.** Dapper

C. Damning   **D.** Sainted

E. No improvement

Q.24 Which of the following fits in the blank labelled (E)?

A. Sacrilege   **B.** Sanctity

C. Fabrication   **D.** Halt

E. No improvement

Ques (25-29):Direction: The question below has two blanks, each blank indicating that something has been omitted. Choose a set of words for each blank that best fits the meaning of the sentence as a whole.

Q.25 There are _____ takers for animal fur today, while ___ of the yesteryear stars were proud owners of mink coats.

A. few, quite a few   **B.** quite a few, a few

C. few, a few   **D.** a few, few

E. quite, few

Q.26 Interest to serve the merchants has been ______ since digitization ______ at the merchant's end.

A. grown, started   **B.** growing, started

C. grow, started   **D.** growing, starting

E. starting, growing

Q.27 The government must now _______ its seriousness by moving away from the _______ policies of the past.

A. ensconce, conscientious

B. masquerade, equitable

C. shelter, scrupulous

D. demonstrate, flawed

E. demonstrate, equitable

Q.28 The traditional practices of yoga lay great __________ on the importance of __________ in the form of pranayama.

A. emphasis, breathing   **B.** stress, exercise

C. faith, controlling   **D.** motion, body

E. strength, games

Q.29 The water availability of a region or nation is largely __________ by hydro-meteorological and geological factors,

and the __________ availability from annual precipitation is well above our requirement.

A. decided, freight

B. determined, utilizable

C. witnessed, lessened

D. governed, qualitative

E. branded, sluggish

Ques (30-39):Direction: Read the following passage carefully and answer the questions given below.

India is known for its rich and varied heritage and cultural diversity, yet much of it remains unknown to the vast majority of people, and in ______ need of preservation and revival. Our belief, at InterGlobe Foundation, is that the promotion of art and culture through heritage conservation is directly linked to the well-being of society. There is much that can and needs to be done in India to **bring forth** the richness of our heritage and weave it into the socio-cultural fabric.

Our efforts are directed (1)/ towards both the tangible (2)/ and the intangible aspects (3)/ of heritage conservation, (4)/ which includes carrying out physical restoration, (5)/ establishing the relevance and importance of sites and creating awareness among communities in close **proximity** as well as the larger public about the value of preservation of culture and heritage.

For us, Heritage Restoration is a holistic concept in which preservation/revival of the "heritage" which may be a monument, a stepwell, a craft, a dance or music form is the central lever around which other aspects like improvement in the quality of life, generation of livelihoods, environment protection go hand in hand. People's ownership of (1)/ conservation processes are (2)/ the key and hence they (3)/ need to be seen as (4)/ repositories of culture and not as beneficiaries of the project (5)/.

While people form the backbone of all the processes, it is critical that Heritage conservation is seen in conjunction with other pressing needs, for example, restoration of a monument will be incomplete without proper waste management in the area so that the monument and its neighborhood is always clean. And no neighborhood can have robust waste management unless the local community owns that process.

affecting the water recharge (1) /and availability in that stepwell (2)/ similarly, the revival of (3)/ an ancient stepwell will be incomplete (4)/ without looking at the factors (5)/. And the value of the beautifully restored stepwell will be sub-optimal if girls and women do not have free and safe access to the stepwell.

holistic perspective makes (1)/ heritage conservation more complicated (2)/, time-consuming and expensive, (3)/ it leads to a more lasting result (4)/ even though this (5)/

We have supported projects in big cities and peri-urban areas, our projects have included reviving the national monuments to documenting some lost dance forms. The key lesson in all these projects has been that heritage revival is a long haul program, it needs respectful partnerships between the Government, NGOs and private investors and **credible**, autonomous on-ground NGOs are key to the successful implementation of any heritage conservation projects. The _______ of such projects is hugely dependent on the implementation process and bringing together of all stakeholders, of which the most important ones are the government and local communities, and it is our persistent effort to bring them together for the _______ of our cultural legacy.

Q.30 Which of the following is the correct meaning of the emboldened word in the given sentence?

it needs respectful partnerships between the Government, NGOs and private investors and **credible**, autonomous on-ground NGOs are key to the successful implementation of any heritage conservation projects.

A. Anger or annoyance provoked by what is perceived as unfair treatment

B. Able to be believed; convincing

C. So great or extreme as to be difficult to believe; extraordinary

D. Strikingly large or obvious

E. Magnificent; very impressive

Q.31 Which of these is closest in meaning to 'proximity'?

A. Approximation **B.** Conspiracy
C. Vicinity **D.** Existence
E. Wrath

Q.32 Fill the blank in the following sentence with the most appropriate word.

the most important ones are the government and local communities, and it is our persistent effort to bring them together for the _______ of our cultural legacy.

A. Succession **B.** Rebate
C. Access **D.** Revival
E. Austere

Q.33 Rearrange the jumbled sentence to make a grammatically correct and meaningful sentence

holistic perspective makes (1)/ heritage conservation more complicated (2)/, time-consuming and expensive, (3)/ it leads to a more lasting result (4)/ even though this (5)/

A. 12345 **B.** 51234 **C.** 12453 **D.** 52134
E. 45123

Q.34 Fill the blank in the following sentence with the most appropriate word.

The _______ of such projects is hugely dependent on the implementation process and bringing together of all stakeholders,

A. Attention **B.** Consideration
C. Sustainability **D.** Cooperation
E. Anonymity

Q.35 The following sentence may or may not contain an error in one of its parts. Identify the part containing the error. If the sentence is correct, select 'no error' as your answer.

People's ownership of (1)/ conservation processes are (2)/ the key and hence they (3)/ need to be seen as (4)/ repositories of culture and not as beneficiaries of the project (5)/.

A. (2) **B.** (3) **C.** (4) **D.** (5)
E. No error

Q.36 The following sentence may or may not contain an error in one of its parts. Identify the part containing the error. If the sentence is correct, select 'no error' as your answer.

Our efforts are directed (1)/ toward both the tangible (2)/ and the intangible aspects (3)/ of heritage conservation, (4)/ which includes carrying out physical restoration (5)/.

A. (1) **B.** (2) **C.** (4) **D.** (5)
E. No error

Q.37 Rearrange the jumbled sentence to make a grammatically correct and meaningful sentence

affecting the water recharge (1) /and availability in that stepwell (2)/ similarly, the revival of (3)/ an ancient stepwell will be incomplete (4)/ without looking at the factors (5)/

A. 34512 **B.** 12345 **C.** 13452 **D.** 34125
E. 12453

Q.38 In the following sentence, correct the emboldened phrase if it is incorrect. If the phrase is correct, select 'no improvement needed' as your answer.

There is much that can and needs to be done in India to **bring forth** the richness of our heritage and weave it into the socio-cultural fabric.

A. Bring up
B. Bring to life
C. Bring it on
D. Bringing up
E. No improvement needed

Q.39 Fill the blank in the following sentence with the most appropriate word.

India is known for its rich and varied heritage and cultural diversity, yet much of it remains unknown to the vast majority of people, and in _______ need of preservation and revival.

A. Consistent **B.** Customary
C. Dread **D.** Tumult
E. Dire

Q.40 Direction: In the given question, a sentence is divided into five parts out of which the last part is correct. Out of the remaining four, three parts have errors. Choose the part which doesn't have an error. If all the four parts are correct, mark E i.e. 'All are correct' as the answer.

Environmental Pollution is an international journal (A)/ that seeks too publish papers that report (B)/ resulting from original, novel research that addresses (C)/ significant environmental pollution issues nor problems (D)/ and contribute new knowledge to science. (E)

A. A **B.** B
C. C **D.** D
E. All are correct

Test of Numerical Ability

Q.41 Direction: In the following number series, the wrong number is given, find out that number.

$100, 221, 77, 245, 50, 275$

A. 245 **B.** 275 **C.** 77 **D.** 100

E. 221

Ques (42-45):Direction: In the following number series, the wrong number is given, find out that number.

Q.42 154, 462, 231, 693, 346.5, 1038
A. 346.5   **B.** 1038   **C.** 154   **D.** 462
E. 231

Q.43 4, 11, 32, 96, 284, 851
A. 851   **B.** 32   **C.** 284   **D.** 11
E. 96

Q.44 4, 8, 17, 33, 58, 95
A. 8   **B.** 17   **C.** 95   **D.** 58
E. 33

Q.45 1440, 240, 48, 16, 4, 2
A. 240   **B.** 2   **C.** 4   **D.** 16
E. 48

Q.46 P and Q started a business together and after 3 months P added $\frac{1}{3}$ of his original investment and after 3 months to that he added same amount he invested at first. Q invested $\frac{1}{4}$ amount of what she originally invested after 4 months. What would the ratio of profits be after 12 months if initial investment by both of them was in ratio 3 : 4?
A. 8 : 9   **B.** 5 : 4   **C.** 9 : 8   **D.** 4 : 5
E. 6 : 5

Q.47 A dishonest shopkeeper professes to sell his goods at the cost price but use faulty measure. His $1kg$ weight measures $950gms$ only. Find his gain percent.
A. $7\frac{3}{19}\%$ **B.** $5\frac{7}{19}\%$ **C.** $5\frac{5}{19}\%$ **D.** $4\frac{5}{19}\%$
E. $3\frac{2}{19}\%$

Q.48 Three taps A, B and C can fill a tank in 12,15 and 20 hours respectively. If A is open all the time and B and C are open for one hour each alternately, the tank will be full in:
A. 6 hours   **B.** $6\frac{2}{3}$ hours
C. 7 hours   **D.** $7\frac{1}{2}$ hours
E. $7\frac{3}{2}$ hours

Q.49 Rs. 68,000 is divided among $A, B,$ and C in the ratio of $\frac{1}{2} : \frac{1}{4} : \frac{5}{16}$. The difference between the greatest part and the smallest part is:
A. Rs. 8000   **B.** Rs. 32000
C. Rs. 9000   **D.** Rs. 12000
E. Rs. 16000

Q.50 The average of 26 articles was found to be 40. On detecting, it was found that two items were wrongly taken as 20 and 18 instead of 40 and 24. Find the correct average.
A. 39   **B.** 40
C. 42   **D.** 41
E. None of these

Ques (51-55):Direction: Study the following line graph and answer the questions based on it.

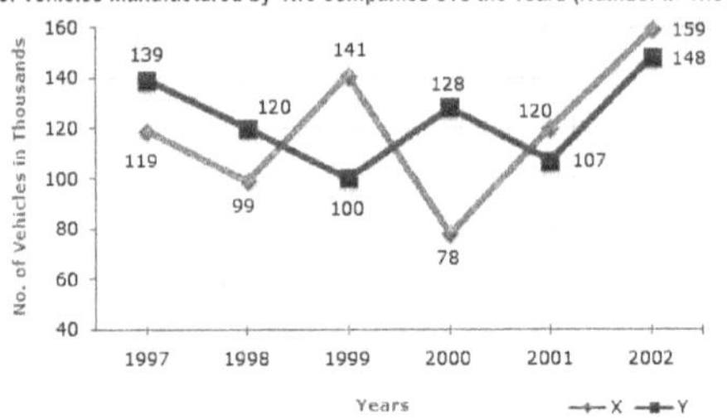

Q.51 What is the difference between the number of vehicles manufactured by Company Y in 2000 and 2001?
A. 50000   **B.** 42000   **C.** 33000   **D.** 21000
E. 23000

Q.52 What is the difference between the total productions of the two Companies in the given years?
A. 19000   **B.** 22000   **C.** 26000   **D.** 28000
E. 29000

Q.53 What is the average number of vehicles manufactured by Company X over the given period? (rounded off to nearest integer)
A. 119333   **B.** 113666   **C.** 112778   **D.** 111223
E. 112231

Q.54 In which of the following years, the difference between the productions of Companies X and Y was the maximum among the given years?
A. 1997   **B.** 1998   **C.** 1999   **D.** 2000
E. 2001

Q.55 The production of Company Y in 2000 was approximately what percent of the production of Company X in the same year?
A. 173   **B.** 164   **C.** 132   **D.** 97
E. 123

Q.56 From three cities A, B and C data is collected. The population of city B is 25% more than the population of city A and population of city C is 80% of the population of city B. What is the population of city B if sum of population of city A and city C is 1,25,000?
A. 72,850   **B.** 78,125   **C.** 74,650   **D.** 82,225
E. 65,980

Q.57 The value of $\dfrac{(0.625 \times 0.0729 \times 28.9)}{(0.0017 \times 0.025 \times 8.1)}$ is:
A. 3825   **B.** 3.825   **C.** 38.25   **D.** 382.5
E. 0.3825

Ques (58-66):Directions: What will come in the place of the question mark (?) in the following question?

Q.58 88.60% of 1500 + 39.25% of 800 + 63.20% of 2500 + 25.40% of 4500 = ?
A. 4856   **B.** 4466
C. 4256   **D.** 4366

E. None of these

Q.59 6.67% of $225 + 6.25\%$ of $1120 = (?)^3 + 3$

A. $(-76)^{\frac{1}{2}}$ **B.** $(76)^{\frac{1}{2}}$ **C.** $(-76)^{\frac{1}{3}}$ **D.** $(76)^{\frac{1}{3}}$

E. $(82)^{\frac{1}{3}}$

Q.60 (999 + 99 + 9) + 5.55% of 90 = ?

A. 1202   **B.** 1022

C. 1122   **D.** 1112

E. None of these

Q.61 $32 + 65 - 16\frac{2}{3}\%$ of $96 = ? + 33\frac{1}{3}\%$ of 120

A. 32   **B.** 52   **C.** 41   **D.** 46

E. 64

Q.62 25% of $7428 + 71.5 \times 2 = 14\frac{2}{7}\%$ of ?

A. 2000   **B.** 5000   **C.** 4000   **D.** 14000

E. 12000

Q.63 31% of $200 + 21\%$ of $300 = 25 \times 5 + ?^2 - 40\%$ of 90

A. 7   **B.** 4   **C.** 6   **D.** 5

E. 8

Q.64 $\sqrt[3]{6859} + \sqrt{441} - \sqrt[3]{4096} - \sqrt{576} = ?$

A. 1   **B.** 48

C. 0   **D.** -42

E. None of these

Q.65 $\dfrac{18 \times \frac{8}{15} + 10\% \text{ of } 624}{?} = 4$

A. 16   **B.** 18   **C.** 22   **D.** 24

E. 26

Q.66 $\left(\sqrt{8} \times \sqrt{8}\right)^{\frac{1}{2}} + 9^{\frac{1}{2}} = ?^3 + \sqrt{8} - 340$

A. 7   **B.** 19   **C.** 18   **D.** 9

E. 8

Q.67 Anikesh travels 30% distance of the total journey by bike and 50% of the remaining by train and taxi in the respective ratio of 4.3 and the remaining distance he covers on foot. If the sum of the distance which he travels by bike and by Taxi is 126 km, then find the total distance which Anikesh travels during his journey?

A. 560 km   **B.** 590 km   **C.** 700 km   **D.** 620 km

E. 656 km

Q.68 After 10 years, the simple interest on a sum of money will be Rs 550. If the rate of interest is made five times after 5 years, then find the total simple interest received at the end of 10th year?

A. Rs. 1550   **B.** Rs. 1600   **C.** Rs. 1625   **D.** Rs. 1850

E. Rs. 1650

Q.69 A sphere is inscribed in a cubical box of side 4 cm in length such that sphere is tangent to all the six surfaces of the cube. Find the percentage of cubical content remaining after in cube other than a sphere?

A. 51.76%   **B.** 49.50%   **C.** 47.64%   **D.** 42%

E. 50.76%

Q.70 The hourly wages of Mohan has increased by 45% and due to that, the daily working hours of Mohan decreased by 25%. If Mohan was earning Rs. 140 per day before the increase then find out the (in Rs.) how much Mohan is earning after the increase?

A. 151.75   **B.** 152   **C.** 149.50   **D.** 152.25

E. 151

Test of Reasoning

Ques (71-76):Direction: Study the following information carefully and answer the question given below.

There are eight boxes which have different colors such as - Black, Blue, Red, Green, White, Pink, Purple and Orange. They are all stacked on top of each other and have a variety of items to be distributed in orphanages such as - books, notebooks, pencils, toys, board games, jeans, T-shirts, shorts, jackets, caps, Raincoats, shoes, belts, bags, sports equipment and cosmetics, all items are placed in such a way that each box contains two items but not necessarily in the same order.

The books are in white boxes and the books are not kept with sports and cosmetics. Toys and bags are kept in red boxes. Four boxes are placed in the center of the pink and black color box in such a way that the pink box is above the black box and the black box has caps and belt. The orange box is placed immediately below the blue box. Jackets and raincoats are placed in the third box from the top. Notebooks and pencils are placed in green boxes. The box with T-shirt and shoes is placed immediately above the box with jeans and shorts and both boxes are placed above the fifth box from the top. The white colored box is placed fourth from the top. The purple and red colored boxes are placed fourth from the base and base respectively.

Q.71 Which box is placed at the third position if starting with the Green box?

A. White box   **B.** Blue box

C. Pink Box   **D.** Black box

E. Red box

Q.72 Which box is in between the Black box and the box with toiletries?

A. The box which contains toys

B. blue box

C. The box which contains jackets

D. The box which contains pencils

E. White box

Q.73 Four of the following are alike in a certain way and so form a group. Which one of the following does not belong to the group?

A. Orange box - board games

B. Pink box - shorts

C. Red box - caps

D. Green box - toiletries

E. Blue box - t-shirts

Q.74 How many boxes are placed between the Orange and the one with the sports equipment?

A. None   **B.** One

C. Two   **D.** Three

E. More than three

Q.75 Which of the following items does the Pink box contains?

A. Board games   **B.** Shorts

C. Shoes   **D.** Toiletries

E. Sport equipment

Q.76 Which of the following statements is true with respect to the given information?

A. Black box is immediately above the box with sports equipment

B. Blue box contains jackets

C. Red box and Green box have three boxes in between them

D. Toiletries are in Orange box

E. None of these

Ques (77-80):Directions: In the following question assuming the given statement to be true, find which of the conclusion(s) among given conclusions is/are definitely true and then give your answers accordingly.

Q.77 Statement: $B < S \leq Q < Y = X > C \geq J$

Conclusion:

I. $S < Y$

II. $X > B$

A. Only I is true

B. Either I or II is true

C. Only II is true

D. Both I and II are true

E. None of these

Q.78 Statements: $A < C = D \leq E; B = A > F$

Conclusions:

I. $D > F$

II. $B > E$

A. Only II is true

B. Only I is true

C. Both are true

D. Neither I nor II is true

E. Either I or II is true

Q.79 Statement: $D = X \geq C > S = F; D > Y \geq H \geq G$

Conclusion:

I. $G \leq X$

II. $D > F$

A. Only conclusion I follows

B. Both conclusion I or II follows

C. Only conclusion II follows

D. Either I or II follows

E. Neither conclusions I nor II follows

Q.80 Statements: $G \geq M = P > C; Q < R = B < C$

Conclusions:

I. $M > R$

II. $G \geq B$

A. Only I follows

B. Only II follows

C. Both follows

D. Either I or II follows

E. None follows

Q.81 Directions: In the following question assuming the given statements to be true, find which of the conclusion among given conclusions is /are definitely true and then give your answers accordingly.

Statements:

$M < N < U; R = T; U \leq R \geq V \geq E$

Conclusions:

I. $T > N$

II. $R \geq E$

III. $M < T$

IV. $T \geq U$

A. All are true

B. None is true

C. Only II is true

D. Only I and either II or IV are true

E. Only I and II are true

Ques (82-87):Direction: Study the information carefully and answer the given questions below.

Seven Students viz. Ganga, Arnav, Swati, Anup, Samita, Prakash, Parul are sitting around a circle to form a circle facing inside. Anup is sitting second to the left of Arnav. Only two students will sit between Samita and Ganga. Parul is not sitting next to Swati and Samita. Arnav is sitting second to the left of Parul. Ganga is not a neighbour of Anup and Swati.

Q.82 Who is sitting to the immediate right of Parul?

A. Ganga   **B.** Arnav

C. Prakash   **D.** No one

E. None of these

Q.83 If they are made to sit in linear arrangement starting from Arnav at the extreme left followed by Ganga, then who will be sitting third from extreme right end.

A. Parul   **B.** Swati   **C.** Samita   **D.** Ganga

E. Prakash

Q.84 Who is sitting between Swati and Samita?

A. Parul   **B.** Anup   **C.** Arnav   **D.** No one

E. Prakash

Q.85 Who is sitting second to left of the one who is immediate right of Anup?

A. Samita   **B.** Swati

C. Parul   **D.** Prakash

E. None of these

Q.86 How many persons are sitting between Prakash and Parul taking clockwise from Parul?

A. One   **B.** Four   **C.** Three   **D.** Five
E. No one

Q.87 Who is sitting between Samita and Parul?

A. Swati   **B.** Prakash   **C.** Anup   **D.** Ganga
E. Arnav

Ques (88-90):Direction: Study the information given below carefully and answer the questions that follow.

From a common starting point O, X and Y move 5 km towards east and west respectively, X moves 5 km towards north and similarly Y moves 5 km south. Then, X moves 10 km toward west and Y moves 10 km toward east.

Q.88 What is the shortest distance between the final positions of X and Y?

A. 5 km   **B.** 25 m
C. $10\sqrt{2}$ km   **D.** 20 m
E. $20\sqrt{2}$ km

Q.89 What is the shortest distance between the final position of X and the starting point?

A. $3\sqrt{2}$ km   **B.** $10\sqrt{2}$ km
C. $5\sqrt{2}$ km   **D.** 50 km
E. 25 km

Q.90 In which direction is the final position of point Y with respect to the final position of X?

A. North   **B.** East
C. South   **D.** North East
E. South East

Ques (91-94):Directions: In the question below are given four statements followed by two conclusions numbered I and II. You have to take the given statements to be true even if they seem to be at variance with commonly known facts. Read all the conclusions and then decide which of the given conclusions logically follows from the given statements disregarding commonly known facts.

Q.91 Statements:

Some C are D.

No C is a E.

All E are F.

Conclusions:

I. No F is a C.

II. At least some D are F.

A. Neither I nor II follows

B. Only I follows

C. Only II follows

D. Either I or II follows

E. Both I and II follow

Q.92 Statement:

No Bad are Good.

All Good are Nice.

Only a few Nice are Sagar.

Conclusions:

I. All Sagar can be Good.

II. Some Nice are not Bad.

A. Only conclusion I follow

B. Only conclusion II follows

C. Either conclusion I or conclusion II follows

D. Neither conclusion I nor conclusion II follows

E. Both conclusion I and conclusion II follows

Q.93 Statement:

No horse is a cat.

Only horse are tiger.

Conclusions:

I. No tiger is cat.

II. Some tiger is cat.

A. Only I follows

B. Only II follows

C. Either I or II follows

D. Neither I nor II follows

E. Both I and II follow

Q.94 Statement:

All belts are leather.

Only a few leather is a bag.

Conclusions:

I. All bags being leather is a possibility.

II. No bag is a belt.

A. Only I follows

B. Only II follows

C. Either I or II follows

D. Neither I nor II follows

E. Both I and II follow

Q.95 Direction: In the question below are given two statements followed by two conclusions I and II. You have to take the given statements to be true even if they seem to be at variance from commonly known facts. Read all the conclusions and then decide which of the given conclusions logically follows from the given statements disregarding commonly known facts.

Statements:

Only a few mango are not green.

No green is yellow.

Conclusions:

I. Some mango can be yellow is a possibility.

II. All green are mango.

A. Only I follows

B. Either I or II follows

C. Only II follows

D. Both I and II follow

E. None follows

Ques (96-100):Direction: Study the following information carefully and answer the given questions.

In a certain code language,

'Shagun knitted mat.' is written as 'Xa Zc Yb',

'Children sat on mat' is written as 'Ax Zc By Dw and

'Shagun taught children 'is written as 'Cx Xa Ax'.

Q.96 What is the possible code for 'children knitted Shawl' in the given code language?

A. Ax Yb Cx

B. Ax Yb Sh

C. Zc Yb Cx

D. Zc Xa Cx

E. Dw By Cx

Q.97 Which of the following is the code for 'taught' in the given code language?

A. By

B. Zc

C. Ax

D. Cx

E. Dw

Q.98 Code 'pi vi fi si' is for which of the following sentence in the following code language?

A. He should do that

B. He should do this

C. Don't do this work

D. They should do that

E. They should do this

Q.99 If 'children on mat' is coded as 'Zc Ax Dw', then what does 'By' mean in the given code language?

A. sat

B. on

C. taught

D. mat

E. knitted

Q.100 What is the code for 'children' in the given code language?

A. By

B. Zc

C. Ax

D. Yb

E. Dw

// Smart Answer Sheet //

Correct — Indicates percentage of students who answered questions correctly.

Skipped — Indicates percentage of students who skipped questions.

Q.	Ans.	Correct / Skipped
1	D	46.31 % / 33.12 %
2	A	28.27 % / 69.3 %
3	B	81.07 % / 12.17 %
4	D	84.56 % / 12.86 %
5	E	79.65 % / 18.44 %
6	E	66.52 % / 32.31 %
7	D	51.99 % / 30.69 %
8	D	57.64 % / 36.97 %
9	C	48.16 % / 33.97 %
10	C	54.48 % / 38.32 %
11	D	42.87 % / 56.72 %
12	C	46.97 % / 32.18 %
13	C	56.27 % / 39.48 %
14	B	55.3 % / 39.73 %
15	B	64.72 % / 31.22 %
16	C	62.91 % / 35.3 %

Q.	Ans.	Correct / Skipped
17	B	44.67 % / 34.52 %
18	D	21.91 % / 67.35 %
19	A	61.85 % / 33.42 %
20	A	49.36 % / 31.69 %
21	D	61.01 % / 35.46 %
22	B	61.93 % / 31.51 %
23	A	66.54 % / 30.6 %
24	C	56.46 % / 43.4 %
25	A	49.01 % / 33.33 %
26	B	45.05 % / 30.62 %
27	D	64.53 % / 34.19 %
28	A	62.43 % / 36.91 %
29	B	44.56 % / 46.27 %
30	B	51.26 % / 35.24 %
31	C	68.96 % / 30.6 %
32	D	61.77 % / 37.94 %

Q.	Ans.	Correct / Skipped
33	B	40.77 % / 57.45 %
34	C	60.04 % / 30.34 %
35	A	46.66 % / 30.21 %
36	D	41.15 % / 50.69 %
37	A	58.09 % / 39.7 %
38	E	59.24 % / 33.0 %
39	E	46.85 % / 30.91 %
40	A	66.86 % / 32.8 %
41	A	83.89 % / 10.38 %
42	B	45.13 % / 31.94 %
43	E	88.53 % / 10.92 %
44	C	89.87 % / 10.1 %
45	B	64.6 % / 31.57 %
46	C	52.72 % / 34.35 %
47	C	47.89 % / 39.76 %
48	C	48.52 % / 45.66 %

Q.	Ans.	Correct / Skipped
49	E	66.26 % / 32.12 %
50	D	78.64 % / 12.71 %
51	D	87.35 % / 12.27 %
52	C	83.61 % / 14.92 %
53	A	79.39 % / 11.61 %
54	D	76.45 % / 19.09 %
55	B	78.81 % / 16.17 %
56	B	48.12 % / 51.1 %
57	A	44.86 % / 36.23 %
58	D	66.92 % / 30.53 %
59	E	56.52 % / 42.24 %
60	D	86.44 % / 10.05 %
61	C	64.43 % / 32.28 %
62	D	80.35 % / 12.61 %
63	C	58.9 % / 32.36 %
64	C	61.53 % / 38.21 %

Q.	Ans.	Correct / Skipped
65	B	68.69 % / 30.03 %
66	A	52.23 % / 38.44 %
67	C	21.61 % / 70.84 %
68	E	22.25 % / 69.96 %
69	E	43.82 % / 34.09 %
70	D	65.71 % / 32.38 %
71	A	18.3 % / 73.25 %
72	D	56.32 % / 41.18 %
73	E	41.49 % / 45.2 %
74	E	64.61 % / 35.33 %
75	C	61.69 % / 35.43 %
76	E	41.06 % / 51.35 %
77	D	69.48 % / 30.01 %
78	B	56.47 % / 38.84 %
79	C	59.66 % / 39.37 %
80	A	48.49 % / 42.85 %

Q.	Ans.	Correct		Q.	Ans.	Correct		Q.	Ans.	Correct		Q.	Ans.	Correct		Q.	Ans.	Correct
		Skipped				Skipped				Skipped				Skipped				Skipped
81	A	49.74 %		85	A	58.3 %		89	C	66.65 %		93	A	59.99 %		97	D	57.38 %
		33.9 %				37.3 %				32.77 %				34.23 %				30.93 %
82	C	44.19 %		86	D	44.22 %		90	E	58.93 %		94	A	40.42 %		98	B	64.09 %
		50.55 %				40.51 %				38.2 %				59.26 %				30.02 %
83	C	64.19 %		87	B	77.7 %		91	A	64.73 %		95	A	56.67 %		99	A	54.63 %
		32.14 %				11.21 %				34.04 %				38.15 %				43.11 %
84	B	62.81 %		88	C	46.56 %		92	E	52.54 %		96	B	53.15 %		100	C	46.94 %
		31.36 %				47.16 %				34.0 %				38.28 %				47.19 %

Performance Analysis

Avg. Score (%)	57.0%
Toppers Score (%)	70.0%
Your Score	

//Hints and Solutions//

1. The first sentence after rearrangement is (B).

The sentence are arranged in the following pattern: (B)-(D)-(C)-(A)-(F)-(E)

- The subject that is being discussed in the passage is the successful launch of 104 satellites in a single mission by the Indian Space Research Organisation and sentence (B) sets the tone by mentioning this achievement in brief.
- (D) follows as it elaborates the details of the satellites launched.
- (C) follows next as it states the further details of the satellites launched.
- 'The United States', 'Israel', 'the UAE', 'the Netherlands', 'Kazakhstan' and 'Switzerland' are foreign countries and keyword that links (C) to (D) is "foreign".
- Now, if we pick sentence (E) as the next sentence, the position of sentence A as either the fifth or the sixth sentence would create absurdity and hence the only available choice for the fourth sentence is sentence (A).
- The sequence made so far is (B)-(D)-(C)-(A).
- The next sentence that should follow is sentence (F) that describes the real purpose of the launch of satellites. Now, the only sentence that is left is (E).

Hence, the correct option is (D).

2. The second sentence after rearrangement is (D).

The sentence are arranged in the following pattern: (B)-(D)-(C)-(A)-(F)-(E)

- The subject that is being discussed in the passage is the successful launch of 104 satellites in a single mission by the Indian Space Research Organisation and sentence (B) sets the tone by mentioning this achievement in brief.
- (D) follows as it elaborates the details of the satellites launched.
- (C) follows next as it states the further details of the satellites launched.
- 'The United States', 'Israel', 'the UAE', 'the Netherlands', 'Kazakhstan' and 'Switzerland' are foreign countries and keyword that links (C) to (D) is "foreign".
- Now, if we pick sentence (E) as the next sentence, the position of sentence A as either the fifth or the sixth sentence would create absurdity and hence the only available choice for the fourth sentence is sentence (A).
- The sequence made so far is (B)-(D)-(C)-(A).
- The next sentence that should follow is sentence (F) that describes the real purpose of the launch of satellites. Now, the only sentence that is left is (E).

Hence, the correct option is (A).

3. The third sentence after rearrangement is (C).

The sentence are arranged in the following pattern: (B)-(D)-(C)-(A)-(F)-(E)

- The subject t\hat is being discussed in the passage is the successful launch of 104 satellites in a single mission by the Indian Space Research Organisation and sentence (B) sets the tone by mentioning this achievement in brief.
- (D) follows as it elaborates the details of the satellites launched.
- (C) follows next as it states the further details of the satellites launched.
- 'The United States', 'Israel', 'the UAE', 'the Netherlands', 'Kazakhstan' and 'Switzerland' are foreign countries and keyword that links (C) to (D) is "foreign".
- Now, if we pick sentence (E) as the next sentence, the position of sentence A as either the fifth or the sixth sentence would create absurdity and hence the only available choice for the fourth sentence is sentence (A).
- The sequence made so far is (B)-(D)-(C)-(A).
- The next sentence that should follow is sentence (F) that describes the real purpose of the launch of satellites. Now, the only sentence that is left is (E).

Hence, the correct option is (B).

4. The fourth sentence after rearrangement is (A).

The sentence are arranged in the following pattern: (B)-(D)-(C)-(A)-(F)-(E)

- The subject that is being discussed in the passage is the successful launch of 104 satellites in a single mission by the Indian Space Research Organisation and sentence (B) sets the tone by mentioning this achievement in brief.
- (D) follows as it elaborates the details of the satellites launched.
- (C) follows next as it states the further details of the satellites launched.
- 'The United States', 'Israel', 'the UAE', 'the Netherlands', 'Kazakhstan' and 'Switzerland' are foreign countries and keyword that links (C) to (D) is "foreign".
- Now, if we pick sentence (E) as the next sentence, the position of sentence A as either the fifth or the sixth sentence would create absurdity and hence the only available choice for the fourth sentence is sentence (A).
- The sequence made so far is (B)-(D)-(C)-(A).
- The next sentence that should follow is sentence (F) that describes the real purpose of the launch of satellites. Now, the only sentence that is left is (E).

Hence, the correct option is (D).

5. The last sentence after rearrangement is (F).

The sentence are arranged in the following pattern: (B)-(D)-(C)-(A)-(F)-(E)

- The subject that is being discussed in the passage is the successful launch of 104 satellites in a single mission by the Indian Space Research Organisation and sentence (B) sets the tone by mentioning this achievement in brief.
- (D) follows as it elaborates the details of the satellites launched.
- (C) follows next as it states the further details of the satellites launched.
- 'The United States', 'Israel', 'the UAE', 'the Netherlands', 'Kazakhstan' and 'Switzerland' are foreign countries and keyword that links (C) to (D) is "foreign".
- Now, if we pick sentence (E) as the next sentence, the position of sentence A as either the fifth or the sixth sentence would create absurdity and hence the only available choice for the fourth sentence is sentence (A).
- The sequence made so far is (B)-(D)-(C)-(A).
- The next sentence that should follow is sentence (F) that describes the real purpose of the launch of satellites. Now, the only sentence that is left is (E).

Hence, the correct option is (E).

6. The given sentence has no grammatically incorrect words.

The meanings of words:

- Detrimental - obviously harmful
- Application - a formal request to be considered for a position or to be allowed to do or have something, submitted to an authority, institution, or organization.
- Operators - a person who operates equipment or a machine.
- Dough - a mixture that consists essentially of flour or meal and a liquid and is stiff enough to knead or roll.

Hence, the correct option is (E).

7. The word "Revolving" is out of context here as the correct word should be "Revolting".

Meaning of "Revolting" and "Revolving":

- Revolting: causing intense disgust; disgusting.
- Revolving: move in a circle on a central axis.

Hence, the correct option is (D).

8. The original sentence is incorrect because as we can observe that the sentence nowhere implies context of a perfect tense and therefore the verb 'has been' should be replaced by 'is' here.

Secondly, the word 'rhetoric' which means 'language designed to have a persuasive or impressive effect' doesn't seem to go well with the context of the sentence. This eliminates options (A) and (C) immediately.

'Retrograde' means 'reverting to an earlier and inferior condition' does make sense in the sentence and therefore must replace the given adjective 'responsive' in the bold part.

Usage of the adjective 'transparent' in the bold phrase is also ungrammatical. It should be replaced by the adverb 'transparently'.

Besides, usage of the preposition 'in' right before the noun 'intent' is absolutely correct.

Evidently, option (D) replaces the bold part most appropriately.

The correct sentence will therefore be: The Bar Council of Delhi's directive to the Big Four accountancy firms not to offer legal services to their clients in India is a retrograde move that is transparently protectionist in intent.

Hence, the correct option is (D).

9. The original sentence is incorrect.

Reason: In the bold part, placement of the phrase 'against the Chief Justice of India' is wrong. It should be immediately followed by the noun 'allegations'.

Secondly, the noun 'finding' which implies 'something that is found' is used in its plural case in general. Therefore, 'findings' will be more suitable here.

Clearly, among the available choices, option (C) replaces the bold part most appropriately.

The correct sentence will therefore be: An ad hoc committee, following an informal procedure, has concluded that the allegations against the Chief Justice of India have no substance, but the findings will not be made public.

Hence, the correct option is (C).

10. The original sentence is erroneous.

Reason: The correct idiomatic expression is 'keep his chin up' and not keep his cheek upwards'.

Keep one's chin up (Idiom):

Meaning: To stay cheerful and hopeful during difficult times.

E.g.: Keep your chin up, we're not lost yet.

So 'keep his chin up' should be used in place of 'keep his cheek upwards' to make the sentence grammatically correct.

Among the given choices, only option (C) replaces the given bold part most appropriately.

The sentence after replacement becomes: It is essential for an entrepreneur to keep his chin up despite failures and setbacks.

Hence, the correct option is (C).

11. The original sentence is erroneous.

Reason: The word 'enemity' must be followed the preposition 'with' instead of 'without' in this context. The expression "enmity with" means 'hostility with'.

So, 'with' should be used in place of 'without' to make the sentence grammatically and contextually correct.

Among the given choices, only option (D) replaces the given bold part most appropriately.

The sentence after replacement becomes: It is not uncommon for politicians to fake their degrees and pass off as highly educated.

Hence, the correct option is (D).

12. There are two errors in the bold part. Firstly, the phrasal verb 'in a bad light' which means 'in a way that makes someone or something look bad' has been written incorrectly. Therefore, 'under a bad light' must be replaced by 'in a bad light' in order to make the sentence correct.

E.g.: The defendants were shown in a bad light by the lawyer.

Secondly, the tense of the word 'showed' is also erroneous. The given sentence is in simple present tense. Therefore, 'showed' should be replaced by 'show' to make it a grammatically correct sentence.

Among the given choices option (C) replaces the bold part most appropriately.

The sentence after replacement becomes: Hecklers generally hurt themselves and their party the most because they show both in a bad light.

Hence, the correct option is (C).

13. Since the sentence begins in the format, 'Subject + helping verb +_______ + object', we know that a Verb in past participle (v3) form needs to come in that place.

The only option that fulfills the requirement is A-D. Therefore, it is the correct option.

So, the correct sentence is: The government has **constituted** a committee of officers to **suggest** measures to **augment** GST revenue **collections** and administration.

Hence, the correct option is (C).

14. In Part A since the article "a" has been used in "a rich" therefore it should be followed by a singular noun. Here the word invaders is not a singular noun therefore it should be replaced. Civilization is a singular noun and fits perfectly well with the context.

In Part C of the sentence, "bands of" is a collective noun and should be followed by a plural noun. Invaders as mentioned above is a plural noun and fits perfectly with the context of part C with proper contextual meaning.

Therefore we replace A with C and vice versa.

"A land with a rich **civilization**, a people reduced to slavery, its wealth **plundered** by successive bands of **invaders** was awakened by the **call** of Vivekananda.

Hence, the correct option is (B).

15. Interchange 'appreciation' and 'result' because the sentence is beginning with the consequence of the depreciation of the rupee so the suitable word is 'result'. The word 'appreciation' means 'estimation or merit of something' which fits in part C because it is talking about the appreciation of the dollar.

Therefore, the correct sentence is 'There is a view that the **depreciation** of the rupee has been the **result** of a general **appreciation** of the dollar **across** all currencies.'

Hence, the correct option is (B).

16. Statement I is wrong due to use of adjective "long" instead of adverb "longer".

Statement II is absolutely correct.

Statement III is wrong due to violation of the rule of subject-verb agreement. According to which, with a plural noun, plural verb is

to be used. Here aftermaths is plural , so the verb "follows" should also be plural i.e. follow.

Hence, the correct option is (C).

17. Statement I is wrong due to omission of article 'the' before '2014 majority'. It is a specific thing before which article 'the' is to be used grammatically.

Statement II is also wrong as it uses wrong preposition. Share is demanded 'in' an alliance and not 'for' an alliance.

Statement III is correct.

Hence, the correct option is (B).

18. In part A, 'Geneva Conventions' need to be preceded by the definite article 'the' as it is unique.

Part B is wrong because there is a faulty construction. 'Serious' is an adjective and should come before the noun 'violations' in order to describe it.

In part C, 'can' is an auxiliary verb and so should be succeeded by the verb 'be' for the part to be grammatically correct.

Hence, the correct option is (D).

19. Let's analyze this sentence carefully:

- Part-B: In this part, the error lies in the usage of the helping verb have instead of has.

- From part A we can deduce that the subject of the sentence, i.e., the investigating team is a singular noun, and according to the Subject-Verb agreement rule, a singular subject follows a singular H.V./Verb and the helping verb has is correct here.

- Part-C: In this part, the error lies in the usage of the preposition 'for' instead of 'of.'

- The usage of the preposition for is grammatically wrong here.

- We have to use the preposition of as it is used to show possession, belonging, or origin, and part B and C implies that the details belong to toolkit documents hence, the preposition of is the correct choice here.

- Part-D: In this part, the error lies in the usage of the pronoun it instead of them.

- Here, the correct pronoun to be used in them as it refers to the plural noun toolkit documents in part C.

Correct sentence: According to the officer, the investigating team has already written to Google seeking details of both the toolkit documents to ascertain where they were actually created, who all drafted and edited them, and to whom all the documents were circulated.

Hence, the correct option is (A).

20. The sentence conveys that the traditional wars do have a possibility of their return. So, the required word must be the same as gradually decreased.

Receded means gradually diminish. This is correct as it has the required meaning.

Susceptible means likely or liable to be influenced or harmed by a particular thing. Wars cannot be harmed or influenced.

Contrived means deliberately created rather than arising naturally or spontaneously. This word does not have the required meaning.

Consorted means habitually associate with (someone), typically with the disapproval of others. This word is inappropriate at this place.

Succumbed means fail to resist pressure, temptation, or some other negative force. Wars cannot fail to resist any pressure. So, this is incorrect.

Hence, the correct option is (A).

21. The sentence conveys that the new weapons introduce a new type of violence which can also be devastating. So, the required word must describe violence.

Capitulate means cease to resist an opponent or an unwelcome demand; yield. This cannot be used to describe violence.

Lascivious means revealing an interest. This is inappropriate with respect to violence.

Congenital means present from birth. This is inappropriate.

Cognitive means based on or capable of being reduced to empirical factual knowledge. This is correct as it describes the violence based on factual knowledge that is threatening.

Languid means having or showing a disinclination for physical exertion or effort. Violence cannot be described with this word.

Hence, the correct option is (D).

22. The sentence conveys that the new warfare is brought into action to harm others. So, the required word should mean the same as bringing into action.

Dandled means move (something) lightly up and down. the warfare cannot move something lightly.

Deployed means bring into effective action. This is correct as it gives the required meaning.

Estranged means no longer close or affectionate to someone; alienated. This word is inappropriate.

Dainty means delicately small and pretty. This is an adjective that is not required.

Instilled means gradually but firmly establish (an idea or attitude) in a person's mind. This is incorrect as the warfare is not firmly established.

Hence, the correct option is (B).

23. It can be concluded that the required word must describe the economics in a negative manner.

Predatory means seeking to exploit others. This is correct as it means the economics that exploits the people.

Dapper means neat and trim in dress and appearance. It is incorrect with context to the passage.

Damning means strongly suggesting guilt or error. Economics cannot suggest guilt or error.

Sainted means worthy of being a saint; very virtuous. This is not the required adjective.

Condone means accept (behaviour that is considered morally wrong or offensive). This is a verb so it is incorrect.

Hence, the correct option is (A).

24. The sentence is highlighting all the negative aspects that harm people. The word manipulation is also used. So, the required word must mean something done to fool people.

Sacrilege means a violation or misuse of what is regarded as sacred. Media is not regarded as sacred, so this is incorrect.

Sanctity means the state or quality of being holy, sacred, or saintly. Again this is incorrect.

Fabrication means done to deceive others. This is correct as fulfils the requirement.

Halt means to bring or come to an abrupt stop. This is a verb and is incorrect.

Latency means the state of existing but not yet being developed or manifest; concealment. This is incorrect with context to the passage.

Hence, the correct option is (C).

25. There are **few** takers for animal fur today, while **quite a few** of the yesteryear stars were proud owners of mink coats.

- Few: a small number of.
- Quite a few: being of a large but indefinite number.

It is appropriate to use 'few' and 'quite a few' respectively in the blanks of the sentence.

Hence, the correct option is (A).

26. The correct answer is growing, started.

The second option is correct as 'growing' is the present participle of the verb, the present perfect continuous is formed using has/have + been + present participle and 'started' is the past tense of the verb.

So, sentence "Interest to serve the merchants has been growing since digitization started at the merchant's end." correct fill in the blank.

Hence, the correct option is (B).

27. The government must now **demonstrate** its seriousness by moving away from the **flawed** policies of the past.

Demonstrate - give a practical exhibition and explanation of (how a machine, skill, or craftworks or is performed).

Flawed - having or characterized by a fundamental weakness or imperfection.

Hence, the correct option is (D).

28. "Pranayama" is a 'breathing exercise' whose importance is greatly 'highlighted' by the "traditional practices of yoga" So, options C, D and E can be eliminated as they are contextually unfit.

The only words that can fit the first blank are either "emphasis" or "stress". For the second blank "breathing" is most appropriate as it specifies the type of exercise that "pranayama" is categorized under. So, it negates the possibility of option (B) as well.

Hence, the correct option is (A).

29. The first blank intends to convey that "water availability" is largely 'dependent' on "hydro-meteorological and geological factors" . In the context of the sentence, the words which are suitable for the first blank are "decided", "determined" and "governed". So, options (C) and (E) are eliminated.

The word in the second blank describes the nature of water available from annual precipitation. The only word that makes the sentence meaningfully correct is "utilizable" which means 'usable'. The words "freight" and "qualitative" are irrelevant to the context of this sentence. This eliminates options (A) and (D) as well.

Hence, the correct option is (B).

30. Credible means able to be believed; convincing; reliable.

Eg- Not many people found my story credible.

Another meaning: capable of persuading people that something will happen or be successful.

Hence, the correct option is (B).

31. Proximity means nearness in space, time, or relationship.

Meanings of the given options are:

- Approximation means a value or quantity that is nearly but not exactly correct.
- Conspiracy means a secret plan by a group to do something unlawful or harmful.
- Vicinity means the area near or surrounding a particular place. Eg- The number of people in the vicinity was large.
- Existence means the fact or state of living or having objective reality.
- Wrath means extreme anger.

Clearly, 'vicinity' is the closest in meaning to 'proximity'.

Hence, the correct option is (C).

32. The sentence talks about the needs and the effort to improve our cultural legacy.

Meanings of the given options are:

- Succession means a number of people or things of a similar kind following one after the other.
- Rebate means a partial refund to someone who has paid too much for tax, rent, or utility.
- Access means the means or opportunity to approach or enter a place.
- Revival means an improvement in the condition, strength, or fortunes of someone or something.
- Austere means severe or strict in manner or attitude.

Clearly, 'revival' is the most appropriate word.

Hence, the correct option is (D).

33. The sentence that comes prior to this jumbled sentence in the passage states that a restored stepwell won't be of the highest standard if women and girls don't have free and safe access to it. The jumbled sentence is connected to this.

Part 5 comes first as it is the most suitable beginning for the sentence. Next is part 1 as it mentions the subject i.e. holistic perspective.

Next is part 2 as it tells what this holistic perspective means for heritage conservation. Next is part 3 as it further describes the results of the holistic perspective mentioned earlier. Part 4 comes at the end as it tells us about the a result which is positive.

The correct sequence is 51234.

Rearranged sentence: Even though this holistic perspective makes heritage conservation more complicated, time-consuming and expensive, it leads to a more lasting result.

Hence, the correct option is (B).

34. The sentence talks about the maintenance of projects which is hugely dependent on the implementation process and bringing together of all stakeholders.

Meanings of the given options are:

- Attention means notice taken of someone or something; the regarding of someone or something as interesting or important.
- Consideration means careful thought, typically over a period of time.
- Sustainability means the ability to be maintained at a certain rate or level.
- Cooperation means the action or process of working together to the same end.
- Anonymity means the condition of being anonymous.

Clearly, 'sustainability' is the appropriate word.

Hence, the correct option is (C).

35. In part (2) of the sentence, we need to use 'is' instead of 'are'. According to the Subject-Verb agreement, subjects and verbs must agree in number. That is, plural verb forms should accompany plural nouns and singular verb forms should accompany singular subjects.

'Are' is used with the plural form of a subject while 'is' is used with the singular form.

Here, 'people's ownership' is a singular subject and therefore 'is' should be used with it.

Corrected sentence: People's ownership of conservation processes is the key and hence they need to be seen as repositories of culture and not as beneficiaries of the project.

Hence, the correct option is (A).

36. There should be a subject-verb agreement in the sentence i.e if the subject is plural we should use the plural form of the verb and if it is singular we should use the singular form of the verb.

'Includes' is the singular form of the verb 'include' and it can only be used with a singular subject. That is why it's wrong here.

Here, the subject is 'efforts' which is plural so we will use 'include' instead of 'includes' in part 5.

Corrected sentence: Our efforts are directed toward both the tangible and the intangible aspects of heritage conservation, which include carrying out physical restoration.

Hence, the correct option is (D).

37. Part 3 comes first as it mentions the subject of the sentence i.e revival of something. Next is part 4 as it tells us to which thing this revival is connected to.

Next is part 5 as it mentions why the revival will be incomplete. Next is part 1 as it mentions what the factors(mentioned in part 5) affect, i.e. water recharge. Part 2 comes at the end as it begins with 'and', and mentions the second thing affected by the factors, i.e. water availability in the stepwell.

The correct sequence is 34512.

Rearranged sentence: Similarly, the revival of an ancient stepwell will be incomplete without looking at the factors affecting the water recharge and availability in that stepwell.

Hence, the correct option is (A).

38. The sentence states that there are a lot of things that need to be done to bring forward the richness of our heritage.

Bring forth something — phrasal verb with bring verb; it means to cause something to happen or be seen or known.

Meanings of the given options are:

- Bring up means to start discussing a subject; to look after a child until he or she becomes an adult.
- Bring to life means to regain or cause to regain consciousness.
- Bring it on is used to express confidence in meeting a challenge.

Clearly, 'bring forth' is correct as the second part of the sentence will mean "to bring forward the richness of Indian heritage so that it can be bonded into the socio-cultural fabric".

Hence, the correct option is (E).

39. The sentence talks about how the rich heritage is in the utmost need of preservation and revival. The required word must be an adjective that describes the need.

Meanings of the given words are:

- Consistent means acting or done in the same way over time, especially so as to be fair or accurate; constant.
- Customary means according to the customs or usual practices associated with a particular society, place, or set of circumstances.
- Dread means anticipate with great apprehension or fear.
- Tumult means a loud, confused noise, especially one caused by a large mass of people; a state of confusion or disorder
- Dire means extremely serious or urgent.

Clearly, 'dire' is the appropriate word.

Hence, the correct option is (E).

40. In part B, the adverb 'too' has been incorrectly used as it means 'excessively' or 'also'. The correct word here should be the preposition 'to'.

In part C, the word 'resulting' has been incorrectly used. It is the present participle form of the verb 'result'. But the part needs a noun to show the outcome from original novel research and hence the noun meaning of 'result' is correct in this part.

In part D, the correlative conjunction 'nor' has been incorrectly used. Since 'neither' is not present in the sentence, it cannot be used. The correct conjunction here is 'and'.

Thus, only A is the correct part.

Hence, the correct option is (A).

41. Considering the above series, the logic should be:

$$100 + (11)^2 = 221$$

$$221 - (12)^2 = 77$$

$$77 + (13)^2 = 246$$

$$246 - (14)^2 = 50$$

$$50 + (15)^2 = 275$$

∴ The wrong term in this series is 245.

Hence, the correct option is (A).

42. The series follows the following pattern:

154 × 3 = 462

462 ÷ 2 = 231

231 × 3 = 693

693 ÷ 2 = 346.5

346.5 × 3 = 1039.5

∴ The wrong term in the series is 1038.

Hence, the correct option is (B).

43. The series follows the following pattern:

4 × 3 - 1 = 11

11 × 3 - 1 = 32

32 × 3 - 1 = 95

95 × 3 - 1 = 284

284 × 3 - 1 = 851

∴ The wrong term in the series is 96.

Hence, the correct option is (E).

44. The series follows the following pattern:

$4 + 2^2 = 8$

$8 + 3^2 = 17$

$17 + 4^2 = 33$

$33 + 5^2 = 58$

$58 + 6^2 = 94$

∴ The wrong term in the series is 95.

Hence, the correct option is (C).

45. The series follows the following pattern:

1440 ÷ 6 = 240

240 ÷ 5 = 48

48 ÷ 4 = 12

12 ÷ 3 = 4

4 ÷ 2 = 2

∴ The wrong term in the series is 16.

Hence, the correct option is (B).

46. Given:

P : Q = 3 : 4

At 9 months = P + $\left(P \times \left(\frac{1}{3} \right) \right)$

At 6 months = P + $\left(P \times \left(\frac{1}{3} \right) \right)$ + P

At 8 months = Q + $\left(Q \times \left(\frac{1}{3} \right) \right)$

Let initial investment by P and Q be 3x and 4x,

The total investment by P $= 3x \times 3 + 4x \times 3 + 7x \times 6 = 63x$

The total investment by Q $= 4x \times 4 + 5x \times 8 = 56x$

The ratio of Profit $= 63x : 56x = 9 : 8$

∴ Profits of P and Q after 12 months would be in ratio 9 : 8

Hence, the correct option is (C).

47. Let, the cost price of $1g$ sugar be $Rs.\ 1$

Assume he sells $1000g$ sugar.

Since he uses false weight he actually sells only $950g$ sugar.

Therefore, the actual cost price for him is Rs. 950.

Selling price $=$ Rs. 1000

Profit percentage $= \dfrac{(1000-950)}{950} \times 100$

$= \dfrac{100}{19}\%$

$= 5\dfrac{5}{19}\%$

Hence, the correct option is (C).

48. Given,

Time taken by tap A to fill the tank = 12 hours

Part filled by tap A in 1 hour = $\dfrac{1}{12}$

Time taken by tap B to fill the tank = 15 hours

Part filled by tap A in 1 hour = $\dfrac{1}{15}$

Time taken by tap C to fill the tank = 20 hours

Part filled by tap C in 1 hour = $\dfrac{1}{20}$

(A + B) 's 1 hour work $= \dfrac{1}{12} + \dfrac{1}{15}$

$= \dfrac{9}{60}$

$= \dfrac{3}{20}$

(A + C) 's 1 hour work $= \dfrac{1}{12} + \dfrac{1}{20}$

$= \dfrac{8}{60}$

$= \dfrac{2}{15}$

Part filled in 2 hours $= \dfrac{3}{20} + \dfrac{2}{15}$

$= \dfrac{17}{60}$

Part filled in 6 hours $= 3 \times \dfrac{17}{60}$

$= \dfrac{17}{20}$

Remaining part $= 1 - \dfrac{17}{20}$

$= \dfrac{3}{20}$

Since the remaining part is $\dfrac{3}{20}$ and this part can be filled by tap A and B in 1 hour.

So, total time taken = 6 + 1

= 7 hours

∴ The total time taken for the tank is 7 hours.

Hence, the correct option is (C).

49. Given:

$$\Rightarrow A:B:C = \frac{1}{2}:\frac{1}{4}:\frac{5}{16}$$

Or, $A:B:C = 8:4:5$

Given amount $=$ Rs. 68,000

Now,

$$\Rightarrow \text{The greatest share } (A) = \left(\frac{68000}{17}\right) \times 8$$

$=$ Rs. 32000

$$\Rightarrow \text{The smallest share } (B) = \left(\frac{68000}{17}\right) \times 4$$

$=$ Rs. 16000

$\Rightarrow$ The difference between the greatest part and the smallest part is $= 32000 - 16000$

$=$ Rs. 16000

Hence, the correct option is (E).

50. We know that,

Sum of observations = Average × Number of Observations

Correct sum of observations = [sum of the observations – (wrong observation) + (correct observation)]

According to the question,

Calculated average of 26 articles = 40

Incorrect sum of 26 articles = 40 × 26 = 1040

Correct sum of 26 articles = Incorrect sum – sum of incorrect articles + sum of correct articles

Correct sum = 1040 – (20 + 18) + (40 + 24)

= 1040 – 38 + 64

= 1066

Correct average = $\dfrac{1066}{26}$ = 41

Hence, the correct option is (D).

51. The number of vehicles manufactured by Company Y in 2000 = 128000

The number of vehicles manufactured by Company Y in 2001 = 107000

Required difference = (128000 - 107000)

= 21000

Hence, the correct option is (D).

52. From the line-graph it is clear that the productions of Company X in the years 1997, 1998, 1999, 2000, 2001 and 2002 are:

119000, 99000, 141000, 78000, 120000 and 159000

and those of Company Y are:

139000, 120000,100000, 128000, 107000 and 148000 respectively.

Total production of Company X from 1997 to 2002

= 119000 + 99000 + 141000 + 78000 + 120000 + 159000

= 716000

and total production of Company Y from 1997 to 2002

= 139000 + 120000 + 100000 + 128000 + 107000 + 148000

= 742000

Difference = (742000 - 716000)

= 26000

Hence, the correct option is (C).

53. Average number of vehicles manufactured by Company X

$$= \tfrac{1}{6} \times (119000 + 99000 + 141000 + 78000 + 120000 + 159000)$$

$$= 119333$$

Hence, the correct option is (A).

54. The difference between the productions of Companies X and Y in various years are:

For 1997 (139000 - 119000) = 20000.

For 1998 (120000 - 99000) = 21000.

For 1999 (141000 - 100000) = 41000.

For 2000 (128000 - 78000) = 50000.

For 2001 (120000 - 107000) = 13000.

For 2002 (159000 - 148000) = 11000.

Clearly, the maximum difference was in 2000.

Hence, the correct option is (D).

55. The production of Company X in 2000 = 78000

The production of Company Y in 2000 = 128000

Required percentage $= \left(\dfrac{128000}{78000} \times 100\right)\% \approx 164\%$

Hence, the correct option is (B).

56. Given:

The population of B is 25% more than population A.

The population of C = 80% of population of B.

Let the Population of city A be 100x.

Then, the population of city B $= \dfrac{125}{100} \times 100x = 125x$

Population of C $= \frac{80}{100} \times 125x = 100x$

∴ According to given question,

100x + 100x = 125000

$\Rightarrow$ 200x = 125000

$\Rightarrow$ x = 625

∴ The population of city B = 125 × 625 = 78,125

∴ The population of city B is 78,125.

Hence, the correct option is (B).

57. This is a simple simplification.

$0.0729 = 8.1 \times 0.009$

$0.625 = 0.025 \times 25$

$28.9 = 0.0017 \times 17000$

$\therefore \frac{(0.625 \times 0.0729 \times 28.9)}{(0.0017 \times 0.025 \times 8.1)}$

$= (0.009 \times 25 \times 17000)$

$= 3825$

Therefore, the value of $\frac{(0.625 \times 0.0729 \times 28.9)}{(0.0017 \times 0.025 \times 8.1)}$ is 3825.

Hence, the correct option is (A).

58. Given:

88.60% of 1500 + 39.25% of 800 + 63.20% of 2500 + 25.40% of 4500 = ?

$\Rightarrow \frac{88.60}{100} \times 1500 + \frac{39.25}{100} \times 800 + \frac{63.20}{100} \times 2500 + \frac{25.40}{100} \times 4500 =?$

$\Rightarrow$ 1329 + 314 + 1580 + 1143 = ?

$\Rightarrow$? = 4366

∴ The value of ? is 4366.

Hence, the correct option is (D).

59. Given:

6.67% of $225 + 6.25\%$ of $1120 = (?)^3 + 3$

$\Rightarrow \frac{1}{15} \times 225 + \frac{1}{16} \times 1120 = (?)^3 + 3$

$\Rightarrow 15 + 70 = (?)^3 + 3$

$\Rightarrow 85 = (?)^3 + 3$

$\Rightarrow (?)^3 = 82$

$\Rightarrow ? = (82)^{\frac{1}{3}}$

The value of $?$ is $(82)^{\frac{1}{3}}$.

Hence, the correct option is (E).

60. Given:

$(999 + 99 + 9) + 5.55\%$ of $90 =?$

We know that value of 5.55% is $\frac{1}{18}$

$1107 + \frac{1}{18}$ of $90 =?$

$\Rightarrow 1107 + 5 =?$

$\Rightarrow 1112 =?$

∴ The value of $?$ is 1112.

Hence, the correct option is (D).

61. Given:

$32 + 65 - 16\frac{2}{3}\%$ of $96 =? +33\frac{1}{3}\%$ of 120

$\Rightarrow 97 - \frac{50}{3}\%$ of $96 =? + \frac{100}{3}\%$ of 120

$\Rightarrow 97 - \frac{50}{(3 \times 100)} \times 96 =? + \frac{100}{(3 \times 100)} \times 120$

$\Rightarrow 97 - 16 =? +40$

$\Rightarrow ? = 97 - 56$

$\Rightarrow ? = 41$

∴ The value of $?$ is 41.

Hence, the correct option is (C).

62. Given:

25% of $7428 + 71.5 \times 2 = 14\frac{2}{7}\%$ of $?$

We know that,

$25\% = \frac{1}{4}$ and $14\frac{2}{7}\% = \frac{1}{7}$

$\Rightarrow \frac{1}{4} \times 7428 + 143 = \frac{1}{7} \times?$

$\Rightarrow ? = 7 \times 2000$

$\Rightarrow ? = 14000$

Hence, the correct option is (D).

63. Given:

31% of $200 + 21\%$ of $300 = 25 \times 5 +?^2 - 40\%$ of 90

$\Rightarrow \frac{31}{100} \times 200 + \frac{21}{100} \times 300 = 125 +?^2 - \frac{40}{100} \times 90$

$\Rightarrow 62 + 63 = 125 +?^2 - 36$

$\Rightarrow ?^2 = 36$

$\Rightarrow ? = 6$

∴ The value of $?$ is 6.

Hence, the correct option is (C).

64. Given:

$$\sqrt[3]{6859} + \sqrt{441} - \sqrt[3]{4096} - \sqrt{576} = ?$$

$\Rightarrow 19 + 21 - 16 - 24 = ?$

$\Rightarrow 19 + 21 - 16 - 24 = ?$

$\Rightarrow 40 - 40 = ?$

$\Rightarrow ? = 0$

$\therefore$ The value of $?$ is 0.

Hence, the correct option is (C).

65. Given:

$$\frac{18 \times \frac{8}{15} + 10\% \text{ of } 624}{?} = 4$$

$\Rightarrow 6 \times \frac{8}{5} + 624 \times \frac{10}{100} = 4 \times ?$

$\Rightarrow 6 \times \frac{8}{5} + 62.4 = 4 \times ?$

$\Rightarrow 6 \times 1.6 + 62.4 = 4 \times ?$

$\Rightarrow 9.6 + 62.4 = 4 \times ?$

$\Rightarrow 72 = 4 \times ?$

$\Rightarrow ? = \frac{72}{4}$

$\Rightarrow ? = 18$

Hence, the correct option is (B).

66. Given:

$$\left(\sqrt{8} \times \sqrt{8}\right)^{\frac{1}{2}} + 9^{\frac{1}{2}} = ?^3 + \sqrt{8} - 340$$

$\Rightarrow \left(\left(\sqrt{8}\right)^2\right)^{\frac{1}{2}} + 9^{\frac{1}{2}} = ?^3 + \sqrt{8} - 340$

$\Rightarrow (8)^{\frac{1}{2}} + 9^{\frac{1}{2}} = ?^3 + \sqrt{8} - 340$

$\Rightarrow (4 \times 2)^{\frac{1}{2}} + 9^{\frac{1}{2}} = ?^3 + \sqrt{(4 \times 2)} - 340$

$\Rightarrow 2\sqrt{2} + 3 = ?^3 + 2\sqrt{2} - 340$

$\Rightarrow 3 = ?^3 + (-340)$

$\Rightarrow ?^3 = 340 + 3$

$\Rightarrow ?^3 = 343$

$\Rightarrow ? = \sqrt[3]{343}$

$\Rightarrow ? = 7$

Hence, the correct option is (A).

67. Let, the total distance travelled by Anikesh $= 100x$

Now according to question,

Distance travelled by bike $= 30\%$ of $100x$

$= \frac{30}{100} \times 100x = 30x$

Distance travelled by train $= \frac{4}{7} \times 50\%$ of $(100x - 30x) = \frac{4}{7} \times \frac{50}{100} \times 70x = 20x$

Distance travelled by taxi $= \frac{3}{7} \times 50\%$ of $(100x - 30x) = \frac{3}{7} \times \frac{50}{100} \times 70x = 15x$

Distance travelled on feet $= 100x - 30x - 20x - 15x = 45x$

Now according to question,

Distance travelled together by bike and taxi $= 315$ km

$30x + 15x = 315$

$45x = 315$

$x = 7$

Now, the total distance travelled by Anikesh will be

Total distance $= 100x = 100 \times 7 = 700$ km

Hence, the correct option is (C).

68. Let, the principal, interest rate be p and r respectively

Now, according to question

Simple interest for 10 years is Rs 550 which is given by,

Simple interest $= \frac{p \times r \times t}{100}$

$550 = \frac{p \times r \times 10}{100}$

$Pr = 5500 \dots \dots (1)$

Now, simple interest for 1 year will be,

Simple interest $= \frac{p \times r \times t}{100}$

$S.I = \frac{p \times r \times 1}{100} = \frac{5500 \times 1}{100} = $ Rs 55 (by using equation (1)

So, the simple interest for 5 years will be

Simple interest for first 5 years $= S.I$ for 1 year $\times 5 = 55 \times 5 = $ Rs. $275 \dots \dots \dots (2)$

Now, according to situation in question after 5 years the principal will be five times so interest will also be five times.

Simple interest for last 5 years $= \text{Rs } 275 \times 5 = \text{Rs.}$ $1375 \quad \ldots \ldots \ldots (3)$

Now , we need to find the simple interest at the end of 10th year which is given by

Simple interest at the end of 10th year $=$ Simple interest for first 5 years $+$ Simple interest for last 5 years

So, by using equation (2) and (3), we get

Simple interest at the end of 10th year $= \text{Rs } 1375 + \text{Rs } 275 = \text{Rs } 1650$

Hence, the correct option is (E).

69. Let, the radius of sphere be $'r'$ cm.

According to question,

A sphere is inscribed in a cubical box so the side of the cube will be equal to the diameter of the sphere inscribed in it

Radius of sphere $= \dfrac{\text{side of cube}}{2} = \dfrac{4}{2} = 2$ cm

So, the volume of the cube and sphere is given by,

Volume of cube $= (\text{ side })^3 = (4)^3 = 64$ cm ^{3}

Volume of sphere $= \dfrac{4}{3} \times \pi r^3 = \dfrac{4}{3} \times \pi \times (2)^3 = 33.51$ cm ^{3}

Now, the required percentage is given by,

Required $\% = \dfrac{\text{Volume of cube } - \text{ Volume of sphere}}{\text{Volume of cube}} \times 100 = \dfrac{64 - 33.51}{64} \times 100$

$= 50.76\%$

So, the correct answer is 50.76%.

Hence, the correct option is (E).

70. Let, the hourly wages and working hours be x and y respectively

According to question,

Since mohan was earning Rs. 140 earlier.

So, daily wages $=$ hourly wages $\times$ working hours

$xy = \text{Rs. } 140 \quad \ldots \ldots \ldots \ldots (i)$

Now, In second case

Mohan hourly wages increased by 45%,

Hourly wages $= x + 45\%$ of x

$= x + \dfrac{45}{100}x = x + 0.45x$

$= 1.45x$

Mohan working hours was decreased by 25%,

Working hours $= y - 25\%$ of y

$= y - \dfrac{25}{100}y = y - 0.25y$

$= 0.75y$

Now, the daily wages of Mohan is given by,

daily wages $=$ hourly wages $\times$ working hours

$1.45x \times 0.75y = 1.0875xy$

Put the value of equation (i) in the above equation,

Daily wages $= 1.0875 \times 140 = \text{Rs. } 152.25$

So, the correct answer is 152.25.

Hence, the correct option is (D).

Ques (71-76): Different colors: Black, Blue, Red, Green, White,Pink, Violet and Orange

Different items: books, notebooks, pencils, toys,board games, jeans, t-shirts, shorts, jackets, caps, rain coats, shoes, belts,bags, sports equipment and toiletries

Boxes placed one above the other.

1) White box is fourth from the top.

2) Toys and bags are in the Red box.

3) The Violet color box and Red colored box are at bottommost place and fourth from bottom respectively.

4) Jackets and raincoats are in the box which is thirdfrom the top.

Color of box	Items in the box
	Jackets, Raincoats
White	
Red	Toys, Bags
Violet	

5) T-shirts and shoes box is immediately above the boxwhich contains jeans and shorts and both these boxes are above the 5th boxfrom the top.

Color of box	Items in the box
	T-shirts, Shoes
	Jeans, Shorts
	Jackets, Raincoats
White	
Red	Toys, Bags
Violet	

6) There are exactly four boxes in between the Pink andBlack box such that Pink is above the Black box.

Case I:

Color of box	Items in the box
Pink	T-shirts, Shoes
	Jeans, Shorts
	Jackets, Raincoats
White	
Red	Toys, Bags
Black	
Violet	

Case II:

Color of box	Items in the box
	T-shirts, Shoes
Pink	Jeans, Shorts
	Jackets, Raincoats
White	
Red	Toys, Bags
Black	
Violet	

7) Orange box is immediately below the Blue box. This isnot possible in case II therefore case II gets eliminated.

8) Black box contains caps and belts.

Color of box	Items in the box
Pink	T-shirts, Shoes
Blue	Jeans, Shorts
Orange	Jackets, Raincoats
White	
Red	Toys, Bags
Black	Caps, Belts
Green	
Violet	

9) Green box contains notebooks and pencils.

Color of box	Items in the box
Pink	T-shirts, Shoes
Blue	Jeans, Shorts
Orange	Jackets, Raincoats
White	
Red	Toys, Bags
Black	Caps, Belts
Green	Notebooks, Pencils
Violet	

10) Books are in the White box and books cannot be in thesame box with sports equipment and toiletries.

Color of box	Items in the box
Pink	T-shirts, Shoes
Blue	Jeans, Shorts
Orange	Jackets, Raincoats
White	Books, Board games
Red	Toys, Bags
Black	Caps, Belts

Green	Notebooks, Pencils
Violet	Sports equipment, Toiletries

71. Clearly, the White box is placed at the third position if starting with the Green box.

Hence, the correct option is (A).

72. Clearly, the Green box which contains pencils is in between the Black box and the box with toiletries.

Hence, the correct option is (D).

73. Clearly, the pair Blue box and t-shirts is the odd one as all the other pairs represents the box given and the item in immediately below box.

Hence, the correct option is (E).

74. Therefore, there are more than three boxes between the Orange box and the box with the sports equipment.

Hence, the correct option is (E).

75. Therefore, the Pink box contains shoes in it.

Hence, the correct option is (C).

76. Therefore, none of the statements is true.

Hence, the correct option is (E).

77. Statement: $B < S \leq Q < Y = X > C \geq J$

I. $S < Y \Rightarrow$ True (as $S \leq Q < Y \Rightarrow S < Y$)

II. $X > B \Rightarrow$ True (as $B < S \leq Q < Y = X \Rightarrow B < X \Rightarrow X > B$)

So, Both I and II are true.

Hence, the correct option is (D).

78. Given statements: $A < C = D < E$; $B = A > F$

On combining: $F < B = A < C = D < E$

I. $D > F \rightarrow$ True (as $F < A < C = D \rightarrow D > F$)

II. $B > E \rightarrow$ False (as $B < C = D < E \rightarrow B < E$)

Thus, the only conclusion I is true.

Hence, the correct option is (B).

79. Given statements: $D = X \geq C > S = F$; $D > Y \geq H \geq G$

On combination: $G \leq H \leq Y < D = X \geq C > S = F$

Conclusions:

I. $G \leq X \rightarrow$ False (as $G \leq H \leq Y < D = X$)

II. $D > F \rightarrow$ True (as $D = X \geq C > S = F$)

So, only conclusion II follows.

Hence, the correct option is (C).

80. Given statements: $G \geq M = P > C$; $Q < R = B < C$

On combining above two statements: $G \geq M = P > C > B = R > Q$

Conclusions:

I. $M > R \rightarrow$ True (as $M = P > C > B = R$)

II. G ≥ B → False (as G ≥ M = P > C > B → G > B)

So, only conclusion I follows.

Hence, the correct option is (A).

81. Given statements: M < N < U; R = T; U ≤ R ≥ V ≥ E

On combining: M < N < U ≤ R = T ≥ V ≥ E

I. T > N → True (as N < U ≤ R = T)

II. R ≥ E → True (as R ≥ V ≥ E)

III. M < T → True (as M < N < U ≤ R = T)

IV. T ≥ U → True (as U ≤ R = T)

Therefore, all are true.

Hence, the correct option is (A).

Ques (82-87):1) Anup is sitting second to the left of Arnav.

2) Arnav is sitting second to the left of Parul.

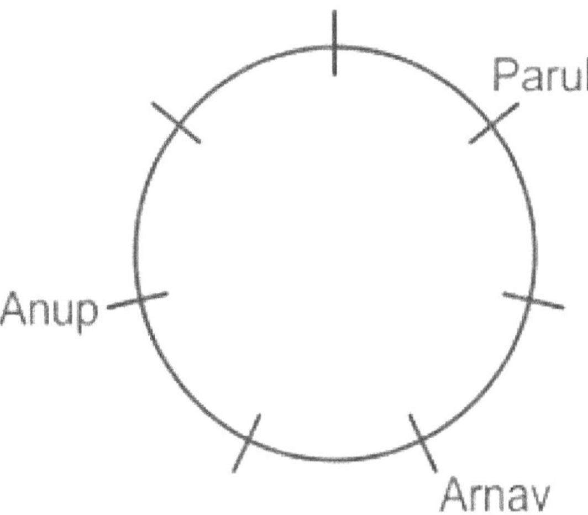

3) Parul is not sitting next to Swati and Samita.

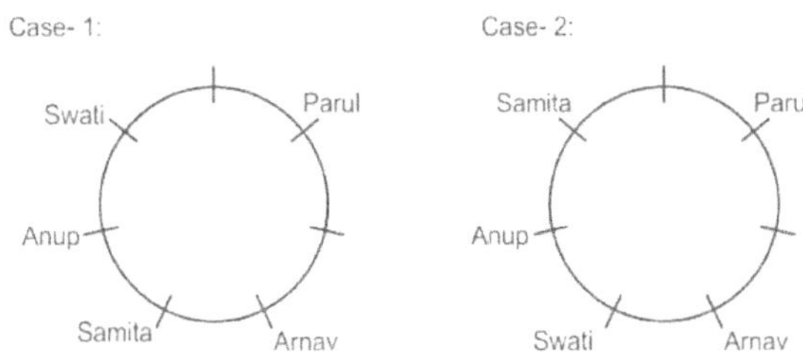

4) Ganga is not a neighbour of Anup and Swati.

5) Only two students will sit between Samita and Ganga.

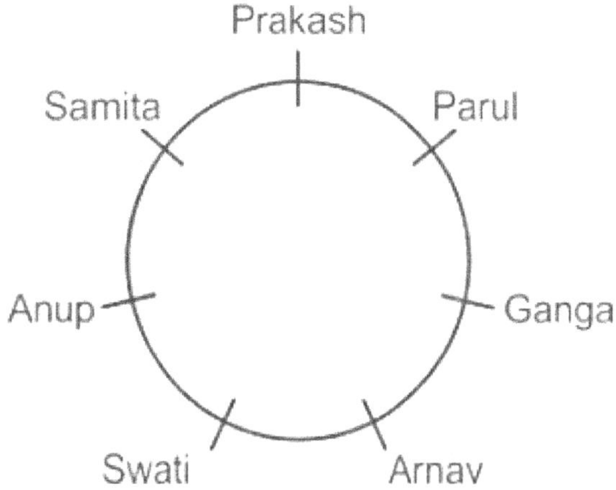

82. So, Prakash is sitting to the immediate right of Parul.

Hence, the correct option is (C).

83. If they are seated in a linear arrangement starting with Arnav at the left end.

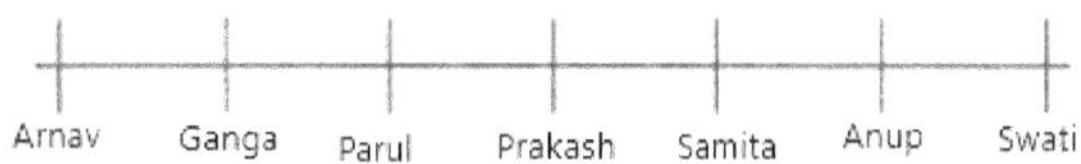

So, Samita is sitting in the third position from the right end.

Hence, the correct option is (C).

84. So, Anup is sitting between Swati and Samita.

Hence, the correct option is (B).

85. Samita is sitting second to the left of the one who is the immediate right of Anup.

Hence, the correct option is (A).

86. Five people are sitting between Prakash and Parul taking clockwise from Parul.

Hence, the correct option is (D).

87. So, Prakash is sitting between Samita and Parul.

Hence, the correct option is (B).

Ques (88-90): The figure according to the information given in the question will be as follows:

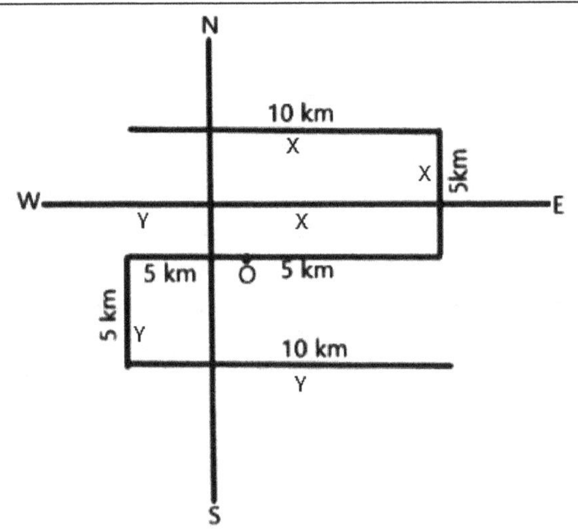

88. We know that, XY = XO + OY where O is the starting point.

By Pythagoras' theorem,

$OY^2 = AO^2 + OY^2$

$OY^2 = 5^2 + 5^2 = 50$

Similarly, $OX^2 = 50$

$\Rightarrow OX = OY = 5\sqrt{2}$

Therefore, $XY = 2 \times 5\sqrt{2} = 10\sqrt{2}$

So, the shortest distance between the final positions of X and Y is $10\sqrt{2}$ km.

Hence, the correct option is (C).

89. We know that, $XY = XO + OY$ where O is the starting point.

By Pythagoras' theorem,

$OX^2 = BO^2 + BX^2$

$OX^2 = 5^2 + 5^2 = 50$

$\Rightarrow OX = 5\sqrt{2}$

So, the shortest distance between the final position of X and the starting point is $5\sqrt{2}$ km.

Hence, the correct option is (C).

90. So, Y is in South East direction with respect to X.

Hence, the correct option is (E).

91. The least possible Venn diagram for the given statements is as follows:

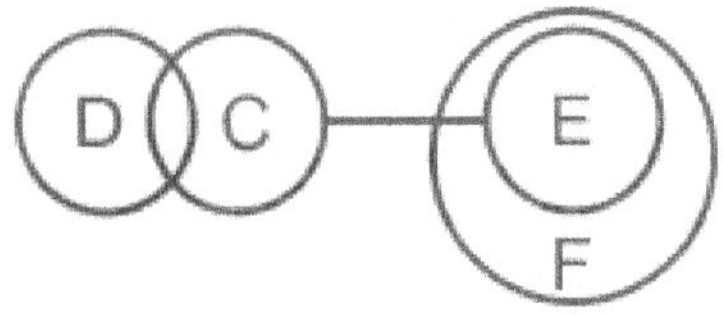

Conclusions:

I. No F is a C → False (It is possible but not definite so its false)

II. At least some D are F → False (It is possible but not definite so its false)

So, Neither I nor II follows.

Hence, the correct option is (A).

92. The least possible diagram is given below:

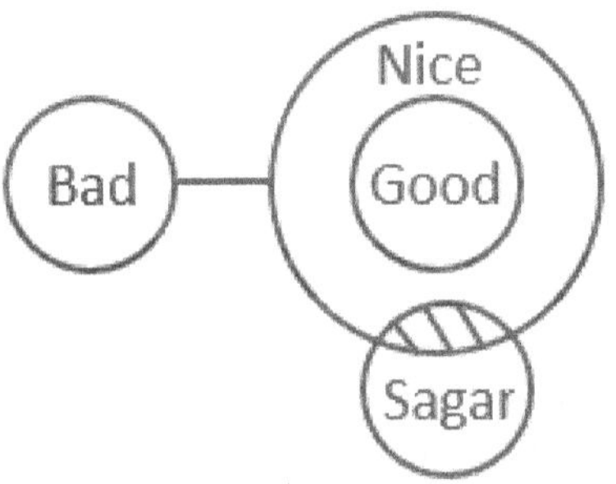

I. All Sagar can be Good → True (In statement it is clearly says Only a few Nice are Sagar and all Good are Nice)

II. Some Nice are not Bad → True (in statement it is clearly says No Bad are Good)

So, Both conclusion I and conclusion II follows.

Hence, the correct option is (E).

93. The least possible diagram for the given statements is as follows:

Conclusions:

I. No tiger is cat → True (It is definite)

II. Some tiger is cat → False (It is not possible as no horse is cat and all tiger is horse)

So, only I follow.

Hence, the correct option is (A).

94. The least possible diagram for the given statements is as follows:

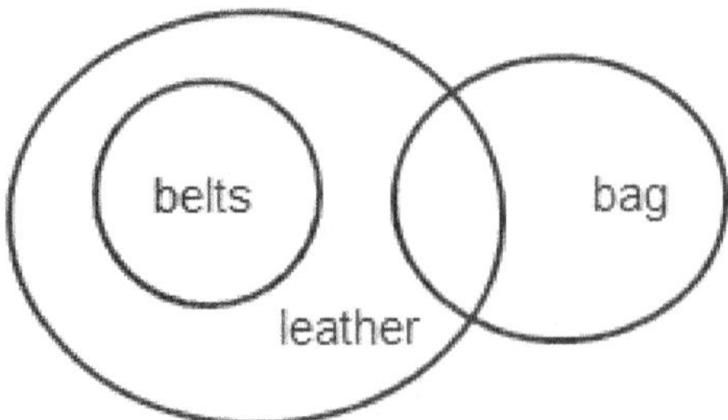

Conclusions:

I. All bags being leather is a possibility. → True (It is possible and in conclusion possibility is given)

II. No bag is a belt → False (It is possible but not definite)

So, only conclusion I follow.

Hence, the correct option is (A).

95. The least possible Venn diagram for the given statements is as follows:

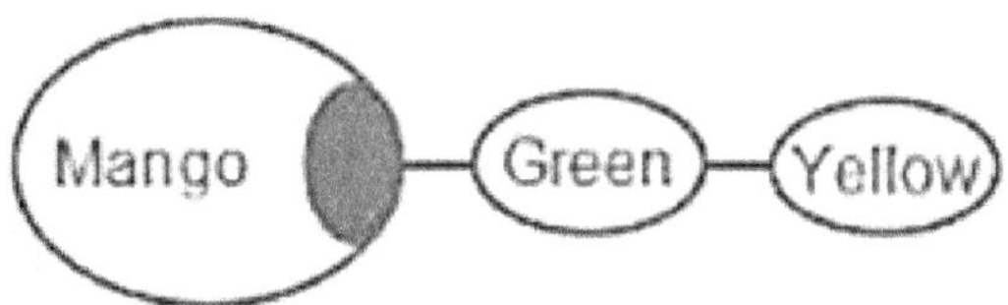

Conclusion:

I. Some mango can be yellow is a possibility → True (Possibility is true as shown below)

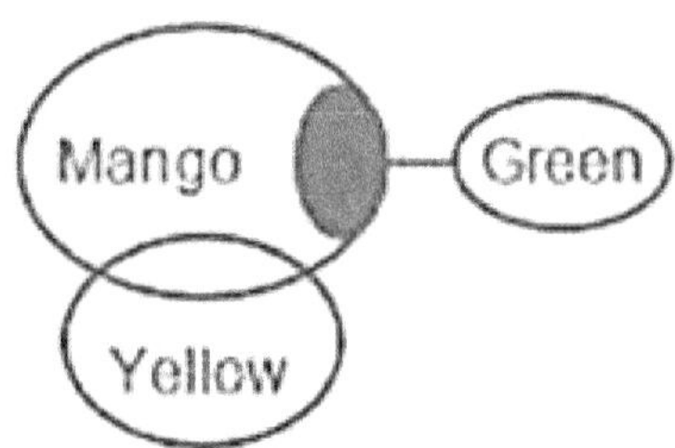

II. All green are mango → False (It is possible but not definite)

Thus, only conclusion I follow.

Hence, the correct option is (A).

Ques (96-100): First, let us decode the words,

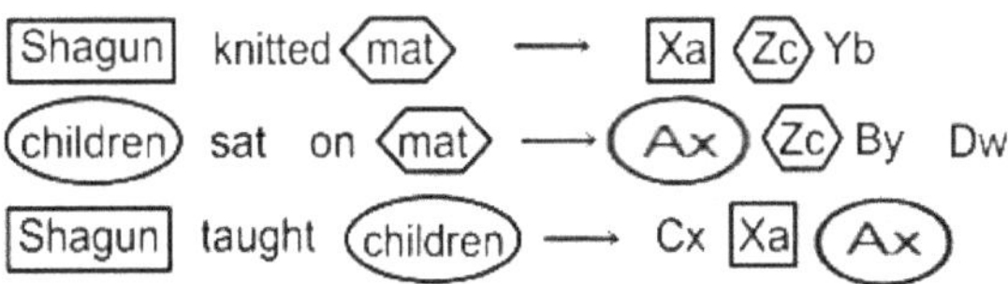

96. So, the possible code for 'children knitted Shawl' in the given code language is Ax Yb Sh.

Hence, the correct option is (B).

97. So, the code for 'taught' in the given code language is Cx.

Hence, the correct option is (D).

98. Code 'pi' represents 'he'

Code 'vi' represents 'should'

Code 'fi' represents 'do'

Code 'si' represents 'this'

So, the code 'pi vi fi si' is for the sentence 'he should do this'.

Hence, the correct option is (B).

99. So, if 'children on mat' is coded as 'Zc Ax Dw', then 'By' mean 'sat' in the given code language.

Hence, the correct option is (A).

100. So, the code for 'children' in the given code language is Ax.

Hence, the correct option is (C).

Test of English Language

Ques (1-5):Direction: In the given question, some part of the sentence may have errors. Find out which part of the sentence has an error and select the appropriate option. If a sentence is free from error, select 'No Error'.

Q.1 He has been (A) / toiling hardly (B) / to be able to (C) / provide for his family. (D) / No Error (E)

A. (A) **B.** (B) **C.** (C) **D.** (D)
E. (E)

Q.2 The brother-in-laws (A) / were very helpful (B) / and supportive of (C) / their choices. (D) / No Error (E)

A. (A) **B.** (B) **C.** (C) **D.** (D)
E. (E)

Q.3 All pieces (A)/ of informations (B) / given by her (C) / were accurate. (D) / No Error (E)

A. (A) **B.** (B) **C.** (C) **D.** (D)
E. (E)

Q.4 Three jawans of District (A) / Reserve Guard were killed (B) / while ten others were injured (C) / in an IED blast on Tuesday. (D) / No Error (E)

A. (A) **B.** (B) **C.** (C) **D.** (D)
E. (E)

Q.5 Despite having lost (A) / the match, the team was receive (B) / at the airport with (C) / a lot of enthusiasm. (D) / No Error (E)

A. (A) **B.** (B) **C.** (C) **D.** (D)
E. (E)

Ques (6-7):Directions: In the following sentence, five words are given in bold, out of which one word is misspelled. Find the misspelled word.

Q.6 Despite(A) the **completion**(B) of the **dilimitation**(C) commission's **exercise**(D), Legislative Assembly elections have still to be **announced**(E).

A. (A) **B.** (B) **C.** (C) **D.** (D)
E. (E)

Q.7 Our popular image of a party is that of the **classical**(A) mass party, which rises from **societal**(B) **movements**(C) and is **essentialy**(D) **internally**(E) democratic.

A. (A) **B.** (B) **C.** (C) **D.** (D)
E. (E)

Ques (8-12):Direction: Read the passage carefully and select the correct answer for the given blank out of the given alternatives.

Agriculture in India needs to become more sustainable even as small and marginal farmers (A) to build resilience against many threats. First, they remain price-takers and economically vulnerable, (B) to traders who set prices, and with limited opportunities to sell at a time of their choice. Further, decades of (C) agriculture have added to water stress and decline soil health. Farmers rely on groundwater for more than 60% of (D) needs. Chemical fertilizers, once used to (E) soil nutrients, have been applied so Intensively that the long-term health of soils is now of deep concern.

Q.8 Pick the appropriate word to be filled in blank (A).

A. Need **B.** Supervise
C. Struggle **D.** Negotiate
E. Address

Q.9 Pick the appropriate word to be filled in blank (B).

A. Naive **B.** Beholden
C. Favorable **D.** Unbound
E. Dominating

Q.10 Pick the appropriate word to be filled in blank (C).

A. Superficial **B.** Tiring
C. Fearless **D.** Undeveloped
E. Intensive

Q.11 Pick the appropriate word to be filled in blank (D).

A. Irrigation **B.** Drink
C. Energy **D.** Cultivate
E. Sow

Q.12 Pick the appropriate word to be filled in blank (E).

A. Grow **B.** Deplete
C. Accelerate **D.** Spread
E. Boost

Ques (13-17):Direction: Which of the option (A), (B), (C), and (D) given below, should replace the phrase printed in bold in the sentence to make it grammatically correct? If the sentence is correct as it is given and no correction is required, mark (E) as the answer.

Q.13 The focus is now on the manner in which the EC **is dealing of complaints** against Mr. Modi.

A. Deal with the complaints
B. Are dealing with the complaints
C. Is dealing with the complaints
D. Deal with the complaints
E. No replacement

Q.14 Bhavana is the only **student by Kerala** to rank among the 13 national toppers who secured 499 marks.

A. Students in Kerala **B.** Student from Kerala
C. Students of Kerala **D.** Student with Kerala
E. No replacement

Q.15 Contract workers in the various departments of the government-owned company have also not been **paid their wages since** the past few months.

A. Paying their wages since
B. Paid there wages for
C. Pay their wages since
D. Paid their wages for
E. No replacement

Q.16 The most relevant **part of the complaint** were the transfer orders and disciplinary inquiry against her.
A. Parts of the complaint
B. Part in the complaints
C. Parts about the complainants
D. Parties of the complaint
E. No replacement

Q.17 The stage is **all set** for the elections to the Mandal and Zilla Parishad territorial constituencies across the State.
A. All sets
B. All setting
C. Set out
D. All setted
E. No replacement required

Ques (18-22):Direction: From the given six sentences A, B, C, D, E and F rearrange the following in the proper sequence to form a meaningful paragraph; then answer the question given below them.

A. Union Law Minister Ravi Shankar Prasad said in the Lok Sabha on Wednesday that while public interest litigation (PIL) for securing the rights of the poor, the workers and against corrupt public servants were to be supported, governance through such petitions should not be done.

B. "Only those voted in by the people and who are accountable to Parliament have the right to govern and frame laws for the country. The High Courts and the Supreme Court do not have that right. This has been clearly stated in our Constitution", he said.

C. Based on the reports submitted by the arrears committee of various High Courts, it was resolved that they would assign top priority to the disposal of cases pending for more than five years and priority should be given for disposal of cases pending in the district courts for more than five years.

D. Mr Prasad owned up to filing several such petitions himself in cases challenging corrupt practices of politicians but said 'with great humility' that it was not the job of the courts to govern the country through them.

E. Responding to a query during Question Hour on the pendency of cases in various courts of law, Mr Prasad was asked by Laxmi Narayan Yadav, BJP MP from Sagar, whether an increase in the number of PIL petitions had contributed to the same.

F. Mr Prasad said more than 5,000 posts in the lower judiciary were lying vacant and the Central government was giving emphasis on filling the posts with fair representation from the SCs, STs, OBCs and minorities so that they could occupy posts in the higher judiciary.

Q.18 Which of the following should be the **SECOND** sentence after rearrangement?

[SBI PO, 2021], [IBPS PO, 2020]

A. E   **B.** D   **C.** B   **D.** F
E. C

Q.19 Which of the following should be the **THIRD** sentence after rearrangement?

[SBI PO, 2021]

A. C   **B.** D   **C.** B   **D.** F
E. E

Q.20 Which of the following should be the **FOURTH** sentence after rearrangement?
A. F   **B.** E   **C.** B   **D.** C
E. D

Q.21 Which of the following should be the **FIFTH** sentence after rearrangement?
A. E   **B.** F   **C.** D   **D.** C
E. B

Q.22 Which of the following should be the **SIXTH** sentence after rearrangement?
A. D   **B.** E   **C.** F   **D.** C
E. B

Ques (23-32):Directions: Read the passage given below and answer the questions that follow by choosing the correct/most appropriate options:

Adrift at the end of the 20th century, the world of the 21st century is proving to be highly **chaotic**. Geopolitical experts in the West confine their findings at present solely to the impact of the Russia-Ukraine **conflict**, believing that this alone would determine not only war and peace but also other critical aspects as well. This tends to be a **myopic** view, for the Ukraine-Russia conflict is only one of the many strands currently altering the **contours** of world governance. Significant developments are also taking place in many other regions of the globe, which will have equal if not more relevance to the future of the international governance system.

What the German Chancellor, Olaf Scholz, said in June 2022 at the end of a three-day gathering of G7 leaders in the Bavarian Alps, sums up the prevailing mood overall, viz., "a time of uncertainty lies ahead of us. We cannot foresee how it will end". In this case, possibly, the German Chancellor was referring only to the fallout from the Ukraine-Russia conflict, for he clearly did not **reckon** with the fact that many other momentous changes were taking place outside Europe, and which are already beginning to dictate the new order of things. The obsession in the West over the outcome ____ the Russia-Ukraine conflict, giving it importance overriding all else, is indeed misleading.

European leaders tending to look inwards is, perhaps, not surprising. Europe has been undergoing several major changes in recent months. Germany, which has steered European politics for almost two decades under Angela Merkel, now has a Chancellor (Olaf Scholz) who has hardly any foreign policy

experience. Without Germany's steadying hand, Europe would be virtually adrift in troubled waters. Emmanuel Macron may have been re-elected as the President of France, but his wings have been clipped with the Opposition now gaining a majority in the French National Assembly. This has damaged his image, and Mr Macron can hardly be expected to provide the kind of leadership that Europe needs at present. The United Kingdom is in deep trouble, if not **disarray**. Consequently, at a time when actual and moral issues require both **deft** and firm handling, Europe appears **rudderless**.

Compounding this situation is the negative economic impact of the war in Ukraine. This is being felt not only in Europe but also across the globe. What is evident already is that apart from the spiralling cost of energy, food and fertilizers, quite a few countries confront the **spectre** of food scarcity given that Ukraine and Russia were generally viewed as the granaries of the world. **Apart from this, nations do face several other problems as well, including, in some case, a foreign exchange crisis.** Many of these problems may have existed earlier but have been **aggravated** by the ongoing conflict. The impact is being felt now well beyond Europe.

Q.23 According to the passage, which country or continent has been undergoing several major changes in recent months?

A. France **B.** Germany
C. Europe **D.** Russia
E. Ukraine

Q.24 According to the passage, what did the German Chancellor, Olaf Scholz, say in June 2022 at the end of a three-day gathering of G7 leaders in the Bavarian Alps?

A. A time of uncertainty lies ahead of us.
B. Changes are beginning to dictate the new order of things.
C. Global developments will relevance to the future of the international governance system.
D. There is a negative economic impact of the war in Ukraine.
E. The impact is being felt now well beyond Europe.

Q.25 What will fit in the blank taken from the passage:

The obsession in the West over the outcome _____ the Russia-Ukraine conflict, giving it importance overriding all else, is indeed misleading.

A. on **B.** at **C.** in **D.** of
E. to

Q.26 In this question, a sentence (in bold) from the passage has been divided into four parts (A), (B), (C) and (D). Read the sentence to find out whether there is any grammatical error in it. The error if any will be in one part of the sentence. If there is no error the answer is 'No Error/(E)'. Ignore the error of punctuation if any.

Apart from this, nations do face (A)/ several other problems as well, (B)/ including, in some case, (C)/ a foreign exchange crisis. (D)/ No Error (E)

A. (A) **B.** (B) **C.** (C) **D.** (D)
E. (E)

Q.27 Which of the following is/are correct according to the given passage?
A. The world of the 21st century is proving to be highly chaotic.

B. Significant developments are also taking place in many other regions of the globe.
C. European leaders tending to look inwards is, perhaps, most surprising.

A. Only A **B.** Only B
C. Only C **D.** Both A and B
E. Both A and C

Q.28 Choose the Antonym of the word 'reckon'.

A. Assume **B.** Believe
C. Conjecture **D.** Disbelieve
E. Bargain

Q.29 Choose the Synonym of the word 'adrift'.

A. Hooked **B.** Rigid
C. Afloat **D.** Anchored
E. Rooted

Q.30 What is the Tone of the passage?

A. Narrative **B.** Introspective
C. Humanistic **D.** Apathetic
E. Expository

Q.31 Which of the following is/are incorrect according to the given passage?

A. The Ukraine-Russia conflict is the only strand currently altering the contour of world governance.

B. Emmanuel Macron's wings have been clipped with the Opposition now gaining a majority in the French National Assembly.

C. Positive Economic impact is being felt not only in Europe but also across the globe.

A. Only A **B.** Only B
C. Both A and B **D.** Both B and C
E. Both A and C

Q.32 What is the central theme of the passage?

A. Changing politics of Europe
B. Global order caught up in chaos.
C. Impact of Russian invasion on Europe
D. Economic impact of the war in Ukraine
E. Geopolitics of the West

Ques (33-37):Directions: The question below has two blanks, each blank indicating that something has been omitted. Choose the set of words for each blank that best fit the meaning of the sentence as a whole.

Q.33 The _____ billionaire had plenty of money but still _____ from anyone who could increase his wealth.

A. crept, content **B.** lurked, sated
C. greedy, stole **D.** crawled, averse
E. slid, impassive

Q.34 The mother-in-law ranted at her daughter-in-law about her _____ for eating and _____ to work.

A. vibrant, able **B.** charge, outlay
C. fondness, aversion **D.** rare, unusual
E. exceptional, vivid

Q.35 The advertisements are ______ to ______ the company's image.

A. abrupt, abuse

B. casual, criticize

C. instinctive, scold

D. intended, improve

E. random, deplete

Q.36 He had been miraculously ______ from almost ______ death.

A. saved, certain

B. ignored, adjustable

C. neglected, changeable

D. disregarded, negotiable

E. damaged, indefinite

Q.37 Fresh food is so ______ that prices have ______.

A. crawled, abundant

B. poked, generous

C. darted, tolerable

D. surged, lavish

E. scarce, rocketed

Ques (38-40):Directions: In the following question, a sentence is given with three words marked as (A), (B) and (C). These words may or may not be placed at their correct places. Four options with different arrangements of these words have been provided. Mark the option with the correct arrangement as the answer. If no rearrangement is required, mark option (E) as your answer.

Q.38 The capacity to form **desires** (A) and to reason allows humans can go **beyond** (B) this minimum state, with a much greater possible range of **concepts** (C) and aversions.

A. BAC

B. BCA

C. CAB

D. CBA

E. No rearrangement required

Q.39 Hedonism, as Socrates **minimize** (A) it, is the motivation wherein a person will **described** (B) in a manner that will maximize pleasure and **behave** (C) pain.

A. BAC

B. BCA

C. CAB

D. CBA

E. No rearrangement required

Q.40 Populations (A) over Japanese ethnic and immigrant groups during the Second World War **Concern** (B) the Canadian and U.S. governments to intern most of their ethnically Japanese **prompted** (C) in the western portions of North America.

A. BAC

B. BCA

C. CAB

D. CBA

E. No rearrangement required

Test of Numerical Ability

Ques (41-43):Direction: What will come in the place of the question mark (?) in the following question?

Q.41 $\sqrt{144} \div 4 \times 6 - \sqrt{196} \div \sqrt{49} + 5 =?$

[SBI Clerk, 2020]

A. 19　　　**B.** 20　　　**C.** 21　　　**D.** 22

E. 23

Q.42 263 – 345 + 180 × 3% of 20 – 1 = ?

A. 30　　　**B.** 24　　　**C.** 25　　　**D.** 26

E. 29

Q.43 $4\frac{1}{5} \times 3\frac{4}{7} \div \frac{5}{3} + 12 =?$

A. 20　　　**B.** 30　　　**C.** 21　　　**D.** 25

E. 40

Ques (44-47):Direction: What should come in place of the question mark (?) in the following question?

Q.44 $15 \times 184 + 27 - 59 = ? + \dfrac{156}{12}$

[SBI Clerk, 2019]

A. 2175　　　**B.** 2517　　　**C.** 2715　　　**D.** 3000

E. 2500

Q.45 $15 + \left\{ \left(2\frac{4}{7} \times 5\frac{4}{2} \right) \div \left(6\frac{2}{9} \times 2\frac{4}{7} \right) \right\} =?$

[SBI Clerk, 2019]

A. 153　　　**B.** $\frac{129}{8}$　　　**C.** $\frac{160}{8}$　　　**D.** $\frac{65}{4}$

E. $\frac{145}{8}$

Q.46 46 + 25% of (? + 1289) = 1340

[SBI Clerk, 2019]

A. 3880　　　　　**B.** 3887

C. 8387　　　　　**D.** 3778

E. None of these

Q.47 $2\frac{1}{9} \times 2\frac{2}{19} \div 6\frac{2}{3} =? -1\frac{1}{2}$

[SBI Clerk, 2019]

A. $1\frac{5}{6}$　　　**B.** $2\frac{1}{6}$　　　**C.** $3\frac{1}{2}$　　　**D.** $2\frac{1}{2}$

E. $2\frac{5}{6}$

Q.48 A man covered a certain distance at some speed. If he had moved 3 kmph faster, he would have taken 40 minutes less. If he had moved 2 kmph slower, he would have taken 40 minutes more. What is the distance in km?

A. 36　　　**B.** 40　　　**C.** 38　　　**D.** 42

E. 50

Q.49 Three numbers are in the ratio of 5 : 4 : 8. The sum of first number and second number is equal to sum of third number and 18. Find the difference between third number and second number.

A. 90　　　**B.** 72　　　**C.** 108　　　**D.** 54

E. 60

Ques (50-54):Direction: In each of the following number series, the wrong number is given, find out that number.

Q.50 5, 7, 11, 19, 36, 67

A. 36　　　B. 11　　　C. 67　　　D. 5
E. 19

Q.51 65, 66, 134, 408, 1624, 8125
A. 8125　　　B. 66　　　C. 134　　　D. 408
E. 1624

Q.52 121, 144, 183, 204, 241, 282
A. 241　　　B. 144　　　C. 204　　　D. 282
E. 183

Q.53 25, 200, 45, 320, 64, 512
A. 200　　　B. 45　　　C. 64　　　D. 512
E. 320

Q.54 25, 13, 14, 22.5, 49, 120
A. 49　　　B. 14　　　C. 22.5　　　D. 120
E. 25

Q.55 The average of (33, 45, 65 and 80) and (21, 9, 11 and 50) is X and Y, respectively. Find the value of 2(X + Y).
A. 54　　　B. 78.5　　　C. 157　　　D. 153
E. 145

Q.56 A boat running upstream takes 8 hours 48 minutes to cover a certain distance, while it takes 4 hours to cover the same distance running downstream. What is the ratio between the speed of the boat and speed of the water current respectively?
A. $2:1$　　　　　　B. $3:2$
C. $8:3$　　　　　　D. $9:5$
E. None of these

Q.57 12 years ago, age of P was 3 times the age of Q. After 12 years, ratio of ages of Q to P will be $2:3$. What is the present age of P?
A. 54 years　　　　　B. 36 years
C. 24 years　　　　　D. 144 years
E. 150 years

Q.58 The area of the four walls of a room is 8460 square metre. If the length and height of the room are in the ratio of 7 : 2 and the height and breadth in the ratio of 5 : 6, then the area of the foot is (in square metre).
A. 3000　　　B. 3200　　　C. 3780　　　D. 4500
E. 4125

Ques (59-63):Direction: Study the given bar graph and answer the following questions accordingly.

The bar graph shows the three different types of pizzas sold by Pizza Hut in four different weeks.

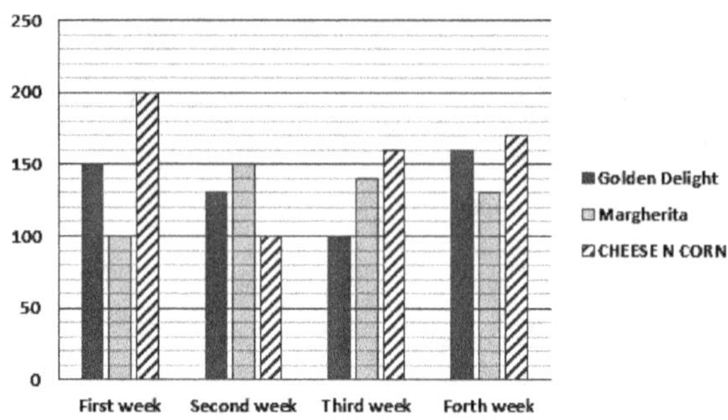

Q.59 The number of Golden Delight pizzas sold in the first and second week is what percent more/less than the number of CHEESE N CORN pizzas sold in the first and second week?
A. 7.14% more　　　　　B. 6.66% less
C. 6.66% more　　　　　D. 7.14% less
E. None of these

Q.60 What is the ratio between the number of Margherita pizzas sold in third and fourth weeks, and the number of CHEESE N CORN pizzas sold in first and third weeks?
A. $3:4$　　　　　　B. $4:3$
C. $1:4$　　　　　　D. $3:5$
E. None of these

Q.61 What is the average number of Margheritas sold in the second, third and fourth weeks?
A. 150　　　　　　B. 160
C. 140　　　　　　D. 120
E. None of these

Q.62 What is the difference between the number of all pizzas sold by Pizza Hut in the first week and the fourth week?
A. 20　　　　　　B. 10
C. 30　　　　　　D. 40
E. None of these

Q.63 What is the total number of all pizzas sold in the first two weeks?
A. 630　　　　　　B. 730
C. 830　　　　　　D. 430
E. None of these

Q.64 A man wants to invest Rs. 40,440 in bank account of his two sons whose age were 12 years and 16 years in such a way that they will get equal amount at age of 20 years@$33\frac{1}{3}$% per annum compounded annually. Find the share of younger son?
A. Rs. 30,720　　　　　B. Rs. 9,720
C. Rs. 10,110　　　　　D. Rs. 9,270
E. Rs. 10,310

Q.65 The cost price of an item is INR 500. The manufacturer sells it to the wholesaler at a profit of 20% and the wholesaler sells it to the retailer at 30% profit and the retailer sells it to the customer at 50% profit. Find the cost price of item for the customer.

A. INR 1100   **B.** INR 1205
C. INR 1170   **D.** INR 1000
E. INR 1060

Ques (66-68):Direction: What will come in place of question mark (?) in the following question?

Q.66 $(3)^{-26} \times (18)^{12} \times (2)^{-11} \times (2)^{2} =?$

A. $\frac{2}{3}$ **B.** $\frac{5}{9}$
C. $\frac{16}{27}$ **D.** $\frac{8}{9}$
E. None of these

Q.67 $10 - 1\frac{2}{9} \text{ of } 3\frac{3}{11} \div \left(6\frac{3}{7} \text{ of } \frac{7}{9}\right) = ?$

A. $\frac{22}{13}$ **B.** $\frac{49}{5}$ **C.** $\frac{42}{5}$ **D.** $\frac{46}{5}$
E. $\frac{73}{5}$

Q.68 $\frac{9}{5} \times 2\frac{3}{4} \div \frac{5}{8} + \frac{9}{2} \times \frac{5}{7} - \frac{18}{25} =?$

A. $\frac{179}{70}$ **B.** $\frac{729}{70}$ **C.** $\frac{269}{70}$ **D.** $\frac{169}{70}$
E. None

Q.69 The ratio of male and female employees in a company is 5 : 3. If 40% of males and 20% of female employees earn more than Rs. 50000 per month, then calculate the percentage of employees who do not earn more than Rs. 50000?

A. 55%   **B.** 50%
C. 60%   **D.** 67.5%
E. None of these

Q.70 Ritu started a business by investing Rs. 4800, after 3-months, Rima joined her by investing Rs. 3600 and after another 3-month Sima joined by investing 5400, if annual profit is 238000. Find difference in profit of Ritu and Sima?

A. 59000   **B.** 49000
C. 29000   **D.** 24000
E. None of these

Test of Reasoning

Q.71 Directions: In the following question assuming the given statements to be true, find which of the conclusion among given conclusions is/are definitely true and then give your answers accordingly.

Statements:

D > A ≥ M ≤ N; M ≥ E < L

Conclusions:

I. D > E

II. N ≤ A

III. A ≥ L

IV. L < D

A. Only III is true
B. Only I is true
C. Only II is true
D. None is true
E. Only I and IV are true

Q.72 Directions: In the following question assuming the given statements to be true, find which of the conclusion among given three conclusions is /are definitely true and then give your answers accordingly.

Statements: A ≥ C; O < C; O = E; E ≥ D

Conclusions:

I. A ≥ O

II. A > O

III. O ≥ D

A. None is true
B. Only I is true
C. Only II and III are true
D. Only I and III are true
E. All are true

Q.73 Directions: In the following question assuming the given statements to be true, find which of the conclusion among given three conclusions is/are definitely true and then give your answers accordingly.

Statements: O ≥ U; Q ≥ S; S ≤ O; G ≤ U

Conclusions:

I. O ≥ G

II. Q ≤ U

III. S ≥ G

A. None is true
B. Only I is true
C. Only I and II is true
D. Only II and III is true
E. Only III is true

Q.74 Direction: In the following question assuming the given statements to be true, find which of the conclusion among given three conclusions is /are definitely true and then give your answers accordingly.

Statements: E ≥ I; I ≥ J; R > J; R = P

Conclusions:

I. E ≥ J

II. I > P

III. J < P

A. Only I and II are true
B. Only I is true
C. Only II and III are true
D. Only III is true
E. Only I and III are true

Q.75 Direction: In the following question assuming the given statements to be true, find which of the conclusion among given conclusions is/are definitely true and then give your answers accordingly.

Statements:

Q = X < R < G; G ≥ T < Y; O > X

Conclusions:

I. O > Q

II. O > G

III. Q = Y

A. Only III is true
B. Only I is true
C. Only I and II are true
D. Either I or III is true
E. Only II is true

Ques (76-81):Direction: Read the following information carefully and answer the questions given below.

Eight persons Ds, Fg, Lm, Ms, Nd, Pe, Ps, and Xy are sitting around a circular table but not necessarily in the same order. Some of them are facing away from centre and some of them are facing towards the centre.

Pe is sitting third to the left of Lm who is facing towards the centre. Ms and Fg are immediate neighbour of Pe. Nd is second to the right of Fg. Fg and Ms face the same direction but opposite to Pe. Ds is not an immediate neighbour of Nd. Xy is second to the right of Ds. Both the immediate neighbour of Nd face the same direction as Ms. Lm faces the same direction as the person who is sitting second to his right.

Q.76 Who is sitting opposite to Nd?
A. Xy   **B.** Ms   **C.** Pe   **D.** Ps
E. Lm

Q.77 How many persons are sitting between Fg and Xy when counting from the left of Xy?
A. Two   **B.** One   **C.** Five   **D.** Three
E. Four

Q.78 How many persons are facing away from centre between Nd and Ds counting from right of Nd?
A. One   **B.** Three   **C.** Four   **D.** Two
E. Zero

Q.79 Who is sitting opposite to Ds?
A. Xy   **B.** Fg   **C.** Pe   **D.** Lm
E. Ps

Q.80 Who sits second to the left of Ps?
A. Pe   **B.** Ms
C. Lm   **D.** Xy
E. None of the above

Q.81 How many persons are facing away from the centre?
A. Five   **B.** Three   **C.** Four   **D.** Two
E. One

Ques (82-84):Direction: Study the information given below carefully and answer the questions that follow.

There are 10 persons A, B, C, D, E, F, G, H, I and J in a family. A is 10 km north of B. E is 16 km south of F. G is 8 km east of F and 6 km north of H. I is situated just in middle of E and D while J is situated in middle of F and E. D is 10 km north of C. E is 8 km west of D. C is 20 km east of B.

Q.82 Which of the following combination forms a straight line?
A. F, J, I   **B.** G, H, B   **C.** F, J, E   **D.** A, B, D
E. A, E, C

Q.83 What is the minimum distance between F and H?

A. 9 km   **B.** 10 km   **C.** 11 km   **D.** 14 km
E. 8 km

Q.84 What is the distance between A and E.
A. 16 km   **B.** 18 km   **C.** 20 km   **D.** 12 km
E. 10 km

Ques (85-88):Direction: In the question below, there are two statements followed by two conclusions numbered I and II. You have to take the given statements to be true even if they seem to be at variance with commonly known facts. Read all the conclusions and then decide which of the given conclusions logically follows from the given statements disregarding commonly known facts.

Q.85 Statements:
Some lime are light.
Only few lemon are light.
Conclusions:
I. Some lemon are lime.
II. All light are lemon.
A. Only conclusion I follows
B. Only conclusion II follows
C. Both I and II follow
D. Neither I nor II follows
E. Either I or II follows

Q.86 Statements:
Some bright are light.
Only few bright are fight.
Conclusions:
I. Some fight are light.
II. All fight are bright.
A. Only conclusion I follows
B. Only conclusion II follows
C. Both I and II follow
D. Neither I nor II follows
E. Either I or II follows

Q.87 Statements:
Some hell are heaven.
Only few heaven are life.
Conclusions:
I. Some hell are life.
II. All life are heaven is a possibility.
A. Only conclusion I follows
B. Only conclusion II follows
C. Both I and II follow
D. Neither I nor II follows
E. Either I or II follows

Q.88 Statements:
Some sea are song.
Only few song are ocean.
Conclusions:
I. Some sea are ocean.
II. All ocean are song.

A. Only conclusion I follows

B. Only conclusion II follows

C. Both I and II follows

D. Neither I nor II follows

E. Either I or II follows

Q.89 Direction: In the question below, there are two statements followed by two conclusions numbered I and II. You have to take the given statements to be true even if they seem to be at variance with commonly known facts. Read all the conclusions and then decide which of the given conclusions logically follows from the given statements disregarding the commonly known facts.

Statements:

Some spades are diamond.

Only few diamond are club.

Conclusions:

I. All diamond are club.

II. Some spades are club.

A. Only conclusion I follows

B. Only conclusion II follows

C. Both I and II follow

D. Neither I nor II follows

E. Either I or II follows

Ques (90-95):Direction: Study the given information carefully and answer the following question below.

There are 8 students chosen for the final round of the 'Fancy Dress Competition. All the students are wearing the costumes of different superheroes. The Student's presenting the character names were written inside the boxes and they need to do mimicry of the character's costume they are wearing. Students presenting these superheroes:- Aquaman, Antman, Batman, Hellboy, Ironman, Spiderman, Superman, and X-men. Each student has taken a box and got the number of their performance. Now, we need to arrange the box according to the order of their performance.

At least six boxes are kept below box Superman. There are four boxes are placed between the box Aquaman and the box Antman. The box Aquaman is placed neither below box Antman nor at an even number. The same number of boxes are placed above the box Hellboy as below the box Spiderman and none of the two boxes is placed at the top or bottom of the stack. The box batman and the box X-Men are placed above the box Ironman but below the box Superman. The box ironman and the box Antman are not placed next to each other. The box Batman is placed in the middle of the boxes starting with the same alphabets.

Q.90 If all boxes are arranged in alphabetic order then how many boxes will remain in it's own place?

A. 3　　　　**B.** 2

C. 1　　　　**D.** 4

E. None of these

Q.91 Which boxes are placed immediate above or below to Box X-Men?

A. Antman and Ironman

B. Hellboy and Ironman

C. Spiderman and Aquaman

D. Only Superman

E. Spiderman and Superman

Q.92 How many students are doing mimicry after Batman?

A. 2　　　**B.** 5　　　**C.** 3　　　**D.** 6

E. 4

Q.93 How many boxes are between the box Spiderman and the box Hellboy?

A. 2　　　　　　　**B.** 4

C. 3　　　　　　　**D.** 0

E. None of these

Q.94 Who is the first person to do mimicry?

A. Spiderman　　　　**B.** Antman

C. Hellboy　　　　　**D.** Aquaman

E. Ironman

Q.95 How many boxes are between the box Superman and the box X-Men?

A. 2　　　**B.** 1　　　**C.** 5　　　**D.** 4

E. 3

Ques (96-100):Directions: Study the following information carefully and answer the questions given below.

In a certain code language:

'India is the biggest country' is written as 'ak bs ct gk np',

'srilanka is the smallest country' is written as 'pk bs ct np st,'

'china is the biggest country' is written as 'ng bs ct gk np' and

'we don't use the glass' is written as 'kt up mx ct ta',

Q.96 What is the code for 'country' in the given code language?

A. bs　　　　　　　**B.** ng

C. np　　　　　　　**D.** Either (A) or (C)

E. None of the above

Q.97 What is the code for 'is the' in the given code language?

A. bs ct　　　　　**B.** np ct

C. bs gk　　　　　**D.** Either (A) or (B)

E. ng bs

Q.98 What is the code for 'china' in the given code language?

A. ak　　　**B.** pk　　　**C.** ng　　　**D.** gk

E. kt

Q.99 What can be the possible code for 'don't use' in the given code language?

A. up mx　　**B.** ct st　　**C.** kt ct　　**D.** up ct

E. mx ct

Q.100 What can be possible code for 'biggest' in the given code language?

A. pk　　　　　　　**B.** st

C. gk　　　　　　　**D.** ng

E. None of these

// Smart Answer Sheet //

| Correct | Indicates percentage of students who answered questions correctly. |
| Skipped | Indicates percentage of students who skipped questions. |

Q.	Ans.	Correct / Skipped	Q.	Ans.	Correct / Skipped	Q.	Ans.	Correct / Skipped	Q.	Ans.	Correct / Skipped	Q.	Ans.	Correct / Skipped
1	B	48.15 % / 33.67 %	17	E	58.89 % / 38.81 %	33	C	45.97 % / 30.07 %	49	B	64.23 % / 32.31 %	65	C	59.82 % / 30.18 %
2	A	77.78 % / 20.28 %	18	A	65.28 % / 30.49 %	34	C	50.92 % / 47.71 %	50	A	53.14 % / 44.69 %	66	D	61.39 % / 34.91 %
3	B	78.44 % / 21.18 %	19	B	51.76 % / 42.41 %	35	D	67.92 % / 30.04 %	51	D	18.4 % / 81.57 %	67	D	56.92 % / 36.56 %
4	E	64.04 % / 32.44 %	20	C	65.68 % / 31.72 %	36	A	50.32 % / 32.56 %	52	E	53.84 % / 36.19 %	68	B	49.54 % / 38.35 %
5	B	22.71 % / 67.69 %	21	B	42.07 % / 56.38 %	37	E	63.7 % / 34.07 %	53	B	15.11 % / 80.67 %	69	D	43.04 % / 55.76 %
6	C	58.08 % / 38.29 %	22	D	55.69 % / 35.22 %	38	D	54.12 % / 38.46 %	54	A	81.34 % / 12.29 %	70	B	50.29 % / 42.29 %
7	D	54.45 % / 41.55 %	23	C	40.42 % / 58.85 %	39	B	47.45 % / 37.09 %	55	C	66.45 % / 31.23 %	71	B	52.57 % / 37.8 %
8	C	55.59 % / 34.02 %	24	A	66.47 % / 33.34 %	40	B	64.14 % / 35.36 %	56	C	47.88 % / 46.12 %	72	C	46.76 % / 36.82 %
9	B	47.42 % / 47.81 %	25	D	48.06 % / 36.21 %	41	C	87.72 % / 10.46 %	57	B	21.39 % / 77.11 %	73	B	43.52 % / 49.94 %
10	E	60.43 % / 30.75 %	26	C	58.14 % / 36.58 %	42	C	40.4 % / 54.39 %	58	C	67.98 % / 30.37 %	74	E	65.69 % / 32.22 %
11	A	68.39 % / 31.41 %	27	D	46.54 % / 53.3 %	43	C	53.93 % / 43.61 %	59	B	10.71 % / 84.9 %	75	B	58.26 % / 33.68 %
12	E	50.88 % / 33.01 %	28	D	61.85 % / 38.02 %	44	C	40.15 % / 57.38 %	60	A	64.75 % / 30.18 %	76	B	46.35 % / 33.22 %
13	C	83.73 % / 11.42 %	29	C	44.97 % / 48.0 %	45	B	11.4 % / 75.39 %	61	C	46.72 % / 36.07 %	77	A	59.15 % / 36.36 %
14	B	55.05 % / 38.82 %	30	E	69.28 % / 30.19 %	46	B	63.71 % / 34.22 %	62	B	54.48 % / 32.74 %	78	B	51.82 % / 40.61 %
15	D	80.32 % / 10.25 %	31	E	49.25 % / 42.88 %	47	B	68.49 % / 30.29 %	63	C	41.0 % / 54.78 %	79	E	57.62 % / 41.95 %
16	A	85.56 % / 14.02 %	32	B	45.44 % / 46.9 %	48	B	53.21 % / 42.44 %	64	B	65.41 % / 33.3 %	80	A	55.92 % / 40.05 %

Q.	Ans.	Correct		Q.	Ans.	Correct		Q.	Ans.	Correct		Q.	Ans.	Correct		Q.	Ans.	Correct
		Skipped				Skipped				Skipped				Skipped				Skipped
81	C	63.03 %		85	D	55.69 %		89	D	62.1 %		93	D	55.75 %		97	D	66.62 %
		31.46 %				39.53 %				30.02 %				32.31 %				32.73 %
82	C	49.15 %		86	D	69.43 %		90	C	46.47 %		94	D	55.94 %		98	C	44.11 %
		46.4 %				30.15 %				39.17 %				33.44 %				35.81 %
83	B	50.46 %		87	B	60.52 %		91	A	44.47 %		95	D	46.6 %		99	A	44.3 %
		45.93 %				34.53 %				54.84 %				37.64 %				38.02 %
84	D	58.3 %		88	D	41.38 %		92	B	66.72 %		96	C	62.44 %		100	C	63.39 %
		37.19 %				37.76 %				32.15 %				32.23 %				35.44 %

Performance Analysis

Avg. Score (%)	60.0%
Toppers Score (%)	60.0%
Your Score	

//Hints and Solutions//

1. In the given sentence, the error in the part is the inappropriate use of the adverb.

Adverbs are words that are used to modify nouns, pronouns, verbs, adjectives, other adverbs, etc.

In the given statement, the word 'hardly' is being used to qualify a statement by saying that it is true to an insignificant degree.

For eg.- The little house in which he lived was hardly bigger than a hut.

Whereas from the sentence we can gather that he works hard to be able to provide for his family.

Therefore, we will replace 'hardly' with 'hard' to make the sentence grammatically correct.

The correct sentence will be: 'He has been toiling hard to be able to provide for his family.'

Hence, the correct option is (B).

2. In the given sentence, the error in the part is the inappropriate use of the noun number.

Nouns are words used to name person, place, animal, thing, emotion, or state.

In the given statement, the incorrect plural form of 'brother-in-law' is being used.

Compound nouns are made plural by adding 's' to the main word.

For eg.- Commander-in-chief - Commanders-in-chief, brother-in-law - brothers-in-law etc.

Therefore, we will replace 'brother-in-laws' with 'brothers-in-law' to make the sentence grammatically correct.

The correct sentence will be: 'The brothers-in-law were very helpful and supportive to their choices'.

Hence, the correct option is (A).

3. In the given sentence, the error in the part is the inappropriate use of the noun number.

Nouns are words used to name person, place, animal, thing, emotion, or state.

In the given statement, the incorrect plural form of 'information' is being used.

Nouns such as jewelry, evidence, information, work, etc are uncountable nouns and can't be made plural by adding 's/es' within a sentence.

Phrases like 'all pieces of', 'many kinds of', 'slices of' etc. are added before uncountable nouns to make them plural.

For eg.- Many kinds of furniture are available in that shop.

Therefore, we will replace 'informations' with 'information' to make the sentence grammatically correct.

The correct sentence will be: 'All pieces of information given by her were accurate.'

Hence, the correct option is (B).

4. The given sentence is in the past tense as can be seen by the use of the verbs 'killed' and 'injured' in the past tense.

There are no errors in the sentence.

Thus, the correct sentence is: 'Three jawans of District Reserve Guard were killed while ten others were injured in an IED blast on Tuesday.'

Hence, the correct option is (E).

5. The sentence is in the past tense as the event is already over, the match has been lost and the team has already arrived at the airport.

This can be seen by the usage of the verb 'lost' and 'was' in the past tense.

This means that the other verbs in the sentence should also be in agreement with this tense of the sentence.

So, 'receive' needs to be replaced with 'received' in order to make the sentence grammatically correct.

Thus, the correct sentence is: 'Despite having lost the match, the team was received at the airport with a lot of enthusiasm.'

Hence, the correct option is (B).

6. 'Despite' means Without being affected by; in spite of.

'Completion' means The action or process of completing or finishing something.

- 'Dilimitation': There is no such word in English or we can say that there is some spelling mistake in this word.

The correct spelling is 'Delimitation' means The action of fixing the boundary or limits of something.

'Exercise' means Activity requiring physical effort, carried out to sustain or improve health and fitness.

'Announced' means To make a formal public statement about a fact, occurrence, or intention.

Correct Sentence: Despite the completion of the delimitation commission's exercise, Legislative Assembly elections have still to be announced.

Hence, the correct option is (C).

7. 'Classical' means Traditional, not modern.

'Societal' means Relating to society or social relations.

'Movements' means General activity or bustle.

'Essentialy': There is no such word in English or we can say that there is some spelling mistake in this word.

- The correct spelling is 'Essentially' means When you consider the basic or most important part of something.

'Internally' means With reference to the inner surface or structure of something; inside.

Correct Sentence: Our popular image of a party is that of the classical mass party, which rises from societal movements and is essentially internally democratic.

Hence, the correct option is (D).

8. In the passage difficulties faced by farmers have been discussed. It mentions the need for agriculture in India to become more sustainable. The reason behind this is to help small and marginal farmers to build resilience against many threats. This means they are facing problems currently. 'Resilience' means capacity to recover quickly from difficulties.

In the context of the passage, only Option (C) i.e. 'struggle' fits in.

Hence, the correct option is (C).

9. In the sentence, the plight of farmers' obligation towards traders has been mentioned. 'Beholden' means feeling you have a duty to someone because they have done something for you. In the given context, it implies the sense of being trapped.

Hence, the correct option is (B).

10. In the blank we need an appropriate adjective for an agriculture practice. Among given options, only suitable word is 'Intensive' which in regard to agricultural practices implies, aiming to achieve maximum production within a limited area, especially by using chemical and technological aids, a practice which has added to water stress and decline in soil health.

Hence, the correct option is (E).

11. We need to fill the blank with a noun. Among the given options, only 'irrigation' is a relevant noun, eliminating options (B), (D) and (E). Farmers use groundwater/water mainly for irrigation.

Hence, the correct option is (A).

12. Farmers use fertilizers to increase the level of nutrients in the soil. 'Boost' means increase. 'Accelerate' means an increase in rate, amount, or extent and hence is inappropriate.

Hence, the correct option is (E).

13. "EC' is singular, thus "is" will be used. Further, as the sentence implies to be made in Present Continous Tense, present participle (Verb + ing) should be used here.

Preposition "of" should also be replaced by preposition 'with' as the phrasal verb 'deal with' means 'to tackle or solve a problem' which is apt in the context of the sentence.

Correct sentence: The focus is now on the manner in which the EC **is dealing with complaints** against Mr. Modi.

Hence, the correct option is (C).

14. The preposition 'by' is incorrect here, thus the phrase needs replacement.

Here the relation between the student and his/her native place is described, thus the only preposition which describes belongingness is "from".

Correct sentence: Bhavana is the only **student from Kerala** to rank among the 13 national toppers who secured 499 marks.

Hence, the correct option is (B).

15. Since is used for a definite point of time, whereas "few months" implies a time period and not a point of time, thus the phrase needs replacement.

For denoting a period of time the preposition "for" is used.

With the helping verb "have" the third form of the verb is used, thus "paid" is correctly placed.

Correct sentence: Contract workers in the various departments of the government-owned company have also not been **paid their wages for** the past few months.

Hence, the correct option is (D).

16. Usage of plural helping verb "were" makes it clear that a plural noun must precede it in order to ensure fulfillment of the subject-verb agreement.

Correct sentence: The most relevant **parts of the complaint** were the transfer orders and disciplinary inquiry against her.

Hence, the correct option is (A).

17. The bold part is already correct, thus no replacement is required.

As the common meaning of the phrase **all set** is "completely ready" or "wholly prepared," or to put it another way "in the proper state for some purpose, use, or activity."

Hence, the correct option is (E).

18. E logically follows the introductory sentence and continues the idea of the Union Law Minister's response to a query raised during his public address on Wednesday.

Thus, the sequence of the sentences after rearrangement is,

Union Law Minister Ravi Shankar Prasad said in the Lok Sabha on Wednesday that while public interest litigation (PIL) for securing the rights of the poor, the workers and against corrupt public servants were to be supported, governance through such petitions should not be done. Responding to a query during Question Hour on the pendency of cases in various courts of law, Mr Prasad was asked by Laxmi Narayan Yadav, BJP MP from Sagar, whether an increase in the number of PIL petitions had contributed to the same.

Hence, the correct option is (A).

19. D logically follows E, i.e. the second sentence after rearrangement.

It continues the query raised by Laxmi Narayan Yadav, BJP MP from Sagar where he asked regarding 'whether an increase in the number of PIL petitions had contributed to the same' and Mr Prasad's action corresponding to the query is evident from the sentence D, i.e. **the third sentence after rearrangement.**

Thus, it can be inferred that **ED is a mandatory pair** where D logically follows E.

Thus, the sequence of the sentences after rearrangement is,

Union Law Minister Ravi Shankar Prasad said in the Lok Sabha on Wednesday that while public interest litigation (PIL) for securing the rights of the poor, the workers and against corrupt public servants were to be supported, governance through such petitions should not be done. Responding to a query during Question Hour on the pendency of cases in various courts of law, Mr Prasad was asked by Laxmi Narayan Yadav, BJP MP from Sagar, whether an increase in the number of PIL petitions had contributed to the same. Mr Prasad owned up to filing several such petitions himself in cases challenging corrupt practices of politicians but said 'with great humility' that it was not the job of the courts to govern the country through them.

Hence, the correct option is (B).

20. DB is a **mandatory pair** where **D** captures the **reaction** of the Minister corresponding to the query and B which is written in double quotes, captures the actual response of the Minister. Moreover, at the end of the sentence in B, 'he said' is also written, which confirms the actual response of the Minister.

Thus, **B is the fourth sentence after** rearrangement as it logically follows the sentences before it in the most appropriate manner.

Thus, the sequence of the sentences after rearrangement is,

Union Law Minister Ravi Shankar Prasad said in the Lok Sabha on Wednesday that while public interest litigation (PIL) for securing the rights of the poor, the workers and against corrupt public servants were to be supported, governance through such petitions should not be done. Responding to a query during Question Hour on the pendency of cases in various courts of law, Mr Prasad was asked by Laxmi Narayan Yadav, BJP MP from Sagar, whether an increase in the number of PIL petitions had contributed to the same. Mr Prasad owned up to filing several such petitions himself in cases challenging corrupt practices of politicians but said 'with great humility' that it was not the job of the courts to govern the country through them. "Only those voted in by the people and who are accountable to Parliament have the right to govern and frame laws for the country. The High Courts and the Supreme Court do not have that right. This has been clearly stated in our Constitution", he said.

Hence, the correct option is (C).

21. F must logically follow B, i.e. the fourth sentence after rearrangement.

F further continues the response of the Minister regarding the query asked by Laxmi Narayan Yadav, BJP MP from Sagar. Thus, it must be used after B only and as B is the fourth sentence after rearrangement, logically **F becomes the fifth sentence after rearrangement.**

Thus, the sequence of the sentences after rearrangement is,

Union Law Minister Ravi Shankar Prasad said in the Lok Sabha on Wednesday that while public interest litigation (PIL) for securing the rights of the poor, the workers and against corrupt public servants were to be supported, governance through such petitions should not be done. Responding to a query during Question Hour on the pendency of cases in various courts of law, Mr Prasad was asked by Laxmi Narayan Yadav, BJP MP from Sagar, whether an increase in the number of PIL petitions had contributed to the same. Mr Prasad owned up to filing several such petitions himself in cases challenging corrupt practices of politicians but said 'with great humility' that it was not the job of

the courts to govern the country through them. "Only those voted in by the people and who are accountable to Parliament have the right to govern and frame laws for the country. The High Courts and the Supreme Court do not have that right. This has been clearly stated in our Constitution", he said. Mr Prasad said more than 5,000 posts in the lower judiciary were lying vacant and the Central government was giving emphasis on filling the posts with fair representation from the SCs, STs, OBCs and minorities so that they could occupy posts in the higher judiciary.

Hence, the correct option is (B).

22. As all the responses by the minister are completed in statement F, i.e. the fifth sentence after rearrangement thus, we are left with only statement C which is further based on the responses of the minister.

It **concludes the flow of ideas** by stating the fact that based on the reports the court has decided to assign top priority to the disposal of cases pending for more than five years. It **concludes the entire flow of ideas** and is thus, the last **sentence in the structure.**

Thus, the sequence of the sentences after rearrangement is,

Union Law Minister Ravi Shankar Prasad said in the Lok Sabha on Wednesday that while public interest litigation (PIL) for securing the rights of the poor, the workers and against corrupt public servants were to be supported, governance through such petitions should not be done. Responding to a query during Question Hour on the pendency of cases in various courts of law, Mr Prasad was asked by Laxmi Narayan Yadav, BJP MP from Sagar, whether an increase in the number of PIL petitions had contributed to the same. Mr Prasad owned up to filing several such petitions himself in cases challenging corrupt practices of politicians but said 'with great humility' that it was not the job of the courts to govern the country through them. "Only those voted in by the people and who are accountable to Parliament have the right to govern and frame laws for the country. The High Courts and the Supreme Court do not have that right. This has been clearly stated in our Constitution", he said. Mr Prasad said more than 5,000 posts in the lower judiciary were lying vacant and the Central government was giving emphasis on filling the posts with fair representation from the SCs, STs, OBCs and minorities so that they could occupy posts in the higher judiciary. Based on the reports submitted by the arrears committee of various High Courts, it was resolved that they would assign top priority to the disposal of cases pending for more than five years and priority should be given for disposal of cases pending in the district courts for more than five years.

Hence, the correct option is (D).

23. The second sentence of the third paragraph clearly says that Europe has been undergoing several major changes in recent months.

The paragraph then continues to paint a picture in which important European leaders like Germany and France are going through changes in their political scenarios.

Hence, the correct option is (C).

24. The first line of the second paragraph says that, What the German Chancellor, Olaf Scholz, said in June 2022 at the end of a

three-day gathering of G7 leaders in the Bavarian Alps, sums up the prevailing mood overall, viz., "a time of uncertainty lies ahead of us. We cannot foresee how it will end".

He was referring to the ongoing Ukraine-Russia conflict.

From the above sentence, we can say that the German Chancellor at the end of the gathering of G7 leaders said, "A time of uncertainty lies ahead of us."

Hence, the correct option is (A).

25. The given sentence is talking about the obsession of the Western countries with the Russia-Ukraine conflict.

Let us explore the given options:

- The preposition 'on' indicates that something is already in the position.
- The preposition 'at' is used to say where something/somebody is or where something happens.
- The preposition 'in' means something inside or enclosed by something else.
- The preposition 'of' means expressing the relationship between a part and a whole.
- The preposition 'to' means We can use to as a preposition to indicate a destination or direction, We also use to with verbs such as give, hand, send, and write, to indicate the person or thing that receives or experiences the object of the verb.
- The proposition 'of' will be used in the above sentence as the sentence talks about the relation between the outcome and the Conflict of the war between Ukraine and Russia.

Hence, the correct option is (D).

26. Correct Sentence: Apart from this, nations do face several other problems as well, including, in some cases, a foreign exchange crisis.

- In the given sentence the use of the singular form of the noun 'case', is incorrect.
- The nations which are facing several problems as mentioned in the sentence are in a plural noun.
- The plural form of the noun 'cases' should be used in this case.

Hence, the correct option is (C).

27. The first sentence of the first paragraph says, 'Adrift at the end of the 20th century, the world of the 21st century is proving to be highly chaotic', so the Sentence A is correct.

The last sentence of the first paragraph says, 'Significant developments are also taking place in many other regions of the globe, which will have equal if not more relevance to the future of the international governance system', so Sentence B is also correct.

The first sentence of the third paragraph says, 'European leaders tending to look inwards is, perhaps, not surprising', so Sentence C is incorrect.

Hence, the correct option is (D).

28. The word 'reckon' means to consider or regard in a specified way.

- Example: The new policy was reckoned as a failure.

Let's look at the meanings of the given options:

Assume- suppose to be the case, without proof.

- Example: I assumed they would be on time, but they didn't turn up.

Believe- accept that (something) is true, especially without proof.

- Example: I believe it will rain today because it is monsoon season.

Conjecture- an opinion or conclusion formed on the basis of incomplete information.

- Example: The conjecture formed for the employee led to his boss demoting him.

Disbelieve- be unable to believe.

- Example: The man looked in disbelief as his house burnt down.

Bargain- an agreement between two or more people or groups as to what each will do for the other.

- Example: The bargain between the political parties led to their political alliance.

Hence, the correct option is (D).

29. The word 'adrift' means to so as to float without being either moored or steered.

- Example: He went adrift from a young age, because of bad company.

Let's look at the meanings of the given options:

Hooked- if you are hooked on something, you find it so attractive or interesting that you want to do it as much as possible.

- Example: The company was hooked on gaining profits every quarter.

Rigid- not able to be changed or adapted.

- Example: Their rigid mentality made it difficult for her to live life on her own terms.

Afloat- out of debt or difficulty.

- Example: The over debt made it difficult for the company to stay afloat.

Anchored- to make something or someone stay in one position by fastening him, her, or it firmly.

- Example: The family head anchored the members by his vision and values.

Rooted- exhausted; worn out.

- Example: We all were rooted by the end of our mountain trek.

Hence, the correct option is (C).

30. A passage is said to be Narrative when the author tries to convey a story or an event. It usually answers the question - "Then what happened?". A narrative type of RC often presents situations like a dispute, conflicts, problems & solutions, motivational events, etc. The basic purpose is to gain a reader's interest and thus, engage the reader.

A passage is said to be Introspective when the tone is employed in the passage so as to self-examine and reflect upon one's actions and feelings.

A passage is said to be Humanistic when the tone of writing is most suitable to issues related to welfare, values and other such human affairs.

A passage is said to be Apathetic when the tone indicates that the written piece is emotionless, the writer is not interested/ concerned and is indifferent and unresponsive towards the topic.

A passage is said to be Expository when the writing is such that it exposes facts. In other words, it's writing that explains and educates its readers, rather than entertaining or attempting to persuade them.

Because in the given passage the writer is shedding light on the way the Ukraine-Russia conflict is having an impact globally and on Europe, the tone of the passage is Expository, as the writer is presenting facts and the effects.

Hence, the correct option is (E).

31. The second last sentence of the first paragraph says, 'The Ukraine-Russia conflict is only one of the many strands currently altering the contours of world governance.' Sentence A is incorrect.

The fourth sentence of the third paragraph says, 'Emmanuel Macron may have been re-elected as the President of France, but his wings have been clipped with the Opposition now gaining a majority in the French National Assembly.' so Sentence B is correct.

The first two lines of the last paragraph say, 'Compounding this situation is the negative economic impact of the war in Ukraine. This is being felt not only in Europe but also across the globe.', so Sentence C is also correct.

Hence, the correct option is (E).

32. 'Changing politics of Europe' means the passage talks about the changing dynamics of the politics in Europe.

'Global order caught up in chaos' means the passage talks about the political, economic, or social situation in the world at a time of chaos because of the invasion of Ukraine and the effect that this has on relationships between different countries.

'Impact of Russian invasion on Europe' means the passage talks about the impact the Russian invasion of Ukraine had on continent of Europe.

'Economic impact of the war in Ukraine' means the passage talks about the impact the war in Ukraine is having on the Economy worldwide.

'Geopolitics of the West' means the passage talks about the study of how the projection of power is effected and affected by the geographic and political landscape of the West.

The entire passage talks about how countries' politics, the relationship between them as well as their economy is suffering because of the ongoing Russia-Ukraine conflict, therefore Global Order caught up in the chaos is a correct theme for the passage.

Hence, the correct option is (B).

33. The given sentence is talking about a billionaire who always looks for increasing his money.

Let us explore the words in the given options:

- 'Greedy' means having or showing an intense and selfish desire for wealth or power.
- 'Stole' means to take something from a person, shop, etc. without permission and without intending to return it or pay for it.

Conclusion: Even though the billionaire had lots of money he still always showed an intense and selfish desire for wealth.

Complete Sentence: The greedy billionaire had plenty of money but still stole from anyone who could increase his wealth.

Hence, the correct option is (C).

34. The given sentence is talking about something related to the reason for the mother-in-law's anger towards her daughter-in-law.

Let us explore the words in the given options:

- 'Fondness' means a liking for somebody or something.
- 'Aversion' means a strong feeling of not liking somebody or something.

Conclusion: Mother-in-law shouting in an angry way at her daughter-in-law for her eating and working habits.

Complete Sentence: The mother-in-law ranted at her daughter-in-law about her fondness for eating and aversion to work.

Hence, the correct option is (C).

35. The given sentence is talking about the role of advertisements in the company's image.

Let us explore the words in the given options:

- 'Intended' means to plan or mean to do something.
- 'Improve' means to become or to make something better.

Conclusion: To make the company's image better, the advertisements are made or planned.

Complete Sentence: The advertisements are intended to improve the company's image.

Hence, the correct option is (D).

36. The given sentence is talking about something that happened in a remarkable and extremely lucky manner related to some kind of death.

Let us explore the words in the given options:

- 'Saved' means to keep somebody or something safe from death, harm, loss, etc.

- 'Certain' means completely sure; without any doubts.

Conclusion: Someone is miraculously rescued from almost completely sure death.

Complete Sentence: He had been miraculously saved from almost certain death.

Hence, the correct option is (A).

37. The given sentence is talking about something related to the prices of fresh food.

Let us explore the words in the given options:

- 'Scarce' means not existing in large quantities; hard to find.
- 'Rocketed' means to increase or rise very quickly.

Conclusion: Increase in the prices of fresh food due to its deficiency.

Complete Sentence: Fresh food is so scarce that prices have rocketed.

Hence, the correct option is (E).

38. Observing the sentence, we see that 'range of desires and aversions' especially because 'desires' and 'aversions' contrast with each other.

So, the word at (C), in place of 'concepts', should be 'desires' (A). This eliminates option (A) and option (C).

Observing option (B), we can say that 'the capacity to form beyond' make no sense. So, option (B) also gets eliminated.

Thus, the correct arrangement becomes: CBA

The sentence after rearrangement:

The capacity to form concepts and to reason allows humans can go beyond this minimum state, with a much greater possible range of desires and aversions.

Hence, the correct option is (D).

39. Observing the sentence, we see that only 'described fits at (A). "Minimize" and "behave" do not make any sense at (A).

This eliminates option (C) and option (D).

Also, "minimize in a manner" does not make much sense. But, "behave in a manner" makes perfect sense. Obviously, "behave" will fit perfectly at (B).

"Maximize pleasure" parallels with "minimize pain" aptly.

Thus, the correct arrangement becomes: BCA

The sentence after rearrangement:

Hedonism, as Socrates described it, is the motivation wherein a person will behave in a manner that will maximize pleasure and minimize pain.

Hence, the correct option is (B).

40. Observing the sentence, we see that only "concern" fits at (A). "Populations" and "prompted" do not make any sense at (A).

This eliminates option (C) and option (D).

Similarly, only "prompted" makes perfect sense after "Second World War".

Also, "Japanese populations" make perfect sense.

Thus, the correct arrangement becomes: BCA

The sentence after rearrangement:

Concern over Japanese ethnic and immigrant groups during the Second World War prompted the Canadian and U.S. governments to intern most of their ethnically Japanese populations in the western portions of North America.

Hence, the correct option is (B).

41. Given,

$$\sqrt{144} \div 4 \times 6 - \sqrt{196} \div \sqrt{49} + 5 =?$$

$$\Rightarrow 12 \div 4 \times 6 - 14 \div 7 + 5 =?$$

$$\Rightarrow 3 \times 6 - 2 + 5 =?$$

$$\Rightarrow 18 - 2 + 5 =?$$

$$\Rightarrow ? = 21$$

$\therefore$ The value of $?$ is 21.

Hence, the correct option is (C).

42. Given,

$$263 - 345 + 180 \times 3\% \text{ of } 20 - 1 =?$$

$$\Rightarrow 263 - 345 + 180 \times \left(\frac{3}{100} \times 20\right) - 1 =?$$

$$\Rightarrow 263 - 345 + 180 \times \frac{60}{100} - 1 =?$$

$$\Rightarrow 263 - 345 + 18 \times 6 - 1 =?$$

$$\Rightarrow 263 - 345 + 108 - 1 =?$$

$$\Rightarrow 263 - 238 =?$$

$$\Rightarrow ? = 25$$

$\therefore$ The value of $?$ is 25.

Hence, the correct option is (C).

43. Given,

$$4\frac{1}{5} \times 3\frac{4}{7} \div \frac{5}{3} + 12 =?$$

$$\Rightarrow \frac{21}{5} \times \frac{25}{7} \div \frac{5}{3} + 12 =?$$

$$\Rightarrow \frac{21}{5} \times \frac{25}{7} \times \frac{3}{5} + 12 =?$$

$$\Rightarrow 9 + 12 =?$$

$$\Rightarrow ? = 21$$

$\therefore$ The value of $?$ is 21.

Hence, the correct option is (C).

44. Rearranging the given problem,

$\Rightarrow (15 \times 184) + 27 - 59 = ? + \left(\dfrac{156}{12}\right)$

$\Rightarrow (15 \times 184) + 27 - 59 = ? + 13$

$\Rightarrow 2760 + 27 - 59 = ? + 13$

$\Rightarrow 2760 + 27 - 59 - 13 = ?$

$\Rightarrow 2760 + 27 - (59 + 13) = ?$

$\Rightarrow 2760 + 27 - 72 = ?$

$\Rightarrow (2760 + 27) - 72 = ?$

$\Rightarrow 2787 - 72 = ?$

$\therefore ? = 2715$

Hence, the correct option is (C).

45. Given expression is:

$15 + \left\{\left(2\dfrac{4}{7} \times 5\dfrac{4}{2}\right) \div \left(6\dfrac{2}{9} \times 2\dfrac{4}{7}\right)\right\} = ?$

$\Rightarrow 15 + \left\{\left(\dfrac{18}{7} \times \dfrac{14}{2}\right) \div \left(\dfrac{56}{9} \times \dfrac{18}{7}\right)\right\} = ?$

$\Rightarrow 15 + \left(\dfrac{18}{16}\right) = ?$

$\Rightarrow 15 + \dfrac{9}{8} = ?$

$\Rightarrow ? = \dfrac{120 + 9}{8} = \dfrac{129}{8}$

$\Rightarrow ? = \dfrac{129}{8}$

Hence, the correct option is (B).

46. Given expression:

46 + 25% of (? + 1289) = 1340

$\Rightarrow 46 + \dfrac{x + 1289}{4} = 1340$

$\Rightarrow \dfrac{x + 1289}{4} = 1294$

$\Rightarrow x + 1289 = 5176$

$\Rightarrow x = 3887$

Hence, the correct option is (B).

47. Now, the given expression:

$\Rightarrow 2\dfrac{1}{9} \times 2\dfrac{2}{19} \div 6\dfrac{2}{3} = ? - 1\dfrac{1}{2}$

$\Rightarrow \dfrac{19}{9} \times \dfrac{40}{19} \div \dfrac{20}{3} = ? - \dfrac{3}{2}$

$\Rightarrow \dfrac{19}{9} \times \dfrac{40}{19} \times \dfrac{3}{20} = ? - \dfrac{3}{2}$

$\Rightarrow \dfrac{2}{3} = ? - \dfrac{3}{2}$

$\Rightarrow \dfrac{2}{3} + \dfrac{3}{2} = ?$

$\Rightarrow ? = \dfrac{13}{6} = 2\dfrac{1}{6}$

So, the required answer is $2\dfrac{1}{6}$

Hence, the correct option is (B).

48. Let distance = x km,

His speed = v kmph

Time taken when moving at normal speed - Time taken when moving 3 kmph faster =40 minutes

$\Rightarrow \dfrac{x}{v} - \dfrac{x}{v+3} = \dfrac{40}{60}$

$\Rightarrow x\left[\dfrac{1}{v} - \dfrac{1}{v+3}\right] = \dfrac{2}{3}$

$\Rightarrow x\left[\dfrac{v+3-v}{v(v+3)}\right] = \dfrac{2}{3}$

$\Rightarrow 2v(v+3) = 9x$ ......(1)

Time taken when moving 2 kmph slower - Time taken when moving at normal speed =40 minutes

$\Rightarrow \dfrac{x}{v-2} - \dfrac{x}{v} = \dfrac{40}{60}$

$\Rightarrow x\left[\dfrac{1}{v-2} - \dfrac{1}{v}\right] = \dfrac{2}{3}$

$\Rightarrow x\left[\dfrac{v-v+2}{v(v-2)}\right] = \dfrac{2}{3}$

$\Rightarrow x\left[\dfrac{2}{v(v-2)}\right] = \dfrac{2}{3}$

$\Rightarrow x\left[\dfrac{1}{v(v-2)}\right] = \dfrac{1}{3}$

$\Rightarrow v(v-2) = 3x$ ......(2)

$\dfrac{(1)}{(2)} \Rightarrow \dfrac{2(v+3)}{(v-2)} = 3$

$\Rightarrow 2v + 6 = 3v - 6$

$\Rightarrow v = 12$

Substituting this value of v in (1)

$\Rightarrow 2 \times 12 \times 15 = 9x$

$\Rightarrow x = \dfrac{2 \times 12 \times 15}{9} = \dfrac{2 \times 4 \times 15}{3}$

$= 2 \times 4 \times 5 = 40$

So, distance $= 40$ km

Hence, the correct option is (B).

49. Given:

Ratio of three numbers = 5 : 4 : 8

Sum of first number and second number = Sum of third number and 18

Let the three numbers be 5x, 4x and 8x respectively

First number + second number = (5x + 4x)

$\Rightarrow$ First number + second number = 9x

Third number + 18 = 8x + 18

Now, 9x = 8x + 18

$\Rightarrow$ x = 18

Difference between third number and second number = 8x – 4x = 4x

$\Rightarrow$ 4x = 4 × 18 = 72

∴ The difference between third number and second number is 72.

Hence, the correct option is (B).

50. Given:

The number series:

5, 7, 11, 19, 36, 67

Number series following a fixed pattern.

The given number series follows the pattern:

$5 + 2^1 = 7$

$7 + 2^2 = 11$

$11 + 2^3 = 19$

$19 + 2^4 = 35$

$35 + 2^5 = 67$

∴ The Wrong Number in the given number series is 36.

Hence, the correct option is (A).

51. The series follows the following pattern:

65 × 1 + 1 = 66

66 × 2 + 2 = 134

134 × 3 + 3 = 405

405 × 4 + 4 = 1624

1624 × 5 + 5 = 8125

∴ The wrong term in the series is 408.

Hence, the correct option is (D).

52. Given:

121, 144, 183, 204, 241, 282

$\Rightarrow$ 121 + 23 = 144

$\Rightarrow$ 144 + 29 = 173

$\Rightarrow$ 173 + 31 = 204

$\Rightarrow$ 204 + 37 = 241

$\Rightarrow$ 241 + 41 = 282

∴ The wrong term is 183.

Hence, the correct option is (E).

53. Given:

25, 200, 45, 320, 64, 512

$\Rightarrow$ 25 × 8 = 200

$\Rightarrow$ 200 ÷ 5 = 40

$\Rightarrow$ 40 × 8 = 320

$\Rightarrow$ 320 ÷ 5 = 64

$\Rightarrow$ 64 × 8 = 512

∴ The wrong term is 45.

Hence, the correct option is (B).

54. Given:

25, 13, 14, 22.5, 49, 120

$\Rightarrow$ 25 × 0.5 + 0.5 = 13

$\Rightarrow$ 13 × 1 + 1 = 14

$\Rightarrow$ 14 × 1.5 + 1.5 = 22.5

$\Rightarrow$ 22.5 × 2 + 2 = 47

$\Rightarrow$ 47 × 2.5 + 2.5 = 120

∴ The wrong term is 49.

Hence, the correct option is (A).

55. Average = $\dfrac{(Sum\ of\ elements)}{(Number\ of\ elements)}$

Given,

The average of (33, 45, 65 and 80) and (21, 9, 11 and 50) is X and Y respectively

$X = \dfrac{(33 + 45 + 65 + 80)}{4} = 55.75$

$Y = \dfrac{(21 + 9 + 11 + 50)}{4} = 22.75$

The value of 2(X + Y) = 2(55.75 + 22.75) = 157

∴ The value of 2(X + Y) is 157.

Hence, the correct option is (C).

56. Given,

Time is taken by boat running upstream to cover certain distance = 8 hours 48 minutes

Time is taken by boat running downstream to cover certain distance = 4 hours

Let the boat's rate upstream be x km/h and that downstream be y km/h.

Then, distance covered upstream in 8 hrs 48 min = Distance covered downstream in 4 hrs.

We know,

$$Speed = \frac{Distance}{Time}$$

$$Distance = Speed \times Time$$

According to question,

$$x \times 8\frac{4}{5} = y \times 4$$

$$\Rightarrow \frac{44}{5}x = 4y$$

$$\Rightarrow y = \frac{11}{5}x$$

Therefore,

Required ratio $= \frac{y+x}{2} : \frac{y-x}{2}$

$$= \left(\frac{16x}{5} \times \frac{1}{2}\right) : \left(\frac{6x}{5} \times \frac{1}{2}\right)$$

$$= \frac{8}{5} : \frac{3}{5}$$

$$= 8 : 3$$

Hence, the correct option is (C).

57. Let us consider $Q's$ present age as K years

12 years ago,

$Q's$ age $= K - 12$ years

So $P's$ age is 3 times $Q's = 3(K - 12)$

$= (3K - 36)$ years

$\rightarrow$ This age of P was 12 years ago

So, $P's$ present age $= (3K - 36) + 12$ years $= (3K - 24)$ years

12 years later from present day,

$Q's$ age $= K + 12$ years

P' sage $= (3K - 24) + 12 = (3K - 12)$ years

Also, $\dfrac{Q's \ age}{p's \ age} = \dfrac{K+12}{3K-12} = \dfrac{2}{3}$

$\therefore K = 20$ years $= Q's$ present age

$\therefore P's$ present age $= 3K - 24 = 3 \times 20 - 24 = 36$ years

Hence, the correct option is (B).

58. Let the length be l, height be h and breadth be b

l : h = 7 : 2

h : b = 5 : 6

$\Rightarrow$ l : h : b = 35 : 10 : 12

$\Rightarrow$ Area of four walls = 2h (l + b) = 2820 m

Let length be 35x, height be 10x, breadth be 12x

$\Rightarrow$ 2 × 10x × (35x + 12x) = 8460

$\Rightarrow$ 20x × 47x = 8460

$\Rightarrow$ 940x2 = 8460

$\Rightarrow$ x = 3

$\Rightarrow$ length = 35 × 3 = 105, height = 10 × 3 = 30 and breadth = 12 × 3 = 36

$\therefore$ Area of floor = lb = 105 × 36 = 3780

Hence, the correct option is (C).

59. According to the given data,

	Different types of pizzas		
Number of weeks	Golden Delight	Margherita	CHEESE N CORN
First week	150	100	200
Second week	130	150	100
Third week	100	140	160
Fourth week	160	130	170

The number of Golden Delight pizzas sold in the first and the second week = 150 + 130 = 280
The number of Golden CHEESE N CORN sold in the second and the fourth week = 200 + 100 = 300
So, difference = (300 - 280) = 20

Required percentage $= \left(\dfrac{20}{300}\right) \times 100 = 6.66\%$

$\therefore$ Golden Delight is sold 6.66% less than CHEESE N CORN.
Hence, the correct option is (B).

60. According to the given data,

	Different types of pizzas		
Number of weeks	Golden Delight	Margherita	CHEESE N CORN
First week	150	100	200
Second week	130	150	100
Third week	100	140	160
Fourth week	160	130	170

The number of Margherita pizzas sold in third and fourth weeks = (140 + 130) = 270
The number of CHEESE N CORN pizzas sold in the first and third weeks = (200 + 160) = 360
So, the ratio between them = 270 : 360 = 3 : 4
$\therefore$ The ratio between the number of Margherita pizzas sold in the third and fourth weeks, and the number of CHEESE N CORN pizzas sold in the first and third weeks is 3 : 4.
Hence, the correct option is (A).

61. According to the given data,

	Different types of pizzas		
Number of weeks	Golden Delight	Margherita	CHEESE N CORN
First week	150	100	200
Second week	130	150	100

| Third week | 100 | 140 | 160 |
| Fourth week | 160 | 130 | 170 |

Total number of Margheritas sold in the second, third and fourth weeks = (150 + 140 + 130) = 420

So, average = $\dfrac{420}{3}$ = 140

∴ The average number of Margheritas sold in the second, third and fourth weeks is 140.

Hence, the correct option is (C).

62. According to the given data,

Number of weeks	Different types of pizzas		
	Golden Delight	Margherita	CHEESE N CORN
First week	150	100	200
Second week	130	150	100
Third week	100	140	160
Fourth week	160	130	170

The total number of pizzas sold in first week = (150 + 100 + 200) = 450

The total number of pizzas sold in fourth week = (160 + 130 + 170) = 460

So, the difference between them = 460 - 450 = 10

∴ The difference between the number of all pizzas sold by Pizza Hut in the first week and the fourth week is 10.

Hence, the correct option is (B).

63. According to the given data,

Number of weeks	Different types of pizzas		
	Golden Delight	Margherita	CHEESE N CORN
First week	150	100	200
Second week	130	150	100
Third week	100	140	160
Fourth week	160	130	170

The total number of all pizzas sold in the first two weeks = 150 + 130 + 100 + 150 + 200 + 100 = 830

∴ The total number of all pizzas sold in the first two weeks is 830.

Hence, the correct option is (C).

64. Given:

Principal $=$ Rs. 40440

Ages of sons $= 12$ years and 16 years

Rate of interest $= 33\frac{1}{3}\%$ per annum compounded annually.

Formula used:

$$A = P\left(\frac{1+r}{100}\right)^n$$

Let the principal for younger son be Rs x

Principal for elder son be Rs y

Interest to be calculated for

Younger son $= (20 - 12) = 8$ years

Elder son $= (20 - 16) = 4$ years

Since, amount will be equally distributed then,

$$\Rightarrow x\left(\frac{1+100}{300}\right)^8 = y\left(\frac{1+100}{300}\right)^4$$

$$\Rightarrow x\left(\frac{4}{3}\right)^8 = y\left(\frac{4}{3}\right)^4$$

$$\Rightarrow \left(\frac{4}{3}\right)^{(8-4)} = \frac{y}{x}$$

$$\Rightarrow \frac{y}{x} = \frac{256}{81}$$

∴ Younger son's share $= \dfrac{81}{337} \times 40,440 =$ Rs. 9,720

Hence, the correct option is (B).

65. Given:

The cost price of an item is INR 500.

The manufacturer sells item to the wholesaler at a profit of 20%

$\Rightarrow$ Manufacturer sells item to the wholesaler at $\dfrac{120}{100} \times 500 =$ INR 600

The Wholesaler sells item to the retailer at a profit of 30%

$\Rightarrow$ Wholesaler sells it to the retailer at $\dfrac{130}{100} \times 600 =$ INR 780

The retailer sells it to the customer at a profit of 50%

$\Rightarrow$ Retailer sells it to the customer at $\dfrac{150}{100} \times 780 =$ INR 1170.

∴, Cost price of item for the customer $=$ INR 1170

Hence, the correct option is (C).

66. Given,

$$? = (3)^{-26} \times (3^2 \times 2)^{12} \times (2)^{-11} \times (2)^2$$

$$\Rightarrow ? = (3)^{-26} \times (3)^{24} \times (2)^{12} \times (2)^{-11} \times (2)^2$$

$$\Rightarrow ? = (3)^{-26+24} \times (2)^{12-11+2}$$

$$\Rightarrow ? = (3)^{-2} \times (2)^3$$

$$\Rightarrow ? = \frac{(2)^3}{(3)^2}$$

$$\Rightarrow ? = \frac{8}{9}$$

Hence, the correct option is (D).

67. Given expression is,

$$\Rightarrow 10 - 1\frac{2}{9} \text{ of } 3\frac{3}{11} \div \left(6\frac{3}{7} \text{ of } \frac{7}{9}\right) = ?$$

$$\Rightarrow 10 - \frac{11}{9} \times \frac{36}{11} \div \frac{45}{7} \times \frac{7}{9} = ?$$

$$\Rightarrow 10 - 4 \div 5 = ?$$

$$\Rightarrow ? = 10 - \frac{4}{5}$$

$$\Rightarrow ? = \frac{46}{5}$$

Hence, the correct option is (D).

68. Given,

$$\frac{9}{5} \times 2\frac{3}{4} \div \frac{5}{8} + \frac{9}{2} \times \frac{5}{7} - \frac{18}{25}$$

$$= \frac{9}{5} \times \frac{11}{4} \div \frac{5}{8} + \frac{9}{2} \times \frac{5}{7} - \frac{18}{25}$$

$$= \frac{9}{5} \times \frac{11}{4} \times \frac{8}{5} + \frac{9}{2} \times \frac{5}{7} - \frac{18}{25}$$

$$= \frac{198}{25} + \frac{45}{14} - \frac{18}{25}$$

$$= \frac{180}{25} + \frac{45}{14}$$

$$= \frac{36}{5} + \frac{45}{14}$$

$$= \frac{36 \times 14 + 45 \times 5}{70}$$

$$= \frac{(504 + 225)}{70}$$

$$= \frac{729}{70}$$

Hence, the correct option is (B).

69. Given:

The ratio of male and female employees in a company is 5 : 3.

If 40% of males and 20% of female employees earn more than Rs. 50000 per month.

Let the total number of employees be 200.

Ratio of male and female employees is 5 : 3.

Therefore, number of male employees will be $= \frac{5}{8} \times 200 = 125$

Similarly, number of female employees $= \frac{3}{8} \times 200 = 75$

It is given that 40% of males and 20% of female employees earn more than Rs. 50000 per month.

Therefore, Number of employees who earn more than Rs. 50000 = (40% of 125 + 20% of 75)

= (50 + 15) = 65

Number of employees who do not earn more than Rs. 50000 = 200 − 65 = 135

Therefore, the percentage of employees who do not earn more than Rs. 50000 $= \frac{135}{200} \times 100 = 67.5$

Hence, the correct option is (D).

70. Given:

Ritu's Investment = 4800

Rima's Investment = 3600

Sima's Investment = 5400

And,

Annual profit = 238000

Calculation:

The Ratio of Ritu, Rima, and Sima's investment

Ritu : Rima : Sima = 4800 × 12 : 3600 × 9 : 5400 × 6

= 16 : 9 : 9

So, the profit ratio will also be the same

Profit of Ritu = 16x

Profit of Rima = 9x

Profit of Sima = 9x

And it is given that annual profit = 238000

Therefore, 16x + 9x + 9x = 238000

Or, 34x = 238000

x = 7000 ... (i)

The Difference in profit between Ritu and Sima is = 16x - 9x

= 7x

Now on putting the value of x from equation (i),

Therefore, the Difference in profit of Ritu and Sima = 7 × 7000

= 49000

Hence, the correct option is (B).

71. Given statements: D > A ≥ M ≤ N; M ≥ E < L

On combining: D > A ≥ M ≥ E < L; M ≤ N

I. D > E → True (as D > A ≥ M ≥ E)

II. N ≤ A → False (as A ≥ M ≤ N → there is no clear relation between A and N)

III. A ≥ L → False (as A ≥ M ≥ E < L → there is clear no relationship between A and L)

IV. L < D → False (as D > A ≥ M ≥ E → there is clear no relationship between D and L)

Therefore, only conclusion I is true.

Hence, the correct option is (B).

72. Important point to remember with these types of questions is if you find the answer to be may be possible then it is not the answer.Now to check the conclusions:

Here, according to the given information: A ≥ C > O = E ≥ D

Conclusions:

I. A ≥ O → False (as A > O)

II. A > O → True (as A > O)

III. O ≥ D → True (as O = E ≥ D)

Therefore, only conclusions II and III are true.

Hence, the correct option is (C).

73. Important point to remember with these types of questions is if you find the answer to be may be possible then it is not the answer.

Now check the conclusions:

Here, according to the given information: Q ≥ S ≤ O ≥ U ≤ G

Conclusions:

I. O ≥ G → True (as O ≥ U ≥ G → clear relation between O and G can be seen)

II. Q ≤ U → False (as Q ≥ S ≤ O ≥ U → clear relation between Q and U cannot be determined)

III. S ≥ G → False (as S ≤ O ≥ U ≤ G → clear relation between S and G cannot be determined)

Hence, the correct option is (B).

74. Given statements: E ≥ I; I ≥ J; R > J; R = P

On combining: E ≥ I ≥ J < R = P

Conclusions:

I. E ≥ J → True (E ≥ I ≥ J; thus E ≥ J)

II. I > P → False (I ≥ J < R = P; the relationship between I and P cannot be determined)

III. J < P → True (J < R = P; thus J < P)

Therefore, only conclusions I and III are true.

Hence, the correct option is (E).

75. Given statements: Q = X < R < G; G ≥ T < Y; O > X

On combining: Q = X < R < G ≥ T < Y; O > X < R < G ≥ T < Y

Conclusions:

I. O > Q → True (as Q = X, O > X → O > Q)

II. O > G → False (as O > X < R < G → hence no relation between O and G can be determined)

III. Q = Y → False (as Q = X < R < G ≥ T < Y → hence no relation between Q and Y can be determined)

Therefore, only conclusion I is true.

Hence, the correct option is (B).

Ques (76-81): Persons: Ds, Fg, Lm, Ms, Nd, Pe, Ps, and Xy

i) Pe is sitting third to the left of Lm who is facing towards the centre.

ii) Ms and Fg are immediate neighbour of Pe.

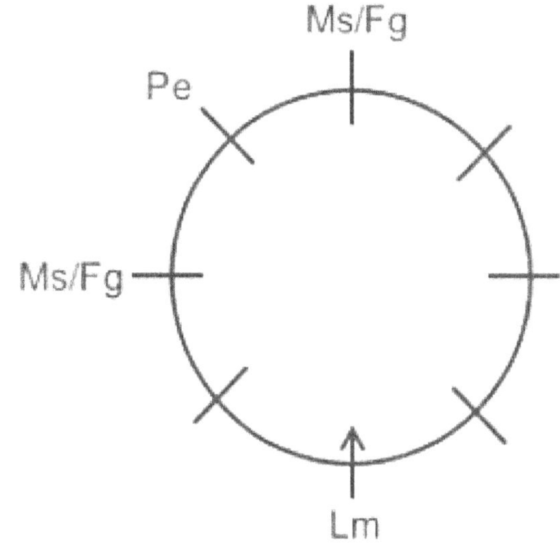

iii) Fg and Ms face the same direction but opposite to Pe.

iv) Nd is second to the right of Fg.

v) Ds is not an immediate neighbour of Nd.

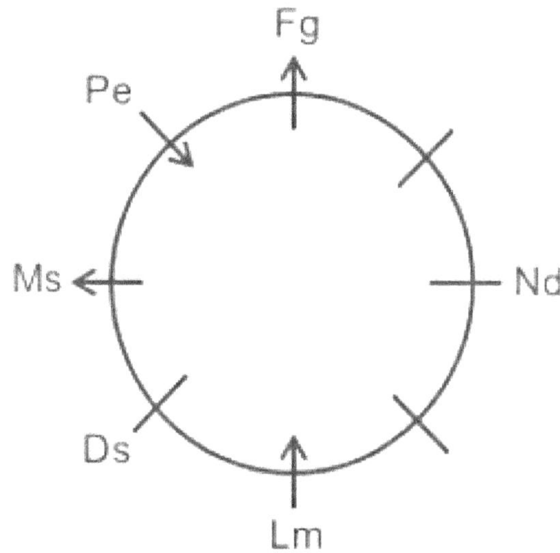

vi) Xy is second to the right of Ds.

vii) Both the immediate neighbour of Nd face the same direction as Ms.

viii) Lm faces the same direction as the person who is sitting second to his right.

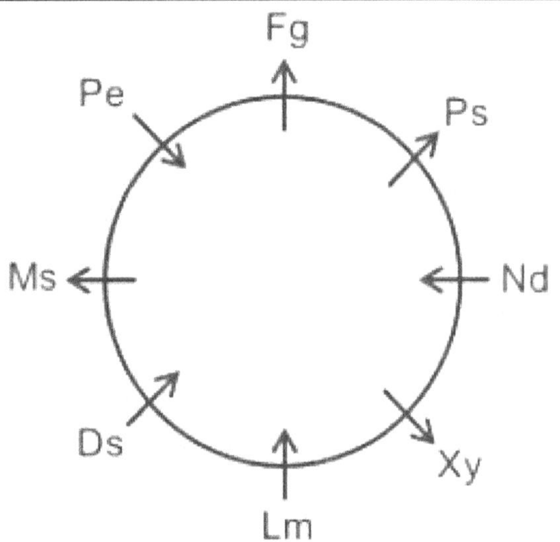

76. So, Ms is sitting opposite to Nd.

Hence, the correct option is (B).

77. So, "Two" persons are sitting between Fg and Xy when counting from the left of Xy.

Hence, the correct option is (A).

78. So, three persons are facing away from centre between Nd and Ds counting from right of Nd.

Hence, the correct option is (B).

79. So, "Ps" is sitting opposite to Ds.

Hence, the correct option is (E).

80. So, "Pe" sits second to the left of Ps.

Hence, the correct option is (A).

81. So, four persons are facing away from the centre.

Hence, the correct option is (C).

Ques (82-84): We have drawn the figure according to the information given in the question,

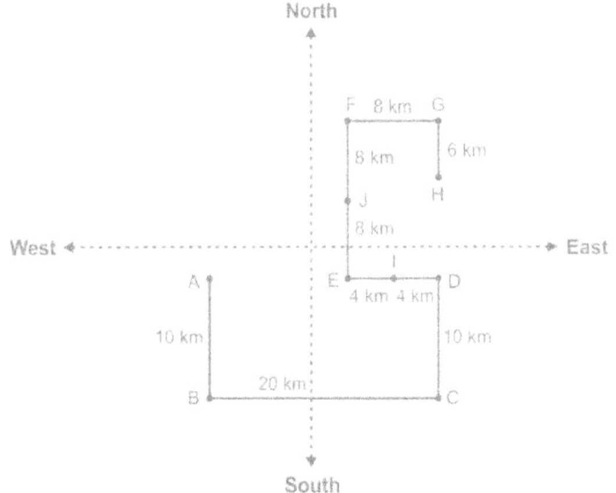

82. Clearly, "F, J, and E" forms a straight line.

Hence, the correct option is (C).

83. Minimum distance between F and H $= \sqrt{(8^2 + 6^2)} = \sqrt{100} = 10$ km.

Thus, the minimum distance between F and H is 10 km.

Hence, the correct option is (B).

84. Distance between A and E = (Distance between B and C) - (Distance between E and D)

Distance between A and E = 20 km - 8 km= 12 km

Thus, the Distance between A and E is 12 km.

Hence, the correct option is (D).

85. The least possible Venn diagram for the given statements is as follows,

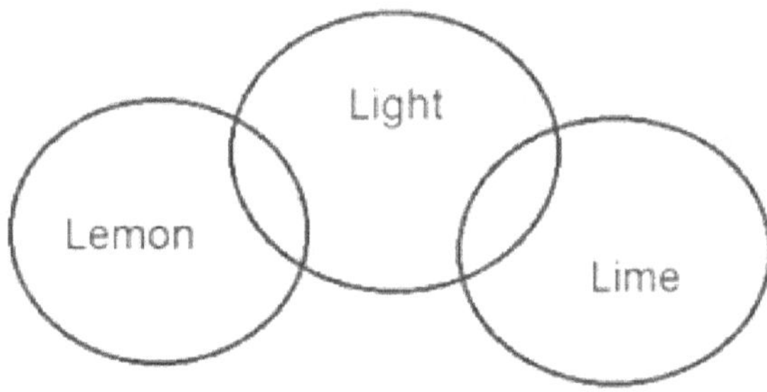

Conclusion:

I. Some lime are light → False (It is possible but not definite)

II. All light are lemon → False (It is possible but not definite)

So, neither conclusion I nor II follows.

Hence, the correct option is (D).

86. The least possible Venn diagram for the given statements is as follows,

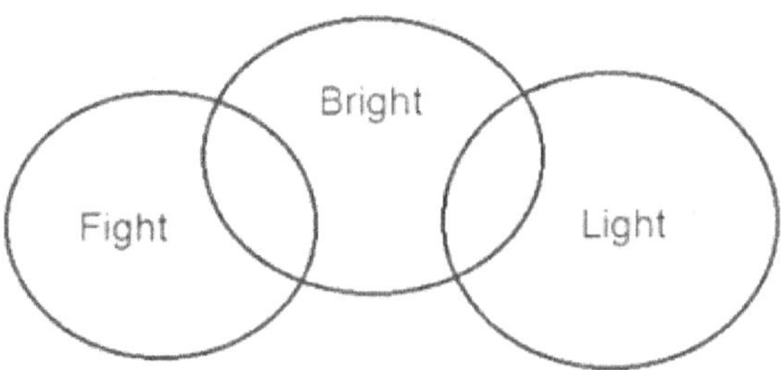

Conclusion:

I. Some fight are light → False (It is possible but not definite)

II. All fight are bright → False (It is possible but not definite)

So, neither conclusion I nor II follows.

Hence, the correct option is (D).

87. The least possible Venn diagram for the given statements is as follows,

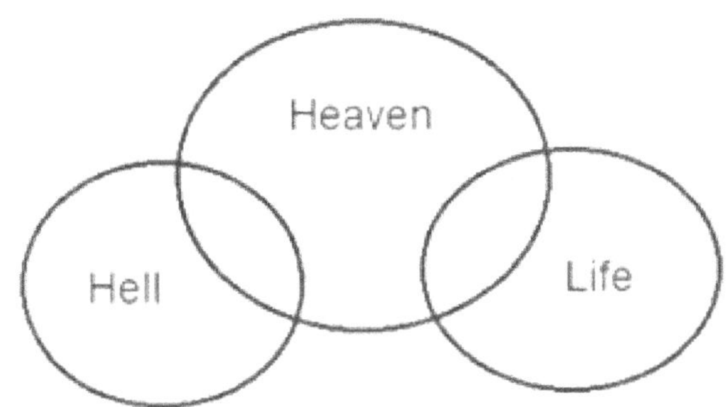

Conclusion:

I. Some hell are life → False (It is possible but not definite)

II. All life are heaven is a possibility → True

So, only conclusion II follows.

Hence, the correct option is (B).

88. The least possible Venn diagram for the given statements is as follows,

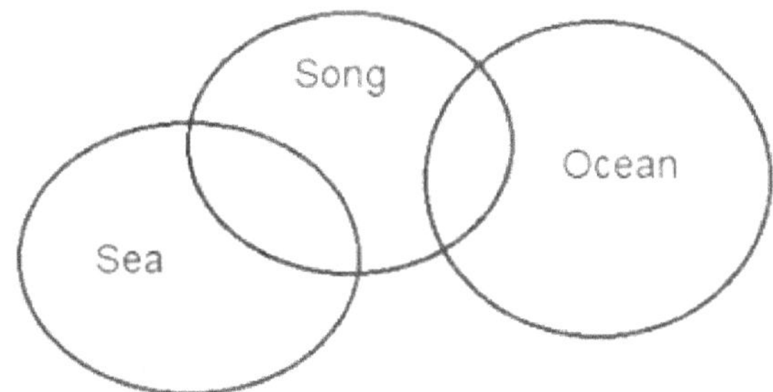

Conclusion:

I. Some sea are ocean → False (It is possible but not definite)

II. All ocean are song → False (It is possible but not definite)

So, neither conclusion I nor II follows.

Hence, the correct option is (D).

89. The least possible Venn diagram for the given statements is as follows,

Conclusion:

I. All diamond are club → False (as only few diamond are club i.e. some diamond must not be club)

II. Some spades are club → False (It is possible but not definite)

Hence, the correct option is (D).

Ques (90-95): Number of the act: 8

Superheroes presented are: Aquaman, Antman, Batman, Hellboy, Ironman, Spiderman, Superman, and X-men

1) The box Aquaman is placed neither below box Antman nor at an even number.

2) There are four boxes are placed between the box Aquaman and the box Antman.

Like the box, Aquaman is not below Antman so it is above Antman and will not be placed on an even number.

	Case 1	Case 2
S. No.	Student	Student
1	Aquaman	
2		
3		Aquaman
4		
5		
6	Antman	
7		
8		Antman

3) At least six boxes are kept below box Superman.

Only two possibilities are there.

4) The same number of boxes are placed above the box Hellboy as below the box Spiderman and none of the two boxes is placed at the top or bottom of the sack.

Only one condition is satisfying in all the cases.

	Case - 1	Case - 2.1	Case - 2.2	Case - 2.3
S. N o.	Student	Student	Student	Student
1	Aquaman	Superman	Superman	
2	Superman		Hellboy/Spiderman	Superman
3		Aquaman	Aquaman	Aquaman
4	Spiderman / Hellboy	Spiderman		Spiderman/Hellboy
5	Hellboy / Spiderman	Hellboy		Hellboy/Spiderman
6	Antman			
7			Spiderman/Hellboy	
8		Antman	Antman	Antman

5) The box batman and X-Men are placed above the box Ironman but below the box Superman.

6) The box ironman and the box Antman are not placed next to each other.

Case 2.2 is eliminated as there will be no empty place where box X-Men can be kept.

S. No.	Student	Student

1	Aquaman	Superman
2	Superman	Hellboy/ Spiderman
3	X-Man/ Batman	Aquaman
4	Spiderman/ Hellboy	X-Man/ Batman
5	Hellboy/Spiderman	X-Man/ Batman
6	Antman	Ironman
7	X-Man/ Batman	Spiderman/ Hellboy
8	Ironman	Antman

7) The box Batman is placed in the middle of the boxes starting with the same alphabets.Case 1.2 and case 2.1 is eliminated because the box Batman will be between box Superman and the box Spiderman because the initials are the same.

The final arrangement:

S. No.	Student
1	Aquaman
2	Superman
3	Batman
4	Spiderman
5	Hellboy
6	Antman
7	X-Men
8	Ironman

The alphabetical order:

S. No.	Student	Alphabetical Order
1	Aquaman	Antman
2	Superman	Aquaman
3	Batman	Batman
4	Spiderman	Hellboy
5	Hellboy	Ironman
6	Antman	Spiderman
7	X-Men	Superman
8	Ironman	X-Men

90. So, Only one box is in the same position.

Hence, the correct option is (C).

91. So, Box Antman is placed just X-Men and Ironman is placed below Ironman.

Hence, the correct option is (A).

92. So, Five students will be doing mimicry after Batman.

Hence, the correct option is (B).

93. So, No box is placed between the box Spiderman and the box Hellboy.

Hence, the correct option is (D).

94. So, The person doing the first mimicry is Aquaman.

Hence, the correct option is (D).

95. So, 4 boxes are placed between the box Superman and the box X-Men.

Hence, the correct option is (D).

Ques (96-100): The codes are as follows:

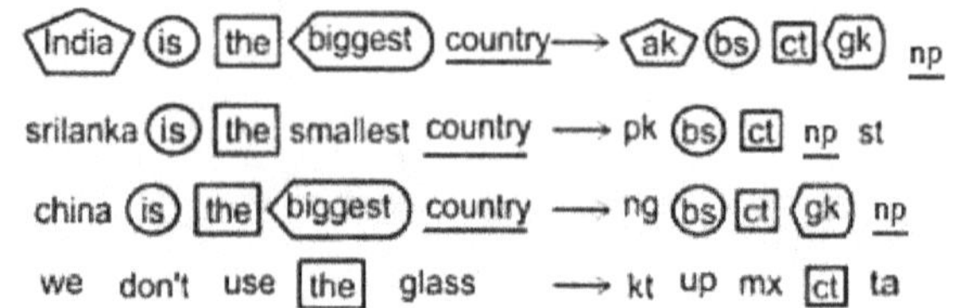

96. So, 'country' will be coded as 'np' or 'bs'.

Hence, the correct option is (C).

97. So, 'is the' will be coded as 'bs ct' or 'ct np'.

Hence, the correct option is (D).

98. So, 'china' will be coded as 'ng'.

Hence, the correct option is (C).

99. So, 'don't use' will be coded as 'up mx'.

Hence, the correct option is (A).

100. So, 'biggest' will be coded as 'gk'.

Hence, the correct option is (C).

Test of English Language

Ques (1-2):Direction: In the following question, a sentence is given with two blanks. You have to find the pair of words from the given options that fit both the blanks in the given order and make the sentence grammatically and contextually correct.

Q.1 Considering the rapid penetration of mobile phones and the rise in use of social media in India, the ____________ of fake news is no longer a problem limited to the online world, especially because it has political, social and economic ____________ on the ground.

A. dissidence, trade
B. dissemination, ramifications
C. devolution, career
D. propagation, transactions
E. None of these

Q.2 The public sector has been called the private sector of politicians, used for creating patronage ____________ and ____________ .

A. networks, kickbacks
B. buildings, hospitals
C. malls, complexes
D. relations, assets
E. None of these

Q.3 Direction: In the following question, a sentence is given with two blanks. You have to find the pair of words from the given options that fit both the blanks in the given order and make the sentence grammatically and contextually correct.

The problem of ____________ journals emerged after the UGC introduced a ____________ scoring system leading to an Academic Performance Indicator in which publishing is a part.

A. qualitative, trade
B. predatory, quantitative
C. rapacious, value
D. exalting, perfect
E. None of these

Ques (4-5):Direction: In the following question, a sentence is given with two blanks. You have to find the pair of words from the given options that fit both the blanks in the given order and make the sentence grammatically and contextually correct.

Q.4 Bankers said the ____________ on rating agencies make their own assessment more important and going ____________ more weightage would be given to the same.

A. suspicions, backward
B. flair, ahead
C. doubts, forward
D. reservations, nether
E. None of these

Q.5 Tuesday's multi-city police raids leading _______ the arrests of five people _______ alleged Maoist links has once again brought the debate on the concept of Urban Naxalism.

A. for, about
B. to, with
C. in, in
D. despite, against
E. None of these

Ques (6-10):Direction: In the following passage, some of the words have been left out. Read the passage carefully and select the correct answer for the given blanks out of the given alternatives.

In Norse mythology, Valhalla is a majestic, enormous hall located in Asgard, ruled over by the God Odin. Chosen by Odin, half of those who die in combat travel to Valhalla upon death, led by Valkyries, while the other half go to the goddess Freyja's field Fólkvangr. In Valhalla, the dead warriors join the masses of those who have died in ___(1)___ and various ___(2)___ Germanic heroes and kings, as they prepare to aid Odin during the events of Ragnarök. Before the hall stands the golden tree Glasir, and the hall's ceiling is ___(3)___ with golden shields. Various creatures live around Valhalla, such as the stag Eikþyrnir and the goat Heiðrún, both described as standing atop Valhalla and consuming the foliage of the tree. Valhalla is ___(4)___ in the Poetic Edda, compiled in the 13th century from earlier traditional sources, in the Prose Edda, in Heimskringla, and in stanzas of an anonymous 10th-century poem ___(5)___ the death of Eric Bloodaxe known as Eiríksmál as compiled in Fagrskinna. Valhalla has inspired various works of art, publication titles, and elements of popular culture, and has become a term synonymous with a martial hall of the chosen dead.

Q.6 Which of the following words fits the blank labelled as (1)?
A. Appeasement
B. Infirm
C. Combat
D. Destiny
E. Lethal

Q.7 Which of the following words fits the blank labelled as (2)?
A. Infamous
B. Predilection
C. Trepidation
D. Vulnerable
E. Legendary

Q.8 Which of the following words fits the blank labelled as (3)?
A. Intermittent
B. Thatched
C. Perpetual
D. Obnoxious
E. Penchant

Q.9 Which of the following words fits the blank labelled as (4)?
A. Attested
B. Arrested
C. Apprehended
D. Futile
E. Interim

Q.10 Which of the following words fits the blank labelled as (5)?
A. Commemorating
B. Corroborating
C. Primed
D. Condescending
E. Triumphing

Ques (11-20):Direction: Read the passage and answer the following question.

The words invention and Innovation are closely linked, but they are not interchangeable. The inventor is a genius who uses his intellect, imagination, time and resources to create something that does not exist. But this invention may or may not be of utility to the masses. It is the enterprising innovator who uses various resources, skills and time to make the invention available for use. The innovator might use the invention as it is, modifies it or even blend two or more inventions to make one marketable product. A great example is that of the iPhone which is a combination of various inventions.

If an invention is the result of countless trials and errors, so can be the case with innovation. Not every attempt to make an invention is successful. Not every innovation sees the light of the day. Benjamin Franklin had the belief that success doesn't come without challenge, mistake, and in a few cases failure.

One of the world's most famous innovators, Steve Jobs says, —Sometimes when you innovate, you make mistakes. It is best to admit them quickly and get on with improving your other innovations.

Thus, inventors and innovators have to be **intrepid** enough to take risks; consider failures as stepping stones and not stumbling blocks.

Some inventions are the result of a keen observation or a simple discovery. The inventor of Velcro, also called the zipless zipper, is the Swiss engineer George de Mestral. He was hiking in the woods when he found burrs clinging to his clothes and his dog's fur. Back at home, he studied the burrs. He discovered that each burr was a collection of tiny hooks which made it cling to another object. A few years later, he made and patented the strips of fabric that came to us like Velcro.

The world of inventions and innovations is a competitive one. But the race does not end here; it is also prevalent in the case of getting intellectual property rights. There have been inventors who failed to get a single patent while there have been some who managed to amass numerous patents in their lifetime. Thomas Edison had 1,093 patents to his credit!'

We relate the telephone with Alexander Graham Bell. It is believed that around the same time, Antonio Meucci had also designed the telephone, but due to lack of resources and various hardships, he could not proceed with the patent of his invention. It is also believed that Elisha Gray had made a design for the telephone and applied for the patent at the U.S. patent office on the same day as Graham Bell did. By sheer chance, Graham's lawyer's turn to file the papers came first. Hence, Graham was granted the first patent for the telephone.

It is not easy, and at times almost impossible, for an inventor to be an innovator too. There are very few like Thomas Edison who graduated from being an incredible inventor to a successful manufacturer and businessman with brilliant marketing skills.

While innovations that have helped to enhance the quality of life are laudable, equally **laudable** are the inventions that laid the foundation of these very innovations.

Q.11 The text in the passage can be best termed as:

A. Narrative   **B.** Descriptive

C. Persuasive   **D.** Expository

E. None of these

Q.12 The main idea of the author is to:

A. Highlight the difficulties faced by innovators.

B. Focus on the hardships of patent -seekers.

C. Compare innovators to inventors.

D. Reveal the importance of inventors.

E. None of these

Q.13 The author believes that:

A. Innovators enhance the utility of inventions.

B. Innovators face fewer challenges than inventors do.

C. Every inventor has a patent for the invention.

D. The invention is the same as innovation.

E. None of these

Q.14 Benjamin Franklin and Steve Jobs, believe that:

A. There is no place for mistakes in the process of making an innovation.

B. Making a mistake before finding success is not unusual.

C. Failure is a permanent stumbling block.

D. All innovators have to go through failure.

E. None of these

Q.15 Velcro can be best described as:

A. A highly-planned and deeply researched invention

B. The fruit of failure

C. The need of the hour

D. An accidental invention

E. None of these

Q.16 It is believed that Graham Bell became the first patent holder of the telephone because of:

A. His ingenuity and good fortune.

B. The carelessness of Elisha's lawyer.

C. The clever trick played by his lawyer.

D. The biased officials in the patent office.

E. None of these

Q.17 Which of the following is Untrue?

[CLAT UG, 2019]

A. Inventors may not be innovators.

B. Innovators are not expected to be enterprising.

C. To get a patent, the applicant has to follow a legal process.

D. Intellectual property rights are not always easy to get.

E. None of these

Q.18 Which of the following texts from the passage clearly indicates failure?

[CLAT UG, 2019]

A. The world of inventions and innovations is a competitive one.

B. Not every innovation sees the light of the day.

C. Thus, inventors and innovators have to be intrepid enough to take risks;

D. Some inventions are the result of a keen observation or a simple discovery.

E. None of the above

Q.19 Which of these words can replace the word intrepid?

A. Hasty   **B.** Intellectual
C. Daring   **D.** Rich
E. None of these

Q.20 Which of these words is the antonym of laudable?

A. Praiseworthy   **B.** Challenging
C. Tiring   **D.** Disgraceful
E. None of these

Ques (21-25):Directions: Rearrange the following six sentences A, B, C, D, E and F in the proper sequence to form a meaningful paragraph and then answer the question given beside.

A. Last June, ISRO had come close to NASA's record by launching 20 satellites in one mission.

B. The Indian Space Research Organisation boosted its reputation further when it successfully launched a record 104 satellites in one mission from Sriharikota a few days ago.

C. Of the 101 foreign satellites launched, 96 were from the U.S. and one each from the other five countries.

D. An earth observation Cartosat-2 series satellite and two other nano satellites were the only Indian satellites launched: the remaining were from the United States, Israel, the UAE, the Netherlands, Kazakhstan and Switzerland.

E. The launch is particularly significant as ISRO now cements its position as a key player in the lucrative commercial space launch market by providing a cheaper yet highly reliable alternative.

F. But ISRO views the launch not as a mission to set a world record but as an opportunity to make full use of the capacity of the launch vehicle.

Q.21 Which of the following would be the FIRST sentence after rearrangement?

A. E   **B.** A   **C.** C   **D.** B
E. D

Q.22 Which of the following would be the SECOND sentence after rearrangment?

A. D   **B.** E   **C.** A   **D.** F
E. B

Q.23 Which of the following would be the THIRD sentence after rearrangement?

A. D   **B.** C   **C.** A   **D.** F
E. E

Q.24 Which of the following would be the FOURTH sentence after rearrangement?

[IDBI Bank Executive, 2019]

A. D   **B.** F   **C.** E   **D.** A
E. C

Q.25 Which of the following would be the LAST but one sentence after rearrangement?

A. A   **B.** C   **C.** D   **D.** E
E. F

Ques (26-30):Directions: In the following question, two columns are given containing three phrases each. In the first column, phrases are A, B, and C, and in the second column, the phrases are D, E, and F. A phrase from the first column may or may not connect with a phrase from the second column to make a grammatically and contextually correct sentence. There are options which display the sequence(s) in which the phrases can be joined to form a grammatically and contextually correct sentence.

Q.26

Column (1)	Column (2)
(A) Differential voting rights enable promoters to retain	(D) ways, all of which involve social engineering tactics to fool end-users.
(B) According to security researchers, this vulnerability could be exploited in three	(E) irrespective of the thunderstorms.
(C) He's young and beautiful	(F) control over company even after many new investors come in.

A. Only B-D   **B.** Only A-F
C. Only A-F, B-D   **D.** A-F, B-D, C-E
E. None of these

Q.27

Column (1)	Column (2)
(A) This surreal experience, of walking along rows of	(D) agreeing to the proposal.
(B) Generally the trend has been to have a design that does not	(E) tea bushes teeming with butterflies, is out of the world.
(C) That isn't how it happened	(F) have any mechanical elements in a smartphone to make them more durable.

A. Only A-E   **B.** Only B-F
C. Only B-F, C-D   **D.** Only A-E, B-F
E. None of these

Q.28

Column (1)	Column (2)
(A) It is a multilateral lending agency	(D) driving, cooking or otherwise have their hands full.
(B) The read-aloud feature is particularly useful when users are	(E) never complain or condemn.
(C) Sarah was great tonight	(F) and regional development bank.

A. Only C-E   **B.** Only A-F
C. Only B-D, C-E   **D.** Only A-F, B-D
E. None of these

Q.29

Column (1)	Column (2)

Column (1)	Column (2)
(A) As part of their role in economic growth, the RBI directed all the commercial	(D) along well with the Jones family.
(B) To demonstrate the severity of the vulnerability, Check Point even created a	(E) banks to provide some percentage of their adjusted net credit as loans to priority sectors.
(C) My father asked me if I got	(F) tool that allows it to decrypt WhatsApp communication and spoof the messages

A. Only C-D   **B.** A-E, C-D, B-F

C. Only B-F   **D.** Only A-E, C-D

E. None of these

Q.30

Column (1)	Column (2)
(A) The guidelines seek to curb sale of counterfeit	(D) data, tall claims by brands fall flat.
(B) In the absence of robust clinical	(E) it was burnt to ashes.
(C) She likes to read everything	(F) products online and unfair trade practices by e-commerce companies.

A. Only A-F, B-D   **B.** Only B-D

C. Only A-F, C-E   **D.** Only B-D, C-E

E. None of these

Ques (31-33):Direction: In the given question, four words are printed in bold and are numbered 1, 2, 3 and 4. Of these, the positions of two of these words may be incorrect and need to be exchanged to make the sentence correct. In case the given sentence is correct, your answer is (E), i.e., 'No correction required'.

Q.31 If you had a short-term goal, then you **(1) provide** a fixed-income **(2) product**, not a market- **(3) linked** product; to **(4) need** return predictability.

A. 1-3 and 2-4

B. 1-2 and 3-4

C. 1-4

D. 2-3

E. No correction required

Q.32 The money would be used for **(1) developing** cutting-edge technologies for high-power, high **(2) repetition** rate lasers, high quality optical **(3) components** and state-of-the-art electronics and **(4) software.**

A. 2-3

B. 1-3 and 2-4

C. 1-2 and 3-4

D. 1-2

E. No correction required

Q.33 While the Bill does point out **(1) recall** of road safety, much-needed **(2) heftier** fines for errant drivers, vehicle **(3) issues** norms, there's no mention of better roads or infrastructure **(4) development.**

A. 1-2 and 3-4

B. 1-3 and 2-4

C. 2-3

D. 1-3

E. No correction required

Ques (34-35):Direction: In each of these questions, a sentence with four words printed in bold type is given. These are numbered as A, B, C and D. One of these four words printed in bold may be either wrongly spelled or inappropriate in context of the sentence. Find out the word which is wrongly spelled or inappropriate if any. The number of that word is your answer. If all the words printed in bold are correctly spelled and also appropriate in the context of the sentence, mark (E) "All are correct" as your answer.

Q.34 Whatsapp **admitted (A)** that hackers remotely installed **spywares (B)** on thousands of smartphones **exploting (C)** a **vulnerability (D)** of the messaging app.

A. Admitted   **B.** Spywares

C. Exploting   **D.** Vulnerability

E. All are correct

Q.35 The **hooligans (A)** could not kidnap the **president (B)** because his **itinerary (C)** was **altared (D)** at the last moment

A. Hooligans   **B.** President

C. Itinerary   **D.** Altared

E. All are correct

Ques (36-38):Directions: The following sentence is divided into 4 parts. Among them, one or more parts may have a grammatical or contextual error. Kindly choose, from the given options, the set of parts that do not have an error and are grammatically and contextually correct.

Q.36 The north-eastern state of Assam (A) / is among the most ethnically, linguistically, (B) / religiously and topographically mixed (C) / bits of India but is also the most combustible. (D)

A. Only A   **B.** Only B and D

C. Only A and C   **D.** Only A, C and D

E. All are correct

Q.37 Not for the first time, an incoming government faces the (A) / balance-of payments crisis were the current-account deficit (B) / has widened, the currency are sliding and the foreign-exchange (C) / reserves are down to just $9bn—barely two months' import cover. (D)

A. Only D   **B.** Only A and B

C. Only B and D   **D.** Only A, B and C

E. All are correct.

Q.38 Few believed President Bashar al-Assad would (A) / survive the rebellion that swept his country seven (B) / years ago and Syria's blood-soaked dictator is (C) / on the brink of defeating those who tried to topple him. (D)

A. Only A

B. Only A and C

C. Only A, B and D

D. Other than the given options

E. All are correct.

Ques (39-40):Direction: Two sentences are given to you. Five options are given for both the sentences. Choose the correct option. Ignore the error of punctuations, if any.

Q.39 1. The guest speaker, Shaina Fishman, had dedicated her new book to her dog who was an archaeologist.

2. Now when I go to a restaurant, I don't order from the menu. I sit down, and they bring me things to trying. The staff is quite firm. If they think you're ordering the wrong wine for the food, they say so.

A. Only sentence (1) has an error

B. Only sentence (2) has an error

C. There is no error in both of the sentences

D. There is an error in both of the sentences

E. There is more than one error in either of the sentences.

Q.40 1. She and I will accompany the students to the picnic on Saturday, everything is planned and sorted already.

2. He, I and you were responsible as a team to the Ministery for the formulation of a new set of laws to curb violence in the parliament

A. If only sentence 1 has error

B. If only sentence 2 has error

C. If there is an error in both 1 and 2

D. If there is no error in both sentences

E. If there is more than one error in either of the two sentences

Test of Numerical Ability

Q.41 A certain sum P when invested for four years at the rate of 15% p.a. simple interest, amounts to Rs. 26240. What will be the interest earned when (P + 1600) is invested at the same rate of simple interest p.a. for four years?

A. Rs. 10000

B. Rs. 10800

C. Rs. 9850

D. Rs. 12800

E. Rs. 10280

Q.42 Direction: Find the wrong term in the series.

589, 1134, 2250, 4482, 8921

A. 1134

B. 589

C. 2250

D. 8921

E. 4482

Ques (43-46):Direction: In each of the following number series, the wrong number is given, find out that number.

Q.43 4,6,18,49,201,1011

A. 1011

B. 201

C. 18

D. 49

E. 6

Q.44 255,435,655,945,1275,1655

A. 1655

B. 1275

C. 435

D. 655

E. 945

Q.45 75,76,156,475,1924,9645

A. 156

B. 76

C. 1924

D. 9645

E. 475

Q.46 198,166,155,142,138,136,135

A. 138

B. 136

C. 142

D. 155

E. 166

Ques (47-48):Direction: What should come in place of the question mark '?' in the following number series?

Q.47 $\sqrt{1444} + \sqrt{1156} + \sqrt{1225} - 80 = ?$

A. 21

B. 27

C. 23

D. 24

E. None of these

Q.48 $11^3 - 16^2 - 15^2 - 14^2 = ?$

A. −556

B. 556

C. −654

D. 654

E. None of these

Q.49 What will come in the place of the question mark '?' in the following question?

37% of 50 − 55% of 250 = ? - {60 (200 − 99 × 2) ÷ 4}

A. 89

B. -89

C. 126

D. 186

E. None of these

Q.50 What will come in the place of the question mark '?' in the following question?

$\sqrt[3]{6859} + \sqrt{441} - \sqrt[3]{4096} - \sqrt{576} = ?$

A. 1

B. 48

C. 0

D. -42

E. None of these

Q.51 What will come in the place of the question mark '?' in the following question?

(999 + 99 + 9) + 5.55% of 90 = ?

A. 1202

B. 1022

C. 1122

D. 1112

E. None of these

Q.52 What will come in the place of the question mark '?' in the following question?

6.67% of 225 + 6.25% of 1120 = (?)³ + 3

A. $(-76)^{\frac{1}{2}}$

B. $(76)^{\frac{1}{2}}$

C. $(-76)^{\frac{1}{3}}$

D. $(76)^{\frac{1}{3}}$

E. None of these

Q.53 What will come in the place of question mark (?) in the given expression?

30% of 120 + ? = 23 × 36 ÷ 46 + 40% of 160

A. 42

B. 46

C. 48

D. 44

E. None of these

Q.54 What should come in place of question mark (?) in the following questions?

(950 + 1750 − 2225 + 1225 + 4250 + 450) ÷ (70 + 60 + 28 − 30) = $\sqrt{?}$

A. 25000

B. 2700

C. 2900

D. 2500

E. None of these

Q.55 What will come in the place of the question mark '?' in the following question?

88.60% of 1500 + 39.25% of 800 + 63.20% of 2500 + 25.40% of 4500 = ?

A. 4856   B. 4466
C. 4256   D. 4366
E. None of these

Q.56 What will come in the place of the question mark '?' in the following question?

25% of $7428 + 71.5 \times 2 = 14\frac{2}{7}\%$ of ?

A. 2000   B. 5000   C. 4000   D. 14000
E. 12000

Q.57 Three pipes A, B, and C can fill a tank in 6 hours. After working at it together for 2 hours, C is closed and A and B can fill the remaining part in 7 hours. The number of hours taken by C alone to fill the tank is:

A. 10 hours   B. 12 hours   C. 14 hours   D. 15 hours
E. 16 hours

Q.58 A train running at a speed of 54 km/h crosses a tree in 13 seconds. In how much time will it cross 75 m long platform?

A. 15 sec   B. 16 sec   C. 17 sec   D. 18 sec
E. 19 sec

Q.59 In a class of 75 students, $\frac{1}{5}$th of the total number of girls and $\frac{3}{5}$th of the total number of boys join a cricket club. If the total number of boys joining the club is 27. What is the respective ratio of the total number of boys to the total number of girls joining the club?

[IDBI Bank Executive, 2017]

A. 9 : 4   B. 3 : 2
C. 5 : 4   D. 8 : 3
E. None of these

Q.60 The average of first three of five number arranged in ascending order is 20 less than the average of the last three of these numbers. If the sum of the last three of these numbers is 65. What is the sum of the first three of the numbers?

A. 15   B. 5   C. 12   D. 9
E. 13

Ques (61-65):Directions: Study the line graph and answer the given questions carefully.

In the line graph shows that turnover(in lakhs) of 2 companies over the years.

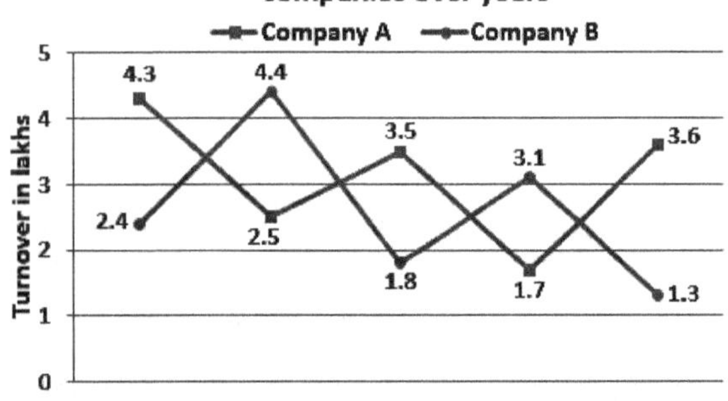

Q.61 The turnover of company B over all the years was approximately what percent of the turnover of company A in all years?

A. 83.33%   B. 75%   C. 66.66%   D. 40%
E. 35%

Q.62 In which year, the difference between turnover of companies A and B was maximum among the given years?

A. 2012   B. 2014   C. 2011   D. 2010
E. 2013

Q.63 What is the average turnover of company A over the given period?

A. 3.12 lakhs   B. 4 lakhs
C. 5 lakhs   D. 4.12 lakhs
E. 5.5 lakhs

Q.64 The turnover of company A in 2011 was approximately what percent of the turnover of company B in the same year?

A. 57%   B. 60%   C. 61%   D. 55%
E. 52%

Q.65 What is the difference between the total turnover of two companies in the given years?

A. 3. 6 lakhs   B. 2.6 lakhs
C. 3 lakhs   D. 5 lakhs
E. 6 lakhs

Q.66 If twice the perimeter of a square is 5.8 cm less than 3 times the sum of its diagonals, then find the side of the square.

A. 8 cm   B. 10 cm   C. 12 cm   D. 15 cm
E. 16 cm

Q.67 When the price of coffee is decreased by 10%. A man could buy 3 kg more for Rs. 540. Find the difference in original and reduced price.

A. Rs. 1   B. Rs. 2   C. Rs. 3   D. Rs. 4
E. Rs. 5

Q.68 Two friends Ravi and Kishan invested Rs. 65000 and Rs. 95000 respectively in a business. After one year, they had got some profit, which they had invested in a bank at the rate of 6% per quarter at simple interest. If they got Rs. 3968 after one year, what would have been the difference of their share of profit had they not invested it again in the bank?

A. Rs. 600   B. Rs. 744
C. Rs. 3300   D. Rs. 1984
E. None of these

Q.69 Remi earns a profit of 20% on selling an article at a certain price If she sells the articles for Rs. 8 more, she will gain 30% What is the original cost price of 16 such articles?

[SSC CGL, 2020]

A. Rs. 1200   B. Rs. 1120
C. Rs. 1152   D. Rs. 1280
E. None of these

Q.70 X can do a work in 9 days and Y in 18 days. How many days they work together to complete the two-third work?

A. 4   **B.** 6   **C.** 8   **D.** 9
E. 10

Test of Reasoning

Q.71 Direction: Study the following information carefully and answer the question given below.

Eight different boxes are kept one above the other, but not necessarily kept in the same order. Each box contains different items Chocolates, Papers, Toys, Books, Medicines, Pens, Pencils, and Ice Creams. The boxes are numbered as 1 to 8. The bottom-most box is numbered as 1 and the box above 1 is numbered as 2 and so on and the topmost box is numbered as 8. Medicines are kept in the lowermost box. Only three boxes kept between Toys and Medicines. Ice Cream box is kept immediately above Pens, which is immediately above Books. Chocolate boxes are kept above Papers but below Pens. Toys are kept above Pencils, which is immediately below Chocolates.

Which of the following is kept at the topmost box?

A. Toys   **B.** Ice Cream
C. Papers   **D.** Pens
E. Pencils

Ques (72-76):Direction: Study the following information carefully and answer the question given below.

Eight different boxes are kept one above the other, but not necessarily kept in the same order. Each box contains different items Chocolates, Papers, Toys, Books, Medicines, Pens, Pencils, and Ice Creams. The boxes are numbered as 1 to 8. The bottom-most box is numbered as 1 and the box above 1 is numbered as 2 and so on and the topmost box is numbered as 8. Medicines are kept in the lowermost box. Only three boxes kept between Toys and Medicines. Ice Cream box is kept immediately above Pens, which is immediately above Books. Chocolate boxes are kept above Papers but below Pens. Toys are kept above Pencils, which is immediately below Chocolates.

Q.72 How many boxes are there between the box in which Books are kept and the box in which Papers are kept?

A. Two   **B.** None   **C.** Four   **D.** Five
E. Three

Q.73 The number of boxes above the box on which Toys is kept is the same as the number of boxes below the box on which __________ is kept.

A. pencils   **B.** pens
C. chocolates   **D.** papers
E. books

Q.74 Four among the five are the same in a certain way which among the following does not belong to that group?

A. Books   **B.** Chocolates
C. Papers   **D.** Pens
E. Ice Cream

Q.75 Which of the following statements is true?
A. Ice Creams are kept in Box 8.
B. Toys are kept in Box 5.
C. Pencils are kept just above the papers.

D. There is one box between pens and toys.
E. All of the above

Q.76 Four among the five are the same in a certain way. Which among the following does not belong to that group?

A. Medicines   **B.** Pencils
C. Chocolates   **D.** Toys
E. Pens

Q.77 Direction: In each of the following question assuming the given statements to be true, find which of the conclusion among given conclusions is/ are definitely true and then give your answers accordingly.

Statements: Q ≤ A < D < K ≤ M = J = F > Z

Conclusions:

I. K > Q

II. F ≥ K

[IBPS RRB Scale I, 2020]

A. Only II is True
B. Only I is True
C. Both I and II are True
D. Either I or II is True
E. None is true

Ques (78-81):Direction: In the following question assuming the given statements to be true, find which of the conclusion(s) among given conclusions is/are definitely true and then give your answers accordingly.

Q.78 Statements:

N ≥ H ≤ T > R = E; E > O < P = I

Conclusion:

I. N > E

II. T > O

A. Only conclusion I follows
B. Both conclusion I or II follows
C. Only conclusion II follows
D. Either I or II follows
E. Neither conclusions I nor II follow

Q.79 Statement: T > P < O = R ≥ U ≥ A > L > W = X > F < J ≤ E ≤ J > K > D

Conclusions:

I. R > F

II. E ≥ L

III. O > D

IV. P > X

A. Only Conclusion I is True
B. Only Conclusion II is True
C. Both Conclusion III and I are True
D. Both Conclusion I and II are True
E. None of these

Q.80 Statements:

H < A > R = D; I ≤ K ≥ P; H < P

Conclusions:

I. K > R

II. D ≤ K
A. Only II is true
B. Only I is true
C. Both I and II are true
D. Either I or II is true
E. None is true

Q.81 Statement:

C < R < I ≤ S ≤ E ≤ A = N > O < G < Y > B ≥ D

Conclusions:

I. C < G

II. R < O

III. I > O

A. Only Conclusion I is true
B. Only Conclusion II is true
C. Only Conclusion III is true
D. Either I or II is True
E. None is True

Ques (82-87):Directions: Read the following information carefully and answer the given questions:

Eight persons - A, E, I, J, K, L, M, and O are sitting in concentric circles in such a way that persons sitting in the inner circle are facing the persons sitting in the outer circle and the persons sitting on the same circle are facing the same direction. They all like different colors - Red, Green, Yellow, Violet, White, Pink, Grey, and Black. The one who likes Black sits immediately left to L who likes Green. The one who likes Pink sits opposite the one who likes Violet in the same circle. The one who likes Yellow faces the one who likes Violet. E sits immediately left to K who likes Grey. The one who likes Black faces the one who likes White. O likes Yellow and sits immediate right to M. The one who likes Pink is facing inside. I sit immediately right of J.

Q.82 Who likes Black?
A. J   **B.** M   **C.** E   **D.** K
E. A

Q.83 Who likes Red?
A. E   **B.** I   **C.** J   **D.** M
E. K

Q.84 Who sits opposite to the one who likes Green in the same circle?
A. E
B. J
C. The one who likes Yellow
D. The one who likes White
E. Cannot be determined

Q.85 Who faces A?
A. I   **B.** M   **C.** J   **D.** L
E. K

Q.86 Who sits immediate right to the one who likes Grey?
A. The one who likes Black
B. The one who likes Pink
C. O
D. E

E. None of these

Q.87 Which of the given statements is true?
A. I and A face each other.
B. M and K face each other.
C. E likes violet.
D. I sits immediate right of J.
E. All of the above

Ques (88-90):

Direction: Read the following information carefully and answer the questions that follow.

A & B means A is 5 km to the south of B.

A % B means A is 5 km to the east of B.

A + B means A is 1 km to the south of B.

A - B means A is 1 km to the east of B.

Q.88 If it is given that: C + B % A; D + E - B. What is the distance between C and D?
A. 1 km   **B.** 2 km   **C.** 3 km   **D.** 4 km
E. 5 km

Q.89 If it is given that: C + B % A; C % D. What is the distance between A and D?
A. 1 km   **B.** 2 km   **C.** 3 km   **D.** 4 km
E. 5 km

Q.90 If it is given that: N % M; N - R - Q; O & Q; O + P. What is the distance between P and M?
A. 4 km   **B.** 5 km   **C.** 6 km   **D.** 8 km
E. 13 km

Q.91 Direction: In the question below are given three statements followed by two conclusions numbered I and II. You have to take the given statements to be true even if they seem to be at variance with commonly known facts. Read all the conclusions and then decide which of the given conclusions logically follows from the given statements disregarding commonly known facts.

Statements:
Only a few rub is pub.
All pub is hub.
Some hub is tub.

Conclusions:

I. All hub being rub is a possibility.

II. Some pub is tub.

A. Only I follows
B. Only II follows
C. Either I or II follows
D. Neither I nor II follows
E. Both I and II follow

Ques (92-95):Direction: In the question below are given four statements followed by four conclusions numbered I, II, III and IV. You have to take the given statements to be true even if they seem to be at variance with commonly known facts. Read all the conclusions and then decide which of the given conclusions logically follows from the given statements disregarding commonly known facts.

Q.92 Statements:

Some fathers are brothers.

All brothers are uncles.

No uncle is a husband.

Some husbands are the son.

Conclusions:

I. Some sons are uncle.

II. No father is a husband.

III. Some uncles are fathers.

IV. Some husbands are brothers.

A. Only conclusion I follows

B. Only conclusion II follows

C. Only conclusion I, II, and III follow

D. Only conclusion III follows

E. None follows

Q.93 Statements:

Some men are singers.

All singers are actors.

No actor is a teacher.

Some teachers are artists.

Conclusions:

I. Some artists are actors.

II. Some men are teachers.

III. Some actors are men.

IV. No singer is a teacher.

A. None follows

B. Either I or III follows

C. Only III & IV follow

D. Only II & III follow

E. All conclusions follow

Q.94 Statements:

Some planets are stars.

Some stars are the moon.

All moon are sun.

Some earth are moon.

Conclusions:

I. Some planets are sun.

II. Some earth are star.

III. No sun is an earth.

IV. Some suns are not Earth.

A. All conclusions follow

B. Either I or IV follows

C. Only III & IV follow

D. Only I, II & III follow

E. None follows

Q.95 Statements:

All sea are oceans.

Some lakes are rivers.

All rivers are ponds.

Some ponds are sea.

Conclusions:

I. Some ocean are river.

II. Some lakes are ponds.

III. Some sea are lakes.

IV. Some ocean being river is possible.

A. Only conclusion I follows

B. Only conclusion II and III follow

C. Only conclusion I, II, and III follow

D. Only conclusion II and IV follow

E. All follow

Ques (96-100):Direction: Study the information given carefully and answer the question given below.

In a certain code language,

"Connect the mobile charger" is coded as " E#2, R#5, T%5, E%3".

"Make sure you win" is coded as "E#2, N$2, U&1, E&2".

"Always study for hours" is coded as "Y&4, S@5, S&3, R%2".

Q.96 What is the code for the word 'mobile'?

A. E%3   **B.** Y&4   **C.** R#5   **D.** T%6

E. E&2

Q.97 In the given code language, what does the code U&1 represents?

A. Win   **B.** Sure   **C.** You   **D.** The

E. Make

Q.98 Which of the following word will have the same code as the word 'the' as per the given code language?

A. Me   **B.** He   **C.** They   **D.** She

E. One

Q.99 What does the code E#2 represents in the code language?

A. The   **B.** You

C. Make   **D.** Both A and B

E. Both A and C

Q.100 What does the code T%5 represents in the code language?

A. Always   **B.** Connect

C. Study   **D.** Make

E. None of the above

// Smart Answer Sheet //

Correct — Indicates percentage of students who answered questions correctly.

Skipped — Indicates percentage of students who skipped questions.

Q.	Ans.	Correct / Skipped	Q.	Ans.	Correct / Skipped	Q.	Ans.	Correct / Skipped	Q.	Ans.	Correct / Skipped	Q.	Ans.	Correct / Skipped
1	B	62.42 % / 35.61 %	17	B	64.09 % / 33.5 %	33	D	58.7 % / 35.05 %	49	B	21.16 % / 75.9 %	65	B	21.77 % / 67.81 %
2	A	56.84 % / 35.54 %	18	B	48.21 % / 33.36 %	34	C	49.91 % / 30.32 %	50	C	82.47 % / 10.51 %	66	C	55.98 % / 35.12 %
3	B	42.1 % / 50.27 %	19	C	41.59 % / 39.34 %	35	D	47.4 % / 49.17 %	51	D	87.18 % / 10.54 %	67	B	58.41 % / 32.26 %
4	C	22.89 % / 69.89 %	20	D	49.93 % / 43.36 %	36	E	43.39 % / 50.28 %	52	E	52.05 % / 39.56 %	68	A	63.02 % / 30.28 %
5	B	78.57 % / 20.14 %	21	D	57.75 % / 32.81 %	37	A	51.16 % / 40.93 %	53	B	88.27 % / 11.51 %	69	D	58.13 % / 34.25 %
6	C	69.54 % / 30.07 %	22	A	46.06 % / 34.13 %	38	C	61.75 % / 33.94 %	54	D	83.93 % / 11.46 %	70	A	54.44 % / 39.15 %
7	E	63.54 % / 34.09 %	23	B	69.3 % / 30.41 %	39	D	55.54 % / 37.88 %	55	D	67.1 % / 30.51 %	71	B	77.67 % / 11.66 %
8	B	66.98 % / 30.77 %	24	D	46.72 % / 47.47 %	40	B	54.87 % / 38.02 %	56	D	31.38 % / 67.92 %	72	E	45.15 % / 51.02 %
9	B	48.05 % / 30.14 %	25	E	45.44 % / 38.4 %	41	B	67.71 % / 31.45 %	57	C	61.0 % / 37.59 %	73	C	46.64 % / 47.81 %
10	A	48.76 % / 48.43 %	26	C	51.88 % / 34.85 %	42	D	47.88 % / 51.79 %	58	D	68.49 % / 30.06 %	74	D	65.89 % / 33.55 %
11	D	50.25 % / 34.25 %	27	D	54.09 % / 35.09 %	43	C	40.24 % / 42.54 %	59	E	44.79 % / 48.75 %	75	E	53.07 % / 35.2 %
12	C	62.04 % / 30.82 %	28	D	66.41 % / 31.11 %	44	D	50.31 % / 31.71 %	60	B	58.29 % / 31.72 %	76	C	64.15 % / 34.49 %
13	A	44.5 % / 53.51 %	29	B	50.12 % / 42.39 %	45	E	25.03 % / 71.76 %	61	A	52.74 % / 37.36 %	77	C	57.87 % / 34.82 %
14	B	49.33 % / 48.63 %	30	A	68.27 % / 30.99 %	46	D	50.16 % / 48.42 %	62	B	60.93 % / 37.37 %	78	C	64.79 % / 31.65 %
15	D	41.17 % / 45.65 %	31	C	45.53 % / 53.12 %	47	B	46.87 % / 30.85 %	63	A	88.11 % / 11.29 %	79	A	68.1 % / 30.16 %
16	A	60.96 % / 37.26 %	32	E	51.82 % / 44.25 %	48	D	50.28 % / 43.3 %	64	A	47.36 % / 48.54 %	80	E	61.57 % / 31.64 %

Q.	Ans.	Correct		Q.	Ans.	Correct		Q.	Ans.	Correct		Q.	Ans.	Correct		Q.	Ans.	Correct
		Skipped				Skipped				Skipped				Skipped				Skipped
81	E	63.55 %		85	D	43.79 %		89	A	87.45 %		93	C	65.82 %		97	C	67.21 %
		32.54 %				52.24 %				11.07 %				32.17 %				31.16 %
82	E	58.73 %		86	B	56.27 %		90	B	47.8 %		94	E	66.79 %		98	D	48.75 %
		37.55 %				32.74 %				49.67 %				31.1 %				40.6 %
83	D	54.06 %		87	E	69.71 %		91	A	61.44 %		95	D	61.19 %		99	E	58.48 %
		38.92 %				30.23 %				32.79 %				38.66 %				38.61 %
84	C	19.91 %		88	A	69.22 %		92	D	42.1 %		96	A	42.84 %		100	B	61.56 %
		75.77 %				30.45 %				48.49 %				50.64 %				31.99 %

Performance Analysis

Avg. Score (%)	66.0%
Toppers Score (%)	73.0%
Your Score	

//Hints and Solutions//

1. The first blank refers to the spreading of fake news which has become easier thanks to the wide reach of mobile phones. In the context of the sentence, the words which are suitable for the first blank are "dissemination", "propagation" and "distribution". So, options (A) and (C) are eliminated.

Out of the remaining choices, the only word that fits in the second blank and makes the sentence meaningfully correct is "ramifications" which means 'complex or unwelcome consequence of an action or event'. The words "transaction" and "transfusion" are irrelevant to the context of this sentence. This eliminates option (D) as well.

Considering the rapid penetration of mobile phones and the rise in use of social media in India, the <u>dissemination</u> of fake news is no longer a problem limited to the online world, especially because it has political, social, and economic <u>ramifications</u> on the ground.
Hence, the correct option is (B).

2. In the context of the sentence, the only appropriate combination of words is that of "networks" and "kickbacks". All other options are either grammatically or contextually incorrect. The sentence says that politicians gain a lot of private favours by sponsoring the public sector through set-ups and bribes.

The public sector has been called the private sector of politicians, used for creating patronage <u>networks</u> and <u>kickbacks</u>.
Hence, the correct option is (A).

3. The word "problem" before the first blank indicates that it is something 'negative' in nature. In the context of the sentence, the words that are suitable for the first blank are "predatory", "rapacious" and "predacious" all of which mean 'greedy'. Hence options (A) and (D) are eliminated.

"Scoring system" after the second blank shows that it has to describe the scoring system as 'measurable' The only word that makes the sentence meaningfully correct is "quantitative". The words "value" and "number" are irrelevant to the context of this sentence. This eliminates options (C).

The problem of <u>predatory</u> journals emerged after the UGC introduced a <u>quantitative</u> scoring system leading to an Academic Performance Indicator in which publishing is a part.
Hence, the correct option is (B).

4. Bankers would have to consider their own assessment methods to be more important only if the rating agencies dedicated for this job have developed a bad reputation. In the context of the sentence, the words which are suitable for the first blank are "suspicions", "doubts" and "reservations". So, option (B) is eliminated.

Out of the remaining choices, the only word that fits in the second blank and makes the sentence meaningfully correct is "forward". The phrase "going forward" means 'moving into the future'. The words "backward" and "nether" are irrelevant to the context of this sentence. This eliminates options (A) and (D) as well.

Bankers said the <u>doubts</u> on rating agencies make their own assessment more important and going <u>forward</u> more weightage would be given to the same.
Hence, the correct option is (C).

5. We know that the verb 'lead' is followed by the preposition 'to'. Therefore, the preposition 'to' should be filled in blank 1.

Ex. Closing the plant will lead to 300 job losses.

Now, if we observe we can find that there is no other option in which 'to' is given as a choice for blank 1. Thus, all other options can get eliminated.

Tuesday's multi-city police raids leading <u>to</u> the arrests of five people <u>with</u> alleged Maoist links has once again brought the debate on the concept of Urban Naxalism.

Hence, the correct option is (B).

6. Combat: active fighting in a war

- The context talks about Valhalla where dead warriors join the masses of those who have died in battle. So, the word <u>Combat</u> fits the blank appropriately.

Word	Meaning
Appeasement	to bring to a state of peace, quiet, ease, calm, or contentment
Infirm	weak; irresolute
Destiny	the events that will necessarily happen to a particular person or thing in the future
Lethal	sufficient to cause death

Hence, the correct option is (C).

7. Legendary: remarkable enough to be famous; very well known

- The context talks about the dead warriors who join the masses of those who have died in battles and also famous Germanic heroes and kings. So, the word <u>Legendary</u> fits the blank appropriately.

Word	Meaning
Infamous	wicked; abominable
Predilection	a preference or special liking for something
Trepidation	a feeling of fear or anxiety about something that may happen
Vulnerable	exposed to the possibility of being attacked or harmed

Hence, the correct option is (E).

8. Thatched: covered (a roof or a building) with straw or a similar material

- The context talks about the hall in Valhalla where the hall's ceiling is covered with golden shields. Hence, the word <u>Thatched</u> fits the blank perfectly.

Word	Meaning
Intermittent	occurring at irregular intervals; not continuous or steady
Perpetual	never-ending or changing
Obnoxious	extremely unpleasant
Penchant	a strong or habitual liking for something or tendency to do something

Hence, the correct option is (B).

9. Attested: provided or served as clear evidence of

- The context talks about the fact that Valhalla is mentioned in the Poetic Edda. So, the word <u>Attested</u> fits the blank perfectly.

Word	Meaning
Arrested	seized (someone) by legal authority and take them into custody
Apprehended	to become aware of; perceive
Futile	incapable of producing any useful result; pointless
Interim	in or for the intervening period; provisional

Hence, the correct option is (B).

10. Commemorating: recalling and showing respect for

- The context talks about recalling and showing respect to the dead Eric Bloodaxe. So, the word <u>Commemorating</u> fits the blank appropriately.

Word	Meaning
Corroborating	confirming or giving support to
Primed	made (something) ready for use or action
Condescending	having or showing an attitude of patronizing superiority
Triumphing	achieving a victory

Hence, the correct option is (A).

11. The text in the passage can be best termed as: Expository.

An expository passage tries to inform by an orderly setting forth of facts and ideas. It includes definitions, comparisons and contradictions.

The passage revolves around innovation and invention. It highlights the difference between innovation and invention. The first paragraph states the definitions of the two terms. The next three paragraphs state that failure plays an important part in innovation and invention. The fourth paragraph states an example of the invention. The next two paragraphs state the biggest challenge in the world of invention and innovation. The last two paragraphs try to merge the lines between the two. Thus, the text of the paragraph can be best termed as expository.

Hence, the correct option is (D).

12. The very first line and the last line of the passage reveal the theme of the passage, "The words invention and Innovation are closely linked, but they are not interchangeable.... While innovations that have helped to enhance the quality of life are laudable, equally laudable are the inventions that laid the foundation of these very innovations." The passage clearly compares innovators to inventors.

Hence, the correct option is (C).

13. The author believes that: Innovators enhance the utility of inventions.

The passage stales "The inventor is a genius who uses his intellect, imagination, time and resources to create something that does not exist. But this invention may or may not be of utility to the masses. It is the enterprising innovator who uses various resources, skills and time to make the invention available for use."

This implies that it is an enterprising innovator that enhances the utility of an invention.

Hence, the correct option is (A).

14. Benjamin Franklin and Steve Jobs, believe that making a mistake before finding success is not unusual.

The passage states "Benjamin Franklin had the belief that success doesn't come without challenge, mistake, and in a few cases failure. . .One of the world's most famous innovators, Steve Jobs says. Sometimes when you innovate, you make mistakes. It is best to admit them quickly and get on with improv ing your other innovations." Thus making a mistake before finding success is not unusual.

Hence, the correct option is (B).

15. Velcro can be best described as an accidental invention.

The passage states "The inventor of Velcro, also cal led the zipless zipper, is the Swiss engineer George de Mestral. He was hiking in the woods when he found burrs clinging to his clothes and his dog's fur. Back at home, he studied the burrs. He discovered that each burr was a collection of tiny hooks which made it cling on to another object. A few years later, he made and patented the strips of fabric that came to us as Velcro." This implies that Velcro was discovered accidentally by George de Mestral. It also implies that besides observing and identifying things, inventors are very creative in using that observation to come up with practical solutions (inventions).

Hence, the correct option is (D).

16. It is believed that Graham Bell became the first patent holder of the telephone because of his ingenuity and good fortune.

It can be deciphered from the following lines, "We relate the telephone with Alexander Graham Bell. It is believed that around the same time, Antonio Meucci had also designed the telephone, but due to lack of resources and various hardships, he could not proceed with the patent of his invention. It is also believed that Elisha Gray had made a design for the telephone and applied for the patent at the U.S. patent office on the same day as Graham Bell did. By sheer chance, Graham's lawyer's turn to tile the papers came first. Hence, Graham was granted the first patent for the telephone."

Hence, the correct option is (A).

17. The passage states "It is the enterprising innovator who uses various resources, skills and time to make the invention available for use. The innovator might use the invention as it is, modify it or even blend two or more inventions to make one marketable product." Thus, this statement is untrue.

Hence, the correct option is (B).

18. The phrase "see the light of the day" means to be made available; or be published, brought out or born. Without this on innovation cannot the called successful. It clearly indicates failure.

Hence, the correct option is (B).

19. 'Intrepid' is an adjective that means fearless; adventurous. Among the options, the synonym of intrepid is 'daring'.

Hence, the correct option is (C).

20. 'Laudable' is an adjective that refers to an action, idea, or aim which deserves praise and commendation. The synonym of laudable is 'praiseworthy' while the antonym is 'disgraceful' which means 'shockingly unacceptable.'

Hence, the correct option is (D).

Ques (21-25): The subject that is being discussed in the passage is the successful launch of 104 satellites in a single mission by the Indian Space Research Organisation and hence sentence B sets the tone by mentioning this achievement in brief.

Important hint to remember:

It is only the sentence B in which the expanded form of the organisation "Indian Space Research Organisation" is being used which further confirms it to be the opening statement.

D follows as it elaborates the details of the satellites launched.

Keyword that links D to B:

"Satellites"

C follows next as it states the further details of the satellites launched.

Keyword that links C to D:

'The United States', 'Israel', 'the UAE', 'the Netherlands', 'Kazakhstan' and 'Switzerland' are foreign countries and keyword that links C to D is "foreign".

Now, if we pick sentence E as the next sentence, the position of sentence A as either the 5th or the 6th sentence would create absurdity and hence the only available choice for the 4th sentence is sentence A.

The sequence made so far is B-D-C-A.

The next sentence that should follow is sentence F that describes the real purpose of the launch of satellites.

Keywords that link F to A:

"ISRO", "launch", "record" and "mission"

Now, the only sentence that is left is E.

21. The correct sequence is B-D-C-A-F-E and the first sentence is clearly B.

Hence, the correct option is (D).

22. The correct sequence is B-D-C-A-F-E and the second sentence is clearly D.

Hence, the correct option is (A).

23. The correct sequence is B-D-C-A-F-E and the third sentence is clearly C.

Hence, the correct option is (B).

24. The correct sequence is B-D-C-A-F-E and the fourth sentence is clearly A.

Hence, the correct option is (D).

25. The correct sequence is B-D-C-A-F-E and the last but one (second from the last) sentence is clearly F.

Hence, the correct option is (E).

26. Checking C-D:

He's young and beautiful irrespective of the thunderstorms.

The sentence is contextually incorrect. The pair C-D is hence invalid.

Checking A-F:

Differential voting rights enable promoters to retain control over company even after many new investors come in.

The above sentence is correct both grammatically and contextually.

Checking B-E:

According to security researchers, this vulnerability could be exploited in three ways, all of which involve social engineering tactics to fool end-users.

The above sentence too is correct both grammatically and contextually.

Hence, the correct option is (C).

27. Checking A-E:

This surreal experience, of walking along rows of tea bushes teeming with butterflies, is out of the world.

The above sentence is correct both grammatically and contextually. Hence, the pair A-E is valid

Checking B-F:

Generally the trend has been to have a design that does not have any mechanical elements in a smartphone to make them more durable.

The above sentence is correct both grammatically and contextually.

Checking C-D:

That isn't how it happened agreeing to the proposal.

The sentence is contextually incorrect. The pair C-D is hence invalid.

Hence, the correct option is (D).

28. Checking C-E:

Sarah was great tonight never complain or condemn.

The sentence doesn't make any sense contextually. The pair C-E is hence invalid.

Checking A-F:

It is a multilateral lending agency and regional development bank.

The above sentence is correct both grammatically and contextually.

Checking B-D:

The read-aloud feature is particularly useful when users are driving, cooking or otherwise have their hands full.

The above sentence is also correct both grammatically and contextually.

Hence, the correct option is (D).

29. Checking A-E:

As part of their role in the economic growth, the RBI directed all the commercial banks to provide some percentage of their adjusted net credit as loans to priority sectors.

The above sentence is correct both grammatically and contextually.

Checking C-D:

My father asked me if I got along well with the Jones family.

The above sentence is correct both grammatically and contextually as well.

Checking B-F:

To demonstrate the severity of the vulnerability, Check Point even created a tool that allows it to decrypt WhatsApp communication and spoof the messages.

The above sentence too is correct both grammatically and contextually.

Hence, the correct option is (B).

30. Checking A-F:

The guidelines seek to curb sale of counterfeit products online and unfair trade practices by e-commerce companies.

The above sentence is correct both grammatically and contextually.

Checking B-D:

In the absence of robust clinical data, tall claims by brands fall flat.

The above sentence is also correct both grammatically and contextually

Checking C-E:

She likes to read everything it was burnt to ashes.

The sentence doesn't make any sense contextually. The pair C-E is hence invalid.

Hence, the correct option is (A).

31. The correct sentence would be:

If you had a short-term goal, then you need a fixed-income product, not a market-linked product; to provide return predictability.

The statement is regarding the financial goals of a person and also the way in which you should handle your finances based on your goals in life. It is regarding aligning your investments with your goals. Short term goals require fixed income products whereas long term goals can be fulfilled with market related

products. If we replace 1 and 4, the sentence will become meaningful. No other replacement is required in the sentence to make it meaningful.

Hence, the correct option is (C).

32. The sentence is correct in the present form and no replacement is required in the present statement in order to make it correct.

Hence, the correct option is (E).

33. The correct sentence would be:

While the Bill does point out issues of road safety, much-needed heftier fines for errant drivers, vehicle recall norms, there's no mention of better roads or infrastructure development.

The given statement is regarding the new law on the road safety and motor vehicles norms in the country. It talks about various important issues but there is no reference to the importance of better roads and infrastructure development. Now if we replace 1-3, the sentence will make sense and no further replacement will be necessary at all.

Hence, the correct option is (D).

34. The word 'exploting' is misspelled in the given sentence.

The correct spelling would be 'exploiting'.

All other words are correct in every aspect.

Admit : confess to be true or to be the case

Spyware : software that enables a user to obtain covert information about another's computer activities by transmitting data covertly from their hard drive

Exploit : make full use of and derive benefit from

Vulnerability : the quality or state of being exposed to the possibility of being attacked or harmed, either physically or emotionally

Hence, the correct option is (C).

35. The usage of the word 'altared' is erroneous in the given sentence.

Altar (noun): a table or flat-topped block used as the focus for a religious ritual, especially for making sacrifices or offerings to a deity

Alter (verb): change in character or composition, typically in a comparatively small but significant way

The correct word in place of '**altared**' would have been 'altered'.

All other words are correct in every aspect.

Hooligan: thug/ ruffian

Itinerary: a planned route or journey

Hence, the correct option is (D).

36. The statement is correct in its original form and has no error.

Hence, the correct option is (E).

37. The use of article 'the' is incorrect as the BOP crisis is a general term and not specific to a nations. Fragment B is incorrect due to the use of 'were' instead of 'where'. Fragment C is incorrect due to use of 'are' instead of 'is' while the currency is singular.

Correct: Not for the first time, an incoming government faces a balance-of payments crisis where the current-account deficit has widened, the currency is sliding and the foreign-exchange reserves are down to just $9bn—barely two months' import cover.

Hence, the correct option is (A).

38. Here, the statement has two fragments- one which talks of how no one expected Syria's President to make it and the other talking about him on the verge of defeating the ones against him. Hence, these fragments are contradictory and the connector 'and' is incorrect and should be replaced by 'but'. The rest of the fragments are correct.

Correct: Few believed President Bashar al-Assad would survive the rebellion that swept his country seven years ago but Syria's blood-soaked dictator is on the brink of defeating those who tried to topple him.

Hence, the correct option is (C).

39. In sentence 1 the error lies in 'misplaced modifier'

- According to the rule regarding placement of modifiers a modifier should be placed as close as possible to what it is modifying.
- Hence as per the rule of placement of modifiers, the modifier 'who was an archaeologist' should be as close as possible to what it modifies 'The guest speaker, Shaina Fishman'

In sentence 2 the error lies in 'things to trying'

- Instead of the gerund 'trying' it should be the to-infinitive 'to try'.
- According to the rule, 'to' always takes V1 form of the verb, i.e. "To + base form of the verb".

Hence, the correct option is (D).

40. If all the three persons or two talks about a mistake, confess about doing anything wrong, or if the pronouns are in plural form, the order is:

- 1st-2nd-3rd

Example: I, you, and he have committed this blunder. (1st-2nd-3rd)

According to the rule and the example is given above, 'I, you and he' will be used instead of 'Him, me and you' in the 1st part of the sentence.

Hence, the correct option is (B).

41. Given:

Amount (A) = Rs. 26240

Rate of Interest (R) = 15%

Concept Used:

$$A = P + \left(\frac{PRT}{100} \right)$$

A = Amount, P = Principal, R = Rate of Interest and T = Time.

Calculation:

According to the question,

In 1st condition,

$$\left[\frac{(P \times 15 \times 4)}{100} \right] + P = 26240$$

$$\Rightarrow \left(\frac{3P}{5} \right) + P = 26240$$

$$\Rightarrow 8P = 26240 \times 5$$

$$\Rightarrow P = Rs.\ 16400$$

In 2nd condition,

$$\frac{[(P+1600) \times 4 \times 15]}{100}$$

$$\Rightarrow \frac{[(16400+1600) \times 15 \times 4]}{100}$$

$$\Rightarrow \frac{(18000 \times 15 \times 4)}{100}$$

$$\Rightarrow 180 \times 15 \times 4$$

$$\Rightarrow Rs.\ 10800$$

∴ The Simple interest on (P + 1600) for 4 years is Rs. 10800.

Hence, the correct option is (B).

42. The pattern of the given series:

(Number - Sum of all digits of the number) × 2 = Next number

$$\Rightarrow (589-(5+8+9)) \times 2 = (589-22) \times 2 = 567 \times 2 = 1134$$

$$\Rightarrow (1134-(1+1+3+4)) \times 2 = (1134-9) \times 2 = 1125 \times 2 = 2250$$

$$\Rightarrow (2250-(2+2+5+0)) \times 2 = (2250-9) \times 2 = 2241 \times 2 = 4482$$

$$\Rightarrow (4482-(4+4+8+2)) \times 2 = (4482-18) \times 2 = 4464 \times 2 = 8928$$

Then,

8928 is the correct term in place of 8921.

∴ 8921 is the wrong term in the series.

Hence, the correct option is (D).

43. The given number series is based on the following pattern:

$$4 \times 1 + 2 = 6$$

$$6 \times 2 + 3 = 15 \neq 18$$

$$15 \times 3 + 4 = 49$$

$$49 \times 4 + 5 = 201$$

$$201 \times 5 + 6 = 1011$$

Thus, The wrong number in the given series is 18.

Hence, the correct option is (C).

44. The given number series is based on the following pattern:

$$15^2 + 30 = 255$$

$$20^2 + 35 = 435$$

$$25^2 + 40 = 665 \neq (655)$$

$$30^2 + 45 = 945$$

$$35^2 + 50 = 1275$$

$$40^2 + 55 = 1655$$

Thus, the wrong number in the given series is 655.

Hence, the correct option is (D).

45. The given number series is based on the following pattern:

$$75 \times 1 + 1^2 = 76$$

$$76 \times 2 + 2^2 = 156$$

$$156 \times 3 + 3^2 = 477 \neq (475)$$

$$477 \times 4 + 4^2 = 1924$$

$$1924 \times 5 + 5^2 = 9645$$

Thus, the wrong number in the given series is 475.

Hence, the correct option is (E).

46. The pattern of the number series is:

$$198 - 32 = 166$$

$$166 - 16 = 150 \neq 155$$

$$150 - 8 = 142$$

$$142 - 4 = 138$$

$$138 - 2 = 136$$

$$136 - 1 = 135$$

Thus, The wrong number in the given series is 155.

Hence, the correct option is (D).

47. Given:

$$\sqrt{1444} + \sqrt{1156} + \sqrt{1225} - 80 =?$$

$$\Rightarrow 38 + 34 + 35 - 80 =?$$

$$\Rightarrow 107 - 80 =?$$

$$\Rightarrow 27 =?$$

$\therefore$ The value of $?$ is 27.

Hence, the correct option is (B).

48. Given:

$$11^3 - 16^2 - 15^2 - 14^2 =?$$

$$\Rightarrow 1331 - 256 - 225 - 196 =?$$

$$\Rightarrow 1331 - 677 =?$$

$$\Rightarrow 654 =?$$

$\therefore$ The value of ? is 654.

Hence, the correct option is (D).

49. Given:

37% of 50 – 55% of 250 = ? - {60 (200 – 99 × 2) ÷ 4}

$$\Rightarrow \frac{37}{100} \text{ of } 50 \ - \frac{55}{100} \text{ of } 250 = ? \text{ - } \{60 (200 – 99 × 2) ÷ 4\}$$

$$\Rightarrow \frac{37}{2} - \frac{11}{20} \text{ of } 250 = ? \text{ - } \{60 (200 – 99 × 2) ÷ 4\}$$

$\Rightarrow$ 18.5 – 137.5 = ? - {60 (200 – 198) ÷ 4}

$\Rightarrow$ -119 = ? - {60 × 2 ÷ 4}

$$\Rightarrow -119 = ? \text{ - } \left\{\frac{60}{2}\right\}$$

$\Rightarrow$ -119 = ? - 30

$\Rightarrow$ -89 = ?

$\therefore$ The value of ? is -89.

Hence, the correct option is (B).

50. Given:

$$\sqrt[3]{6859} + \sqrt{441} - \sqrt[3]{4096} - \sqrt{576} =?$$

$\Rightarrow$ 19 + 21 – 16 – 24 = ?

$\Rightarrow$ 40 – 40 = ?

$\Rightarrow$? = 0

$\therefore$ The value of ? is 0.

Hence, the correct option is (C).

51. Given:

(999 + 99 + 9) + 5.55% of 90 = ?

$$\Rightarrow 1107 + \frac{1}{18} \text{ of } 90 = ?$$

$\Rightarrow$ 1107 + 5 = ?

$\Rightarrow$ 1112 = ?

$\therefore$ The value of ? is 1112.

Hence, the correct option is (D).

52. Given:

6.67% of 225 + 6.25% of 1120 = (?)³ + 3

$$\Rightarrow \frac{1}{15} \times 225 \ + \frac{1}{16} \text{ of } 1120 = (?)^3 + 3$$

$\Rightarrow$ 15 + 70 = (?)³ + 3

$\Rightarrow$ 85= (?)³ + 3

$\Rightarrow (?)^3 = 82$

$\Rightarrow ? = (82)^{\frac{1}{3}}$

Hence, the correct option is (E).

53. Given:

30% of 120 + ? = 23 × 36 ÷ 46 + 40% of 160

$\Rightarrow \left(\dfrac{30}{100}\right) \times 120 + ? = \dfrac{36}{2} + \left(\dfrac{40}{100}\right) \times 160$

$\Rightarrow 36 + ? = 18 + 64$

$\Rightarrow ? = 82 - 36 = 46$

∴ The value of ? is 46.

Hence, the correct option is (B).

54. Given:

$\Rightarrow (950 + 1750 - 2225 + 1225 + 4250 + 450) \div (70 + 60 + 28 - 30) = \sqrt{?}$

$\Rightarrow (2700 - 2225 + 5925) \div (158 - 30) = \sqrt{?}$

$\Rightarrow (8625 - 2225) \div 128 = \sqrt{?}$

$\Rightarrow 6400 \div 128 = \sqrt{?}$

$\Rightarrow 50 = \sqrt{?}$

$\Rightarrow 2500 = ?$

∴ The value of ? is 2500.

Hence, the correct option is (D).

55. Given:

88.60% of 1500 + 39.25% of 800 + 63.20% of 2500 + 25.40% of 4500 = ?

$\Rightarrow 1500 \times \frac{88.60}{100} + 800 \times \frac{39.25}{100} + 2500 \times \frac{63.20}{100} + 4500 \times \frac{25.40}{100} = ?$

$\Rightarrow 1329 + 314 + 1580 + 1143 = ?$

$\Rightarrow ? = 4366$

∴ The value of ? is 4366.

Hence, the correct option is (D).

56. We know that 25% = $\dfrac{1}{4}$ and $14\dfrac{2}{7}\% = \dfrac{1}{7}$

$\Rightarrow \dfrac{1}{4} \times 7428 + 143 = \dfrac{1}{7} \times ?$

$\Rightarrow ? = 7 \times 2000$

$\Rightarrow ? = 14000$

Hence, the correct option is (D).

57. Given,

Total time taken by pipe A, B and C to fill the tank = 6 hours

Part filled by A, B and C in 1 hour = $\dfrac{1}{6}$

Part filled by A, B and C in 2 hour = $\dfrac{2}{6}$

$= \dfrac{1}{3}$

Remaining part $= 1 - \dfrac{1}{3}$

$= \dfrac{2}{3}$

(A + B)'s 7 hours' work = $\dfrac{2}{3}$

(A + B)'s 1 hours' work = $\dfrac{2}{21}$

C's 1 hour's work = (A + B + C) 's 1 hour's work - (A + B)'s 1 hour's work

$\dfrac{1}{C} = \dfrac{1}{(A+B+C)} - \dfrac{1}{(A+B)}$

$= \dfrac{1}{6} - \dfrac{2}{21}$

$= \dfrac{1}{14}$

∴ C alone can fill the tank in 14 hours.

Hence, the correct option is (C).

58. Given:

Speed of train = 54 km/h

Time train takes to cross a tree = 13 sec

Length of a platform = 75 m

Formula used:

Speed = $\dfrac{Distance}{Time}$

Speed of the train in m/sec = 54 × $\left(\dfrac{5}{18}\right)$ = 15 m/sec

$\Rightarrow$ Length of the train = 15 × 13 = 195 m

Time taken to cross the platform = $\dfrac{(195 + 75)}{15}$

$\Rightarrow$ Time taken to cross the platform = $\dfrac{270}{15}$ = 18 sec

∴ The time train will take to cross the platform is 18 sec.

Hence, the correct option is (D).

59. Total student $= 75$

$\dfrac{3}{5} th$ of the total number of boys $= 27$

∴ Total number of boys $= 27 \times \dfrac{3}{5} = 45$

∴ Total number of girls $= 75 - 45 = 30$

$\left(\dfrac{1}{5}\right)$th of the total number of girls $= 6$

So, required ratio $= 27:6 = 9:2$

Hence, the correct option is (E).

60. Given:

The average of first three of five number arranged in ascending order is 20 less than the average of the last three of these numbers.

If the sum of the last three of these numbers is 65

Assumption:

Let the numbers be p, q, r, s and t

Calculation:

According to question

$\Rightarrow \dfrac{(p+q+r)}{3} = \dfrac{(r+s+t)}{3} - 20$

$\Rightarrow p + q + r = r + s + t - 60$

$\Rightarrow p + q = s + t - 60$ 1

Given,

$\Rightarrow r + s + t = 65$

$\Rightarrow s + t = 65 - r$ 2

Putting the value of s + t in 1 we get

$\Rightarrow p + q = 65 - r - 60$

$\therefore p + q + r = 5$

Hence, the correct option is (B).

61. Given:

Company A:

2010 = 4.3, 2011 = 2.5, 2012 = 3.5, 2013 = 1.7, 2014 = 3.6

Company B:

2010 = 2.4, 2011= 4.4, 2012 = 1.8, 2013 = 3.1, 2014 = 1.3

Formula:

Percentage = $\left(\dfrac{Required\ data}{Total\ data}\right) \times 100$

Required % = $\left(\dfrac{13}{15.6}\right) \times 100$

= 83.33%

$\therefore$ Turnover of company B over all the years was approximately 83.33% of company A.

Hence, the correct option is (A).

62. Given:

In 2010 : company A = 4.3, company B = 2.4

In 2011 : company A = 4.4, company B = 2.5

In 2012 : company A = 3.5, company B = 1.8

In 2013 : company A = 3.1, company B = 1.7

In 2014 : company A = 3.6, company B = 1.3

Formula:

Required difference = Turnover of company A – Turnover of company B

Calculation:

In 2010: 4.3 – 2.4 = 1.9

In 2011: 4.4 – 2.5 = 1.9

In 2012: 3.5 – 1.8 = 1.7

In 2013: 3.1 – 1.7 = 1.4

In 2014: 3.6 – 1.3 = 2.3

$\therefore$ In 2014 difference between turnover is maximum.

Hence, the correct option is (B).

63. Given:

Company A turnover for all the years

In 2010 = 4.3

In 2011 = 2.5

In 2012 = 3.5

In 2013 = 1.7

In 2014 = 3.6

Formula:

Average = $\dfrac{Sum\ of\ data}{Number\ of\ data}$

Calculation:

Sum = 4.3 + 2.5 + 3.5 + 1.7 + 3.6 = 15.6

Average = $\dfrac{15.6}{5}$ = 3.12 lakhs

$\therefore$ Average turnover of company A over the given period is 3.12 lakhs.

Hence, the correct option is (A).

64. Given:

Turnover of company A in 2011 = 2.5

Turnover of company B in 2011 = 4.4

Formula:

Percentage = $\left(\dfrac{Required\ data}{Total\ data}\right) \times 100$

Calculation:

Required % = $\left(\dfrac{2.5}{4.4}\right) \times 100 = 56.81\%$

$\therefore$ Turnover of company A in 2011 was approximately 57% of the turnover of company B in the same year.

Hence, the correct option is (A).

65. Given:

Company A:

2010 = 4.3, 2011= 2.5, 2012 = 3.5, 2013=1.7, 2014= 3.6

Company B:

2010 = 2.4, 2011= 4.4, 2012 = 1.8, 2013=3.1, 2014= 1.3

Formula:

Difference = Total turnover of company A – Total turnover of company B

Calculation:

Total turnover of company A from 2010 to 2014.

= 4.3 + 2.5 + 3.5 + 1.7 + 3.6 = 15.6 lakhs

Total turnover of company B from 2010 to 2014

= 2.4 + 4.4 + 1.8 + 3.1 + 1.3 = 13 lakhs

Difference = 15.6 – 13 = 2.6 lakhs

∴ Difference between total turnover of two companies is 2.6 lakh.

Hence, the correct option is (B).

66. Let the side of the square be 'a' cm

Perimeter of square = 4a cm

Diagonal of square = $a\sqrt{2}$ cm

Now,

⇒ 2 × 4a = 3 × 2 × $a\sqrt{2}$ – 5.8

⇒ 8a = 8.48a – 5.8

⇒ 0.48a = 5.8

⇒ a = $\dfrac{5.8}{0.48}$ ≅ 12 cm

∴ The side of the square is 12 cm

Hence, the correct option is (C).

67. Given:

A man could buy 3 kg more = Rs. 540

Reduced Price of 3 kg coffee = 540 × $\dfrac{10}{100}$ = Rs. 54

Reduced Price of 1 kg coffee = $\dfrac{54}{3}$ = Rs. 18

Original price of 1 kg coffee = 18 × $\dfrac{100}{90}$ = Rs. 20

Difference in Original and reduced price = Rs. 20 – Rs. 18 = Rs. 2

∴ Difference in Original and reduced price is Rs. 2.

Hence, the correct option is (B).

68. Ratio of investments made by Ravi and Kishan $= \dfrac{65000}{95000} =$
$\dfrac{13}{19}$

After one year, they got Rs. 3968 at an interest of 6% per quarter.

Annual rate of interest = 6 × 4 = 24%

Total amount = Principle × (1 + Rate%)

⇒ 3968 = Principle × (1 + 0.24)

⇒ Principle = $\dfrac{3968}{1.24}$ = 3200

The profit before investing into bank was Rs. 3200.

⇒ Ravi's share $= 3200 \times \dfrac{13}{32} = 1300$

Kishan's share $= 3200\dfrac{19}{32} = 1900$

∴ Difference of their share of profits = Rs. (1900 - 1300) = Rs. 600

Hence, the correct option is (A).

69. Given:

Profit $= 20\%$

New profit if sells Rs. 8 more $= 30\%$

As we know,

Selling price $= (100 + \text{Profit})\%$ of C.P.

Let the C.P. of an article be Rs. x.

According to the question,

120% of C.P. $+8 = 130\%$ of C.P.

⇒ 130% of $x - 120\%$ of $x = 8$

⇒ 10% of $x = 8$

⇒ $\dfrac{10}{100} \times x = 8$

⇒ $x = 80$

Original C.P. of 16 article $= 16x$

Required C.P. $= 16 \times 80$

$= $ Rs. 1280

∴ The original cost price of 16 such articles is Rs. 1280 .

Hence, the correct option is (D).

70. X complete work in 9 days.

X's 1-day work $= \dfrac{1}{9}$

Y complete work in $= 18$ days

Y's 1-day work $= \dfrac{1}{18}$

Both working together for 1 hour $= \dfrac{1}{9} + \dfrac{1}{9}$

Both working together for 1 hour $= \dfrac{(2+1)}{18}$

Time to complete the work together $= \dfrac{18}{3} = 6$ days

$\therefore$ Time to complete $\left(\dfrac{2}{3}\right)$ of total work together $=$

$6 \times \left(\dfrac{2}{3}\right) = 4$ days

Hence, the correct option is (A).

Q.71 Eight boxes: 1 to 8

Eight items: Chocolates, Papers, Toys, Books, Medicines, Pens, Pencils, and Ice Creams

1) Medicines are kept in the lowermost box.

2) Only three boxes kept between Toys and Medicines.

3) Ice Cream box is kept immediately above Pens, which is immediately above Books.

Case 1	
Box	Items
8	Ice Creams
7	Pens
6	Books
5	Toys
4	
3	
2	
1	Medicines

Case 2	
Box	Items
8	
7	
6	
5	Toys
4	Ice Creams
3	Pens
2	Books
1	Medicines

4) Chocolate boxes are kept above Papers but below Pens. (This eliminates case 2)
5) Toys are kept above Pencils, which is immediately below Chocolates. (This eliminates case 2)

Case 1	
Box	Items
8	Ice Creams
7	Pens
6	Books
5	Toys
4	Chocolates
3	Pencils
2	Papers
1	Medicines

So, 'Ice Cream' is kept at the topmost box.

Hence, the correct option is (B).

Ques (72-76): Eight boxes: 1 to 8

Eight items: Chocolates, Papers, Toys, Books, Medicines, Pens, Pencils, and Ice Creams

1) Medicines are kept in the lowermost box.

2) Only three boxes kept between Toys and Medicines.

3) Ice Cream box is kept immediately above Pens, which is immediately above Books.

Case 1	
Box	Items
8	Ice Creams
7	Pens
6	Books
5	Toys
4	
3	
2	
1	Medicines

Case 2	
Box	Items
8	
7	
6	
5	Toys
4	Ice Creams
3	Pens
2	Books
1	Medicines

4) Chocolate boxes are kept above Papers but below Pens. (This eliminates case 2)
5) Toys are kept above Pencils, which is immediately below Chocolates. (This eliminates case 2)

Case 1	
Box	Items
8	Ice Creams
7	Pens
6	Books
5	Toys
4	Chocolates
3	Pencils
2	Papers
1	Medicines

72. So, 'three' boxes are there between the box in which Books are kept and the box in which Papers are kept.

Hence, the correct option is (E).

73. The number of boxes above the box on which Toys is kept is 3, the same as the number of boxes below the box on which Chocolates is kept.

Hence, the correct option is (C).

74. All the boxes are kept in even number boxes except Pens, while Pens are kept in the odd number boxes.

So, 'Pen' does not belong to that group.

Hence, the correct option is (D).

75. After analysing the above table, we can conclude that all the statements given above are true.

Hence, the correct option is (E).

76. All the boxes are kept in odd number boxes except Chocolates. Chocolates are kept in the even number box.

Hence, Chocolates do not belong to that group.

Hence, the correct option is (C).

77. Given statements: Q ≤ A < D < K ≤ M = J = F > Z

Conclusions:

I. K > Q → True (as **Q ≤ A < D < K** ≤ M = J = F > Z → K > Q)

II. F ≥ K → True (as Q ≤ A < D < **K ≤ M = J = F** > Z → F ≥ K)

Therefore, both I and II are true.

Hence, the correct option is (C).

78. Given statements: N ≥ H ≤ T > R = E; E > O < P = I

On combination: N ≥ H ≤ T > R = E > O < P = I

Conclusion

I. N > E → False (as N ≥ H ≤ T > R = E)

II. T > O → True (as T > R = E > O)

So, only conclusion II follows.

Hence, the correct option is (C).

79. Given Statement: T > P < O = R ≥ U ≥ A > L > W = X > F < J ≤ E ≤ J > K > D

Conclusions:

I. R > F → True (As, R ≥ U ≥ A > L > W = X > F → R > F).

II. E ≥ L → False (As, definite relationship between the two cannot be determined).

III. O > D → False (As, definite relationship between the two cannot be determined).

IV. P > X → False (As, definite relationship between the two cannot be determined).

Hence, the correct option is (A).

80. Given Statements: H < A > R = D; I ≤ K ≥ P; H < P

On Combining: I ≤ K ≥ P > H < A > R = D

Conclusions:

I. K > R → False (As, K ≥ P > H < A > R → Clear relation between K and R cannot be determined)

II. D ≤ K → False (As, K ≥ P > H < A > R = D→ Clear relation between D and K cannot be determined)

So, none of the conclusion is true

Hence, the correct option is (E).

81. Statement:

C < R < I ≤ S ≤ E ≤ A = N > O < G < Y > B ≥ D

Conclusions:

I. C < N → False (C < R < I ≤ S ≤ E ≤ A = N > O < G → No definite relation between the two can be determined)

II. R < O → False (R < I ≤ S ≤ E ≤ A = N > O → No definite relation between the two can be determined)

III. I > O → False (I ≤ S ≤ E ≤ A = N > O → No definite relation between the two can be determined)

Hence, the correct option is (E).

Ques (82-87): Eight Persons: A, E, I, J, K, L, M, and O

Colors: Red, Green, Yellow, Violet, White, Pink, Grey, and Black

1) The one who likes Black sits immediately left to L who likes Green.

As it is not clear, if L sits on the inner circle or the outer circle, two cases will be formed.

Case 1:

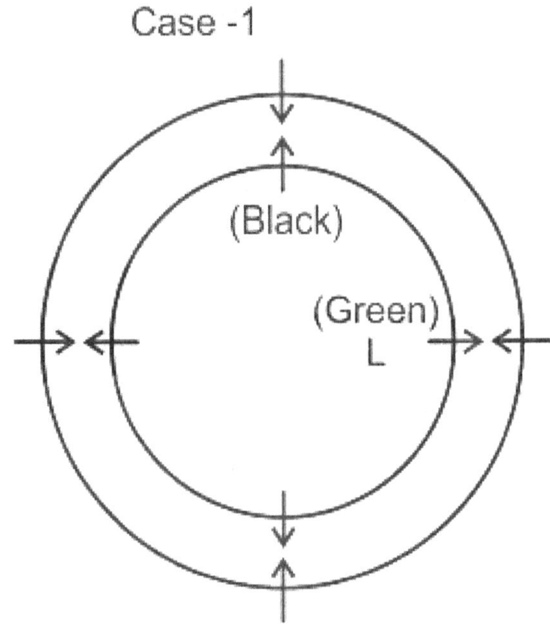

Case 2:

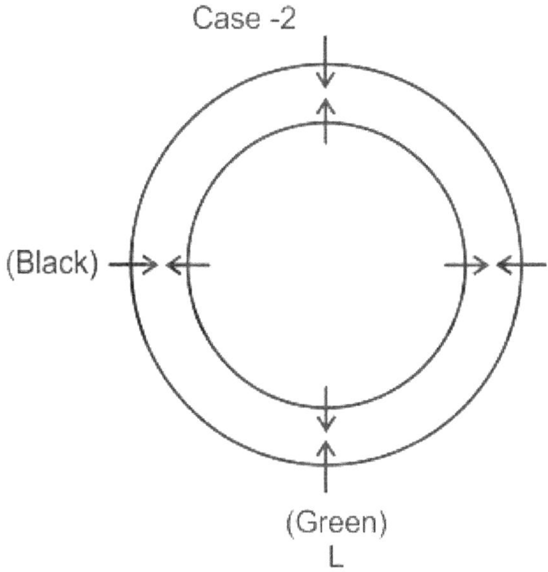

2) The one who likes Black faces the one who likes White.

Case 1:

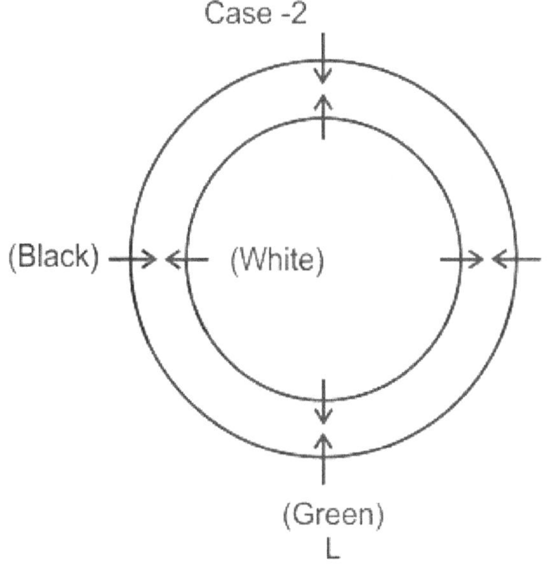

Case 2:

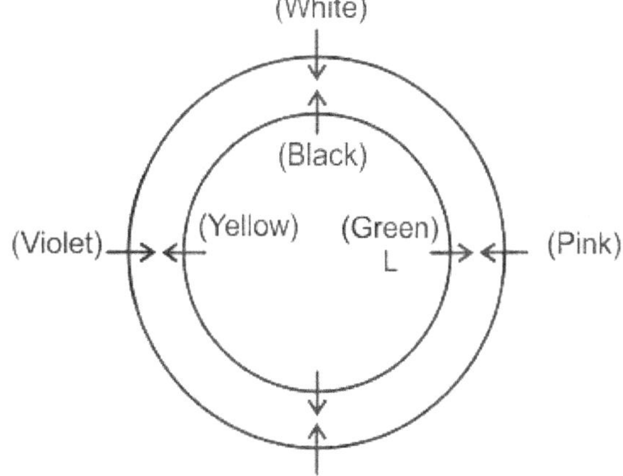

3) The one who likes Pink sits opposite the one who likes Violet in the same circle.

4) The one who likes Pink is facing inside.

As the above condition is not satisfied in case 2, it will get canceled.

5) The one who likes Yellow faces the one who likes Violet.

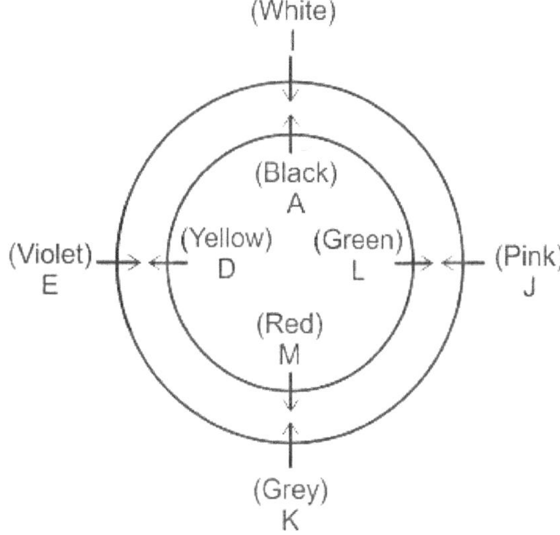

6) E sits immediately left to K who likes Grey.

7) O likes Yellow and sits immediate right to M.

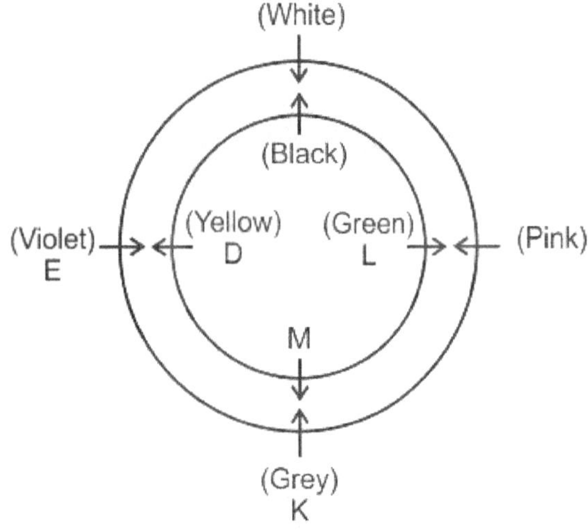

8) I sits immediate right of J.

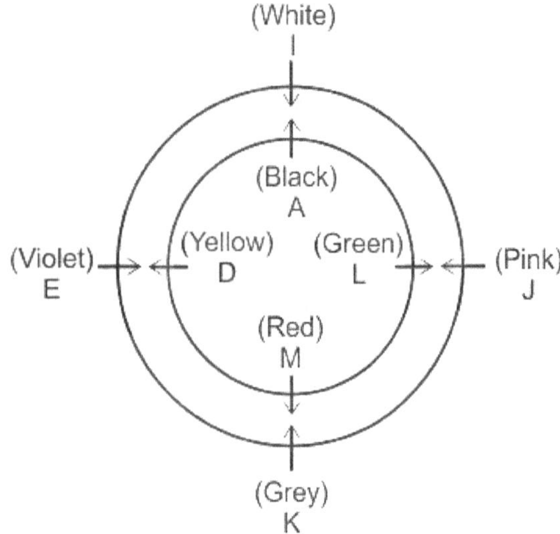

82. So, A likes Black.

Hence, the correct option is (E).

83. So, M likes Red.

Hence, the correct option is (D).

84. So, the one who likes Yellow sits opposite the one who likes Green.

Hence, the correct option is (C).

85. So, L faces J.

Hence, the correct option is (D).

86. So, the one who likes Pink sits immediately right to the one who likes Grey.

Hence, the correct option is (B).

87. After analysing the above information, we can conclude that all the given statements are true.

Hence, the correct option is (E).

88. Following the above instructions will lead to the below diagram:

C + B % A= C is 1 km to the south of B which is 5 km to the east of A

D + E - B → D is 1 km to the south of E which is 1 km to the east of B

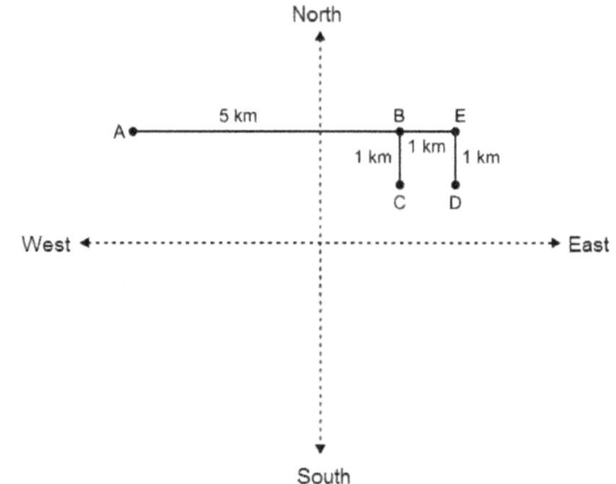

The distance between C and D is 1 km.

Hence, the correct option is (A).

89. Following the above instructions will lead to the below diagram:

C + B % A → C is 1 km to the south of B which is 5 km to the east of A.

C % D → C is 5 km to the east of D.

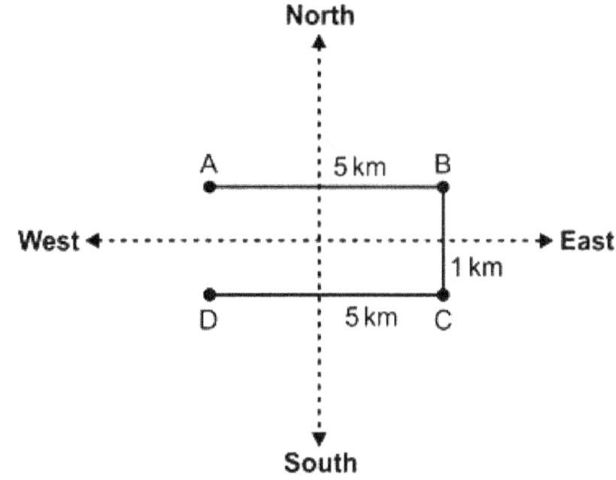

The distance between A and D is 1 km.

Hence, the correct option is (A).

90. Following the above instructions will lead to the below diagram:

N % M → N is 5 km to the east of M

N - R - Q → N is 1 km to the east of R which is 1 km to the east of Q

O & Q → O is 5 km to the south of Q

O + P → O is 1 km to the south of P

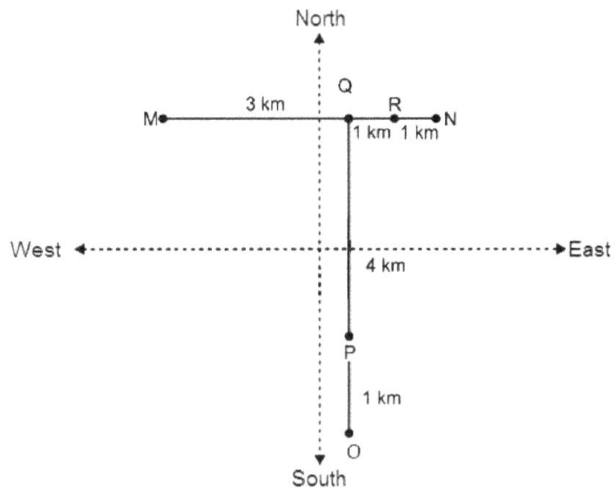

By, using Pythagoras theorem,

$PM^2 = 4^2 + 3^2$

$PM^2 = 25$

$PM = 5$

The distance between P and M is 5 km.

Hence, the correct option is (B).

91. The least possible Venn diagram for the given statements is as follows,

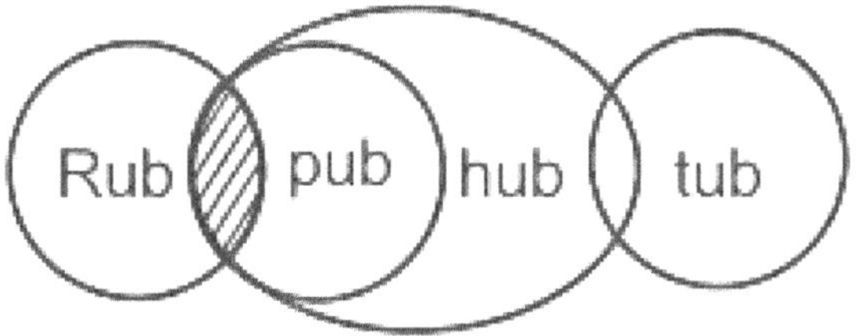

Conclusions:

I. All hub being rub is a possibility → True (possibility is true as shown below)

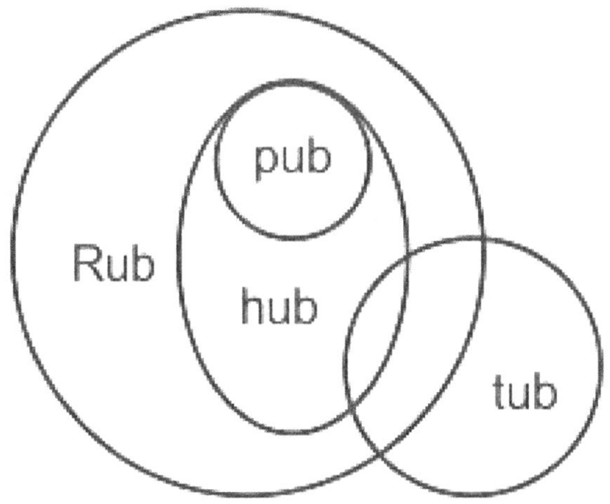

II. Some pub is tub → False (it is possible but not definite, as direct relation between pub and tub is not given)

So, Only I follows is the correct answer.

Additional Information:

Only a few rub is pub means Some rub is pub + some rub is not pub

But all rub/hub can be pub.

Hence, the correct option is (A).

92. The best possible Venn diagram for the given statements is as follows:

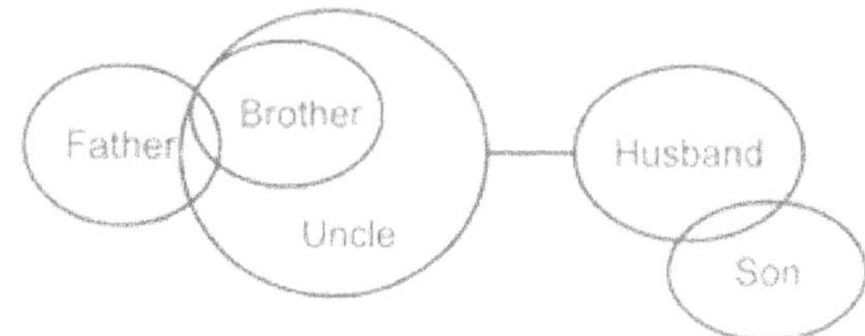

Conclusions:

I. Some sons are uncle → It is possible but not definite, therefore false.

II. No father is a husband → It is possible but not definite, so false.

III. Some uncles are fathers → It is true.

IV. Some husbands are brothers → It is false.

Therefore, only conclusion III follows.

Hence, the correct option is (D).

93. The best possible Venn diagram for the given statements is as follows,

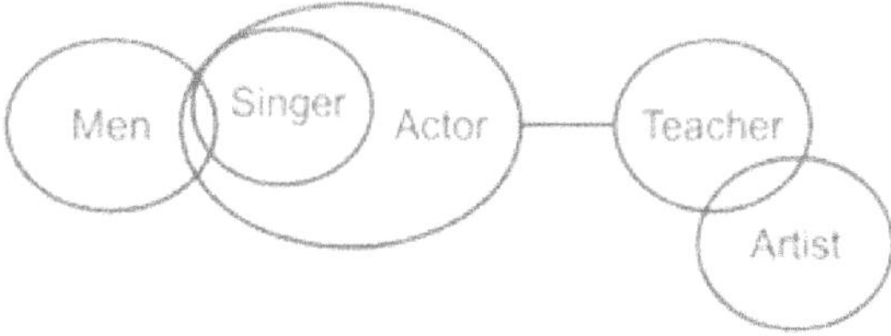

Conclusions:

I. Some artists are actors → It is possible but not definite, therefore false.

II. Some men are teachers → It is possible but not definite, so false.

III. Some actors are men → It is true.

IV. No singer is teacher → It is true.

Therefore, only conclusions III and IV follow.

Hence, the correct option is (C).

94. The best possible Venn diagram for the given statements is as follows:

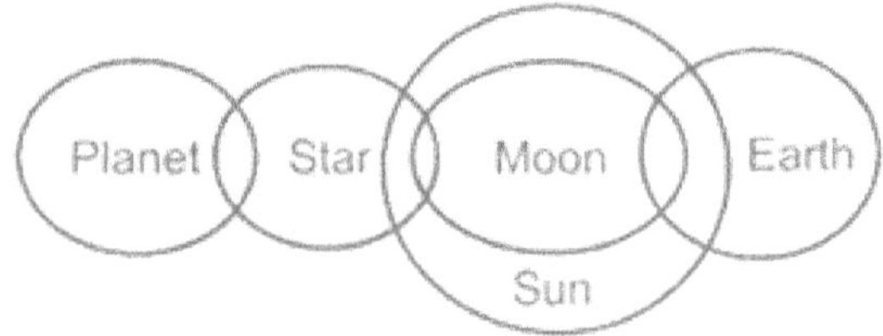

Conclusions:

I. Some planets are sun → It is possible but not definite, so false.

II. Some earth are stars → It is possible but not definite, therefore false.

III. No sun is earth → It is false.

IV. Some suns are not Earth → It is possible but not definite, so false.

Conclusion III and IV form a complementary pair.

Therefore, none is follows

Hence, the correct option is (E).

95. The best possible Venn diagram for the given statements is as follows:

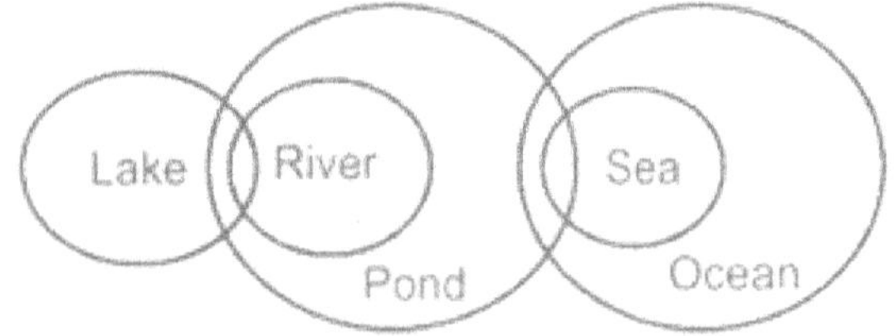

Conclusions:

I. Some oceans are rivers → It is false.

II. Some lakes are ponds → It is true.

III. Some sea are lakes → It is possible but not definite, so false.

IV. Some oceans being lake is possible → Possibility is true.

Therefore, conclusions II and IV follow.

Hence, the correct option is (D).

Ques (96-100):1) The first element of each code is a letter that represents the last letter of each word.

2) The second element of each code is a symbol that represents the highest vowel in the word.

After a careful observation we can easily determine the following:

A	E	I	O	U
@	#	$	%	&

3) The last element of each code is a number that represents the number of consonants in each word.

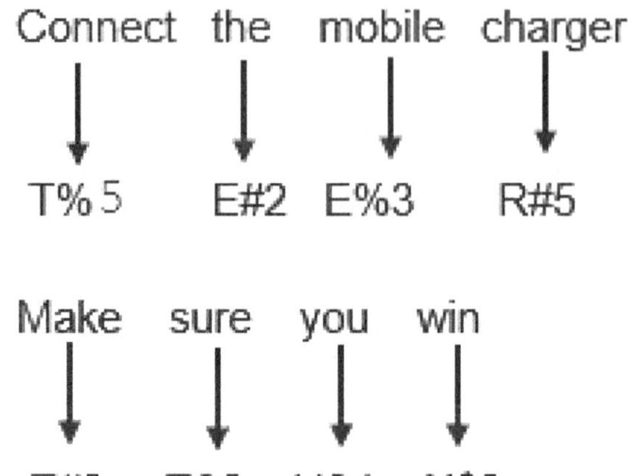

96. Clearly, the code for the word 'mobile' is E%3.

Hence, the correct option is (A).

97. Clearly, the code U&1 represents 'you' in the given code language.

Hence, the correct option is (C).

98. Clearly, the code for the word 'the' is E#2. To have the same code, the last letter of the word must be 'E', the highest vowel in the word should be 'E' and there should be two consonants in the word. Clearly, only 'she' satisfies this criteria. Thus, the code of 'she' is same as the code of 'the'.

Hence, the correct option is (D).

99. Clearly, the code E#2 represents both 'the' and 'make'.

Hence, the correct option is (E).

100. Clearly, the code T%5 represents 'Connect'.

Hence, the correct option is (B).

Ques (1-2):Direction: In the following sentence, some parts have been printed in bold. One of the bold parts is incorrectly spelt. Pick up that part and choose that word. If there is no error in the bold parts, choose option (E) i.e., No error as the answer.

Q.1 The ill and the **mentally** unstable have been **dumped** into this remote corner of the city, this act clearly shows a **delibarate** lack of **empathy.**

A. Mentally
B. Dumped
C. Delibarate
D. Empathy
E. No error

Q.2 Lathargy has taken over his entire **existence** and he spends his day **languishing** in **idleness.**

A. lathargy
B. Existence
C. Llanguishing
D. Idleness
E. No error

Q.3 Direction: The following question has two blanks, each blank indicating that something has been omitted. Choose the set of words for each blank that best fits in the context of the sentence.

The Reserve Bank of India on Monday _______ Draft Variation Margin Directions, 2020 and asked the stakeholders to _______ their suggestions and comments.

A. releasing, submit
B. release, submitted
C. released, submitting
D. released, submit
E. realize, submission

Q.4 Direction: In the following question, a sentence is given with two blanks. You have to find the pair of words from the given options that fit both the blanks in the given order and make the sentence grammatically and contextually correct.

If you look at the number of districts, then the areas under the _______ of left - wing extremism have shrunk _______ more than 40% in the last three years.

A. existence, with
B. influence, by
C. ecstasy, about
D. confidence, off
E. None of these

Ques (5-9):Direction: A passage is given below with five blanks labelled (A)-(E). Below the passage, five options are given for each blank. Choose the word that fits each blank most appropriately in the context of the passage, and mark the corresponding answer.

Oddly enough, events like this drove me to __(A)__. I reluctantly pursued a career in research. But, because these events are not going away, I, like a __(B)__, was drawn to research of widely publicized racially __(C)__ events on everyone, but especially on people of color. While I am heartbroken at the events themselves, I am glad to be doing research that might __(D)__ to better understanding, if not some __(E)__, of the wounds that separate us.

Q.5 Which of the following words most appropriately fits the blank labelled (A)?

A. narcotics
B. academia
C. blacks
D. cinema
E. psychiatry

Q.6 Which of the following words most appropriately fits the blank labelled (B)?

A. rock
B. particle
C. feather
D. slave
E. magnet

Q.7 Which of the following words most appropriately fits the blank labelled (C)?

A. charged
B. abused
C. challenged
D. mentored
E. ambiguous

Q.8 Which of the following words most appropriately fits the blank labelled (D)?

A. delude
B. excel
C. indemnify
D. secure
E. lead

Q.9 Which of the following words most appropriately fits the blank labelled (E)?

A. exaggeration
B. enhancement
C. healing
D. cure
E. therapy

Q.10 Direction: In the questions given below, there is a sentence in which one part is given in bold. The part given in bold may or may not be grammatically correct. Choose the best alternative among the four given which can replace the part in bold to make the sentence grammatically correct. If the part given in bold is already correct and does not require any replacement, choose option (E), i.e. "No replacement required" as your answer.

The High Court has **sought a response from** the state government regarding the dearness allowance dues of the state government employees.

A. Sought a response to
B. Sought a response off
C. Sought a response of
D. Sought a response about
E. No replacement required

Q.11 Direction: Which of the option (A), (B), (C) and (D) given below, should replace the phrase printed in bold in the sentence to make it grammatically correct? If the sentence is correct as it is given and no correction is required, mark (E) as the answer.

The composition of **the Council of Ministers throw light** on Mr. Modi's thinking regarding the agenda that will develop the country.

A. The Council of Ministers throws light
B. The Council of Ministers threw light
C. The Council of Ministers has throw light
D. The Council of Ministers throwing light
E. No correction required

Ques (12-16):Direction: Below, a set of eight statements is given, out of which the first sentence, given in bold, is fixed. The rest are jumbled in any random order. Out of the remaining seven statements, one does not belong to the passage. Rearrange the remaining sentences in the correct order and then answer the questions.

A. Until the early 2000s, Bollywood remained the main source of entertainment for the Himalayan monarchy of Bhutan.

B. As the industry continues to boom, a new parallel cinema movement, made mostly for an international audience, is emerging.

C. Arun Bhattarai's The Next Guardian, a bittersweet documentary set in a remote monastery, also features a character going through a sexual identity crisis.

D. Passionate, self-taught film-makers, armed with themes ranging from magical realism to social justice and sexual identity, have begun to appear in major international film festivals in recent years.

E. The advent of the internet brought along a tidal wave of new content and a nascent parallel voice has also begun taking shape.

F. It was a love triangle about two college boys falling for the same girl, that birthed the commercial Bhutanese film industry.

G. Two decades later, commercial Bhutanese films continue to ride on Bollywood influences, with staple themes of mawkish drama, syrupy duets and acrobatic action sequences featuring prominently.

H. It was in 1999 when the late Tshering Wangyel released the first Dzongkha-language movie called Rewaa (Hope).

Q.12 Which of the following sentences is SECOND in the correct order?
A. B   **B.** G   **C.** E   **D.** H
E. F

Q.13 Which of the following sentences is FOURTH in the correct order?
A. E   **B.** C   **C.** G   **D.** B
E. H

Q.14 Which of the following sentences does not belong in the given passage?
A. E   **B.** F   **C.** G   **D.** H
E. C

Q.15 Which of the following sentences is FIFTH in the correct order?
A. C   **B.** E   **C.** B   **D.** F
E. H

Q.16 Which of the following sentences is SIXTH in the correct order?
A. E   **B.** D   **C.** C   **D.** B
E. G

Ques (17-19):Direction: In each of the questions given below, three words are given in bold. These three words may or may not be in their correct positions. The sentence is then followed by options with the correct combination of words that should replace each other in order to make the sentence grammatically and contextually correct. Find the correct combination of words that replace each other. If the sentence is correct as it is, select '(E)' as your option.

Q.17 The **dynamics** (A) story 'A Shadow' gives a subtle **picture** (B) of the **famous** (C) of relationships in an Indian family.
[IBPS PO, 2021]

A. CBA   **B.** ACB   **C.** CAB   **D.** BCA
E. No error

Q.18 In this utter **wasteland**(A) of human remains, two robots **decided**(B) to decode the fall of the greatest **species**(C) that ever existed.
[IBPS PO, 2021]

A. ACB   **B.** BAC   **C.** CBA   **D.** CAB
E. No error

Q.19 Union minister M.J. Akbar **newspapers** (A) to take legal action against several women **journalists** (B) who had **accused** (C) him of sexual harassment at two **threatened** (D) where he had been an editor.
[IBPS PO, 2021]

A. Both (A)-(B) and (C)-(D)
B. Only (C)-(D)
C. Only (A)-(B)
D. Only (A)-(D)
E. No improvement

Ques (20-22):Direction: In the following sentence, some parts have errors and some are correct. Find out which part has an error and mark it as your answer. If there is no error, mark 'No error' as your answer.

Q.20 The challenge before India is (A)/ to deepening the tactical (B)/ engagement with China (C)/ keeping strategic glitches at bay (D)/. No error.
[IBPS PO, 2019]

A. (A)   **B.** (B)   **C.** (C)   **D.** (D)
E. No error

Q.21 The trip to the airport and the (A)/ flight to Singapore was both uneventful, (B)/ the hotel accommodations were better than they (C)/ could have expected on such short notice. (D)/ No error (E)
[IBPS PO, 2019]

A. (A)   **B.** (B)   **C.** (C)   **D.** (D)
E. No error

Q.22 I have no difficulty in making it clear (A)/ to her that if plants and animals didn't produces (B)/ offspring of their kind, they would cease (C)/ to exist, and everything in the world would soon die. (D)/ No error (E).

[IBPS PO, 2019]

A. (A)   **B.** (B)   **C.** (C)   **D.** (D)
E. No error

Ques (23-24):Direction: Each question contains three statements, one or more of which may not be grammatically correct. You are required to identify the incorrect statements from the options given below and mark that as your answer.

Q.23 I. There should be special places in hell for those which promoted Brexit.

II. The reason May's plan failed was her effort to avoid any possibility of a hard border.

III. A soft border was an essential feature of the agreement that ended 30 years of terrorist violence.

A. Only II   **B.** Only I and II
C. Only I and III   **D.** Only I
E. All are correct

Q.24 I. Global warming is on track to transform the frigid mountain peaks in bare rocks shortly.

II. People living in the downstream areas of this river basins benefit directly and indirectly from its resources.

III. The projected reductions in pre-monsoon river flows will hit the hardest.

A. Only II   **B.** Only I and II
C. Only I and III   **D.** Only III
E. All are correct

Ques (25-27):Direction: In each of the questions below, a sentence is given with two blanks that indicate that some parts are missing. Identify the correct pair of words that fit in the sentence to make it grammatically and contextually correct.

Q.25 What the ruling by the International Court of Justice __________ , is that should Pakistan decide to retry Jadhav, the Indian naval officer will be properly __________ by Indian counsel.

A. enacts, guided
B. explains, ingrained
C. guarantees, represented
D. enshrines, represented
E. means, feared

Q.26 They fear that any original thinking or non-conformist initiative may attract accusations of __________ , making PSU managers shun risk and stick to procedures and __________ rather than break out boldly in new directions.

A. transgression, peculiarities
B. malfeasance, precedents
C. excellence, patients
D. wrongdoing, projects
E. exuberance, patents

Q.27 Insurance law has to be revisited to also ensure that there is a guaranteed __________ of policies, that age is no bar for __________ , and pre-existing conditions are uniformly covered.

A. renewal, entry
B. relapse, coming
C. review, exit
D. enhancement, bringing
E. robustness, viewing

Ques (28-30):Direction: In the questions given below, there is a sentence in which one part is given in bold. The part given in bold may or may not be grammatically correct. Choose the best alternative among the four given which can replace the part in bold to make the sentence grammatically correct. If the part given in bold is already correct and does not require any replacement, choose option (e), i.e. "No replacement required" as your answer.

Q.28 He is quite a right in his approach towards solving this issue but the higher management disagrees with him.

A. He is quite right
B. He is quite alright
C. He is quiet right
D. He is all quite right
E. No replacement required

Q.29 Though he will never admit this in front of his friends, the loss of his parents is **much too painful for him**.

A. Too much pain for him
B. Much too pain for him
C. Much too pains for him
D. Too much pains for him
E. No replacement required

Q.30 The Supreme Court decided to refer **the unusual complicated issue** to a larger bench of the apex court so that proper justice is meted out to the citizens of the country.

A. The unusual complicatedly issues
B. The unusually complicated issue
C. The unusual complicating issue
D. The unusual complications issue
E. No replacement required

Ques (31-40):Direction: Read the passage given below and answer the questions that follow by choosing the correct/most appropriate options.

In a substantial blow in favor of free speech, the Supreme Court has effectively suspended the operation of the sedition provision in the country's penal law. "All pending trials, appeals, and proceedings with respect to the charge framed under Section 124A be kept in abeyance", it has said in an order that will bring some welcome relief to those calling for the abrogation of Section 124A of the IPC, which criminalizes any speech, writing or representation that "excites disaffection against the government". The Court has recorded its hope and expectation that governments at the Centre and the States will refrain from registering any fresh case of sedition under Section 124A of the IPC, or continuing with any investigation or taking any coercive measure under it. The hope and the expectation arise from the Union government's own submission that it has decided to re-examine and reconsider the provision as part of the Prime Minister's efforts to scrap outdated laws and compliance burdens. Perhaps, realizing that its order may not

be enough to deter thin-skinned and vindictive governments and politically pliant police officers from invoking it against detractors and dissenters, the Court has given liberty to the people to approach the jurisdiction courts if any fresh case is registered for sedition and cite in their support the present order, as well as the Union government's stand.

That the **sedition** law is being **persistently** misused has been **recognized** years ago, and courts have pointed out that the police authorities are not **heeding** the **limitation** imposed by a 1962 Constitution Bench of the Supreme Court on what constitutes sedition. The Court had upheld the section only by reading it down to mean that it is applicable only to "acts involving intention or tendency to create disorder, or disturbance of law and order, or incitement to violence". **In practice, the police has been using the broad definition of sedition to book anyone who criticized the Government in strong and strident language.** The question now before the Court is whether it ought to overrule a decision rendered by a five-judge Bench 60 years ago. If it chooses to do so and strikes down Section 124A as an unconstitutional restriction on free speech, it may help the larger cause of preventing misuse of provisions relating to speech-based offenses. However, the Government may choose to prevent such a situation by amending it so that the offense is narrowly defined to cover only acts that affect the sovereignty, integrity, and security of the state, as reportedly recommended by a panel of experts. When the Government submitted that it was revisiting the provision on its own, it was expecting only an indefinite postponement of the hearing on the constitutional validity of Section 124A, but it must now heed the spirit of the order and take effective steps to prevent its misuse.

Q.31 Choose the most appropriate meaning of the given idiom from the passage:

Pointed out

A. To show that something is likely to exist, happen or be true.

B. To face or be turned in a particular direction.

C. A distinctive feature or characteristic.

D. To direct or aim something at someone or something.

E. To bring attention to something or someone.

Q.32 Choose the antonym of the word 'Abeyance'.

A. Suspension **B.** Dormancy

C. Resuscitation **D.** Quiescence

E. Latency

Q.33 Choose the synonym of the word 'Abrogation'.

A. Institution **B.** Repudiation

C. Establishment **D.** Launch

E. Introduction

Q.34 In this question, a sentence (in bold) from the passage has been divided into five parts (A), (B), (C), (D), and (E). Read the sentence to find out whether there is any grammatical error in it. The error if any, will be in one part of the sentence. If there is no error, the answer is 'No error'. Ignore the error of punctuation if any.

In practice, the police has been using (A)/ the broad definition of sedition to book (B)/ anyone who criticized the Government (C)/ in strong and strident language. (D)/ No error (E)

A. (A) **B.** (B) **C.** (C) **D.** (D)

E. (E)

Q.35 Select the word from the passage that can be used as a one-word substitute for the given group of words.

To pay attention to advise, a warning, etc.

A. Sedition **B.** Persistently

C. Recognized **D.** Heeding

E. Limitation

Q.36 What will fit in the blank taken from the passage:

"The Court has _______ its hope and expectation that governments at the Centre and the States will refrain from registering any fresh case of sedition under Section 124A of the IPC, or continuing with any investigation or taking any coercive measure under it"

A. Record **B.** Records

C. Recorded **D.** Recording

E. Recorder

Q.37 According to the passage, if the Supreme Court abolishes Section 124A:

A. It may help encourage the misuse of provisions relating to speech-based offenses.

B. It may help encourage the misuse of government properties.

C. It may help in encouraging terrorist activities.

D. It may help prevent the misuse of provisions relating to sexual offenses.

E. It may help prevent the misuse of provisions relating to speech-based offenses.

Q.38 Which of the following is/are incorrect according to the given passage?

A. People cannot approach the jurisdiction courts if any fresh case is registered for sedition.

B. The Supreme Court has suspended the operation of the sedition provision in the country's penal law.

C. Section 124A criminalizes any speech, writing, or representation that excites disaffection against the government.

A. Only A **B.** Both A and B

C. Only B **D.** Both B and C

E. Only C

Q.39 Which of the following is/are correct according to the given passage?

A. The Court has an expectation that governments at the Centre and the States will effectively register fresh cases of sedition.

B. The Supreme Court's order is enough to deter vindictive governments and politically pliant police officers.

C. The police used the sedition law to arrest anyone who criticized the Government.

A. Only A **B.** Both A and B

C. Only B **D.** Both B and C

E. Only C

Q.40 What is the central theme of the passage?

A. Encouraging misuse of sedition law.
B. Restricting people from approaching the jurisdiction courts.
C. Intention or tendency to create disorder
D. Preventing misuse of sedition law.
E. The Government must disregard the spirit of the SC order.

// Smart Answer Sheet //

Correct Indicates percentage of students who answered questions correctly.

Skipped Indicates percentage of students who skipped questions.

Q.	Ans.	Correct / Skipped
1	C	88.79 % / 10.6 %
2	A	68.39 % / 31.03 %
3	D	57.93 % / 32.79 %
4	B	88.67 % / 10.83 %
5	B	63.59 % / 35.83 %
6	E	60.27 % / 36.74 %
7	A	64.59 % / 31.31 %
8	E	61.72 % / 30.67 %
9	C	68.68 % / 30.1 %
10	E	45.35 % / 39.08 %
11	A	77.93 % / 12.21 %
12	D	55.88 % / 35.15 %
13	C	59.63 % / 32.44 %
14	E	57.25 % / 39.3 %
15	B	41.08 % / 33.77 %
16	D	47.81 % / 47.01 %
17	A	62.03 % / 37.84 %
18	E	64.76 % / 30.33 %
19	D	12.45 % / 70.75 %
20	B	46.01 % / 44.71 %
21	B	50.88 % / 48.64 %
22	B	58.07 % / 30.77 %
23	D	53.54 % / 34.8 %
24	B	42.94 % / 51.44 %
25	C	58.02 % / 41.52 %
26	B	61.72 % / 34.65 %
27	A	61.8 % / 33.57 %
28	A	54.58 % / 36.0 %
29	E	68.14 % / 31.59 %
30	B	44.84 % / 37.18 %
31	E	48.98 % / 30.51 %
32	C	52.31 % / 42.48 %
33	B	44.12 % / 32.93 %
34	A	19.73 % / 71.62 %
35	D	53.38 % / 34.44 %
36	C	24.65 % / 68.35 %
37	E	51.0 % / 39.93 %
38	A	57.42 % / 35.45 %
39	E	40.59 % / 57.16 %
40	D	58.54 % / 35.08 %

Performance Analysis	
Avg. Score (%)	37.5%
Toppers Score (%)	65.0%
Your Score	

//Hints and Solutions//

1. In the sentence, out of all the bold parts '**delibarate**' is the word that has no meaning. So, '**delibarate**' is an incorrectly spelt word. The correct spelling is '**deliberate**' which means done consciously and intentionally. Therefore, the correct answer is **delibarate** as it is wrongly spelt.

Hence, the correct option is (C).

2. In the sentence, out of all the bold parts '**lathargy**' is the word that has no meaning. So, '**lathargy**' is an incorrectly spelt word. The correct spelling is '**lethargy**' which means a lack of energy and enthusiasm. Therefore, the correct answer is **lathargy** as it is wrongly spelt.

Hence, the correct option is (A).

3. Complete Sentence: The Reserve Bank of India on Monday released Draft Variation Margin Directions, 2020, and asked the stakeholders to submit their suggestions and comments.

From the context of the sentence, the verbs should be used in the given blanks.

The fourth option is correct as the form of both the verbs is correct. 'Released' is the past form of the verb and 'submit' is the base form of the verb to be used with a to-infinitive.

Hence, the correct option is (D).

4. The given sentence is about the data regarding the influence of Left-wing extremism in India in the last three years in which it has seen a downfall.

Among the given options, option (A) is not correct since existence does not fit in the context and the same can be said about the second word also. Option (C) is not correct since both the words are not fit for the blanks in the sentence. The same can be said about options (D). Only option (B) implies the actual meaning intended in the sentence and it explains the meaning that the number of districts affected by left-wing extremism has decreased in the last few years.

If you look at the number of districts, then the areas under the influence of left-wing extremism have shrunk by more than 40% in the last three years.

Hence, the correct option is (B).

5. As mentioned, events like this drove him to something that was associated with a career in research. Thus, 'narcotics', 'cinema' and 'psychiatry' are irrelevant here.

The narrator later mentions that he was drawn to research on people of color, which is a wider term than blacks.

Thus, 'academia', which refers to 'the environment or community concerned with the pursuit of research, education, and scholarship', is the correct answer.

Hence, the correct option is (B).

6. The concerned sentence mentions that the narrator was drawn to research.

This indicates that something which has the property to get attract and get attracted must be mentioned in the blank space.

Clearly, 'magnet' is the best fit answer.

Hence, the correct option is (E).

7. The word in the blank space has been modified by the adverb 'racially' and the blank space is followed by the word 'events'.

This indicates that the word in the blank must signify that the events were loaded with racism.

This meaning is served by 'charged'.

'Ambiguous' does not give the desired meaning.

A person can be said to be racially 'abused' or 'challenged' but not an event.

Hence, the correct option is (A).

8. Lead: to guide someone or something along a way

Delude: mislead, fool

Excel: to be very good at doing something

Indemnify: reimburse, compensate

Secure: free from worry or doubt, confident

Hence, the correct option is (E).

9. Since the concerned sentence mentions the word 'wounds', 'healing' is the best fit answer.

Therapy is inappropriate in the context of 'wounds'.

Also note that cure is not the answer because if we use it the rule of parallelism suffers. According to this rule all the verbs in a single sentence must follow a similar form. Since understanding has been used, the verb in the blank should end in -ing.

Hence, the correct option is (C).

10. The given phrase in bold in correct in the given context and no replacement is required to be carried out in case of this sentence.

Hence, the correct option is (E).

11. The statement in the present form is not correct due to the fact that the subject-verb agreement is not correct here. We are talking about the composition of the Council of Ministers and it is practically a singular subject and that is why the singular verb will follow. In this case throws should have been used.

The correct statement would have been:

The composition of **the Council of Ministers throws light** on Mr. Modi's thinking regarding the agenda that will develop the country.

Hence, the correct option is (A).

12. The first sentence of a paragraph gives an introduction, which is then elaborated in the following sentences.

A is given as the first, introductory sentence. So, logically, the next sentence must give more information about the Bhutanese cinema circa 2000.

This is only shown by H, which talks about the first commercially successful Bhutanese film. **So, H is the second sentence.**

Sentence F gives more information about the film in H. **So, F is the third sentence.**

The next sentences talk about the current state of commercial cinema. **So, G must be fourth.**

E talks about the emergence of current parallel cinema. **So, E must be fifth.**

It is followed logically by B, which talks about its audience. **So, B is the sixth sentence.**

The remaining sentence, **D, is then, the seventh.**

The correct order is : **AHFGEBD**

Hence, the correct option is (D).

13. The first sentence of a paragraph gives an introduction, which is then elaborated in the following sentences.

A is given as the first, introductory sentence. So, logically, the next sentence must give more information about the Bhutanese cinema circa 2000.

This is only shown by H, which talks about the first commercially successful Bhutanese film. **So, H is the second sentence.**

Sentence F gives more information about the film in H. **So, F is the third sentence.**

The next sentences talk about the current state of commercial cinema. **So, G must be fourth.**

E talks about the emergence of current parallel cinema. **So, E must be fifth.**

It is followed logically by B, which talks about its audience. **So, B is the sixth sentence.**

The remaining sentence, **D, is then, the seventh.**

The correct order is : **AHFGEBD**

Hence, the correct option is (C).

14. The context of most sentences is the emergence of Bhutanese cinema.

Only C talks about Anil Bhattarai's documentary. **So, C is out of context.**

The first sentence of a paragraph gives an introduction, which is then elaborated in the following sentences.

A is given as the first, introductory sentence. So, logically, the next sentence must give more information about the Bhutanese cinema circa 2000.

This is only shown by H, which talks about the first commercially successful Bhutanese film. **So, H is the second sentence.**

Sentence F gives more information about the film in H. **So, F is the third sentence.**

The next sentences talk about the current state of commercial cinema. **So, G must be fourth.**

E talks about the emergence of current parallel cinema. **So, E must be fifth.**

It is followed logically by B, which talks about its audience. **So, B is the sixth sentence.**

The remaining sentence, **D, is then, the seventh.**

The correct order is : **AHFGEBD**

Hence, the correct option is (E).

15. The first sentence of a paragraph gives an introduction, which is then elaborated in the following sentences.

A is given as the first, introductory sentence. So, logically, the next sentence must give more information about the Bhutanese cinema circa 2000.

This is only shown by H, which talks about the first commercially successful Bhutanese film. **So, H is the second sentence.**

Sentence F gives more information about the film in H. **So, F is the third sentence.**

The next sentences talk about the current state of commercial cinema. **So, G must be fourth.**

E talks about the emergence of current parallel cinema. **So, E must be fifth.**

It is followed logically by B, which talks about its audience. **So, B is the sixth sentence.**

The remaining sentence, **D, is then, the seventh.**

The correct order is : **AHFGEBD**

Hence, the correct option is (B).

16. The first sentence of a paragraph gives an introduction, which is then elaborated in the following sentences.

A is given as the first, introductory sentence. So, logically, the next sentence must give more information about the Bhutanese cinema circa 2000.

This is only shown by H, which talks about the first commercially successful Bhutanese film. **So, H is the second sentence.**

Sentence F gives more information about the film in H. **So, F is the third sentence.**

The next sentences talk about the current state of commercial cinema. **So, G must be fourth.**

E talks about the emergence of current parallel cinema. **So, E must be fifth.**

It is followed logically by B, which talks about its audience. **So, B is the sixth sentence.**

The remaining sentence, **D, is then, the seventh.**

The correct order is : **AHFGEBD**

Hence, the correct option is (D).

17. Reading the given sentence we find that:

The first part of the sentence wrongly uses the word dynamics and should be replaced with the word famous.

The sentence is talking about a famous story therefore A should be replaced with C.

The word B is correctly used in the sentence i.e subtle picture means presenting the proper idea in a fine manner.

Therefore the correct sequence will be CBA.

The correct sentence will be: The famous story 'A Shadow' gives a subtle picture of the dynamics of relationship in an Indian family.

Hence, the correct option is (A).

18. Reading the given sentence we find that:

All the emboldened words are placed in the correct order. Thus the sentence does not require any changes and is contextually correct. Therefore the correct answer is no error.

Hence, the correct option is (E).

19. The given statement, is not correct. It does not make any sense.

- Though it may seem that with some changes, the sentence would imply something.

- Here, we have to understand the context of the statement which is talking about the action to be taken by the Union Minister against others.

- Now, coming to the options, Option (A) can be ruled out since it is clear that with this option being implemented, the resultant statement would not make any sense whatsoever.

- With Option (B) also, the same may be said since it also does not make any sense.

- Option (C) can be ruled out since it does imply anything.

- Option (D) is the right pick since if we interchange the words according to this option, the resultant statement will make sense. 'Threatened' should be used along with the term 'legal action', and with further part of the sentence 'two newspapers' fitting in well.

Correct sentence: Union minister M.J. Akbar threatened to take legal action against several women journalists who had accused him of sexual harassment at two newspapers where he had been the editor.

Hence, the correct option is (D).

20. The error lies in part (B) of the sentence. The usage of 'deepening' is incorrect. Use 'deepen' in place of deepening.

According to grammar, whenever we have an infinitive phrase we need to use the base form of the verb with the preposition 'to' i.e., 'to + V1'

Example- I decided not to go to London.

So, the correct sentence is: The challenge before India is to deepen the tactical engagement with China keeping strategic glitches at bay.

Hence, the correct option is (B).

21. The error lies in part (B) of the sentence.

In Part (B), replace 'was' with were because here two individual subjects are connected by 'and' so the subject is in the plural and the verb should also be in plural.

When the subject of the sentence is composed of two or more nouns or pronouns connected by and, use a plural verb.

So, the correct sentence is: The trip to the airport and the flight to Singapore were both uneventful, the hotel accommodations were better than they could have expected on such short notice.

Hence, the correct option is (B).

22. The error lies in part (B) of the sentence.

In part (B), replace 'produces' with 'produce' because the subject 'plants and animals' are in plural so the verb should also be in plural form.

RULE: When the subject of the sentence is composed of two or more nouns or pronouns connected by and, use a plural verb.

So, the correct sentence is: I have no difficulty in making it clear to her that if plants and animals didn't produce offspring of their kind, they would cease to exist, and everything in the world would soon die.

Hence, the correct option is (B).

23. I. is grammatically incorrect. As the ones who have promoted Brexit were the human beings and for living-beings 'who' is used instead of 'which'.

Correct sentence: There should be special places in hell for those who promoted Brexit.

And, II and III are correct.

Hence, the correct option is (D).

24. I. is grammatically incorrect as it uses incorrect preposition with the verb 'transform', which is accompanied by prepositions 'to' or 'into'.

Correct sentence: Global warming is on track to transform the frigid mountain peaks into bare rocks shortly.

II. is also grammatically incorrect with respect to use of singular pronoun 'this' along with the plural subject basins.

Correct sentence: People living in the downstream areas of these river basins benefit directly and indirectly from its resources.

And III is absolutely correct.

Hence, the correct option is (B).

25. In the context of the sentence, the only appropriate combination of words is that of "guarantees" and "represented".

This makes the sentence meaningfully correct. All other options are either grammatically or contextually incorrect.

Therefore, options (A), (B), (D) and (E) are eliminated.

Hence, the correct option is (C).

26. The word "accusations" before the first blank indicates that it is something 'negative' in nature. In the context of the sentence, the words that are suitable for the first blank are "transgression", "malfeasance" and "wrongdoing". So, options (C) and (E) are eliminated.

"Rather than" after the second blank shows that it has to be the opposite of "break out boldly in new directions" ,i.e., 'following standards that have already been set'. The only word that makes the sentence meaningfully correct is "precedents" which means 'an earlier event or action that is regarded as an example or guide to be considered in subsequent similar circumstances'. The words "peculiarities" and "projects" are irrelevant to the context of this sentence. This eliminates options (A) and (D) as well.

Hence, the correct option is (B).

27. In the context of the sentence, the only combination of words that lead to a meaningful sentence is "renewal" and "entry". All other options are incorrect either contextually or grammatically.

The sentence wants to convey that insurance policies should be renewed compulsorily and that there should be no age restriction.

Hence, the correct option is (A).

28. In the given sentence, the part given in bold has error in it. Usage of 'a' before 'right' is erroneous as 'right' is an adjective and not a noun.

The correct sentence would be: **He is quite right** in his approach towards solving this issue but the higher management disagrees with him.

Quiet right in option (C) is incorrect since quiet means calm and composed and it is completely out of context in the given statement.

It makes option (A) the correct choice among the given options.

Hence, the correct option is (A).

29. There is no error in the bold part of the sentence and correct phrase has been used in this context. Had it been too much, it would have been followed by a noun but in case of much too, it is always followed by an unpleasant adjective.

In this case, we are talking about the loss of his parents for him and that is painful for him. It is an unpleasant adjective used in the given context. No replacement is required in the phrase given in bold in this sentence.

This makes option (E) the correct choice among the given options.

Hence, the correct option is (E).

30. The bold part of the statement has error since proper parts of speech has not been used in this part of the sentence. If we want to modify an adjective, we should use an adverb to do the same rather than having another adjective preceding it. Unusual complicated is not the correct usage since both are adjectives and they cannot be used like this. An adverb should have been placed before complicated to modify the same. Unusually complicated would have been the correct usage in this context.

The correct sentence would be:

The Supreme Court decided to refer **the unusually complicated issue** to a larger bench of the apex court so that proper justice is meted out to the citizens of the country.

This makes option (B) the correct choice among the given options.

Hence, the correct option is (B).

31. The correct meaning of Pointed out is 'To bring attention to something or someone.'

Given Idiom: Pointed out means To bring attention to something or someone.

Example: The error was pointed out to her by one of her colleagues.

From the given options, the fifth option is the most appropriate meaning of the given idiom.

Hence, the correct option is (E).

32. The word 'Abeyance' means A state of temporary disuse or suspension.

Example: The law was held in abeyance for well over twenty years.

Let's look at the meaning of the given options:

Suspension - A state of temporary inactivity.

Example: These events have led to the suspension of talks.

Dormancy - The state of being temporarily inactive or inoperative.

Example: The volcano erupted after years of dormancy.

Resuscitation - The action of making something active or vigorous again.

Example: The economy needs vigorous resuscitation.

Quiescence - Inactivity or dormancy.

Example: Although the inactive volcano has been in a state of quiescence for quite some time, it could erupt again very soon.

Latency - A state of temporary inactivity.

Example: Patients usually become symptomatic after a latency period of hours to days.

Hence, the correct option is (C).

33. The word 'Abrogation' means The repeal or abolition of a law, right, or agreement.

Example: The abrogation of the death penalty embodies the humanization of law.

Let's look at the meaning of the given options:-

Institution - The action of instituting something.

Example: The institution of the Freedom of Information Act has had a significant effect.

Repudiation - Rejection of a proposal or idea.

Example: They were surprised by his sudden repudiation of all his former beliefs.

Establishment - The action of establishing something or being established.

Example: The establishment of new international economic order is the essence of his article.

Launch - An act or instance of launching something.

Example: They managed to launch a new business.

Introduction - The act of introducing a system, policy, etc., or of starting a process.

Example: With the introduction of independent taxation, a married woman's position is much clearer.

Hence, the correct option is (B).

34. In the first part of the given sentence, the singular form of the verb 'has' is incorrect.

In the given sentence, the noun 'police' is a noun that describes a collection of police officers.

This means it has no singular form and always uses a plural verb.

We know that a plural subject always takes a plural verb.

The plural form of the verb 'have' should be used with the noun 'police'.

Therefore, the plural form of the verb 'have' should be used in place of the singular form of the verb 'has'.

Correct sentence: In practice, the police have been using the broad definition of sedition to book anyone who criticized the Government in strong and strident language.

Hence, the correct option is (A).

35. Let's see the meanings of the given words:-

Heeding - To pay attention to advise, a warning, etc.

Example: They acknowledge their sin in heeding the warnings and the wild stories of the majority of the spies.

Sedition - Conduct or speech inciting people to rebel against the authority of a state or monarch.

Example: Trade Union leaders were charged with sedition.

Persistently - In a persistent manner; continuously.

Example: They have persistently denied claims of illegal dealing.

Recognized - To accept that something is true.

Example: Many employers have recognized that age discrimination is unfair.

Limitation - A limiting rule or circumstance; a restriction.

Example: They would resist any limitation of their powers.

Hence, the correct option is (D).

36. The given sentence is in the present perfect tense as it links the past to the present in some way.

The present perfect tense refers to an action or state that either occurred at an indefinite time in the past or began in the past and continued to the present time.

This tense is formed by have/has + the past participle (here, recorded).

Therefore, the past participle form of the verb 'recorded' should be used in the blank.

Complete Sentence: The Court has **recorded** its hope and expectation that governments at the Centre and the States will refrain from registering any fresh case of sedition under Section 124A of the IPC, or continuing with any investigation or taking any coercive measure under it.

Hence, the correct option is (C).

37. The correct answer is 'It may help prevent the misuse of provisions relating to speech-based offenses.'

The fifth sentence of the second paragraph says "If it chooses to do so and strikes down Section 124A as an unconstitutional restriction on free speech, it may help the larger cause of preventing misuse of provisions relating to speech-based offenses.''

From the above sentence, we can say that according to the passage, if the Supreme Court abolishes Section 124A it may help prevent the misuse of provisions relating to speech-based offenses.

Hence, the correct option is (E).

38. The last sentence of the first paragraph says "Perhaps, realizing that its order may not be enough to deter thin-skinned and vindictive governments and politically pliant police officers from invoking it against detractors and dissenters, the Court has given liberty to the people to approach the jurisdiction courts if any fresh case is registered for sedition and cite in their support the present order, as well as the Union government's stand.''

- From the above sentence, we can say that statement A is incorrect according to the given passage.

The first sentence of the passage says "In a substantial blow in favor of free speech, the Supreme Court has effectively suspended the operation of the sedition provision in the country's penal law'' and the second sentence of the first paragraph says "All pending trials, appeals, and proceedings with respect to the charge framed under Section 124A be kept in abeyance, it has said in an order that will bring some welcome relief to those calling for the abrogation of Section 124A of the IPC, which criminalizes any speech, writing or representation that excites disaffection against the government''.

- From the above sentences, we can say that statements B and C are correct according to the given passage.

Hence, the correct option is (A).

39. The third sentence of the first paragraph says "The Court has recorded its hope and expectation that governments at the Centre and the States will refrain from registering any fresh case of sedition under Section 124A of the IPC, or continuing with any investigation or taking any coercive measure under it'' and the last sentence of the first paragraph says ''Perhaps, realizing that its order may not be enough to deter thin-skinned and vindictive governments and politically pliant police officers from invoking it against detractors and dissenters, the Court has given liberty to the people to approach the jurisdiction courts if any fresh case is registered for sedition and cite in their support the present order, as well as the Union government's stand".

- From the above sentences, we can say that statements A and B are incorrect according to the given passage.

The third sentence of the second paragraph says "In practice, the police have been using the broad definition of sedition to book anyone who criticized the Government in strong and strident language."

- From the above sentence, we can say that statement C is correct according to the given passage.

Hence, the correct option is (E).

40. The first sentence of the passage says "In a substantial blow in favor of free speech, the Supreme Court has effectively suspended the operation of the sedition provision in the country's penal law", the last sentence of the first paragraph says "Perhaps, realizing that its order may not be enough to deter thin-skinned and vindictive governments and politically pliant police officers from invoking it against detractors and dissenters, the Court has given liberty to the people to approach the jurisdiction courts if any fresh case is registered for sedition and cite in their support the present order, as well as the Union government's stand" and the last sentence of the passage, concludes "When the Government submitted that it was revisiting the provision on its own, it was expecting only an indefinite postponement of the hearing on the constitutional validity of Section 124A, but it must now heed the spirit of the order and take effective steps to prevent its misuse".

From the above sentences, we can say that the central theme of the passage is "Preventing misuse of sedition law".

Hence, the correct option is (D).

Ques (1-3):Direction: Read the following sentence and determine whether there is any error in it. The error, if any, will be in one part of the sentence. If the sentence is error-free, select 'No error' as your answer.

Q.1 Many a doubt on History/(A) were cleared in the remedial class,/(B) thus proving the maximum/(C) utility of such initiatives./(D)

[IBPS Clerk, 2021]

A. (A)   **B.** (B)   **C.** (C)   **D.** (D)
E. No error

Q.2 After spending (A)/ three years of our (B)/ college life together (C)/ we parted with our friends. /(D)
A. (A)   **B.** (B)   **C.** (C)   **D.** (D)
E. No error

Q.3 I lived here (A)/ in New York since 1980 (B)/, so I know everything about the city (C)/, its culture, and famous places for tourism. /(D)
A. (A)   **B.** (B)   **C.** (C)   **D.** (D)
E. No Error

Q.4 Direction: The question below has two blanks, each blank indicating that something has been omitted. Choose a set of words for each blank that best fits the meaning of the sentence as a whole.

Satellite data confirm _____ on protected lands as Indigenous people fight for their rights and recognition of their _____ in conserving forests.

[SBI Clerk, 2021]

A.   revolution, destroy
B.   floating, signal
C.   incursions, role
D.   inclusions, commendable
E.   degrade, performance

Ques (5-8):Direction: In the following question, a sentence is given with two blanks. You have to find the pair of words from the given options that fit both the blanks in the given order and make the sentence grammatically and contextually correct.

Q.5 Tropical cyclones laden with moisture and accumulated energy _____ a growing challenge, as they have a propensity to _____ heavy damage to lives and property.

[SBI Clerk, 2021]

A. demand, act   **B.** calculate, condemn
C. indicate, withdraw   **D.** pose, inflict
E. helpful, experience

Q.6 _____ in pastoralism, one of the world's most sustainable food systems, could help Spain _____ to climate change and revitalize depopulated rural areas.

[SBI Clerk, 2021]

A. Resurgence, adapt   **B.** Trial, continue
C. Switching, reach   **D.** Rise, adopt
E. Renaming, rush

Q.7 The _____ of genetically modified foods being grown and sold in the UK has come a step closer after changes to farming _____ that allow field trials of gene-edited crops in England.

[SBI Clerk, 2021]

A.   writing, seasons
B.   teaching, freedom
C.   prospect, regulations
D.   idea, working
E.   category, introduction

Q.8 A house that miraculously _____ an erupting volcano on La Palma in the Spanish Canary Islands for days has now been _____ by lava.

[SBI Clerk, 2021]

A.   spew, operating
B.   helped, strengthened
C.   endured, annihilated
D.   generated, nourished
E.   released, devoid

Q.9 Direction: Which of the option (A), (B), (C) and (D) given below, should replace the phrase printed in bold in the sentence to make it grammatically correct? If the sentence is correct as it is given and no correction is required, mark (E) as the answer.

Medical treatment here is **very expensive that** they had to sell off their land to pay for it.
A.   Quite expensive and
B.   Too expensive for
C.   So expensive but
D.   More expensive
E.   No correction required

Ques (10-19):Direction: Read the passage and answer the following question.

Child labor is an important topic that is being debated as a serious social issue all around the world. Keeping the society aware of this issue will help to avoid such illegal and **inhuman** activity from destroying the lives of many children. Child labor is something that replaces the normal activities of a child, like education, playing, etc., with economic activities. These economic activities may be paid or unpaid work, which benefits the family of the child or the owner the child works for. The age limit is restricted to fourteen years or even seventeen years in case of dangerous works.

Children may be forced to do child labor because of poverty and financial problems in their family. Many owners accept child labors since they only need a less amount as salary or even some accept non-monetary jobs too. Children are often made to do such hard jobs by their irresponsible parents. They send their kids for domestic works for the money as well as for the food they get through these works. These demanding works often spoil the childhood and give a harder way of living to the kid.

Parents allow their children for such jobs because of lack of awareness too. When they are too poor to take admissions in schools and the lack of good schools in their locality may also lead to such activities. Not all forms of jobs done by children are considered as child labor, but there are some things to note while categorizing them. Whether the job is done mentally, morally, physically and socially, does it affects the child in a dangerous way? Does the job done affect their education and other childhood activities like playing? The job they do shouldn't be both tiring and excessive that they are forced to avoid other activities they should be doing in their age. These are the characteristics of Child Labor.

In extreme ways, there are owners who treat children like slaves and separate them from their families to do such hard jobs. Whatever be the job done, child labor depends on the age of the kid involved, type of activity and hours of work they do per day. As a conclusion, children are meant to be enjoying their childhood and should be allowed to educate themselves at early ages. There are many **schemes** introduced by the government to reduce such child labors like providing free education and taking severe actions against those who promote child labor.

Q.10 Which of the following statements is true in terms of child labor?

A. Children cannot get admissions to school and should continue earning money through labor

B. Children are meant to be enjoying their childhood and should not be allowed to do these jobs

C. Children below 17 are more active and can provide better productivity as laborers.

D. Since they only need a less amount as salary, they should continue to do these jobs

E. None of these is true

Q.11 What do the government schemes include to reduce child labor?

(A). Providing free education.

(B). Taking severe actions against those who promote child labor.

(C). Encouraging more wages for child laborers.

A. Only (A)　　　　**B.** Only (B)

C. all except (A)　　　　**D.** all except (C)

E. None of these

Q.12 What are the characteristics to look for to identify child labor?

(A). Whether the job affects the child in a dangerous way

(B). Whether the jobs done affect their education and other childhood activities like playing.

(C). Whether the jobs are fun and not risky.

A. Only (A)　　　　**B.** Only (B)

C. Only (C)　　　　**D.** All except (B)

E. All except (C)

Q.13 Why do parents push their children into doing child labor?

(A). lack of awareness

(B). lack of good schools in the area

(C). too poor to admit their children to schools

A. All of these　　　　**B.** All except (A)

C. All except (B)　　　　**D.** All except (C)

E. None of these

Q.14 According to the passage, **'schemes'** refers to-

A. Make plans, especially in a devious way or with intent to do something illegal or wrong

B. Not properly planned and controlled

C. Involving or contributing to a breakdown of peaceful and law-abiding behavior

D. A large-scale systematic plan or arrangement for putting a particular idea into effect

E. Not done or acting according to a fixed plan or system

Q.15 According to the passage, **'inhuman'** refers to -

A. Having or showing compassion

B. Having or showing a friendly, generous, and considerate nature

C. Lacking human qualities of compassion and mercy

D. Having or showing an intense and selfish desire for wealth or power

E. Neither good nor bad

Q.16 Why do owners prefer child labors?

Because -

(A). They are cute

(B). They need less salary or wages

(C). They do not throw tantrums

A. Only (A)　　　　**B.** Only (B)

C. Only (C)　　　　**D.** All of the above

E. None of the above

Q.17 Why are children forced into child labor?

(A). Poverty

(B). Financial problems

(C). To gain experience

A. Only (A)　　　　**B.** Only (B)

C. Only (C)　　　　**D.** all except (A)

E. all except (C)

Q.18 What age limit is child labor restricted to?

A. 14 years　　　　**B.** 18 years

C. 20 years　　　　**D.** 5 to 10 years

E. None of these

Q.19 Which activities does child labor replace?

(A). Education

(B). Playing

(C). Earning money

A. Only (A)　　　　**B.** Only (B)

C. Only (C)　　　　**D.** All except (A)

E. All except (C)

Q.20 Direction: In the following question, a sentence is given with four words marked as (A), (B) (C), and (D). These words may or may not be placed in the correct order. Four options with different arrangements of these words have been provided.

The **acquired(A)** of the **collection(B)** of social statistics by the state is in itself much older, but it **practice(C)** its modern form towards the end of the eighteenth **century(D)**.

A. (B)-(D) **B.** (B)-(C) **C.** (C)-(D) **D.** (A)-(C)
E. (A)-(D)

Ques (21-22):Direction: In each of the questions given below, three words are given in bold. These three words may or may not be in their correct positions. The sentence is then followed by options with the correct combination of words that should replace each other in order to make the sentence grammatically and contextually correct. Find the correct combination of words that replace each other. If the sentence is correct as it is, select '(E)' as your option.

Q.21 The **received** (A) birthday party was the best **surprise** (B) Andrew could have **gift**. (C)

[IBPS PO, 2021]

A. (A)(B)(C) **B.** (B)(A)(C)
C. (B)(C)(A) **D.** (C)(A)(B)
E. No Rearrangement

Q.22 The **blared** (A) parlour's owner **night** (B) really loud music all **tattoo** (C) long.

[IBPS PO, 2021]

A. (B)(C)(A) **B.** (A)(B)(C)
C. (C)(A)(B) **D.** (B)(A)(C)
E. No Rearrangement

Ques (23-27):Direction: In the following passage there are blanks, each of which has been numbered. These members are printed below the passage and against each, five words are suggested, one of which fits the blank appropriately. Find out the appropriate words.

Pompeii was an ___(1)___ city located in what is now the comune of Pompei near Naples in the Campania region of Italy. Pompeii, along with Herculaneum and many villas in the surrounding area (e.g. at Boscoreale, Stabiae), was buried under 4 to 6 m (13 to 20 ft) of volcanic ash and pumice in the ___(2)___of Mount Vesuvius in AD 79.

Largely preserved under the ash, the excavated city offered a unique snapshot of Roman life, ___(3)___ at the moment it was buried, and extraordinarily detailed insight into the everyday life of its inhabitants, although much of the evidence was lost in the early excavations. It was a wealthy town, enjoying many fine public buildings and ___(4)___ private houses with lavish decorations, furnishings and works of art which were the main attractions for the early excavators. Organic remains, including wooden objects and human bodies, were entombed in the ash. Over time, they decayed, leaving voids that archaeologists found could be used as moulds to make plaster casts of unique — and often ___(5)___ figures in their final moments of life.

Q.23 Which of the following is the most appropriate answer for blank no. (1)?

[IBPS Clerk, 2021]

A. former **B.** artificial
C. ancient **D.** advanced
E. fraudulent

Q.24 Which of the following is the most appropriate answer for blank no. (2)?

[IBPS Clerk, 2021]

A. tremors **B.** eruption
C. crash **D.** depletion
E. inflation

Q.25 Which of the following is the most appropriate answer for blank no. (3)?

[IBPS Clerk, 2021]

A. flowed **B.** melting
C. terminate **D.** frozen
E. created

Q.26 Which of the following is the most appropriate answer for blank no. (4)?

[IBPS Clerk, 2021]

A. despondent **B.** modest
C. defective **D.** imitation
E. luxurious

Q.27 Which of the following is the most appropriate answer for blank no. (5)?

[IBPS Clerk, 2021]

A. gruesome **B.** pleasant
C. magnificent **D.** generous
E. faulty

Ques (28-32):Direction: Rearrange the following five segments A, B, C, D and E in the proper sequence to form a meaningful paragraph; then answer the questions given below them.

A. NPCIL is a dividend-paying company with the highest credit rating of AAA by CRISIL and CARE

B. At present, NPCIL operates 22 nuclear power reactors with an installed capacity of 6780 MW.

C. NPCIL is responsible for siting, design, construction, commissioning and operation of nuclear power reactors.

D. Nuclear Power Corporation of India Limited (NPCIL), formed in 1987, is a Public Sector Enterprise under the administrative control of Department of Atomic Energy (DAE).

E. Safety is given overriding priority in all facets of nuclear power reactors.

Q.28 Which is the first sentence according to the paragraph?

[SBI Clerk, 2021], [IBPS Clerk, 2021]

A. A   **B.** B   **C.** C   **D.** D
E. E

Q.29 Which is the second sentence according to the passage?
[SBI Clerk, 2021], [IBPS Clerk, 2021]

A. A   **B.** B   **C.** C   **D.** D
E. E

Q.30 Which is the third sentence according to the paragraph?
[SBI Clerk, 2021], [IBPS Clerk, 2021]

A. A   **B.** B   **C.** C   **D.** D
E. E

Q.31 Which is the fourth sentence according to the paragraph?
[SBI Clerk, 2021], [IBPS Clerk, 2021]

A. A   **B.** B   **C.** C   **D.** D
E. E

Q.32 Which is the fifth sentence according to the paragraph?
[SBI Clerk, 2021], [IBPS Clerk, 2021]

A. A   **B.** B   **C.** C   **D.** D
E. E

Q.33 Direction: Three sentences are given. You need to find if they are grammatically correct or incorrect and mark the answer accordingly.

P. It was the first time this important scientific journal had ever published the work of college students.

Q. In sports, that would be like making the big leagues at the age of fifteen and hitting a home run your first-time at-bat.

R. For Richard Ebright, it was the first in long string of achievements in science and other fields.

A. Only P is incorrect
B. Only Q is incorrect
C. Both Q and R are incorrect
D. Only R is incorrect
E. All are correct

Q.34 Direction: Three sentences are given. You need to find if they are grammatically correct or incorrect and mark the answer accordingly.

P. Did you complete your homework?

Q. When he saw a couple of them approaching, he panicked and begun to run.

R. In the end, he was able to escape only by quickly taking off his newly found clothes.

A. Only P is incorrect
B. Only Q is incorrect
C. Both P and Q are incorrect
D. Only R is incorrect
E. All are correct

Ques (35-38):Direction: Which of the option (A), (B), (C) and (D) given below, should replace the phrase printed in bold in the sentence to make it grammatically correct? If the sentence is correct as it is given and no correction is required, mark (E) as the answer.

Q.35 He will continue to lead the Likud in the September elections and a**ppears better-place than his rivals** to form a coalition government.
A. Appeared bitterly-placing than his rivals
B. Appearing bitterly placed than his rivals
C. Appears better-placed than his rivals
D. Appearing better-placedly than his rivals
E. No correction required

Q.36 A comedian analyzes the mundane from a variety of angles and **find the thread among two points.**
A. Found the threading between two points
B. Finds the thread between two points
C. Finding the thread among two points
D. Is finding the thread between more than two points
E. No correction required

Q.37 The Delhi Congress has constituted a five-member committee **to prove in-depth, the reasons** behind the defeat of the Congress candidates in the Capital.
A. Proving in-depth, the reasons
B. Proved in-depth, the reasons
C. Probing in-depth, the reasons
D. To probe in-depth, the reasons
E. No correction required

Q.38 The Indian banking system is beleaguered **with non-performing assets.**
A. In non-performing assets
B. For non-performing assets
C. From non-performing assets
D. Under non-performing assets
E. No correction required

Ques (39-40):Direction: In the following sentence, four words are given in bold out of which one word is misspelled. Find the misspelled word. If the words are correct as it is given and no error, mark (E) as the answer.

Q.39 Shopping for that perfect **memmento (A)** has become almost as popular as **touring (B)** the famous **aquarium (C)** and taking photos of the **native (D)** seals.
[SBI Clerk, 2021]

A. A   **B.** B   **C.** C   **D.** D
E. No error

Q.40 He set the metaphysical mode by **vibrancy(A)** of language and **startling(B)** imagery, and a preference for a **diction(C)** modeled on direct **uteerances(D)**
[SBI Clerk, 2021]

A. A   **B.** B   **C.** C   **D.** D
E. No error

// Smart Answer Sheet //

Correct   Indicates percentage of students who answered questions correctly.

Skipped   Indicates percentage of students who skipped questions.

Q.	Ans.	Correct / Skipped
1	B	49.9 % / 42.53 %
2	D	80.48 % / 13.68 %
3	A	89.58 % / 10.02 %
4	C	85.56 % / 10.36 %
5	D	76.89 % / 21.62 %
6	A	67.98 % / 31.02 %
7	C	46.24 % / 33.84 %
8	C	50.29 % / 35.35 %
9	A	31.23 % / 68.16 %
10	B	88.29 % / 11.57 %
11	D	85.01 % / 10.53 %
12	E	49.89 % / 35.71 %
13	A	57.61 % / 33.04 %
14	D	62.15 % / 30.09 %
15	C	60.67 % / 37.84 %
16	B	66.88 % / 30.92 %
17	E	42.93 % / 32.07 %
18	A	41.11 % / 41.26 %
19	E	44.89 % / 36.82 %
20	D	80.72 % / 17.21 %
21	C	86.66 % / 11.43 %
22	C	81.6 % / 15.59 %
23	C	84.58 % / 10.28 %
24	B	76.08 % / 14.61 %
25	D	76.0 % / 16.02 %
26	E	86.24 % / 12.89 %
27	A	57.6 % / 38.86 %
28	D	84.64 % / 11.96 %
29	A	89.04 % / 10.94 %
30	C	88.88 % / 10.06 %
31	E	78.38 % / 16.44 %
32	B	87.82 % / 10.49 %
33	D	76.39 % / 11.43 %
34	B	87.39 % / 10.14 %
35	C	49.8 % / 44.32 %
36	B	58.97 % / 35.51 %
37	D	43.26 % / 44.03 %
38	E	66.29 % / 30.14 %
39	A	64.71 % / 32.82 %
40	D	54.6 % / 37.59 %

Performance Analysis

Avg. Score (%)	47.5%
Toppers Score (%)	65.0%
Your Score	

//Hints and Solutions//

1. The error lies in the wrong usage of the verb 'were' in Part (B).

'Were' should be replaced by 'was' because a singular verb always comes after 'many a', 'each', 'either', 'neither', 'everyone'.

Therefore, the singular verb 'was' should be used instead of the plural verb 'were' to make the sentence correct.

So, the correct sentence is:

"Many a doubt on History **was** cleared in the remedial class, thus proving the maximum utility of such initiatives."

Hence, the correct option is (B).

2. The error is in part (D) of the sentence.

The preposition should be 'from' instead of 'with'.

The tense used in the sentence talks about an action which has already been carried out previously which refers to past continuous tense.

The pronouns used in the sentence is the first person along with the subject, for example, we is used with 'our'.

Hence, the correct option is (D).

3. There is an error in part (A) of the sentence.

There is a use of a time adverbial since in this sentence.

Since is used to talk about action from the past which still continues in the present. So, we have to use the present perfect tense in part (A).

Therefore, in part, (A) of the sentence 'have' should be inserted before 'lived'.

Correct sentence: I have lived here in New York since 1980, so I know everything about the city, its culture and famous places for tourism.

Hence, the correct option is (A).

4. Satellite data confirm **incursions** on protected lands as Indigenous people fight for their rights and recognition of their **role** in conserving forests.

- The first blank in the sentence is followed by 'on protected lands'. As we read the sentence carefully, we can infer that the satellite data plausibly indicates a violation of the rights of indigenous people. Besides, these people are fighting for their recognition regarding forest conservation.

- For the first blank, we need to look for a word that is similar to 'violate/invade'. 'Revolution' is inappropriate as it does not indicate anything related to it; 'floating' and 'degrade' are out of context; 'inclusions' is inappropriate considering 'on protected lands'. Therefore, the correct word is 'incursions' (meaning: invasion).

- For the second blank, we need a word that means 'part or function'. From the given options, we can infer that 'role' is the most appropriate word.

Hence, the correct option is (C).

5. Tropical cyclones laden with moisture and accumulated energy **pose** a growing challenge, as they have a propensity to **inflict** heavy damage to lives and property.

- The given sentence talks about the attributes of Tropical cyclones laden with moisture and accumulated energy. The effect of these cyclones on lives and property is mentioned.

- For the first blank, we need to find a word that means 'to place/present'. From the given options, 'pose' that means 'to set forth' is the correct word. The other words 'Demand', 'calculate', 'indicate' and 'helpful' are irrelevant in the context.

- For the second blank, we need to find a word that means 'impact or induce'. From the given options, 'inflict' that means 'to cause' is the correct answer.

Hence, the correct option is (D).

6. Resurgence in pastoralism, one of the world's most sustainable food systems, could help Spain **adapt** to climate change and revitalize depopulated rural areas.

- The sentence talks about pastoralism and its role in helping Spain to deal with climate change.

- For the first blank, we need to find a word that means 'rise/ revival'. From the given options, both 'resurgence' and 'rise' are correct and fit in the context.

- For the second blank, we need to find a word that means 'adjust or suit'. From the given options, 'adapt' is the correct answer. Hence, considering the option with the word 'adapt', 'resurgence' is the most appropriate word for the first blank. Though 'rise' is correct as mentioned above, 'adopt' is incorrect.

Hence, the correct option is (A).

7. The **prospect** of genetically modified foods being grown and sold in the UK has come a step closer after changes to farming **regulations** that allow field trials of gene-edited crops in England.

- The given sentence talks about the aspect of genetically modified foods and it's field trials.

- For the first blank, we need to find a word that conveys the meaning outlook'. It is evident that genetically modified foods are being considered by the UK. From the given options, 'prospect' that means 'possibility, vision or outlook' is the appropriate word.

- For the second blank, we need to find a word that means 'rules'. It can be inferred that there have been changes to farming rules or farming supervision. Owing to these changes in the rules, the prospect of genetically modified crops has come a step closer. From the given options, 'regulations' is the correct word.

Hence, the correct option is (C).

8. A house that miraculously **endured** an erupting volcano on La Palma in the Spanish Canary Islands for days has now been **annihilated** by lava.

- Reading the given sentence, we can infer that the house has miraculously sustained the lava of an erupting volcano.

- The word 'miraculously' emphasizes the surprise. As it is normal that buildings are damaged by volcanic lava, this is an instance of surprise.

- For the first blank, we need to find a word that means 'sustained or tolerated', Thus, the correct word is 'endured'.

- The latter part of the sentence indicates the contrasting picture to the former part. We can infer that the house that miraculously sustained the volcanic lava has now been destroyed by lava. Thus, we need to find a word that means 'destroyed or consumed'. From the given options, 'annihilated' is the correct word.

Hence, the correct option is (C).

9. Option (A) replaces the bold part appropriately and thus becomes the best replacement among all.

Option (B) can be eliminated because 'too' must be followed by an infinitive (to + verb1) which is not the case here.

Option (C) gets eliminated too because 'so' must be followed by 'that' which is again not the case here.

Option (D) gets eliminated because no comparison is made in the sentence and it gets confirmed by the absence of the preposition 'than' in the sentence.

Hence, the correct option is (A).

10. The passage speaks of child labor as an inhuman aspect.

It generally describes the reasons as well as the effects of child labor.

Hence, the correct option is (B).

11. The passage speaks of child labor as an inhuman aspect.

It generally describes the reasons as well as the effects of child labor.

Hence, the correct option is (D).

12. The passage speaks of child labor as an inhuman aspect.

It generally describes the reasons as well as the effects of child labor.

The sentences in the passage clearly mention "...does it affects the child in a dangerous way?" and "Does the job done affect their education and other childhood activities?"

The job they do shouldn't be both tiring and excessive that they are forced to avoid other activities they should be doing in their age.

Other than point (C), the rest are mentioned in the passage.

Hence, the correct option is (E).

13. The passage speaks of child labor as an inhuman aspect.

It generally describes the reasons as well as the effects of child labor.

The sentences in the passage clearly mention "Parents allow their children for such jobs because of lack of awareness too. When they are too poor to take admissions in schools and the lack of good schools in their locality may also lead to such activities".

These demanding works often spoil their childhood and give a harder way of living to the kid.

Hence, the correct option is (A).

14. The passage speaks of child labor as an inhuman aspect.

It generally describes the reasons as well as the effects of child labor.

The sentence in the passage containing the above word is "There are many schemes introduced by the government to reduce such child labors like providing free education and taking severe actions against those who promote child labor".

Here, it refers to the planning or arrangement of putting a law into action against the people who employee child laborers.

An example of 'schemes' is: The government is dusting off schemes for supporting creative industries.

Hence, the correct option is (D).

15. The passage speaks of child labor as an inhuman aspect.

It generally describes the reasons as well as the effects of child labor.

The sentence in the passage containing the above word is "Keeping the society aware of this issue will help to avoid such illegal and inhuman activity from destroying the lives of many children".

Here, it refers to the lack of compassion and mercy shown to children in order to use them as cheap labor. It is an 'inhuman' act that destroys the lives of many children.

An example of 'inhuman' is: The slaughter of whales is unnecessary and inhuman.

Hence, the correct option is (C).

16. The passage speaks of child labor as an inhuman aspect.

It generally describes the reasons as well as the effects of child labor.

The sentence in the passage clearly mentions "Many owners accept child labors since they only need a less amount as salary or even some accept non-monetary jobs too".

Here, points (B) and (C) are not mentioned in the passage or in the above sentence as well. Therefore, they are invalid.

Hence, the correct option is (B).

17. The passage speaks of child labor as an inhuman aspect.

It generally describes the reasons as well as the effects of child labor.

The sentence in the passage clearly mentions "Children may be forced to do child labor because of poverty and financial problems in their family".

Here, 'gaining experience' is the downside of child labor. Children are expected to play and study, not earn money or gain experience in working at that age.

Therefore, only points (A) and (B) are valid.

Hence, the correct option is (E).

18. The passage speaks of child labor as an inhuman aspect.

It generally describes the reasons as well as the effects of child labor.

The sentence in the passage clearly mentions "The age limit is restricted to fourteen years or even seventeen years in case of dangerous works".

Child Labor is something that replaces the normal activities a child, like education, playing, etc., by economic activities.

These economic activities may be paid or unpaid work, which benefits the family of the child or the owner the child work's for.

Hence, the correct option is (A).

19. The passage speaks of child labor as an inhuman aspect.

It generally describes the reasons as well as the effects of child labor.

The sentence in the passage clearly mentions "Child Labor is something that replaces the normal activities a child, like education, playing, etc., by economic activities".

Here, 'earning money' is the downside of child labor. Children are expected to play and study, not earn money.

Therefore, only points (A) and (B) are valid.

Hence, the correct option is (E).

20. The words 'acquired' and 'practice' have been placed incorrectly, they have to be replaced with each other to make the sentence meaningful and contextually correct.

- Acquired means to buy or obtain (an asset or object) for oneself.
- Practice means the act of doing something again and again in order to learn.

The correct sentence is: The practice of the collection of social statistics by the state is in itself much older, but it acquired its modern form towards the end of the eighteenth century.

Hence, the correct option is (D).

21. (B)(C)(A) is the correct combination of words that replace each other.

- Received: Given or presented with something. A 'birthday party' is not an object that can be 'received'.
- Surprise: An unexpected or astonishing thing - object or event.

- Gift: A present that is willingly given to someone without any payment. The sentence requires a verb in the past tense and 'gift' is in the present tense.

Correct Sentence: The surprise birthday part was the best gift Andrew could have received.

Hence, the correct option is (C).

22. (C)(A)(B) is the correct combination of words that replace each other.

- Blared: Made or caused a loud noise. 'Blared' is a verb (an action), it is grammatically and contextually incorrect to say "blared parlour".
- Night: The time between the sunset and the sunrise every day. 'Night' is a noun and not a verb, so it cannot cause loud music.
- Tattoo: An ink mark made on the body that is permanent and is done by puncturing the skin. A 'tattoo' is a noun and not a time period (like night) during which one can do anything.

Correct Sentence: The tattoo parlour's owner blared really loud music all night long.

Hence, the correct option is (C).

23. The meaning of the given words:

- Ancient: belonging to the very distant past and no longer in existence
- Former: of or occurring in the past or an earlier period
- Artificial: made or produced by human beings rather than occurring naturally, especially as a copy of something natural
- Advanced: modern and recently developed
- Fraudulent: obtained, done by, or involving deception, especially criminal deception

The sentence with the first blank talks about how there 'was' a city, this use of the verb 'was' in the past tense is very important as it lets the reader know that the city does not exist anymore.

- The passage mentions that the destruction of Pompeii happened in 79 AD, by any standard this is a very long time ago meaning that Pompeii is a really old city.
- Any adjective used to describe such a city should represent that.
- The blank is also preceded by an article, and the article is 'an' meaning that the word in the blank must start with a vowel sound. So, ancient is appropriate here.

Hence, the correct option is (C).

24. The meaning of the given words:

- Eruption: a sudden outbreak of something, typically something unwelcome or noisy
- Tremors: a slight earthquake
- Crash: fall from the sky and violently hit the land or sea
- Depletion: reduction in the number or quantity of something

- Inflation: a general increase in prices and fall in the purchasing value of money

The sentence with the second blank talks about how the city of Pompeii was buried under 4-6 meters of volcanic and pumice in an event that happened at Mount Vesuvius in 79 AD.

- The sentence talks about volcanic ash, pumice and a mountain. All of these elements point towards a volcano.

- The noun in the blank will have to describe the event that happened at Mount Vesuvius which involved a sudden and dangerous spread of volcanic ash and pumice that kills hundreds of people. So, eruption is appropriate here.

Hence, the correct option is (B).

25. The meaning of the given words:

- Frozen (past tense): stop (a moving at a particular time)

- Flowed (past tense): move along or out steadily and continuously in a current or stream

- Melting (present continuous tense): becoming liquefied by heat

- Terminate (present tense): bring to an end

- Create (present tense): bring (something) into existence

The sentence with the third blank talks about how the city of Pompeii was major preserved under ash and its excavation led to a rare insight into life in those days all because of the descent of such large heaps of ash, which made everything come to a standstill.

- The sentence mentions the verb 'preserved' which means 'maintained in its original and existing stage'.

- If a whole city were to be preserved under ash and then years later the ash was to be moved - through the process of excavation - the entire part buried under the ash would be as it is.

- An idiom to describe this phenomenon would be 'frozen in time' because even though volcanoes have nothing to do with ice 'frozen' here means becoming fixed in place.

- Since this event happened many years ago, the verb in the blank will be in the past tense. So, frozen is appropriate here.

Hence, the correct option is (D).

26. The meaning of the given words:

- Luxurious: extremely comfortable, elegant, or enjoyable, especially in a way that involves great expense

- Despondent: in low spirits from loss of hope or courage

- Modest: relatively moderate, limited, or small

- Defective: imperfect or faulty

- Imitation: a thing intended to simulate or copy something else

The sentence with the fourth blank talks about the excavation of Pompeii showed that it was a rich town and that it had good public buildings, houses with extravagant decorations, furniture and art.

- The blank is followed by the noun 'houses' meaning that the blank most likely requires an adjective the describes the houses.

- The sentence mentions that the houses had rich furniture and a lot of artwork, meaning that the houses themselves were extravagant and would have a lot of luxury.

- The adjective in the blank should represent this extravagance and elegance. So, luxurious is appropriate here.

Hence, the correct option is (E).

27. The meaning of the given words:

- Gruesome: causing repulsion or horror; grisly; extremely unpleasant.

- Pleasant: giving a sense of happy satisfaction or enjoyment

- Magnificent: very good; excellent

- Generous: (of a thing) larger or more plentiful than is usual or necessary

- Faulty: working badly or unreliably because of imperfections

The sentence with the fifth blank talks about how the bodies of living beings underneath the ash decayed and this left empty holes that acted as moulds to recreate the final moments of people as they were buried under the ash.

- The sentence talks about the recreation of the final moments in the lives of the citizens of Pompeii, the moment when they knew death was imminent.

- This is a very morbid (unpleasant and disturbing) event, the capturing of the final moment of someone's life, like the picture of a car or plane crash.

- The blank requires an adjective that can describe this situation, something that captures how painful and depressing that image would be. So, gruesome is appropriate here.

Hence, the correct option is (A).

Ques (28-32): Reading the given sentences we find that:

- The paragraph starts by introducing the Nuclear Power Corporation of India Limited, and my mentioning what it is; which is D.

- Then statement A provides us more information regarding NPCIL that it is a dividend-paying company.

- This is soon followed by statement C which elaborates on what NPCIL does, its responsibilities.

- This is elaborated using the second statement that is the overriding priority given to safety as mentioned in E.

- The paragraph ends by concluding the present operation of NPCIL i.e the number of power reactors and it's capacity, which is B.
- Therefore the correct sequence is DACEB.

28. So, D is the first sentence according to the paragraph.

Hence, the correct option is (D).

29. So, A is the second sentence according to the passage.

Hence, the correct option is (A).

30. So, C is the third sentence according to the paragraph.

Hence, the correct option is (C).

31. So, E is the fourth sentence according to the paragraph.

Hence, the correct option is (E).

32. So, B is the fifth sentence according to the paragraph.

Hence, the correct option is (B).

33. In sentence R:

- There is an article missing before the word 'long'.
- The article 'a' should be added before the word long.
- An article (a, an, or the) is a type of determiner.
- Single countable nouns usually require a determiner.
- Therefore, the correct sentence is,

For Richard Ebright, it was the first in a long string of achievements in science and other fields.

So, Only R is incorrect.

Hence, the correct option is (D).

34. In sentence Q:

- The form of the verb used here is incorrect.
- The correct verb that should be used here is 'began'.
- begun is past participle form of begin
- The tense of the sentence is simple past for which the past form of the verb should be used.
- The past form of the verb begin is began
- Therefore, the correct sentence is

When he saw a couple of them approaching, he panicked and began to run.

So, only Q is incorrect.

Hence, the correct option is (B).

35. There is an error in the bold part of the sentence because the usage is not correct here. From the context, it is clear that the leader is well placed to lead the new government because his party will be able to beat the rivals to form the next coalition government.

Option (C) is our pick since better-placed is correct.

The correct sentence would have been:

He will continue to lead the Likud in the September elections and **appears better-placed than his rivals** to form a coalition government.

Option (A) is not correct since bitterly-placed is not correct and Option (B) is also not correct for the same reason. Option D is not correct since better-placedly is not the correct usage.

Hence, the correct option is (C).

36. Reason: The verb 'find' is not in agreement with the subject 'A comedian' which is singular in number. Besides, 'for two points' usage of 'among' is erroneous. Instead of 'among' 'between' must be used to make the sentence grammatically correct.

Clearly, among the given choices option (B) replaces the bold part most appropriately.

The sentence after replacement becomes:

A comedian analyzes the mundane from a variety of angles and **finds the thread between two points.**

Hence, the correct option is (B).

37. There is an error in the bold part of the given statement since according to the context we are talking about the committee that has been constituted in order to understand the reasons behind the defeat of the Congress candidates in Delhi.

The correct statement would have been:

The Delhi Congress has constituted a five-member committee **to probe in-depth, the reasons** behind the defeat of the Congress candidates in the capital.

Options (A) and (B) are eliminated since prove is not correct in the given context whereas Option (C) will not be correct because of the grammatical structure here. Since infinitive has been used here, we should use the present indefinite form only i.e. to probe.

Hence, the correct option is (D).

38. Non-performing asset (NPA) refers to a classification for loans or advances in default or arrears.

So, the original sentence is absolutely correct.

Hence, the correct option is (E).

39. The word 'memmento' has been incorrectly spelled in the given sentence.

The correct spelling and its meaning:

Memento: an object kept as a reminder of a person or event. Example - An exclusive range of gifts will provide your guests with a lasting memento of the evening.

Hence, the correct option is (A).

40. The word 'uteerances' is spelled incorrectly in the given sentence.

The correct spelling and meaning:

Utterances: a spoken word, statement, or vocal sound For Example: There is always a story behind utterances.

Hence, the correct option is (D).

Q.1 Direction: What will come in place of question mark (?) in the following equation?

$$950 + 50 \times 15 - 14 \times 22 + \sqrt{?} = 11^3 + 9^2$$

A. 200 **B.** 240 **C.** 320 **D.** 400 **E.** 420

Q.2 Direction: What will come in place of question mark '?' in the following question?

74% of 159 – [36.5% of 142 + 25.4% of 203] = 13.5% of ? – 10.5% of 120

A. 129.05 **B.** 149.22 **C.** 179.03 **D.** 199.02 **E.** None of the above

Q.3 Direction: What should come in place of the question mark '?' in the following question?

$$9\frac{10}{2} \times \left(\frac{3}{8} \times \frac{16}{9}\right) - 6\frac{5}{3} = 5\frac{5}{2} + 4\frac{1}{2} - ?$$

A. $\frac{14}{3}$ **B.** $\frac{31}{3}$ **C.** $\frac{28}{3}$ **D.** $\frac{33}{5}$ **E.** $\frac{31}{5}$

Q.4 Direction: What should come in place of the question mark (?) in the following question?

$$\sqrt[3]{12167} \times \sqrt[3]{5832} = ?$$

A. 416 **B.** 394 **C.** 414 **D.** 396 **E.** None of these

Q.5 Direction: What should come in place of the question mark (?) in the following question?

(8.2% of 365) – (1.75% of 108) = ?

A. 16.02 **B.** 28.04 **C.** 42.34 **D.** 53.76 **E.** None of these

Q.6 Direction: What should come in place of the question mark (?) in the following question?

$$\sqrt{64 \times 49} \div (4)^2 \times 12 = ?$$

A. 56 **B.** 49 **C.** 63 **D.** 42 **E.** None of these

Q.7 A man sells two books for Rs. 1110. He earns 15% loss on the first book and 25% profit on the second book. If the cost price of the first book is equal to the selling price of the second book, find the cost price of the two books.

A. Rs. 700 and Rs. 400 **B.** Rs. 600 and Rs. 480 **C.** Rs. 450 and Rs. 650 **D.** Rs. 500 and Rs. 600 **E.** Rs. 800 and Rs. 300

Q.8 Joseph wants to use Nitrogen, Potassium, and Phosphorus in his field as fertilizers. When any of them is mixed in the field, its quantity reduces by $1\ kg$ every day due to chemical reactions. He mixed Nitrogen, Potassium, and Phosphorus on 7th November, 9th November, and 15th November, respectively. He spent equal amounts on buying each of the three. What should be the ratio of prices of Nitrogen, Potassium, and Phosphorus, so that there is an equal quantity of each of them in the field on 16th November, and that quantity is $11\ kg$?

A. $9:10:15$ **B.** $15:9:7$ **C.** $7:9:15$ **D.** $7:12:15$ **E.** $11:9:16$

Q.9 The average of eleven distinct positive integers is 21. If the average of the first 6 is 23 and the average of the last six is 22, find the sixth integer.

A. 29 **B.** 39 **C.** 49 **D.** 59 **E.** 69

Q.10 A boat covers $24\ km$ upstream and $36\ km$ downstream in 6 hours, while it covers $36\ km$ upstream and $24\ km$ downstream in $6\frac{1}{2}$ hours. The speed of the current is?

A. $1\ km/hr$ **B.** $2\ km/hr$ **C.** $1.5\ km/hr$ **D.** $2.5\ km/hr$ **E.** $3.5\ km/hr$

Q.11 Average age of a family of 4 members was 19 years, 4 years back. Birth of a new child kept the average age of the family same even today. How old is the child today?

A. 4 years **B.** 1 year **C.** 2 years **D.** 3 years **E.** 5 years

Q.12 The volumes of two cones are in the ratio of 11 : 10 and the radius of cones are in the ratio of 3 : 2. what is the ratio of their vertical heights.

A. 22 : 45 **B.** 50 : 21 **C.** 22 : 37 **D.** 45 : 22 **E.** None of these

Q.13 If a number is increased by 10% and then reduced by 50%, further increased by 50%, the resulting number would be what percentage of an original number?

A. 80% **B.** 82.5% **C.** 85% **D.** 90% **E.** 125%

Ques (14-18):Direction: Study the following data and answer the following questions.

Following table shows the number of officers and workers of a company in five departments.

Q.14 The number of officers in the department I is approximately what percent more than the number of officers in department IV?

[SBI Apprentice, 2019]

A. 65%   **B.** 75%   **C.** 70%   **D.** 80%
E. 72%

Q.15 Find the ratio between officers and workers in departments III.

[SBI Apprentice, 2019]

A. 3 : 4   **B.** 4 : 5   **C.** 2 : 7   **D.** 1 : 5
E. 2 : 9

Q.16 Find the difference between total workers and officers in five departments.

[SBI Apprentice, 2019]

A. 280   **B.** 320   **C.** 210   **D.** 180
E. 150

Q.17 Find the average number of workers in five departments.

[SBI Apprentice, 2019]

A. 142   **B.** 130   **C.** 180   **D.** 145
E. 140

Q.18 The number of workers in department V is approximately what percent of total workers in five departments?

[SBI Apprentice, 2019]

A. 20%   **B.** 28%   **C.** 26%   **D.** 30%
E. 35%

Q.19 The principal is 10500, Simple Interest is 12% and Time is 10 years. $\dfrac{1^{rd}}{3}$ of interest earned from A invested in B for 5 years at 12% rate. Find the amount received from B after 5 years.

[IBPS Clerk, 2021]

A. Rs. 7240   **B.** Rs. 5480
C. Rs. 6720   **D.** Rs. 2520
E. Rs. 6250

Q.20 Direction: What will come in the place of the question mark?

$$25\% \times 676 - 10\% \times 810 + 60 \div 6 = ? \times 70 \div 5$$

A. 35   **B.** 7   **C.** 16   **D.** 19
E. 23

Q.21 Direction: What will come in the place of the question mark ' ?' in the following question?

$$240 \div 6 + \sqrt{529} \times 17 = ? + 150\% \text{ of } 80$$

A. 311   **B.** 310   **C.** 309   **D.** 312
E. 320

Q.22 Direction: What will come in the place of the question mark ' ?' in the following question?

$$35\% \text{ of } 520 + 33.33\% \text{ of } 216 + 45\% \text{ of } 120 = ?$$

A. 890   **B.** 375   **C.** 308   **D.** 400
E. 775

Q.23 It takes 10 hours for a person to travel a distance. If he reduces his speed by 20%, then what is the percentage increase in the time taken to cover the same distance?

[UP Police Sub Inspector, 2017]

A. 33.33%   **B.** 20%   **C.** 25%   **D.** 35%
E. 40%

Q.24 A and B invest in a business in a ratio 3 : 2. If 30% of total profit goes to charity and A investment 18 months and B investment 15 months. If A profit is Rs. 1800 then find the profit of B.

A. Rs. 1000   **B.** Rs. 1200   **C.** Rs. 1400   **D.** Rs. 1800
E. Rs. 2000

Ques (25-29):Direction: In each of the following number series, the wrong number is given, find out that number.

Q.25 40,41,37,46,29,55
A. 41   **B.** 29   **C.** 37   **D.** 66
E. 46

Q.26 100,104,112,126,160,224
A. 112   **B.** 126   **C.** 104   **D.** 160
E. 224

Q.27 28,30,33,38,45,56,67
A. 30   **B.** 67   **C.** 38   **D.** 56
E. 45

Q.28 142,119,100,83,65,59,52
A. 65   **B.** 100   **C.** 59   **D.** 119
E. 52

Q.29 4,11,39,163,823,4947,34639
A. 11   **B.** 4   **C.** 163   **D.** 34639
E. 823

Q.30 Direction: What will come in the place of the question mark '?' in the following question?

$$40\% \text{ of } 820 + 60\% \text{ of } 390 - 511 = 49 + ?$$

A. 8   **B.** 1   **C.** 3   **D.** 2
E. 7

// Smart Answer Sheet //

Correct — Indicates percentage of students who answered questions correctly.

Skipped — Indicates percentage of students who skipped questions.

Q.	Ans.	Correct / Skipped
1	D	43.17 % / 37.61 %
2	D	49.85 % / 34.6 %
3	B	62.86 % / 32.56 %
4	C	79.59 % / 13.45 %
5	B	51.78 % / 44.18 %
6	D	49.38 % / 45.03 %

Q.	Ans.	Correct / Skipped
7	B	13.5 % / 75.01 %
8	A	65.04 % / 33.46 %
9	B	42.18 % / 40.17 %
10	B	16.05 % / 81.79 %
11	D	51.77 % / 47.34 %
12	A	43.43 % / 49.58 %

Q.	Ans.	Correct / Skipped
13	B	81.61 % / 10.48 %
14	B	45.42 % / 45.59 %
15	B	87.6 % / 11.61 %
16	C	42.66 % / 48.87 %
17	A	67.9 % / 31.66 %
18	B	64.63 % / 33.36 %

Q.	Ans.	Correct / Skipped
19	C	21.59 % / 74.38 %
20	B	42.27 % / 53.98 %
21	A	58.58 % / 30.11 %
22	C	54.0 % / 39.54 %
23	C	62.21 % / 34.83 %
24	A	56.54 % / 38.32 %

Q.	Ans.	Correct / Skipped
25	B	49.89 % / 40.53 %
26	B	52.69 % / 45.34 %
27	B	45.23 % / 40.7 %
28	A	55.03 % / 41.92 %
29	B	55.98 % / 35.84 %
30	D	55.48 % / 38.73 %

Performance Analysis

Avg. Score (%)	53.33%
Toppers Score (%)	73.33%
Your Score	

//Hints and Solutions//

1. Given:

$$950 + 50 \times 15 - 14 \times 22 + \sqrt{?} = 11^3 + 9^2$$

$$\Rightarrow 950 + 750 - 308 + \sqrt{?} = 1331 + 81$$

$$\Rightarrow 1392 + \sqrt{?} = 1412$$

$$\Rightarrow \sqrt{?} = 20$$

$$\Rightarrow ? = 400$$

Hence, the correct option is (D).

2. Follow the BODMAS rule to solve the question,

Step-1: Parts of an equation enclosed in 'Brackets' must be solved first, and in the bracket, the BODMAS rule must be followed,

74% of 159 – [36.5% of 142 + 25.4% of 203] = 13.5% of ? – 10.5% of 120

$$\Rightarrow 74\% \text{ of } 159 - \left\{ \left[\left(\tfrac{36.5}{100} \right) \times 142 \right] + \left[\left(\tfrac{25.4}{100} \right) \times 203 \right] \right\} = \left[\left(\tfrac{13.5}{100} \right) \times ? \right] - \left[\left(\tfrac{10.5}{100} \right) \times 120 \right]$$

$$\Rightarrow 74\% \text{ of } 159 - [51.83 + 51.56] = [0.135 \times ?] - 12.6$$

$$\Rightarrow 74\% \text{ of } 159 - 103.39 = 0.135 \times ? - 12.6$$

Any mathematical 'Of' or 'Exponent' must be solved,

$$\Rightarrow \left[\left(\tfrac{74}{100} \right) \times 159 \right] - 103.39 = 0.135 \times ? - 12.6$$

$$\Rightarrow 117.66 - 103.39 = 0.135 \times ? - 12.6$$

$$\Rightarrow 14.27 = 0.135 \times ? - 12.6$$

$$\Rightarrow 14.27 + 12.6 = 0.135 \times ?$$

$$\Rightarrow 26.87 = 0.135 \times ?$$

$$\therefore ? = 199.02$$

Hence, the correct option is (D).

3. Given expression is,

$$9\tfrac{10}{2} \times \left(\tfrac{3}{8} \times \tfrac{16}{9} \right) - 6\tfrac{5}{3} = 5\tfrac{5}{2} + 4\tfrac{1}{2} - ?$$

According to the question,

$$\Rightarrow \left(\tfrac{28}{2} \right) \times \left[\left(\tfrac{3}{8} \right) \times \left(\tfrac{16}{9} \right) \right] - \tfrac{23}{3} = \tfrac{15}{2} + \tfrac{9}{2} - ?$$

$$\Rightarrow 14 \times \left(\tfrac{2}{3} \right) - \tfrac{23}{3} = \tfrac{15}{2} + \tfrac{9}{2} - ?$$

$$\Rightarrow \tfrac{28}{3} - \tfrac{23}{3} = \tfrac{15}{2} + \tfrac{9}{2} - ?$$

$$\Rightarrow \tfrac{28}{3} - \tfrac{23}{3} = \tfrac{24}{2} - ?$$

$$\Rightarrow \tfrac{5}{3} = 12 - ?$$

$$\Rightarrow ? = 12 - \tfrac{5}{3}$$

$$\Rightarrow ? = \tfrac{31}{3}$$

Hence, the correct option is (B).

4. Given:

$$\sqrt[3]{12167} \times \sqrt[3]{5832} = ?$$

$$\sqrt[3]{12167} = 23$$

Also $\sqrt[3]{5832} = 18$

So, $\sqrt[3]{12167} \times \sqrt[3]{5832} = 23 \times 18$

$$= 414$$

Hence, the correct option is (C).

5. Given:

(8.2% of 365) – (1.75% of 108) = ?

$$\Rightarrow \left[\left(\tfrac{8.2}{100} \right) \times 365 \right] - \left[\left(\tfrac{1.75}{100} \right) \times 108 \right] = ?$$

$$\Rightarrow \frac{[(8.2 \times 365) - (1.75 \times 108)]}{100} = ?$$

$$\Rightarrow \frac{(2993 - 189)}{100} = ?$$

$$\Rightarrow ? = \frac{2804}{100} = 28.04$$

Hence, the correct option is (B).

6. Given:

$$\sqrt{64 \times 49} \div (4)^2 \times 12 = ?$$

Let the ? be x.

$$\sqrt{64 \times 49} \div (4)^2 \times 12 = ?$$

Factoring the terms under the square root and squaring 4 we get,

$$x = \sqrt{(8 \times 8 \times 7 \times 7)} \div 16 \times 12$$

Square rooting the given term, we get,

$$x = 8 \times 7 \div 16 \times 12$$

Applying BODMAS rule and simplifying we get,

$$x = \frac{(8 \times 7 \times 12)}{16} = 42$$

Hence, the correct option is (D).

7. Given:

Selling price two books = Rs. 1110

Loss % on 1st book = 15%

Profit % on 2nd book = 25%

We know that:

SP = [CP + (CP × profit%)]

SP = [CP – (CP × loss%)]

SP = selling price

CP = cost price

Let CP of two books be Rs. $20x$ and Rs. $20y$

SP of 1 st book $= $ Rs. $20x \times \dfrac{85}{100}$

$\Rightarrow$ Rs. $17x$

SP of 2 nd book = Rs. $20y \times \dfrac{125}{100}$

$\Rightarrow$ Rs. $25y$

According to the question,

$20x = 25y$

$\Rightarrow \dfrac{x}{y} = \dfrac{5}{4}$

CP of 1st book $= 100$

SP of 1st book $= 85$

CP of 2nd book $= 80$

So, Total $CP = 100 + 80$

$\Rightarrow 180$

Total $SP = 85 + 100$

$\Rightarrow 185$

$\Rightarrow 185 \rightarrow 1110$

$\Rightarrow 1 \rightarrow 6$

$\Rightarrow 100 \rightarrow 600$

$\Rightarrow 80 \rightarrow 480$

$\therefore$ Cost price of both the books is Rs. 600 and Rs. 480

Hence, the correct option is (B).

8. Quantities of each of Nitrogen, Potassium and Phosphorus in field on 16th November are $11\ kg$.

Nitrogen was mixed on 7th November.

Quantity of Nitrogen when it was mixed $= 11 + (16 - 7) = 20\ kg$

Potassium was mixed on 9th November.

Quantity of Potassium when it was mixed $= 11 + (16 - 9) = 18\ kg$

Phosphorus was mixed on 15th November.

Quantity of Phosphorus when it was mixed $= 11 + (16 - 15) = 12kg$

Expenditure = Amount bought $\times$ Price per unit

$\Rightarrow$ If equal amounts are spent on buying them, the ratio of their prices will be inverse of ratios of their amounts.

$\Rightarrow$ Ratio of their prices $= \left(\dfrac{1}{20}\right) : \left(\dfrac{1}{18}\right) : \left(\dfrac{1}{12}\right) = 9 : 10 : 15$

Hence, the correct option is (A).

9. Given:

The average of eleven distinct positive integers is 21.

The average of the first 6 is 23 and the average of the last six is 22.

Total sum of 11 numbers = 21 × 11 = 231

The average of the first 6 is 23

Sum of first 6 numbers = 23 × 6 = 138

The average of the last 6 is 22

Sum of last 6 numbers = 22 × 6 = 132

6th number = 138 + 132 – 231

= 270 – 231

= 39

Hence, the correct option is (B).

10. Given,

Time taken by boat to cover 24 km downstream and 36 km upstream = 6 hours

Time taken by boat to cover 36 km downstream and 24 km upstream = $6\dfrac{1}{2}$ hours

let speed of boat in still water = $x\ km/h$

Speed of stream current = y km/h

According to question,

$\dfrac{24}{x-y} + \dfrac{36}{x+y} = 6h$ (i)

$\dfrac{36}{x-y} + \dfrac{24}{x+y} = \dfrac{13}{2}h$ (ii)

In these type of questions, make factor of 24 and 36 and choose the common values which satisfy the above equations.

$24 = 2,3,4,6,8,12$

$36 = 3,4,9,12$

Choose the common factor i.e. Put this value in equation (i)

$\dfrac{24}{x-y} + \dfrac{36}{12} = 6$

$\dfrac{24}{x-y} + 3 = 6$

$x - y = 8$

$\therefore x + y = 12$

$\therefore x = 10, \quad y = 2$

Speed of the current, $y = 2\ km/h$

Hence, the correct option is (B).

11. 4 years back, Average age of family $= 19$ years

Sum or Total of all ages of all 4 family members $= 19 \times 4 = 76$ years

In present day, that means after 4 years,

Sum or Total of present ages of these 4 family members $= 76 + (4 \times 4) = 92$ years.

Let the child's present age be K years.

Now family is of 5 members (because a child has been added some years back)

Present average age of family $=$ Sum of present ages of 4 members $+$ Child $'$ s present age Average remains same as it was 4 years back

$\therefore 19 = \dfrac{92+K}{5}$

$\Rightarrow 95 = 92 + K$

$\therefore 95 - 92 = K$

$\therefore K = 3$ years $=$ This is the present age of the child.

Hence, the correct option is (D).

12. Given that:

The ratio between the volume of two cones = 11 : 10

The ratio between the radius of two cones = 3 : 2

We know that,

Volume of cone $= \dfrac{1}{3}\pi r^2 h$

According to the question,

$\dfrac{V_1}{V_2} = \left(\dfrac{r_1}{r_2}\right)^2 \times \left(\dfrac{h_1}{h_2}\right)$

$\Rightarrow \dfrac{h_1}{h_2} = \dfrac{11}{10} \times \left(\dfrac{2}{3}\right)^2$

$\dfrac{h_1}{h_2} = \dfrac{22}{45}$

$\therefore$ ratio between vertical heights of cone is $22:45$.

Hence, the correct option is (A).

13. Let the original number be 100, then

First, it is increased by 10%;

$\Rightarrow 100 \times \dfrac{110}{100} = 110$

Further, it is decreased by 50%;

$\Rightarrow 110 \times \dfrac{50}{100} = 55$

Now, it is increased by 50%;

$\Rightarrow 55 \times \dfrac{150}{100} = 82.5$

$\therefore$ Required % $= \dfrac{82.5}{100} \times 100 = 82.5\%$

Hence, the correct option is (B).

14. Given:

Number of officers in department I = 70

Number of officers in department IV = 40

Required percentage = $\dfrac{(70-40)}{40} \times 100\%$

Required percentage = $\dfrac{(30)}{40} \times 100\%$

Required percentage = 75%

$\therefore$ Required percentage is 75%.

Hence, the correct option is (B).

15. Given:

Total officers in department III = 120

Total workers in department III = 150

Required ratio = 120 : 150 = 4 : 5

$\therefore$ The required the ratio between officers and workers in departments III is 4 : 5.

Hence, the correct option is (B).

16. Given:

Total officers in five departments = 70 + 90 + 120 + 40 + 180 = 500

Total workers in five departments = 110 + 160 + 150 + 90 + 200 = 710

Required difference = 710 – 500 = 210

$\therefore$ The required difference between total workers and officers in five departments is 210.

Hence, the correct option is (C).

17. Given:

Total workers in five departments = 110 + 160 + 150 + 90 + 200 = 710

Required average = $\dfrac{710}{5}$ = 142

$\therefore$ The average number of workers in five departments is 142.

Hence, the correct option is (A).

18. Given:

Total workers in five departments = 110 + 160 + 150 + 90 + 200 = 710

Number of workers in department V = 200

Required percentage = $\dfrac{200}{710} \times 100 = 28.16\%$

∴ The number of workers in department V is approximately 28% of total workers in five departments.

Hence, the correct option is (B).

19. Given,

Principal $=$ Rs. 10500

Rate $= 12\%$

Time $= 10$ years

As we know,

Amount $=$ Principal $+$ Interest

$SI = \dfrac{(P \times R \times T)}{100}$

$= \dfrac{(10500 \times 12 \times 10)}{100}$

$=$ Rs. 12600

Now, according to question,

$\dfrac{1}{3}^{rd}$ of interest earned from A invested in B for 5 years $=$ Rs. $\dfrac{12600}{3}$

$=$ Rs. 4200

SI earned from A invested in B for 5 years $= \dfrac{(4200 \times 12 \times 5)}{100}$

$=$ Rs. 2520

Amount received from B after 5 years $=$ Principal $+$ Interest $= 4200 + 2520$

$= 6720$

∴ The amount received from B after 5 years is Rs. 6720.

Hence, the correct option is (C).

20. Given,

$25\% \times 676 - 10\% \times 810 + 60 \div 6 =? \times 70 \div 5$

$\Rightarrow 169 - 81 + 10 =? \times 14$

$\Rightarrow 98 =? \times 14$

$\Rightarrow \dfrac{98}{14} =?$

$\Rightarrow ? = 7$

∴ The value of $?$ is 7.

Hence, the correct option is (B).

21. Given,

$240 \div 6 + \sqrt{529} \times 17 =? + 150\%$ of 80

$\Rightarrow 40 + 23 \times 17 =? + 120$

$\Rightarrow 40 + 391 =? + 120$

$\Rightarrow 431 - 120 =?$

$\Rightarrow ? = 311$

∴ The value of $?$ is 311.

Hence, the correct option is (A).

22. Given,

35% of $520 + 33.33\%$ of $216 + 45\%$ of $120 =?$

$\Rightarrow \left(\dfrac{35}{100}\right) \times 520 + \left(\dfrac{1}{3}\right) \times 216 + \left(\dfrac{45}{100}\right) \times 120 =?$

$\Rightarrow 182 + 72 + 54 =?$

$\Rightarrow ? = 308$

∴ The value of $?$ is 308.

Hence, the correct option is (C).

23. Given:

Let, speed be x km/hour.

It takes 10 hours to travel the distance.

That means total distance = 10x km

Latter speed $= x \left\{ \dfrac{(100-20)}{100} \right\} = \left(\dfrac{4x}{5}\right)$ km/hour

Time taken to cover the whole distance at this speed
$= \dfrac{10x}{\left(\dfrac{4x}{5}\right)} = 12.5$ hour

Time increase = (12.5 − 10) hours = 2.5 hours

Percentage increase in time taken $= \left(\dfrac{2.5}{10}\right) \times 100 = 25\%$

Hence, the correct option is (C).

24. Given:

Share's ratio A and B is 3 : 2 for 18 months and 15 months

Profit of A is Rs. 1800

Let total profit be = 100 unit

30% profit is given to charity

100 × 30% = 30 unit

So, remaining is = 70 unit

Then A' and B share = 3 : 2 in 18 months and 15 months

3 × 18 : 2 × 15 = 54 : 30

New ratio of A and B is = 9 : 5

Profit of A's = $\dfrac{9}{14}$ × 70 = 45 unit

So, profit of B is = 70 - 45 = 25 unit

Given Rs. 1800 profit = 45 unit

1 unit = 40

B profit = 40 × 25 = Rs. 1000

Profit of B is Rs. 1000.

Hence, the correct option is (A).

25. The pattern of the given number series:

$\Rightarrow 40 + 1^2 = 41$

$\Rightarrow 41 - 2^2 = 37$

$\Rightarrow 37 + 3^2 = 46$

$\Rightarrow 46 - 4^2 = 30$

$\Rightarrow 30 + 5^2 = 55$

$\therefore$ The wrong number in the series $= 29$

Hence, the correct option is (B).

26. The series follows the following pattern:

$100 + 4 = 104$

$104 + 8 = 112$

$112 + 16 = 128$

$128 + 32 = 160$

$160 + 64 = 224$

$\therefore$ The wrong term in the series is 126.

Hence, the correct option is (B).

27. The pattern of the above series is as follows:

$28 + 2 = 30$

$30 + 3 = 33$

$33 + 5 = 38$

$38 + 7 = 45$

$45 + 11 = 56$

$56 + 13 = 69$

$\therefore$ The wrong term in the series is 67.

Hence, the correct option is (B).

28. The pattern of the number series is:

$142 - 23 = 119$

$119 - 19 = 100$

$100 - 17 = 83$

$83 - 13 = 70 \neq 65$

$70 - 11 = 59$

$59 - 7 = 52$

So, 65 is Wrong Number.

Hence, the correct option is (A).

29. Given:

$4,11,39,163,823,4947,34639$

The pattern is:

3	11	39	163	823	4947	34639
	×2+5	×3+6	×4+7	×5+8	×6+9	×7+10

So, the wrong number is 4.

Hence, the correct option is (B).

30. Given:

40% of $820 + 60\%$ of $390 - 511 = 49 +?$

$\Rightarrow \dfrac{40}{100} \times 820 + \dfrac{60}{100} \times 390 - 511 = 49+?$

$\Rightarrow 4 \times 82 + 6 \times 39 - 511 - 49 =?$

$\Rightarrow ? = 328 + 234 - 560$

$\Rightarrow ? = 2$

$\therefore$ The value of ? is 2.

Hence, the correct option is (D).

Q.1 Direction: What will come in place of question mark(?) in the following question?

$$6153 \div \sqrt{?} \times 53 = 4028$$

A. 6889 **B.** 6241
C. 5929 **D.** 6561
E. None of these

Q.2 Direction: What will come in place of question mark(?) in the following question?

$$(38)^2 + (63)^2 + (?)^2 = 6089$$

A. 26 **B.** 24
C. 28 **D.** 32
E. None of these

Q.3 Direction: What will come in place of the question mark (?) in the following equation?

$$27 - [16^2 - (273 + 281) \div 2] =?$$

A. 52 **B.** 58 **C.** 32 **D.** 48
E. 38

Q.4 Two sports bikes were sold for Rs. 18,750 each, gaining 25% on one and losing 25% on the other. The gain or loss percent on the whole transaction is:

A. Neither loss nor gain
B. 6% profit
C. $7\frac{1}{4}\%$ profit
D. 6% loss
E. None of these

Q.5 The average salary of male workers in a firm is Rs 4100 and that of the female workers is Rs 4800. If the mean salary of all the employees is Rs 4345, Then find the percentage of male employees in the firm.

A. 35% **B.** 65% **C.** 45% **D.** 55%
E. 40%

Q.6 A man can row at a speed of $4\frac{1}{2}$ km/hr in still water. If he takes 2 times as long to row a distance upstream as to row the same distance downstream, then the speed of stream (in km/hr) is:

A. 1 **B.** 1.5 **C.** 2 **D.** 2.5
E. 3

Q.7 At present, the ratio between the ages of Amit and Dhiraj is $5:4$. After 6 years, Amit's age will be 26 years. What is the age of Dhiraj at present?

A. 12 years **B.** 16 years
C. $19\frac{1}{2}$ years **D.** 21 years
E. 22 years

Q.8 As Jio entered into market, other telecom sectors have to struggle alot in order to remain in the market. The effect is also seen on the share price of the companies. A survey is being conducted for share price fluctuation of Airtel. It has been observed that share price of Airtel rose by 10% from July to August. Then, it has been dropped 20% from August to September and again rose by 50% from September to October. What was the percentage increase for the whole quarter in 2017?

A. 31% **B.** 24% **C.** 26% **D.** 32%
E. 23%

Q.9 A invests Rs.400, B invests Rs.600 into a partnership. After 5 months, B adds Rs.100 and C joined them with Rs.800. After 10 months, A adds Rs.300 to his investment. Their total profit is Rs. 2079 after 1 year. Find the difference between the profit shares of C and A.

A. Rs. 30 **B.** Rs. 22 **C.** Rs. 18 **D.** Rs. 40
E. Rs. 36

Ques (10-14):Direction: The following graph represents the number of students studying three different subjects individually in four colleges. Study the graph carefully and answer the question given below.

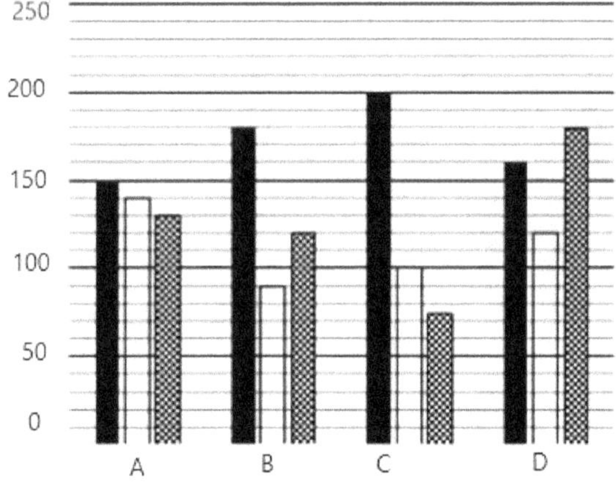

Q.10 Find the ratio between 40% of total number of students studying math in all colleges together to 30% of total number of students studying English in all colleges together?

[IDBI Bank Executive, 2017]

A. 172 : 101 **B.** 173 : 103
C. 184 : 101 **D.** 183 : 103
E. None of these

Q.11 What is the ratio of the number of students studying math in college B to that studying English in college C?

[IDBI Bank Executive, 2017]

A. 7 : 3 **B.** 8 : 5
C. 12 : 5 **D.** 5 : 1
E. None of these

Q.12 Find the difference between number of students studying math in college C and D together and number of students studying Science in college A and B together:

[IDBI Bank Executive, 2017]

A. 115
B. 110
C. 140
D. 130
E. None of these

Q.13 25% of total number of students studying math in all college together is approximately what percent more than that of 20% of total number of students studying Science in all college together?

[IDBI Bank Executive, 2017]

A. 88%
B. 98%
C. 90%
D. 91.67%
E. None of these

Q.14 Number of students studying English in college D is what percent of number of students studying Science in college A?

[IDBI Bank Executive, 2017]

A. 128.57
B. 129.57
C. 120
D. 130
E. None of these

Ques (15-17):Direction: In each of the following number series, a wrong number is given, find out that number.

Q.15 23,45,89,177,363,705

[IBPS Clerk, 2021]

A. 177
B. 45
C. 89
D. 363
E. 705

Q.16 100800,14400,2400,480,240,40

[IBPS Clerk, 2021]

A. 40
B. 240
C. 14400
D. 480
E. 2400

Q.17 540,540,270,135,22.5,4.5

[IBPS Clerk, 2021]

A. 540
B. 270
C. 22.5
D. 135
E. 4.5

Q.18 Direction: What will come in the place of the question mark '?' in the following question?

14.28% of 490 − 71.43% of 63 = ?

A. 25
B. 49
C. 64
D. 81
E. 35

Q.19 Simplify $\dfrac{2\frac{3}{4}}{1\frac{5}{6}} \div \dfrac{7}{8} \times \left(\dfrac{1}{3} + \dfrac{1}{4}\right) + \dfrac{5}{7} \div \dfrac{3}{4} \times \dfrac{3}{4}$

A. $\dfrac{56}{77}$
B. $\dfrac{49}{80}$
C. $\dfrac{12}{7}$
D. $3\dfrac{2}{9}$
E. $\dfrac{37}{81}$

Q.20 Direction: What will come in the place of the question mark '?' in the following question?

$(18)^{7.9} \times (3)^{0.1} \times (6)^{0.1} \div \{(3)^4 \times (6)^4\} = (18)^?$

A. 8
B. 4
C. 3
D. 9
E. 5

Q.21 Direction: What will come in the place of the question mark '?' in the following question?

$2^{-2} \times 4^{-3} \div 8^{-4} = 2^?$

A. 12
B. 18
C. 20
D. −4
E. 4

Q.22 Direction: What will come in the place of the question mark '?' in the following question?

$\sqrt{324} + 9^2 - 7^2 = 2 \times (?)^2$

A. 25
B. 5
C. 10
D. 125
E. 20

Q.23 For how many minutes does a bus stop per hour, if including the stoppages the bus travels at a speed of 67.96 kmph and excluding stoppages the speed of the bus is 81.57 kmph.

A. 10.011
B. 10.110
C. 10.119
D. 10.991
E. 10.911

Q.24 A square sheet of paper is converted into a cylinder by rolling it along its length. What is the ratio of the base radius to the side of the square?

A. $\dfrac{1}{2\pi}$
B. $\dfrac{\sqrt{2}}{\pi}$
C. $\dfrac{1}{\sqrt{2}\pi}$
D. $\dfrac{1}{\pi}$
E. $\dfrac{1}{\sqrt{3}\pi}$

Q.25 Direction: What will come in place of question mark (?) in the following question?

28% of 640 + 34% of 720 = ? × 54

A. 6.82
B. 8.55
C. 4.90
D. 7.85
E. 10.6

Q.26 Three businessmen rent a company for Rs. 7000 per annum. P puts 120 computers in company for 3 months, Q puts 160 computers for next 6 months and R puts 440 computers in company for next 3 months. What percentage of total expenditure should P pay?

A. 10%
B. 13.6%
C. 20.20%
D. 25%
E. 33.33%

Q.27 Direction: In the following number series, one of the numbers is wrong. Find out the wrong number.

19, 24, 33, 43, 55, 69, 85

A. 24
B. 19
C. 33
D. 55
E. 85

Q.28 Direction: In the following number series, one of the numbers is wrong. Find out the wrong number.

4866, 2432, 1218, 610, 306, 154, 78

A. 4866
B. 306
C. 78
D. 154
E. 610

Q.29 Ankit borrowed Rs. 3.5 lakh from a bank to purchase one bus. If the rate of interest be 6% per annum compounded annually, what payment he will have to make after 2 years 8 months?

A. 378689.50

B. 378600

C. 387966.55

D. 396890

E. 405687.25

Q.30 Direction: What will come in the place of the question mark '?' in the following question?

$$215 + 369 - 60\% \text{ of } 900 + 5 = ?^2$$

A. 8

B. 7

C. 6

D. 9

E. 10

// Smart Answer Sheet //

Correct Indicates percentage of students who answered questions correctly.

Skipped Indicates percentage of students who skipped questions.

Q.	Ans.	Correct / Skipped		Q.	Ans.	Correct / Skipped		Q.	Ans.	Correct / Skipped		Q.	Ans.	Correct / Skipped		Q.	Ans.	Correct / Skipped
1	D	79.59 % / 15.9 %		7	B	79.74 % / 11.71 %		13	D	17.23 % / 78.35 %		19	C	50.55 % / 42.8 %		25	D	47.48 % / 37.05 %
2	A	66.73 % / 32.4 %		8	D	54.08 % / 32.07 %		14	A	51.95 % / 44.5 %		20	B	62.29 % / 32.72 %		26	B	64.46 % / 32.5 %
3	D	10.71 % / 79.33 %		9	B	54.5 % / 36.13 %		15	D	66.57 % / 33.36 %		21	E	52.42 % / 40.41 %		27	A	45.62 % / 41.67 %
4	E	52.48 % / 42.49 %		10	C	69.91 % / 30.02 %		16	B	56.2 % / 34.6 %		22	B	49.74 % / 49.37 %		28	C	65.36 % / 32.18 %
5	B	52.87 % / 32.76 %		11	C	65.1 % / 31.92 %		17	D	58.88 % / 31.22 %		23	A	45.85 % / 33.51 %		29	A	68.18 % / 30.96 %
6	B	61.84 % / 37.97 %		12	D	83.7 % / 12.37 %		18	A	41.47 % / 54.56 %		24	A	56.95 % / 32.85 %		30	B	53.93 % / 32.56 %

Performance Analysis	
Avg. Score (%)	56.67%
Toppers Score (%)	70.0%
Your Score	

//Hints and Solutions//

1. Given,

$$6153 \div \sqrt{?} \times 53 = 4028$$

$$\Rightarrow \frac{(6153 \times 53)}{\sqrt{?}} = 4028$$

$$\Rightarrow \sqrt{?} = 80.96 \approx 81$$

$$\Rightarrow ? = 6561$$

Hence, the correct option is (D).

2. Given,

$$(38)^2 + (63)^2 + (?)^2 = 6089$$

$$\Rightarrow ?^2 = 6089 - 1444 - 3969$$

$$= 676$$

$$? = 26$$

Therefore, the value of '?' is 26.

Hence, the correct option is (A).

3. Follow BODMAS rule to solve this question, as per the order given below,

$$27 - [16^2 - (273 + 281) \div 2]$$

$$= 27 - [256 - \frac{554}{2}]$$

$$= 27 - 256 + 277$$

$$= 48$$

Hence, the correct option is (D).

4. Let the two sports bikes be A & B.

Total S.P. of the two sports bikes = 18750 × 2 = Rs. 37,500

C.P. of sports bike A (C.P.₁) = S.P. of sports bike A – Profit

⇒ C.P.₁ = 18750 – (25% of C.P.₁)

⇒ C.P.₁ + 0.25 C.P.₁ = 18750

$$\Rightarrow \text{C.P.}_1 = \frac{18750}{1.25} = \text{Rs. } 15,000$$

∴ C.P. of sports bike A = C.P.₁ = Rs. 15,000

C.P. of sports bike B (C.P.₂) = S.P. of sports bike B + Loss

⇒ C.P.₂ = 18750 + (25% of C.P.₂)

⇒ C.P.₂ – 0.25C.P.₂ = 18750

$$\Rightarrow \text{C.P.}_2 = \frac{18750}{0.75} = \text{Rs. } 25,000$$

∴ C.P. of sports bike B = C.P.₂ = Rs. 25,000

C.P. of the two sports bikes = 15000 + 25000 = Rs. 40,000

∵ S.P. of the whole transaction < C.P. of the whole transaction, there is loss.

∴ Loss % on the whole transaction = $\frac{C.P. - S.P.}{C.P.} \times 100 = $

$$\frac{40,000 - 37,500}{40,000} \times 100 = 6.25$$

Hence, the correct option is (E).

5. Given:

Average salary of Males = Rs 4100

Average salary of Females = Rs 4800

Average salary of all the workers = Rs 4345

We know that,

$$\text{Average} = \frac{Sum\ of\ observations}{Total\ number\ of\ observations}$$

Let the males be x and the females be y

Total salary of males = 4100x

Total salary of females = 4800y

Total salary of all the workers = 4345(x + y)

So, 4100x + 4800y = 4345x + 4345y

⇒ 245x = 455y

$$\Rightarrow \frac{x}{y} = \frac{13}{7}$$

So, percentage of males = $\frac{13}{20} \times 100 = 65\%$

∴ The males are 65%.

Hence, the correct option is (B).

6. Given,

Speed at which man can row in still water = $4\frac{1}{2}$ km/hr

let speed of stream $= y$ km/hr

Speed in downstream $= \frac{9}{2} + y$

Speed in upstream $= \frac{9}{2} - y$

According to question,

$$2 \times \left(\frac{9}{2} - y\right) = \left(\frac{9}{2} + y\right)$$

$$\Rightarrow 9 - 2y = \frac{9}{2} + y$$

$$\Rightarrow 3y = \frac{9}{2}$$

$$\Rightarrow y = 1.5 \text{ km/hr}$$

Hence, the correct option is (B).

7. Let the present ages of Amit and Dhiraj be $5x$ years and

$4x$ years respectively. Then,

$5x + 6 = 26$

$5x = 20$

$x = 4$

Dhiraj's age $= 4x = 16$ years

Hence, the correct option is (B).

8. First we calculate multiplier for various percentage changes

$\Rightarrow$ Multiplier for 10% increase = 1 + 0.10 = 1.1

$\Rightarrow$ Multiplier for 20% decrease = 1.1 – 0.20 × 1.1 = 1.1 – 0.22 = 0.88

$\Rightarrow$ Multiplier for 50% increase = 0.88 + 0.50 × 0.88 = 0.88 + 0.44

$\Rightarrow$ Overall Percentage change = 1.32

$\therefore$ Answer is 32%.

Hence, the correct option is (D).

9. Given:

Total profit = Rs. 2079

We know that,

Profit ratio = Investment × Time period

Total investment of A = 400 × 10 + 700 × 2 = Rs. 5400

Total investment of B = 600 × 5 + 700 × 7 = Rs. 7900

Total investment of C = 800 × 7 = Rs. 5600

Ratio between their profit shares = 5400 : 7900 : 5600

= 54 : 79 : 56

$\therefore$ Required difference = $\dfrac{56}{189}$ × 2079 – $\dfrac{54}{189}$ × 2079

= Rs. 22

Hence, the correct option is (B).

10. 40% of $690 : 30\%$ of 505

$= 276 : 151.5$

$= 184 : 101$

Hence, the correct option is (C).

11. Number of students studying math in college B = 180

Number of students studying English in college C = 75

So, required ratio = 180 : 75

=12:5

Hence, the correct option is (C).

12. Required difference = (200 + 160) – (140 + 90)

= 360 - 230

= 130

Hence, the correct option is (D).

13. Total number of students studying Maths = 690

Total number of students studying science = 450

25% of 690 = 172.5

20% of 450 = 90

So, required percentage= $\dfrac{(172.5-90)\times100}{90}$

$= \dfrac{825}{9}$

= 91.67

Hence, the correct option is (D).

14. Required percentage = $\dfrac{180}{140} \times 100$

= 128.57%

Hence, the correct option is (A).

15. The series follows following pattern:

$\Rightarrow 23 \times 2 - 1 = 45$

$\Rightarrow 45 \times 2 - 1 = 89$

$\Rightarrow 89 \times 2 - 1 = 177$

$\Rightarrow 177 \times 2 - 1 = 353 \neq 363$

$\Rightarrow 353 \times 2 - 1 = 705$

There should be 353 instead of 363.

$\therefore 363$ is the wrong number in the series.

Hence, the correct option is (D).

16. The series follows following pattern:

$\Rightarrow 100800 \div 7 = 14400$

$\Rightarrow 14400 \div 6 = 2400$

$\Rightarrow 2400 \div 5 = 480$

$\Rightarrow 480 \div 4 = 120 \neq 240$

$\Rightarrow 120 \div 3 = 40$

There should be 120 instead of 240.

$\therefore 240$ is the wrong number in the series.

Hence, the correct option is (B).

17. The series follows following pattern:

$\Rightarrow 540 \div 1 = 540$

$\Rightarrow 540 \div 2 = 270$

$\Rightarrow 270 \div 3 = 90$

$\Rightarrow 90 \div 4 = 22.5$

$\Rightarrow 22.5 \div 5 = 4.5$

$\therefore$ 135 is the wrong number in the series.

Hence, the correct option is (D).

18. Given:

14.28% of 490 – 71.43% of 63 = ?

According to the BODMAS Rule,

Converting given percentages into fraction,

$\Rightarrow 14.28\% = \dfrac{1}{7}$

$\Rightarrow 71.43\% = \dfrac{5}{7}$

According to the given equation,

$\Rightarrow \dfrac{1}{7} \times 490 - \dfrac{5}{7} \times 63 = ?$

$\Rightarrow 70 - 45 = ?$

$\Rightarrow 25 = ?$

$\therefore$ The value of ? is 25.

Hence, the correct option is (A).

19. Given:

$\Rightarrow ? = \dfrac{2\frac{3}{4}}{1\frac{5}{6}} \div \dfrac{7}{8} \times \left(\dfrac{1}{3} + \dfrac{1}{4}\right) + \dfrac{5}{7} \div \dfrac{3}{4} \times \dfrac{3}{4}$

$\Rightarrow ? = \dfrac{\frac{11}{4}}{\frac{11}{6}} \div \dfrac{7}{8} \times \left(\dfrac{1}{3} + \dfrac{1}{4}\right) + \dfrac{5}{7} \div \dfrac{3}{4} \times \dfrac{3}{4}$

$\Rightarrow ? = \dfrac{6}{4} \div \dfrac{7}{8} \times \left(\dfrac{7}{12}\right) + \dfrac{5}{7} \div \dfrac{3}{4} \times \dfrac{3}{4}$

$\Rightarrow ? = \dfrac{12}{7} \times \left(\dfrac{7}{12}\right) + \dfrac{20}{21} \times \dfrac{3}{4}$

$\Rightarrow ? = 1 + \dfrac{5}{7}$

$\Rightarrow ? = \dfrac{12}{7}$

$\therefore ? = \dfrac{12}{7}$

Hence, the correct option is (C).

20. Given:

$(18)^{7.9} \times (3)^{0.1} \times (6)^{0.1} \div \{(3)^4 \times (6)^4\} = (18)^?$

$\Rightarrow (18)^{7.9} \times (18)^{0.1} \div (18)^4 = (18)^?$

Comparing powers from both sides, we get

$\Rightarrow 7.9 + 0.1 - 4 = ?$

$\Rightarrow ? = 8 - 4$

$\Rightarrow ? = 4$

$\therefore$ The value of (?) is 4.

Hence, the correct option is (B).

21. Given:

$2^{-2} \times 4^{-3} \div 8^{-4} = 2^?$

$\Rightarrow 2^{-2} \times (2^2)^{-3} \div (2^3)^{-4} = 2^?$

$\Rightarrow 2^{-2} \times 2^{-6} \div 2^{-12} = 2^?$

$\Rightarrow 2^{-2} \times 2^{-6-(-12)} = 2^?$

$\Rightarrow 2^{-2} \times 2^6 = 2^?$

$\Rightarrow 2^{(-2+6)} = 2^?$

$\Rightarrow 2^4 = 2^?$

$\Rightarrow ? = 4$

$\therefore$ The value of (?) is 4.

Hence, the correct option is (E).

22. Given:

$\sqrt{324} + 9^2 - 7^2 = 2 \times (?)^2$

$\Rightarrow 18 + 81 - 49 = 2 \times (?)^2$

$\Rightarrow 50 = 2 \times (?)^2$

$\Rightarrow \dfrac{50}{2} = (?)^2$

$\Rightarrow 25 = (?)^2$

$\Rightarrow ? = \sqrt{25}$

$\Rightarrow ? = 5$

$\therefore$ The value of (?) is 5.

Hence, the correct option is (B).

23. From the question it's known that the bus travels at a speed of 67.96 kmph including stoppages and without stoppages 81.57 kmph.

So it's very clear that some time is wasted due to decrease in speed of the bus

Decrease in speed of bus = 81.57 kmph – 67.96 kmph = 13.61 kmph

Every hour 13.61 km is wasted due to stoppages, we know that

$$\text{Time} = \dfrac{\text{Distance}}{\text{Speed}}$$

So if it would have travelled this 13.61 km with a speed of 81.57 kmph, it would have saved

$\Rightarrow \dfrac{13.61}{81.57} = 0.1668\text{hrs} = 10.011 \text{ minutes}$

$\therefore$ The bus stops 10.011 minutes per hour due to these stoppages.

Hence, the correct option is (A).

24. The surface area of the cylinder = Surface area of the square

Here height 'h' of the cylinder = Side of the square since it is rolled along its length

$$\therefore\ h\ =\ a$$

$$\Rightarrow\ 2\pi r a\ =\ a^2$$

$\Rightarrow$ Base radius r $=\ \dfrac{a}{2\pi}$

$\Rightarrow$ The ratio of base radius to the side of square $=\ \dfrac{a}{2\pi} : a = \dfrac{1}{2\pi}$

$\therefore$ The required ratio is $\dfrac{1}{2\pi}$.

Hence, the correct option is (A).

25. Given:

28% of 640 + 34% of 720 = ? × 54

$$\Rightarrow \frac{28}{100} \times 640 + \frac{34}{100} \times 720 = ? \times 54$$

$$\Rightarrow 179.2 + 244.8 = ? \times 54$$

$$\Rightarrow 424 = ? \times 54$$

$$\Rightarrow ? = \frac{424}{54}$$

$$\therefore ? = 7.85$$

Hence, the correct option is (D).

26. According to question,

Ratio of computers for $P, Q, R = 120:160:440 = 3:4:11$

Ratio of months for which computers were kept in godown $= 3:6:3 = 1:2:1$

$\Rightarrow$ Compounding both the ratio $= (3 \times 1):(4 \times 2):(11 \times 1) = 3:8:11$

Total Amount $=$ Rs. 7000

Expenditure paid by $P = \dfrac{3}{3+8+11} \times 100$

$$= \frac{3}{22} \times 100$$

$$= 13.6\%$$

Hence, the correct option is (B).

27. Given series:

19, 24, 33, 43, 55, 69, 85

The pattern is:

$$\begin{array}{ccccccc}
19 & \boxed{25} & 33 & 43 & 55 & 69 & 85 \\
& +6 & +8 & +10 & +12 & +14 & +16
\end{array}$$

So, the wrong number is 24.

Hence, the correct option is (A).

28. Given series:

4866, 2432, 1218, 610, 306, 154, 78

The pattern is:

$$\begin{array}{ccccccc}
4866 & \boxed{2434} & 1218 & 610 & 306 & 154 & 78 \\
& \div2+1 & \div2+1 & \div2+1 & \div2+1 & \div2+1 & \div2+1
\end{array}$$

So, the wrong number is 2432.

Hence, the correct option is (C).

29. Let the rate of interest be 'r' and time period be $'t'$ years

Now, according to question

Now, Compound Interest (CI) for 2 years 8 months at the rate of 6%, calculating net rate $\%$ for 2 years

$$CI \text{ for } 2 \text{ years} = 6 + 6 + \frac{6 \times 6}{100} = 12.36\%$$

Now, Rate of interest for 8 months $= \dfrac{8}{12} \times 6 = 4\%$

$$CI \text{ for next } 8 \text{ months} = 12.36 + 4 + \frac{12.36 \times 4}{100} = 16.85\%$$

Now, the amount to be paid after 2 years 8 month is

$$\text{Amount} = p\left(1 + \frac{r}{100}\right)^t$$

$$\text{Amount} = 250000(0.11685)^{\frac{8}{3}}$$

$$\text{Amount} = 378689.49 \sim 378689.50$$

Hence, the correct option is (A).

30. Given:

$$215 + 369 - 60\% \text{ of } 900 + 5 = ?^2$$

$$\Rightarrow 584 - \frac{60}{100} \times 900 + 5 = ?^2$$

$$\Rightarrow 584 - 540 + 5 = ?^2$$

$$\Rightarrow 589 - 540 = ?^2$$

$$\Rightarrow 49 = ?^2$$

$$\Rightarrow ? = 7$$

$\therefore$ The value of ? is 7.

Hence, the correct option is (B).

Ques (1-4):Direction: In the following question assuming the given statements to be true, find which of the conclusion(s) among given conclusions is/are definitely true and then give your answers accordingly.

Q.1 Statements: Z > Y ≥ X ≥ K; K = L ≥ M;

Which of the following are definitely true?

A. X > L
B. Z > L
C. K = Z
D. K < Y
E. None of the above

Q.2 Statements: T ≥ C ≥ F; E = A < D; X > T; D < F = T

Conclusions:

I. F < E

II. C = F

III. A > T

A. Only I is True
B. Only II is True
C. Only III is True
D. Only I and III are True
E. None is True

Q.3 Statements: Y < Z > X; W > D < R; Y > T = R; X > W

Conclusions:

I. R < Z

II. X > D

III. T < W

A. Only I is True
B. Only II is True
C. Only I and II are True
D. Only II and III are True
E. Only III and I are True

Q.4 Statements: E ≥ U = D; R < A < F; W ≤ D; W > F

Conclusions:

I. U < R

II. E = W

III. E > W

A. Only II is True
B. Only III is True
C. Only I and II are True
D. Either I or II is True
E. Either II or III is True

Q.5 Direction: In the question, assuming the given statements to be true, find which of the conclusion (s) among given two conclusions is /are definitely true and then give your answer accordingly.

Statements: $M \leq K < L;\quad N \leq M < P < Q$

Conclusions:

I. $L > P$

II. $N < L$

A. Either conclusion I or II is true.
B. Only conclusion II is true.
C. Only conclusion I is true.
D. Both conclusions I and II are true.
E. None of the conclusions is true

Ques (6-11):Direction: Study the following information carefully and answer the questions based on it.

Eight persons A, D, H, I, J, R, S, and V sitting around the circular table but not necessarily in the same order and all are facing towards the center.

There are 2 persons sitting between R and V. J is sitting third to the right of S. A is sitting in the opposite direction of R. J and V are immediate neighbors. There are 2 persons sitting between H and D. H and R are immediate neighbors and neither of them is immediate neighbors of S.

Q.6 Who are the neighbors of person I?

A. D, I
B. V, A
C. V, D
D. R, D
E. R, H

Q.7 Which of the following pairs are sitting opposite each other?

A. D – A
B. V – R
C. H – S
D. J – I
E. R – D

Q.8 How many persons are sitting between A and J (when counted from right of A)?

A. One
B. Two
C. Three
D. Four
E. More than Four

Q.9 Who are the neighbors of person S?

A. D, I
B. V, A
C. V, D
D. D, A
E. R, H

Q.10 Who sits opposite to person I?

A. H
B. A
C. V
D. J
E. S

Q.11 Who sits second to the right of the person who is sitting opposite to A?

A. V
B. D
C. I
D. S
E. H

Ques (12-14):Direction: Study the following information carefully and answer the question given below.

A man starts from the initial point A towards west and reaches point B after covering the distance of 6 km. He then takes a left turn and walks another 2 km to reach point C. He then realizes his mistake that he has taken a wrong left turn so he returns back to point B and walks 4 km again towards west and reaches point D. From point D, he takes a left turn and walks 4 km to reach point E. After taking a right turn from E, he finally reaches point F which is 2 km away from E.

Q.12 Which direction is he facing now?

A. East **B.** North

C. West **D.** South

E. None of these

Q.13 How many kilometers has the man walked?

A. 50 km **B.** 40 km **C.** 18 km **D.** 20 km

E. 28 km

Q.14 If from the point F the man walks 4 km more in the same direction and stops, how far is he now from the point D?

A. 12 km **B.** $\sqrt{52}$ km **C.** 28 km **D.** 54 km

E. 15 km

Ques (15-18):Direction: In the question below are given two statements followed by two conclusions numbered I and II. You have to take the given statements to be true even if they seem to be at variance with commonly known facts. Read all the conclusions and then decide which of the given conclusions logically follows from the given statements disregarding commonly known facts.

Q.15 Statement:

Some huts are mud.

No mud is iron.

Conclusion:

I. Some huts are iron.

II. Some huts are not iron.

A. Only I follows

B. Only II follows

C. Either I or II follows

D. Neither I nor II follows

E. Both I and II follow

Q.16 Statement:

Some oranges are lemons.

Only a few lemons are sweet.

Conclusion:

I. Some oranges are sweet.

II. No orange is sweet.

A. Only I follows

B. Only II follows

C. Either I or II follows

D. Neither I nor II follows

E. Both I and II follow

Q.17 Statement:

All fighters are women.

All women are mothers.

Conclusion:

I. All mothers are fighters.

II. All women are fighters.

A. Only I follows

B. Only II follows

C. Either I or II follows

D. Neither I nor II follows

E. Both I and II follow

Q.18 Statement:

All trams are trains.

Only a few trains are bullet.

Conclusion:

I. Some trams can be bullet.

II. All bullet can be trains.

A. Only I follows

B. Only II follows

C. Either I or II follows

D. Neither I nor II follows

E. Both I and II follow

Q.19 Direction: In each of the following questions three statements are given and these statements are followed by two conclusions numbered I and II. Taking the given statements to be true even if they seem to be at variance from commonly known facts. Read the conclusions and then decide which of the given conclusions logically follows from the two given statements:

Statement:

All mango are papaya

No papaya is apple

Some papaya are watermelon

Conclusions:

I. Some apple are mango

II. Some watermelon are not papaya

[SBI PO, 2021]

A. Only I follows **B.** Only II follows

C. Both follow **D.** Either I or II follow

E. None follow

Ques (20-25):Direction: Study the following information carefully and answer the questions that follow.

Nine boxes A, B, C, D, E, F, G, H, and I are kept one above the other not necessarily in the same order.

Three boxes are kept between A and B. Equal number of boxes are kept above and below A. Number of boxes kept above B is same as the number of boxes kept below C. Only two boxes are kept between C and I. One box is kept between A and G, which is not kept immediate above I. No box is kept between F and D, which is not kept above F. E is placed below H, which is kept immediate below D.

Q.20 How many boxes are kept between F and A?

[IBPS PO, 2021]

A. None **B.** Two

C. One **D.** Three

E. More than three

Q.21 Which box is kept immediately below H?

[IBPS PO, 2021]

A. I **B.** F

C. D **D.** E

E. None of these

[SBI Clerk, 2021]

Q.22 Four of the following five are alike in a certain way and so form a group, find the one which does not belong to the group.

[IBPS PO, 2021]

A. AG   **B.** BD   **C.** FH   **D.** IC
E. DA

Q.23 Which of the following pairs represent the lowermost and the topmost box?

[IBPS PO, 2021]

A. EF   **B.** EB
C. CB   **D.** CF
E. None of these

Q.24 Which of the following statement is / are true?

[IBPS PO, 2021]

A. Only one box is kept between F and A
B. All of the given statements are true
C. Three boxes are kept between E and H
D. I is kept immediately below G
E. None of the given statement is true

Q.25 How many boxes are kept below D?
A. 6   **B.** 7   **C.** 1   **D.** 2
E. 3

Ques (26-30):Direction: Study the following information and answer the questions given below.

In a certain code language,

"focus on economic development" is written as "vl no py su"

"greater growth more development" is written as "wr ea vl om"

"more focus is important" is written as "su ta nx ea"

"economic growth is important" is written as "ta py om nx"

Q.26 What is the code for 'economic'?

[SBI Clerk, 2021]

A. no   **B.** py   **C.** nx   **D.** ta
E. su

Q.27 'su' is the code for which of the following?

[SBI Clerk, 2021]

A. more   **B.** development
C. focus   **D.** on
E. important

Q.28 What is the code for "growth is important"?

[SBI Clerk, 2021]

A. om ta py
B. om ta nx
C. wr ta nx
D. ea nx py
E. Cannot be determined

Q.29 What is the code for 'important'?

A. ta
B. py
C. nx
D. om
E. Cannot be determined

Q.30 What is the code for 'greater'?

[SBI Clerk, 2021]

A. wr   **B.** ea   **C.** vl   **D.** om
E. no

// Smart Answer Sheet //

Correct Indicates percentage of students who answered questions correctly.

Skipped Indicates percentage of students who skipped questions.

Q.	Ans.	Correct / Skipped		Q.	Ans.	Correct / Skipped		Q.	Ans.	Correct / Skipped		Q.	Ans.	Correct / Skipped		Q.	Ans.	Correct / Skipped
1	B	46.52 % / 44.53 %		7	C	51.33 % / 40.67 %		13	D	78.31 % / 13.81 %		19	E	58.19 % / 33.67 %		25	A	78.8 % / 16.15 %
2	E	54.05 % / 41.93 %		8	A	57.74 % / 31.17 %		14	B	86.92 % / 11.89 %		20	B	89.16 % / 10.02 %		26	B	41.51 % / 54.33 %
3	C	68.56 % / 30.24 %		9	D	12.45 % / 79.97 %		15	B	86.6 % / 10.39 %		21	E	18.23 % / 73.79 %		27	C	64.37 % / 32.61 %
4	E	43.58 % / 47.05 %		10	C	68.21 % / 31.74 %		16	C	82.53 % / 10.7 %		22	D	56.21 % / 30.3 %		28	B	84.87 % / 13.47 %
5	B	83.26 % / 12.84 %		11	B	57.81 % / 30.08 %		17	D	68.9 % / 30.13 %		23	C	50.26 % / 44.09 %		29	E	80.75 % / 16.13 %
6	D	29.31 % / 68.66 %		12	C	41.94 % / 38.74 %		18	E	13.97 % / 76.39 %		24	C	26.14 % / 68.74 %		30	A	47.24 % / 39.85 %

Performance Analysis

Avg. Score (%)	56.67%
Toppers Score (%)	60.0%
Your Score	

//Hints and Solutions//

1. Given statements: Z > Y ≥ X ≥ K; K = L ≥ M;

On combining: Z > Y ≥ X ≥ K = L ≥ M;

Conclusions:

I. X > L → False (as X ≥ K and K = L implies X ≥ L, thus a clear relation cannot be determined)

II. Z > L → True (as Z > Y ≥ X ≥ K; K = L implies Z > L)

III. K = Z → False (as Z > Y ≥ X ≥ K implies K < Z)

IV. K < Y → False (as Z > Y ≥ X ≥ K implies Y ≥ K, thus a clear relation cannot be determined)

Hence, the correct option is (B).

2. Given statements: T ≥ C ≥ F; E = A < D; X > T; D < F = T

On combining: E = A < D < F ≤ C ≤ T < X; F = T

Conclusions:

I. F < E → False (as E = A < D < F → E < F)

II. C = F → False (as per the given information F = T & T ≥ C ≥ F)

III. A > T → False (as A < D < F ≤ C ≤ T → A < F ≤ C ≤ T → A < C ≤ T → A < T)

Hence, the correct option is (E).

3. Given statements: Y < Z > X; W > D < R; Y > T = R; X > W

On combining: D < R = T < Y < Z > X > W > D

Conclusions:

I. R < Z → True (as R = T < Y < Z → R < Z)

II. X > D → True (as X > W > D → X > D)

III. T < W → False (as T < Y < Z > X > W → T < Z > W → thus clear relation between T and W cannot be determined)

Hence, the correct option is (C).

4. Given statements: E ≥ U = D; R < A < F; W ≤ D; W > F

On combining: E ≥ U = D ≥ W > F > A > R

Conclusions:

I. U < R → False (as U = D ≥ W > F > A > R → U ≥ W > R → U > R)

II. E = W → False (as E ≥ U = D ≥ W → E ≥ D ≥ W → E ≥ W)

III. E > W → False (as E ≥ U = D ≥ W → E ≥ D ≥ W → E ≥ W)

Since, conclusion II and III form complementary pair and E ≥ W.

Hence, the correct option is (E).

5. Given statements: $M \leq K < L; N \leq M < P < Q$

On combining, we get

$L > K \geq M < P < Q; N \leq M \leq K < L$

Conclusions:

I. $L > P \to$ False (As $L > K \geq M < P < Q$ thus, the relation between L and P cannot be determined)

II. $N < L \to$ True (As $N \leq M \leq K < L$, so $N < L$)

Hence, the correct option is (B).

Ques (6-11):Persons: A, D, H, I, J, R, S, and V

1) J is sitting third to the right of S.

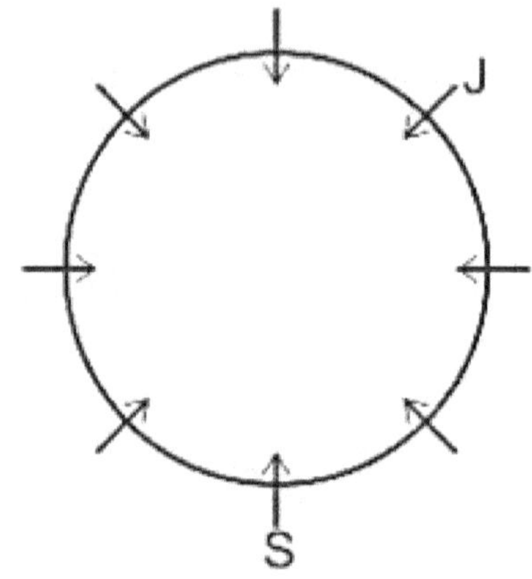

2) J and V are immediate neighbors.

Case 1:

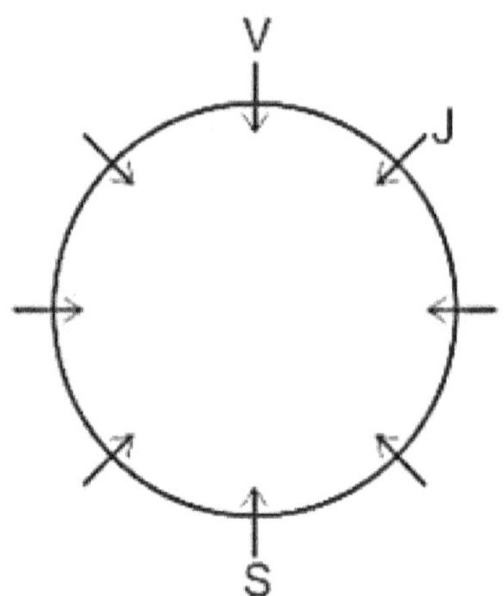

Case 2:

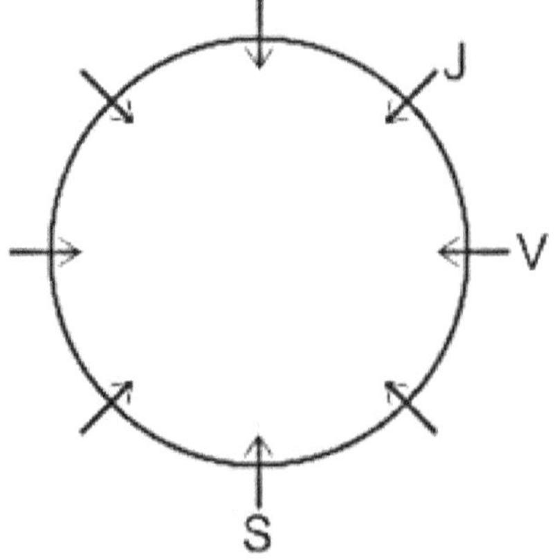

3) There are 2 persons sitting between R and V.

4) H and R are not immediate neighbors of S.

Case 1 cannot satisfy the above conditions. So, gets eliminated.

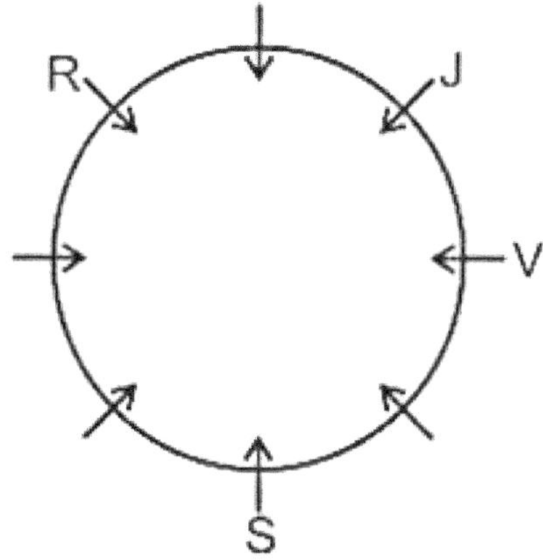

5) A is facing in the opposite direction of R.

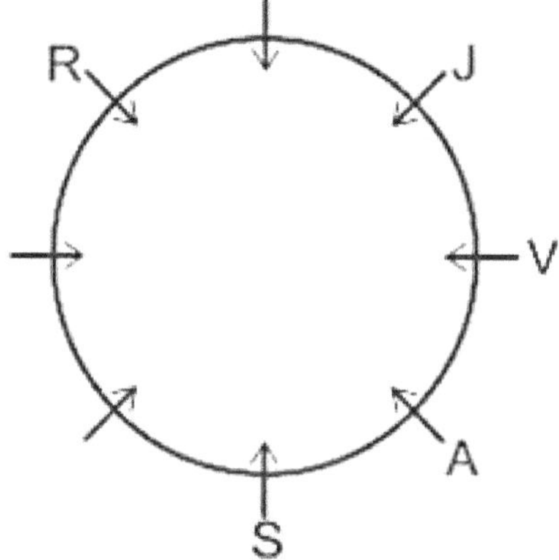

6) There are 2 persons sitting between H and D.

7) H and R are immediate neighbors.

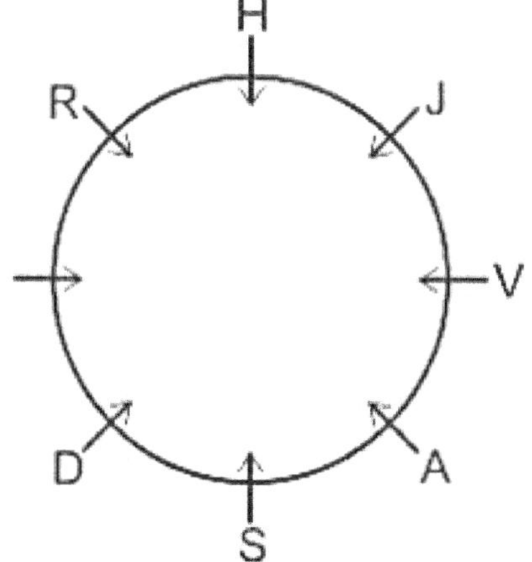

So, I will sit between R and D.

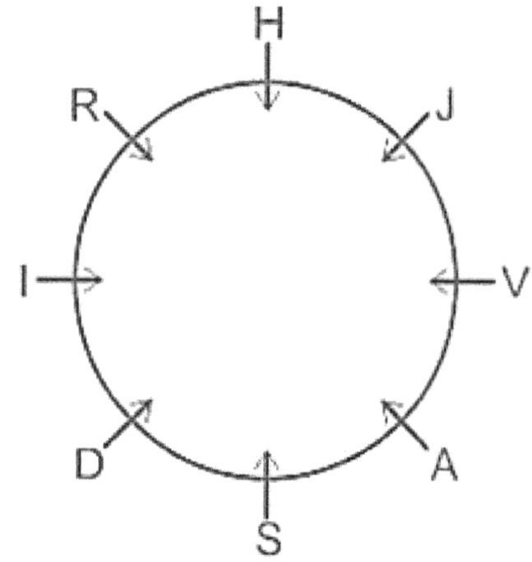

6. So, "R, D" are the neighbors of I.

Hence, the correct option is (D).

7. So, "H – S" are sitting opposite to each other.

Hence, the correct option is (C).

8. One persons are sitting between A and J (when counted from right of A).

Hence, the correct option is (A).

9. So, "D, A" are the neighbors of S.

Hence, the correct option is (D).

10. So, V sits opposite to person I.

Hence, the correct option is (C).

11. D sits second to the right of the person who is sitting opposite to A.

Hence, the correct option is (B).

Ques (12-14): The information given can be represented as follows,

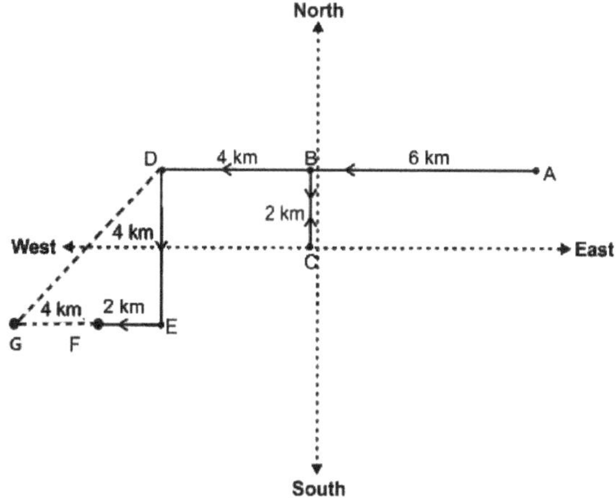

12. Therefore, he is facing the west direction.

Hence, the correct option is (C).

13. Clearly, the man has walked a total of 20 km (6 + 2 + 2 + 4 + 4 + 2).

Hence, the correct option is (D).

14. $(DG)^2 = (GE)^2 + (ED)^2$

$= (6)^2 + (4)^2$

$= 36 + 16$

$= \sqrt{52}$

Thus if from the point F the man walks 4 km more in the same direction and stops, he will be $\sqrt{52}$ km away from point D.

Hence, the correct option is (B).

15. The least possible diagram for the given statements is as follows.

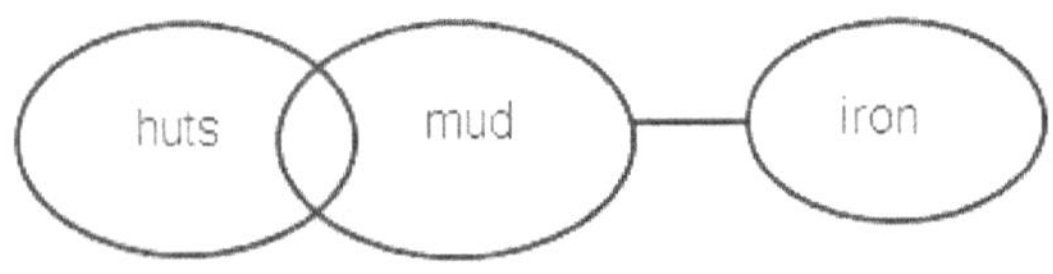

Conclusions:

I. Some huts are iron. → False (It is possible but not definite).

II. Some huts are not iron. → True (Part of huts which is mud is definitely not iron).

Hence, the correct option is (B).

16. The least possible diagram for the given statements is as follows.

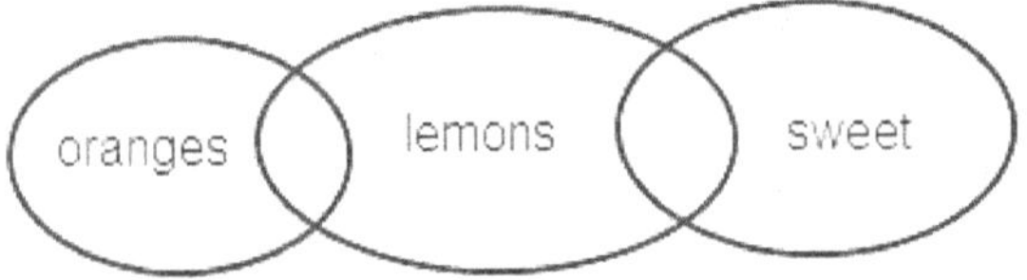

Conclusions:

I. Some oranges are sweet.→ False (It is possible but not definite).

II. No orange is sweet. → False (It is possible but not definite)

Both are complementary conclusions.

Hence, the correct option is (C).

17. The least possible diagram for the given statements is as follows:

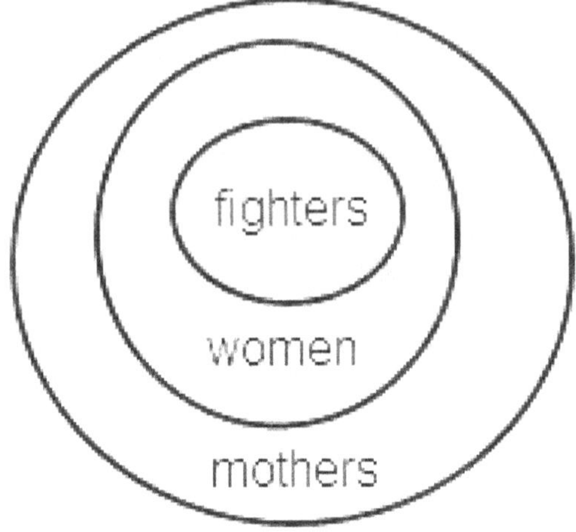

Conclusions:

I. All mothers are fighters. → False (It is possible but not definite).

II. All women are fighters. → False (It is possible but not definite).

Hence, the correct option is (D).

18. The least possible diagram for the given statements is as follows.

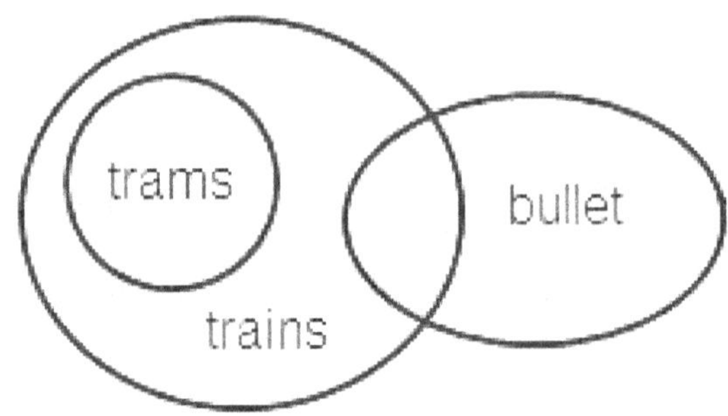

Conclusions:

I. Some trams can be bullet. → True (It is not definite. Possibility with non definite conclusion makes conclusion true).

II. All bullet can be trains. → True (It is not definite. Possibility with non definite conclusion makes conclusion true).

Hence, the correct option is (E).

19.

Conclusions:

I. Some apple are mango → False (All mango are papaya and No papaya is apple. So, apple cannot be mango)

II. Some watermelon are not papaya → False (As given some watermelon are papaya. So negative conclusion not follow)

Thus, None of the conclusion are follow.

Hence, the correct option is (E).

Ques (20-25):1. Equal number of boxes are kept above and below A.

2. Three boxes are kept between A and B.

Case 1	Case 2
B	
A	A
	B

3. The number of boxes kept above B is the same as the number of boxes kept below C.

4. Only two boxes are kept between C and I.

Case 1	Case 2
B	C
	I
A	A
I	
C	B

5. One box is kept between A and G, which is not kept immediate above I.

Case 1	Case 1.1	Case 2
B	B	C
G		
		I
A	A	A
I	I	
	G	G
C	C	B

6. No box is kept between F and D, which is not kept above F → D is kept immediately below F.

7. E is placed below H, which is kept immediate below D → Case 1 and Case 2 gets canceled because the given statement will not be satisfied.

So, the final arrangement will be

Case 1.1
B

F
D
H
A
I
G
E
C

20. So, only two boxes are kept between F and A.

Hence, the correct option is (B).

21. So, A is kept immediately below H.

Hence, the correct option is (E).

22. There are two boxes between I and C, whereas there is only one box between other pairs.

So, IC does not belong to the group.

Hence, the correct option is (D).

23. So, CB represent the lowermost box and topmost box.

Hence, the correct option is (C).

24. So, three boxes are kept between E and H.

Hence, the correct option is (C).

25. So, 6 boxes are kept below D.

Hence, the correct option is (A).

Ques (26-30): According to the given information,

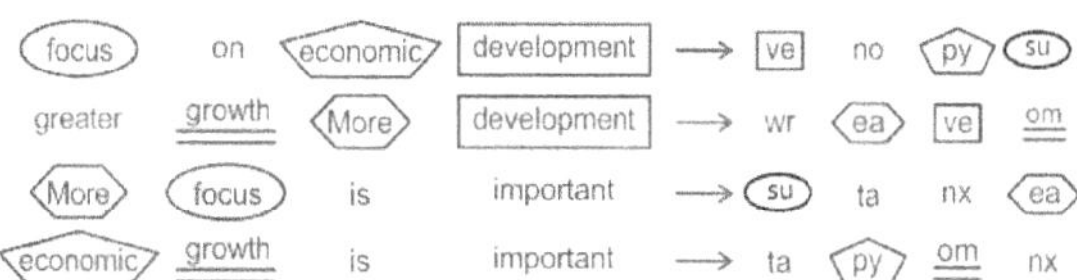

26. So, code for 'economic' is 'py'.

Hence, the correct option is (B).

27. So, 'su' is the code for focus.

Hence, the correct option is (C).

28. Code for growth is 'om'.

Code for 'is important' is 'ta nx'

So, code for 'growth is important' is 'om ta nx'.

Hence, the correct option is (B).

29. Code for 'important' is either 'ta' or 'nx'.

So, answer is cannot be determined.

Hence, the correct option is (E).

30. So, 'wr' is the code for greater.

Hence, the correct option is (A).

Ques (1-3):Direction: In the following question assuming the given statements to be true, find which of the conclusion among given conclusions is/are definitely true and then give your answers accordingly.

Q.1 Statements: Y ≥ R < E; R > P ≥ C = A

Conclusions:

I. Y > A

II. E ≥ C

A. Only I is True

B. Neither I nor II is True

C. Both I and II are True

D. Either I or II is True

E. Only II is True

Q.2 Statements: W > Q ≥ M; H ≤ T = M

Conclusions:

I. H ≤ Q

II. W > T

A. Only I is True

B. Neither I nor II is True

C. Both I and II are True

D. Either I or II is True

E. Only II is True

Q.3 Statements: J < E ≥ O; Y < P ≤ H < O

Conclusions:

I. J > P

II. Y < E

A. Only II is True

B. Neither I nor II is True

C. Both I and II are True

D. Either I or II is True

E. Only I is True

Ques (4-8):Direction: Study the following information carefully and answer the given questions.

In a certain code language

'da mi ge he' means 'David is going school'

'da ta ri' means 'David stays there'

'he mi ri' means 'school is there'

'ra ta li he' means 'Roshni stays in school'

Q.4 What does 'mi' mean in that language?

A. is

B. school

C. there

D. stays

E. None of these

Q.5 How will 'Roshni is going there' be written in that code language?

A. ra mi ge ri

B. li mi ge ri

C. Either (A) or (B)

D. da mi ge ri

E. None of the above

Q.6 What is the meaning of 'li' in that language?

A. Roshni

B. David

C. in

D. stays

E. Either (A) or (C)

Q.7 What does 'ta' mean in that language?

A. there

B. David

C. is

D. stays

E. school

Q.8 What does 'ri mi da ge he' mean In that language?

A. There is Roshni going school

B. Roshni is going to school

C. There is David going school

D. David stays there in school

E. David and Roshni are going

Ques (9-12):Direction: In the question below are given three statements followed by two conclusions. You have to take the given statements to be true even if they seem to be at variance with commonly known facts. Read all the conclusions and then decide which of the given conclusions logically follows from the given statements disregarding commonly known facts.

Q.9 Statement:

I. All cars are bikes

II. No bikes are track

III. Only few tracks are laps

Conclusions:

I. Some cars are laps.

II. No cars are track.

A. Only conclusion I follows

B. Only conclusion II follows

C. Either conclusion I or II follows

D. Neither conclusion I nor II follows

E. Both conclusion I and II follows

Q.10 Statement:

I. Only a few switches are USB

II. Only a few USB are wires

III. Some switches are not chargers

Conclusion:

I. Some chargers are wires

II. Few USB are chargers

A. Only I follows

B. Only II follows

C. Either I or II follows

D. Neither I nor II follows

E. Both I and II follows

Q.11 Statement:

I. No brick is cement

II. All cement is soil

III. No soil is a rod

Conclusion:

I. Some soil is not brick

II. No rod is brick

A. Only I follows

B. Only II follows

C. Either I or II follows

D. Neither I nor II follows

E. Both I and II follows

Q.12 Statement:

I. Only a few caps are hats.

II. All hats are masks.

III. Some masks are covers.

Conclusion:

I. Some masks are hats.

II. No caps are covers is a possibility.

A. Only I follows

B. Only II follows

C. Either I or II follows

D. Neither I nor II follows

E. Both I and II follow

Q.13 Directions: In the question given below, three statements of I, II, and III are followed by four statements. You have to take the given statements to be true even if they are in variance with commonly known facts. Read all the conclusions and then decide which of the given conclusions logically follows from the given statement disregarding commonly known facts.

Statements:

1) No Poet is Artists

2) All Artists are Singer

3) All Singers are Writer

4) No Writer is Father

Conclusion:

I) Only Writers are Artists.

II) No Singer is a Poet.

III) Only Artists is Writer

A. Only conclusion II follows

B. Only conclusion III follows

C. Both conclusion I and III follow

D. Only Conclusion I follows

E. None follows

Ques (14-15):Direction: In each of the following questions assuming the given statements to be true, find which of the conclusion among given conclusions is/ are definitely true, and then give your answers accordingly.

Q.14 Statements: A < Z ≥ P > Q < L ≤ M < R = S

Conclusions:

I. M > P

II. L < S

[IBPS Clerk, 2021]

A. Only I follow

B. Only II follow

C. Either I or II follow

D. Neither I nor II follows

E. Both I and II follows

Q.15 Statements:

A < B = C > E ≥ D ≥ F

Conclusions:

I. E > F

II. E = F

[IBPS Clerk, 2021]

A. Either Conclusion I or II is true.

B. Both Conclusions I and II are true.

C. Neither Conclusion I nor II is true.

D. Only Conclusion I is true.

E. Only Conclusion II is true.

Ques (16-18):Direction: Read the following information carefully and answer the questions given below.

P is 9m to the west of R. R is 7m to the north of T, who is 5m to the east of S. S is 4m north of Q. Q is 14m to the south of U, Where V is the midpoint of U and S.

Q.16 What is the distance between V and Q?

[IBPS Clerk, 2021]

A. 14m

B. 9m

C. 10m

D. 15m

E. None of these

Q.17 Point P is in which direction with respect to V?

[IBPS Clerk, 2021]

A. Northeast

B. North

C. Southwest

D. Southeast

E. Northwest

Q.18 If a point W is drawn 7m to the south of point P, then what will be the distance between W and S?

[IBPS Clerk, 2021]

A. 9m

B. 10m

C. 8m

D. 12m

E. None of these

Ques (19-24):Direction: Study the following information carefully and answer the question given below.

Eight chocolate boxes namely Fivestar, Dairy Milk, KitKat, Snicker, Twix, Bournville, Cadbury and Candy are placed one above the other but not necessarily in the same order. Three chocolate boxes are placed between Dairy Milk and Snicker. Two boxes are placed between Twix and Dairy Milk. Twix is placed below Dairy Milk. Four boxes are placed between Twix and Cadbury. The number of boxes above Cadbury is the same as the number of boxes below Candy. Bournville is placed above Kitkat but below Fivestar. Bournville is not placed just above KitKat.

Q.19 Which of the following chocolate box is placed between Bournville and Fivestar?

A. Cadbury   **B.** Dairy Milk
C. Candy   **D.** KitKat
E. Twix

Q.20 Which of the following box is placed at the top?

A. Fivestar   **B.** Cadbury   **C.** KitKat   **D.** Twix
E. Snicker

Q.21 How many boxes are placed between Twix and Snicker?

A. None   **B.** Two
C. Three   **D.** Four
E. More than four

Q.22 Which of the following box is placed immediately below the box of Candy?

A. KitKat   **B.** Dairy Milk
C. Bournville   **D.** Snicker
E. None of these

Q.23 How many boxes are placed above Cadbury?

A. None   **B.** One   **C.** Two   **D.** Three
E. Four

Q.24 Which box is kept at the bottom?

A. Cadbury   **B.** Twix
C. Dairy Milk   **D.** Snicker
E. Kitkat

Ques (25-30):Direction: Study the following information carefully to answer the given question.

Ten friends - A, B, C, D, E, F, G, H, I and J are sitting around a circular table, but not necessarily in the same order. All friends are facing inside. Adjacent name as in alphabetical series are not sitting nearby to each other in the circle.

There are two person sitting between the J and A when count to the left of A. More than three person are sitting between the I and A when count both left and right of A. J sits just to the left of F who sits third to the left of C. More than four person sit between G and B when counted to the left of B. B who sits near to I. D does not sit near to B. H sits just right of E.

Q.25 How many persons are sitting between C and I when counted to the right of C?

[SBI Clerk, 2021]

A. Two   **B.** Three   **C.** Four   **D.** Five
E. Six

Q.26 Who is sitting fourth to the left E?

[SBI Clerk, 2021]

A. F   **B.** G   **C.** H   **D.** I
E. J

Q.27 Who is sitting just to the near of F and G?

[SBI Clerk, 2021]

A. D   **B.** I   **C.** A   **D.** C
E. J

Q.28 How many persons are sitting between D and G when counted to the right of D?

[SBI Clerk, 2021]

A. Four   **B.** Five   **C.** Six   **D.** Seven
E. Eight

Q.29 Who sits third to the right of H?

[SBI Clerk, 2021]

A. J   **B.** F   **C.** D   **D.** G
E. I

Q.30 Who sits just near the H?

A. B   **B.** E
C. C   **D.** D
E. Both (A) and (B)

// Smart Answer Sheet //

Correct Indicates percentage of students who answered questions correctly.

Skipped Indicates percentage of students who skipped questions.

Q.	Ans.	Correct / Skipped
1	A	42.0 % / 42.73 %
2	C	68.84 % / 31.16 %
3	A	45.95 % / 49.39 %
4	A	84.27 % / 11.87 %
5	C	54.42 % / 38.34 %
6	E	65.31 % / 32.17 %

Q.	Ans.	Correct / Skipped
7	D	58.64 % / 38.06 %
8	C	87.92 % / 10.42 %
9	B	46.67 % / 40.93 %
10	D	54.41 % / 44.74 %
11	A	42.38 % / 32.24 %
12	E	86.12 % / 12.88 %

Q.	Ans.	Correct / Skipped
13	E	59.81 % / 37.38 %
14	B	86.34 % / 13.09 %
15	A	85.97 % / 13.29 %
16	B	86.65 % / 13.07 %
17	E	55.42 % / 34.62 %
18	E	53.75 % / 39.08 %

Q.	Ans.	Correct / Skipped
19	A	78.23 % / 13.12 %
20	E	80.85 % / 12.88 %
21	E	76.85 % / 21.3 %
22	A	76.26 % / 15.14 %
23	C	89.86 % / 10.13 %
24	B	79.74 % / 12.92 %

Q.	Ans.	Correct / Skipped
25	B	86.33 % / 11.82 %
26	A	87.04 % / 10.73 %
27	E	60.14 % / 34.82 %
28	C	88.05 % / 11.16 %
29	D	45.67 % / 37.79 %
30	E	84.88 % / 13.18 %

Performance Analysis	
Avg. Score (%)	46.67%
Toppers Score (%)	66.67%
Your Score	

//Hints and Solutions//

1. Given statements: Y ≥ R < E; R > P ≥ C = A

On combining: Y ≥ R > P ≥ C = A; E > R > P ≥ C = A

Conclusions:

I. Y > A → True (as Y ≥ R > P ≥ C = A → Y > A)

II. E ≥ C → False (as E > R > P ≥ C → E > C)

Hence, the correct option is (A).

2. Given statements: W > Q ≥ M; H ≤ T = M

On combining: W > Q ≥ M = T ≥ H

Conclusions:

I. H ≤ Q → True (as Q ≥ M = T ≥ H → Q ≥ H)

II. W > T → True (as W > Q ≥ M = T → W > T)

Hence, the correct option is (C).

3. Given statements: J < E ≥ O; Y < P ≤ H < O.

On combining: J < E ≥ O > H ≥ P > Y.

Conclusions:

I. J > P → False (as J < E ≥ O > H ≥ P thus clear relation between J and P cannot be determined).

II. Y < E → True (as E ≥ O > H ≥ P > Y → E > Y).

Hence, the correct option is (A).

Ques (4-8): The given information can be analyzed as follows:

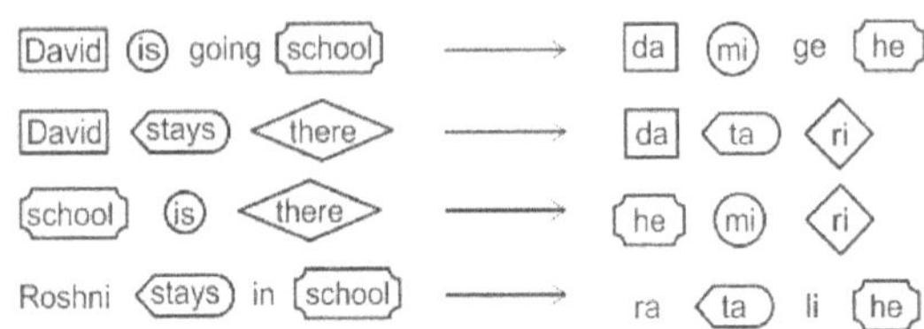

Therefore, in the given code language,

'da' means 'David'

'mi' means 'is'

'he' means 'school'

'ge' means 'going'

'ta' means 'stays'

'ri' means 'there'

4. Therefore, 'mi' means 'is'.

Hence, the correct option is (A).

5. Either 'ra' or 'li' means 'Roshni' or 'in'

Therefore, either 'ra mi ge ri' or 'li mi ge ri' means 'Roshni is going there'.

Therefore, 'Either (A) or (B)' is the correct answer.

Hence, the correct option is (C).

6. Therefore, 'li' means either 'Roshni' or 'in' in that language.

So, 'either (A) or (C)' is the correct answer.

Hence, the correct option is (E).

7. Therefore, 'ta' means 'stays' in that code language.

Hence, the correct option is (D).

8. Therefore, 'ri mi da ge he' means 'there is David going school'.

Hence, the correct option is (C).

9. The least possible Venn diagram for the given statements is as follows:

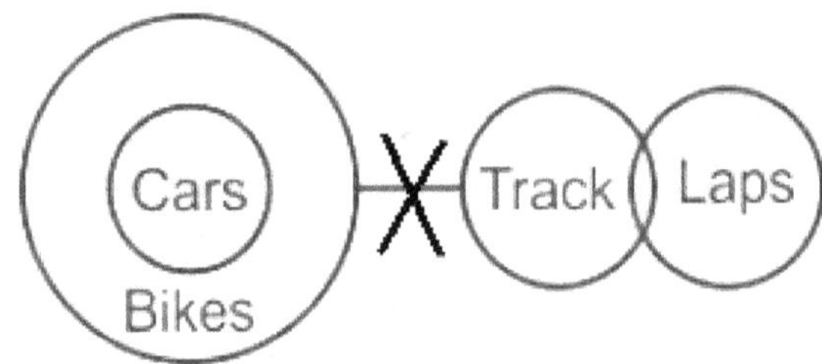

Conclusions:

I. Some cars are laps → False (It is possible, but there is no definite positive or negative relation is given between the elements, therefore it is false)

II. No cars are track → True (Because all cars are bikes and no bikes are track → no cars are track)

So, only conclusion II follows.

Hence, the correct option is (B).

10. The least possible Venn diagram for the given statements is as follows:

Conclusion:

I. Some chargers are wires → False (As there is no definite relation between chargers and wires, We cannot determine some chargers are wires or not)

II. Few USB are chargers → False (As there is no definite relation between chargers and USB, We cannot determine few USB are chargers or not)

So, Neither I nor II follows.

Hence, the correct option is (D).

11. The least possible Venn diagram for the given statements is as follows:

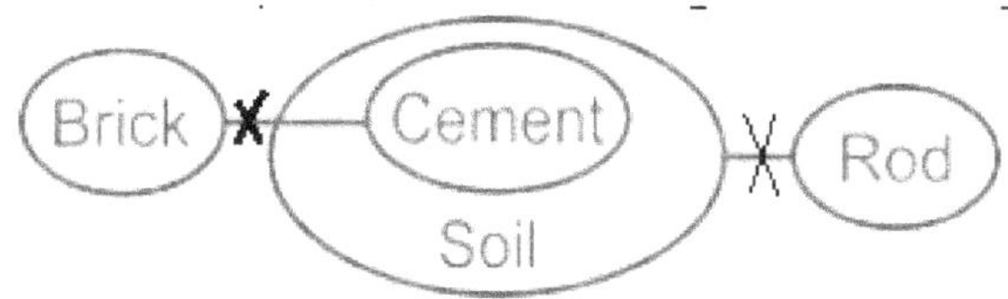

Conclusion:

I. Some soil is not brick → True (As all cement is oil and no cement is brick so the part of the soil which is cement is not brick, So, it is true)

II. No rod is brick → False (As there is no relation between rod and brick)

So, Only I follows.

Hence, the correct option is (A).

12. The least possible Venn diagram for the given statements is as follows:

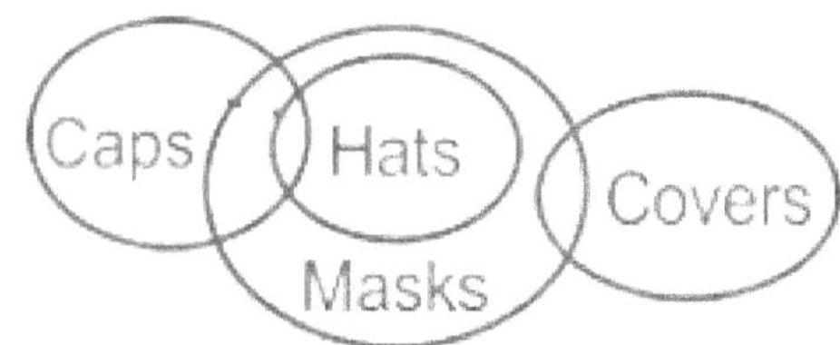

Conclusion:

I. Some masks are hats → True (As all hats are masks so, Some hats are definitely masks)

II. No caps are covers is a possibility → True (As there is no relation between caps and covers so we cannot say anything here but any possibility can follow here, So it is true)

So, Both I and II follow.

Hence, the correct option is (E).

13.

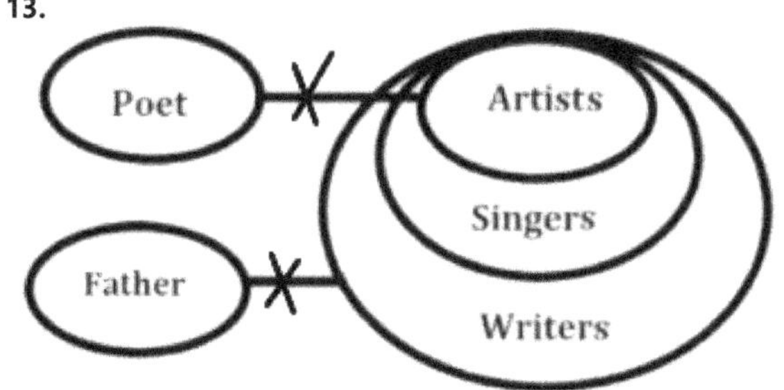

(I) Only Writers are artists means Except Writers nothing can be Artists. So, This Conclusion doesn't follow.

(II) No Singer is a Poet. False (As It is possible but not definite).

(III) Only artists are Writers means Except Artists nothing can be writers. So, This Conclusion doesn't follow.

Hence, the correct option is (E).

14. Given statement: A < Z ≥ P > Q < L ≤ M < R = S

Conclusions:

I. M > P → False (As A < Z ≥ P > Q < L ≤ M < R = S, there is no relation between M and P because there are opposite signs between M and P. So, it is false)

II. L < S → True (As A < Z ≥ P > Q < L ≤ M < R = S → L < S. So, it is true)

So, Only II follow.

Hence, the correct option is (B).

15. Given statements:

A < B = C > E ≥ D ≥ F

Conclusions:

I. E > F → False (as E ≥ D ≥ F → E ≥ F)

II. E = F → False (as E ≥ D ≥ F → E ≥ F)

Conclusion I and II are complementary pairs.

So, either conclusion I or II is true.

Hence, the correct option is (A).

Ques (16-18): According to the given information,

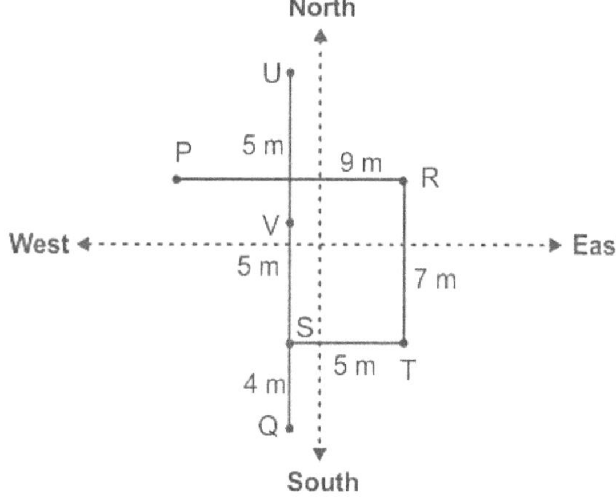

16. Distance between V and Q = VS + SQ

$$= 5 + 4$$

$$= 9m$$

So, the distance between V and Q is 9m.

Hence, the correct option is (B).

17. So, Point P is northwest of point V.

Hence, the correct option is (E).

18. Distance between point S and T $= 5m$

Distance between point P and R $= 9m$

So, Distance between point S and W $= (9 - 5)m = 4\,m$

The total distance covered by man to reach point W from point S is 4m.

Hence, the correct option is (E).

Ques (19-24): Eight chocolate boxes namely Fivestar, Dairy Milk, KitKat, Snicker, Twix, Bournville, Cadbury and Candy.

1) Three chocolate boxes are placed between Dairy Milk and Snicker.

2) Two boxes are placed between Twix and Dairy Milk.

3) Twix is placed below Dairy Milk.

Case 1	Case 2
Snicker	Dairy Milk
	Twix
Dairy Milk	Snicker
Twix	

4) Four boxes are placed between Twix and Cadbury.5) The number of boxes above Cadbury is the same as the number of boxes below Candy.

Case 1	Case 2
Snicker	Cadbury
Cadbury	Dairy Milk
Dairy Milk	
Candy	Twix
	Snicker
Twix	Candy

6)Bournville is placed above Kitkat but below Fivestar.

Case 1	Case 2
Snicker	Cadbury
Fivestar	Fivestar
Cadbury	Dairy Milk
Bournville	Bournville
Dairy Milk	Kitkat
Candy	Twix
Kitkat	Snicker
Twix	Candy

7) Bournville is not placed just above KitKat. (This eliminates case 2)

Final arrangement:

Case 1
Snicker
Fivestar
Cadbury
Bournville
Dairy Milk
Candy
Kitkat
Twix

19. Therefore, Cadbury is placed between Bournville and Fivestar.

Hence, the correct option is (A).

20. Therefore, Snicker is placed at the top.

Hence, the correct option is (E).

21. Six boxes are placed between Twix and Snicker.

Therefore, more than four boxes are placed between Twix and Snicker.

Hence, the correct option is (E).

22. Therefore, Kitkat is placed just below the Candy.

Hence, the correct option is (A).

23. Therefore, 'two' boxes are placed above Cadbury.

Hence, the correct option is (C).

24. So, twix is kept at the bottom.

Hence, the correct option is (B).

Ques (25-30): Persons: Ten friends - A, B, C, D, E, F, G, H, I and J

Facing : Inside

1. There are two person sitting between the J and A when count to the left of A.

2. More than three person are sitting between the I and A when count both left and right of A.

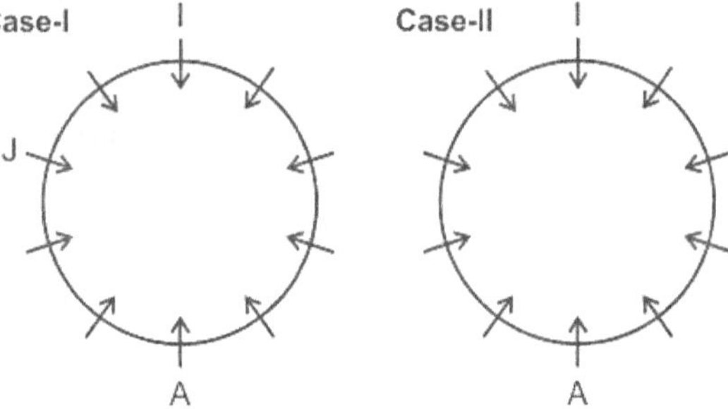

3. J sits just to the left of F who sits third to the left of C.

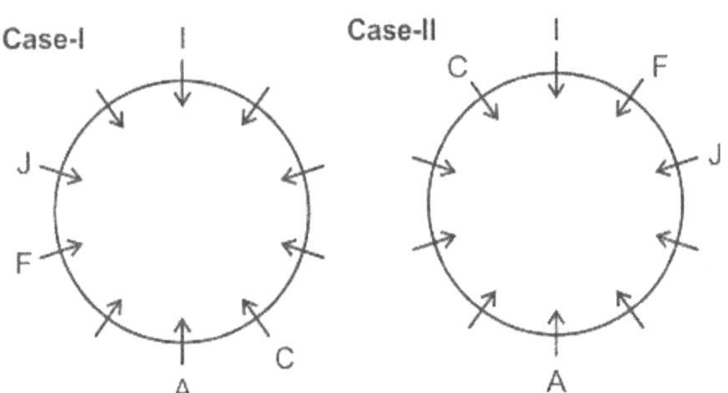

4. More than four person sit between G and B when counted to the left of B.

5. B who sits near to I. so here case II gets eliminated as C and F are already sitting near to I so that we can not place B near to I.

After elimination of case II, case I again has 2 case (a) and (b).

Case-I(a)   **Case-I(b)**

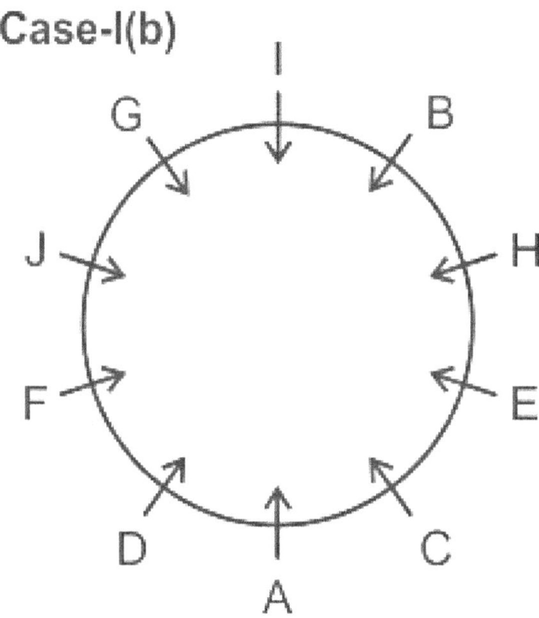

30. So, B and E sits just near the H.

Hence, the correct option is (E).

6. D does not sit near to B. Here case I(a) gets eliminated as F and G are near but condition given that nearby alphabet can not sit together.

7. D does not sit near to B. So only one place left for D between F and A as D will also not sits near to C.

8. H sits just right of E.

The final arrangement is:

Case-I(b)

25. So, three persons sitting between C and I when counted to the right of C.

Hence, the correct option is (B).

26. So, F is sitting fourth to the left E.

Hence, the correct option is (A).

27. So, J is sitting just to the near of F and G.

Hence, the correct option is (E).

28. So, six persons are sitting between D and G when counted to the right of D.

Hence, the correct option is (C).

29. So, G sits third to the right of H.

Hence, the correct option is (D).

// Notes //

// Notes //